Neural Networks and Natural Intelligence

Neural Networks and Natural Intelligence

edited by
Stephen Grossberg

A Bradford Book
The MIT Press
Cambridge, Massachusetts
London, England

PUBLISHER'S NOTE

This format is intended to reduce the cost of publishing certain works in fook form and to shorten the gap between editorial preparation and final publication. Detailed editing and composition have been avoided by photographing the text of this book directly from the authors' prepared copy.

Library of Congress Cataloging-in-Publication Data

Neural networks and natural intelligence.

Includes index.
1. Neural circuitry. 2. Neural computers.
3. Artificial intelligence. 4. Intellect.
I. Grossberg, Stephen, 1939-
QP363.3.N44 1988   612'.81 88-2942
ISBN 0-262-07107-X

TABLE OF CONTENTS

LIST OF AUTHORS

Professor Daniel Bullock
Center for Adaptive Systems
Boston University
111 Cummington Street
Boston, MA 02215

Professor Gail A. Carpenter
Department of Mathematics
Northeastern University
360 Huntington Avenue
Boston, MA 02115
and
Center for Adaptive Systems
Boston University
111 Cummington Street
Boston, MA 02215

Professor Michael A. Cohen
Center for Adaptive Systems
Boston University
111 Cummington Street
Boston, MA 02215

Professor Stephen Grossberg
Center for Adaptive Systems
Boston University
111 Cummington Street
Boston, MA 02215

Professor William Gutowski
Department of Psychology
Merrimack College
North Andover, MA 01845

Professor Daniel Levine
Department of Mathematics
University of Texas
P.O. Box 19408
Arlington, TX 76019

Dr. Ennio Mingolla
Center for Adaptive Systems
Boston University
111 Cummington Street
Boston, MA 02215

Dr. Nestor A. Schmajuk
Center for Adaptive Systems
Boston University
111 Cummington Street
Boston, MA 02215

Professor Gregory O. Stone
Department of Psychology
Arizona State University
Tempe, AZ 85287

Professor Dejan Todorović, Ph.D.
Univerzitet u Beogradu
Filozofski Fakultet
Odeljenje za Psihologiju
čika Ljubina 16–18
11000 Beograd
Yugoslavia

PREFACE

This volume brings together recent research contributions of ten authors to the field that is variously called neural networks, connectionism, parallel distributed processing, or biological information processing. All of the articles were carried out through collaborative work with members of the Center for Adaptive Systems (CAS) at Boston University.

The CAS carries out two types of theoretical activities which, although conceptually independent, have turned out to be mutually reinforcing in our case. One type of activity studies the fundamental design principles and mechanisms needed to explain and predict large data bases about brain and behavior. The other type of activity generates novel architectures for implementation as intelligent machines in technological applications.

There is no necessary reason why all studies of biological intelligence should go technological, or conversely. To validly advance understanding of biological intelligence, one must explain and predict lots of biological data. To advance understanding of machine intelligence, one must solve outstanding technological problems. Diminishing returns set in when a flimsy technological advance is propped up by saying it works just like the brain, or when a metaphorical brain theory devoid of data implications is heralded as the next hi-tech sensation.

Why, then does the type of research done at CAS lend itself to both biological and technological applications? The research at CAS is grounded in its sustained analyses of biological data. This research has proved to be relevant to technology both because of the types of problems we study and the methods that we use to solve them.

In particular, we study problems requiring real-time adaptive responses of individuals to unexpected changes in complex environments. These are the types of problems that humans and mammals need to solve in order to survive. These are also among the types of technological problems that traditional scientific and engineering approaches have not already well-handled.

Our methods for attacking such problems are systematic and rigorous. We typically begin by analysing a huge interdisciplinary data base within a prescribed problem area. In our work on preattentive vision, for example (Chapters 1–4), we have studied data from many parts of the vision literature—data about boundary completion, texture segmentation, surface perception, depth perception, motion perception, illusory figures, stabilized images, hyperacuity, brightness and color paradoxes, multiple scale filtering, and neurophysiology and anatomy from retina to prestriate cortex. Only through the sustained analysis of many hundreds or even thousands of such experiments can one accumulate enough data constraints to discard superficial modelling ideas and to discern a small number of fundamental design principles and circuits.

Such concepts do not make themselves known, however, through a purely bottom-up shifting among huge heaps of data. They come into view by thinking about how these data could arise as emergent, or interactive, properties of a real-time process engaged moment-by-moment by the external environment. Being able to think about an immense mass of static data in terms of the real-time processes that generate these data is an art. It is, I believe, the rate-limiting skill in our work. These real-time processes gradually become discernable through the active confrontation of a huge data mass with known theoretical principles, mechanisms, and computations about real-time neural network processes to test for matches and mismatches. Through this approach, a series of design paradoxes, or trade-offs, come into view which balance many data and computational requirements against one another. Gradually the accumulated impact of these design tradeoffs creates such an intense intellectual pressure within the emerging scheme of ideas that every fact and hypothesis ramifies through it with multiple implications. By this point, a well-defined family of real-time neural network architectures has usually come into view, supported by a new computational theory that is often quite invisible to a merely passive compilation of the data.

We develop and test these architectures using rigorous mathematical techniques and systematic parametric series of computer simulations in order to gain a complete formal understanding of their emergent, or interactive, properties. The combination of working on problems for which both biology and technology need answers, and developing these answers into rigorously characterized computational structures, makes such work equally applicable to quantitative data analysis and to efficient technology transfer.

This rigorous approach has led to real-time neural network architectures that provide explicit examples of intelligent systems which overcome classical bottlenecks in stability, adaptability, scalability, capacity, and speed that have hampered the further development of AI algorithms. Because the demonstrations that guarantee these properties take the form of rigorous mathematical theorems and parametric computational analyses, they provide a firm foundation upon which software and hardware applications may confidently be supported.

What kind of problem can such a neural network architecture solve? Each architecture is being developed to supply a general-purpose solution within a focussed problem domain—what has been called a solution of a *modal problem*. A modal architecture is less general than a general-purpose digital computer but much more general than a typical AI algorithm.

The modal problems analysed in this volume form part of the answer to a central question about real-time adaptive behavior: How does a freely moving human or robot learn to approach an affectively valued object? Despite the apparent simplicity of this question, its complete answer would require an understanding of at least four types of modal problems. Contributions to analysing all these types of modal problems are represented herein, including problems of:

perception (Chapters 1–4), including architectures for biological and machine vision, which clarify how processes of emergent boundary segmentation and featural filling-in can cooperatively utilize scenic data about boundaries, textures, surfaces, multiple spatial scales, and stereopsis to generate a hyperacute preattentive representation of 3-dimensional form in which variable illumination conditions are discounted;

cognitive information processing (Chapters 5–8), including architectures for adaptive pattern recognition, nonstationary hypothesis testing, self-adjusting parallel memory search, updating of working memory, and automatic reallocation of attentional resources;

cognitive-emotional interactions (Chapters 9–11), including architectures for rapidly focussing attention on environmental events and hypotheses which predict behavioral success based upon prior satisfaction of internal constraints, as in the action of rewards, punishments, homeostatic rhythms, or the unexpected nonoccurrence of expected goals, leading to new insights concerning how such adaptive mechanisms may generate irrational behavior when confronted with environments requiring decision making under risk; and

goal-oriented motor control and robotics (Chapter 12), including architectures which circumvent classical combinatorial explosions to show how invariant properties of flexible arm trajectories can be generated as emergent real-time properties of nonlinear neural interactions, rather than as explicitly pre-planned commands, and how self-calibration of movement command parameters can be learned automatically after partial accidents or other unexpected environmental feedback.

Although each of these projects can, at least in part, be carried out independently, they can also collectively benefit from efficiencies of cooperation, interfacing, and scale when they are organized as part of a coordinated research program aimed at the design of intelligent machines capable of autonomous adaptive real-time operation in unanticipated environmental situations, as they are at an interdisciplinary institute such as CAS.

In order to partially cope with the interdisciplinary demands that are commonplace in analysing such modal problems, each staff member at the CAS typically has training in at least three of the four fields: computer science, mathematics, psychology, and neurobiology (the 3/4 Rule) so that every individual has both good design intuition and technical ability to carry out advanced modelling. It is really quite futile to ask people who individually know the data, or have strong computational technique, but not both, to understand each other, let alone to collaborate effectively with each other. Key scientists in such collaborations need to individually possess both design intuition and appropriate formal technique. Consequently, despite its relatively small size, Center scientists hold advanced degrees in mathematics, computer science, psychology, neurobiology, engineering, and physics.

Research is carried out in small cooperative groups and each scientist works on multiple projects which often cut across fields. The unifying impact of available neural network theories and methods make such diversity possible, since results discovered in one problem domain often bring new insights to seemingly unrelated problem domains; for example, results about reinforcement mechanisms have shed new light on mechanisms of vision, mechanisms of circadian rhythms, and mechanisms of motor control because all these mechanisms use specialized variants of a general design for opponent processing (fear-relief, red-green, awake-asleep, push-pull) that is called a *gated dipole field* (see Chapters 2, 10, and 11). Such cooperative interdisciplinary research teams may become the norm in future theoretical investigations of intelligent architectures due to the sheer complexity of the scientific and technological problems.

If you ask my CAS colleagues how they got trained to satisfy the 3/4 Rule, you should not, however, expect to get a straightforward reply. The answer may vary from "accidentally" to "against all odds" to "I'm a very unusual person." It simply is not easy to get systematic training in the major data domains and computational techniques that are needed to do advanced theoretical work on mind and brain topics. That is why several universities, including our own, have begun to put together new interdisciplinary programs or degrees to make it easier for students to enjoy learning about this field.

I hope that volumes such as the present one, which bring together research that includes a variety of the problems, models, and methods at the forefront of neural network research, will make it easier for individuals at all levels to acquire the interdisciplinary knowledge needed to appreciate and contribute to this exciting field of scientific inquiry.

The work reported within this volume has been supported by the Air Force Office of Scientific Research, the Army Research Office, the National Science Foundation, and the Office of Naval Research. We are grateful to these agencies for making this work possible.

We are also grateful to Cynthia Suchta for doing a wonderful job of typing and formatting the text.

Stephen Grossberg
Boston, Massachusetts
August, 1987

Neural Networks and Natural Intelligence

Perception and Psychophysics
1987, **41** (2), 87–116
©1987 Psychonomic Society, Inc.

CORTICAL DYNAMICS OF THREE-DIMENSIONAL FORM, COLOR, AND BRIGHTNESS PERCEPTION, I: MONOCULAR THEORY

Stephen Grossberg†

ABSTRACT

A real-time visual processing theory is developed of how three-dimensional form, color, and brightness percepts are coherently synthesized. The theory describes how several fundamental uncertainty principles which limit the computation of visual information at individual processing stages are resolved through parallel and hierarchical interactions among several processing stages. The theory hereby provides a unified analysis and many predictions of data about stereopsis, binocular rivalry, hyperacuity, McCollough effect, textural grouping, border distinctness, surface perception, monocular and binocular brightness percepts, filling-in, metacontrast, transparency, figural aftereffects, lateral inhibition within spatial frequency channels, proximity-luminance covariance, tissue contrast, motion segmentation, and illusory figures, as well as about reciprocal interactions among the hypercolumns, blobs, and stripes of cortical areas V1, V2, and V4. Monocular and binocular interactions between a Boundary Contour (BC) System and a Feature Contour (FC) System are developed. The BC System, defined by a hierarchy of oriented interactions, synthesizes an emergent and coherent binocular boundary segmentation from combinations of unoriented and oriented scenic elements. These BC System interactions instantiate a new theory of stereopsis, and of how mechanisms of stereopsis are related to mechanisms of boundary segmentation. Interactions between the BC System and FC System explain why boundary completion and segmentation processes become binocular at an earlier processing stage than color and brightness perception processes. The new stereopsis theory includes a new model of how chromatically broad-band cortical complex cells can be adaptively tuned to multiplex information about position, orientation, spatial frequency, positional disparity, and orientational disparity. These binocular cells input to spatially short-range competitive interactions (within orientations and between positions, followed by between orientations and within positions) which initiate suppression of binocular double images as they complete boundaries at scenic line ends and corners. The competitive interactions interact via both feedforward and feedback pathways with spatially long-range oriented cooperative gating interactions which generate a coherent, multiple-scale 3-D boundary segmentation as they complete the suppression of double image boundaries. The completed BC System boundary segmentation generates output signals, called Filling-In Generators (FIGs) and Filling-In Barriers (FIBs), along parallel pathways to two successive FC System stages: the Monocular Syncytium and the Binocular Syncytium. FIB signals at the Monocular

---

† Supported in part by the Air Force Office of Scientific Research (AFOSR 85-0149 and AFOSR F49620-86-C-0037), the Army Research Office (ARO DAAG-29-85-K-0095), and the National Science Foundation (NSF IRI-84-17756).

Syncytium suppress monocular color and brightness signals which are binocularly inconsistent and select binocularly consistent, monocular Feature Contour signals as outputs
to the Binocular Syncytium. Binocular matching of these Feature Contour signals further suppresses binocularly inconsistent color and brightness signals. Binocular Feature
Contour signals which survive these multiple suppressive events interact with FIB signals
at the Binocular Syncytium to fill-in a multiple scale representation of form-and-color-in-
depth. To achieve these properties distinct syncytia correspond to each spatial scale of the
BC System. Each syncytium is composed of opponent subsyncytia which generate output
signals through a network of double opponent cells. Although composed of unoriented
wavelength-sensitive cells, double opponent networks detect oriented properties of form
when they interact with FIG signals, yet also generate nonselective properties of binocular rivalry. Electrotonic and chemical transmitter interactions within the syncytia are
formally akin to interactions in H1 horizontal cells of turtle retina. The cortical syncytia
are hypothesized to be encephalizations of ancestral retinal syncytia. In addition to double opponent cell networks, electrotonic syncytial interactions, and resistive gating signals
due to BC System outputs, FC System processes also include habituative transmitters
and non-Hebbian adaptive filters that maintain the positional and chromatic selectivity
of Feature Contour interactions. Alternative perceptual theories are evaluated in light
of these results. The theoretical circuits provide qualitatively new design principles and
architectures for computer vision applications.

1. Introduction

When we gaze upon a scene, our brains combine many types of locally ambiguous visual
information to rapidly generate a globally unambiguous representation of form-and-color-
in-depth. In contrast, many models of visual perception are specialized models which deal
with only one type of information—for example, boundary, disparity, curvature, shading,
color, or spatial frequency information. For such models, other types of signals are often
contaminants, or noise elements, rather than cooperative sources of ambiguity-reducing
information. This state of affairs raises the basic question: What new principles and
mechanisms are needed to understand how multiple sources of visual information preattentively cooperate to generate a percept of 3-D form?

This article describes a single neural network architecture for 3-D form, color, and
brightness perception. The model has been developed to analyse and predict behavioral
and neural data about such diverse phenomena as boundary detection, sharpening, and
completion; textural segmentation and grouping; surface perception, notably shape-from-
shading; stereopsis; multiple scale filtering; hyperacuity; filling-in of brightness and color;
and perceptual aftereffects. The macrocircuit diagram to which these studies have led,
and which is introduced and developed herein, is depicted in Figure 1.

This macrocircuit represents a synthesis of two parallel lines of theoretical inquiry.
One line of theory focused upon problems concerning monocular brightness, color, and
form perception (Cohen and Grossberg, 1984a; Grossberg, 1980, 1983a, 1983b, 1984, 1987;
Grossberg and Mingolla, 1985a, 1985b, 1987a, 1987b). The other line of theory focused
upon problems concerning binocular depth, brightness, and form perception (Cohen and
Grossberg, 1984a, 1984b; Grossberg, 1981, 1983a, 1983b, 1987). Each theory used its new
behavioral and neural concepts and mechanisms to qualitatively explain and to quantitatively simulate on the computer large but distinct classes of perceptual and neural data.
The present theory builds upon the concepts of these previous theories to generate a unified

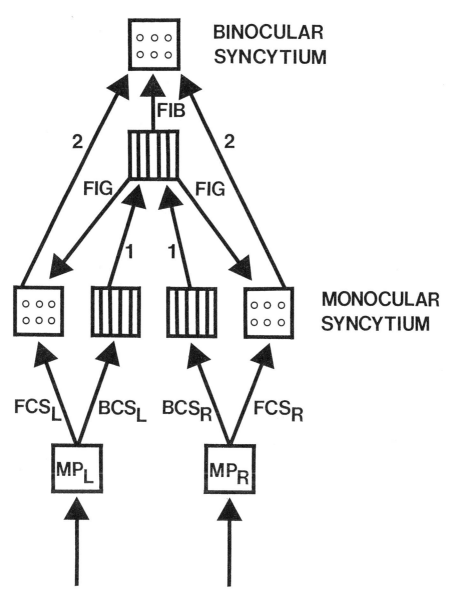

Figure 1. Macrocircuit of monocular and binocular interactions within the Boundary Contour System (BCS) and the Feature Contour System (FCS): Left and right monocular preprocessing stages (MP$_L$ and MP$_R$) send parallel monocular inputs to the BCS (boxes with vertical lines) and the FCS (boxes with three pairs of circles). The monocular BCS$_L$ and BCS$_R$ interact via bottom-up pathways labelled 1 to generate a coherent binocular boundary segmentation. This segmentation generates output signals called filling-in generators (FIGs) and filling-in barriers (FIBs). The FIGs input to the monocular syncytia of the FCS. The FIBs input to the binocular syncytia of the FCS. The text describes how inputs from the MP stages interact with FIGs at the monocular syncytia to selectively generate binocularly consistent Feature Contour signals along the pathways labelled 2 to the binocular syncytia. Part II of the text describes how these monocular Feature Contour signals interact with FIB signals to generate a multiple scale representation of form-and-color-in-depth within the binocular syncytia.

monocular and binocular theory with a far reaching explanatory and predictive range.

2. The Heterarchical Resolution of Uncertainty

The previous and present theories begin with an analysis of the sensory uptake process. Such an analysis shows that there exist fundamental limitations of the visual measurement process at each stage of neural processing. The theory shows how the nervous system *as a whole* can compensate for these uncertainties using both parallel and hierarchical stages of neural processing. Thus the visual nervous system is designed to achieve *heterarchical compensation for uncertainties of measurement*.

I suggest that many of the subtleties in understanding the visual system derive from the following general fact: When a neural processing stage eliminates one type of uncertainty in the input patterns that it receives, it often generates a new type of uncertainty in the outputs that it passes along to the next processing stage. Uncertainties beget uncertainties. It is not the case that informational uncertainty is progressively reduced by every stage of neural processing. This striking property of neural information processing invites comparisons with fields other than visual perception and neurobiology, such as quantum statistical mechanics, the foundations of geometry, and artificial intelligence.

The identification of several new uncertainty principles which visual interactions are designed to surmount has led to a qualitatively new computational theory of how visual systems are designed. Although Figure 1 contains a number of distinct macrostages, the microscopic circuit designs that comprise each macrostage take on functional meaning only in terms of the circuit designs within other macrostages. In earlier work, for example, rules for monocular boundary segmentation and featural filling-in were discovered through an analysis of how each type of process interacts with, and complements deficiencies of, the other. The present work became possible when it was noticed that these rules for monocular boundary segmentation and filling-in also provide a basis for analysing stereopsis and the suppression of binocular double images. Such results suggest that the popular hypothesis of independent modules in visual perception is both wrong and misleading. Specialization exists, to be sure, but its functional significance is not captured by the concept of independent modules.

3. The Boundary Contour System and the Feature Contour System

The present article specifies both the functional meaning and the mechanistic interactions of the model microcircuits which comprise the macrocircuit schematized in Figure 1. This macrocircuit is built up from two systems, the Boundary Contour System (BC System) and the Feature Contour System (FC System). Previous articles have developed rules for these systems in a monocular setting. The present article shows that and how these rules can be generalized to explain both monocular and binocular data.

The BC System controls the emergence of a 3-D segmentation of a scene. This segmentation process is capable of detecting, sharpening, and completing boundaries; of grouping textures; of generating a boundary web of form-sensitive compartments in response to smoothly shaded regions; and of carrying out a disparity-sensitive and scale-sensitive binocular matching process. The outcome of this 3-D segmentation process is perceptually invisible within the BC System. Visible percepts are a property of the FC System.

A completed segmentation within the BC System elicits topographically organized output signals to the FC System. These completed BC Signals regulate the hierarchical processing of color and brightness signals by the FC System (Figure 1). Notable among FC System processes are the extraction of color and brightness signals that are relatively uncontaminated by changes in illumination conditions. These Feature Contour signals interact within the FC System with the output signals from the BC System to control featural filling-in processes. These filling-in processes lead to visible percepts of color-and-form-in-depth at the final stage of the FC System, which is called the Binocular Syncytium (Figure 1).

In order to achieve a self-contained presentation, the basic monocular properties of the BC System and the FC System will be reviewed before they are used to explain more data and as a foundation for developing a binocular theory.

4. Preattentive versus Postattentive Color-Form Interactions

The processes summarized in Figure 1 are preattentive and automatic. These preattentive processes may, however, influence and be influenced by attentive, learned object recognition processes. The macrocircuit depicted in Figure 2 suggests, for example, that a preattentively completed segmentation within the BC System can directly activate an Object Recognition System (ORS), whether or not this segmentation supports visible contrast differences within the FC System. The ORS can, in turn, read-out attentive learned priming, or expectation, signals to the BC System. In response to familiar objects in a scene, the final 3-D segmentation within the BC System may thus be *doubly* completed, first by automatic preattentive segmentation processes and then by attentive learned expectation processes. This doubly completed segmentation regulates the filling-in processes within the FC System that lead to a percept of visible form. The FC System also interacts with the ORS. The rules whereby such parallel inputs from the BC System and the FC System are combined within the ORS have been the subject of active experimental investigation (Garner, 1974; Pomerantz, 1981, 1983; Pomerantz and Schwaitzberg, 1975; Stefurak and Boynton, 1986; Treisman, 1982; Treisman and Gelade, 1980; Treisman and Schmidt, 1982; Treisman, Sykes, and Gelade, 1977).

The present theory hereby clarifies two distinct types of interactions that may occur among processes governing segmentation and color perception: preattentive interactions from the BC System to the FC System (Figure 1) and attentive interactions between the BC System and the ORS and the FC System and the ORS (Figure 2). In support of this distinction, Houck and Hoffman (1986) have described McCollough aftereffects which were independent of whether the adaptation stimuli were presented inside or outside the focus of spatial attention. Part II of the present article suggests an explanation of McCollough aftereffects in terms of interactions of the BC System with the FC System. This explanation clarifies the data of Houck and Hoffman (1986) showing that McCollough aftereffects may be preattentively generated, but also notes the possibility that modulatory effects may sometimes occur via the attentionally controlled pathway ORS→BC System→FC System (Figure 2). For recent analyses of such attentive top-down priming effects, see Carpenter and Grossberg (1987a, 1987b) and Grossberg and Stone (1986).

The remainder of the article develops the model mechanisms whereby the BC System and the FC System preattentively interact. Part I of the article provides a self-contained review of the monocular theory and uses it to analyse results from a number of perceptual and neural experiments that were not discussed in Cohen and Grossberg (1984a) or Grossberg and Mingolla (1985a, 1985b, 1987b). Since several of these experiments were

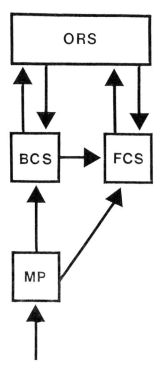

Figure 2. A macrocircuit of processing stages: Monocular preprocessed signals (MP) are sent independently to both the Boundary Contour System (BCS) and the Feature Contour System (FCS). The BCS preattentively generates coherent boundary structures from these MP signals. These structures send outputs to both the FCS and the Object Recognition System (ORS). The ORS, in turn, rapidly sends top-down learned template signals to the BCS. These template signals can modify the preattentively completed boundary structures using learned information. The BCS passes these modifications along to the FCS. The signals from the BCS organize the FCS into perceptual regions wherein filling-in of visible brightnesses and colors can occur. This filling-in process is activated by signals from the MP stage. The completed FCS representation, in turn, also interacts with the ORS.

performed after the monocular theory was published, they illustrate the theory's predictive competence. Part II of the article uses this foundation to derive the theory's binocular mechanisms, which are then applied to the analysis of both binocular phenomena and monocular phenomena that engage binocular mechanisms.

5. Discounting the Illuminant: Extracting Feature Contours

One form of uncertainty with which the nervous system deals is due to the fact that the visual world is viewed under variable lighting conditions. When an object reflects light to an oberver's eyes, the amount of light energy within a given wavelength that reaches the eye from each object location is determined by a product of two factors. One factor is a fixed ratio, or reflectance, which determines the fraction of incident light that is reflected by that object location to the eye. The other factor is the variable intensity of the light which illuminates the object location. Two object locations with equal reflectances can reflect different amounts of light to the eye if they are illuminated by different light intensities.

Spatial gradients of light across a scene are the rule, rather than the exception, during perception, and wavelengths of light that illuminate a scene can vary widely during a single day. If the nervous system directly coded into percepts the light energies which it received, it would compute false measures of object colors and brightnesses, as well as false measures of object shapes. This problem was already clear to Helmholtz (1962). It demands an approach to visual perception that points away from a simple Newtonian analysis of colors and white light.

Land (1977) and his colleagues have sharpened contemporary understanding of this issue by carrying out a series of remarkable experiments. In these experiments, a picture constructed from overlapping patches of colored paper, called a McCann Mondrian, is viewed under different lighting conditions. If red, green, and blue lights simultaneously illuminate the picture, then an observer perceives surprisingly little color change as the intensities of illumination are chosen to vary within wide limits. The stability of perceived colors obtains despite the fact that the intensity of light at each wavelength that is reflected to the eye varies linearly with the incident illumination intensity at that wavelength. This property of color stability indicates that the nervous system "discounts the illuminant," or suppresses the "extra" amount of light in each wavelength, in order to extract a color percept that is invariant under many lighting conditions.

In an even more striking experimental demonstration of this property, inhomogeneous lighting conditions were devised such that spectrophotometric readings from positions within the interiors of two color patches were the same, yet the two patches appeared to have different colors. The perceived colors were, moreover, close to the colors that would be perceived when viewed in a homogeneous source of white light.

These results show that the signals from within the interiors of the colored patches are significantly attenuated in order to discount the illuminant. This property makes ecological sense, since even a gradual change in illumination level could cause a large cumulative distortion in perceived color or brightness if it were allowed to influence the percept of a large scenic region. In contrast, illuminant intensities typically do not vary much across a scenic edge. Thus the ratio of light signals reflected from the two sides of a scenic edge can provide an accurate local estimate of the relative reflectances of the scene at the corresponding positions. We have called the color and brightness signals which remain unattenuated near scenic edges FC signals.

The neural mechanisms which "discount the illuminant" overcome a fundamental uncertainty in the retinal pickup of visual information. In so doing, however, they create a new problem of uncertain measurement, which illustrates one of the classical uncertainty principles of visual perception. If color and brightness signals are suppressed except near scenic edges, then why do not we see just a world of colored edges? How are these local FC signals used by later processing stages to synthesize global percepts of continuous forms, notably of color fields and of smoothly varying surfaces?

Land (1977, 1983) developed his Retinex model to formally show how FC signals could be combined to generate veridical color and brightness percepts within the patches of McCann Mondrians. Although his model was an important step forward that showed the sufficiency of using FC signals to build up a color or brightness percept in response to McCann Mondrians, its operations do not translate directly into a neurally plausible model, and it cannot explain many brightness and color percepts outside the domain of McCann Mondrians (Grossberg and Mingolla, 1985a, 1985b). An important task of perceptual theory is thus to explain why the Retinex model works so well on McCann Mondrians, but fails in general.

Figure 3. A classical example of featural filling-in: When the edges of the large circle and the vertical line are stabilized on the retina, the red color (dots) outside the large circle envelopes the black and white hemidisks except within the small red circles whose edges are not stabilized (Yarbus, 1967). The red inside the left circle looks brighter and the red inside the right circle looks darker than the enveloping red.

6. Featural Filling-In and Stabilized Images

Our monocular theory has developed mechanisms whereby contour-sensitive FC signals activate a process of lateral spreading, or filling-in, of color and brightness signals within the FC System. This filling-in process is contained by topographically organized output signals from the BC System to the FC System (Figure 1). Where no BC signals obstruct the filling-in process, its strength is attenuated with distance. Our monocular model for this filling-in process was developed and tested using quantitative computer simulations of paradoxical brightness data (Cohen and Grossberg, 1984a).

Many examples of featural filling-in and its containment by BC signals can be cited. A classical example of this phenomenon is described in Figure 3. The image in Figure 3 was used by Yarbus (1967) in a stabilized image experiment. Normally the eye jitters rapidly in its orbit, and thereby is in continual relative motion with respect to a scene. In a stabilized image experiment, prescribed regions in an image are kept stabilized, or do not move with respect to the retina. Stabilization is accomplished by the use of a contact lens or an electronic feedback circuit. Stabilizing an image with respect to the retina can cause the perception of the image to fade (Krauskopf, 1963; Pritchard, 1961; Pritchard, Heron, and Hebb, 1960; Riggs, Ratliff, Cornsweet, and Cornsweet, 1953; Yarbus, 1967). The adaptive utility of this property can be partially understood by noting that, in humans, light passes through retinal veins before it reaches the photosensitive retina. The veins form stabilized images with respect to the retina, hence are fortunately not visible under ordinary viewing conditions.

In the Yarbus display shown in Figure 3, the large circular edge and the vertical edge are stabilized with respect to the retina. As these edge percepts fade, the red color outside

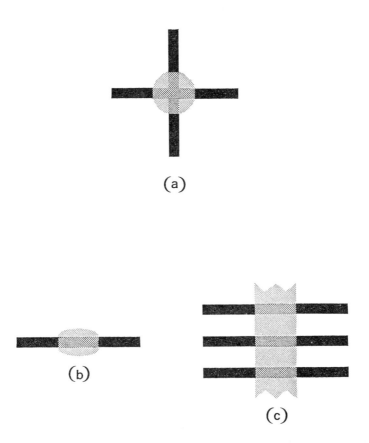

(a)

(b)   (c)

Figure 4. Neon color flanks and spreading: (a) When a colored cross is surrounded by an Ehrenstein figure, the red color can flow out of the cross until it hits the illusory boundary induced by the Ehrenstein figure. (b) When a colored line spans a gap in a black line, the spread of neon color is confined to a narrow diffuse streak which flanks the colored line on either side. (c) When several such colored lines are arranged along a smooth path, then the neon flanks are replaced by a wide band of neon color. The stippled areas schematize the regions in which neon is seen.

the large circle is perceived to flow over and envelop the black and white hemi-discs until it reaches the small red circles whose edges are not stabilized. This percept illustrates how FC signals can spread across, or fill-in, a scenic percept until they hit perceptually significant boundaries.

In summary, the uncertainty of variable lighting conditions is resolved by discounting the illuminant and extracting contour-sensitive FC signals. The uncertainty created within the discounted regions is resolved at a later processing stage via a featural filling-in process that is activated by the FC signals.

7. Neon Color Flanks and Neon Color Spreading

Filling-in of color and brightness can be seen without using stabilized image techniques. The theory suggests explanations of many such filling-in reactions through its analyses of how emergent segmentations within the BC System can inhibit some BC signals that would otherwise be activated by local scenic contrasts. When these segmentations generate BC signals to the FC System, the inhibited boundary segments cannot contain the flow of color or brightness across their positions. Then color or brightness can flow out of regions which contain all of their inducing FC signals. The flow of color or brightness tends to fill-in whatever FC region is bounded by a compartment of the segmentation, subject to the attenuation of filling-in with distance. Such a filled-in percept thus provides visible evidence of how BC signals can both compete and cooperate to form an emergent segmentation whose topographically organized output signals to the FC System define the compartments which contain the featural filling-in process.

Using such analyses, the theory suggests explanations (Grossberg and Mingolla, 1985a, 1985b, 1987b) of many properties of neon color flanks and neon color spreading (Ejima, Redies, Takahashi, and Akita, 1984; Redies and Spillmann, 1981; Redies, Spillmann, and Kunz, 1984; van Tuijl, 1975; van Tuijl and de Weert, 1979; van Tuijl and Leeuwenberg, 1979). For example, when a suitably sized and contrastive red cross is placed within a black Ehrenstein figure, as in Figure 4a, the redness is perceived to fill-in the emergent boundary, or illusory figure, generated by the Ehrenstein figure. When a suitably sized and contrastive horizontal red line segment is placed colinear to flanking horizontal black line segments, as in Figure 4b, then color fills-in approximately colinear neon flanks. When several such horizontal red line segments are arranged so that their line ends are aligned, as in Figure 4c, then color fills-in the vertical region that bounds these horizontal red line segments.

Thus an emergent segmentation can generate a colinear grouping, as in Figure 4b, a perpendicular grouping, as in Figures 4a and 4c, or even a diagonal grouping, as occurs if the image in Figure 4a is periodically repeated (Redies and Spillmann, 1981). In every case, certain BC signals are inhibited which are perpendicular to, or at least non-colinear with, the direction of the strongest cooperative groupings at chromatic-achromatic boundaries. Neon color phenomena thus provide visible evidence of *oriented* cooperative-competitive interactions within the BC System. In contrast, the fact that color or brightness can fill-in whatever compartments may emerge illustrates that featural filling-in within the FC System is an unoriented process, unlike the segmentation process which contains it. This is one of the rule differences that may be used to distinguish the BC System from the FC System.

8.   The Boundary Contour System and the Feature Contour System Obey Different Rules

Figure 5 provides another type of evidence that Feature Contour and Boundary Contour information is extracted by separate, but parallel, neural subsystems before being integrated at a later stage into a unitary percept. The total body of evidence for this new insight takes several forms: the two subsystems obey different rules; they can be used to explain a large body of perceptual data that has received no other unified explanation; they can be perceptually dissociated; when they are interpreted in terms of different neural substrates (the cytochrome-oxydase staining blob system and the hypercolumn system of the striate cortex and their prestriate cortical projections), their rules are consistent with known cortical data and have successfully predicted new cortical data (Grossberg, 1984; Grossberg and Mingolla, 1985a).

Figure 5 illustrates several more rule differences between the BC System and the FC

Figure 5. A reverse-contrast Kanizsa square: An illusory square is induced by two black and two white pac-man figures on a grey background. Illusory contours can thus join edges with opposite directions of contrast. (This effect may be weakened by the photographic reproduction process.)

System. The reproduction process may have weakened the percept of an "illusory" square. The critical percept is that of the square's vertical boundaries. The black-grey vertical edge of the top-left pac-man figure is, relatively speaking, a dark-light vertical edge. The white-grey vertical edge of the bottom-left pac-man figure is, relatively speaking, a light-dark vertical edge. These two vertical edges possess the same orientation but opposite directions-of-contrast. The percept of the vertical boundary that spans these opposite direction-of-contrast edges shows that the BC System is sensitive to boundary orientation but is indifferent to direction-of-contrast. This observation is strengthened by the fact that the horizontal boundaries of the square, which connect edges of like direction-of-contrast, group together with the vertical boundaries to generate a unitary percept of a square. Opposite direction-of-contrast and same direction-of-contrast boundaries both input to the same BC System.

The FC System must, by contrast, be exquisitely sensitive to direction-of-contrast. If FC signals were insensitive to direction-of-contrast, then it would be impossible to detect which side of a scenic edge possesses a larger reflectance, as in dark-light and red-green discriminations. Thus the rules obeyed by the two contour-extracting systems are not the same.

The BC System and the FC System differ in their spatial interaction rules in addition to their rules of contrast. For example, in Figure 5, a vertical illusory boundary forms between the Boundary Contours generated by a pair of vertically-oriented and spatially aligned pac-man edges. Thus the process of boundary completion is due to an *inwardly* directed and *oriented* interaction whereby *pairs* of inducing BC signals can trigger the formation of an intervening boundary of similar orientation. In contrast, in the filling-in reactions of Figures 3 and 4, featural quality can flow from each FC signal in all directions until it hits a Boundary Contour or is attenuated by its own spatial spread. Thus featural filling-in is an *outwardly* directed and *unoriented* interaction that is triggered by *individual* FC signals. The manner in which the FC System can achieve both sensitivity to direction-of-contrast and unoriented filling-in is clarified in Section 24.

9. Illusory Percepts as Probes of Adaptive Processes

The adaptive value of a featural filling-in process is clarified by considering how the nervous system discounts the illuminant. The adaptive value of a boundary completion process with properties capable of generating the percept of a Kanizsa square (Figure 5) can be understood by considering other imperfections of the retinal uptake process. For example, as noted in Section 5, light passes through retinal veins before it reaches retinal photoreceptors. Human observers do not perceive their retinal veins in part due to the action of mechanisms that attenuate the perception of images that are stabilized with respect to the retina. Mechanisms capable of generating this adaptive property of visual percepts can also generate paradoxical percepts, as during the perception of stabilized images or ganzfelds (Pritchard, 1961; Pritchard, Heron, and Hebb, 1960; Riggs, Ratliff, Cornsweet, and Cornsweet, 1953; Yarbus, 1967), including the percept of Figure 3.

Suppressing the perception of stabilized veins is insufficient to generate an adequate percept. The images that reach the retina can be occluded and segmented by the veins in several places. Somehow, broken retinal contours need to be completed, and occluded retinal color and brightness signals need to be filled-in. Holes in the retina, such as the blind spot or certain scotomas, are also not visually perceived (Gerrits, de Haan, and Vendrick, 1966; Gerrits and Timmermann, 1969; Gerrits and Vendrick, 1970) due to a combination of boundary completion and filling-in processes (Kawabata, 1984). These completed boundaries and filled-in colors are illusory percepts, albeit illusory percepts with an important adaptive value. Observers are not aware which parts of such a completed figure are "real" (derived directly from retinal signals) or "illusory" (derived by boundary completion and featural filling-in). Thus in a perceptual theory capable of understanding such completion phenomena, "real" and "illusory" percepts exist on an equal ontological footing. Consequently, we have been able to use the large literature on illusory figures, such as Figure 5, and filling-in reactions, such as Figures 3 and 4, to help us discover the distinct rules of BC System segmentation and FC System filling-in (Arend, Buehler, and Lockhead, 1971; Day, 1983; Gellatly, 1980; Kanizsa, 1974; Kennedy, 1978, 1979, 1981; Parks, 1980; Parks and Marks, 1983; Petry, Harbeck, Conway, and Levey, 1983; Redies and Spillmann, 1981; van Tuijl, 1975; van Tuijl and de Weert, 1979; Yarbus, 1967).

10. Boundary Contour Detection and Grouping Begins with Oriented Receptive Fields

Having distinguished the BC System from the FC System, I now more closely scrutinize the rules whereby boundaries are synthesized. This analysis leads to two of the theory's most important conclusions concerning how the visual system solves problems of uncertain measurement.

In order to build up boundaries effectively, the BC System must be able to determine the orientation of a boundary at every position. To accomplish this, the cells at the first stage of the BC System possess orientationally tuned receptive fields, or oriented masks. Such a cell, or cell population, is selectively responsive to oriented contrasts that activate a prescribed small region of the retina, and whose orientations lie within a prescribed band of orientations with respect to the retina. A collection of such orientationally tuned cells is assumed to exist at every network position, such that each cell type is sensitive to a different band of oriented contrasts within its prescribed small region of the scene, as in the hypercolumn model of Hubel and Wiesel (1977).

These oriented receptive fields illustrate that, from the very earliest stages of BC System processing, image contrasts are grouped and regrouped in order to generate configurations of ever greater global coherence and structural invariance. For example, even the oriented masks at the earliest stage of BC System processing regroup image contrasts (Figure 6). Such masks are oriented *local contrast* detectors, rather than edge detectors. This property enables them to fire in response to a wide variety of spatially nonuniform image contrasts that do not contain edges, as well as in response to edges. In particular, such oriented masks can respond to spatially nonuniform densities of unoriented textural elements, such as dots. They can also respond to spatially nonuniform densities of surface gradients. Thus by sacrificing a certain amount of spatial resolution in order to detect oriented local contrasts, these masks achieve a general detection characteristic which can respond to boundaries, textures, and surfaces.

The fact that these receptive fields are *oriented* greatly reduces the number of possible groupings into which their target cells can enter. On the other hand, in order to detect oriented local contrasts, the receptive fields must be elongated along their preferred axis of symmetry. Then the cells can preferentially detect differences of average contrast across this axis of symmetry, yet can remain silent in response to differences of average contrast that are perpendicular to the axis of symmetry. Such receptive field elongation creates even greater positional uncertainty about the exact locations within the receptive field of the image contrasts which fire the cell. This positional uncertainty becomes acute during the processing of image line ends and corners.

11. A Basic Uncertainty Principle: Orientational Certainty Implies Positional Uncertainty at Line Ends and Corners

Oriented receptive fields cannot easily detect the ends of thin scenic lines or scenic corners. This positional uncertainty is illustrated by the computer simulation in Figure 7. The scenic image is a black vertical line (colored grey for illustrative purposes) against a white background. The line is drawn large to represent its scale relative to the receptive fields that it activates. The activation level of each oriented receptive field at a given position is proportional to the length of the line segment at that position which possesses the same orientation as the corresponding receptive field. The relative lengths of line segments across all positions encode the relative levels of receptive field activation due to different parts of the input pattern. We call such a spatial array of oriented responses an *orientation field*. An orientation field provides a concise statistical description of an image as seen by the receptive fields that it can activate.

In Figure 7, a strong vertical reaction occurs at positions along the vertical sides of the input pattern that are sufficiently far from the bottom of the pattern. The contrast needed

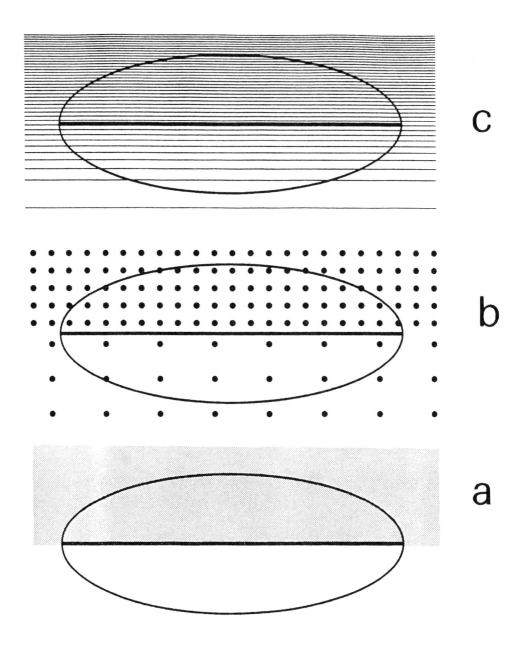

Figure 6. Oriented masks respond to amount of luminance contrast over their elongated axis of symmetry, regardless of whether image contrasts are generated by (a) luminance step functions, (b) differences in textural distribution, or (c) smooth luminance gradients (indicated by the spacings of the lines).

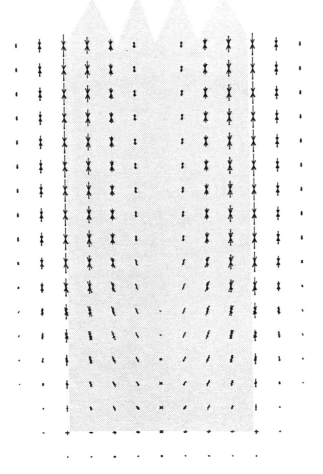

Figure 7. An orientation field: Lengths and orientations of lines encode the relative sizes of the activations and orientations of the input masks at the corresponding positions. The input pattern, which is a vertical line end as seen by the receptive fields, correspond to the shaded area. Each mask has total exterior dimension of 16×8 units, with a unit length being the distance between two adjacent lattice positions. (Reprinted with permission from Grossberg and Mingolla, 1985b.)

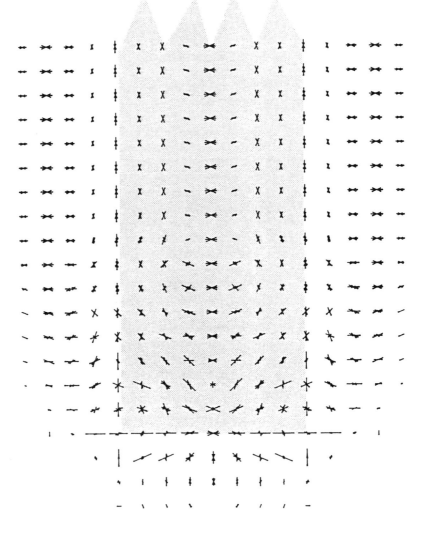

Figure 8. Response of the second competitive stage, defined in Section 14, to the orientation field of Figure 7: End cutting generates horizontal activations at line end locations that receive small and orientationally ambiguous input activations. (Reprinted with permission from Grossberg and Mingolla, 1985b).

to activate these receptive fields was chosen low enough to allow cells with close-to-vertical orientations to be significantly activated at these positions. Despite the fact that cells were tuned to respond to relatively low contrasts, the cell responses at positions near the end of the line are very small. Figure 7 thus illustrates a basic uncertainty principles which says: Orientational "certainty" implies positional "uncertainty" at the ends of scenic lines.

Why does not the nervous system overcome this difficulty by restricting itself to perceiving objects which are wide enough to offset the positional uncertainty depicted in Figure 7? This could be done only at the cost of a large loss of acuity, since only object dimensions that are wider than the elongated receptive fields could then be perceived. Were such a restriction enforced, the nervous system would have to somehow prevent the processing of the long edges of scenic lines and curves, which are well within receptive field capabilities, as in Figure 7, whenever the ends of the lines were too thin. Since scenic lines and curves can be arranged in very complex configurations, such a restriction could not be implemented without an extremely complex interaction scheme. Alternatively, one might ask why the nervous system bothers at all to offset the positional uncertainty at line ends and corners. The next section shows that a perceptual disaster would ensue in the absence of such compensation.

Thus a strong selective pressure exists towards the design of visual systems possessing a discriminative capability finer than that of their individual receptive fields. Such *hyperacuity* is, of course, well known to exist (Badcock and Westheimer, 1985a, 1985b; Beck and Schwartz, 1979; Ludvigh, 1953; Watt and Campbell, 1985; Westheimer, 1981; Westheimer and McKee, 1977). In Section 30, I show that the type of hyperacuity which we have modelled to compensate for positional uncertainty at line ends and corners has also predicted properties of recent data about hyperacuity that possess no other explanation at the present time.

12. Boundary-Feature Trade-Off: A New Organizational Principle

The perceptual disaster in question becomes clear when Figure 7 is considered from the viewpoint of the featural filling-in process that compensates for discounting the illuminant. If no BC signals are elicited at the ends of lines and at object corners, then in the absence of further processing within the BC System, Boundary Contours will not be synthesized to prevent featural quality from flowing out of all line ends and object corners within the FC System. Many percepts would hereby become badly degraded by featural flow. In fact, as Sections 6 and 7 indicated, such featural flows occasionally do occur despite compensatory processing, notably in percepts of neon color flanks and spreading and during stabilized image experiments.

Thus basic constraints upon visual processing seem to be seriously at odds with each other. The need to discount the illuminant leads to the need for featural filling-in. The need for featural filling-in leads to the need to synthesize boundaries capable of restricting featural filling-in to appropriate perceptual domains. The need to synthesize boundaries leads to the need for orientation-sensitive receptive fields. Such receptive fields are, however, unable to restrict featural filling-in at scenic line ends or sharp corners. Thus, orientational certainty implies a type of positional uncertainty, which is unacceptable from the perspective of featural filling-in requirements. Indeed, an adequate understanding of how to resolve this uncertainty principle is not possible without considering featural filling-in requirements. That is why perceptual theories which have not clearly distinguished the BC System from the FC System have not adequately characterized how perceptual boundaries are formed. We call the design balance that exists between BC System and FC System design requirements the *Boundary-Feature Trade-Off*.

I now summarize how later stages of BC System processing compensate for the positional uncertainty that is created by the orientational tuning of receptive fields.

13. All Line Ends Are Illusory

Figure 8 depicts the reaction of the BC System's next processing stages to the input pattern depicted in Figure 7. Strong horizontal activations are generated at the end of the scenic line by these processing stages. These horizontal activations are capable of generating a horizontal boundary within the BC System whose output signals prevent flow of featural quality from the end of the line within the FC System. These horizontal activations form an "illusory" boundary, in the sense that this boundary is not directly extracted from luminance differences in the scenic image. The theory suggests that the perceived ends of *all* thin lines are generated by such "illusory" line end inductions, which we call *end cuts*. This conclusion is sufficiently remarkable to summarize it with a maxim: *All line ends are illusory*. This maxim suggests how fundamentally different are the rules which generate geometrical percepts, such as lines and surfaces, from the axioms of geometry that one finds in the great classics of Euclid, Gauss, and Riemann.

14. The OC Filter and the Short-Range Competitive Stages

The processing stages that are hypothesized to generate end cuts are summarized in Figure 9. First, oriented receptive fields of like position and orientation, but opposite direction-of-contrast, cooperate at the next processing stage to activate cells whose receptive fields are sensitive to the same position and orientation as themselves, but are insensitive to direction-of-contrast. These target cells maintain their sensitivity to *amount* of oriented contrast, but not to the *direction* of this oriented contrast, as in our explanation of Figure 5. Such model cells, which play the role of complex cells in Area 17 of the visual cortex, pool inputs from receptive fields with opposite directions-of-contrast in order to generate boundary detectors which can detect the broadest possible range of luminance or chromatic contrasts, as described in greater detail in Sections 23 and 31 . These two successive stages of oriented contrast-sensitive cells are called the OC Filter (Grossberg and Mingolla, 1985b).

The output from the OC Filter successively activates two types of short-range competitive interaction whose net effect is to generate end cuts. First, a cell of prescribed orientation excites like-oriented cells corresponding to its location and inhibits like-oriented cells corresponding to nearby locations at the next processing stage. In other words, an on-center off-surround organization of like-oriented cell interactions exists around each perceptual location. The outputs from this competitive mechanism interact with the second competitive mechanism. Here, cells compete that represent different orientations, notably perpendicular orientations, at the same perceptual location. This competition defines a push-pull opponent process. If a given orientation is excited, then its perpendicular orientation is inhibited. If a given orientation is inhibited, then its perpendicular orientation is excited via disinhibition.

These competitive rules generate end cuts as follows. The strong vertical activations along the edges of a scenic line, as in Figure 7, inhibit the weak vertical activations near the

TO COOPERATION

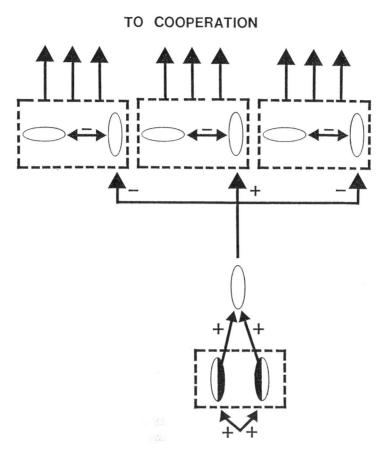

Figure 9. Early stages of Boundary Contour processing: At each position exist cells with elongated receptive fields of various sizes which are sensitive to orientation, amount-of-contrast, and direction-of-contrast. Pairs of such cells sensitive to like orientation but opposite directions-of-contrast (lower dashed box) input to cells that are sensitive to orientation and amount-of-contrast but not to direction-of-contrast (white ellipses). Collectively, these two stages consist of the OC Filter, as in Figure 15. These cells, in turn, excite like-oriented cells corresponding to the same position and inhibit like-oriented cells corresponding to nearby positions at the first competitive stage. At the second competitive stage, cells corresponding to the same position but different orientations inhibit each other via a push-pull competitive interaction.

line end. These inhibited vertical activations, in turn, disinhibit horizontal activations near the line end, as in Figure 8. Thus the positional uncertainty generated by orientational certainty is eliminated by the interaction of two short-range competitive mechanisms.

The properties of these competitive mechanisms help to explain many type of perceptual data. For example, they contribute to an explanation of neon color flanks and spreading (Grossberg and Mingolla, 1985a) by showing how some BC signals are inhibited by boundary completion processes. They also clarify many properties of perceptual grouping, notably of the "emergent features" that group textures into figure and ground (Grossberg and Mingolla, 1985b). Such percepts can be explained by the end cutting mechanism when it interacts with the next processing stage of the BC System.

15. Long-Range Cooperation: Boundary Completion and Emergent Features

The outputs from the competition input to a spatially long-range cooperative process, called the *boundary completion* process. This cooperative process helps to build up sharp coherent global boundaries and emergent segmentations from noisy local boundary fragments. In the first stage of this boundary completion process, outputs from the second competitive stage from (approximately) like-oriented cells that are (approximately) aligned across perceptual space cooperate to begin the synthesis of an intervening boundary. For example, such a boundary completion process can span the blind spot and the faded stabilized images of retinal veins. The same boundary completion process is used to complete the sides of the Kanizsa square in Figure 5. Thus the boundary completion process can scale itself to span different distances in response to different combinations of scenic inducers. To understand further details about this boundary completion process, it is important to understand that the boundary completion process overcomes a different type of informational uncertainty than is depicted in Figure 7.

This type of uncertainty is clarified by considering Figures 10 and 11. In Figure 10a, a series of radially directed black lines induce an illusory circular contour. This illusion can be understood as a byproduct of four processes: Within the BC System, perpendicular end cuts at the line ends (Figure 8) cooperate to complete a circular boundary which separates the visual field into two domains. This completed boundary structure sends topographically organized boundary signals into the FC System (Figure 1), thereby dividing the FC System into two domains. If different filled-in contrasts are induced within these domains due to the FC signals generated by the black scenic lines, then the illusory circle can become visible. No circle is perceived in Figure 10b because the perpendicular end cuts cannot cooperate to form a closed boundary contour. Hence the FC System is not separated into two domains capable of supporting different filled-in contrasts.

Figure 11a shows that the tendency to form boundaries that are perpendicular to line ends is a strong one; the completed boundary forms sharp corners to keep the boundary perpendicular to the inducing scenic line ends. Figure 11b shows, however, that the boundary completion process can generate a boundary that is not perpendicular to the inducing line ends under certain circumstances.

16. Orientational Uncertainty and the Initiation of Boundary Completion

A comparison of Figures 11a and 11b indicates the nature of the other problem of uncertain measurement that I will discuss. Figures 11a and 11b show that boundary completion can occur within a *band* of orientations. These orientations include the orientations that are perpendicular to their inducing line ends (Figure 11a), as well as nearby orientations that are not perpendicular to their inducing line ends (Figure 11b). Figure 8 illustrates how such a band of end cuts can be induced at the end of a scenic line. Such a band of possible orientations increases the probability that spatially separated boundary segments can group cooperatively into a global boundary. If only a single orientation at each spatial location were activated, then the probability that these orientations could precisely line up across perceptual space to initiate boundary completion would be small. The (partial) orientational uncertainty that is caused by bands of orientations is thus a useful property for the initiation of the perceptual grouping process that controls boundary completion and textural segmentation.

Such orientational uncertainty can, however, cause a serious loss of acuity in the absence of compensatory processes. If *all* orientations in each band could cooperate with

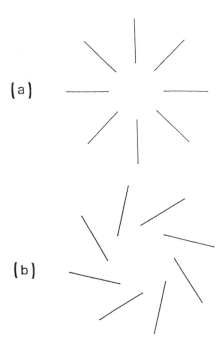

Figure 10. (a) Bright illusory circle induced perpendicular to the ends of the radial lines. (b) Illusory circle becomes less vivid as line orientations are chosen more parallel to the illusory contour. Thus illusory induction is strongest in an orientation perpendicular to the ends of the lines, and its strength depends on the global configuration of the lines relative to one another. (From **Perception and Pictorial Representation**, p.182, C.F. Nodine and D.F. Fisher (Eds.). New York: Praeger, 1979. ©1979 by Praeger. Adapted by permission.)

all approximately aligned orientations in nearby bands, then a fuzzy band of completed boundaries, rather than a single sharp boundary, could be generated. The existence of such fuzzy boundaries would severely impair visual clarity. Figure 11 illustrates that only a single sharp boundary usually becomes visible despite the existence of oriented bands of boundary inducers. How does the nervous system resolve the uncertainty produced by the existence of orientational bands? How is a single global boundary chosen from among the many possible boundaries that fall within the local oriented bandwidths?

Our answer to these questions suggests a basic reason why later stages of Boundary Contour processing must send feedback signals to earlier stages of Boundary Contour processing. This cooperative feedback provides a particular grouping of orientations with a competitive advantage over other possible groupings.

17. Boundary Completion by Cooperative-Competitive Feedback Networks: The CC Loop

We assume, as is illustrated by Figure 5, that pairs of similarly oriented and spatially aligned cells of the second competitive stage are needed to activate the cooperative cells that subserve boundary completion (Figure 12). These cells, in turn, feed back excitatory

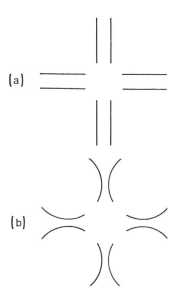

Figure 11. (a) Illusory square generated by changing the orientations, but not the end-points, of the lines in Figure 7a. In (b), an illusory square is generated by lines with orientations that are not exactly perpendicular to the illusory contour. (From **Perception and Pictorial Representation**, p.186, C.F. Nodine and D.F. Fisher (Eds.). New York: Praeger, 1979. ©1979 by Praeger. Adapted by permission.)

signals to like-oriented cells at the first competitive stage, which feeds into the competition between orientations at each position of the second competitive stage. Thus, in Figure 12, positive feedback signals are triggered in pathway 2 by a cooperative cell if sufficient activation simultaneously occurs in both of the feedforward pathways labelled 1 from similarly oriented cells of the second competitive stage. Then both pathways labelled 3 can trigger feedback in pathway 4. This feedback exchange can rapidly complete an oriented boundary between pairs of inducing scenic contrasts via a spatially discontinuous bisection process.

Such a boundary completion process realizes a new type of real-time statistical decision theory. Each cooperative cell is sensitive to the position, orientation, density, and size of the inputs that it receives from the second competitive stage. Each cooperative cell performs like a type of statistical "and" gate, since it can only fire feedback signals to the first competitive stage if both of its branches are sufficiently activated. We call such cooperative cells *bipole* cells. The entire cooperative-competitive feedback network is called the CC Loop. The CC Loop can generate a sharp emergent boundary from a fuzzy band of possible boundaries for the following reason (Grossberg and Mingolla, 1985a, 1985b).

As in Figure 8, certain orientations at given position are more strongly activated than other orientations. Suppose that the cells which encode a particular orientation at two or more approximately aligned positions can more strongly activate their target bipole cells than can the cells which encode other orientations. Then competitive cells of similar orientation at intervening positions will receive more intense excitatory feedback from

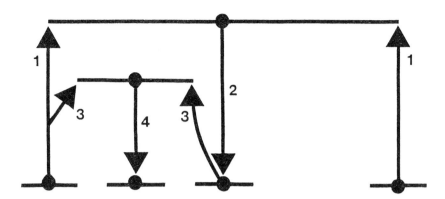

Figure 12. A cooperative-competitive feedback exchange leading to boundary completion: Cells at the bottom row represent like-oriented cells at the second competitive stage whose orientational preferences are approximately aligned across perceptual space. The cells in the top two rows are bipole cells in the cooperative layer whose receptive field pairs are oriented along the axis of the competitive cells. Suppose that simultaneous activation of the pair of pathways 1 activates positive boundary completion feedback along pathway 2. Then pairs of pathways such as 3 activate positive feedback along pathways such as 4. Rapid completion of a sharp boundary between the locations of pathways 1 can hereby be generated by a spatially discontinuous bisection process.

these bipole cells. This excitatory feedback enhances the activation of these competitive cells relative to the activation of cells which encode other orientations. This advantage enables the favored orientation to suppress alternative orientations due to the orientational competition that occurs at the second competitive stage (Figure 9). Cooperative feedback hereby provides the network with autocatalytic, or contrast-enhancing, properties that enable it to choose a single sharp boundary from among a band of possible boundaries by using the short-range competitive interactions. In particular, if in response to a particular image region there are many small-scale oriented contrasts but no *preferred* orientations in which long-range cooperative feedback can act, then the orientational competition can annihilate an emergent long-range cooperative grouping between these contrasts before it can fully form. Thus the CC Loop is designed to sense and amplify the preferred orientations for grouping, and to actively suppress less preferred orientations of potential groupings in which no orientations are preferred. This property is designed into the CC Loop using theorems which characterize the factors that enable cooperative-competitive feedback networks to contrast-enhance their input patterns, and in extreme cases to make choices (Ellias and Grossberg, 1975; Grossberg, 1973; Grossberg and Levine, 1975).

18. Dynamic Geometry of Curves: Metacontrast

A preattentive BC System representation emerges when CC Loop dynamics approach a non-zero equilibrium activity pattern. The nonlinear feedback process whereby an emergent line or curve is synthesized need not even define a connected set of activated cells until equilibrium is approached. This property can be seen in Figure 13, which illustrates how a sharp boundary is rapidly completed between a pair of noisy inducing elements by

REAL TIME BOUNDARY COMPLETION

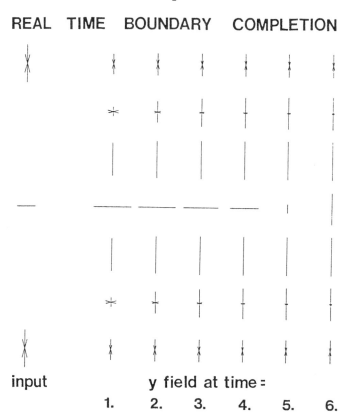

Figure 13. Each column depicts the same band of positions at the second competitive stage (y field) at a different time during the boundary completion process. The input (leftmost column) consists of two noisy but vertically biased inducing line elements and an intervening horizontal line element. Line lengths are proportional to the activities of cells with the represented positions and orientational preferences. The competitive-cooperative feedback exchange triggers transient almost horizontal end cuts before attenuating all nonvertical elements as it completes a sharp emergent vertical boundary.

the spatially discontinuous bisection process in Figure 12. This process sequentially interpolates boundary components within progressively finer spatial intervals until a connected configuration is attained.

The property of transient disconnectedness is perceptually important. Until a boundary can form a connected set, it cannot separate the perceptual space into two distinct regions. Unless such a separation occurs, the boundary cannot support a visible featural difference within the FC System, as a comparison of Figures 10a and 10b illustrates. Thus only boundaries which are activated by enough visual evidence, and hence possess enough statistical inertia to drive the boundary completion process towards a non-zero stable equilibrium, can have a significant effect on conscious perception. Initial surges of boundary activation can be competitively squelched before a conscious percept can be generated. The phenomenon of metacontrast provides an important set of examples wherein visual inputs can be competitively squelched by a later event before they can organize a conscious percept (Breitmeter, 1978, 1980; Gellatly, 1980; Kaufman, 1974; Reynolds, 1981).

Thus, the CC Loop behaves like an on-line statistical decision machine in response to its input patterns. It senses only those groupings of perceptual elements that possess enough "statistical inertia" to drive its cooperative-competitive feedback exchanges towards a non-zero stable equilibrium configuration. After a boundary structure does emerge from the cooperative-competitive feedback exchange, it is stored in short term memory by the feedback exchange until it is actively reset by the next perceptual cycle. While the boundary is active, it possesses hysteretic and coherent properties due to the persistent suppression of alternative groupings by the competition, the persistent enhancement of the winning grouping by the cooperation, and the self-sustaining activation by the feedback. In addition, the conjoint action of the OC Filter and the CC Loop reconcile two ostensibly conflicting types of perceptual computation. Inputs from the OC Filter to the CC Loop retain their "analog" sensitivity to amount-of-contrast in order to properly bias its operation to favor statistically important image groupings. Once the CC Loop responds to these inputs, it uses its nonlinear feedback loops and long-range cooperative bandwidths to generate a more structural and "digital" representation of the form within the image. Such a boundary structure is not even remotely like classical definitions of lines and curves in terms of connected sets of points or tangents to these points.

19. Spatial Impenetrability and Textural Grouping: Gated Dipole Field

Figure 14 depicts the results of computer simulations which illustrate how these properties of the CC Loop can generate a perceptual grouping or emergent segmentation of figural elements (Grossberg and Mingolla, 1985b). Figure 14a depicts an array of nine vertically oriented input clusters. Each cluster is called a Line because it represents a caricature of how a field of OC Filter output cells respond to a vertical line. Figure 14b displays the equilibrium activities of the cells at the second competitive stage of the CC Loop in response to these Lines. The length of an oriented line at each position is proportional to the equilibrium activity of a cell whose receptive field is centered at that position with that orientation. The input pattern in Figure 14a possesses a vertical symmetry: Triples of vertical Lines are colinear in the vertical direction, whereas they are spatially out-of-phase in the horizontal direction. The BC System senses this vertical symmetry, and generates emergent vertical boundaries in Figure 14b. The BC System also generates horizontal end cuts at the ends of each Line, which can trap the featural contrasts of each Line within the FC System. Thus the emergent segmentation simultaneously supports a vertical macrostructure and a horizontal microstructure among the Lines.

In Figure 14c, the input Lines are moved so that triples of Lines are colinear in the vertical direction and their Line ends are lined up in the horizontal direction. Both vertical and horizontal boundary groupings are generated in Figure 14d. The segmentation distinguishes between Line ends and the small horizontal inductions that bound the sides of each Line. Only Line ends have enough statistical inertia to activate horizontal boundary completion via the CC Loop.

In Figure 14e, the input Lines are shifted so that they become non-colinear in a vertical direction, but triples of their Line ends remain aligned. The vertical symmetry of Figure 14c is hereby broken. Consequently, in Figure 14f the BC System groups the horizontal Line ends, but not the vertical Lines.

Figure 14h depicts the emergence of diagonal groupings where no diagonals exist in the input pattern. Figure 14g is generated by bringing the three horizontal rows of vertical Lines close together until their ends lie within the spatial bandwidth of the cooperative interaction. In Figure 14h, the BC System senses diagonal groupings of the Lines. Diagonally oriented receptive fields are activated in the emergent boundaries, and these activations,

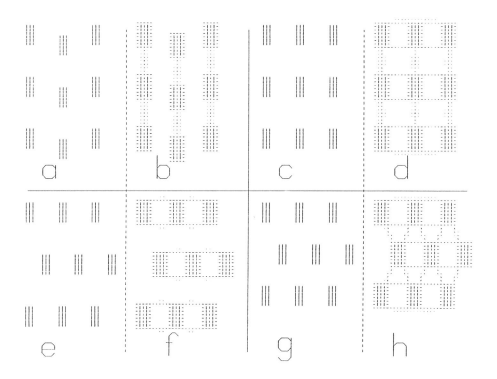

Figure 14. Computer simulations of processes underlying textural grouping: The length of each line segment is proportional to the activation of a network node responsive to one of twelve possible orientations. Parts (a), (c), (e), and (g) display the activities of oriented cells which input to the CC Loop. Parts (b), (d), (f), and (h) display equilibrium activities of oriented cells at the second competitive stage of the CC Loop. A pairwise comparison of (a) with (b), (c) with (d), and so on indicates the major groupings sensed by the network.

as a whole, group into diagonal bands. Thus these diagonal groupings emerge on both microscopic and macroscopic scales.

The computer simulations illustrated in Figure 14 show that the CC Loop can generate large-scale segmentations without a loss of positional or orientational acuity. In order to achieve this type of acuity, the CC Loop is designed to realize the *postulate of spatial impenetrability* (Grossberg and Mingolla, 1985b, 1986). This postulate was imposed to prevent the long-range cooperative process from leaping over all intervening images and grouping together inappropriate combinations of inputs. The mechanism which realizes the postulate must not prevent like-oriented responses from cooperating across spatially aligned positions, since such grouping is a primary function of the cooperation. The mechanism does, however, need to prevent like-oriented responses from cooperating across a region of (approximately) *perpendicularly* oriented responses. In particular, it prevents the horizontal end cuts in Figure 14 which are separated by the vertically oriented responses to each Line from activating a receptive field of a dipole cell. As a result, only end cuts at the Line *ends* can cooperate to form horizontal boundaries which span two or more Lines.

The postulate of spatial impenetrability can be realized by modelling the second competitive stage as a gated dipole field (Grossberg, 1976, 1980). Figure 15 joins together the OC Filter with a CC Loop whose second competitive stage is a gated dipole field. Such a circuit was used to generate the computer output illustrated by Figure 14. Specialized gated dipole fields are also useful in models of double-opponent color fields (Part II) and in models of movement segmentation (Section 32). Thus they seem to realize a general cortical design which can be specialized to accomplish a variety of functions.

In the gated dipole field of Figure 15, the first competitive stage delivers inputs to the on-cells of the field. As previously described, such an input excites like-oriented on-cells at its own position and inhibits like-oriented on-cells at nearby positions. As previously described, on-cells at a given position compete among orientations at the second competitive stage. In addition to on-cells, a gated dipole field also possesses an off-cell population corresponding to each on-cell population. In the network in Figure 15, on-cells inhibit off-cells which represent the same position and orientation. Off-cells at each position, in turn, compete among orientations. Both on-cells and off-cells are driven by a source of tonic activity, which is kept under control by their inhibitory interactions. Thus an input which excites vertically oriented on-cells at a given position can also inhibit vertically-oriented off-cells and horizontally-oriented on-cells at that position. In addition, due to the inhibition of like-oriented on-cells at nearby positions, vertically-oriented off-cells and horizontally-oriented on-cells can be excited due to disinhibition at these nearby positions.

Spatial impenetrability is achieved by assuming that active on-cells send excitatory signals, whereas active off-cells send inhibitory signals, to the similarly oriented receptive fields of bipole cells (Figure 15). Consequently, if horizontally oriented on-cells are active at a given position, they will not be able to activate a horizontally oriented bipole receptive field if sufficiently many vertically oriented on-cells are also active at positions within this receptive field. Each bipole receptive field can help to activate its bipole cell only if its *total* input is sufficiently positive. A bipole cell can only fire if *both* of its receptive fields receive positive total inputs. Sufficiently strong net positive activation of both receptive fields of a bipole cell enables the cell to generate feedback to like-oriented on-cells at the first competitive stage via an on-center off-surround interaction. Thus both bottom-up inputs and top-down cooperative feedback access the first competitive stage via an on-center off-surround interaction among like-oriented on-cells. On-cells which receive the most favorable combination of bottom-up inputs and top-down signals remain active within the emergent boundary segmentation, as in Figure 14.

The ability of the CC Loop to group fuzzy local orientational bands into sharp emergent boundaries illustrates how the imposition of simple perceptual constraints can lead to unsuspected mechanistic conclusions. The need to generate end cuts (Figure 8) capable of preventing the flow of featural quality out of line ends leads to the hypothesis that orientational competition occurs corresponding to each perceptual location (Figure 9) at a prescribed stage of boundary processing. Once orientational competition is available, the cooperative process which it feeds can use the *same* orientational competition to also help generate sharp boundary segmentations. I will furthermore suggest that the filtering and competitive stages described in Figure 9 generate properties of hyperacuity (Section 30) and border distinctness (Section 31), and provide a new basis for understanding of how binocular double images are suppressed and of how stereopsis and segmentation mechanisms work together (Part II). These competitive stages, which are new to our theory, have thus already proved their usefulness in helping to explain much data about vision, and can thus be multiply tested using several different experimental paradigms.

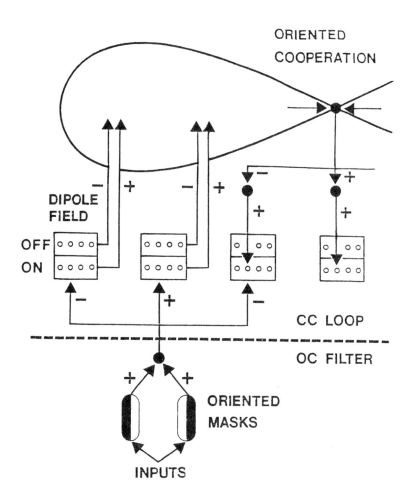

Figure 15. Circuit diagram of the Boundary Contour System: Inputs activate oriented masks of opposite direction-of-contrast which cooperate at each position and orientation before feeding into an on-center
off-surround interaction. This interaction excites like-orientations at the same position and inhibits like-
orientations at nearby positions. The affected cells are on-cells within a dipole field. On-cells at a fixed
position compete among orientations. On-cells also inhibit off-cells which represent the same position and
orientation. Off-cells at each position, in turn, compete among orientations. Both on-cells and off-cells are
tonically active. Net excitation of an on-cell excites a similarly oriented cooperative receptive field at a location corresponding to that of the on-cell. Net excitation of an off-cell inhibits a similarly oriented cooperative
receptive field of a bipole cell at a location corresponding to that of the off-cell. Thus, bottom-up excitation
of a vertical on-cell, by inhibiting the horizontal on-cell at that position, disinhibits the horizontal off-cell at
that position, which in turn inhibits (almost) horizontally oriented cooperative receptive fields that include
its position. Sufficiently strong net positive activation of both receptive fields of a cooperative cell enables
it to generate feedback via an on-center off-surround interaction among like-oriented cells. On-cells which
receive the most favorable combination of bottom-up signals and top-down signals generate the emergent
perceptual grouping.

20. Self-Similar Cooperative Scales: Δ-Neighborhoods and Colinear Boundary Completion during Recognition

Many perceptual properties also follow from the conception of the boundary completion process described in Sections 17–19. For one, the process explicates what is meant by saying that boundary completion is an *inwardly* directed process (Section 8). This type of boundary completion also mechanistically clarifies the empirically derived concept of Δ-neighborhood which Julesz (1985) has used to explain his textural grouping data. The Δ-neighborhood is the domain around individual textural elements across which they can group with other texture elements. Julesz has shown that this neighborhood is a factor 2–3 times the size of his individual textural elements. The factor of 2–3 is consistent with the idea that grouping can proceed *inwards* when *both* branches of a bipole cell are sufficiently activated. The fact that the same factor 2–3 approximately holds across textural element sizes follows if the bipole cells are assumed to satisfy a *self-similarity* property: A bipole cell with larger receptive fields requires larger total inputs to these receptive fields in order to fire. Thus a small number of like-oriented image contrasts may be able to supraliminally activate a receptive field of a small bipole cell, but not of a large bipole cell. The self-similarity constraint hereby prevents large groupings from forming in response to insufficient scenic evidence.

Such a self-similarity property among bipole cells clarifies how large-scale illusory figures can sometimes fail to form in images built up from textural elements that are nearly isoluminant (Cavanagh, 1985). Due to the sensitivity of the BC System to amount-of-contrast, as isoluminance is approached, bipole cells with large receptive fields may receive insufficient total inputs to fire, even if small bipole cells continue to fire.

The self-similarity property also suggests why increasing the overall scale of a line drawing in which gaps occur between colinear scenic edges does not damage rapid recognition of the drawing, within certain limits (Biederman, 1985). By increasing the scale both of the inducing figural elements and of the gaps between these elements, bipole cells with larger receptive fields can be activated to initiate boundary completion across the larger gaps. These colinear boundaries preattentively complete the image boundaries before the completed boundary segmentation inputs to the Object Recognition System (Figure 2). The completed segmentation hereby facilitates recognition of the image even if the emergent boundaries do not support visible contrast differences within the FC System. Many other grouping data have also been analysed using this conception of the grouping process (Grossberg and Mingolla, 1985a, 1985b, 1987b).

21. Comparison of Boundary Contour Operations with Striate and Prestriate Cortical Data

Despite the fact that our theory was derived from perceptual data and concepts, after it reached a certain stage in its development, striking formal similarities with recent neurophysiological data became apparent. Some of our perceptually-derived neural predictions were already supported by known neural data, albeit data that took on new meaning in the light of the perceptual theory. Most of the predictions were not known, however, and several of them have since been supported by neurophysiological and anatomical experiments. In this section, I begin to describe some of these neural contacts, and continue to do so with increasing frequency in later sections.

Figure 16 reproduces the theoretical macrocircuit that was introduced in Grossberg (1983b). This article associated the early stage of left-monocular preprocessing (MP_L) and

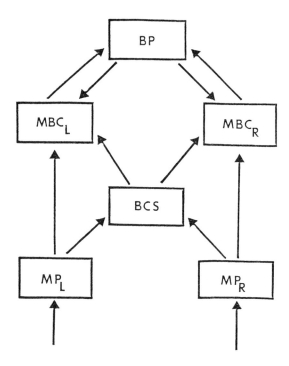

Figure 16. Macrocircuit of processing stages: Boundary Contour formation is assumed to occur within the BCS stage. Its output signals to the monocular MBC_L and MBC_R stages define boundaries within which Feature Contour signals from MP_L and MP_R, respectively, can trigger the spreading, or diffusion, of featural quality.

right-monocular preprocessing (MP_R) with the dynamics of the lateral geniculate nucleus, the first cortical stages in the BC System with the hypercolumns in striate cortex (Hubel and Wiesel, 1977), and the first cortical stages in the FC System with the blobs in striate cortex (Hendrickson, Hunt, and Wu, 1981; Horton and Hubel, 1981). This interpretation is compatible with and anticipated some recent cortical data: The LGN projects directly to the hypercolumns as well as to the blobs (Livingstone and Hubel, 1982). The blobs are sensitive to color but not to orientation (Livingstone and Hubel, 1984a), whereas the hypercolumns are sensitive to orientation but not to color (Hubel and Wiesel, 1977; Livingstone and Hubel, 1984b).

Given this neural labelling, the theory predicted that the blobs and the hypercolumns activate testably different types of cortical interactions. These interactions were not required to all occur within the striate cortex, although they were predicted to be triggered by signals from the blobs and the hypercolumns.

Neural data that support our conception of processing stages within the BC System are summarized below. Within the OC Filter, hypercolumn cells which are sensitive to orientation, to amount-of-contrast, and to direction-of-contrast are hypothesized to activate cells which are sensitive to orientation and to amount-of-contrast, but not to direction-of-contrast (Figure 9). Simple cortical cells that are sensitive to orientation and to direction-of-contrast have been studied by many authors. "Contour-sensitive" complex cells that are sensitive to orientation but insensitive to direction-of-contrast are also well-known to occur in area 17 of monkeys (DeValois, Albrecht, and Thorell, 1982; Gouras and Krüger, 1979; Hubel and Wiesel, 1968; Schiller, Finlay, and Volman, 1976; Tanaka, Lee, and Creutzfeldt, 1983) and cats (Heggelund, 1981; Hubel and Wiesel, 1962; Spitzer and Hochstein, 1985). Spitzer and Hochstein (1985) have, moreover, used their cortical data from cats to develop a quantitative model of complex cells which is very similar to the one which we independently developed from perceptual data (Grossberg, 1984; Grossberg and Mingolla, 1985a, 1985b).

Such complex cells are predicted by the theory to trigger on-center off-surround interactions among cells of like orientation (Figure 9). Experimental data from monkeys which are consistent with this prediction have been reported by Livingstone and Hubel (1984a), who wrote that "After interstripe injections in area 18 the labeling in the labeled part of area 17...formed a regular periodic pattern of parallel stripes with a separation not very different from that of the blobs...The ordered sequence of orientation shifts found in area 18...make it also certain that cells of like orientation are grouped in columns" (p.339). To more completely test this prediction, it is necessary to record whether excitation of these like-oriented area 18 cells by complex cells of area 17 is correlated with inhibition of like-oriented area 18 cells corresponding to nearby perceptual positions.

Strong experimental support for the theory's predictions concerning the competitive and cooperative stages in Figures 9 and 12 was reported by von der Heydt, Peterhans, and Baumgartner (1984). Recall that these processing stages control competitive end cutting and cooperative-competitive boundary completion within the theory. Given the previous cellular interpretations, the theory suggests that, although the contour-sensitive complex cells in area 17 may not be able to respond to thin line ends that are perpendicular to their preferred receptive field orientation, as in Figure 7, their target cells in area 18 can respond to line ends that are perpendicular to their preferred receptive field orientation, as in Figure 8. Such responses occur among the cells at both the competitive and the cooperative stages of Figure 12. Moreover, the cooperative cells respond like logical "and" gates to pairs of scenic edges that are similarly oriented and spatially aligned with their receptive fields over a wide perceptual domain, and can relay this excitation back to the corresponding competitive cells, as in Figure 12.

The data of von der Heydt, Peterhans, and Baumgartner (1984) supported all of these predictions. These authors reported the existence of cells in area 18 of the visual cortex that help to "extrapolate lines to connect parts of the stimulus which might belong to the same object" (p.1261). The investigators found these cells by using visual images which induce a percept of illusory figures in humans, as in Figures 5 and 11. Concerning the existence of a cooperative boundary competition process between similarly oriented and spatially aligned cells (Figure 12), they wrote: "Responses of cells in area 18 that required appropriately positioned and oriented luminance gradients when conventional stimuli were used could often be evoked also be the corresponding illusory contour stimuli...The way widely separated picture elements contribute to a response resembles the function of logical gates" (pp.1261-1262). Concerning the existence of a competitive end-cutting process, they wrote: "the responses to stimuli with lines perpendicular to the cell's preferred orientation reveal an unexpected new receptive field property" (p.1262). The deep issues raised by these data can be expressed as follows. Why do cells in area 18 which usually react to scenic edges that are parallel to their orientational preference also react to line ends that are perpendicular to their orientational preference, whereas cells in area 17 do not? Why do the same area 18 cells act as logical gates? Our theory predicted and provides principled explanations of all of these properties.

If we put these several types of experimental evidence together, the theory suggests that the complex cells in area 17 input to the cells which von der Heydt *et al.* have discovered in area 18. A large number of physiological experiments can be designed to test this hypothesis using stimuli such as those in Figures 3, 5, 10, and 11. Some of these experiments are described in Grossberg and Mingolla (1985a).

The collective impact of these cortical data is promising. When the theory was being formulated, direct neural data concerning the predicted hypercolumn-activated competitive and cooperative interactions were lacking, data concerning the color coding within cortical blobs were lacking, and data concerning independence-of-contrast within complex cells were well-known but used more as a criterion for cell classification than as a functionally meaningful property. The present neural data base is much more supportive of the theory. The meaning of these data that the theory has proposed is not, however, evident within the experimental articles themselves.

For example, the beautiful experiments of Livingstone and Hubel (1984a, 1984b) led them to distinguish a color system within the blobs and an orientation system within the hypercolumns. In contrast, our theory suggests that cortical hypercolumns in area 17 form part of a boundary completion and segmentation system, rather than part of an orientation system. This difference of emphasis is needed to explain how perceived boundaries can occur corresponding to parts of the visual field in which no oriented receptive fields in area 17 respond at all, as in Figures 5 and 11. This capacity for boundary completion is, moreover, a fundamental one, because it lets the visual system compensate for the retinal veins and blind spot, enables perceptual segmentation into figure and ground to occur, helps to inhibit binocular double images, and prevents flow of colors from line ends and corners. I therefore suggest that the hypercolumns be viewed as part of a boundary system, not an orientation system. From this perspective, properties such as independence of direction-of-contrast, multiple types of competition, and oriented cooperative interactions are at least as important as orientational tuning.

22. Invisible Boundaries: Contrast-Sensitivity Does Not Imply Visibility

This difference of emphasis reflects a major difference in our theory's conception of the global constraints that have molded cortical design. This difference leads to a prediction of our theory which has not yet been physiologically tested. The theory predicts that all BC activations are perceptually invisible within the BC System. Boundary Contours are predicted to gain visibility by separating the FC System into perceptual domains which can support different levels of filled-in featural activity. We claim that large activations of contrast-sensitive hypercolumn cells may have no effect whatsoever on conscious perception. In short, *contrast-sensitivity does not imply visibility*. Cohen and Grossberg (1984a) and Grossberg and Mingolla (1985a, 1985b, 1987b) have analysed many paradoxical percepts which are consistent with this hypothesis.

The widespread assumption that a hypercolumn cell's contrast-sensitivity is simply related to a visible brightness percept has caused a long-standing confusion in the neurophysiological literature. For many years, the wavelength sensitivity of most LGN cells stood in stark contrast to the report of Hubel and Wiesel (1968) that most Area 17 cells are insensitive to wavelength. The question "Where did the color go?" weighed heavily on visual neurophysiology for a long time. The elegant discoveries by Zeki (1983a, 1983b) of color-sensitive cells in area V4 of the prestriate cortex did not settle this issue, because V4 receives the bulk of its inputs from area V1 (or 17) and V2 (part of area 18). The discovery of color coding within the blobs (Livingstone and Hubel, 1984a) relieved part of this concern by suggesting that electrode sampling bias may have been to blame for not previously noticing that many cells in V1 are indeed wavelength-sensitive.

The Livingstone and Hubel (1984a) data have, however, replaced a dirth of wavelength-sensitive cells with an embarrassment of riches that has not been adequately appreciated within the experimental literature. "Too little" has been replaced by "too much." This is because the Livingstone and Hubel (1984a) data reveal a three-fold Red-Green Blue-Yellow, and White-Black system in each blob, as Hering (1964) would have desired. If, however, there is already a contrast-sensitive White-Black system in each blob, then why does the visual system also need a contrast-sensitive White-Black system in each hypercolumn? Do *both* of these White-Black systems give rise to brightness percepts? To merely say that the hypercolumns form an orientation system does not explain how the contrast-sensitivity that subserves orientational tuning contributes to a visible brightness percept.

Widespread acceptance of the term "feature detector" for all cells which are sensitive to luminance or hue differences within scenic images has contributed to this type of confusion. Within our theory, both the BC System and the FC System contain "feature detectors," if only because both systems need to detect contrasts in scenic images. However, we would argue that these "feature detectors" are used within the BC System to generate boundaries, not visible "features." Boundary Contours do contribute to visible "featural" percepts, but only indirectly, by defining the perceptual domains within the FC System wherein FC signals can initiate the filling-in of featural activities which may, or may not, lead to visible contrast differences.

Thus our theory accomodates parallel "feature detector" systems by characterizing the role of one system in generating coherent boundary structures to organize featural filling-in, and the role of the other system in discounting the illuminant to extract the luminance and color contours which trigger featural filling-in within these boundary structures.

23. Simple and Complex Striate Cells Revisited

The assumption that "contrast sensitivity implies visibility" has strongly influenced the interpretation of recent striate cortical data. For example, DeValois, Albrecht, and Thorell (1982) provided a lucid discussion of the fact that a fundamental property of a simple cell is its dependence on direction-of-contrast and of a complex cell is its independence of direction-of-contrast: "The fundamental property of a simple cell, in Hubel and Wiesel's scheme, is that the RF [receptive field] is composed of spatially discrete excitatory and inhibitory regions...The fundamental property of a complex cell, on the other hand, is that it fires similarly to a stimulus regardless of its location within the RF" (p.553). Since, in addition, simple cells are slightly more narrowly tuned than complex cells in both spatial frequency and orientation, they also noted that "it is what one might expect if complex cells were just summing simple cells in a hierarchical manner" (p.555), as was assumed in Hubel and Wiesel's original classification and was also assumed based upon perceptual evidence (Figure 5) in the present theory (Figure 9). DeValois *et al.* also noted that "simple cells are phase specific: they respond in opposite direction to white and black...Complex cells...are not phase specific: they respond identically to white and black in the same location. The phase specificity of human vision and our ability to tell white from black cannot be explained if complex cells carry the sole output from the striate cortex" (p.555).

The conclusion that complex cells do not carry the sole output from the striate cortex has proved to be correct. These considerations also led DeValois *et al.* to challenge the hierarchical organization of simple cells into complex cells. Such a challenge is strongly indicated if one also assumes that "contrast-sensitivity implies visibility," since then the contrast-sensitivities of the simple cells and complex cells in hypercolumns are naturally viewed as direct sources of visible percepts. If, however, these contrast-sensitivities are used to generate invisible boundary structures, then the hierarchical organization of simple cells and complex cells may coexist with a separate parallel system for processing visible featural qualities, which has proved to be the blob-activated system, at least in monkeys.

Wavelength-sensitive cells of the lateral geniculate nucleus (LGN) are the input sources to both the FC System and the BC System (Figures 1 and 15). This fact sheds new light on recent data concerning responses of striate simple cells and complex cells to color-varying and luminance-varying patterns of different spatial frequencies (Thorell, deValois, and Albrecht, 1984). The FC System must process its LGN inputs in such a way that double-opponent spectral sensitivities become elaborated and remain segregated in different cell populations. Sections 24–27 and Part II say more about the processing of FC signals. In contrast, the BC System needs to pool its LGN inputs in such a way that boundary signals will be generated in response to the broadest possible combination of luminance and color differences due to scenic contrasts. In particular, boundaries need to be generated at all locations where a luminance or color contrast must be maintained against the smoothing effects of featural filling-in. Since the striate simple cells of the BC System receive their inputs from wavelength-sensitive LGN cells, the responses of these simple cells will be restricted to stimuli capable of activating the corresponding wavelength-sensitive LGN cells. On the other hand, the model complex cells of the BC System pool together inputs from like-oriented cells of opposite direction-of-contrast as well as from like-oriented cells of different spectral sensitivities. Thus the output signals from these complex cells can generate BC inputs to the subsequent competitive and cooperative stages (Figure 9) in response to scenic contrasts arising from a wide range of luminance and color differences. Although they pool together wavelength-sensitive LGN signals to act as broad-band boundary detectors, the complex cells are segregated in terms of their spatial frequency selectivity in order to generate a 3-D segmentation that can distinguish image size on the retina from object size and distance (Part II).

Thorell, deValois, and Albrecht (1984) have reported important data from macaque cortex which support all of these expectations. They showed that "simple cells...are distinguished by relatively narrow color specificity" (p.761), and moreover that a significant fraction of their simple cells exhibited double-opponent properties. In contrast, "complex color cells...responded uniformly to many (or, in the extreme, all) equiluminant wavelength changes...The RF's of many of these cells (15/31, 48%) were composed of overlapping color-regions" (p.762). Just as Boundary Contour outputs need to be insensitive to direction-of-contrast, "these cells always responded with the same polarity to all colors tested. This was in keeping with one of the criterial features of complex cell behavior: their lack of phase specificity" (p.764).

Thorell *et al.* (1984) went on to conclude that these complex cells "must surely be considered color cells in the broadest sense. They clearly use color information to detect the presence of spatial patterns" (p.768). From the perspective of the present theory, these complex cells seem easiest to understand as part of the BC System. They do "detect the presence of spatial patterns," but this detection, in itself, does not imply that a visible color or brightness percept will be generated. Visible percepts are, I claim, generated within the FC System. Thus these complex cells should not "be considered color cells" in any psychophysically traditional sense.

Despite this pooling of luminance and color information, "individual cells tend to have similar spatial frequency preferences for color and luminance patterns" (p.757). In summary, the present theory suggests that the pooling of chromatic information by complex cells enables these cells to provide broad-band BC signals to subsequent processing stages, whereas the segregation of spatial frequency information provides a substrate for multiple scale binocular processing of these boundary signals.

24. Feature Contours and Diffusive Filling-In: Syncytial Coupling

As discussed in Section 5, the FC System first preprocesses visual signals in order to discount the illuminant. The output of these preprocessing stages takes the form of color edges (Red-Green, Blue-Yellow, White-Black). These color edge signals form the inputs to the processing stages at which featural filling-in occurs (Figure 1). I will describe a theory of this filling-in process in ever greater mechanistic detail as I proceed.

The existence of two distinct contour-sensitive processes is best demonstrated by the differences that exist between their processing rules. The rules of contrast obeyed by the FC System are different from those obeyed by the BC System.

Contrast: The receptive fields of FC System cells are not oriented, but they maintain their sensitivity to both the *amount* of contrast and the *direction* of contrast in an image at all processing stages, unlike the cells of the BC System. For example, to compute the relative brightness across a scenic boundary, it is obviously important to keep track of which side of the scenic boundary has a larger reflectance. Sensitivity to direction-of-contrast is also needed to determine which side of a red-green scenic boundary is red and which is green. Sensitivity to both amount-of-contrast and direction-of-contrast is needed to enable FC signals to "discount the illuminant."

The rules of spatial interaction that govern the FC System are also different from those that govern the BC System.

Diffusive Filling-In: Boundary Contours activate a boundary completion process that synthesizes the boundaries that define perceptual domains. Feature Contours activate a diffusive filling-in process that spreads featural qualities, such as brightness or color, across these perceptual domains. Figure 17 depicts the main properties of this filling-in process.

It is assumed that featural filling-in occurs within a syncytium of cell compartments. By a syncytium of cells, I mean a regular array of cells in such an intimate relationship to one another that contiguous cells can easily pass electrotonic signals between each other's compartment membranes. In the present instance, an FC input signal to a cell of the syncytium activates that cell. Due to the syncytial coupling of this cell with its neighbors, the activity can rapidly spread to neighboring cells, then to neighbors of the neighbors, and so on. Since the spreading occurs via an electrotonic diffusion of activity, it tends to average the activity that was triggered by the FC input signal across the cells that receive this spreading activity. The activity spreads across the syncytium with a space constant that depends upon the electrical properties of both the cell interiors and their membranes. The electrical properties of the cell membranes can be altered by BC signals in the following way.

A BC signal is assumed to decrease the diffusion constant of its target cell membranes

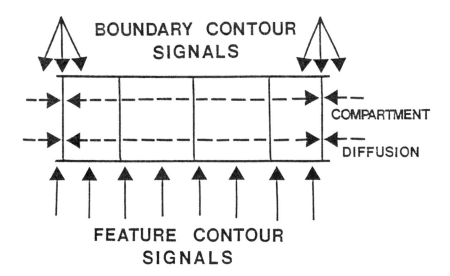

Figure 17. A monocular syncytium, or filling-in domain, within the FC System: Feature Contour signals activate cell compartments which permit rapid lateral diffusion of activity, or potential, across their compartment boundaries, except at those compartment boundaries which receive Boundary Contour signals from the BC System. Consequently, the FC signals are smoothed except at boundaries that are completed within the BC System stage.

within the cell syncytium. It does so by acting as an inhibitory gating signal that causes an increase in cell membrane resistance. At the same time that a BC signal creates a barrier to the filling-in process at its target cells, it also acts to inhibit the activity of these cells. Thus, due to the physical process whereby a Boundary Contour limits featural spreading across the syncytium, a BC input also acts as an FC input to its target syncytial cells.

Such a diffusive filling-in reaction is hypothesized to instantiate featural filling-in over the blind spot, over the faded images of stabilized retinal veins, and over the illuminants that are discounted by Feature Contour preprocessing.

Our mechanistic model of these qualitative concepts, which was introduced in Grossberg (1983a, 1983b), has been developed by Cohen and Grossberg (1984a) to quantitatively simulate on the computer such paradoxical brightness data as versions of the Craik-O'Brien-Cornsweet effect (Arend, Buehler, and Lockhead, 1971; Cornsweet, 1970; O'Brien, 1958) and its exceptions (Coren, 1983; Heggelund and Krekling, 1976; Todorović, 1983; van den Brink and Keemink, 1976), the Bergström demonstrations comparing the brightness profiles of smoothly modulated and step-like luminance profiles (Bergström, 1966, 1967a, 1967b), and the demonstrations of Hamada (1980) showing nonclassical differences between the perception of luminance decrements and increments. In addition, this filling-in model helps to physically explain the brightness and color phenomena for which the Land (1977) retinex theory was developed, and suggests explanations of many phenomena that the Land theory cannot explain, such as neon color spreading and "illusory" brightness and color phenomena as in Figures 3, 4, and 11 (Grossberg, 1984; Grossberg and Mingolla, 1985a).

Of course, no behaviorally derived mathematical model can impose a unique physiological and biochemical interpretation upon its formal operations. Our theory does, however, make strong functional demands upon possible physiological substrates of filling-in. In particular, a dense array of Boundary Contours must be able to parse a filling-in domain into very small, and sharply delineated, spatial compartments. This property suggests that the individual cellular units which comprise these compartments are also very small. On the other hand, widely separated Boundary Contours must also be able to define large filling-in compartments. This property suggests that contacts between the individual small cells are able to pass filling-in signals easily to their neighboring cells in the absence of boundary obstructions. In addition, the filling-in process is an averaging process which is attenuated at a determinate rate with distance. All of these constraints suggest the existence of small, diffusively coupled cells whose membranes can be gated shut by BC signals. Finer model details were derived through a process of quantitative computer simulation of psychophysical brightness data (Cohen and Grossberg, 1984a). Any physiological realization of such a featural filling-in process must therefore obey the highly constraining functional properties which are satisfied by the present instantiation.

25. Chemical and Electrotonic Signalling at Gap Junctions

Recent physiological and pharmacological data lend support to the particular physiological mechanisms that we have used to interpret our featural filling-in model. We suggest that the cortical filling-in process is functionally homologous to the types of interactions that have been reported in the horizontal cell layers of vertebrate retinas (Piccolino, Neyton, and Gershenfeld, 1984; Skrzypek, 1984; Usui, Mitarai, and Sakakibara, 1983). In our model and in these data, electrotonic interactions between contiguous cell membranes mediate the filling-in reaction. *In vivo*, the electrotonically interacting cells are often separated by gap junctions. Chemical transmitters alter the ability of the gap junctions to pass electrotonic signals by functionally decoupling the cells. The Piccolino *et al.* (1984) results on the turtle retina are most closely related to our filling-in model. These authors reported that "the axon terminals of the H1 horizontal cells of the turtle retina are electrically coupled by extensive gap junctions. Dopamine...induces a narrowing of the receptive field profile of the H1 horizontal cell axon terminals, increases the coupling resistance between them, and decreases the diffusion of the dye Lucifer Yellow in the network formed by the coupled axon terminals" (p.2477).

This description is consistent with the formal filling-in model that we derived from perceptual data about brightness perception. It also refines our model by suggesting that axo-axonal interactions, but not soma-soma interactions (Skrzypek, 1984), may mediate the electrotonic flow. We originally speculated that dendro-dendritic interactions may have played this role, but the formal structure of our model would not change if axo-axonal interactions were reported in the predicted cortical syncytium. If, in addition, the formal homolog between retinal and cortical syncytia extends to the pharmacological level, then the transmitter which mediates BC signals to the FC syncytia is expected to be a catecholamine. The existence and properties of such cortical filling-in mechanisms can be experimentally tested by using the analysis in Part II to suggest where in the cortex the formal FC System stages schematized in Figure 1 should be found.

26. Retinal versus Cortical Filling-In

If a homolog indeed exists between filling-in within the retina and filling-in within the cortex, then why is cortex necessary, especially given the recent report that goldfish can make many of the color discriminations required by the Land experiments (Ingle, 1985)? I suggest that this process of encephalization permits more elaborately processed BC signals to input topographically to the FC System. In particular, the multiple scale, binocular boundary interactions that support depth percepts (Part II) and the top-down "cognitive" boundary signals that help to complete form percepts of familiar objects (Figure 2) both require the additional stages of processing that cortex permits. The process of monocular discounting of illuminants does not require this degree of preprocessing.

Striate and prestriate cortical data concerning color interactions are far from complete, but are consistent with our theory as far as they go (Desimone, Schein, Moran, and Ungerleider, 1985; Livingstone and Hubel, 1984a, 1984b; Zeki, 1983a, 1983b). Before suggesting explanations and predictions concerning such data, I will use BC System and FC System properties to clarify five illustrative percepts. Then, in Part II, I will address the question of how binocular boundaries are synthesized, and how they regulate visible depth, brightness, color, and form percepts to build up a modelling framework in which further cortical data can be analysed.

27. Tissue Contrast

The tissue contrast experiment was already familiar to Helmholtz (1962). I suggest that its deceptive simplicity hides a deep property of cortical processing.

To perform the experiment, place a grey circular disk on top of a red background. Cover the whole figure with a white piece of tissue paper that lets the colors be seen but attenuates the contrast at the red-grey edge. Then the grey area looks green. Draw a circle with a black pen on the tissue to divide the circular area from the background. The grey area looks grey again.

I suggest the following explanation of this classical phenomenon. The tissue does not totally obliterate Boundary Contour activation at the red-grey interface. In fact, if no boundary could form, then the image would become a functional ganzfeld and no chromatic difference could be perceived. The tissue does, however, alter the processing within both the BC System and the FC System. It creates a good approximation to a sharp red-grey spatial transition. Thus the boundary formed at this interface within the BC System is very thin. In addition, double opponent color processing of Feature Contours within the FC System enables the red input to activate green channels at positions just interior to the circle. These green FC signals can fill-in the entire circle within their cell syncytium due to the absence of boundary obstructions within this syncytial domain.

Drawing the black circle on the tissue has coordinated effects on both Boundary Contour and Feature Contour processing. To understand these effects, recall from Figure 7 that a scenic line generates a complex spatially structured activation pattern, with a determinate thickness, across the receptive fields of the BC System. A black scenic line can therefore replace the thin boundary that forms in response to the tissue-covered image with a thicker boundary structure which possesses a determinate interior. A black scenic line can also dramatically alter the reaction of double opponent color cells within the FC System. Double opponent cells at the outer edge of the black line respond to a red-black contrast. Double opponent cells at the inner edge of the black line respond to an achromatic black-grey contrast, rather than the chromatic red-grey contrast of the tissue condition. Consequently, no complementary color induction occurs within the interior of the circle. In addition, the boundary structure induced by the black line separates the cell syncytium into three, rather than two, separate filling-in domains. The inner domain fills-in achromatic FC signals, rather than the green FC signals of the tissue condition.

28. Perception of Continuously Shaded Curved Surfaces: Boundary Webs

The next example consistently applies the idea that colors flow down electrotonic gradients unless barriers are generated within their cell syncytia by BC signals. Given this hypothesis, how can we perceive the smoothly shaded interiors of curved surfaces? Why do not the color signals interior to such a surface flow until the surface is perceived to be flat? In order to answer such questions, we are led to a concept of a surface percept that is just as nonclassical as our concept of a line or a curve.

To begin an explanation of surface perception, recall that oriented receptive fields within the BC System are local *contrast* detectors, not merely *edge* detectors (Section 10). If the luminance gradient of the shaded surface is sufficiently steep and oriented, then it can preferentially activate complex cells whose orientations are aligned along the luminance gradient. These activated complex cells can then engage the cooperative-competitive feedback loops of the CC Loop, just as if they had been activated by scenic edges. If the luminance gradient exists over a large spatial domain, then it can generate a form-sensitive mesh, coordinate system, or *boundary web*, of completed Boundary Contours. Most of the boundaries in a boundary web are illusory boundaries, as in Figures 5, 10, and 11. Such a boundary web can partition the region of the BC System which corresponds to the surface into a large number of compartments whose size and shape reflect the form of the inducing image or scene. Within the full 3-D theory, the BC System is divided into several parallel subsystems, such that each subsystem corresponds to a different spatial scale, or range of receptive field sizes (Figure 6). Each receptive field size is sensitive to a different range of continuous changes in image contrast across the surface image, and each spatial scale possesses its own CC Loop. Consequently, each spatial scale of the BC System can generate its own distinct boundary web. In Part II of the article, I discuss how such a multiple scale boundary structure can be the basis for a 3-dimensional form percept.

If a boundary web can indeed be generated by sufficiently steep luminance gradients, then why cannot we see these boundaries? At this juncture, I depend heavily upon the theory's radical claim that *all* boundaries are invisible until they can support different filled-in featural contrasts within the FC System (Section 22). This claim is radical because it reverses the dictates of lay intuition. Instead of taking for granted that all boundaries can be seen, we now must actively explain why some boundaries can ever become visible.

When a fine boundary web divides the FC System into small syncytial compartments, the filled-in contrasts between neighboring compartments are often similar. Thus the boundary web reveals itself through the very fact that it can support a percept of an approximately continuous brightness or color gradient which is much less uniform than would be expected were unobstructed filling-in to occur.

The hypothesis that a boundary web supports percepts of surface gradients immediately makes many facts intuitively clearer. A boundary web can bridge surface regions where highlights occur using its colinear boundary completion properties. It can resist distortion due to local changes in illuminant intensities using the hysteretic and coherent "structural" properties of the CC Loop. Although the boundary web may maintain its coherent structure as illuminant intensities vary, the FC signals which activate featural filling-in of boundary web compartments can remain sensitive to changes in scenic reflectances. Thus the problem of explaining the simultaneous apprehension of a stable shape and of the volatile surface appearances which are perceived as occurring on this shape is translated by the theory into an analysis of how a coherent 3-D segmentation, which is generated by a surface within the BC System, supports the filling-in percept of surface form-and-color-in-depth, which is generated within the FC System (see Part II).

Grossberg and Mingolla (1987b) further develop this theory of surface perception and describe computer simulations which show how boundary webs within multiple spatial scales can support a 3-D percept of a continuously shaded object. Todd and Akerstrom (1986) have used the theory to quantitatively explain their data concerning shape-from-texture; namely, how the grouping of textural elements can impart a depthful appearance to an otherwise ambiguous 2-D image of a surface. Such successful comparisons between theory and data highlight the ability of a spatially discrete boundary web to simultaneously encode both smooth shading and discrete boundary and textural elements into a single form-sensitive network of boundary compartments.

29. Sine Wave Gratings as Surface Images: Lateral Inhibition between Spatially Adjacent Spatial-Frequency Channels

The concept of the visual system as a spatial frequency filter has enjoyed such enormous success that it need not be reviewed again here. On the other hand, a suprathreshold image of a sine wave grating is also a 2-D image of a possible 3-D surface, and thus it must activate many of the same processes as more complex surface images. Many of the most useful psychophysical images, such as sine wave gratings, are not salient cues for raising issues about image segmentation and filling-in. However, once the generality of these issues becomes clear through an analysis of other types of perceptual data, these issues must also be raised for the case of sine wave gratings too. In particular, we suggest that a sine wave image, no less than any other surface image, generates a boundary web within the BC System that supports a percept of its nonuniform brightness distribution within the FC System. Thus at suprathreshold luminances, a number of perceptual effects may be expected to occur in response to sine wave gratings, as well as other psychophysical stimuli, that cannot be explained using a classical modulation transfer function approach. In more mechanistic terms, such data indicate the limits of otherwise successful psychophysical models based entirely on internal receptive field structure and nonlinear transduction of receptive field responses, such as the model of Wilson and Bergen (1979) and Wilson (1986).

A number of experiments on sine wave gratings point to the types of segmentation interactions which are posited within our theory. These experiments have analysed how perceived contrast and spatial frequency change as a function of physical contrast for different spatial frequencies. Quinn (1985) has reviewed and confirmed a number of studies which demonstrate a perceived contrast equivalence at low and intermediate spatial frequencies; yet at high spatial frequencies, perceived contrast surpasses that at an intermediate spatial frequency. Sagi and Hochstein (1984) have reported similar data. They explain their data in terms of "A new lateral inhibitory phenomenon ... between spatially neighboring channels that detect similar spatial frequencies ... At high contrasts, the effect is an enhancement of grating contrast near its border, whereas at near threshold contrasts, an opposite effect, edge contrast diminution, is seen ... This shift may also be responsible for the phenomenon of contrast constancy" (Sagi and Hochstein, 1985, p.315). In the contrast constancy phenomenon (Georgeson and Sullivan, 1975), the apparent contrast of intermediate frequencies rises gradually with stimulus contrast, whereas the apparent contrast of higher spatial frequencies rises more rapidly. In their model of these phenomena, Sagi and Hochstein (1985) posit the existence of a processing stage, subsequent to their model's receptive field stage, at which lateral inhibition occurs across perceptual locations but within each spatial frequency channel.

We link our theory to the Sagi and Hochstein (1985) model by noting that the first competitive stage (Figure 9) contains lateral inhibitory interactions subsequent to the receptive fields of the OC Filter. In the full 3-D theory that is developed in Part II, receptive fields of different sizes (Figure 6) exist in separate copies of the OC Filter. These distinct OC Filters interact with distinct copies of the CC Loop to generate a multiple-scale segmentation of the scenic image. Thus the lateral inhibitory stage described by Sagi and Hochstein (1985) is consistent with our model's earliest stage of CC Loop processing.

30. Spatial Localization and Hyperacuity

The model's posited interactions between receptive field and segmentation mechanisms are also supported by recent psychophysical data about spatial localization and hyperacuity. In Section 11, it was pointed out that a selective pressure towards hyperacuity exists in nervous systems which are capable of processing the long edges of thin lines. In order to prevent featural flow from occurring out of line ends and corners, spatially short-range competitive interactions (Section 14) are needed to generate end cuts at the positions corresponding to line ends. These end cuts exhibit properties of hyperacuity (Figure 8), because they are localized at the position of a line end with a much finer spatial resolution than could have been expected from the larger sizes of individual elongated receptive fields alone (Figure 7).

In a series of experiments studying spatial localization and hyperacuity, Badcock and Westheimer (1985a, 1985b) have presented psychophysical evidence which strongly support our conception of how oriented receptive fields average scenic luminances, pool their inputs to become independent of direction-of-contrast, and then excite like-oriented cells at the same position while inhibiting like-oriented cells at nearby positions (Figure 9). Badcock and Westheimer (1985a) used flanking lines to influence the perceived location of a test line. They varied the position of the flank with respect to the test line as well as the direction-of-contrast of flank and test lines with respect to the background. They found that two separate underlying mechanisms were needed to explain their data: a mechanism concerned with the luminance distribution within a restricted region, and a mechanism reflecting interactions between features. Within the central zone defined by the first mechanism, sensitivity to direction-of-contrast was found, as would be expected within an individual receptive field. On the other hand, a flank within the surround region always caused a repulsion which is independent of direction-of-contrast. Thus "when flanks are close to a target line, it is pulled towards the flank for a positive flank contrast but they push each other apart if the flank has a negative contrast. A flank in the surround region always causes repulsion under the conditions presented" (p.1263). To further test independence of direction-of-contrast due to the surround, they also found that "the effect of a bright flank on one side can be cancelled by a dark flank on the other. Within the central zone this procedure produces a substantial shift of the mean of a positive contrast target line towards the positive contrast flank" (p.1266).

Badcock and Westheimer (1985a) noted that the averaging of luminance within the central zone is sensitive to amount-of-contrast and direction-of-contrast in a way that is consistent with a Difference-of-Gaussian model. Such a computation also occurs at the elongated receptive fields, or input masks, of the BC System (Figure 6). Pairs of simple cells with like positions and orientations but opposite directions-of-contrast then add their rectified outputs at complex cells which are, as a consequence, insensitive to direction-of-contrast (Figure 9). Such cells provide the inputs to the first competitive stage. The oriented short-range lateral inhibition at the first competitive stage is thus insensitive to direction-of-contrast, has a broader spatial range than the central zone, and, being inhibitory, would always cause repulsion—all properties of the Badcock and Westheimer (1985a) data. In summary, all the main effects in these data mirror properties of the circuit in Figure 9.

In further tests of the existence and properties of these distinct mechanisms, Badcock and Westheimer (1985b, p.3) noted that "in the surround zone the amount of repulsion obtained was not influenced by vertical separation of the flank halves, even when they were several minutes higher (or lower) than the target line. In the central zone attraction was only obtained when the vertical separation was small enough to provide some overlap of lines in the horizontal direction." These data further support the idea that the central zone consists of individual receptive fields, whereas the surround zone is due to interactions across receptive fields which are first processed to be independent of direction-of-contrast, as in Figure 9. In our computer simulations of boundary completion and segmentation (Grossberg and Mingolla, 1985a, 1985b), it was assumed that the lateral inhibition within the first competitive stage is not restricted to any preferred orientation, as is also true of the surround repulsion effect in the Badcock and Westheimer (1985b) data.

Badcock and Westheimer (1985) also compared their data with results of earlier workers who were studying figural after-effects. They reviewed experiments in which "The amount of repulsion also increases as luminance contrast increases (Pollack, 1958) although contrast polarity is not an important factor (Ganz, 1964) as was found in the current study employing hyperacuity tasks" (p.1267). This result is consistent with the model property that the input to the first competitive level is sensitive to amount-of-contrast but not direction-of-contrast. They also noted that "both Köhler and Wallach (1944) and Ganz and Day (1965) have demonstrated that repulsion can be obtained using dichoptic presentation while the latter failed to find interocular transfer for the attraction effect. These results suggest that attraction seems to reflect properties of the monocular pathways while repulsion involves at least some binocular components" (p.1267). These properties are consistent with the analysis in Part II which suggests that the complex cells which generate inputs to the first competitive level are binocular cells, in fact disparity-sensitive cells, whereas the simple cell receptive fields which define the center zone are more monocular.

The integration of several types of experimental results using BC System interactions suggests that the competitive bandwidth that has been identified in the above hyperacuity and figural after-effect studies is the same bandwidth which controls many examples of neon color spreading (Redies and Spillmann, 1981), the end cuts found by von der Heydt, Peterhans, and Baumgartner (1984) at cells within cortical area 18, the initiation of preattentive textural grouping by colinear line ends (Beck, Prazdny, and Rosenfeld, 1983), and the lateral inhibition that occurs within spatial frequency channels (Sagi and Hochstein, 1985). The theory suggests that all these phenomena reflect the nervous system's compensation for the fact that "orientational certainty implies positional uncertainty at line ends and corners" (Section 11). In addition, it is suggested in Part II that these competitive interactions play an important role in the binocular suppression of double images and in binocular rivalry phenomena. Now that so many different types of data have been mechanistically related as manifestations of this design, a large number of new types of experiments can be carried out to discover finer details of these BC System mechanisms.

A number of other psychophysical experiments on hyperacuity implicate segmentation mechanisms in addition to the more familiar receptive field mechanisms. For example, in their studies of vernier acuity, Watt and Campbell (1985) have systematically varied the lengths of a pair of thin comparison bars as well as the sizes and location of gaps within these bars. They concluded that the effect of gap size "is consistent with the suggestion that the cue is the orientation of an imaginary line [read, emergent segmentation] joining the inner ends of the two bars" (p.36), that "line terminations [read, end cuts] segment a line prior to accurate shape analysis" (p.37), and in general that "experiments on Vernier acuity demonstrate a piecewise and structural analysis of the target" (p.38).

Once the relevance of BC System mechanisms to an analysis of hyperacuity data is acknowledged, it also becomes clear that the psychophysical literature has not fully analysed the cues subjects can use to make their discriminations. As Figure 2 indicates, an emergent segmentation within the BC System may sometimes be used to recognize a discrimination within the Object Recognition System even if it does not support a large visible contrast difference. Psychophysical measurements of visible contrast changes probe primarily the outcome of FC System processes and their projections to the Object Recognition System. Although such visible contrast changes often covary with contrast-sensitive changes in the BC System, sometimes they do not, as when an "imaginary line" influences vernier acuity. To deal with such properties of psychophysical data, theoretical analyses will need to distinguish between the FC System processes which directly control visible contrast differences via the progressive elaboration and filling-in of FC signals, and the BC System processes which indirectly control visible contrast differences via the emergent segmentations which select the FC signals and filling-in domains that will influence conscious perception.

Another type of psychophysical data which is clarified by BC System and FC System properties is summarized in the next section.

31. Border Distinctness, Blue Cones, and Neon Color Spreading

Boynton, Eskew, and Olson (1985) have recently performed psychophysical experiments to further test the role of blue cones in the "melting" of borders that was previously reported by Tansley and Boynton (1976, 1978). Their studies are consistent with the hypothesis that wavelength-sensitive opponent inputs from the lateral geniculate nuclei to the BC System are combined together to generate a chromatically broad-band boundary signal (Section 23), whereas opponent inputs from the lateral geniculate nuclei to the FC System are kept separate and further articulated to generate double-opponent color percepts (Part II).

In support of this general conception, Boynton, Eskew, and Olson (1985) reported that, in their experiments, "changes in contour are much more obvious than changes in color, and that in the main experiment we were attending not to differences in color but, as intended, to variations in the strength of contour" (p.1350). Moreover "blue cones may form contours directly and ... in addition they form contours indirectly by influencing the effects of red-cone excitation" (p.1351). In summary, these studies support the hypothesis that opponent information from the lateral geniculate nuclei is used in parallel in two different ways: to generate color and brightness signals and to generate broad-band boundary signals.

Our model of how broad-band boundary signals are synthesized is supported by the model of Tansley, Robertson, and Maughan (1983) which posits that luminance and chromatic signals converge upon common target cells to generate "perception of edges" or "edge distinctness." In this model, only L and M cones are assumed to play a role. The luminance channel processes an $(L + M)$ input and the chromatic channel processes an $(L - M)$ input. The magnitude of the edge signal is assumed to increase with the $\log_{10}$ of the difference between the $(L + M)$ signals or the $(L - M)$ signals arising from either side of the border in the scenic image. The data of Boynton, Eskew, and Olson (1985) suggest that blue cones also input to this boundary detection system.

Tansley, Robertson, and Maughan (1983, p.452) also went on to suggest, however, that "the results of McCollough-type experiments should be predictable" from their model. I believe that this suggestion confuses BC System properties with FC System properties. It does not clearly distinguish between boundary formation *per se* within the BC System and its role in supporting visible contrast differences within the FC System. An explanation of many McCollough effect properties is developed in Part II, and makes major use of differences between BC System and FC System processes.

Ejima, Redies, Takahashi, and Akita (1984) have reported psychophysical data which support our analysis of how neon color spreading (Section 7) is related to border distinctness. These authors used variants of the stimulus pattern in Figure 4a in which the wavelengths of the Ehrenstein pattern and the crosses were independently varied from 460 to 680nm in 20nm steps. Observers were asked to judge the strength of the illusory spread of neon color around the center crosses for each wavelength combination. The results led the authors to draw an explicit connection with the Tansley and Boynton (1978) study on border distinctness. They concluded that the strength of the neon color effect is correlated with the spectral purity difference $P_{crosses} - P_{E\ pattern}$. This quantity provides a good first approximation to our theoretical explanation of how well the Boundary Contour formed by the Ehrenstein pattern can inhibit the contiguous Boundary Contour formed by the cross, thereby allowing FC signals to flow across the corresponding region within the corresponding syncytium of the FC System (Grossberg and Mingolla, 1985a).

Various other data properties reported by Ejima *et al.* (1984) are consistent with the model. Thus the strength of the neon effect is "independent of the illuminance level of the crosses when the illuminance ratio to the Ehrenstein pattern is maintained" (p.1726). This property supports the hypothesis that inhibition at the first competitive stage is of shunting, or divisive, type (Grossberg and Mingolla, 1985a). When achromatic line patterns are used, an illuminance ratio of the Ehrenstein pattern to the crosses that is greater than 1 is needed to generate the effect (van Tuijl and de Weert, 1979). This fact is consistent with the properties that (1) inhibition of the cross boundary by the Ehrenstein pattern helps to initiate the effect, and (2) the inhibition is sensitive to amount-of-contrast of the inducing scenic figures to their respective grounds. When chromatic line patterns are used, "a just noticeable effect requires luminance ratios of less than 1 ... for wavelengths of the crosses eliciting weaker effects ... the illuminance ratios required for a just noticeable effect are higher than for wavelengths of the crosses eliciting stronger effects" (p.1725). This fact supports the concept that achromatic and chromatic signals are pooled within the BC System to generate a broad-band boundary signal.

Further studies aimed at consciously separating the influence of lateral geniculate opponent signals on parallel color and boundary systems are needed and can profitably employ the Boynton paradigm. In particular, isoluminance in a scenic image does not necessarily imply zero contrast detection by the complex cells which input to the CC Loop. Indeed, if no receptive fields could generate inputs to the CC Loop, then the CC Loop would detect a functional ganzfeld, and could not support any pre-attentive form or color percept whatsoever. It would therefore be most useful to have parametric physiological data concerning the manner in which complex cells respond to isoluminant scenes that are constructed from different chromatic scenic combinations. Such data could form a secure basis for deriving conclusions about the distinctness of boundaries and of perceptual groupings, uncontaminated by the perceived color or brightness differences which these boundaries support within the FC System.

32. Motion Segmentation

Although the OC Filter and CC Loop circuits were developed to explain percepts of static images, they also respond well to a variety of moving images. This observation does not challenge the well-documented role of cortical systems, such as MT, which are specialized for the processing of motion (Albright, Desimone, and Gross, 1984; Maunsell and Van Essen, 1983; Newsome, Gizzi, and Movshon, 1983; Zeki, 1974a, 1974b). It merely notes that a single cortical system may be used to represent aspects of 3-D form in response to both static and moving images. In addition, although the cortical systems which process form and motion information may be anatomically distinct, model mechanisms which have been proposed to derive form-from-motion bear striking resemblances to CC Loop mechanisms. Thus the CC Loop may be a specialized version of a more general cortical design.

The above assertions are illustrated by considering how the CC Loop responds to differentially moving random dots (Braddick, 1974; Julesz, 1971; Lappin and Bell, 1976; Nakayama, 1985; Nakayama, Silverman, MacLeod, and Mulligan, 1985; Nakayama and Tyler, 1981). As illustrated by Figure 6, an oriented receptive field of the CC Loop responds best if a dot density difference that is parallel to the preferred receptive field orientation moves in a direction perpendicular to the preferred receptive field orientation (Nakayama, Silverman, MacLeod, and Mulligan, 1985). Where local random dot motions are superimposed upon such statistical drifts, the system could fail to respond well were it not for CC Loop mechanisms. In particular, orientational competition within the second competitive stage (Figure 9) amplifies the preferred combination of dot density orientation and direction of movement while suppressing less preferred combinations. Then the co-operation can begin to group together these preferred combinations of dots into emergent segmentations of the image.

Both competitive stages of the CC Loop are formally analogous to model mechanisms that Nakayama and Loomis (1974) have proposed for the extraction of a figural boundary moving relative to a ground, and could be used to generate the properties of cells that Frost and Nakayama (1983) have discovered within the intermediate and deeper layers of the pigeon optic tectum. Figure 18 describes two variants of this model. In both variants, cells which respond to the same direction-of-motion interact via an on-center off-surround network. If the preferred direction-of-motion of a cell is perpendicular to its preferred orientation, then the model is consistent with the existence of a short-range inhibitory interaction among like-oriented cells, as in the first competitive stage depicted in Figures 9 and 12.

If cells with the same preferred orientation, but opposite directions-of-motion, feed the on-cells and off-cells, respectively, of a dipole field (Figure 12), then opposite directions-of-motion are also inhibitory, as in the model of Figure 18b. Thus a first competitive stage that inputs to a second competitive stage which is organized as a gated dipole field can realize the spatial interactions required by the Nakayama and Loomis model. In addition to the interactions suggested by Nakayama and Loomis, such a dipole field contains interactions between orientations at each position, with mutually perpendicular orientations competing and sufficiently similar orientations cooperating to synthesize a best net orientation (Grossberg and Mingolla, 1987b). Using these orientational interactions, non-optimal random motions can be suppressed and a best local direction-of-motion chosen, thereby facilitating the detection of the figural boundary. In summary, the same general types of short-range competition and dipole field mechanisms which this article has linked to a wide range of data about static form perception may also play an important role in the neural circuits which process form-from-motion.

On the other hand, differences in the preprocessing of inputs to these form-extracting mechanisms can also be cited, and thereby clarify the need for separate anatomical circuits to carry out such preprocessing. For example, unlike the CC Loop depicted in Figure 12, the competitive stages of a motion-detecting dipole field do not receive inputs from an OC Filter whose receptive fields are independent of direction-of-contrast. Rather, the inputs to such a dipole field are derived from directionally-sensitive cells (Barlow and Levick, 1965; Nakayama, 1985; Reichardt, 1961; van Santen and Sperling, 1984, 1985). Thus BC System cells may input to parallel circuits for extracting different aspects of contrast-sensitive form information before these parallel circuits combine their outputs into a single completed boundary segmentation for further processing by the FC System into a unitary percept of form-and-color-in-depth. Illusory contours generated by inducers defined solely by spatiotemporal correlation (Prazdny, 1986) can be explained by such a network if its dipole field interacts with oriented dipole cells such as those which exist within the CC Loop. Such a mechanism may also contribute to figure-ground segregation that is induced by motion contrast between object and background (Regan and Beverley, 1984).

33. Concluding Remarks

This article illustrates how the OC Filter and the CC Loop of the BC System can be used to analyse a wide variety of perceptual and neural data about monocular form perception. This unification permits these model circuits to be experimentally tested in multiple ways and thereby refined and modified by data focused upon this task. Although such modifications are to be expected, it would seem that the uncertainty principles which are resolved by these mechanisms will be part of the foundation of any future theory. Indeed, the very possibility of analysing discrete boundaries and textures as well as continuous surfaces using a single computational theory suggests that these uncertainty principles have probed a basic level of brain design.

One of the main themes of the article is that psychophysical paradigms often activate mechanisms which control percepts of emergent form. The hypothesis that all boundaries are invisible within the BC System, yet can nonetheless strongly influence the recognition of form, suggests that the analysis of psychophysical data in terms only of the contrast sensitivity and nonlinear transduction of receptive field properties is insufficient in general.

Part II of the article builds upon this foundation by showing that these mechanisms of monocular form perception provide a computational foundation upon which a neural theory of 3-D form perception, including by not restricted to binocular percepts, can be built.

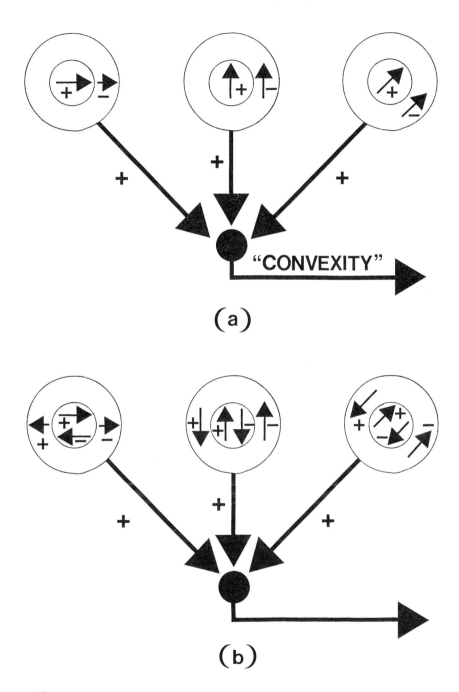

Figure 18. Variants of the Nakayama and Loomis (1974) model of "convexity" detecting units for extracting edges of 3-D objects for an observer translated through a rigid environment: (a) Units with like-preferred direction inhibit each other via an on-center off-surround interaction. All orientations at a given position summate their outputs to compute a "convexity" value which measures relative motion near figure-ground boundaries. (b) The model of (a) is augmented between opponent interactions between opposing directions of motion at each position.

REFERENCES

Albright, T.D., Desimone, R., and Gross, C.G., Columnar organization of directionally sensitive cells in visual area MT of the macaque. *Journal of Neurophysiology*, 1984, **51**, 16–31.

Arend, L.E., Buehler, J.N., and Lockhead, G.R., Difference information in brightness perception. *Perception and Psychophysics*, 1971, **9**, 367–370.

Badcock, D.R. and Westheimer, G., Spatial location and hyperacuity: The centre/surround localization contribution function has two substrates. *Vision Research*, 1985, **25**, 1259–1267 (a).

Badcock, D.R. and Westheimer, G., Spatial location and hyperacuity: Flank position within the centre and surround zones. *Spatial Vision*, 1985, **1**, 3–11 (b).

Barlow, H.B. and Levick, W.R., The mechanism of directionally selective units in rabbit's retina. *Journal of Physiology*, 1965, **178**, 447–504.

Beck, J., Prazdny, K., and Rosenfeld, A., A theory of textural segmentation. In J. Beck, B. Hope, and A. Rosenfeld (Eds.), **Human and machine vision**. New York: Academic Press, 1983.

Beck, J. and Schwartz, T., Vernier acuity with dot test objects. *Vision Research*, 1979, **19**, 313–319.

Bergström, S.S., A paradox in the perception of luminance gradients, I. *Scandinavian Journal of Psychology*, 1966, **7**, 209–224.

Bergström, S.S., A paradox in the perception of luminance gradients, II. *Scandinavian Journal of Psychology*, 1967, **8**, 25–32 (a).

Bergström, S.S., A paradox in the perception of luminance gradients, III. *Scandinavian Journal of Psychology*, 1967, **8**, 33–37 (b).

Biederman, I., Personal communication, 1985.

Boynton, R.M., Eskew, R.T. Jr., and Olson, C.X., Research Note: Blue cones contribute to border distinctness. *Vision Research*, 1985, **25**, 1349–1352.

Braddick, O.J., A short range process in apparent motion. *Vision Research*, 1974, **14**, 519–527.

Breitmeyer, B.G., Disinhibition in metacontrast masking of vernier acuity targets: Sustained channels inhibit transient channels. *Vision Research*, 1978, **18**, 1401–1405.

Breitmeyer, B.G., Unmasking visual masking: A look at the "why" behind the veil of the "how". *Psychological Review*, 1980, **87**, 52–69.

Carpenter, G.A. and Grossberg, S., Neural dynamics of category learning and recognition: Attention, memory consolidation, and amnesia. In J. Davis, R. Newburgh, and E. Wegman (Eds.), **Brain structure, learning, and memory**. AAAS Symposium Series, in press, 1987 (a).

Carpenter, G.A. and Grossberg, S., A massively parallel architecture for a self-organizing neural pattern recognition machine. *Computer Graphics and Image Processing*, 1987, **37**, 54–115 (b).

Cavanagh, P., Paper delivered at the Third Workshop on Human and Machine Vision, Boston, 1985.

Cohen, M.A. and Grossberg, S., Neural dynamics of brightness perception: Features, boundaries, diffusion, and resonance. *Perception and Psychophysics*, 1984, **36**, 428–456 (a).

Cohen, M.A. and Grossberg, S., Some global properties of binocular resonances: Disparity matching, filling-in, and figure-ground synthesis. In P. Dodwell and T. Caelli (Eds.), **Figural synthesis**. Hillsdale, NJ: Erlbaum, 1984 (b).

Coren, S., When "filling-in" fails. *Behavioral and Brain Sciences*, 1983, **6**, 661–662.

Cornsweet, T.N., **Visual perception**. New York: Academic Press, 1970.

Day, R.H., Neon color spreading, partially delineated borders, and the formation of illusory contours. *Perception and Psychophysics*, 1983, **34**, 488–490.

Desimone, R., Schein, S.J., Moran, J., and Ungerleider, L.G., Contour, color, and shape analysis beyond the striate cortex. *Vision Research*, 1985, **25**, 441–452.

DeValois, R.L., Albrecht, D.G., and Thorell, L.G., Spatial frequency selectivity of cells in macaque visual cortex. *Vision Research*, 1982, **22**, 545–559.

Ejima, Y., Redies, C., Takahashi, S. and Akita, M., The neon color effect in the Ehrenstein pattern: Dependence on wavelength and illuminance. *Vision Research*, 1984, **24**, 1719–1726.

Ellias, S.A. and Grossberg, S., Pattern formation, contrast control, and oscillations in the short term memory of shunting on-center off-surround networks. *Biological Cybernetics*, 1975, **20**, 69–98.

Frost, B.J. and Nakayama, K., Single visual neurons code opposing motion independent of direction. *Science*, 1983, **220**, 744–745.

Ganz, L., Lateral inhibition and the location of visual contours: An analysis of figural after-effects. *Vision Research*, 1964, **4**, 465–481.

Ganz, L. and Day, R.H., An analysis of the satiation-fatigue mechanism in figural after-effects. *American Journal of Psychology*, 1965, **78**, 345–361.

Garner, W.R., **The processing of information and structure**. Hillsdale, NJ: Erlbaum, 1974.

Gellatly, A.R.H., Perception of an illusory triangle with masked inducing figure. *Perception*, 1980, **9**, 599–602.

Georgeson, M.A. and Sullivan, G.D., Contrast constancy: Deblurring in human vision by spatial frequency channels. *Journal of Physiology (London)*, 1975, **252**, 627–656.

Gerrits, H.J.M., de Haan, B., and Vendrick, A.J.H., Experiments with retinal stablized images: Relations between the observations and neural data. *Vision Research*, 1966, **6**, 427–440.

Gerrits, H.J.M. and Timmerman, J.G.M.E.N., The filling-in process in patients with retinal scotomata. *Vision Research*, 1969, **9**, 439–442.

Gerrits, H.J.M. and Vendrick, A.J.H., Simultaneous contrast, filling-in process and information processing in man's visual system. *Experimental Brain Research*, 1970, **11**, 411–430.

Gouras, P. and Krüger, J., Responses of cells in foveal visual cortex of the monkey to pure color contrast. *Journal of Neurophysiology*, 1979, **42**, 850–860.

Grossberg, S., Contour enhancement, short-term memory, and constancies in reverberating neural networks. *Studies in Applied Mathematics*, 1973, **52**, 217–257.

Grossberg, S., Adaptive pattern classification and universal recoding, II: Feedback, expectation, olfaction, and illusions. *Biological Cybernetics*, 1976, **23**, 187–202.

Grossberg, S., How does a brain build a cognitive code? *Psychological Review*, 1980, **87**, 1–51.

Grossberg, S., Adaptive resonance in development, perception, and cognition. In S. Grossberg (Ed.), **Mathematical psychology and psychophysiology**. Providence, RI: American Mathematical Society, 1981.

Grossberg, S., The quantized geometry of visual space: The coherent computation of depth, form, and lightness. *Behavioral and Brain Sciences*, 1983, **6**, 625–692 (a).

Grossberg, S., Neural substrates of binocular form perception: Filtering, matching, diffusion, and resonance. In E. Basar, H. Flohr, H. Haken, and A.J. Mandell (Eds.), **Synergetics of the brain**. New York: Springer-Verlag, 1983 (b).

Grossberg, S., Outline of a theory of brightness, color, and form perception. In E. Degreef and J. van Buggenhaut (Eds.), **Trends in mathematical psychology**. Amsterdam: North-Holland, 1984.

Grossberg, S., **The adaptive brain, II: Vision, speech, language, and motor control**. Amsterdam: North-Holland, 1987.

Grossberg, S. and Levine, D.S., Some developmental and attentional biases in the contrast enhancement and short term memory of recurrent neural networks. *Journal of Theoretical Biology*, 1975, **53**, 341–380.

Grossberg, S. and Mingolla, E., Neural dynamics of form perception: Boundary completion, illusory figures, and neon color spreading. *Psychological Review*, 1985, **92**, 173–211 (a).

Grossberg, S. and Mingolla, E., Neural dynamics of perceptual grouping: Textures, boundaries, and emergent segmentations. *Perception and Psychophysics*, 1985, **38**, 141–171 (b).

Grossberg, S. and Mingolla, E., Computer simulation of neural networks for perceptual psychology. *Behavior Research: Methods, Instruments, and Computers*, 1986, **18**, 601–607.

Grossberg, S. and Mingolla, E., The role of illusory contours in visual segmentation. In S. Petry and G. Meyer (Eds.), **The perception of illusory contours**. New York: Springer-Verlag, 1987, 116–125 (a).

Grossberg, S. and Mingolla, E., Neural dynamics of surface perception: Boundary webs, illuminants, and shape-from-shading. *Computer Graphics and Image Processing*, 1987, **37**, 116–165 (b).

Grossberg, S. and Stone, G., Neural dynamics of word recognition and recall: Attentional priming, learning, and resonance. *Psychological Review*, 1986, **93**, 46–74.

Hamada, J., Antagonistic and non-antagonistic processes in the lightness perception. **Proceedings of the XXII international conference of psychology**, Leipzig, July 6–12, 1980.

Heggelund, P., Receptive field organisation of complex cells in cat striate cortex. *Experimental Brain Research*, 1981, **42**, 99–107.

Heggelund, P. and Krekling, S., Edge dependent lightness distributions at different adaptation levels. *Vision Research*, 1976, **16**, 493–496.

Helmholtz, H.L.F. von, **Treatise on physiological optics**, J.P.C. Southall (translator). New York: Dover Press, 1962.

Hendrickson, A.E., Hunt, S.P., and Wu, J.-Y., Immunocytochemical localization of glutamic acid decarboxylase in monkey striate cortex. *Nature*, 1981, **292**, 605–607.

Hering, E., **Outlines of a theory of the light sense**. Cambridge, MA: Harvard University Press, 1964.

Horton, J.C. and Hubel, D.H., Regular patchy distribution of cytochrome oxidase staining in primary visual cortex of macaque monkey. *Nature*, 1981, **292**, 762–764.

Houck, M.R. and Hoffman, J.E., Conjunction of color and form without attention: Evidence from an orientation-contingent color aftereffect. *Journal of Experimental Psychology: Human Perception and Performance*, 1986, **12**, 186–199.

Hubel, D.H. and Wiesel, T.N., Receptive fields, binocular interaction and functional architecture in the cat's visual cortex. *Journal of Physiology*, 1962, **160**, 106–154.

Hubel, D.H. and Wiesel, T.N., Receptive fields and functional architectures of monkey striate cortex. *Journal of Physiology*, 1968, **195**, 215–243.

Hubel, D.H. and Wiesel, T.N., Functional architecture of macaque monkey visual cortex. *Proceedings of the Royal Society of London (B)*, 1977, **198**, 1–59.

Ingle, D.J., The goldfish as a retinex animal. *Science*, 1985, **227**, 651–654.

Julesz, B., **Foundations of cyclopean perception**. Chicago: University of Chicago Press, 1971.

Julesz, B., Paper delivered at the Third Workshop on Human and Machine Vision, Boston, 1985.

Kanizsa, G., Contours without gradients or cognitive contours? *Italian Journal of Psychology*, 1974, **1**, 93–113.

Kaufman, L., **Sight and mind: An introduction to visual perception**. New York: Oxford University Press, 1974.

Kawabata, N., Perception at the blind spot and similarity grouping. *Perception and Psychophysics*, 1984, **36**, 151–158.

Kennedy, J.M., Illusory contours and the ends of lines. *Perception*, 1978, **7**, 605–607.

Kennedy, J.M., Subjective contours, contrast, and assimilation. In C.F. Nodine and D.F. Fisher (Eds.), **Perception and pictorial representation**. New York: Praeger, 1979.

Kennedy, J.M., Illusory brightness and the ends of petals: Change in brightness without aid of stratification or assimilation effects. *Perception*, 1981, **10**, 583–585.

Köhler, W. and Wallach, H., Figural after-effects: An investigation of visual processes. *Proceedings of the American Philosophical Society*, 1944, **88**, 269–357.

Krauskopf, J., Effect of retinal image stabilization on the appearance of heterochromatic targets. *Journal of the Optical Society of America*, 1963, **53**, 741–744.

Land, E.H., The retinex theory of color vision. *Scientific American*, 1977, **237**, 108–128.

Land, E.H., Color vision and the natural image, III: Recent advances in Retinex theory and some implications for cortical computations. *Proceedings of the National Academy of Sciences USA*, 1983, **80**, 5163–5169.

Lappin, J.S. and Bell, H.H., The detection of coherence in moving random-dot patterns. *Vision Research*, 1976, **16**, 161–168.

Livingstone, M.S. and Hubel, D.H., Thalamic inputs to cytochrome oxidase-rich regions in monkey visual cortex. *Proceedings of the National Academy of Sciences*, 1982, **79**, 6098–6101.

Livingstone, M.S. and Hubel, D.H., Anatomy and physiology of a color system in the primate visual cortex. *Journal of Neuroscience*, 1984, **4**, 309–356 (a).

Livingstone, M.S. and Hubel, D.H., Specificity of intrinsic connections in primate primary cortex. *Journal of Neuroscience*, 1984, **4**, 2830–2835 (b).

Ludvigh, E., Direction sense of the eye. *American Journal of Ophthalmology*, 1953, **36**, 139–143.

Maunsell, J.H.R. and Van Essen, D.C., Response properties of single units in middle temporal visual area of the macaque. *Journal of Neurophysiology*, 1983, **49**, 1127–1147.

Nakayama, K., Biological image motion processing: A review. *Vision Research*, 1985, **25**, 625–660.

Nakayama, K. and Loomis, J.M., Optical velocity patterns, velocity-sensitive neurons, and space perception: A hypothesis. *Perception*, 1974, **3**, 63–80.

Nakayama, K., Silverman, G.H., MacLeod, D.I.A., and Mulligan, J., Sensitivity to shearing and compressive motion in random dots. *Perception*, 1985, **14**, 225–238.

Nakayama, K. and Tyler, C.W., Psychophysical isolation of movement sensitivity by removal of familiar position cues. *Vision Research*, 1981, **21**, 427–433.

Newsome, W.T., Gizzi, M.S., and Movshon, J.A., Spatial and temporal properties of neurons in macaque MT. *Investigative Ophthalmology and Visual Science*, 1983, **24**, 106.

O'Brien, V., Contour perception, illusion, and reality. *Journal of the Optical Society of America*, 1958, **48**, 112–119.

Parks, T.E., Subjective figures: Some unusual concomitant brightness effects. *Perception*, 1980, **9**, 239–241.

Parks, T.E. and Marks, W., Sharp-edged vs. diffuse illusory circles: The effects of varying luminance. *Perception and Psychophysics*, 1983, **33**, 172–176.

Petry, S., Harbeck, A., Conway, J., and Levey, J., Stimulus determinants of brightness and distinctness of subjective contours. *Perception and Psychophysics*, 1983, **34**, 169–174.

Piccolino, M., Neyton, J., and Gerschenfeld, H.M., Decrease of gap junction permeability induced by dopamine and cyclic adenosine 3':5'-monophosphate in horizontal cells of turtle retina. *Journal of Neuroscience*, 1984, **4**, 2477–2488.

Pollack, R.H., Figural after-effects: Quantitative studies of displacement. *Aust. Journal of Psychology*, 1958, **10**, 269–277.

Pomerantz, J.R., Perceptual organization in information processing. In M. Kubovy and J.R. Pomerantz (Eds.), **Perceptual organization**. Hillsdale, NJ: Erlbaum, 1981.

Pomerantz, J.R., Global and local precedence: Selective attention in form and motion perception. *Journal of Experimental Psychology: General*, 1983, **112**, 516–540.

Pomerantz, J.R. and Schwaitzberg, S.D., Grouping by proximity: Selective attention measures. *Perception and Psychophysics*, 1975, **18**, 355–361.

Prazdny, K., Illusory contours from inducers defined solely by spatiotemporal correlation. *Perception and Psychophysics*, 1986, **39**, 175–178.

Pritchard, R.M., Stabilized images on the retina. *Scientific American*, 1961, **204**, 72–78.

Pritchard, R.M., Heron, W., and Hebb, D.O., Visual perception approached by the method of stabilized images. *Canadian Journal of Psychology*, 1960, **14**, 67–77.

Quinn, P.C., Suprathreshold contrast perception as a function of spatial frequency. *Perception and Psychophysics*, 1985, **38**, 408–414.

Regan, D. and Beverley, K.I., Figure-ground segregation by motion contrast and by luminance contrast. *Journal of the Optical Society of America*, 1984, 1, 433–442.

Redies, C. and Spillmann, L., The neon color effect in the Ehrenstein illusion. *Perception*, 1981, **10**, 667–681.

Redies, C., Spillmann, L., and Kunz, K., Colored neon flanks and line gap enhancement. *Vision Research*, 1984, **24**, 1301–1309.

Reichardt, W., Autocorrelation, a principle for the evaluation of sensory information by the central nervous system. In W.A. Rosenblith (Ed.), **Sensory communication**. New York: Wiley, 1961.

Reynolds, R.I., Perception of an illusory contour as a function of processing time. *Perception*, 1981, **10**, 107–115.

Riggs, L.A., Ratliff, F., Cornsweet, J.C., and Cornsweet, T.N., The disappearance of steadily fixated visual test objects. *Journal of the Optical Society of America*, 1953, **43**, 495–501.

Sagi, D. and Hochstein, S., The contrast dependence of spatial frequency channel interactions. *Vision Research*, 1984, **24**, 1357–1365.

Sagi, D. and Hochstein, S., Lateral inhibition between spatially adjacent spatial-frequency channels? *Perception and Psychophysics*, 1985, **37**, 315–322.

Schiller, P.H., Finlay, B.L., and Volman, S.F., Quantitative studies of single-cell properties in monkey striate cortex, I: Spatiotemporal organization of receptive fields. *Journal of Neurophysiology*, 1976, **39**, 1288–1319.

Skrzypek, J., Electrical coupling between horizontal cell bodies in the tiger salamander retina. *Vision Research*, 1984, **24**, 701–711.

Spitzer, H. and Hochstein, S., A complex-cell receptive field model. *Journal of Neurophysiology*, 1985, **53**, 1266–1286.

Stefurak, D.L. and Boynton, R.M., Independence of memory for categorically different colors and shapes. *Perception and Psychophysics*, 1986, **39**, 164–174.

Tanaka, M., Lee, B.B., and Creutzfeldt, O.D., Spectral tuning and contour representation in area 17 of the awake monkey. In J.D. Mollon and L.T. Sharpe (Eds.), **Colour vision**. New York: Academic Press, 1983.

Tansley, B.W. and Boynton, R.M., A line, not a space, represents visual distinctness of borders formed by different colors. *Science*, 1976, **191**, 954–957.

Tansley, B.W. and Boynton, R.M., Chromatic border perception: The role of the red- and green-sensitivity cones. *Vision Research*, 1978, **18**, 683–697.

Tansley, B.W., Robertson, A.W., and Maughan, K.E., Chromatic and achromatic border perception: A two-cone model accounts for suprathreshold border distinctness judgments and cortical pattern-evoked response amplitudes to the same stimuli. In J.D. Mollon and L.T. Sharpe (Eds.), **Colour vision**. New York: Academic Press, 1983.

Thorell, L.G., DeValois, R.L., and Albrecht, D.G., Spatial mapping of monkey V1 cells with pure color and luminance stimuli. *Vision Research*, 1984, **24**, 751–769.

Todd, J.T. and Akerstrom, R., The perception of 3-D form from patterns of optical texture. In preparation, 1986.

Todorović, D., Brightness perception and the Craik-O'Brien-Cornsweet effect. Unpublished M.A. Thesis. Storrs: University of Connecticut, 1983.

Usui, S., Mitarai, G., and Sakakibara, M., Discrete nonlinear reduction model for horizontal cell response in the carp retina. *Vision Research*, 1983, **23**, 413–420.

van den Brink, G. and Keemink, C.J., Luminance gradients and edge effects. *Vision Research*, 1976, **16**, 155–159.

van Santen, J.P.H. and Sperling, G., Temporal covariance model of human motion perception. *Journal of the Optical Society of America*, 1984, **1**, 451–473.

van Santen, J.P.H. and Sperling, G., Elaborated Reichardt detectors. *Journal of the Optical Society of America*, 1985, **2**, 300–321.

van Tuijl, H.F.J.M., A new visual illusion: Neonlike color spreading and complementary color induction between subjective contours. *Acta Psychologica*, 1975, **39**, 441–445.

van Tuijl, H.F.J.M. and de Weert, C.M.M., Sensory conditions for the occurrence of the neon spreading illusion. *Perception*, 1979, **8**, 211–215.

van Tuijl, H.F.J.M. and Leeuwenberg, E.L.J., Neon color spreading and structural information measures. *Perception and Psychophysics*, 1979, **25**, 269–284.

von der Heydt, R., Peterhans, E., and Baumgartner, G., Illusory contours and cortical neuron responses. *Science*, 1984, **224**, 1260–1262.

Watt, R.J. and Campbell, F.W., Vernier acuity: Interactions between length effects and gaps when orientation cues are eliminated. *Spatial Vision*, 1985, **1**, 31–38.

Westheimer, G., Visual hyperacuity. *Progress in Sensory Physiology*, 1981, **1**, 1–30.

Westheimer, G. and McKee, S.P., Integration regions for visual hyperacuity. *Vision Research*, 1977, **17**, 89–93.

Wilson, H.R., Responses of spatial mechanisms can explain hyperacuity. *Vision Research*, 1986, **26**, 453–469.

Wilson, H.R. and Bergen, J.R., A four mechanism model for threshold spatial vision. *Vision Research*, 1979, **19**, 19–32.

Yarbus, A.L., **Eye movements and vision**. New York: Plenum Press, 1967.

Zeki, S., Functional organization of a visual area in the posterior bank of the superior temporal sulcus of the rhesus monkey. *Journal of Physiology (London)*, 1974, **236**, 549–573 (a).

Zeki, S., Cells responding to changing image size and disparity in the cortex of the rhesus monkey. *Journal of Physiology (London)*, 1974, **242**, 827–841 (b).

Zeki, S., Colour coding in the cerebral cortex: The reaction of cells in monkey visual cortex to wavelengths and colours. *Neuroscience*, 1983, **9**, 741–765 (a).

Zeki, S., Colour coding in the cerebral cortex: The responses of wavelength-sensitive and colour coded cells in monkey visual cortex to changes in wavelength composition. *Neuroscience*, 1983, **9**, 767–791 (b).

Perception and Psychophysics
1987, **41** (2), 117–158
©1987 Psychonomic Society, Inc.

CORTICAL DYNAMICS OF THREE-DIMENSIONAL FORM, COLOR, AND BRIGHTNESS PERCEPTION, II: BINOCULAR THEORY

Stephen Grossberg†

ABSTRACT

A real-time visual processing theory is developed of how three-dimensional form, color, and brightness percepts are coherently synthesized. The theory describes how several fundamental uncertainty principles which limit the computation of visual information at individual processing stages are resolved through parallel and hierarchical interactions among several processing stages. The theory hereby provides a unified analysis and many predictions of data about stereopsis, binocular rivalry, hyperacuity, McCollough effect, textural grouping, border distinctness, surface perception, monocular and binocular brightness percepts, filling-in, metacontrast, transparency, figural aftereffects, lateral inhibition within spatial frequency channels, proximity-luminance covariance, tissue contrast, motion segmentation, and illusory figures, as well as about reciprocal interactions among the hypercolumns, blobs, and stripes of cortical areas V1, V2, and V4. Monocular and binocular interactions between a Boundary Contour (BC) System and a Feature Contour (FC) System are developed. The BC System, defined by a hierarchy of oriented interactions, synthesizes an emergent and coherent binocular boundary segmentation from combinations of unoriented and oriented scenic elements. These BC System interactions instantiate a new theory of stereopsis, and of how mechanisms of stereopsis are related to mechanisms of boundary segmentation. Interactions between the BC System and FC System explain why boundary completion and segmentation processes become binocular at an earlier processing stage than color and brightness perception processes. The new stereopsis theory includes a new model of how chromatically broad-band cortical complex cells can be adaptively tuned to multiplex information about position, orientation, spatial frequency, positional disparity, and orientational disparity. These binocular cells input to spatially short-range competitive interactions (within orientations and between positions, followed by between orientations and within positions) which initiate suppression of binocular double images as they complete boundaries at scenic line ends and corners. The competitive interactions interact via both feedforward and feedback pathways with spatially long-range oriented cooperative gating interactions which generate a coherent, multiple-scale 3-D boundary segmentation as they complete the suppression of double image boundaries. The completed BC System boundary segmentation generates output signals, called Filling-In Generators (FIGs) and Filling-In Barriers (FIBs), along parallel pathways to two successive FC System stages: the Monocular Syncytium and the Binocular Syncytium. FIB signals at the Monocular

† Supported in part by the Air Force Office of Scientific Research (AFOSR 85-0149 and AFOSR F49620-86-C-0037), the Army Research Office (ARO DAAG-29-85-K-0095), and the National Science Foundation (NSF IRI-84-17756).

Syncytium suppress monocular color and brightness signals which are binocularly inconsistent and select binocularly consistent, monocular Feature Contour signals as outputs
to the Binocular Syncytium. Binocular matching of these Feature Contour signals further suppresses binocularly inconsistent color and brightness signals. Binocular Feature
Contour signals which survive these multiple suppressive events interact with FIB signals
at the Binocular Syncytium to fill-in a multiple scale representation of form-and-color-in-
depth. To achieve these properties, distinct syncytia correspond to each spatial scale of
the BC System. Each syncytium is composed of opponent subsyncytia which generate
output signals through a network of double opponent cells. Although composed of unoriented wavelength-sensitive cells, double opponent networks detect oriented properties
of form when they interact with FIG signals, yet also generate nonselective properties of
binocular rivalry. Electrotonic and chemical transmitter interactions within the syncytia
are formally akin to interactions in H1 horizontal cells of turtle retina. The cortical syncytia are hypothesized to be encephalizations of ancestral retinal syncytia. In addition to
double opponent cell networks, electrotonic syncytial interactions, and resistive gating signals due to BC System outputs, FC System processes also include habituative transmitters
and non-Hebbian adaptive filters that maintain the positional and chromatic selectivity
of Feature Contour interactions. Alternative perceptual theories are evaluated in light
of these results. The theoretical circuits provide qualitatively new design principles and
architectures for computer vision applications.

1. Introduction: From Filling-In Resonant Exchange to Boundary-Feature Trade-Off

Part II of this article builds a neural theory of 3-D form perception using as a foundation
the mechanisms of monocular form perception that were summarized and applied in Part I
(Grossberg, 1987b). A macrocircuit of this 3-D theory is shown in Figure 1. One of the
main purposes of the article is to suggest how mechanisms of stereopsis and of boundary
segmentation work together to generate an emergent percept of form-and-color-in-depth.
Another general goal of the article is to explain why mechanisms of boundary segmentation
within the BC System become binocular at an earlier processing stage than the mechanisms
of Feature Contour extraction and filling-in within the FC System (Figure 1). Yet another
contribution is to show how networks of unoriented double-opponent wavelength-sensitive
cells can compute oriented form-sensitive properties when they interact with BC signals.

As noted in Part I (Grossberg, 1987b), the present theory is a synthesis of two previous
theories. Both theories got their start through an analysis of binocular perceptual data
which required a combination of cooperative and competitive interactions for their analysis (Grossberg, 1980, 1981, 1983a). These data suggested how a single contour-sensitive
process could control featural filling-in. This filling-in process was called a *filling-in resonant exchange*, or FIRE. Properties of the FIRE process enabled qualitative explanations
and quantitative computer simulations of binocular perceptual data to be made (Cohen
and Grossberg, 1984a, 1984b; Grossberg, 1983b). However, the quantitative analysis of
FIRE properties also led to the realization that a distinct type of filling-in—called diffusive, or electrotonic, filling-in—was needed to preprocess visual inputs before they were
transformed by the FIRE itself.

This insight opened the way to distinguishing between two distinct types of contour-
sensitive processes–the Boundary Contour System and the Feature Contour System (Grossberg, 1983b, 1984). At first, the BC System and the FC System were used to analyse

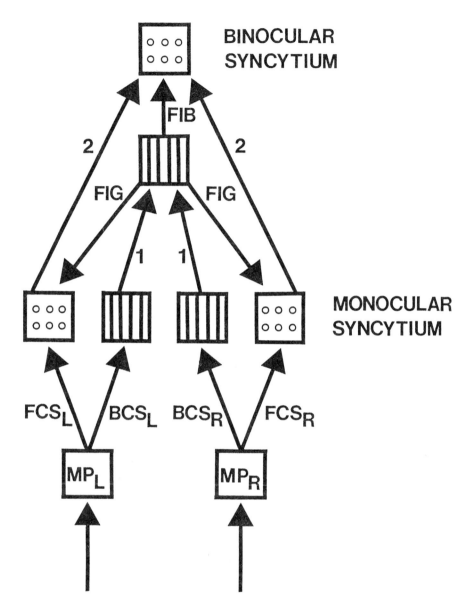

Figure 1. Macrocircuit of monocular and binocular interactions within the Boundary Contour System (BCS) and the Feature Contour System (FCS): Left and right monocular preprocessing stages (MP_L and MP_R) send parallel monocular inputs to the BCS (boxes with vertical lines) and the FCS (boxes with three pairs of circles). The monocular BCS_L and BCS_R interact via bottom-up pathways labelled 1 to generate a coherent binocular boundary segmentation. This segmentation generates output signals called filling-in generators (FIGs) and filling-in barriers (FIBs). The FIGs input to the monocular syncytia of the FCS. The FIBs input to the binocular syncytia of the FCS. The text describes how inputs from the MP stages interact with FIGs at the monocular syncytia to selectively generate binocularly consistent Feature Contour signals along the pathways labelled 2 to the binocular syncytia. The text also describes how these monocular Feature Contour signals interact with FIB signals to generate a multiple scale representation of form-and-color-in-depth within the binocular syncytia.

data about monocular percepts, as in Part I of this article (Grossberg, 1987b). However, the theory as a whole then used two different types of filling-in—one monocular (diffusive) and the other binocular (FIRE)—and two different types of cooperative-competitive interactions—one monocular (CC Loop) and the other binocular (FIRE). In addition, as the FIRE theory began to be used to analyse complex 2-dimensional images, the analysis seemed to become unnecessarily complicated.

These inelegances ultimately focused attention upon the following demanding problem: How could the FIRE process be replaced by a *binocular* theory of the BC System and FC System while preserving all of the good properties of the FIRE process within a unified theory with an expanded predictive range? Why did the FIRE process work so well if it could be replaced in such a fashion? The present theory is the result of this quest, and satisfies the above requirements. The theory suggests, moreover, that the FIRE explanations were all qualitatively, if not mechanistically, correct.

This article will not redevelop all of the data which were analysed using properties of the FIRE process in Cohen and Grossberg (1984a, 1984b) and Grossberg (1983a). Instead, I will cut a steep path to neural architectures. Along the way, I will sketch explanations of some binocular data which the FIRE theory could explain to show how previous explanations carry over to the present theory. I will also develop explanations of several important data bases which the FIRE theory could not explain.

2. Two Types of Binocular Rivalry: The Kaufman Stereogram

Just as percepts of neon color spreading provide a vivid guide to conceptualizing key monocular processes (Grossberg, 1987b; Grossberg and Mingolla, 1985a), percepts of binocular rivalry provide crucial clues concerning the mechanisms of binocular processing. In particular, two mechanistically distinct types of binocular rivalry can be identified by comparing properties of rivalry data with formal properties of the BC System circuits depicted in Figures 2 and 3.

Figure 2 schematizes early stages of filtering and short-range competition within the monocular BC System. Figure 3 joins these early stages to a later stage of long-range cooperation. Together the entire monocular BC System is broken into two subsystems (Figure 3): an OC Filter and a CC Loop, which were used in Grossberg (1987b) to analyse properties of monocular data. The discussion below of binocular rivalry data motivates how these monocular mechanisms can be generalized to the binocular case. The possibility of carrying out such a generalization cannot be taken for granted. In particular, the competition and cooperation mechanisms shown in Figures 2 and 3 are new to our theory, and possess properties which are essential for carrying out the generalization from monocular to binocular processing.

The Kaufman stereogram (Kaufman, 1974) illustrates the first type of binocular rivalry (Figure 4). In this stereogram, the left picture is constructed from 45°-oblique dark parallel lines bounded by an imaginary square, which is surrounded by 135°-oblique lighter parallel lines. The right picture is constructed from 135°-oblique dark parallel lines bounded by an imaginary square whose position in the picture is shifted relative to the square in the left picture. This imaginary square is surrounded by 45°-oblique lighter parallel lines. When these pictures are viewed through a stereoscope, a single fused square is seen in depth relative to the background. Superimposed upon the continuous percept of a square-in-depth is a rivalrous percept due to the dark oblique lines. At any given moment, an observer can perceive either a 45°-oblique dark line or a 135°-oblique dark line at a

TO COOPERATION

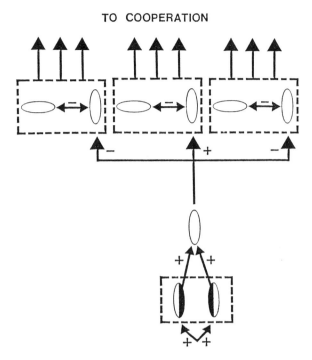

Figure 2. Early stages of BC System processing: At each position exist cells with elongated receptive fields of various sizes which are sensitive to orientation, amount-of-contrast, and direction-of-contrast. Pairs of such cells sensitive to like orientation but opposite directions-of-contrast (lower dashed box) input to cells that are sensitive to orientation and amount-of-contrast but not to direction-of-contrast (white ellipses). These cells, in turn, excite like-oriented cells corresponding to the same position and inhibit like-oriented cells corresponding to nearby positions using the first competitive stage. At the second competitive stage (upper dashed boxes), cells corresponding to the same position but different orientations inhibit each other via a push-pull competitive interaction.

given position, but not both. The percept switches intermittently between these mutually perpendicular lines.

This rivalrous percept illustrates that images which can be clearly seen under monocular viewing conditions may not be visible under binocular viewing conditions when the other eye is viewing a discordant image. These mutually perpendicular lines tend to pop into and out of conscious perception with coherent properties: If several short 45°-oblique line elements start to be perceived, then the whole 45°-oblique line segment between them is also often perceived. Thus binocular rivalry provides striking illustrations of how binocular grouping processes regulate visible percepts of 3-D form. Further consideration of this percept of simultaneous fusion and rivalry implicates binocular versions of the mechanisms summarized in Figures 2 and 3.

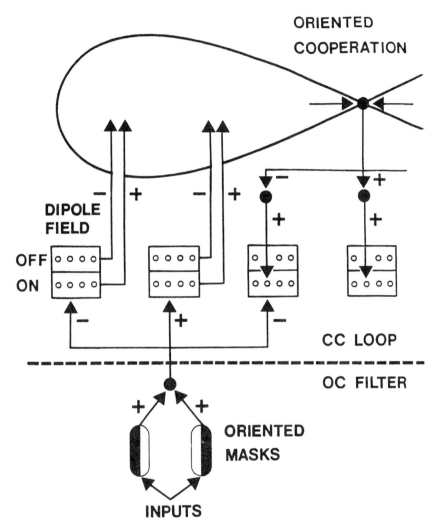

Figure 3. Circuit diagram of the Boundary Contour System: Inputs activate oriented masks of opposite direction-of-contrast which cooperate at each position and orientation before feeding into an on-center off-surround interaction. This interaction excites like-orientations at the same position and inhibits like-orientations at nearby positions. The affected cells are on-cells within a dipole field. On-cells at a fixed position compete among orientations. On-cells also inhibit off-cells which represent the same position and orientation. Off-cells at each position, in turn, compete among orientations. Both on-cells and off-cells are tonically active. Net excitation of an on-cell excites a similarly oriented receptive field of a cooperative bipole cell at a location corresponding to that of the on-cell. Net excitation of an off-cell inhibits a similarly oriented receptive field of a bipole cell at a location corresponding to that of the off-cell. Thus, bottom-up excitation of a vertical on-cell, by inhibiting the horizontal on-cell at that position, disinhibits the horizontal off-cell at that position, which in turn inhibits (almost) horizontally oriented cooperative receptive fields that include its position. Sufficiently strong net positive activation of both receptive fields of a bipole cell enables it to generate feedback via an on-center off-surround interaction among like-oriented cells. On-cells which receive the most favorable combination of bottom-up signals and top-down signals generate the emergent perceptual grouping.

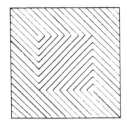 

Figure 4. The Kaufman stereogram induces a percept of a square in depth even while the perpendicular line patterns are rivalrous. (From Sight and mind: An introduction to visual perception by L. Kaufman, 1974, New York, Oxford University Press. Copyright 1974 by Oxford University Press. Reprinted with permission.)

3. Interaction between Segmentation and Stereopsis Mechanisms within the CC Loop

Percepts of the Kaufman stereogram illustrate one sense in which multiple spatial scales are operative during binocular perception: A square can be perceived continuously in depth while perpendicular lines are rivalrous at the same positions in perceptual space. The Kaufman percept also emphasizes the intimate linkage that exists between mechanisms of segmentation and mechanisms of stereopsis. Although a square is perceived continuously in depth, neither image in Figure 4 contains a square. A square is synthesized from each image as an emergent illusory boundary. This illusory boundary interpolates the corner discontinuities at the ends of the oblique line segments in each image. Grossberg (1987b) described a mechanism for generating such an emergent illusory boundary at line ends and corners. This process is initiated by end cuts at the second competitive stage of the OC Filter. These end cuts interact via the long-range cooperative process of the CC Loop to generate a sharp emergent boundary from the fuzzy bands of end cuts that exist at each line corner.

Given this linkage with CC Loop mechanisms, the percept of a square-in-depth suggests that these mechanisms are binocular. In particular, the imaginary squares of the two images are positionally disparate with respect to the frame of each image. Consequently, when each image of the stereogram is monocularly viewed, each square boundary emerges at a different perceptual location. In contrast, under binocular viewing conditions, only a single fused square boundary is perceived. Thus the CC Loop must combine the pair of positionally disparate, monocular emergent boundaries into a single, fused binocular boundary. In order for this to occur, a binocular matching process must occur within the CC Loop. This binocular matching process operates upon the emergent boundaries generated by the images to each eye, rather than upon the individual local contrasts within these images. The process whereby a single fused square-in-depth is generated from pairs of emergent boundaries thus combines mechanisms of segmentation with mechanisms of stereopsis.

Of course, there exist many images whose emergent boundary disparities covary with the disparities of their image contrasts. The Kaufman stereogram reminds us, however, that this is just as often false. When it is false, emergent segmentations can override local image disparities during the synthesis of a 3-D percept, as has been shown by a number of experimental studies (Ramachandran and Nelson, 1976; Tauch, 1953; Wilde, 1950).

4. The Second Competitive Stage is Binocular: Correlated Emergence and Suppression of Coherent Boundaries

Finer conclusions can be drawn by considering the rivalry which is perceived when viewing the Kaufman stereogram. This rivalry occurs between perpendicular orientations at each position of perceptual space (Figure 4). This is the very sort of competition which occurs at the second competitive stage of the CC Loop (Figure 2). The linking hypothesis that the second competitive stage is responsible for the orientational competition that occurs during rivalry will be used to help explain a large binocular data base below. This linking hypothesis provides my first example of the fact that the segmentation laws governing the CC Loop, which were derived from an analysis of monocular data, generalize directly to the binocular case.

The linking hypothesis implies that *the second competitive stage is binocular*, so that perpendicular boundary signals from both eyes can compete by the time they reach this stage. The linking hypothesis also helps to explain how whole boundary segments can coherently pop into and out of consciousness. Suppose that several colinear 45°-oriented cells at the second competitive stage get simultaneously activated by the image to one eye. These cells can excite like-oriented bipole cells at the cooperative stage of the CC Loop (Figure 3). The activated bipole cells can use cooperative feedback to excite 45°-oriented cells at the second competitive stage at positions between the originally excited cells. These newly excitaed cells can inhibit 135°-oriented cells at their positions via the orientational competition that takes place at the second competitive stage (Figure 2). Thus the fact that boundary completion is an *inwardly* directed process between *pairs* of inducing elements enables whole boundary segments to emerge in response to spatially separated inducers. The fact that orientational competition is engaged by the same cooperative feedback which controls boundary completion shows how the emergence of a given boundary can cause the suppression of perpendicular boundaries that intersect the same perceptual locations.

In summary, if a sufficient number of like orientations from one scenic image can momentarily suppress the perpendicular orientations from the other scenic image, then these winning orientations can colinearly cooperate to complete the oriented boundary at intervening positions. The oriented cooperative feedback can inhibit any perpendicularly oriented cells at the intervening positions by using the second competitive stage. This combination of competition between orientations at each position and colinear cooperation between positions helps to explain why whole segments of the rivalrous interior edges of the square seem to pop coherently into and out of conscious perception.

5. The Kulikowski Stereogram

The second type of binocular rivalry is exemplified by the percepts seen in response to the Kulikowski (1978) stereograms. The Kulikowski stereograms consist of two pairs of pictures which differ in their spatial frequencies. Each picture is bounded by the same frame, which includes a pair of short vertical reference lines to help viewers fuse the frames binocularly. In one pair of pictures, spatially blurred alternating black and white vertical bars of a fixed spatial frequency are 180° out of phase (Figure 5a). In the other pair of pictures (Figure 5b), sharp black and white vertical bars of the same spatial extent are 180° out of phase. The latter pair of pictures contains high spatial frequency components (edges) as well as the low spatial frequency components of the first pair.

During binocular viewing, subjects can fuse the two spatially blurred pictures. They perceive the fused image continuously in depth relative to the fused images of the two

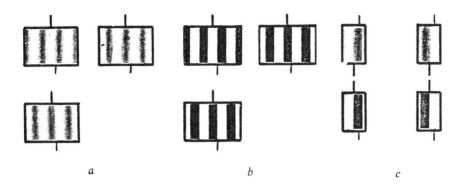

Figure 5. The Kulikowski stereograms illustrate the action of multiple spatial frequency sensitive scales during simultaneous fusion and rivalry: (a) Sinusoidal gratings in antiphase can be fused to yield a percept of a grating in depth. (b) Bar gratings in antiphase yield a percept of depth even though their edges are rivalrous. (c) Similar percepts are seen when single sinusoids or bars are viewed. (From J.J. Kulikowski, 1978, *Nature*, **275**, 126–127. Copyright 1978 by Macmillan Journals. Reprinted with permission.)

frames. Subjects experience a more complex percept when they view the stereogram composed from out-of-phase sharp bars. As in the case of viewing the blurred bars, a fused form-in-depth is again perceived continuously. However, superimposed upon the fused percept of form-in-depth is a percept of binocular rivalry. The spatially out-of-phase edges of the bars in the left and right images are rivalrous and appear to pop alternately into and out of conscious perception.

6. Simultaneous Fusion and Rivalry: Multiple Spatial Scales

This percept of simultaneous fusion and rivalry illustrates the operation of multiple spatial scales: The lower spatial frequency components of the two images can be binocularly fused into a continuously seen percept-in-depth at the same time that the high spatial frequency edges are seen to be rivalrous. Thus the high spatial frequency scales which process the edges cannot fuse these image properties at the same disparity at which the low spatial frequency scales can fuse the low spatial frequency contents of the two images. In contrast, the frames of both images can be fused by all spatial scales because the frames can be spatially aligned with respect to both eyes. Thus the Kulikowski stereogram provides visible evidence of the classical fact (Julesz, 1971) that a relative depth percept can be generated when different parts of two images are fused by different combinations of binocular spatial scales.

The relative depth percept that is generated by the Kaufman stereogram (Figure 4) can also be analysed from this perspective. As described in Section 3, the formation of an emergent boundary around the illusory square region is initiated by end cuts at the corners where the oblique line ends of the square join its surround. Due to the horizontal disparity of the end cuts formed in response to the left and right images, not all of the BC System spatial scales can form fused images of these emergent boundaries. In contrast, the scenic edges which frame the image pair have zero disparity with respect to each other and can thus form fused boundary responses within all spatial scales of the BC System. The selective activation of a subset of BC System scales by the disparate image figures provides the basis for a relative depth difference of the figure with respect to the ground.

As described in Section 3, end cuts, in themselves, are insufficient to generate an illusory square boundary. The CC Loop chooses and completes an illusory boundary that passes through all of the line corners. More precisely, a *multiple scale* CC Loop reaction chooses and completes several illusory boundaries, one for each spatial scale at which end cuts due to the two images can be binocularly fused. Thus several copies of the CC Loop exist within the BC System, one for each spatial scale.

7. Suppression of Double Images by the First Competitive Stage

In the Kaufman stereogram, *perpendicular* scenic edges that excite the two eyes at the *same* positions are rivalrous, thereby implicating the second competitive stage. In the Kulikowski stereogram, *parallel* scenic edges that excite the two eyes at *disparate* positions are rivalrous. This is the type of competition which occurs at the first competitive stage (Figures 2 and 3). The rivalry between the disparate vertical edges of the Kulikowski stereogram is initiated when the first competitive stage causes parallel, but disparate, orientations from both eyes to compete at the second competitive stage. Thus the Kulikowski and Kaufman stereograms are mechanistically differentiated by the way in which they differentially engage the first and second competitive stages, respectively.

The suppressive action of the first competitive stage seems paradoxical when it is perceived in demonstrations of binocular rivalry. The same mechanism, however, is used to help suppress monocular information that cannot be fused into a binocularly consistent 3-D percept. Thus the first competitive stage is one of the mechanisms whereby binocular double images, or the many possible combinations of false binocular matches (Julesz, 1971; Sperling, 1970), are suppressed before they can generate completed binocular boundary segmentations within the CC Loop. In summary, the mechanisms of the first and second competitive stages begin to explain how the percept of a monocularly viewed image can be suppressed by viewing a binocularly discordant image through the other eye.

Further consideration of the Kulikowski percept begins to shed light on other important issues: Why are fusion and rivalry alternative binocular modes? How does fusion at one spatial scale coexist with rivalry at a different spatial scale that represents the same region of visual space? Why can certain lower spatial frequency components be fused whereas certain higher spatial frequencies cannot be fused at a fixed disparity? What definition of spatial scale can accomodate all of these properties?

8. The Complex Cells of the OC Filter are Binocular: A Positionally Sharp but Deformable Binocular Space

The role of the first competitive stage in initiating suppression of binocular double images leads towards an understanding of these properties. In particular, why does not the first competitive stage cause rivalry between the disparate monocular images in *all* spatial scales? How can some spatial scales binocularly fuse images at the same disparity that at other spatial scales leads to binocular rivalry? In order for this to happen, disparate monocular images which are fused within a given scale must both input to the on-center of the scale's first competitive stage (Figure 6a). In contrast, disparate monocular images which are rivalrous within a given scale must compete via the off-surrounds of that scale's first competitive stage (Figure 6b).

This distinction suggests several conclusions: The output cells of the OC Filter are themselves already binocular. Section 21 of Grossberg (1987b) identifies these cells with contour-sensitive complex cells in Area 17 of the striate cortex. Complex cells are, in fact, well-known to be binocular (Hubel and Wiesel, 1962, 1968, 1970, 1977; Poggio, Motter, Squatrito, and Trotter, 1985). Thus the second competitive stage is binocular because its inputs from the complex cells are already binocular. Figure 6 suggests that there exist disparities at which low spatial frequency scales can fuse monocular image elements (Figure 6a) but high spatial frequency scales cannot (Figure 6b). As a result, there exist disparities at which complex cells tuned to low spatial frequencies can excite the on-center of the corresponding second competitive stage (Figure 6a) but complex cells tuned to high spatial frequencies generate mutually inhibitory signals to the second competitive stage (Figure 6b). I return in Section 24 to the question of how this relationship between spatial frequency, disparity, fusion, and rivalry can be mechanistically realized. For the moment, Figure 6 provides a pictorial way to understand how some spatial scales can fuse images which other spatial scales cannot, and how CC Loop mechanisms can inhibit binocularly discordant boundary signals within those scales which are incapable of fusion.

Figure 6 also hints at how another important property of binocular space is realized. In order to fuse pairs of monocular images which are spatially disparate, the binocular space must be *deformable*: Two images must be deformed into one image, much as in the phenomenon of *displacement*, or *allelotropia* (von Tschermak-Seysenegg, 1952; Werner, 1937). In this phenomenon, when a pattern *AB C* is viewed through one eye and a pattern *A BC* is viewed through the other eye, the letter *B* can be seen in depth at a position halfway between *A* and *C*. Although deformability implies that there exists a certain degree of positional uncertainty at early stages of binocular processing, the final binocular percept is often positionally sharp. In Section 24, I describe mechanisms whereby the ostensibly conflicting properties of deformability and positional sharpness are realized within a binocular space that is built up using a multiple scale, binocular version of OC Filter and CC Loop mechanisms.

9. Binocular Switching, Boundary Frames, and Negative Afterimages

Yet another test of the hypothesis linking binocular rivalry to CC Loop mechanisms concerns the issue of why rivalrous percepts switch suddenly, and approximately periodically, between representations of left image and right image. I trace this type of switching to the existence of habituating chemical transmitter substances which are hypothesized to multiply, or gate, signals within the CC Loop. I assume that these transmitters occur along the feedback pathways from the cooperative stage to the dipole field (Figure 3). Thus the CC Loop contains a specialized type of *gated dipole field* (Grossberg, 1976b, 1980, 1983b).

Spontaneous switching behavior has previously been shown to be a property of a gated dipole field in response to image pairs which create approximately balanced, but competitive, input patterns (Grossberg, 1976b, 1980). Periodic switching occurs because the habituating transmitters within a winning channel weaken the competitive advantage of that channel by causing a decrease in the size of its positive feedback signals. The inhibited channel can then win the competition because its transmitters are able to accumulate while it is being inhibited. Then the cycle of rivalry repeats itself, leading to cyclic recovery and habituation of transmitter gates as a given channel periodically loses and wins the

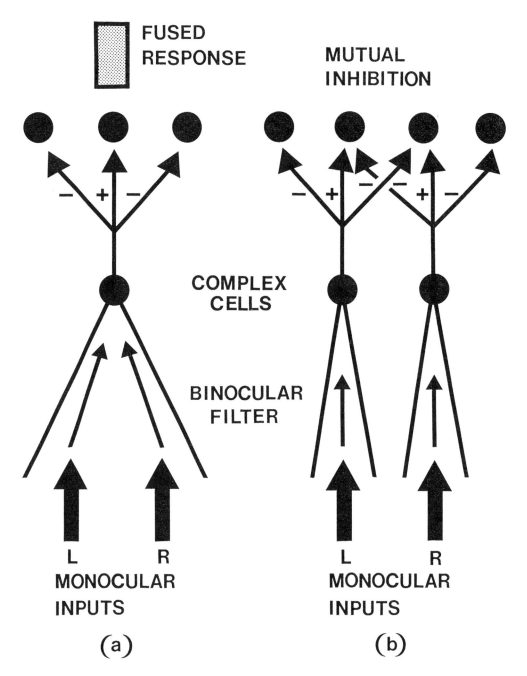

Figure 6. Initial processing stages leading to fusion or rivalry: (a) Spatially disparate monocular images from left (L) and right (R) eyes activate a shared population of complex cells, which in turn activate a "fused" locus of cells within an on-center of the second competitive stage. (b) At a smaller spatial scale, the same monocular images may activate spatially disjoint sets of complex cells, which input to off-surrounds at the second competitive stage, thereby initiating rivalry between the images.

competition.

In order to explain the binocular rivalry which occurs in response to the Kulikowski stereogram, the positive feedback must influence the stage at which the competing inputs are registered. This stage is the second competitive stage (Figure 3). Thus the CC Loop, which was derived from constraints about monocular boundary completion and segmentation, possesses feedback pathways which are correctly placed to explain binocular rivalry.

In Grossberg (1980), the habituating gates within a gated dipole field were shown to be an important mechanism for dynamically stabilizing the adaptive tuning of cortical filters against persistant recoding by irrelevant cues (also see Section 23 below). In the special case of the gated dipole field within the CC Loop, another useful function can be noted. Consider a moving vertical scenic edge which activates, then passes over, a vertically oriented cell of the CC Loop dipole field. The offset of the vertically-oriented input to these cells can trigger a momentary activation of horizontally oriented cells corresponding to the same position. This opponent reaction, or antagonistic rebound, helps to prevent a blurring of the vertical edge as it moves across the BC System by rebalancing the orientational competition in readiness for the next oriented input. The importance of registering moving edges as successive boundary frames, rather than as a blurred optical flow, has been emphasized in the classical studies of Johannsen (1973, 1975, 1978). Such an antagonistic rebound within a gated dipole field is mediated by its habituating transmitter gates. The theory hereby traces the periodic nature of binocular rivalry, as well as other metastable percepts such as the Necker cube (Grossberg, 1980), to mechanisms for dynamically stabilizing cortical learning and for dynamically rebalancing cortical competitive mechanisms.

When a Boundary Contour is kept active long enough for its transmitter gates to significantly habituate, a larger and more sustained antagonistic rebound is caused by offset of the inducing image, thereby causing a negative afterimage. Parametric properties of the negative afterimages due to dipole field rebounds have been compared with monocular and binocular perceptual data in Grossberg (1976b, 1980). A more detailed understanding of oriented afterimages can be derived from properties of the feedback interaction which occurs between the second competitive stage and the cooperative stage of the CC Loop (Figure 7). MacKay (1957) has reported that, when an image with radial symmetry (Figure 7a) is inspected for a long time, then offset of the pattern can generate a negative afterimage with radial symmetry (Figure 7c). This is explained by CC Loop mechanisms as follows. Each position and orientation which is activated by the image habituates its transmitter gates within the CC Loop. Since the gated dipole field is tonically active (Grossberg, 1987b, Section 19), offset of the image triggers antagonistic rebounds within the gated dipole field. In particular, because *orientational* competition occurs within the second competitive stage, offset of an orientation at a given position can activate the *perpendicular* orientation at that position via such an antagonistic rebound (Figure 7b). These perpendicular orientations can then colinearly cooperate with the cooperative stage to complete bands of circular negative afterimages (Figure 7c).

The above discussion suggests how circular boundary segmentations can be induced by offset of a radially organized scenic image. It does not, however, explain how we *see* these circular bands, since all boundaries are invisible within the BC System (Grossberg, 1987b, Section 22). The FC System also contains gated dipole fields, which are specialized as double opponent networks of color-sensitive cells. These double opponent color fields can also experience antagonistic rebounds when a sustained inducing image is shut off. Below it is explained how these two types of gated dipole fields interact to generate visible

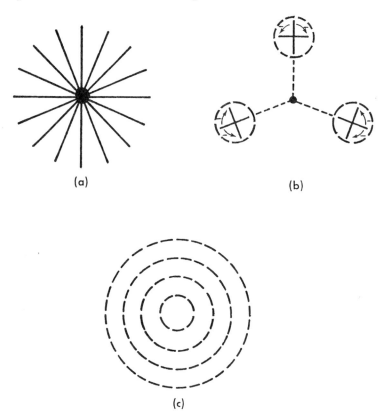

Figure 7. Negative aftereffects in orientation: (a) A pattern with radial symmetry is inspected for a long time. (b) Orientational competition occurs at each position of the second competitive stage. (c) Offset of the radial pattern elicits antagonistic rebounds that activate the perpendicular orientations, which thereupon colinearly cooperate with bipole cells of the CC Loop to form circular emergent boundaries.

percepts of form-and-color-in-depth, including visible percepts of negative afterimages. In order to reach this insight, I momentarily turn away from the delightful phenomena of binocular rivalry to follow a conceptual path whereby a number of additional mechanistic insights about 3-D perception can efficiently be motivated and derived. Several simple gedanken experiments (Grossberg, 1983a) guide the choice of this path.

10. Scenic Edges and Fixations: Binocular Boundary Matches Support Depth Percepts

Suppose that an observer attempts to fixate a perceptually uniform rectangle hovering in space in front of a discriminable but perceptually uniform background. How does the observer know where to fixate the rectangle? Suppose, for example, that each of the observer's eyes independently fixates a different point of the rectangle's interior. Both eyes will register identical input patterns near their fixation points due to the rectangle's uniformity. The monocular visual patterns near the fixation points *match* no matter how large a disparity exists between the chosen fixation points, just so long as both fixation points fall well within the rectangle.

This simple example shows that binocular visual matching between spatially homogeneous regions contains no information about where the eyes are pointed, since all binocular matches between homogeneous regions are equally good no matter where the eyes are pointed. Many false matches will be generated if spatially homogeneous visual data can influence percepts of depth.

The only binocular visual matches which stand out above the baseline of multiple false homogeneous matches are those which correlate spatially nonuniform, or "edge-like," data to the two eyes. Once one has distinguished Boundary Contours from Feature Contours, it becomes clear that the binocular matches in question occur within the BC System.

It is well accepted that the disparities of contours within the two monocular images registered by the eyes provide information about the depths of perceived objects. The above argument also shows, however, that disparity information is insufficient. Even if one computes disparities from binocular matches of Boundary Contours, the disparities will depend upon the fixation points of the two eyes. Thus disparity information combines with information about the vergeance angle of the two eyes to determine where an object is in space (Foley, 1980; Sperling, 1970). The present article will not discuss the role of vergeance in establishing absolute percepts of depth. Instead, mechanisms leading to relative percepts of depth will be analysed.

Once one agrees that binocular matches within the BC System help to generate such relative percepts of depth, it becomes vital to explain how such a binocular match is computed. In particular, data on binocular rivalry such as we have just considered lead us to raise the question: How can a binocular *mismatch* within the BC System suppress the visibility of monocular image data whose boundaries lose the binocular competition? This question leads to a related question: From a functional viewpoint, why *should* a binocular mismatch suppress the percept of the monocular image which loses the binocular competition? The second gedanken experiment helps to answer this question.

11. Multiple Spatial Scales: Distinguishing Size from Depth

The second gedanken experiment suggests the need for multiple spatial scales, such that only those scales capable of supporting a match can be allowed to generate a visible percept. This gedanken experiment can also be phrased in terms of the fixation process.

As a rigid object approaches an observer, the binocular disparities between its non-fixated features increase proportionally. In order to maintain the fixation process and to achieve a percept of object permanence, mechanisms capable of correlating these progressively larger disparities are needed. Other things being equal, the largest disparities will lie at the most peripheral points on the retina. The cortical magnification factor, whereby cortical regions of fixed size process larger retinal regions as a function of retinal eccentricity, is one mechanism whereby this may be accomplished (Hubel and Wiesel, 1977; Schwartz, 1980).

It is not sufficient, however, for a single spatial scale to exist at each retinal position, such that scale size increases with retinal eccentricity. This is because objects of different size can approach an observer. The observer can confuse object size with object depth unless multiple scales exist corresponding to each retinal position which can correlate information about object size with information about object depth. In particular, objects of different sizes can generate the same monocular retinal image if they lie at different distances from an observer, with larger objects further away. On the other hand, the boundary disparities of their paired retinal images carry information about their depth since objects at different depths generate different binocular disparities. Multiple spatial scales corresponding to each retinal position can carry out these multiple disparity computations and disambiguate image size from image depth.

This gedanken experiment suggests the functional utility of suppressing monocular image data which cause binocularly mismatched boundaries. Each monocular image can excite more spatial scales corresponding to each retinal position than can binocularly match. Only the monocular boundaries which are capable of being binocularly matched provide correct information concerning form-in-depth. Consequently, the mismatched boundaries must be prevented from contributing to percepts of 3-D form.

The gedanken experiment also clarifies the utility of allowing lower spatial frequencies to match and be fused at disparities such that higher spatial frequencies are suppressed or rivalrous (Section 6). As an object approaches an observer, the sizes of its monocular retinal images and their binocular disparities increase together. Other things being equal, larger spatial scales (lower spatial frequencies) should therefore be able to binocularly match pairs of images with larger disparities than can be fused by smaller spatial scales (higher spatial frequencies).

12. Monocular Self-Matches: Gradient Depth and Motion Depth

When an observer closes one eye, vivid perception is still possible. Moreover, monocular percepts can retain a significant impression of depth. Thus a binocular match within the BC System is not necessary to generate a conscious percept, let alone a depthful percept. What is needed is the absence of a binocular mismatch. Because the visual world can vividly be perceived through a single eye, certain BC System cells must be capable of being monocularly activated. I call such activation a *monocular self-match* to distinguish it from a binocular match (Grossberg, 1983a).

In the absence of binocular mismatches, more monocular self-matches can occur than under binocular viewing conditions. This property helps to explain why, when viewed under reduction conditions (one eye looks through a small aperture in dim light), depth percepts can be ambiguous (Gogel, 1956, 1965, 1970). On the other hand, the existence of more monocular self-matches raises the question of why depth is ever perceived under monocular viewing conditions? One factor is the correlation between scale size and fusable disparities that was discussed in Sections 6 and 11. Larger scales can, other things being equal, preferentially respond to larger image elements. Under binocular viewing conditions, larger images are often closer and generate larger disparities. Due to the preferential response of larger scales to large image elements, a monocularly viewed image which contains spatial gradients (Figure 8) can be parsed among multiple spatial scales in a manner similar to its parsing during binocular viewing conditions. Gibson (1950) is notable among classical perceptual theorists for his many illustrations of how spatial gradients can influence depth perception.

A monocularly viewed moving object can activate a succession of monocular self-matches which are capable of matching or mismatching previous self-matches before they can be reset. Temporally staggered pairs of monocular self-matches can hereby generate matches or mismatches across the multiple spatial scales, which are akin to the matches due to binocular image disparities. Due to the correlation between scale size and maximal fusable disparity, faster motions can preferentially activate larger spatial scales. Thus moving objects can cause preferential activation of some spatial scales over others, thereby enhancing a percept of depth.

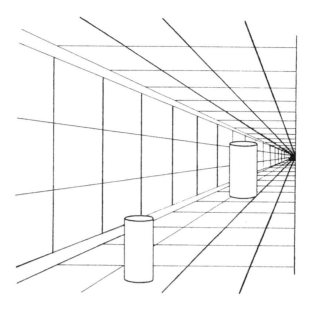

Figure 8. The corridor illusion: Due to the spatial gradients within the figure, the upper cylinder looks larger than the lower cylinder, although both cylinders are the same size. (From **Sight and mind: An introduction to visual perception** by L. Kaufman, 1974, New York, Oxford University Press. Copyright 1974 by Oxford University Press. Reprinted with permission.)

The present theory suggests, more generally, that any visual operations which cause equivalent activations of multiple scale BC System computations tend to generate equivalent depth percepts, whether they be due to monocular spatial gradients, monocular motion cues, binocular disparities, or top-down "cognitive contours." This tenet of the theory is called *the principle of scale equivalence.* Scale equivalence does not deny the possibility, outlined in Section 32 of Grossberg (1987b), that separate BC subsystems process distinct aspects of static form and form-from-motion (Beverley and Regan, 1979; Regan and Beverley, 1979; Regan and Cynader, 1982) before integrating these computations into a final 3-D percept. On the other hand, scale equivalence emphasizes that the BC System of primary interest in this article can generate depthful segmentations in response to multiple sources of monocular and binocular visual information, rather than being restricted to a single informational source—such as binocular disparity or monocular gradients—as is the case in many models of image processing.

13. Continuous Modulation of Multiple Scale Activity

As an observer moves within a scene, the scenic forms and their depths seem to change continuously. On the other hand, at most a finite number of spatial scales can exist in the brain. In many contemporary models of binocular depth perception, depth jumps discretely between a few values as an observer moves about. Moreover, these binocular models do not explain how the computation of disparity values leads to a percept of form-and-color-in-depth. Grossberg (1983a) summarizes and analyses a number of these models.

The present theory suggests that multiple spatial scales exist within the BC System and that these scales can be simultaneously activated, by a monocularly or binocularly viewed scene, albeit by different amounts corresponding to different scenic positions. As an observer moves about a scene, the relative and absolute degree to which each of these multiple boundary scales is activated changes. These changes in the energy balance across multiple boundary scales alters the ability of the corresponding FC signals to generate a visible percept. I suggest that multiple FC syncytia exist corresponding to the multiple BC System spatial scales, each syncytium capable of contributing to a visible percept, but to different degrees. In the limiting case wherein no BC signal within a given spatial scale excites the corresponding FC syncytium, that FC syncytium cannot contribute to a visible percept.

This type of multiple scale concept supports the strong kernel of truth that exists within the Fourier theory of spatial perception (Graham, 1981; Graham and Nachmias, 1971), but also replaces the Fourier theory by one with a greater explanatory range.

14. To Have Your Edge and Fill-In Too: The Julesz 5% Solution

The type of interactions which occur between the BC System and the FC System to generate a depthful percept can be motivated in several ways: The suppression of spatially uniform input patterns to extract informative signals for binocular matching (Section 10) follows from the contrast-sensitivity of the BC System. It also illustrates that reduction of one type of informational uncertainty can cause a new type of informational uncertainty. For example, in response to monocular viewing of a perceptually uniform rectangle hovering in space above a perceptually uniform background, the BC System generates a rectangular boundary and suppresses the uniform parts of both figure and ground. Why, then, do we not perceive a world of discrete boundaries, or at best a world of cartoon-like boundary segmentations? How do we perceive continuous forms?

As mentioned above, the theory suggests that boundary segmentations regulate diffusive filling-in events within multiple cell syncytia of the FC System, such that a different syncytium corresponds to each spatial scale of the BC System. Indeed, a spatial scale of the BC System is *defined* to be the set of BC System receptive field sizes whose CC Loop output pathways project to a single syncytium of the FC System. I show below how the locations where unambiguous depth computations can be performed, such as at the fused binocular boundaries of the BC System, regulate the multiple scale filling-in reaction within the FC System. The selectivity of this filling-in reaction across spatial scales enables ambiguous regions, such as the interior of a homogeneous rectangle, to inherit the relative depth values computed by the fused binocular boundaries.

A beautiful example of the role of multiple-scale filling-in mechanisms in depth perception is provided by what I like to call the Julesz 5% solution (Julesz, 1971, p.336). This is a stereogram whose left "figure" and "ground" are both constructed from a 5% density of randomly placed black dots on white paper. In the right picture, the "figure" of dots is shifted, as a whole, with respect to its position in the left picture. As usual, the background dots in both pictures have identical positions, except for positions that are covered or created by shifting the "figure". When viewed through a stereoscope, the whole figure, including the entire 95% of white background between its dots, appears to hover as a planar surface above a planar ground.

How does the white region of the "figure" inherit the depth arising from the binocular disparities of the meagerly distributed black dots within the "figure"? How does the white region of the "ground" inherit the depth due to binocular matching of its meagerly distributed dots? What mechanism organizes the locally ambiguous white patches that dominate 95% of the pictures into two distinct planar regions in depth?

This is not simply a matter of computing different disparity values for the two white regions, as many models have suggested (Dev, 1975; Marr and Poggio, 1976, 1979; Sperling, 1970). Instead, the *entire featural landscape* of black dots on white background is split into two planar regions. An adequate explanation must show how all the filled-in featural qualities, such as black and white, can inherit the depth values computed by a sparse BC System segmentation that is itself indifferent to figural qualities because it is generated by broad-band boundary detectors that are insensitive to direction-of-contrast (Grossberg, 1987b, Section 23).

15. Surface Curvature and Multiple Syncytial Scales: The $2\frac{1}{2}$-D Sketch Does Not Exist

That interactions between disparity-sensitive BC System segmentations and FC System filling-in events are needed to generate a completed 3-D percept can also be seen through the following examples. When both eyes focus on a single point within a patterned planar surface viewed in depth, the fixation point is a point of zero disparity. Points of the surface that are increasingly far from the fixation point have increasingly large binocular disparities. Why does such a plane not recede towards optical infinity at the fixation point and curve towards the observer at the periphery of the visual field? Why does the plane not become distorted in a new way every time our eyes fixate on a different point within its surface? If the relative sizes of boundary disparities control relative depth percepts, then how do we ever perceive planar surfaces? How do we even perceive rigid surfaces?

The severity of this problem is further indicated by the fact that perceived depth does, under certain circumstances, depend upon the choice of fixation point. Staring at one point in a Julesz stereogram can result in a gradual loss of depth (Kaufman, 1974). Also, in a stereogram composed of three vertical lines to the left eye and just the two outmost lines to the right eye, the depth of the middle line depends upon whether the left line or the right line is fixated (Kaufman, 1974). If depth can depend on the fixation point when discrete lines are viewed, then why do not observers perceive planar surfaces as being highly curved? What is the crucial difference between the way we perceive the depths of curves and of surfaces?

These examples raise the fundamental issue of how an observer knows that a planar surface is being viewed, not just whether the observer can estimate the depths of some parts of the surface. As noted in Section 10, when a homogeneous planar surface is being viewed, it is not possible to compute *any* unambiguous disparity computation within the interior of the plane. Determining that such a surface is planar thus cannot just be a matter of showing that the same disparity can be computed at all interior points of the surface. In fact, the BC System suppresses the interior of the plane in order to successfully match its boundaries.

The present theory suggests that when a particular Boundary Contour scale is strongly activated by a given scene, this Boundary Contour activation can trigger a strong filling-in reaction within the corresponding syncytium of the FC System. By definition, featural filling-in within a syncytium is restricted to the spatial scale in which this syncytium resides. I suggest that a surface percept will appear flat if it is generated by a pair of bounding Boundary Contours within a single spatial scale, because featural filling-in is restricted to the single syncytial scale that these Boundary Contours activate. A surface will appear curved if a multiple scale Boundary Contour reaction causes the distribution of filled-in featural activity to be "curved" among several syncytial scales as perceptual space is traversed. Several scales can be coactivated at each perceptual location. The distribution across space of which scales are activated imparts an impression of relative depth.

This explanation of perceived surface flatness and curvature suggests that FC signals corresponding to a fixed retinal position send inputs to the filling-in syncytia of *all* the multiple spatial scales. Only those scales that also receive BC signals can, however, convert these FC signals into visible percepts. One of the fundamental tasks of the present binocular theory is to explain how such an interaction between BC signals and FC signals can convert some, but not all, of the FC signals into filled-in percepts.

The above considerations suggest that the hypothesis that a $2\frac{1}{2}$-D sketch exists, distinct from a full 3-D representation, is incorrect (Marr and Nishihara, 1978). Such a $2\frac{1}{2}$-D sketch is an "orientation and depth map of the visible surfaces around a viewer" (Marr and Poggio, 1979, p.306). In contrast, the above considerations suggest that "ambiguous" regions of a scene, whose positions do not possess their own Boundary Contours, derive a relative depth value from the energy balance of their filled-in featural activities across all the spatial scales at that position. In other words, a depth map is completed by the multiple-scale featural filling-in process which generates a full 3-D representation of form-and-color-in-depth. Even in many filled-in 3-D representations there exist positions with indeterminate orientations because the featural filling-in process is unoriented, unlike the boundary completion process.

Although multiple-scale filling-in events within the FC System play an important role in the present theory towards imparting a relative depth value to ambiguous positions which do not possess their own binocular Boundary Contours, these events are surely not the only mechanisms used in depth perception. As noted in Section 10, vergeance angle is one of perhaps several additional factors that contribute to an absolute depth percept. In addition, the mechanisms which generate a percept of 3-D form need not be identical with the mechanisms used to reach objects in space, just as the mechanisms which generate a percept of 3-D form are not identical with the mechanisms which govern the recognition of objects (Grossberg, 1987b, Section 4).

16. Emmert's Law and Fechner's Paradox

Even without a detailed mechanistic analysis, many paradoxical percepts are clarified by these concepts. The classical Emmert's law, for example, is consistent with the theory. Emmert (1881) showed that a monocular afterimage seems to be located on *any* surface which a subject binocularly fixates while the afterimage is active. Moreover, the perceived size of the afterimage increases as the perceived distance of the surface increases. The present theory suggests that binocular viewing selectively activates certain BC System spatial scales more than others, whereas the monocular afterimage may excite all scales more equally. The energetic loading of certain BC System scales selectively activates the corresponding syncytia, and thereby shifts the apparent depth of the afterimage to those syncytia in which featural filling-in can most strongly occur.

The hypothesis that scale-specific Boundary Contours can selectively trigger featural filling-in reactions requires further development to explain how the Feature Contour signals from the two eyes contribute to the final binocular percept. One of the virtues of the FIRE process was its ability to quantitatively simulate paradoxical properties of binocular brightness percepts (Cohen and Grossberg, 1984a), such as Fechner's paradox, binocular brightness summation, binocular brightness averaging, and aspects of binocular rivalry (Blake, Sloane, and Fox, 1981; Cogan, 1982, Cogan, Silverman, and Sekuler, 1982; Curtis and Rule, 1980; Legge and Rubin, 1981; Levelt, 1965). Fechner's paradox illustrates the type of Feature Contour interactions that must be developed within an adequate theory of binocular form perception. In its simplest version, Fechner's paradox notes that the world does not look half as bright when one eye is closed, despite the fact that half as much light activates the brain. In fact, suppose that a scene is viewed through both eyes but that one eye sees it through a neutral density filter (Hering, 1964). When the filtered eye is entirely occluded, the scene looks brighter and more vivid despite the fact that less total light reaches the two eyes. The explanation below of how Boundary Contours trigger featural filling-in explains all the binocular phenomena that the FIRE theory could explain, and clarifies the properties of the FIRE theory which led to these successes.

17. Filling-In Generators and Filling-In Barriers: Blobs, Stripes, and Reciprocal Striate-Prestriate Connections

I can now outline a theory of how binocular interactions occur within the BC System and the FC System, and how the totality of the interactions within these systems lead to a representation which joins depth, brightness, color, and form information together within the model network which I compare to prestriate area V4. This model is consistent with recent experimental evidence that "many V4 cells exhibit length, width, orientation, direction of motion and spatial frequency selectivity. In the spectral domain, many V4 cells are also tuned to wavelength. Thus, V4 is not specialized to analyse one particular attribute of a visual stimulus; rather V4 appears to process both spatial and spectral information in parallel" (Desimone, Schein, Moran, and Ungerleider, 1985, p.441).

Such a multiple representation was also suggested within the FIRE theory (Cohen and Grossberg, 1984a, 1984b; Grossberg, 1983a). The present theory agrees with the assumption of the FIRE theory that the control of featural filling-in requires multiple processing stages. The present theory makes a break with the FIRE theory by showing how these stages can all use a diffusive mechanism of featural filling-in, rather than diffusive filling-in for monocular interactions and FIRE filling-in for binocular interactions.

In both the FIRE theory and the present work, it is necessary to distinguish between Filling-In Generators (FIGs) and Filling-In Barriers (FIBs). First I will sketch the functional ideas that necessitate this distinction and draw some general conclusions. Then I will analyse each of the mechanisms in greater detail.

Figure 1 summarizes the main property of FIGs and FIBs. In Figure 1, boxes with vertical lines stand for stages of Boundary Contour processing. Boxes with three pairs of circles stand for stages of Feature Contour processing. The lines symbolize the orientational tuning within the BC System. The pairs of circles symbolize the organization of the FC System into opponent and double-opponent cells (Red-Green, Blue-Yellow, White-Black). In Figure 1, oriented monocular cells from the left eye (BCS_L) and the right eye (BCS_R) interact along the pathways labelled 1 to activate oriented binocular BC System cells. This interaction requires the processing stages that are schematized in Figures 3 and 6. For the moment, it suffices to say that this interaction take places, in parallel, within multiple spatial scales, and that it generates oriented binocular cells some of which are precisely tuned to binocular disparity. The outputs from this binocular stage generate both FIGs and FIBs. Both types of signals are assumed to operate using the same mechanism. Their different functional effects are due to their different locations within the network as a whole. FIG signals are top-down signals to a prior level of processing. Their targets are cells within the FC System which process monocular Feature Contour signals. FIB signals do not project to a prior level of processing. Their targets are cells within the FC System which process binocular Feature Contour signals.

Figure 9 schematizes the effect of a FIG signal. Contour-sensitive FC System inputs which discount the illuminant are segregated within separate double-opponent channels (R–G, B–Y, W–B). These double-opponent channels are replicated so that FIG signals from each spatial scale of the BC System can interact with its own complete set of double-opponent cells and their corresponding syncytia. In Figure 9a, such an FC System input activates its target cell. This activation spreads laterally, or diffusively fills-in, from cell to cell. As in Section 24 of Grossberg (1987b), such a filling-in reaction is assumed to be accomplished by electrotonic interactions across gap junctions. Also as in Grossberg (1987b), I continue to call such a filling-in reaction a syncytial interaction. The network as a whole is called a *monocular syncytium*. Each FC input is distributed topographically to all the syncytia of the FC System, such that one complete set of double-opponent syncytia corresponds to each spatial scale of the BC System. Each FIG input from the BC System is distributed topographically to all the double-opponent syncytia of its spatial scale. In all, an FC input is broadcast in a wavelength-selective and positionally-selective way to the syncytia of all spatial scales, whereas a FIG input is broadcast in a scale-selective and positionally-selective way across syncytia which code different wavelengths (Figure 9b).

In the absence of BC System signals, the lateral syncytial interactions elicit a spatial pattern of activation such that nearby cells have similar activity levels (Figure 9c). The syncytial cells output through a spatially short-range shunting on-center off-surround network (Grossberg, 1983a). Such a network is sensitive to spatial discontinuities, or edges, in the activity pattern. Due to the smoothing action of the lateral interactions, the shunting on-center off-surround network does not allow any output signals to be generated.

Thus, in the absence of FIG signals from the BC System, the FC inputs to the monocular syncytium cannot generate contour-sensitive output signals from the monocular syncytium. Since only the FC System syncytia which also receive FIG signals can elicit output signals, one can begin to see how the FC System can generate scale-selective visible representations despite the fact that all of its syncytia receive the same FC inputs at an early processing stage. I now explain how FIG signals enable some of the contour-sensitive FC inputs to generate contour-sensitive FC outputs to the next processing stage.

When an FC input occurs at the same time as a contiguous FIG signal from the BC System, the FIG signal acts, as described in Figure 17 of Grossberg (1987b), to prevent the lateral spread of activation across its target cells (Figure 9d). A spatial discontinuity is hereby created in the spatial pattern of activation. The shunting on-center off-surround network senses this spatial discontinuity, and generates an output signal from the locations where it occurs. Due to properties of such shunting networks, the size of this output signal is sensitive to both the relative and absolute size of the spatial discontinuity as compared to the level of background activity (Grossberg, 1983a, 1987a). Thus these FC output signals have useful properties for building up ecologically useful color percepts (Cohen and Grossberg, 1984a).

In summary, a FIG signal from the BC System allows an FC input to generate an

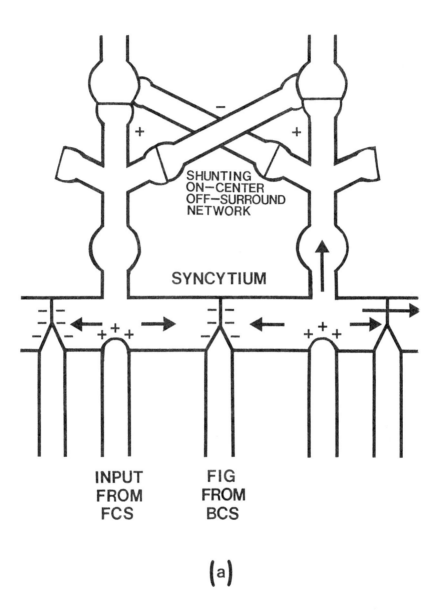

Figure 9. How filling-in generators (FIGs) control FC output signals: (a) FC inputs excite the monocular syncytium, which carries activation electrotonically to neighboring syncytial cells, except at cell membranes which receive FIG inputs. Syncytial cells activate a shunting on-center off-surround network that is sensitive to spatial discontinuities in the filled-in syncytial activity profile. Thus if no FIG input prevents lateral spread of the FC input, then no FC output signal occurs, as in (c). (b) Each FC input is broadcast in a wavelength-selective and positionally-selective way to the syncytia of all spatial scales. Each FIG input is broadcast in a scale-selective and positionally-selective way across syncytia which code different wavelengths. In (d), an FC output signal is generated because a FIG input causes a spatial discontinuity in the filled-in activity profile.

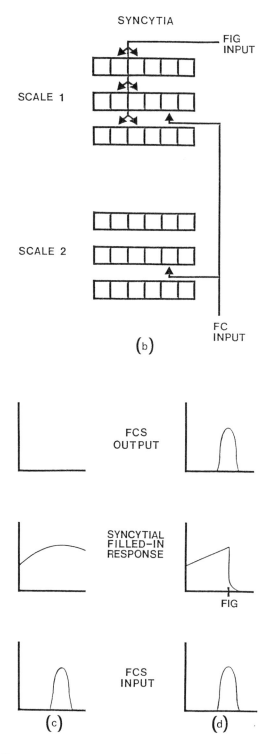

(b)

Figure 9 (continued).

output from the monocular syncytium by creating a spatial discontinuity in the spatial patterning of activity that is caused by the input. No FC output can occur, even in response to a large FC input, unless such a FIG, or binocular boundary signal, is received from the BC System. This property will be crucial in my explanation of how we typically see a globally self-consistent binocular percept uncontaminated by the existence of many binocularly discordant monocular inputs.

The type of featural filling-in which occurs within the monocular syncytium can be effective even if its interaction range, or spatial bandwidth, is relatively narrow. It need only smooth the FC input over a spatial domain that is wider than the spatial bandwidth of the short-range shunting on-center off-surround network, so that the filled-in activities are not processed as "edges" by this network.

Rockland and Lund (1983) and Livingstone and Hubel (1984a, 1984b) have both reported lateral interactions among the cytochrome oxydase staining blobs of area 17. Several facts are consistent with the interpretation that the monocular syncytium may include the blobs: Many of the blob cells are monocular (Livingstone and Hubel, 1984a). The interblob interactions are of relatively short range. Livingstone and Hubel (1984a, p.353) go so far as to comment that "the blob cells...are probably too short range in their spatial coverage to generate the long-range interactions that occur in color perception." If this anatomical interpretation of the monocular syncytium is correct, then two types of heretofore unreported interactions should exist: (1) prestriate-to-blob signals capable of gating shut the lateral interblob interactions; (2) post-processing of blob cells such that only spatially discontinuous, or edge-like, blob activity patterns can generate output signals to the area 18 stripes to which the area 17 blobs project (Livingstone and Hubel, 1984b). If this syncytial interaction does not occur among the blobs, then it should occur at target cells of the blobs.

18. Binocular Matching of Color Edges and Featural Filling-In

The output signals from the left and right monocular syncytia are labelled 2 in Figure 1. These output signals play the role of color contours in the theory. In order to generate percepts of color fields and surfaces, these color contours must also trigger a featural filling-in reaction. To this end, the color contour signals project topographically to binocular double-opponent cells which are hypothesized to exist within the *binocular syncytium* of Figure 1. A separate complete set of double-opponent binocular syncytia exists corresponding to every spatial scale of the BC System. The discussion in Section 17 showed that a binocular syncytium within the FC System receives a color contour signal only at those positions which can generate a binocular boundary signal within the BC System. As in the monocular syncytium, FC inputs to the binocular syncytium trigger a lateral spreading, or diffusive filling-in, of featural activity which spreads until it runs down its own electrotonic gradient, or until it hits a cell membrane that acts as a high resistance barrier.

Signals from the BC System generate such barriers in a binocular syncytium much as they do within a monocular syncytium. Within a binocular syncytium, boundary signals from the BC System are called filling-in barriers (FIBs) rather than filling-in generators (FIGs), even though their local mechanisms are assumed to be identical. How is a FIB signal generated within the binocular syncytium at every position which may receive an FC output from a monocular syncytium? The answer suggested in Figure 1 is that both FIGs and FIBs are elicited by the same BC System segmentation. Since FC outputs are regulated by the positions of FIG signals to the monocular syncytia, FIB signals will exist at all positions of the binocular syncytia which may be expected to receive these FC outputs.

Pairs of monocular FC signals input topographically to that binocular syncytium which corresponds to their own color and spatial scale. Because these inputs are processed by a network of double opponent cells, chromatically similar inputs which are spatially disparate may inhibit one another, whereas inputs that are sufficiently well matched spatially can elicit a synergetic reaction. I assume that the double opponent network is a specialized *gated dipole field* (Grossberg, 1976b, 1980, 1983b). In such a network, shunting on-center off-surround interactions within a color channel coexist with shunting off-center on-surround interactions within the opponent color channel, and the opponent color channels compete with each other at each position. (Also see Section 26.) Cohen and Grossberg (1984a) have demonstrated that monocular and binocular featural inputs to such a shunting on-center off-surround network generate activity patterns whose properties are strikingly similar to data about monocular and binocular brightness perception. In the Cohen and Grossberg (1984a) article, a FIRE process fills-in between the color contours. The FIRE process acts to binocularly summate and fill-in activities within perceptive regions between binocularly matched boundaries. Since a FIRE process is defined by a shunting on-center off-surround network, its monocular and binocular activity levels are the same as those generated by the shunting on-center off-surround network which defines a color channel. In the present theory, filling-in of these values by FIRE is replaced by diffusive filling-in of these values under the enabling influences of FIGs and FIBs. Since the filling-in values generated by a FIRE and those generated by diffusive filling-in both average the values computed by the shunting network, the Cohen and Grossberg (1984a) computer simulations of monocular and binocular brightness data are also valid in the present theory. However, the present theory uses only a single mechanism of featural filling-in, namely electrotonic or diffusive filling-in, for both monocular and binocular featural interactions.

19. A Representation of Form-and-Color-in-Depth

Even in the absence of further details, the perceptual representations that arise within the binocular syncytium can be seen to be sensitive to such factors as orientation, spatial frequency, depth, form, and color, as Desimone, Schein, Moran, and Ungerleider (1985) and Zeki (1983a, 1983b) have reported in V4. The sensitivity to orientation is due in part to the orientation-sensitive inputs from the BC System (but also see Section 29). Sensitivity to spatial frequency is due to the parsing of both BC System and FC System subnetworks into separate spatial frequency-sensitive channels. Sensitivity to depth is due to the disparity-sensitive inputs from the BC System, as well as to the possibility that spatially disparate monocular FC System inputs can mismatch within a double-opponent network. Sensitivity to form follows from the ability of the BC System to preattentively complete boundaries and to segment textures, as well as to receive learned and attentionally-modulated boundary completion signals from the Object Recognition System, before generating FIG signals and FIB signals to the FC System (Grossberg, 1987b, Figure 2). Sensitivity to color derives from the fact that successive stages of FC System processing progress from opponent to double-opponent processing. A single cell within the binocular syncytium can thus be sensitive to all of these factors. Such a cell is also sensitive to featural filling-in across a spatial domain that is determined by the global configuration of all BC and FC signals.

Neurophysiological data have not yet disentangled the separate input and interaction pathways that can give rise to such a complicated cellular response. In particular, direct evidence is lacking for the existence of a binocular cortical cell syncytium or, for that matter, for lateral interactions, although interactions of some type are known to influence V4 cells over regions corresponding to as much as 30° on the retina. Although direct evidence is, as yet, lacking, some indirect evidence has been found. The evidence of Zeki (1983b) is sufficiently important to quote at length:

> "...it has been very difficult to determine the extent and the disposition of the critical surround...Adding middle or short wave light...led to a response, but only after a delay of about 4s. The reverse sequence of stimulation also led to a response, but again with a delay. Compared to the almost instantaneous reactions of...cells in V1, this in itself suggests indirectly that the cell is responding only after integrating information from large parts of the field of view... The actual position of the rest of the...display...did not make a difference to the cell's response" (pp.775–776).

Both the long delay before the cell responded (which may be considerably shortened in an unanesthetized animal) and the cell's insensitivity to changes in the positioning of the rest of the display are consistent with the existence of a lateral filling-in reaction which averages its activations from all the color edge inputs that are contained within the surrounding boundary.

20. Interactions between Brightness and Depth Information

The concept that multiple scale filling-in inparts a relative depth value to ambiguous regions implies that brightness and depth information can mutually influence one another. Grossberg (1983a) reviews classical data which are consistent with this assertion. Two types of more recent data are summarized in this section for illustrative purposes.

Schwartz and Sperling (1983) and Dosher, Sperling, and Wurst (1986) have analysed influences of luminance differences upon both perceived depth and perceived rigidity of form. In their studies they consider *proximity luminance covariance* (PLC) as a factor influencing percepts of depth and form. To manipulate PLC, the luminance of each line in a 2-D projection of an object was made to depend on the 3-D depth of that line. A larger luminance was used to signal a closer object projection. PLC's that confirm and that conflict with the 3-D depth were analysed. The interaction of PLC with stereo information was also analysed. Both studies concluded that PLC is a powerful factor in determining a depth percept and that, moreover, stereo and PLC information combine in a way that can be summarized by a weighted linear model.

Egusa (1983) has studied the effects of luminance differences on perceived depth by constructing stimuli consisting of two hemifields of different colors, and asking the subject to state which appeared nearer and to judge the perceived depth between them. When both hemifields were achromatic, the perceived depth increased with increasing brightness difference. With chromatic-chromatic combinations, the perceived depth depended upon the hue combination. In terms of decreasing frequency of "nearer" judgments, the hue order was red, green, and blue.

21. Transparency

Transparency phenomena (Beck, Prazdny, and Ivry, 1984; Metelli, 1974; Metelli, da Pos, and Cavedon, 1985; Meyer and Senecal, 1983) provide another type of data which support the concept that multiple syncytia exist corresponding to different spatial scales, and that filling-in of FC signals within some of these syncytia but not others can generate a percept of form-and-color-in-depth. In percepts of transparency, a phenomenal scission occurs which replaces the percept of a single color at a fixed perceptual location with the simultaneous perception of two colors: the color of the object seen through the transparency and the color of the transparent layer. Within the theory, such a scission is analysed by considering how one color elicits filling-in within a syncytium of one spatial scale, whereas the other color elicits filling-in within a syncytium of a different spatial scale. Such an analysis is possible due to the hypothesis that each FC signal is topographically broadcast to the syncytia of all spatial scales, and that the spatial distribution of BC signals among the several scales determines which of the syncytia will react to such an FC signal by triggering a filling-in reaction.

The formal rules which Metelli (1974) has articulated for predicting the occurrence of transparency are similar to the conditions under which the BC system triggers neon color spreading (Redies and Spillman, 1981; van Tuijl, 1975; van Tuijl and de Weert, 1979) within the FC System. This relationship is perhaps best seen from the study of Meyer and Senecal (1983) using a variant of the Kanizsa (1976, 1979) subjective contour configuration. Unlike Figure 5 of Grossberg (1987b), some of the pac-man figures which they used to induce a rectangular subjective contour were completed into circles within the rectangle using faintly colored wedge shaped regions. Meyer and Senecal (1983) showed that a percept of transparency covaried with the percept of a chromatically filled-in rectangle surrounded by a strong rectangular subjective contour. In our explanation of neon color spreading (Grossberg and Mingolla, 1985a), the strength of such a subjective contour also regulates the strength of chromatic filling-in reactions by inhibiting boundaries that would otherwise prevent filling-in from escaping from the colored inducing wedge-shaped regions. Thus these data are consistent with the idea that transparency is due to featural filling-in reactions across some, but not all, of the syncytia corresponding to each fixed perceptual location, and that these differential filling-in reactions are associated with a percept of a relative difference in depth.

22. Generating Disparity Sensitive and Spatial Frequency Sensitive Cells using Positionally Ambiguous Inputs: Inhibitory Interneurons and Multiplexed Complex Cells

I now outline the theory's conception of how monocular inputs to the BC System generate the binocular and disparity-sensitive complex cells which input to the CC Loop, as in Figure 6. I also suggest how these complex cells can become sensitive to orientational disparity at each position as well as to positional disparity (Shinkman and Bruce, 1977; von der Heydt, Hänny, and Dürsteler, 1981). Indeed, I show how individual complex cells can become sensitive to position, orientation, spatial frequency, positional disparity, and orientational disparity, yet also be broad-band with respect to color in order to function as boundary detectors (DeValois, Albrecht, and Thorell, 1982; Poggio, Motter, Squatrito, and Trotter, 1985; Thorell, DeValois, and Albrecht, 1984). Thus individual complex cells *multiplex* many different types of perceptual information. Then spatial arrays of such complex cells input to the competitive and cooperative mechanisms of the CC Loop, which sort out all of these different types of information into a binocularly consistent segmentation capable of suppressing many possible double images. Thus the BC System's cells become binocular, indeed multiplexed, at an early stage to provide a processing substrate from which the CC Loop's mechanisms can synthesize stereo information into its emergent segmentations. This scheme of binocular preprocessing followed by competitive and co-operative interactions will be seen to sharpen my explanation of the Kaufman (1974) and Kulikowski (1978) data about binocular rivalry (Sections 2–9), in addition to various other data about interactions between form and color processing. In order to reach these con-clusions, I briefly consider the role of developmental plasticity and intracortical inhibitory interactions in setting up the binocular BC System computation.

Figure 10a schematizes the fact that a certain amount of positional uncertainty is caused in order to form an oriented receptive field: To detect the orientation of a scenic contrast difference, the receptive field needs to collect inputs corresponding to small regions of the retinal mosaic. Thus in response to a monocularly viewed, vertical figural edge, a *spatial pattern* of reactions can be generated at the earliest stage of oriented BC System processing, which I identify with the simple cells of striate cortex (Hubel and Wiesel, 1977). This type of positional uncertainty is functionally related to the well-known relationship between receptive field scatter and the cortical magnification factor (Daniel and Whit-teridge, 1961; Dow, Snyder, Vautin, and Bauer, 1981; Hubel and Wiesel, 1977). This type of positional uncertainty may also contribute to the binocular sensitivity of some striate simple cells (Poggio, Motter, Squatrito, and Trotter, 1985) by contributing to the overlap of ocular dominance columns.

The positional uncertainty property raises the following basic issue. The receptive fields of simple cells enable them to respond selectively to properties of orientation and spatial frequency within a scene. These receptive fields also, however, suffer a loss of posi-tional information, since receptive fields corresponding to several retinal positions may be activated by a single scenic position. How can subsequent cortical interactions compen-sate for the loss of positional information that is required to design orientationally selective receptive fields? I suggest below how the processes which restore a greater measure of po-sitional certainty also generate binocular complex cells whose tuning curves are sensitive to positional disparity, orientational disparity, and spatial frequency.

The technical challenge met by a network capable of this task can be seen by comparing Figures 10b–e, which show that as the positional disparity or the orientational disparity of a binocularly perceived edge varies, it elicits a different spatial pattern of activation across the network of oriented receptive fields. As the input disparity changes, the pattern of excitation can change not only its internal structure, but also its spatial scale. How can such spatial patterns be used to activate binocular cells that are sensitive to positional disparity, orientational disparity, and spatial frequency? Several models for the develop-ment of binocular tuning in cortical cells have been advanced; for example, by Bienenstock, Cooper, and Munro (1982), Grossberg (1980, 1983b), Singer (1983, 1985), and Willshaw and von der Malsburg (1976). None of these models has, however, dealt directly with the problem schematized in Figure 10. A solution is suggested by the use of a general neural network design—called a *masking field*—that has heretofore been applied to explain data concerning visual masking (Grossberg and Levine, 1975) and context-sensitive encoding of speech sounds and cognitive recognition codes (Cohen and Grossberg, 1986, 1987; Gross-berg, 1978, 1987a). I suggest that variants of the masking field design may be used by the nervous system wherever functional properties of the following type are needed.

In a masking field model, a level F_1 of cells sends input pathways to a second level F_2 of cells. Level F_1 generates spatial patterns of activation that can vary both in their internal structuring and in their spatial scale, as in Figure 10. These spatial patterns of activation across F_1 generate spatially distributed inputs to F_2 (Figure 11). In particular, each active F_1 cell can send signals to many F_2 cells along pathways whose connection

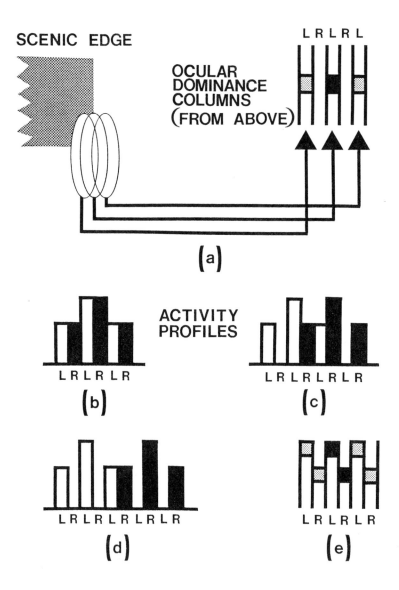

Figure 10. Translation of scenic contour information into spatial patterns of cortical activity: (a) Overlapping like-oriented receptive fields generate a spatial pattern of activity at left-monocular representations in response to a left-monocularly viewed scenic edge. The figure portrays a view from above of cortical ocular dominance columns for the left (L) and right (R) eyes, and portrays increased cell activation with darker areas. (b)-(d) Binocular inputs due to a scenic edge viewed by the two eyes at increasing positional disparities creates distinct, expanding activity patterns, across the ocular dominance columns. Here bar heights code activities. (e) Binocular viewing can cause an orientational disparity that is coded by a positional shift in the activity pattern caused by the left eye relative to that caused by the right eye. This shift is perpendicular to the shift caused by positional disparity, which separates activity patterns caused by the two eyes in a horizontal, rather than a vertical direction.

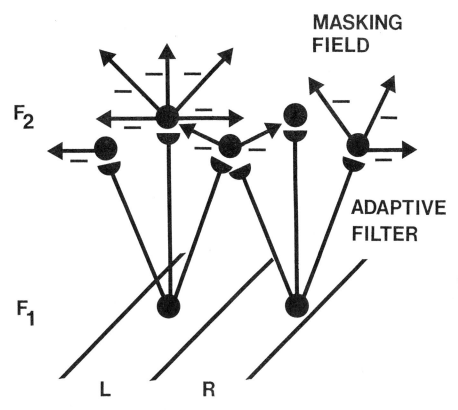

Figure 11. Output signals from oriented monocular representations (L and R in level F_1) converge via an adaptive filter at cells which compete via a masking field (level F_2). Only cells whose inputs survive the masking field competition to generate a short term memory (STM) activation can trigger learned changes in the abutting LTM traces which are found in the $F_1 \rightarrow F_2$ pathways.

strengths decrease with the lengths of the pathways. Thus the positional uncertainty of the responses by F_1 cells in Figure 10 is rendered even more ambiguous by the divergence of signal pathways from each cell in F_1 to F_2. Despite this fact, level F_2 can generate spatially localized activations in response to the distributed input patterns from F_1. Moreover, these spatially localized F_2 activations represent narrowly tuned reactions to positional disparity, orientational disparity, and spatial frequency information (Grossberg and Marshall, 1987).

These formal properties are due to three types of network interactions: First, the divergence of signals from each cell of F_1 to F_2 implies a convergence of F_1 signals at each cell of F_2 (Figure 11). Such a convergence of signals enables F_2 to *filter* the activation pattern across F_1.

Second, level F_2 contains a network of intrinsic inhibitory interneurons. The design of this network enables it to suppress, or mask, the activations of all F_2 cells except those which best represent the total activation pattern across F_1. In particular, many cells in F_2 receive input combinations which represent subpatterns of the total activation pattern across F_1. These cells are inhibited by masking field interactions. Only those F_2 cells which respond best to the total activation across F_1 can survive these inhibitory interactions. Figures 12 and 13 illustrate this type of selectivity using computer simulations from Cohen and Grossberg (1986). These simulations illustrate that a masking field can selectively activate different F_2 cells in response to input patterns across F_1 which differ either in their spatial scale (compare Figures 12, 13a, and 13c) or in the patterning of activation across a fixed set of cells (compare Figures 13a with 13b and 13c with 13d).

These general purpose properties of a masking field give rise to complex cells in F_2 with desired coding properties when the simple cells of F_1 are spatially organized into alternating ocular dominance columns containing hypercolumns whose cell receptive fields undergo regular orientation shifts as the hypercolumn is traversed (Hubel and Wiesel, 1977). Then the *total activation pattern* across F_1 unambiguously represents such factors as monocular position, binocular positional disparity, binocular orientation disparity, and spatial frequency (Figures 10 and 14). The selective response of F_2 to F_1 translates the information within the total activation pattern across F_1 into selective tuning curves for all of these factors within *individual cells* of F_2. In summary, although individual cells of F_1 generate positionally ambiguous responses, the spatial patterning of F_1 cell activations carries unambiguous information about position, disparity, and spatial scale. The interaction between F_1 and F_2 converts the unambiguous spatially distributed information across F_1 into unambiguous reactions of individual cells in F_2. In this way, the transformation $F_1 \rightarrow F_2$ enables individual cells in F_2 to *multiplex* the data which is spatially distributed across F_1.

These masking field properties are consistent with the fact that many receptive field properties of striate cells are interactive properties which require inhibitory interneurons for their normal expression. In particular, application of the GABA antagonist bicuculline produces striking reductions in the selectivity of striate cell receptive field properties (Sillito, 1974, 1975a, 1975b, 1977, 1979; Sillito, Salt, and Kemp, 1985), notably a reduction of orientational tuning. This type of property is consistent with the model, since the divergent inputs from F_1 to F_2 are shaped by the inhibition across F_2. The model is also consistent with the fact that striate complex cells (in F_2) exhibit true cyclopean depth reactions, whereas striate simple cells do not (Poggio, Motter, Squatrito, and Trotter, 1985).

Using the same mechanisms, complex cells in F_2 may multiplex an even greater number of image properties just so long as F_1 is able to represent these properties as part of its total spatial pattern of activation. Letting individual cells in F_2 receive converging inputs from F_1 cells which respond to opposite direction-of-contrast and several ranges of wavelength sensitivity (Grossberg, 1987b; Thorell, DeValois, and Albrecht, 1984) does not create new problems of principle, although it does raise as yet unanswered questions about the spatial organization of such information.

Sensitivity to spatial frequency information (DeValois, Albrecht, and Thorell, 1982) is a characteristic of masking field cells, whether or not the individual input cells from F_1 are sensitive to spatial frequency (Figures 12, 13a, and 13c). This type of spatial frequency sensitivity enables F_2 to preferentially activate cells that best encode the total F_1 activity pattern, even if these patterns excite narrower or broader expanses of F_1 cells, as in Figure 14. This property suggests possible differences in the mechanisms whereby simple cells and complex cells achieve spatial frequency sensitivity. Individual simple cells in F_1 may be made sensitive to lower spatial frequencies by increasing the size of their receptive fields, or input-averaging domains. Due to the organization of F_1 into ocular dominance columns, such a size increase can also cause an increase in the positional uncertainty with which networks of these simple cells respond (Figure 14). This increase in positional uncertainty can generate more widespread spatial patterns of activation across the F_1 network. The F_1 spatial pattern can, in turn, generate spatial-frequency selective responses of individual F_2 cells using the spatial frequency-sensitive F_2 properties that enable F_2 to best encode

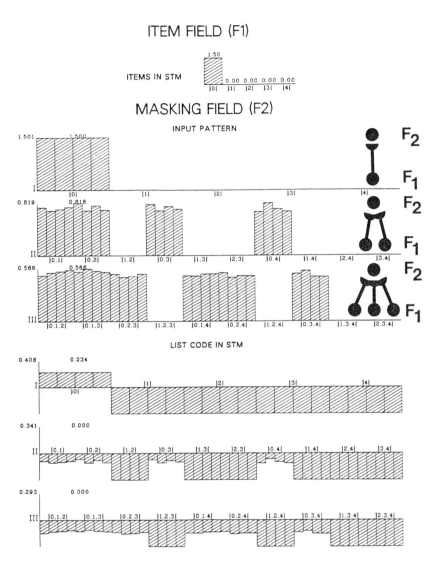

Figure 12. Multiplexing of spatial patterns of activity across F_1 into selective STM activations of individual cell populations at F_2: The item field depicts the spatial pattern of activity across F_1. The first three rows under Masking Field, labelled Input Pattern, depict the inputs from F_1 to cells across F_2. The inputs to the cell populations of the masking field F_2 are arranged in three rows. In this computer simulation, the cell population in the ith $(i = 1, 2, 3)$ row receive inputs from exactly i populations of F_1. Thus, in row 1, there are 4 cell populations in F_2, labelled $\{0\}$, which receive an input from only the population in F_1 which codes item $\{0\}$. In row 2, there are 4 cell populations in F_2, labelled $\{0, 3\}$, which receive an input from the populations in F_1 which code items $\{0\}$ and $\{3\}$. The number above the bars which represent input size designates the maximal input to that row. Bar heights represent input intensities. The inputs are broadly distributed across F_2 cells. The Code in STM depicts the selective STM activation of the corresponding F_2 cell populations to these broadly distributed inputs. In this simulation, only a single population generates a positive response to the broadly distributed input pattern. All other activations are negative, or inhibited, and hence are not large enough to exceed the nonnegative output threshold of the cells.

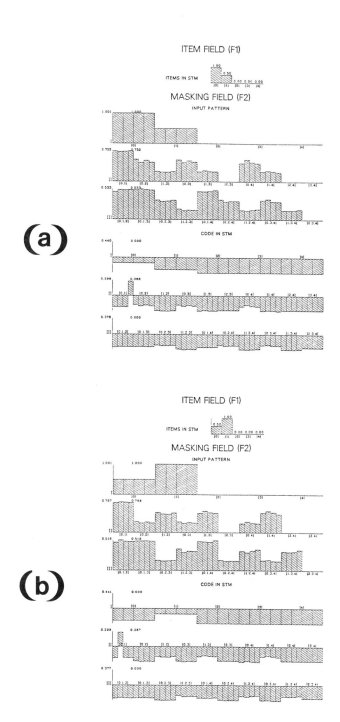

Figure 13. Multiplexing of spatial patterns of activity across F_1 into selective activations of individual cell populations at F_2. In (a)–(d), four different activity patterns across F_1, varying in spatial scale and internal structuring, generate distinct selective reactions at F_2.

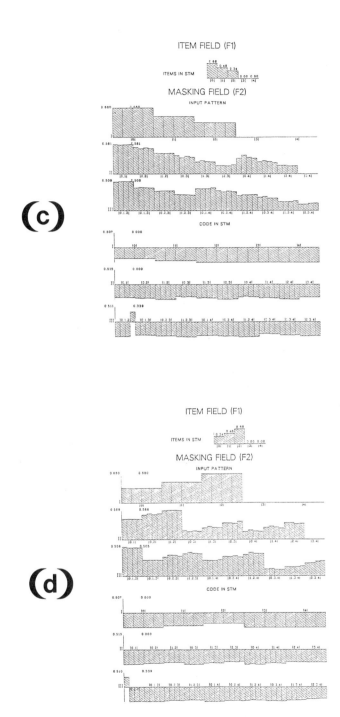

Figure 13 (continued).

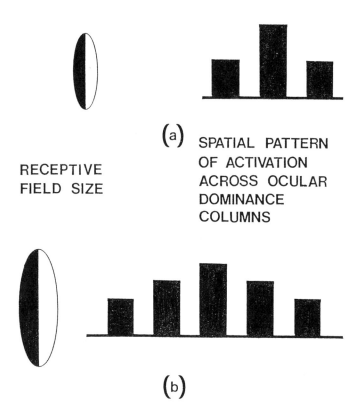

Figure 14. Early stages of spatial frequency sensitivity are represented by covariation of receptive field size with the spatial pattern of activity generated by cells of this size across F_1: Small receptive fields generate more localized patterns (a) than large receptive fields (b). Bar height represents activity at each cell position.

any F_1 activity pattern.

Thus within a masking field model, the same multiplexing mechanism can be used to generate disparity-sensitive cells (Figure 10) and spatial frequency-sensitive cells (Figure 14). In fact, replacing a monocular pattern (Figure 10a) by a binocular pattern (Figure 10d) is an operation formally analogous to replacing a high spatial frequency pattern (Figure 14a) by a low spatial frequency pattern (Figure 14b). This observation indicates that cells sensitive to different spatial frequencies need not, in principle, be segregated from cells sensitive to different disparities in order to achieve selective F_2 tuning curves.

In summary, the masking field model suggests how individual striate complex cells may multiplex the selective encoding of spatial position, orientation, binocular positional disparity, binocular orientational disparity, and spatial frequency, while lumping together direction-of-contrast and wavelength sensitivity. From the perspective of the present theory, these cells function to generate chromatically broad-band, but spatially focused, spatially frequency-selective and disparity-selective binocular boundary signals to the binocular segmentation mechanisms of the CC Loop.

23. Adaptive Tuning of the Complex Cell Filter by a Non-Hebbian Associative Law: Spatial Patterns as the Units of Learning

The third factor which is used by the masking field model is adaptive tuning of the $F_1 \rightarrow F_2$ filter, and thus of the complex cell tuning curves, to the activation patterns which are experienced most regularly across F_1 (Cohen and Grossberg, 1987). Such adaptive tuning is mediated by associative long term memory (LTM) traces which exist at the synaptic terminals of each $F_1 \rightarrow F_2$ pathway, and which multiply, or gate, the signals in these pathways before the gated signals can influence target cells in F_2. In the present application, these adaptive tuning properties form part of the machinery which regulates the critical period of developmental plasticity for binocular cortical cells (Blakemore and Cooper, 1970; Braastad and Heggelund, 1985; Frégnac and Imbert, 1978; Hirsch and Spinelli, 1970; Hubel and Wiesel, 1977; Singer, 1985; von der Heydt, Hänny, and Dürsteler, 1981). The theory uses an associative law which allows the long-term memory traces to either increase or decrease in strength in response to the correlated activities of their presynaptic F_1 neuron and postsynaptic F_2 neuron (Grossberg, 1968, 1969, 1976a).

Such an associative law does not obey the familiar Hebbian associative law (Hebb, 1949), which assumes that correlated activities always lead to an increase of associative strength. Figure 10 suggests why a Hebbian law is inadequate. Due to adaptive tuning, each F_2 cell becomes more strongly and selectively activated by its "trigger" spatial pattern across F_1. *All* the LTM traces in pathways from F_1 to such an activated F_2 cell change as a result of the tuning process. In order for these LTM traces to learn the optimal *spatial pattern* of activation across the F_1 network, an LTM trace in an $F_1 \rightarrow F_2$ pathway must be able to decrease if its F_1 activity is small and to increase if its F_1 activity is large. The Hebbian associative law, which mandates an increase due to associative pairing, is thus not suitable for learning spatial patterns. It was based on the idea that activities in individual pathways, rather than spatial patterns of activation across a network of cells, are the functional units of associative learning. Several investigators (Levy, 1985; Levy, Brassel, and Moore, 1983; Levy and Desmond, 1985; Rauschacker and Singer, 1979; Singer, 1983, 1985) have presented neurophysiological evidence concerning cortical plasticity that are consistent with this type of non-Hebbian associative law.

Suppose that such non-Hebbian LTM traces multiply the signals within the pathways converging from simple cells to complex cells, and that the complex cells interact via a masking field. Such a competitive learning system is competent to selectively tune complex cells to those activation patterns which occur regularly across F_1 (Cohen and Grossberg, 1987; Grossberg, 1976a). For example, due to normal viewing conditions, certain complex cells may be preferentially tuned to different orientations from the left eye and the right eye (Figure 10e), if these correlations are persistent ones within their spatial scale and retinal position (von der Heydt, Hänny, and Dürsteler, 1981). Tuning of disparity-selectivity may be sharper for vertically oriented than horizontally oriented complex cells, due to the breadth of the F_1 spatial pattern that is caused by left eye and right eye representations of a horizontal contour. This property may help to explain the greater number of vertical than horizontal disparity-sensitive cells that Hubel and Wiesel (1970) found in V2, and the fact that complex cells may be either disparity sensitive (depth neurons) or disparity insensitive (flat neurons) (Poggio, Motter, Squatrito, and Trotter, 1985).

The existence of disparity insensitive neurons is not considered an imperfection of cortical design within the theory. Disparity-sensitive cells are herein regarded as part of a 3-D boundary segmentation system, rather than as part of a disembodied stereopsis computation. From this perspective, it is obvious that boundaries must be computed

within all spatial scales in a manner that prevents spurious featural filling-in from occurring (Grossberg, 1987b). If only finely tuned disparity-sensitive cells could input to
this boundary computation, then horizontally oriented binocular cells would necessarily
be excluded. The full burden of completing horizontal boundaries would then fall upon
responses of the end cutting mechanism (Grossberg, 1987b, Section 13) to nearly vertical
image contrasts. Non-vertically oriented cells with lesser degrees of disparity-insensitivity
overcome this possible problem. In particular, disparity-insensitive horizontally tuned cells
can complete a rectangular boundary within a spatial scale capable of binocularly fusing
the vertical boundaries of the rectangle. Such a completed rectangle could generate a filled-
in representation within the corresponding syncytium within the FC System, and thereby
contribute to the final percept. In contrast, disparity-insensitive horizontally tuned cells
would have little influence on the syncytia of scales in which they could not complete a
boundary grouping capable of supporting a filled-in percept.

This summary has suggested mechanisms capable of giving rise to the multiplexed
tuning curve properties which are characteristic of individual striate complex cells. It
hereby provides enough detail to address the question of how binocular complex cells which
vary in their position, orientation, spatial frequency, and disparity-sensitive properties
influence a boundary completion within the BC System. Sections 2–9 indicated that the
same competitive and cooperative interactions within the CC Loop which were suggested
in Grossberg (1987b) to complete monocularly-activated boundaries are also competent to
complete binocularly-activated boundaries. By putting together these two lines of evidence,
the theory can begin to analyse a large data base about binocular perception. I begin by
refining my analysis of how these mechanisms suppress binocular double images.

Julesz (1971) and Sperling (1970) have analysed how spurious binocular correlations between pairs of monocular images can be suppressed before they enter conscious perception.
Their important pioneering models of binocular disparity detection and the suppression
of spurious double images led to the active development of several models for binocular
matching of edges (Dev, 1975; Marr and Poggio, 1976, 1979). I have elsewhere discussed
some basic weaknesses of these models (Grossberg, 1983a). Herein I suggest a different
solution to this problem which avoids these weaknesses. The main new insight is as follows: The processes which compensate for the positional uncertainty due to orientational
tuning (masking field) combine with boundary completion processes (CC Loop) in such a
way as to synthesize disparity-sensitive boundaries which suppress double images. Neither
of these processes was incorporated into the earlier models. Hence the present model is
genuinely new.

24. Suppression of Double Images: Self-Similar Interaction between Mask Scale, Filter Scale, Competition Scale, and Cooperation Scale

Four stages of network interactions lead to the suppression of boundary signals that could
otherwise have led to percepts of double images. At the first stage (simple cells), input
masks average inputs over an oriented receptive field. One half of this field inhibits the
other half. The output signal is rectified. Consequently each mask can generate an output
only if the net mask activity, after inhibition acts, is positive. Pairs of such input masks,
each sensitive to opposite contrasts of luminance or wavelength, cooperate at the second
stage (complex cells) to generate an output signal which is sensitive to position, orientation,
amount-of-contrast, disparity, and spatial frequency, but not to direction-of-contrast.

The sensitivity to spatial frequency is particularly important for an understanding of depth perception and the suppression of false images. As mentioned in Section 22, two distinct sources of spatial frequency sensitivity are operative at the first, or input mask, stage. One source is the different sizes of the masks, or receptive fields (Figure 14), across the multiple spatial scales of the network. Despite the variability in total input mask size, the masks within *all* the spatial scales are designed to respond to sufficiently large and sharp contrasts in the scenic inputs which share their position and orientation. In particular, sufficiently contrastive bounding edges of a scene are monocularly detectable by oriented receptive fields in all the BC System spatial scales. Monocular detectability of bounding edges by all scales provides the most important example of how multiple scales can simultaneously be active in generating a 3-D form percept. Such multiple detectability of bounding edges "grounds" the remainder of the 3-D form computation and enables all spatial frequencies to share this feature of stereo resolution.

In contrast, only the largest masks can respond to the most gradual oriented changes in contrast. Such gradual contrast changes may occur, for example, within the interior luminance gradients of a smoothly shaded, nearby surface. Thus the smallest masks can react to the most narrow range of spatial frequencies; in particular, to high spatial frequencies. The largest masks can react to high spatial frequencies as well as to lower spatial frequencies. This type of spatial frequency sensitivity is, in itself, insufficient to distinguish whether size differences of retinal inputs are due to different object sizes or depths (Section 11). The remaining spatial frequency sensitive mechanisms interact with the spatial frequency sensitivity of the input masks to make this distinction.

A second source of spatial frequency sensitivity at the input mask stage derives from the positional uncertainty which subserves orientational tuning of the input masks. Such positional uncertainty smoothes the input from each retinal position and can thereby, within a cortex organized into interleaved ocular dominance columns, give rise to multiple periodic receptive fields for the simple cells of the model (Figures 10 and 14). Multiple simple cell receptive fields have, for example, been reported in the experiments of Mullikin, Jones, and Palmer (1984) on cat visual cortex. The theory suggests that larger individual input masks are generated by a more widespread scatter of the input pathways corresponding to each retinal position across the field of input masks (Figure 14). This periodic distance-dependent and spatial-frequency sensitive smoothing of the input provides a framework for rationalizing the successful use of the Gabor transform for analysis of the spatial frequency properties of visual cortex (Daugman, 1979; Gabor, 1946; Kulikowski and Kranda, 1986; Kulikowski, Marčelja, and Bishop, 1982; Pollen, Andrews, and Feldon, 1978; Pollen and Ronner, 1975, 1981, 1983).

I assume that the adaptive filter which carries outputs from the first stage F_1 to the second stage F_2 is *self-similar*: that is, larger receptive fields at F_1 can broadcast their outputs across a broader expanse of cells at F_2. As a result of this correlation, there exist disparities at which pairs of large input masks can converge upon individual binocular cells at F_2 whereas pairs of small input masks cannot converge upon individual binocular cells at the second stage (Figure 15). In other words, there exist disparities at which large input masks activate a single spatial locus of cells in the masking field, whereas small input masks activate a pair of disparate spatial loci in the masking field. By combining the different spatial frequency sensitivities of input masks and binocular cells, the following conclusion may be drawn: Image contrasts which are sharp enough to activate a pair (left eye, right eye) of high frequency input masks may be too disparate to activate individual binocular complex cells. At the same disparity, image contrasts which are either sharp or gradual may activate a pair of low frequency input masks which can activate individual binocular complex cells. This interaction begins to correlate size differences with disparity differences, but it does not yet cope with the many pairs of left and right monocular input masks which cannot activate individual binocular cells. The CC Loop solves this problem as follows.

Outputs from the masking field input to the first competitive stage. A single spatial locus of activation at the masking field can excite a single spatial locus within the corresponding spatial scale of the first competitive stage of the CC Loop (Figure 15a). In contrast, a pair of disparate spatial loci at the masking field can mutually inhibit each other's signals using the first competitive stage (Figure 15b). Thus the first competitive stage can suppress the boundary signals due to pairs of monocular boundary signals which are incapable of fusing at the masking field stage (double images). If, for any reason, one of a pair of disparate masking field activations is stronger than the other, then its Boundary Contour signal can inhibit the other one at the first competitive stage.

In summary, a self-similar hierarchical interaction between multiple-scale input masks, masking fields, and short-range oriented competition sets the stage for computing fused binocular boundaries versus rivalrous monocular boundaries, thereby mechanistically explicating the concept of binocular filter depicted in Figure 6. Moreover, although all spatial scales can respond well to high spatial frequency contrasts, the larger scales can fuse large binocular disparities which the smaller scales cannot fuse. All of the interactions summarized above use relatively short-range spatial interactions. As indicated in Section 4, feedback interactions between the short-range competition and the long-range cooperation of the CC Loop endows the selection of binocularly consistent boundaries and the suppression of binocularly discordant boundaries with properties of completion and coherence. In Section 20 of Grossberg (1987b), it was furthermore suggested that the bipole cells of the CC Loop exhibit a property of self-similarity which enables them to fire only in response to enough scenic evidence. In this section, it was suggested that the simple cells and their $F_1 \rightarrow F_2$ pathways within the OC Filter also possess a self-similarity property that helps to distinguish between object size and object depth. The property of self-similarity may thus be a rather general principle of cortical design which is worthy of more experimental investigation.

Many type of data relating stereopsis mechanisms to emergent boundary segmentation mechanisms are clarified by the binocular BC System design that is summarized above. For example, Russell (1979) reanalysed the data of Lu and Fender (1972), who studied the chromatic input to stereopsis by using pairs of random dot stereograms built up from arrays of small colored squares. These authors varied the luminance of all squares of one color until depth was perceived. Russell (1979, p.834) concluded that "depth was perceived when there was enough signal from the enhanced edge detector [read: chromatically broad-band boundary detector] to allow the stereopsis process to calculate depth [read: generate emergent binocular boundaries] from the disparity of the edges detected." Russell calculated that the opponent L–M signal is an important component of this boundary detector, which is consistent with the discussion of complex cell properties in Section 31 of Grossberg (1987b).

Earle (1985, p.551) has shown that the "introduction of stereoscopic depth effects can destroy the perceptual salience of both local and global Glass pattern structure present in a two-dimensional projection ..., can be used to create novel three-dimensional Glass patterns ..., and can lead to the perception of both local and global Glass pattern structure when none is apparent in the two-dimensional projection." Such data can be explained as the result of several interacting BC System processes, notably the OC Filter and short-

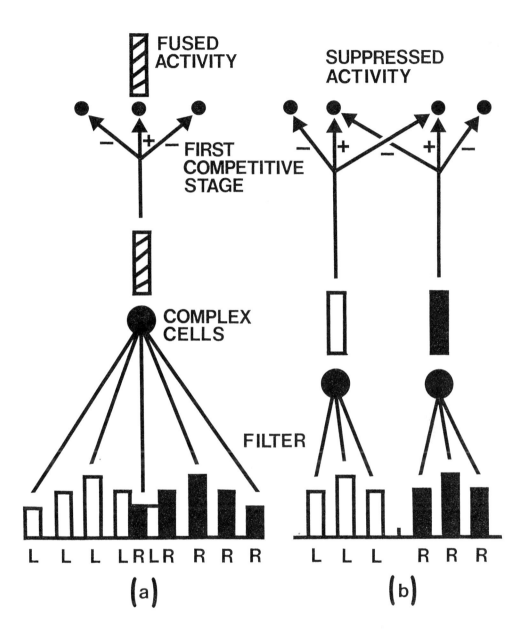

Figure 15. Early stages of binocular fusion and rivalry: A low spatial frequency channel in (a) can binocularly fuse a pair of monocular images at a fixed disparity that cannot be fused by the high spatial frequency channel in (b). The fused input in (a) generates a focal excitation at the first competitive stage. The disparate monocular inputs in (b) can cancel each other at the first competitive stage. These circuits show how the distinction made in Figure 6 can be mechanistically realized.

range competitive processes through which binocular viewing can selectively fuse binocular boundaries from spatially disparate pairs of monocular boundaries, parse the fused
boundaries into the CC Loop spatial scales capable of supporting the fusion, and initiate
scale-specific boundary completion and grouping with the other binocular boundaries that
are processed within that scale. Earle (1985, p.551) went on to say that his data "are in
contradiction of the [primal sketch] proposals advanced by Marr."

25. Interaction of Binocular Boundaries with Monocular Syncytia during Binocular Fusion and Rivalry

Having provided a framework for discussing how binocular boundary signals are selected
and generate outputs from the BC System to the FC System, I can now deepen the
analysis of how these boundary signals selectively enable some, but not necessarily all,
FC signals to generate the filling-in events that lead to visible percepts. This analysis
suggests several new functional reasons why the FC System is organized into networks of
double opponent cells interleaved with networks of syncytia. It also supportes a neural
model of double opponent color fields that takes the form of a specialized gated dipole
field (Grossberg, 1976b, 1980). I also show that, whereas individual double opponent
cells may have unoriented receptive fields, when a *network* of such cells processes oriented
BC signals and oriented scenic contrasts, it acts like a *form*-selecting mechanism, not
merely as a source of veridical color signals. Thus the several stages of the FC System
elaborate progressively more sophisticated properties of color *and* form together due to
their interactions with the BC System. These properties are thus emergent properties of
FC System and BC System interactions, and cannot be understood by an analysis of either
system as an independent module.

The starting point of this analysis was outlined in Sections 17 and 18. In Section
17, I suggested how a binocular BC signal can generate both filling-in generators (FIGs)
and filling-in barriers (FIBs). It was shown how monocular FC signals to the monocular
syncytia can be prevented from eliciting output signals unless they interacted with topographically matched FIGs. Thus although FC signals are topographically broadcast to the
syncytia which process their wavelengths across all spatial scales, only scales in which a
topographic match with boundary signals from the BC System occurs can elicit output
signals to the binocular syncytium.

In Section 18, I noted that even the existence of output signals from a spatial scale of a
monocular syncytium does not guarantee that a percept will be generated by that spatial
scale. Within each scale of a binocular syncytium, pairs of FC output signals from the
corresponding monocular syncytia of the left and right eyes are topographically matched.
Approximately matched FC signals can binocularly summate. A monocular FC signal
in the absence of any input from the other eye can also be registered by the binocular
syncytium. However, pairs of FC signals which are spatially too disparate, or mismatched,
can inhibit each other before they can activate the binocular syncytium. This type of
lateral inhibition is mediated by the organization of the binocular syncytium into double
opponent cells: Spatially mismatched FC signals of like wavelength can inhibit each other
due to the on-center off-surround interaction among like wavelength-sensitive cells within
a double opponent field.

In summary, Sections 17 and 18 described two different ways in which disparity-
sensitive processes can contribute to a percept of form-and-color-in-depth. I now show
that these interactions of binocular BC signals with multiple scale monocular and binoc-

ular syncytia also possess other properties which help to explain difficult perceptual data if the syncytia are interleaved with networks of double opponent cells.

A core issue can be stated as follows. Suppression of double images is a fundamental property of binocular vision. Thus it is an appealing idea that output signals from the BC System to the FC System occur only after the BC System has already undergone a binocular matching process that internally suppresses many boundaries that could otherwise have supported percepts of binocular double images (Section 24). A formidable difficulty could arise from the very property of the BC System that seems so desirable. The process of suppressing binocular double images synthesizes a single coherent binocular boundary segmentation. If, however, a *single* binocular boundary structure outputs to the FC System, then how can this segmentation simultaneously suppress a percept from one eye while supporting a percept from the other eye, as occurs during binocular rivalry? Moreover, even if one wished to overturn the idea that a single binocular BC System exists, how could one then explain the large data base concerning the preponderance of binocularly tuned orientation-selective cells at both early and late stages of visual cortical processing?

This issue has already drawn the attention of several visual scientists (Cogan, 1982; Savoy, 1984). Savoy (1984) has provided a particularly clear discussion of the issue as a basis for some of his important experiments on interocular transfer of the McCollough effect. These experiments led Savoy (1984) to reject a model in which a single "binocular achromatic spatial system" (read BC System) inputs to a pair of monocular "pre-color systems" (read FC System). Savoy (1984, p.575) went on to write "There is also no way to account for binocular rivalry in either spatial or color systems ... Some of these connections might have other implications, such as might be relevant to another major issue that is beyond the scope of the present class of models—stereopsis."

I support Savoy's intuitions below by showing how a theory capable of analysing binocular rivalry and stereopsis can also account for interocular transfer properties of the McCollough effect (Section 29). On the other hand, I do this using a variant of the very type of model that Savoy has rejected. The possibility of reconciling these ostensibly contradictory elements arises from the detailed properties of the microprocesses and hierarchical interactions of the BC System and FC System, notably from the way in which binocular FIGs and FIBs regulate filling-in syncytia interleaved with double opponent fields.

To see how to proceed, let us focus upon the following example. Consider a time when the left eye input due to a Kaufman stereogram (Section 2) is being suppressed due to binocular rivalry. The 45°-oblique dark parallel lines of the left image are then suppressed while the 135°-oblique dark parallel lines of the right image are visible. In Section 4, I argued that, when this happens, the 135°-oblique BC signals suppress the 45°-oblique BC signals within the CC Loop. Then the 135°-oblique BC signals generate FIGs to both the left monocular syncytium and the right monocular syncytium (Section 17). Why cannot the 135°-oblique FIGs generate output signals from the left monocular syncytium in response to its 45°-oblique FC input signals? Why can the 135°-oblique FIGs generate output signals from the right monocular syncytium in response to its 135°-oblique FC input signals? Since the syncytial interactions within the monocular syncytium are unoriented, how can the FC System act *as if* it contains orientation-specific cells when it receives oriented BC signals? Figure 16 schematizes my solution of this basic problem.

Opponent processing occurs among the wavelength-sensitive FC cells that input to the monocular syncytium. Consequently, a spatial contrast in the wavelengths to which the cells are sensitive can cause an FC ON input as well as a spatially contiguous FC OFF input (Figure 16a). These ON and OFF signals generate inputs to distinct monocular ON

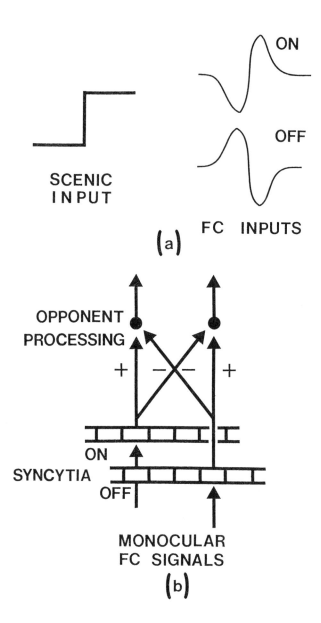

Figure 16. Spatial correlation between ON and OFF FC input signals with FIG signals determines whether FC output signals will be generated: (a) A spatial discontinuity in the scenic input pattern causes correlated ON and OFF reactions within opponent FC input pathways. (b) These opponent reactions excite opponent ON and OFF syncytia at spatially contiguous positions. Lateral filling-in due to these ON and OFF inputs occurs within the ON and OFF syncytia (connected rectangles) except across locations where FIG inputs are registered. Opponent competition between the ON and OFF syncytia at each position determines the net FC output signal.

and OFF syncytia, where they initiate featural filling-in. If a FIG inputs to a syncytial position that is located between the ON and OFF FC inputs, then filling-in due to the ON signal will occur to one side of the FIG, while filling-in due to the OFF signal will occur to the other side of the FIG. If no FIG signal is interpolated between the ON and OFF inputs, however, then filling-in due to both signals will spread over similar positions within the ON and OFF syncytia.

Each syncytium gives rise to topographically organized output signals. The output signals of ON and OFF syncytia compete *at each position* before generating a net FC output signal to the binocular syncytium (Figure 16b). If a FIG is spatially interpolated between the ON and OFF input signals, then a net FC ON signal can be generated to the binocular syncytium (Figure 17a). If no FIG interpolates the ON and OFF input signals, then the ON FC output signal can be inhibited by opponent competition from the filled-in activity pattern within the OFF monocular syncytium (Figure 17b).

Figure 17 shows how opponent processing at *each* position of the inputs and outputs of the ON and OFF syncytia can generate output signals or not depending upon the location of a FIG input signal to both syncytia. Figure 18 uses these properties to help explain the rivalrous percept seen during inspection of the Kaufman stereogram, and more generally the nonselective nature of rivalry suppression. Two cases arise: The boundary synthesized by the BC System is either perpendicular to or parallel to the contour of ON and OFF FC inputs received by the monocular syncytia.

When the FIG signals and the FC input signals are spatially in-phase (Figure 18a), the ON monocular syncytium can generate FC output signals to the binocular syncytium all along the extent of the FIG, as in Figure 17a. When the FIG signals and the FC input signals are perpendicular (Figure 18b), the filled-in activities within the ON and OFF syncytia can mutually inhibit each other's output signals via opponent processing, as in Figure 17b. Thus, whereas the receptive fields of individual syncytial and opponent processing cells may be unoriented, networks of these cells respond to oriented combinations of FC and BC input patterns with orientation- and form-sensitive properties. In particular, if the boundary selected at a given moment by the BC System parallels the monocular FC data from a given eye, then these data can generate input signals to the binocular syncytium for further processing into a visible percept. If this boundary is perpendicular to, or even sufficiently oblique, with respect to the monocular FC data from the other eye, then these data are suppressed before they can input to the binocular syncytium. If the orientation of the boundary flips due to habituative-competitive-cooperative interactions within the CC Loop (Section 9), then the previously suppressed eye's FC data can activate the binocular syncytium.

26. Interaction of Double Opponent Networks with Binocular Boundary Signals

The opponent processing properties illustrated in Figures 16–18 can be used to analyse a variety of paradoxical psychophysical data about binocular rivalry and the McCollough effect. To form a bridge to these data, it is first necessary to integrate the opponent processing properties of the ON and OFF syncytia into a more complete scheme of double opponent processing. This can be done by combining the analyses of monocular syncytial interactions found in Sections 17 and 25.

Section 17 argued that spatial discontinuities of the filled-in activity pattern across a monocular syncytium can generate FC output signals by being passed through a shunting

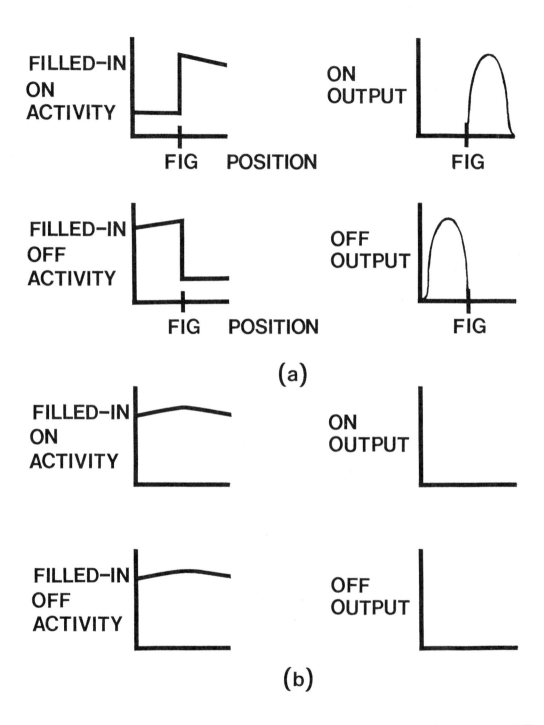

Figure 17. Opponent processing of filled-in activity patterns in on- and off-syncytia generates spatially adjacent on- and off-output signals if a FIG signal is properly placed, as in (a), but not if filling-in proceeds unimpeded, as in (b).

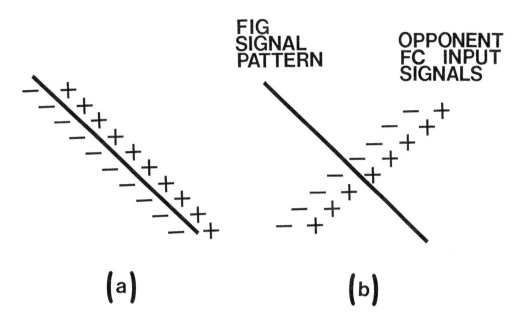

Figure 18. Two-dimensional overlap of a FIG contour and a contour of correlated ON and OFF inputs to opponent ON and OFF syncytia determines whether output signals will be emitted by the syncytia: (a) If a FIG input (solid line) interpolates ON (+) and OFF (−) inputs, then FC output signals from the ON syncytium and the OFF syncytium, respectively, can be generated from opposite sides of the FIG. (b) If ON (+) and OFF (−) FC inputs are not interpolated by a FIG input (solid line), then the filled-in activities within the ON and OFF syncytia can cancel each other's output signals.

on-center off-surround network filter. This type of lateral inhibition prevents the filter from generating outputs to the binocular syncytium unless a FIG is present to generate such a spatial discontinuity. Shunting lateral inhibition *across* positions and *within* a single syncytial channel mediate this property. Section 25 argued that, in addition, subtractive lateral inhibition *within* positions and *across* opponent syncytial channels mediate spatially correlated ON and OFF reactions. These reactions prevent the filter from generating outputs to the binocular syncytium unless a FIG interpolated the spatial pattern of ON and OFF FC inputs to the monocular syncytium. This total network architecture for processing the inputs and outputs of the monocular syncytium obeys the rules of a gated dipole field: shunting on-center off-surround interactions occur within the ON subfield and within the OFF subfield; subtractive opponent interactions occur between positionally matched ON and OFF cells.

If a pair of ON and OFF subfields is identified with an opponent channel for (Red, Green), (Blue, Yellow), or (White, Black) processing, then such a gated dipole field possesses the properties of a network of double-opponent cells. For example, identifying Red with the ON channel and Green with the OFF channel enables us to conclude that a red ON activation inhibits nearby red ON activations via shunting lateral inhibition within the ON subfield. In addition, a red ON activation also inhibits a green OFF activation at the same position via subtractive opponent inhibition. Thus our analysis of the functional properties needed to suppress binocularly discordant FC signals has led to a totally new viewpoint for understanding why color processing is organized into networks of double-opponent cells. This analysis also suggests that three pairs (Red, Green), (Blue, Yellow), (Black, White) of monocular syncytia and double-opponent networks exist within each spatial scale of the FC System, and that FIG signals from each spatial scale of the BC System are topographically registered at all six monocular syncytia of that spatial scale.

The interpretation of ON and OFF processing in terms of double-opponent cells suggests that the terms ON and OFF are relative. For example, a red (green) signal is an ON signal to its own syncytium and an OFF signal to the green (red) syncytium. Only in the case of the chromatically broad-band White-Black system does the terminology ON and OFF have an absolute significance, since only the White system is activated by external inputs. Output signals from the Black system are activated due to disinhibition of internally generated tonic activity. Thus, whereas there exists a tendency to symmetry in the double-opponent network of Red vs. Green and Blue vs. Yellow, the White vs. Black system contains a manifest asymmetry due to the fact that only the White subsystem is activated by external inputs. One manifestation of this asymmetry was observed by Livingstone and Hubel (1984a, p.321), who reported that "On-center cells outnumbered off-center cells by more than two to one."

Modelling double-opponent networks as gated dipole fields also clarifies how negative aftereffects of color or luminance can be generated by antagonistic rebounds due to sudden offset of previously sustained inputs (Grossberg, 1976b, 1980). Correlated rebounds within the gated dipole fields of the CC Loop (Section 9) and the gated dipole fields of the FC System are both needed to initiate the boundary completion, double-opponent, and filling-in events that organize the negative afterimage into a visible percept.

In summary, each FC input to the monocular syncytium is topographically broadcast to all the subsyncytia, across all spatial scales, which process its wavelength. Thus red FC inputs activate the red syncytia of all spatial scales. In contrast, each FIG is topographically broadcast to all the syncytia within its spatial scale, irrespective of their wavelength sensitivity. Thus a FIG output from a high spatial frequency BC System scale is registered at all the (R,G), (B,Y), and (W,B) syncytia corresponding to that spatial scale. Then double opponent networks process the outputs from all pairs of opponent syncytia on their way to the binocular syncytium.

27. Psychophysical Properties of Binocular Rivalry

It has been shown that the depth of suppression during binocular rivalry is independent of a variety of properties of the contralateral eye's rivalry target, such as its orientation (Blake and Lema, 1978), its contrast (Blake and Camisa, 1979), its luminance (Hollins and Bailey, 1981), and the time during the suppression phase when a test probe is presented (Fox and Check, 1972). These data refine the conclusion of Wales and Fox (1970, p.90) that "rivalry suppression…nonselectively attenuates all classes of inputs falling within the spatial boundaries of the suppressed target." On the other hand, the average duration of a suppression phase varies inversely with the strength of the suppressed image. Doubling the contrast of a rivalry stimulus can almost halve the length of time that the image is suppressed (Blake, 1977) and adding strength to an already suppressed image can abbreviate the duration of suppression (Blake and Fox, 1974). A viable theory of binocular rivalry must explain how a variable duration of suppression can coexist with a constant depth of suppression over a wide range of stimulus conditions.

The present theory explains the variable duration of suppression as a consequence of five interacting factors. First, the oriented receptive fields of the BC System are sensitive to amount of contrast near scenic edges. Thus more contrastive scenic edges generate larger BC System signals, other things being equal. Second, the rate of habituation of the transmitter gates in active feedback pathways of the CC Loop (Section 9) depends upon the size of the signals in these active pathways. Habituation takes place more rapidly if the signals are larger. Thus CC Loop pathways that are activated by larger contrasts will tend to habituate faster. This property clarifies why switching rate is sensitive to contrast, but it also brings into focus the mechanistic issue which makes these data hard to explain.

Why does not the amount of rivalry suppression also vary continuously with the amount of habituation? How can habituation take place continuously and in an activity-dependent fashion, yet switching itself be an all-or-none process? These questions motivate my third point. The property of all-or-none switching is controlled by the nonlinear feedback dynamics of short term memory storage within the CC Loop. The transmitter gates multiply the positive feedback signals to the competing orientations within the CC Loop (Section 9). As a transmitter gate habituates within its active pathway, the amount of positive feedback which the pathway supplies to its orientation decreases continuously through time. On the other hand, this process is only one of several factors that controls the switching properties of the CC Loop. The feedback interactions which enable the CC Loop to overcome initial orientational uncertainty and to choose a globally sharp and coherent boundary also endow the CC Loop with properties of hysteresis. Consequently, the winning orientations do not gradually shut off due to habituation; rather, a time is reached when the cumulative habituation of the transmitter gates in the active pathways has so attenuated the transmitter-gated feedback signals in these pathways that the network's hysteresis is suddenly overcome. The previously suppressed orientations can then win the competition and begin to cooperatively group into a new boundary configuration. Extensive computer and mathematical analyses of all-or-none switching due to continuous habituation of transmitter gates are found in Carpenter and Grossberg (1983, 1984, 1985), where a physically distinct but functionally related model of a gated dipole field is characterized. In summary, although the transmitter habituation within the CC Loop is continuous, its switching behavior is discrete.

Fourth, the FIG signals are nonlinear functions, in fact S-shaped functions, of BC System activity (Cohen and Grossberg, 1984a). After a boundary segmentation becomes active within the CC Loop, its FIG signals to the FC System approximate binary on-off signals. Fifth, whenever FIG signals do not interpolate the spatial pattern of FC inputs to the monocular syncytium, the output signals from the syncytium are nonspecifically attenuated (Section 25). In particular, Figure 18 illustrates that *all* orientations of monocular FC input patterns which are not parallel to, and even interpolated by, a FIG contour are suppressed. Thus, due to interactions between the BC System and the FC System, binocular rivalry can exhibit perceptual properties of nonspecific suppression even though the computations within the BC System are oriented.

Another possible cause of unoriented suppression can arise directly from BC System properties. The first competitive stage inhibits *like* orientations at nearby positions whereas the second competitive stage inhibits *perpendicular*, and close-to-perpendicular, orientations at the same position (Figure 2). Thus, a rivalry paradigm which does not control the relative spatial phases of its images may generate inhibition that seems to be unoriented because the combined effects of both competitive stages in response to such a paradigm can inhibit a broad band of orientations.

In summary, the theory suggests explanations of a number of important psychophysical results about binocular rivalry using properties whereby the BC System generates sharp coherent boundaries with hysteretic properties which selectively attenuate binocularly discordant features via interactions with FC System filling-in syncytia interleaved with double-opponent networks. Other properties of rivalry are explained below using the same mechanisms.

28. Chromatic Suppression and Achromatic Sparing during Binocular Rivalry

Smith, Levi, Harwerth, and White (1982) have described psychophysical data concerning the suppression of colored flashes during binocular rivalry. They discovered that binocular rivalry nonspecifically attenuates opponent-color information but spares achromatic information. To clarify the issues raised by their data, a brief summary of the experiment is given.

Their rivalry stimuli were high-contrast square wave gratings with a fundamental spatial frequency of 2.8 cycles per degree that were presented separately to the two eyes at perpendicular orientations of 45° and 135°. A rectangular test stimulus, .4° by .8° in size, was projected as 20-msec flashes to the center of the left eye. An ascending method of limits was used to estimate detection thresholds for each of three viewing conditions: (1) monocular nonrivalry: the right eye was occluded with a black patch; (2) binocular rivalry during the left-eye dominance phase; and (3) binocular rivalry during the left-eye suppression phase. The spectral sensitivity functions for the non-rivalry control condition and the dominance phase of binocular rivalry were similar, with three sensitivity peaks at about 440nm (blue), 530nm (green), and 610nm (red). The spectral sensitivity curve during the suppression phase of binocular rivalry was unimodal with a single broad peak near 550nm and a shape that fits the mean spectral sensitivity function determined by a flicker method under nonrivalry conditions. This sensitivity function implicates an active achromatic channel during the suppression phase.

The nonspecific attenuation of double-opponent signals can be explained as in Section 26. The sparing of achromatic signals raises a number of subtle issues concerning differences between the temporal and spatial parameters of chromatic and achromatic channels and their interactions even at early processing stages (King-Smith, 1975). I mention herein one theoretical property which may significantly contribute to this result: The asymmetry within the White-Black achromatic system that was noted in Section 26. If OFF signals from the Black syncytium cannot completely inhibit ON signals from the White syncytium, then FC signals may be generated from an achromatic monocular syncytium even if no FIG is colinear with the achromatic input. On the other hand, in order for a FC output signal to be generated from the White syncytium, the filled-in activity within the White syncytium due to the test flash must be significantly larger than the resting syncytial activity within the White syncytium on the other side of some FIG. This is true because of the basic property that a syncytium cannot generate an output signal unless there is a spatial discontinuity in its filled-in activity pattern. This FIG may be generated by activation of the other eye and need not be colinear with the test flash. The explanation thus uses, in an essential way, the property that binocular FIG signals reach the monocular syncytia of both eyes.

The explanation also clarifies why varying properties such as the duration of a brief test flash during the suppression phase does not significantly influence its detectability (Hollins and Bailey, 1981; Wales and Fox, 1970). The criterion for detectability is essentially "structural": Is an FC output signal generated from a monocular syncytium after syncytial filling-in and double-opponent competition occur? Unless the flash can overcome the hysteresis of the active binocular boundary, the answer will not substantially change.

29. The McCollough Effect: Monocular and Binocular Properties

In this section, I use the same mechanisms to suggest a unified explanation of the following phenomena: Why under monocular presentation conditions the McCollough effect does not transfer interocularly (McCollough, 1965; Murch, 1972; White, Petry, Riggs, and Miller, 1978); why subsequent viewing of achromatic gratings of the same spatial frequency and orientation speeds up the decay, or "extinction", of the effect (Savoy, 1984; Skowbo, Timney, Gentry, and Morant, 1975); why this type of "extinction" does not transfer interocularly (Savoy, 1984); and why the McCollough effect depends upon the duration of exposure, rather than upon the number of exposures to inducing stimuli (Skowbo and White, 1983). All of the data emphasize monocular properties of the McCollough effect. Explaining the McCollough effect is complicated by the following types of binocular properties.

Vidyasagar (1976) has shown that individuals may be trained to experience opposite McCollough effects in response to monocularly and binocularly presented images. White, Petry, Riggs, and Miller (1978) have reported four experiments which discovered a number of demanding binocular effects. In experiment I (Figure 19a), they compared binocular rivalry and no-rivalry conditions of inspection. In both conditions, subjects focussed upon a fixation point as their left eye was exposed to magenta verticals alternating with green horizontals. In the no-rivalry group, the right eye was exposed to an achromatic homogeneous field. In the binocular rivalry group, the right eye was exposed to an achromatic "jazzy" pattern of varying contrastive shapes. The strength of aftereffect tested with the left eye depended upon the duration of the inspection phase, regardless of the subject's failure to see the colored grating during binocular suppression by the jazzy pattern. These data raise the issue of whether there exists a wavelength-sensitive stage prior to the stage at which a rivalry-sensitive conscious percept is generated. Moreover, if such a stage does exist, then why are its adaptational mechanisms still active during the suppression phase of rivalry?

In experiment II (Figure 19b), binocular "different color" and "like color" conditions were studied. In both conditions, the left eye was exposed to alternating magenta verticals and green horizontals. In the like color condition, the right eye was exposed to homogeneous colored fields whose color matched that of the stripes presented simultaneously to the left eye. In the different color condition the right eye was exposed to homogeneous colored fields whose color was opposed to that of the stripes presented simultaneously to the right eye. The right eye was then tested with achromatic striped patterns. In the like color condition, normal aftereffects were observed; for example, a green aftereffect to achromatic vertical lines was observed if the left eye inspected magenta verticals while the right eye inspected a homogeneous magenta field. In the different color condition, reversed aftereffects were observed; for example, a magenta aftereffect to achromatic vertical lines was observed if the left eye inspected magenta verticals while the right eye inspected a homogeneous green field. The strength and persistence of this reversed aftereffect were not as great as those of normal aftereffects.

White et al. (1978) compared this result to the reports of MacKay and MacKay (1973, 1975) that if an achromatic grating is presented to one eye and a homogeneous colored field is presented to the other eye, then testing of the former eye led to a reversed aftereffect whereas testing of the latter eye led to a normal aftereffect. White et al. (1978) discuss

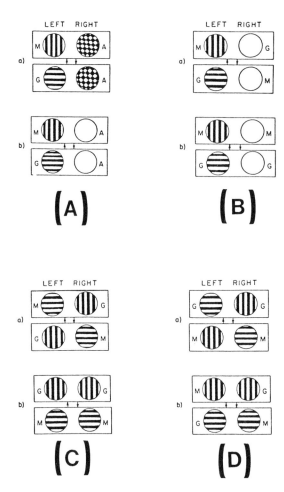

Figure 19. Stimuli used by White, Petry, Riggs, and Miller (1978): (A) Inspection conditions of Experiment I: In either condition, the left eye views alternating magenta (M) and green (G) gratings. In condition (a) (rivalry), the right eye views an achromatic "jazzy" pattern. In condition (b) (no rivalry), the right eye views an achromatic homogeneous field. (B) Inspection conditions of Experiment II: (a) "Different color" condition. Presentation of a magenta (M) vertical grating to the left eye paired with a homogeneous green (G) field to the right eye, alternated with a green grating paired with a homogeneous magenta field. (b) "Like color" condition. Magenta vertical grating paired with a homogeneous magenta field alternates with a green grating paired with a homogeneous green field. (C) Inspection conditions of Experiment III: (a) "Different color/different orientation" condition. Presentation of a magenta (M) horizontal grating to the left eye paired with a green (G) vertical grating to the right eye alternated with a green vertical grating paired with a magenta horizontal grating. (b) "Like color/like orientation" condition. Green vertical gratings alternated with magenta horizontal gratings. (D) Inspection conditions of Experiment IV: (a) "Like color/different orientation" condition. Presentation of a green (G) horizontal grating to the left eye paired with a green vertical grating to the right eye, alternated with a magenta (M) vertical grating paired with a magenta horizontal grating. (b) "Different color/like orientation" condition. Magenta vertical grating paired with a green vertical grating alternated with a green horizontal grating paired with a magenta horizontal grating. (From White *et al.*, *Vision Research*, 1978, **18**, 1201–1215. Copyright 1978 by Pergamon Press. Reprinted with permission.)

some of the problems which other investigators have had in replicating these results. Savoy (1985) has replicated these data.

The results of Experiment II raise the issue of how a homogeneous colored field can energize aftereffects which are sensitive to orientations presented through the other eye, and which thus are strongly influenced by binocular rivalry, unlike the aftereffects found in Experiment I. Moreover, why do these binocularly mediated orientations generate aftereffects which are contingent upon the color of the homogeneous colored field, rather than upon the color of the inspection grating? In other words, why does the orientation transfer binocularly but not the color? On the other hand, why in studies which use achromatic gratings to one eye, such as the MacKay and MacKay (1973, 1975) experiments, is there a tendency for the opposite color to transfer binocularly?

These issues are dramatized by Experiment III (Figure 19c), in which a "different color/different orientation" condition is compared with a "like color/like orientation" condition. Subjects were tested with monocular achromatic gratings as well as with binocular achromatic gratings. The binocular test score was greater than each of the monocular test scores following inspection in the like color/like orientation condition. In contrast, the monocular scores were both greater than the binocular score following the different color/different orientation inspection condition. These data illustrate that rivalry both of orientations and of colors need to be taken into account in order to analyse binocular transfer effects.

Experiment IV (Figure 19d) provided more information about this interaction by also considering "like color/different orientation" and "different color/like orientation" conditions. Monocularly tested aftereffects were weakest after inspection in the "like color/different orientation" condition.

My discussion builds upon previous analyses (Grossberg, 1980, 1983a) in which I showed how interactions between an adaptive filter and a double-opponent gated dipole field could generate long-term color-contingent aftereffects. These analyses linked the existence of McCollough-type effects to general mechanisms of visual information processing before the BC System and FC System were discovered. I now outline how these general mechanisms can explain all of the above data properties when they are embedded within the network in Figure 1 that is introduced herein.

Adaptational properties consistent with McCollough effect data are generated within the FC System pathways from the monocular preprocessing stages to the monocular syncytia and from the monocular syncytia to the binocular syncytia (Figure 1). The total network architecture modulates the processing within these FC System pathways. To understand how these properties arise, first one needs to know what the adaptational mechanisms are, and then one needs to know how the total network modulates these mechanisms.

These mechanisms have been described elsewhere and are the same mechanisms which have been used to discuss negative afterimages in this article: "Pattern-contingent colored aftereffects can also be generated in a dipole field. Suppose that a prescribed field of feature detectors is color coded. Let the on-cells be maximally turned on by red light and the off-cells be maximally turned on by green light for definiteness. Then white light will excite both on-cells and off-cells; that is, white light acts like an adaptation level in this situation. Suppose that a red input whose features are extracted by the field is turned on long enough to substantially deplete its transmitter. What happens if a white light replaces the red input on test trials? The depletion caused by the prior red input now causes the white adaptation level to generate a larger gated signal to the green channel, so a green pattern-contingent aftereffect will be generated" (Grossberg, 1980, p.22).

How can the long duration of McCollough after-effects be explained? Before the BC System and FC System were discovered, two types of mechanisms were suggested to explain how the persistence of these aftereffects could extend long beyond the time of recovery from the transmitter habituation process. One of these mechanisms used the contrast enhancement and short term memory properties of recurrent on-center off-surround networks (Grossberg, 1980, p.22). These properties are now relegated to the CC Loop of the BC System. The other mechanism is advocated here for the FC System: "The imbalance due to asymmetric habituation can also be encoded in the LTM traces due to the property that a decrease in postsynaptic STM activity can cause a decrease in LTM strength. Such an LTM change is not a case of associative learning due to CS–UCS (conditioned stimulus, unconditioned stimulus) contiguity. Rather it is a case of retuning feature detectors to their trigger input patterns. Thus habituation within a nonclassical opponent process interacting with a non-Hebbian adaptive filter [cf. Section 23] can explain McCollough effect properties as manifestations of a basic processing design" (Grossberg, 1983a, p.680).

These general mechanisms are specialized within the FC System as follows. The pathways from the monocular preprocessing stages to the monocular syncytia and from the monocular syncytia to the binocular syncytia are assumed to contain non-Hebbian LTM traces that multiplicatively gate the signals in their respective pathways (cf. Section 23). The collection of all the adaptive pathways from a monocular preprocessing stage to a monocular syncytium comprises an adaptive fiter. So too does the collection of all the adaptive pathways from a monocular syncytium to a binocular syncytium. These adaptive filters work together with double opponent networks to process output signals on their way to the next syncytial stage. The primary function of the adaptive filters is to maintain selective contacts between FC System cells which code the same positions and colors; thus red cells map into red cells, green cells map into green cells, and so on, at corresponding positions due to the adaptive tuning carried out by the LTM traces.

Since each double opponent network is a gated dipole field, its pathways contain habituative transmitters that multiplicatively gate the signals carried by the pathway. Thus the adaptive filter pathways are *doubly* gated: first by habituative transmitters that regulate the opponent balance between coupled ON and OFF channels, notably their antagonistic rebounds; and second by non-Hebbian LTM traces which slowly track the habituatively gated signals and doubly gate these signals on their way to their target syncytium.

Using this combination of double opponent and non-Hebbian adaptive filter processing, I now show how the global anatomy of BC System and FC System interactions enables different scenic inputs to activate combinations of FC System pathways which are sensitive to the orientations of scenic contrasts. Since each FC System pathway is also selective for color (red→red, green→green, etc.), a pathway that is activated by a particular scenic orientation automatically correlates that orientation with the color system in which the pathway is found. This type of correlated adaptation is not classical conditioning, in agreement with previous experimental work on the McCollough effect (McCarter and Silver, 1977; Savoy, 1984; Skowbo, 1984; Skowbo and Forster, 1983; Skowbo and White, 1983).

Some McCollough effect data can be analysed using properties of the adaptive reactions within individual FC System pathways, without regard to the spatial patterning of these pathways. For example, persistent input to an FC System pathway can habituate its transmitter gate. The total amount of habituation covaries with the duration of the input, since the total habituation is a cumulative process. This property is consistent with the data of Skowbo and White (1983), who showed that the strength of the McCollough effect depends upon the duration, not the number, of exposures. If the input to a pathway persists long enough for a cumulative habituation to occur within its transmitter gate, then—because it obeys a non-Hebbian associative law—the slowly varying LTM trace along the pathway senses the persistent decrease in its transmitter-gated signal and also begins to decrease (Figure 20). Thus the LTM change is also sensitive to the duration of the signal. This LTM change can, however, endure long after the transmitter habituation recovers.

The opponent organization of the FC System pathways clarifies how an achromatic input can elicit a long-term opponent-color aftereffect, yet how repeated presentation of the achromatic input can extinguish the aftereffect (Savoy, 1984; Skowbo et al., 1975). Suppose, for definiteness, that prior input to an ON pathway has previously caused substantial transmitter habituation and decrease of the pathway's LTM trace. Suppose that the transmitter has already recovered from its habituation but that the LTM trace has not been retrained (Figure 21). Let an achromatic scenic edge generate equal signals within the ON pathway and its corresponding OFF pathway. Then the smaller LTM trace gates the signal in the previously habituated pathway. Consequently, the opponent OFF pathway delivers a larger LTM-gated input, and a long-term opponent-color aftereffect is generated. Suppose that this white input is persistently presented. Then equal amounts of cumulative transmitter habituation are caused in the opponent channels and their LTM traces equalize by tracking these equalized transmitter-gated signals. In this way, a white input trains equal LTM-gated signals within the opponent channels, and the aftereffect is actively extinguished.

I now discuss how different combinations of scenic images can selectively activate different subsets of FC System pathways in a manner that mimmicks monocular and binocular McCollough effect data. The core issue is, of course, why the McCollough effect is orientation-sensitive. Remarkably, orientation-sensitive aftereffects can be generated even if none of the FC System cells possesses an oriented receptive field. In the subsequent discussion, I separate those properties of orientation-sensitive aftereffects which can arise from non-oriented FC System cells from those properties of orientation-sensitive aftereffects which can arise from oriented FC System cells. This separation is conceptually necessary because the relative proportion of non-oriented to oriented FC System cells may vary across species, or oriented cells may be totally absent, without our denying the existence of orientation-sensitive aftereffects.

Oriented receptive fields can, in principle, exist within the FC System at any of several stages. For example, a double-opponent gated dipole field transforms the activities of a monocular syncytium to output signals to a binocular syncytium (Section 26). This gated dipole field may, in principle, possess orientation-sensitive cells. Evidence for this possibility could, for example, include the discovery of orientation-sensitive cells which receive inputs from area 17 blobs and which output to color-coded area 18 stripes. Such orientational tuning could facilitate the binocular matching of monocular inputs from pairs of monocular syncytia before the matched inputs could activate the binocular filling-in process (Section 18). If the output signals from the monocular syncytia are both orientationally tuned and chromatically tuned, then the habituative and LTM trace changes described above would all depend upon both the orientation and the color of the stimuli, yet would not be due to classical conditioning of orientation to color.

Oriented receptive fields can also exist in the pathways from the monocular preprocessing stages to the monocular syncytia. Oriented cells are, for example, known to exist in

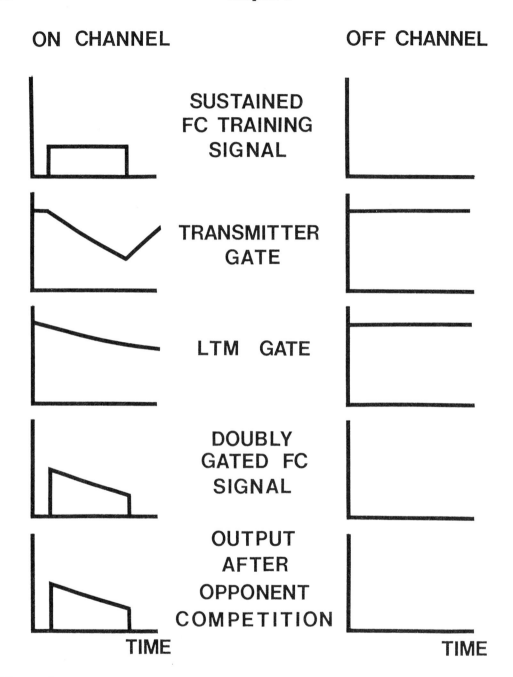

Figure 20. Interaction between sustained FC signal, habituating transmitter gate, long-term memory (LTM) trace, and opponent competition between ON and OFF channels: A sustained FC training signal to the ON channel causes a cumulative habituation of its transmitter. The LTM trace slowly tracks the transmitter-gated FC signal—(FC signal) times (transmitter)—and also decreases. The LTM trace remains small even after the transmitter recovers. The net signal from this pathway equals (FC signal) times (transmitter) times (LTM trace). Net signals from the ON and OFF channels compete subtractively to generate outputs to the next FC stage.

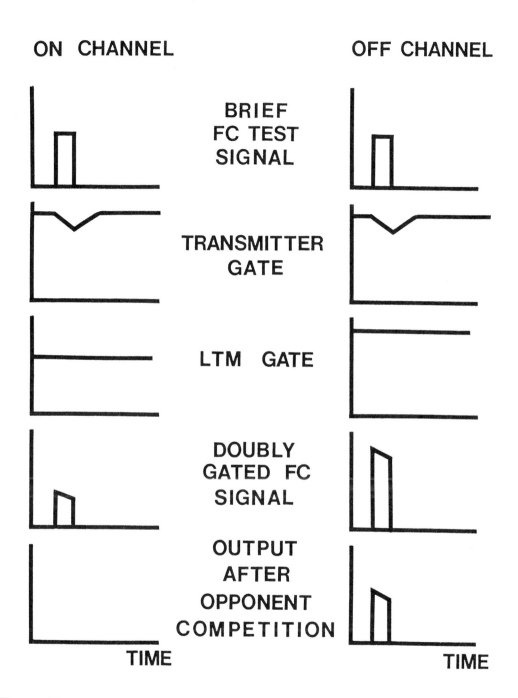

Figure 21. Generation of a long-term color after-effect: After the transmitter in Figure 20 recovers, the LTM trace in the ON channel can remain small. A brief test signal that equally excites both opponent channels (e.g., white) can cause minor, but equal, habituation of the transmitters. However, gating of the signal by the LTM traces generates a larger net signal in the OFF channel than the ON channel. After opponent competition, the OFF channel generates an output FC signal.

cat retinal ganglion cells (Leventhal and Schall, 1983; Levick and Thibos, 1982), cat lateral geniculate cells (Daniels, Norman, and Pettigrew, 1977; Vidyasagar and Urbas, 1982), and monkey lateral geniculate cells (Lee, Creutzfeldt, and Elepfandt, 1979).

Orientation-sensitive responses within the FC System may be generated in either of two ways if all FC System cells possess unoriented receptive fields. The first mechanism can influence only pathways from the monocular syncytia to the binocular syncytia. The second mechanism can influence pathways from the monocular preprocessing stages to the monocular syncytia and from the monocular syncytia to the binocular syncytia. The first mechanism is based upon the fact that the BC System is organized into ocular dominance columns and orientationally tuned hypercolumns (Section 22 and Figure 10). Different orientations corresponding to a given retinal position are coded at slightly different hypercolumn positions. Different orientations thus send FIG signals to slightly different cells within the monocular syncytium. These cells can, in turn, activate slightly different FC System pathways to the binocular syncytium. Consequently, the orientational tuning within the BC System may indirectly cause orientationally sensitive retuning of the adaptive filter between the monocular and binocular syncytia by causing statistically significant differences in the spatial patterning of FC System pathways that are activated by different orientations. This type of mechanism can also operate when BC System cells are selectively activated by oriented edges moving in prescribed directions.

The second mechanism cannot cause orientationally sensitive adaptation in response to moving scenic edges. It is only effective when static images are presented in a prescribed spatial relation to a fixation point. This mechanism uses the property that orientationally sensitive FIG signals can group the color signals from adapted and non-adapted pathways into oriented regions for featural filling-in. Figure 22 schematizes regions in which red, or magenta (M), green (G), or both (A) adaptations occur within the FC System due to alternate monocular presentations of red verticals and green horizontals. When achromatic verticals are presented, they cause vertical FIG signals to divide the syncytia into vertical filling-in domains. Due to adaptation of the red-coded FC System pathways, the red filling-in is weaker than the green filling-in. After opponent processing occurs, a green vertical aftereffect can be generated. For the same reason, a red horizontal aftereffect can be generated. The achromatic (A) regions do not contribute to the aftereffects because their pathways are equally adapted in both directions (assuming all FC System cells are nonoriented). The FIG-induced organization of the syncytia into vertical or horizontal domains enables opposite chromatic aftereffects to fill-in over the chromatically neutral (A and Bl) regions when the orientation of the FIG signals is reversed. Because of these mechanisms, opposite monocular aftereffects can be trained in the same individual using, say, green verticals and red horizontals because these stimuli preferentially activate, and therefore adapt, positionally disjoint subsets of pathways between different syncytia, whether or not any FC System cells have oriented receptive fields.

The acquisition of the McCollough effect does not transfer interocularly (McCollough, 1965; Murch, 1972; White *et al.*, 1978) and extinction of the McCollough effect does not transfer interocularly (Savoy, 1984) for the following reason in these networks: Monocular presentation of oriented chromatic or achromatic stimuli activates the BC System which, in turn, sends FIG signals to both the left and the right monocular syncytia. On the other hand, only the eye which receives the monocular stimulus receives FC System inputs to its monocular syncytia, and only these monocular syncytia can generate FC output signals to the binocular syncytia. The monocular preprocessing stage and monocular syncytia of the unstimulated eye cannot activate their FC System output pathways, hence cannot

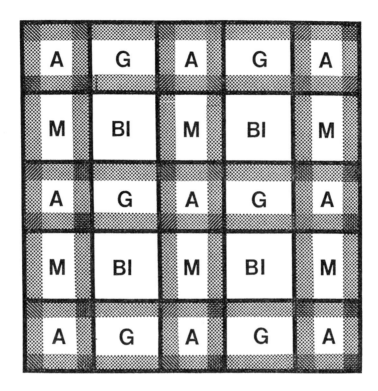

Figure 22. Alternate viewing of green (G) and black horizontal bars and magenta (M) and black vertical bars can cause a lattice of chromatically adapted regions to emerge: R, G, achromatic or equally adapted (A), and black (Bl). The stipled regions indicate positions where chromatic adaptation occurs. Horizontal hatched areas adapt to green and vertical hatched areas adapt to magenta. Viewing of achromatic horizontal test bars can generate boundary contours which enable G and A regions to fill-in over each white bar within the G syncytium, thereby generating an uninterrupted band of green monocular syncytial activity. In addition, the white input enables M and A regions to fill-in over each white bar within the M syncytium. Because the green FC pathways are adapted, after opponent processing takes place, horizontal bands of magenta FC output signals are generated. A similar analysis shows how vertical bands of green FC output signals are generated in response to vertical achromatic white and black bars.

undergo the adaptational LTM changes which are contingent upon sustained activation of these pathways.

A similar argument suggests how a single individual can acquire opposite monocular and binocular McCollough effects in response to cyclic presentation for 30 minutes of the following sequence of stimuli: red vertical, binocular; blue vertical, right eye; red horizontal, right eye; blue horizontal, binocular; red horizontal, left eye; blue vertical, left eye (Vidyasagar, 1976). The primary property needed to explain this result is that binocular viewing of these images excites a different spatial distribution of binocular FIG pathways and monocular-to-binocular FC System pathways than does monocular viewing. This property is one of the basic means whereby double images are suppressed and a coherent representation of form-and-color-in-depth is generated. The multiple spatial scales of the BCS typically react differently to monocular versus binocular viewing of simple pairs of images (Sections 2–9 and 24). In addition, binocular mismatch of pairs of monocular FC signals from the monocular syncytia can prevent activation of cells that would have responded to just one monocular syncytium (Section 25). Since adaptive tuning of an LTM trace is controlled by activation of its pathway's postsynaptic cell, certain pathways which could have adapted in response to monocular viewing may not adapt to binocular viewing.

30. Interocular Transfer Properties of McCollough Effect

The data from Experiment I of the White *et al.* (1978) study are consistent with the fact that transmitter habituation and LTM changes can occur continuously in the pathways from the monocular preprocessing stages to the monocular syncytia, even when the percept from the corresponding eye is suppressed due to binocular rivalry. Binocular rivalry influences the FC System only from the monocular syncytia onwards. Thus comparison of the amount of adaptation in the rivalry and no-rivalry conditions when both conditions are equated for the time that the percept is seen should yield higher levels of adaptation in the rivalry condition, as found in the data. A number of subtle interactions can also occur due to rivalry at the binocular syncytia. The properties of these interactions are best seen through consideration of Experiments II–IV.

The data from Experiment II of the White *et al.* (1978) study show that, although the McCollough effect does not transfer interocularly under monocular acquisition conditions, it does transfer interocularly if the non-adapted eye is presented with a homogeneous colored field during adaptation. This type of interocular transfer can be explained by adaptation occurring subsequent to the monocular syncytia, as follows. Although transmitter habituation and LTM adaptation can occur in the adaptive filter from the right monocular preprocessing stage to the monocular syncytia, due to the homogeneity of the right eye training image, such adaptation cannot be sensitive to the orientation of an achromatic test grating. Moreover, alternate presentation of magenta and green homogeneous training images to the right eye tend to cause equal levels of adaptation in the corresponding opponent color systems. These balanced adaptations would tend to cancel any aftereffect. The interocular transfer effects reported in Experiment II must therefore be traced to adaptation effects subsequent to the monocular syncytia.

A homogeneous colored field does not, however, contain interior edges. If spatially discontinuous inputs are needed to elicit FC outputs from a monocular syncytium, yet there are no interior edges in a homogeneous field with which to generate spatially discontinuous inputs, then why does a homogeneous colored field have any effect whatsoever on interocular transfer?

A possible explanation of these data arises from consideration of how a FIG signal restricts filling-in within a monocular syncytium. As noted in Section 24 of Grossberg (1987b), a FIG signal acts as an inhibitory gating signal that causes an increase in the membrane resistance of its target syncytial cells. Thus, a FIG signal also acts as an inhibitory FC input to its target syncytial cells. When no other inputs reach the monocular syncytia, this inhibitory signal cannot create excitatory output signals from the monocular syncytia. When excitatory inputs do activate the monocular syncytium, a FIG signal can cause a spatial discontinuity in the syncytium's filled-in activity due to the fact that it can trap its own inhibitory signals within the cells whose membrane resistance it has increased.

The size of this spatial discontinuity may increase, albeit nonlinearly, with the luminance of the homogeneous colored field.

We have now reached a crucial point in the argument. If homogeneous colored fields can generate FC outputs to the binocular syncytium, then why cannot all mismatched monocular images do so? Why does not the entire theoretical structure for preventing double images collapse? Why is not the whole argument about suppression during binocular rivalry invalid? There is a "safe" answer that cannot explain the intraocular transfer data, and a more interesting answer that can.

The safe answer posits that the spatial scale of a FIG is too fine to be detected by the on-center off-surround interactions of a double-opponent gated dipole field. A spatial discontinuity in filled-in syncytial activities must occur across a wider domain than the thickness of a FIG in order to generate FC output signals. Hence FIG discontinuities surrounded by equal filled-in syncytial activities cannot generate FC output signals and thus do not influence perception.

The interesting answer builds from the observation that homogeneous colored fields are essentially the only colored images that do not excite any nontrivial opponent color reactions. Given essentially any colored inhomogeneous image, an ON input to one region is associated with an opponent OFF input to a contiguous region. After filling-in takes place, the ON and OFF outputs at every position of the monocular syncytium, including positions along the FIG, tend to inhibit each other if the FIG does not spatially interpolate the ON and OFF inputs. Thus the previous explanations hold for colored images which contain contrastive contours despite the fact that a homogeneous colored image can support interocular transfer of the McCollough effect.

It is nonetheless probable that a FIG signal to a homogeneously activated monocular syncytium cannot generate an FC output signal that is as large as one generated from an inhomogeneously activated monocular syncytium. The bandwidth of a FIG signal may be detectable by the on-center off-surround gated dipole field, but may be too narrow to generate optimal output signals to the binocular syncytium. Thus the aftereffects generated by the right eye may involve fewer pathways, whose transmitters habituate less and whose LTM traces adapt less. The interocular transfer aftereffects reported by White et al. (1978) were, in fact, weak and less persistent than the aftereffects generated through the left eye.

It remains to say why the right eye aftereffect was in the opponent color to the color of the homogeneous test field. In the like color condition, this property can be explained using the usual mechanism: When the right eye inspected a homogeneous magenta field while the left eye inspected magenta verticals, orientationally tagged red cells inputting to the binocular syncytium were binocularly activated. The active input pathways underwent the usual habituation and LTM tuning, therefore favoring a green aftereffect in response to achromatic verticals. In the different color condition, the aftereffect can be traced to binocular rivalry within the double-opponent network that inputs to the binocular syncytium: When the right eye inspected a homogeneous green field while the left eye inspected magenta verticals, both green and red orientationally tagged pathways to the binocular syncytia would be activated and would compete. The right eye green pathways would habituate and retune their LTM traces when these pathways won the opponent competition, thereby generating a magenta aftereffect in response to achromatic verticals.

The tendency to get reversed aftereffects, as reported by MacKay and MacKay (1973, 1975) and Savoy (1985), can be explained as follows. This explanation ignores the sources of binocular suppression that may weaken this tendency. Suppose that an achromatic grating is presented to the left eye and a homogeneous magenta field is presented to the right eye. The achromatic grating generates binocular FIGs which enable FC output signals to be generated from red-coded monocular syncytia of the right eye. These signals habituate the transmitter gates in the active red-coded right eye pathways *and* activate the binocular red-coded cells that input into the binocular red-coded syncytia. The achromatic left eye input tends to equally activate both the red-coded and the green-coded pathways from the left monocular syncytia to the binocular syncytia. The transmitters in these pathways thus tend to undergo an equal amount of habituation. On the other hand, the red-coded binocular cells are more active than the green-coded binocular cells due to the summation of inputs from left eye and right eye at the red-coded cells. Consequently the LTM traces in the red-coded left eye pathways to these binocular cells tend to become larger than the LTM traces in the green-coded active left eye pathways. During test trials, an achromatic grating to the right eye tends to generate a green aftereffect, whereas an achromatic grating to the left eye tends to generate a red aftereffect.

In Experiments III and IV, the pathways from the monocular preprocessing stages to the monocular syncytia experience similar levels of adaptation in all experimental conditions. Adaptation within these monocular pathways determines an adaptational baseline which is augmented to different degrees in the four experimental conditions by the adaptation which occurs in the pathways from the monocular syncytia to the binocular syncytia. Thus my explanations of these data depend upon the hierarchical organization of FC System pathways from the monocular preprocessing stages to the binocular syncytia, which enables a cumulative adaptation effect to be registered at the binocular syncytia.

In the like color/like orientation condition of Experiment III (Figure 19Cb), left eye and right eye inputs can cooperate both at binocular BC System cells and at binocular FC System cells which input to the binocular syncytia. In contrast, the different color/different orientation condition (Figure 19Ca) causes rivalry to occur both within the BC System and at the binocular FC System cells. Consequently, binocular test gratings lead to stronger aftereffects than monocular test gratings in the like color/like orientation condition, whereas the opposite is true in the different color/different orientation condition.

In order to explain the main finding of Experiment IV that monocular testing of the like color/different orientation condition (Figure 19Da) yields the weakest aftereffect, a finer analysis of the different color/different orientation of Experiment III is needed. Consider a time when horizontal FIG signals are activated by magenta horizontals to the left eye. The FIG signals activate red-coded horizontally-sensitive pathways from the left monocular syncytia to the binocular syncytia. The FIG signals also divide the right monocular syncytia into horizontal strips. Due to the narrow bandwidth of the FIG signals, weak activation of green-coded horizontally-sensitive pathways from the right monocular syncytia to the binocular syncytia occurs. Rivalry between these opponent-color pathways can occur at the binocular syncytia, leading to both red and green adaptation in horizontally-sensitive pathways. These opponent adaptations lead to a weakened net adaptive effect, but the red-horizontal correlation may nonetheless tend to be stronger than the green-horizontal correlation. For a similar reason, the green-vertical correlation tends to be stronger than the red-vertical correlation.

In contrast, consider a time during the like color/different orientation condition (Figure 19Da) when horizontal FIG signals are activated by green horizontals to the left eye. The FIG signals activate green-coded horizontally-sensitive pathways from *both* the left and the right monocular syncytia. There is no color rivalry at the binocular syncytia. Hence the green-coded horizontally-sensitive pathways from the right eye can adapt more in this condition than in the comparable different color/different orientation condition. Under achromatic monocular right eye testing, these pathways can therefore more effectively inhibit the red-coded horizontally-sensitive pathways which adapted in response to presentation of magenta horizontal stripes to the right eye. In summary, in the like color/different orientation condition, color rivalry at the binocular syncytium cannot spare the correlation between orientation and color that is endangered in pathways from the monocular syncytia to the binocular syncytia by the orientation rivalry taking place within the BC System.

A variety of other data concerning McCollough-type aftereffects can be analysed in terms of such interactions. For example, Broerse and Crassini (1986) have shown that McCollough-type adaptation can be used to render ambiguous displays, such as the diamond-rectangles figure, unambiguous. These data can be analysed, as in the above discussion, by a combination of BC System and FC System rivalry and adaptational mechanisms.

31. Concluding Remarks

This article introduces a perceptual theory which explains in a principled and unified way a large body of data about 3-D form, color, and brightness perception. Many of these data have received no previous explanation, let alone an explanation as part of a general perceptual theory. The article also describes a neural architecture whose interactive properties generate the theory's explanations of perceptual data. This architecture is well enough characterized to test it in multiple ways through experiments on striate and prestriate visual cortex. Mathematical and computer analyses of different pieces of this architecture are developed in a number of other articles (Cohen and Grossberg, 1984a, 1984b, 1986; Grossberg and Marshall, 1987; Grossberg and Mingolla, 1985a, 1985b, 1986, 1987), and further quantitative analyses are presently underway.

Underlying these detailed mechanisms and data explanations are a number of new design principles and concepts about visual perception. Concepts such as monocular syncytium and binocular syncytium, gated dipole field, filling-in generator and filling-in barrier, OC Filter and CC Loop, orientation field, masking field, orthogonal end cut, and non-Hebbian adaptive filter can guide the theoretical development of a more complete visual theory. Details concerning anatomical connections may, for example, be different across species without requiring such concepts to be abandoned. Design principles such as Boundary-Feature Trade-Off and the several new uncertainty principles which govern the organization of successive processing stages within the BC System and the FC System may also be used as a foundation for building a more complete theory. Another general foundational theme is that mechanisms of boundary segmentation and featural filling-in, and of stereopsis and boundary segmentation can best be understood through an analysis of their interactions, rather than as independent modules. This approach led to the discovery that double-opponent networks of unoriented color cells can compute oriented form-sensitive properties when they interact with Boundary Contour signals, and that, paradoxically, this particular type of orientational sensitivity helps to explain the nonspecific suppression that occurs during binocular rivalry. The explanations of why the BC System becomes binocular at an earlier processing stage than the FC System; of how the CC Loop generates a globally consistent, sharp yet deformable, binocular segmentation from the multiplexed signals of binocular complex cells; and of how perceptually invisible Boundary Contours can influence object recognition are among the other general results that promise to persist in a more complete theory.

Even as it stands, however, the theory suggests explanations of an unusually large perceptual and neural data base, and provides tools for explaining a large body of perceptual data that I have not considered in detail, but for which a direct attack is now clearly indicated; for example, data about metacontrast and stereoscopic capture. The theory has also already articulated qualitatively new mathematical designs for parallel machines capable of rapidly synthesizing coherent and informative global visual representations of the external world. It remains to be seen just how far these ideas can carry us towards a complete perceptual and neural theory of form-and-color-in-depth and a new generation of real-time context-sensitive massively parallel vision machines.

REFERENCES

Beck, J., Prazdny, K., and Ivry, R., The perception of transparency with achromatic colors. *Perception and Psychophysics*, 1984, **35**, 407–422.

Beverley, K.I. and Regan, D., Separable aftereffects of changing-size and motion-in-depth: Different neural mechanisms. *Vision Research*, 1979, **19**, 727–732.

Bienenstock, E.L., Cooper, L.N., and Munro, P.W., Theory for the development of neuron selectivity: Orientation specificity and binocular interaction in visual cortex. *Journal of Neuroscience*, 1982, **2**, 32–48.

Blake, R., Threshold conditions for binocular rivalry. *Journal of Experimental Psychology: Human Perception and Performance*, 1977, **3**, 251–257.

Blake, R. and Camisa, J., On the inhibitory nature of binocular rivalry suppression. *Journal of Experimental Psychology: Human Perception and Performance*, 1979, **5**, 315–323.

Blake, R. and Fox, R., Binocular rivalry suppression: Insensitive to spatial frequency and orientation change. *Vision Research*, 1974, **14**, 687–692.

Blake, R. and Lema, S.A., Inhibitory effect of binocular rivalry suppression is independent of orientation. *Vision Research*, 1978, **18**, 541–544.

Blake, R., Sloane, M., and Fox, R., Further developments in binocular summation. *Perception and Psychophysics*, 1981, **30**, 266–276.

Blakemore, C. and Cooper, G.F., Development of the brain depends on the visual environment. *Nature*, 1970, **228**, 477–478.

Braastad, B.O. and Heggelund, P., Development of spatial receptive-field organization and orientation selectivity in kitten striate cortex. *Journal of Neurophysiology*, 1985, **53**, 1158–1178.

Broerse, J. and Crassini, B., Making ambiguous displays unambiguous: The influence of real colors and colored aftereffects on perceptual alternation. *Perception and Psychophysics*, 1986, **39**, 105–116.

Carpenter, G.A. and Grossberg, S., A neural theory of circadian rhythms: The gated pacemaker. *Biological Cybernetics*, 1983, **48**, 35–59.

Carpenter, G.A. and Grossberg, S., A neural theory of circadian rhythms: Aschoff's rule in diurnal and nocturnal mammals. *American Journal of Physiology*, 1984, **247**, R1067–R1082.

Carpenter, G.A. and Grossberg, S., A neural theory of circadian rhythms: Split rhythms, after-effects, and motivational interactions. *Journal of Theoretical Biology*, 1985, **113**, 163–223.

Cogan, A.I., Monocular sensitivity during binocular viewing. *Vision Research*, 1982, **22**, 1–16.

Cogan, A.I., Silverman, G., and Sekuler, R., Binocular summation in detection of contrast flashes. *Perception and Psychophysics*, 1982, **31**, 330–338.

Cohen, M.A. and Grossberg, S., Neural dynamics of brightness perception: Features, boundaries, diffusion, and resonance. *Perception and Psychophysics*, 1984, **36**, 428–456 (a).

Cohen, M.A. and Grossberg, S., Some global properties of binocular resonances: Disparity matching, filling-in, and figure-ground synthesis. In P. Dodwell and T. Caelli (Eds.), **Figural synthesis**. Hillsdale, NJ: Erlbaum, 1984 (b).

Cohen, M.A. and Grossberg, S., Neural dynamics of speech and language coding: Developmental programs, perceptual grouping, and competition for short term memory. *Human Neurobiology*, 1986, **5**, 1–22.

Cohen, M.A. and Grossberg, S., Masking fields: A massively parallel neural architecture for learning, recognizing, and predicting multiple groupings of patterned data. *Applied Optics*, 1987, **26**, 1866–1891.

Curtis, D.W. and Rule, S.J., Fechner's paradox reflects a nonmonotone relation between binocular brightness and luminance. *Perception and Psychophysics*, 1980, **27**, 263–266.

Daniel, P.M. and Whitteridge, D., The representation of the visual field in the cerebral cortex of monkeys. *Journal of Physiology (London)*, 1961, **159**, 302–321.

Daniels, J.D., Norman, J.L., and Pettigrew, J.D., Biases for oriented moving bars in lateral geniculate nucleus neurons of normal and stripe-reared cats. *Experimental Brain Research*, 1977, **29**, 155–172.

Daugman, J.G., Two-dimensional spectral analysis of cortical receptive field profiles. *Vision Research*, 1979, **20**, 847–856.

Desimone, R., Schein, S.J., Moran, J., and Ungerleider, L.G., Contour, color, and shape analysis beyond the striate cortex. *Vision Research*, 1985, **25**, 441–452.

Dev, P., Perception of depth surfaces in random-dot stereograms: A neural model. *International Journal of Man-Machine Studies*, 1975, **7**, 511–528.

Dosher, B., Sperling, G., and Wurst, S., Tradeoffs between stereopsis and proximity luminance covariance as determinants of perceived 3D structure. *Vision Research*, 1986, **26**, 973–990.

Dow, B.M., Snyder, A.Z., Vautin, R.G., and Bauer, R., Magnification factor and receptive field size in foveal striate cortex of the monkey. *Experimental Brain Research*, 1981, **44**, 213–228.

DeValois, R.L., Albrecht, D.G., and Thorell, L.G., Spatial frequency selectivity of cells in macaque visual cortex. *Vision Research*, 1982, **22**, 545–559.

Earle, D.C., Perception of Glass pattern structure with stereopsis. *Perception*, 1985, **14**, 545–552.

Egusa, H., Effects of brightness, hue, and saturation on perceived depth between adjacent regions in the visual field. *Perception*, 1983, **12**, 167–175.

Emmert, E., Grössenverhaltnisse der Nachbilder. *Klin. Monatsbl. d. Augenheilk.*. 1881, **19**, 443–450.

Foley, J.M., Binocular distance perception. *Psychological Review*, 1980, **87**, 411–434.

Fox, R. and Check, R., Independence between binocular rivalry suppression duration and magnitude of suppression. *Journal of Experimental Psychology*, 1972, **93**, 283–289.

Frégnac, Y. and Imbert, M., Early development of visual cortical cells in normal and dark-reared kittens: Relationship between orientation selectivity and ocular dominance. *Journal of Physiology*, 1978, **278**, 27–44.

Gabor, D., Theory of communication. *IEEE*, 1946, **93**, 429–457.

Gibson, J.J., **Perception of the visual world**. Boston: Houghton Mifflin, 1950.

Gogel, W.C., The tendency to see objects as equidistant and its reverse relations to lateral separation. *Psychological Monograph*, 1956, **70**, whole no. 411.

Gogel, W.C., Equidistance tendency and its consequences. *Psychological Bulletin*, 1965, **64**, 153–163.

Gogel, W.C., The adjacency principle and three-dimensional visual illusions. *Psychonomic Monograph Supplement*, 1970, **3** (whole no. 45), 153–169.

Gouras, P. and Krüger, J., Responses of cells in foveal visual cortex of the monkey to pure color contrast. *Journal of Neurophysiology*, 1979, **42**, 850–860.

Graham, N., The visual system does a crude Fourier analysis of patterns. In S. Grossberg (Ed.), **Mathematical psychology and psychophysiology**. Providence, RI: American Mathematical Society, 1981.

Graham, N. and Nachmias, J., Detection of grating patterns containing two spatial frequencies: A test of single-channel and multiple channel models. *Vision Research*, 1971, **11**, 251–259.

Grossberg, S., Some physiological and biochemical consequences of psychological postulates. *Proceedings of the National Academy of Sciences*, 1968, **60**, 758–765.

Grossberg, S., On learning and energy-entropy dependence in recurrent and nonrecurrent signed networks. *Journal of Statistical Physics*, 1969, **1**, 319–350.

Grossberg, S., Contour enhancement, short-term memory, and constancies in reverberating neural networks. *Studies in Applied Mathematics*, 1973, **52**, 217–257.

Grossberg, S., Adaptive pattern classification and universal recoding, I: Parallel development and coding of neural feature detectors. *Biological Cybernetics*, 1976, **23**, 121–134 (a).

Grossberg, S., Adaptive pattern classification and universal recoding, II: Feedback, expectation, olfaction, and illusions. *Biological Cybernetics*, 1976, **23**, 187–202 (b).

Grossberg, S., A theory of human memory: Self-organization and performance of sensory-motor codes, maps, and plans. In R. Rosen and F. Snell (Eds.), **Progress in theoretical biology**, Vol. 5. New York: Academic Press, 1978.

Grossberg, S., How does a brain build a cognitive code? *Psychological Review*, 1980, **87**, 1–51.

Grossberg, S., Adaptive resonance in development, perception, and cognition. In S. Grossberg (Ed.), **Mathematical psychology and psychophysiology**. Providence, RI: American Mathematical Society, 1981.

Grossberg, S., The quantized geometry of visual space: The coherent computation of depth, form, and lightness. *Behavioral and Brain Sciences*, 1983, **6**, 625–692 (a).

Grossberg, S., Neural substrates of binocular form perception: Filtering, matching, diffusion, and resonance. In E. Basar, H. Flohr, H. Haken, and A.J. Mandell (Eds.), **Synergetics of the brain**. New York: Springer-Verlag, 1983 (b).

Grossberg, S., Outline of a theory of brightness, color, and form perception. In E. Degreef and J. van Buggenhaut (Eds.), **Trends in mathematical psychology**. Amsterdam: North-Holland, 1984.

Grossberg, S., **The adaptive brain, II: Vision, speech, language, and motor control**. Amsterdam: North-Holland, 1987 (a).

Grossberg, S., Cortical dynamics of three-dimensional form, color, and brightness perception, I: Monocular theory. *Perception and Psychophysics*, 1987, **41**, 87–116 (b).

Grossberg, S. and Levine, D.S., Some developmental and attentional biases in the contrast enhancement and short term memory of recurrent neural networks. *Journal of Theoretical Biology*, 1975, **53**, 341–380.

Grossberg, S. and Marshall, J., A computational model of how cortical complex cells multiplex information about position, contrast, orientation, spatial frequency, and disparity. In preparation, 1987.

Grossberg, S. and Mingolla, E., Neural dynamics of form perception: Boundary completion, illusory figures, and neon color spreading. *Psychological Review*, 1985, **92**, 173–211 (a).

Grossberg, S. and Mingolla, E., Neural dynamics of perceptual grouping: Textures, boundaries, and emergent segmentations. *Perception and Psychophysics*, 1985, **38**, 141–171 (b).

Grossberg, S. and Mingolla, E., Computer simulation of neural networks for perceptual psychology. *Behavior Research Methods, Instruments, and Computers*, 1986, **18**, 601–607.

Grossberg, S. and Mingolla, E., Neural dynamics of surface perception: Boundary webs, illuminants, and shape-from-shading. *Computer Vision, Graphics, and Image Processing*, 1987, **37**, 116–165.

Hebb, D.O., **The organization of behavior**. New York: Wiley and Sons, 1949.

Hering, E., **Outlines of a theory of the light sense**. Cambridge, MA: Harvard University Press, 1964.

Hirsch, H.V.B. and Spinelli, D.N., Visual experience modifies distribution of horizontally and vertically oriented receptive fields in cats. *Science*, 1970, **168**, 869–871.

Hollins, M. and Bailey, G.W., Rivalry target luminance does not affect suppression depth. *Perception and Psychophysics*, 1981, **30**, 201–203.

Hubel, D.H. and Wiesel, T.N., Receptive fields, binocular interaction and functional architecture in the cat's visual cortex. *Journal of Physiology*, 1962, **160**, 106–154.

Hubel, D.H. and Wiesel, T.N., Receptive fields and functional architectures of monkey striate cortex. *Journal of Physiology*, 1968, **195**, 215–243.

Hubel, D.H. and Wiesel, T.N., Stereoscopic vision in macaque monkey. *Nature*, 1970, **225**, 41–42.

Hubel, D.H. and Wiesel, T.N., Functional architecture of macaque monkey visual cortex. *Proceedings of the Royal Society of London (B)*, 1977, **198**, 1–59.

Johansson, G., Visual perception of biological motion and a model for its analysis. *Perception and Psychophysics*, 1973, **14**, 201–211.

Johansson, G., Visual motion perception. *Scientific American*, June, 1975, 76–88.

Johannson, G., About the geometry underlying spontaneous visual decoding of the optical message. In E.L.J. Leeuwenberg and H.F.J.M. Buffart (Eds.), **Formal theories of visual perception**. New York: Wiley and Sons, 1978.

Julesz, B., **Foundations of cyclopean perception**. Chicago: University of Chicago Press, 1971.

Kanizsa, G., Subjective contours. *Scientific American*, 1976, **234**, 48–52.

Kanizsa, G., **Organization in vision**. New York: Praeger, 1979.

Kaufman, L., **Sight and mind: An introduction to visual perception**. New York: Oxford University Press, 1974.

King-Smith, P.E., Visual detection analysed in terms of luminance and chromatic signals. *Nature*, 1975, **255**, 69–70.

Kulikowski, J.J., Limit of single vision in stereopsis depends on contour sharpness. *Nature*, 1978, **275**, 126–127.

Kulikowski, J.J. and Kranda, K., In J.D. Pettigrew, K.J. Sanderson, and W.R. Levick (Eds.), **Visual neuroscience.** Cambridge: Cambridge University Press, 1986.

Kulikowski, J.J., Marčelja, S., and Bishop, P.O., Theory of spatial position and spatial frequency relations in the receptive fields of simple cells in the visual cortex. *Biological Cybernetics*, 1982, **43**, 187–198.

Lee, B.B., Creutzfeldt, O.D., and Elepfandt, A., The response of magno-and-parvocellular cells of the monkey's lateral geniculate body to moving stimuli. *Experimental Brain Research*, 1979, **35**, 547–557.

Legge, G.E. and Rubin, G.S., Binocular interactions in suprathreshold contrast perception. *Perception and Psychophysics*, 1981, **30**, 49–61.

Levelt, W.J.M., **On binocular rivalry.** Soesterberg, The Netherlands: Institute for Perception, RVO-TNO, 1965.

Leventhal, A.G. and Schall, J.D., Structural basis of orientation sensitivity of cat retinal ganglion cells. *Journal of Comparative Neurology*, 1983, **220**, 465–475.

Levick, W.R. and Thibos, L.N., Analysis of orientation bias in cat retina. *Journal of Physiology (London)*, 1982, **329**, 243–261.

Levy, W.B., Associative changes at the synapse: LTP in the hippocampus. In W.B. Levy, J. Anderson, and S. Lehmkuhle (Eds.), **Synaptic modification, neuron selectivity, and nervous system organization.** Hillsdale, NJ: Erlbaum, 1985, pp.5–33.

Levy, W.B., Brassel, S.E., and Moore, S.D., Partial quantification of the associative synaptic learning rule of the dentate gyrus. *Neuroscience*, 1983, **8**, 799–808.

Levy, W.B. and Desmond, N.L., The rules of elemental synptic plasticity. In W.B. Levy, J. Anderson, and S. Lehmkuhle (Eds.), **Synaptic modification, neuron selectivity, and nervous system organization.** Hillsdale, NJ: Erlbaum, 1985, pp.105–121.

Livingstone, M.S. and Hubel, D.H., Anatomy and physiology of a color system in the primate visual cortex. *Journal of Neuroscience*, 1984, **4**, 309–356 (a).

Livingstone, M.S. and Hubel, D.H., Specificity of intrinsic connections in primate primary cortex. *Journal of Neuroscience*, 1984, **4**, 2830–2835 (b).

Lu, C. and Fender, D.H., The interaction of color and luminance in stereoscopic vision. *Investigative Ophthalmology*, 1972, **11**, 482–490.

MacKay, D.M., Moving visual images produced by regular stationary patterns. *Nature*, 1957, **180**, 849–850.

MacKay, D.M. and MacKay, V., Orientation-sensitive aftereffects of dichoptically presented colour and form. *Nature*, 1973, **242**, 477–479.

MacKay, D.M. and MacKay, V., Dichoptic induction of McCollough-type effects. *Quarterly Journal of Experimental Psychology*, 1975, **27**, 225–233.

Marr, D. and Nishihara, H.K., Representation and recognition of the spatial organization of three-dimensional shapes. *Proceedings of the Royal Society of London (B)*, 1978, **200**, 269–294.

Marr, D. and Poggio, T., Cooperative computation of stereo disparity. *Science*, 1976, **194**, 283–287.

Marr, D. and Poggio, T., A computational theory of human stereo vision. *Proceedings of the Royal Society of London (B)*, 1979, **204**, 301–328.

McCarter, A. and Silver, A.I., The McCollough effect: A classical conditioning phenomenon? *Vision Research*, 1977, **17**, 317–319.

McCollough, C., Color adaptation of edge-detectors in the human visual system. *Science*, 1965, **149**, 1115–1116.

Metelli, F., The perception of transparency. *Scientific American*, 1974, **230**, 90–98.

Metelli, F., DaPos, O., and Cavedon, A., Balanced and unbalanced, complete and partial transparency. *Perception and Psychophysics*, 1985, **38**, 354–366.

Meyer, G.E. and Senecal, M., The illusion of transparency and chromatic subjective contours. *Perception and Psychophysics*, 1983, **34**, 58–64.

Mullikin, W.H., Jones, J.P., and Palmer, L.A., Periodic simple cells in cat area 17. *Journal of Neurophysiology*, 1984, **52**, 372–387.

Murch, G.M., Binocular relationships in a size and color orientation specific aftereffect. *Journal of Experimental Psychology*, 1972, **93**, 30–34.

Poggio, G.F., Motter, B.C., Squatrito, S., and Trotter, Y., Responses of neurons in visual cortex (V1 and V2) of the alert macaque to dynamic random-dot stereograms. *Vision Research*, 1985, **25**, 397–406.

Pollen, D.A., Andrews, B.W., and Feldon, S.E., Spatial frequency selectivity of periodic complex cells in the visual cortex of the cat. *Vision Research*, 1978, **18**, 665–682.

Pollen, D.A. and Ronner, S.F., Periodic excitability changes across the receptive fields of complex cells in the striate and parastriate cortex of the cat. *Journal of Physiology (London)*, 1975, **245**, 667–697.

Pollen, D.A. and Ronner, S.F., Phase relationships between adjacent simple cells in the visual cortex. *Science*, 1981, **212**, 1409–1411.

Pollen, D.A. and Ronner, S.F., Visual cortical neurons as localized spatial frequency filters. *IEEE Transactions on Systems, Man, and Cybernetics*, 1983, **SMC-13**, 907–916.

Ramachandran, V.S. and Nelson, J.I., Global grouping overrides point-to-point disparities. *Perception*, 1976, **5**, 125–128.

Rauschecker, J.P. and Singer, W., Changes in the circuitry of the kitten's visual cortex are gated by postsynaptic activity. *Nature*, 1979, **280**, 58–60.

Redies, C. and Spillmann, L., The neon color effect in the Ehrenstein illusion. *Perception*, 1981, **10**, 667–681.

Regan, D. and Beverley, K.I., Binocular and monocular stimuli for motion in depth: Changing-disparity and changing-size feed the same motion-in-depth stage. *Vision Research*, 1979, **19**, 1331–1342.

Regan, D. and Cynader, M., Neurons in cat visual cortex tuned to the direction of motion in depth: Effect of stimulus speed. *Investigative Ophthalmology and Visual Science*, 1982, **22**, 535–550.

Rockland, K.S. and Lund, J.S., Intrinsic laminar lattice connections in primate visual cortex. *Journal of Comparative Neurology*, 1983, **216**, 303–318.

Russell, P.W., Chromatic input to stereopsis. *Vision Research*, 1979, **19**, 831–834.

Savoy, R.L., "Extinction" of the McCollough effect does not transfer interocularly. *Perception and Psychophysics*, 1984, **36**, 571–576.

Savoy, R.L., Personal communication, 1985.

Schwartz, E.L., Computational anatomy and functional architecture of striate cortex: A spatial mapping approach to perceptual coding. *Vision Research*, 1980, **20**, 645–669.

Schwartz, B.J. and Sperling, G., Luminance controls the perceived 3-D structure of dynamic 2-D displays. *Bulletin of the Psychonomic Society*, 1983, **21**, 456–458.

Shinkman, P.G. and Bruce, C.J., Binocular differences in cortical receptive fields of kittens after rotationally disparate binocular experience. *Science*, 1977, **197**, 285–287.

Sillito, A.M., Modification of the receptive field properties of neurons in the visual cortex by bicuculline, a GABA antagonist. *Journal of Physiology*, 1974, **239**, 36P–37P.

Sillito, A.M., The effectiveness of bicuculline as an antagonist of GABA and visually evoked innhibition in the cat's striate cortex. *Journal of Physiology*, 1975, **250**, 287–304 (a).

Sillito, A.M., The contribution of inhibitory mechanisms to the receptive field properties of neurones in the striate cortex of the cat. *Journal of Physiology*, 1975, **250**, 305–329 (b).

Sillito, A.M., Inhibitory processes underlying the directional specificity of simple, complex and hypercomplex cells in the cat's visual cortex. *Journal of Physiology*, 1977, **271**, 699–720.

Sillito, A.M., Inhibitory mechanisms influencing complex cell orientation selectivity and their modification at high resting discharge levels. *Journal of Physiology*, 1979, **289**, 33–53.

Sillito, A.M., Salt, T.E., and Kemp, J.A., Modulatory and inhibitory processes in the visual cortex. *Vision Research*, 1985, **25**, 375–381.

Singer, W., Neuronal activity as a shaping factor in the self-organization of neuron assemblies. In E. Basar, H. Flohr, H. Haken, and A.J. Mandell (Eds.), **Synergetics of the brain**. New York: Springer-Verlag, 1983.

Singer, W., Central control of developmental plasticity in the mammalian visual cortex. *Vision Research*, 1985, **25**, 389–396.

Skowbo, D., Are McCollough effects conditioned responses? *Psychological Bulletin*, 1984, **96**, 215–226.

Skowbo, D. and Forster, T., Further evidence against the classical conditioning model of McCollough effects. *Perception and Psychophysics*, 1983, **34**, 552–554.

Skowbo, D., Timney, B.N., Gentry, T.A., and Morant, R.B., McCollough effects: Experimental findings and theoretical accounts. *Psychological Bulletin*, 1975, **82**, 497–510.

Skowbo, D. and White, K., McCollough effect acquisition depends on duration of exposure to inducing stimuli, not number of stimulus presentations. *Perception and Psychophysics*, 1983, **34**, 549–551.

Smith, E.L. III, Levi, D.M., Harwerth, R.S., and White, J.M., Color vision is altered during the suppression phase of binocular rivalry. *Science*, 1982, **218**, 802–804.

Sperling, G., Binocular vision: A physical and a neural theory. *American Journal of Psychology*, 1970, **83**, 461–534.

Tausch, R., Die beidäugige Raumwahrnehmung—ein Prozess auf Grund der Korrespondenz und Disparation von Gestalten anstelle der Korrespondenz oder Disparation einzelner Netzhautelemente. *Zeitschrift für experimentelle und angewandte Psychologie*, 1953, **1**, 394–421.

Thorell, L.G., DeValois, R.L., and Albrecht, D.G., Spatial mapping of monkey V1 cells with pure color and luminance stimuli. *Vision Research*, 1984, **24**, 751–769.

van Tuijl, H.F.J.M., A new visual illusion: Neonlike color spreading and complementary color induction between subjective contours. *Acta Psychologica*, 1975, **39**, 441–445.

van Tuijl, H.F.J.M. and de Weert, C.M.M., Sensory conditions for the occurrence of the neon spreading illusion. *Perception*, 1979, **8**, 211–215.

Vidyasagar, T.R., Orientation specific colour adaptation at a binocular site. *Nature*, 1976, **261**, 39–40.

Vidyasagar, T.R. and Urbas, J.V., Orientation sensitivity of cat LGN neurones with and without inputs from visual cortical areas 17 and 18. *Experimental Brain Research*, 1982, **46**, 157–169.

von der Heydt, R., Hänny, P., and Dürsteler, M.R., The role of orientation disparity in stereoscopic perception and the development of binocular correspondence. In E. Grastyán and P. Molnár (Eds.), **Advances in physiological science, Vol. 16: Sensory functions**. Elmsford, NY: Pergamon Press, 1981.

von Tschermak-Seysenegg, A., **Introduction to physiological optics**, (P. Boeder, translator). Springfield, IL: C.C. Thomas, 1952.

Wales, R. and Fox, R., Incremental detection thresholds during binocular rivalry suppression. *Perception and Psychophysics*, 1970, **8**, 90–94.

Werner, H., Dynamics in binocular depth perception. **Psychological Monograph** (whole no.218), 1937.

White, K.D., Petry, H.M., Riggs, L.A., and Miller, J., Binocular interactions during establishment of McCollough effects. *Vision Research*, 1978, **18**, 1201–1215.

Wilde, K., Der Punktreiheneffekt und die Rolle der binocularen Querdisparation beim Tienfenshen. *Psychologische Forschung*, 1950, **23**, 223–262.

Willshaw, D.J. and Malsburg, C. von der, How patterned neural connections can be set up by self-organization. *Proceedings of the Royal Society of London (B)*, 1976, **194**, 431–445.

Zeki, S., Colour coding in the cerebral cortex: The reaction of cells in monkey visual cortex to wavelengths and colours. *Neuroscience*, 1983, **9**, 741–765 (a).

Zeki, S., Colour coding in the cerebral cortex: The responses of wavelength-sensitive and colour coded cells in monkey visual cortex to changes in wavelength composition. *Neuroscience*, 1983, **9**, 767–791 (b).

NEURAL DYNAMICS OF 1-D AND 2-D BRIGHTNESS PERCEPTION:
A UNIFIED MODEL OF CLASSICAL AND RECENT PHENOMENA

Stephen Grossberg† and Dejan Todorović‡

ABSTRACT

Computer simulations of a neural network model of 1-D and 2-D brightness phenomena are presented. The simulations indicate how configural image properties trigger interactions among spatially organized contrastive, boundary segmentation, and filling-in processes to generate emergent percepts. They provide the first unified mechanistic explanation of this set of phenomena, a number of which have received no previous mechanistic explanation. Network interactions between a Boundary Contour System (BCS) and a Feature Contour System (FCS) comprise the model. The BCS consists of a hierarchy of contrast-sensitive and orientationally tuned interactions, leading to a boundary segmentation. On and Off geniculate cells and simple and complex cortical cells are modelled. Output signals from the BCS segmentation generate compartmental boundaries within the FCS. Contrast-sensitive inputs to the FCS generate a lateral filling-in of activation within FCS compartments. The filling-in process is defined by a nonlinear diffusion mechanism. Simulated phenomena include network responses to stimulus distributions which involve combinations of luminance steps, gradients, cusps, and corners of various sizes. These images include impossible staircases, bull's eyes, nested combinations of luminance profiles, and images viewed under nonuniform illumination conditions. Simulated phenomena include variants of brightness constancy, brightness contrast, brightness assimilation, the Craik-O'Brien-Cornsweet effect, the Koffka-Benussi ring, the Kanizsa-Minguzzi anomalous brightness differentiation, the Hermann grid, and a Land Mondrian viewed under constant and gradient illumination which cannot be explained by Retinex theory.

_____

† Supported in part by the Air Force Office of Scientific Research (AFOSR 85-0149 and AFOSR F49620-86-C-0037) and the Army Research Office (ARO DAAG-29-85-K-0095).

‡ Supported in part by the Army Research Office (ARO DAAG-29-85-K-0095).

1. Introduction: Interactions between Form and Appearance

The sensitivity to ambient differences in light energy is the most basic discriminative ability of visual systems. The distribution of light energy reaching an animal's eyes is often characterized by regions of slow or zero gradients bordered by abrupt changes such as edges or contours. Correspondingly, one important tradition of psychophysical investigation has intensively studied the perceptual properties of juxtaposed homogeneous regions, leading to such classical contributions as Weber's ratio and Fechner's law (Fechner, 1889), Metzger's Ganzfeld (Metzger, 1930), and the analysis of brightness constancy and contrast (Hess and Pretori, 1894; Katz, 1935). A parallel line of psychophysical investigation has emphasized the processing of luminance discontinuities, notably edges and textures (Beck, 1966a, 1966b; Julesz, 1971; Ratliff, 1965).

Each type of investigation has provided essential data and concepts about visual perception, but nonetheless, taken in isolation, is inherently incomplete. For example, the output of an edge processing model produces only an outline of its visual environment and provides insufficient information about either the form or the appearance of the structures within the outline.

The nature of the incompleteness of vision concepts and models which focus only one type of process at the expense of the other can be understood from two different perspectives. On the one hand, there exist large data bases which support the hypothesis that the processes which control the perception of form and appearance strongly interact before generating a final percept. Data concerning 1-dimensional and 2-dimensional brightness perception provide a particularly rich and constraining set of phenomena of this type. A number of key phenomena from this data base are given a unified explanation herein. In our model these brightness phenomena are generated as emergent properties of a neural network theory of preattentive visual perception (Cohen and Grossberg, 1984; Grossberg, 1987a, 1987b; Grossberg and Mingolla, 1985a, 1985b, 1987a, 1987b).

The anomalous brightness differentation (Kanizsa and Minguzzi, 1986) which is induced by the image shown in Figure 1 is one of the many brightness phenomena that can be explained by this theory. As Kanizsa and Minguzzi (1986, p.223) have noted "this unexpected effect is not easily explained. In fact, it cannot be accounted for by any simple physiological mechanism such as lateral inhibition or frequency filtering. Furthermore, it does not seem obvious to invoke organzational factors, like figural belongingness or figure-ground articulation." We agree with these authors, but also show that this brightness phenomenon can be explained by the same theory that we use to explain many other brightness phenomena.

The properties of this theory clarify a deeper sense in which models which consider only form or appearance are incomplete. The perceptual theory which we apply suggests that the neural systems which process form or appearance each compensate for limitations of the other systems with which they interact. In other words, complete articulation of the processing rules for *either* system requires an analysis of the processing rules of the other system and of how the systems offset each other's complementary inadequacies through their *interactions*. Such an analysis has led to the identification of several new uncertainty principles which these systems overcome through parallel and hierarchical interactions (Grossberg, 1987a, 1987b).

The theory suggests that two parallel contour-sensitive processes interact to generate a percept of brightness. The Boundary Contour System, defined by a network hierarchy of oriented interactions, synthesizes an emergent binocular boundary segmentation from combinations of oriented and unoriented scenic elements. The Feature Contour System

Figure 1. The Kanizsa-Minguzzi anomalous brightness differentiation. The bright annulus is divided into two unequal segments. The smaller segment looks slightly brighter.

triggers a diffusive filling-in of featural quality within perceptual domains whose boundaries are determined by output signals from the Boundary Contour System. Neurophysiological and anatomical data from lateral geniculate nucleus and visual cortex which have been analysed and predicted by the theory are summarized in Grossberg (1987a, 1987b).

Herein we use a simplified version of the model to explain brightness data. The simplified model does not include Boundary Contour System and Feature Contour System mechanisms of emergent segmentation, multiple scale filtering, binocular interactions, and double-opponent processing. We focus on that large domain of brightness data whose qualitative properties can be explained by a single scale, monocular version of the model. Our computer simulations of 1-dimensional phenomena use a single set of numerical parameters, as do our simulations of 2-dimensional brightness phenomena. We also show how parameter changes influence quantitative details of the simulation results. Since many visual images activate multiple spatial scales, binocular interactions, and emergent segmentations, our goal herein is to provide the type of quantitative understanding of model mechanisms that can achieve a unified qualitative explanation of difficult brightness data. The explanations of brightness phenomena within this reduced model are easily seen to be valid within the full theory, and provide necessary information for future studies of quantitative matches between simulations and data in a multiple scale, binocular setting.

The present article is organized as follows. In Section 2 we describe the neural network model which we use to simulate brightness phenomena. This model generalizes to two dimensions the types of processes which Cohen and Grossberg (1984) used to simulate 1-dimensional brightness phenomena. This generalization joins together processing concepts and mechanisms from Cohen and Grossberg (1984) with those from Grossberg and Mingolla (1985b, 1987a). Section 3 defines and illustrates model properties through computer simulations of the model's reactions to a particular 2-dimensional luminance distribution called the yin-yang square. The next two sections provide a unified account, through computer simulations, of several classical and recent varieties of brightness phenomena. Section 4 contains the 1-dimensional simulations and Section 5 contains the 2-dimensional simulations. Section 6 discusses how the model's concepts and mechanisms are related to other concepts and mechanisms of the theory which have been developed to analyse different data bases.

2. The Model: A Hierarchy of Spatially Organized Network Interactions

Figure 2 provides an overview of the neural network model that we have analysed. The model has six levels depicted as thick-bordered rectangles numbered from 1 to 6. Levels 1 and 2 are preprocessing levels prior to the Boundary and Feature Contour Systems. Output signals from Level 2 generate inputs to both of these Systems. Levels 3–5 are processing stages within the Boundary Contour System. Level 6, which models the Feature Contour System, receives inputs from both Level 2 and Level 5.

Each level contains a different type of neural network. The type of network is indicated by the symbol inside the rectangle. The symbols provide graphical mnemonics for the processing characteristics at a given level, and are used in the figures which present the computer simulations of the two-dimensional implementation of the model. The arrows connecting the rectangles depict the flow of processing between the levels. The type of signal processing between different levels is indicated inside thin-bordered insets attached by dotted lines to appropriate arrows, and coded by letters from "A" to "E". The sketch inside the inset coded "F" depicts the complex interactions between Levels 2, 5, and 6. The properties of different levels and transformations will be discussed in detail in the following pages. To explain the working of the system, we repeatedly refer to Figure 2, and present a number of computer simulations of network dynamics. The mathematical equations of the model are described in the Appendix.

2.1. Level 1: The Stimulus Distribution

The first level of the model consists of a set of units that sample the luminance distribution. In the one-dimensional version of the model, the units are arranged on a line, and in the two-dimensional version, they form a square grid.

2.2. Level 2: Circular Concentric On and Off Units (LGN Cells)

Level 2 of the network models cells with the type of circular concentric receptive fields found at early levels of the visual system, such as ganglion retinal cells or lateral geniculate cells. These cells come in two varieties: the on-center-off-surround, or on-cells, and the off-center-on-surround cells, or off-cells. In Figure 2, the on-units are symbolized with a white center and a black annulus, and the off-units with a black center and a white annulus. The mathematical specification of the receptive field (see the Appendix) uses feedforward shunting equations (Grossberg, 1983) because of their sensitivity to input reflectances. Thus the model utilizes the simplest physiological mechanism that discounts the illuminant and is sufficient to explain key properties of the targeted brightness percepts.

The one-dimensional cross-sections of these receptive fields are presented in insets "A" and "B" in Figure 2. In two dimensions, these profiles have the shape of sombreros for on-units and inverted sombreros for off-units. The activity level of such cells correlates with the size of the center-surround luminance contrast. More luminance in the center than in the surround induces increased activity in on-cells and decreased activity in off-cells. Inverse luminance conditions result in inverse activation levels. Due to the shunting interaction, the cells are sensitive to relative contrast in a manner approximating a Weber law (Grossberg, 1983). In addition, the cells are tuned to display nonnegligible activity levels even for homogeneous stimulation, as do retinal ganglion cells (Enroth-Cugell and Robson, 1984). This property enables such a cell to generate output signals which are sensitive to both excitatory and inhibitory inputs.

2.3. Level 3: Oriented Direction-of-Contrast Sensitive Units (Simple Cells)

Level 3 consists of cell units that share properties with cortical simple cells. The symbol for these units in Figure 2 expresses their sensitivity to luminance contrast of a

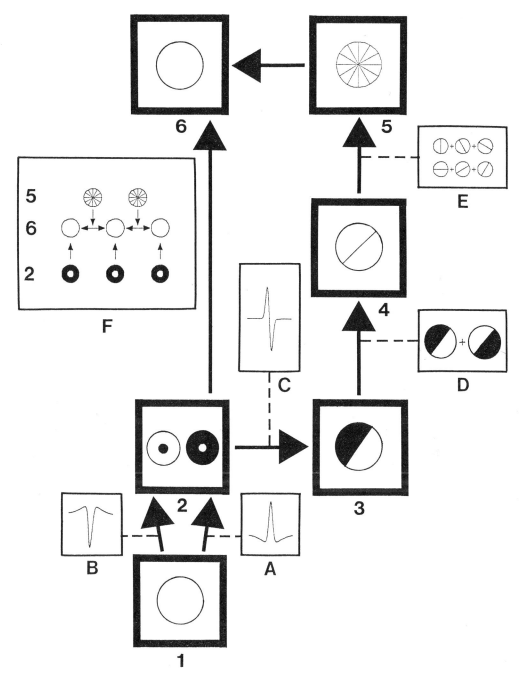

Figure 2. Overview of the model. The thick-bordered rectangles numbered from 1 to 6 correspond to the levels of the system. The symbols inside the rectangles are graphical mnemonics for the types of computational units residing at the corresponding model level. The arrows depict the interconnections between the levels. The thin-bordered rectangles coded by letters A through E represent the the type of processing between pairs of levels. Inset F illustrates how the activity at Level 6 is modulated by outputs from Level 2 and Level 5. See text for additional details.

given orientation and given direction-of-contrast. Inset "C" depicts the one-dimensional cross-section of the receptive field of such units, taken with respect to the network of on-cells.

In our two-dimensional simulations, the function we used to generate this receptive field profile was the difference of two identical bivariate Gaussians whose centers were shifted with respect to each other (see the Appendix). A similar formalization was used by Heggelund (1981a, 1985). As yet, neither anatomical not physiological studies have unequivocally demonstrated the manner in which orientational sensitivity arises in cortical cells (Braitenberg and Braitenberg, 1979; Nielsen, 1985; Sillito, 1984). Our ambition was not to resolve this issue, but to find a simple yet acceptable arrangement which realizes the desired functional properties. In our current implementation, Level 3 units are activated by Level 2 on-units.

In order to represent a number of different orientation sensitivities, Level 3 consists of 12 different cell types, each sensitive to a different orientation and direction-of-contrast. A convenient "hour code" was used to denote these units. For example, a cell tuned to detect vertical left-to-right light-dark edges is denoted a "12 o'clock unit", whereas a cell with the same axis orientation but reversed contrast preference is a "6 o'clock unit" (See Figure 7). In the one-dimensional implementation, only two directions were used.

2.4. Level 4: Oriented Direction-of-Contrast Insensitive Units (Complex Cells)

Level 3 units are sensitive to oriented contrasts in a specific direction. However, there is both physiological and psychophysical evidence for the existence of complex cell units sensitive to contrasts of specific orientation regardless of contrast polarity are well-known to occur in area 17 of monkeys (DeValois, Albrecht, and Thorell, 1982; Gouras and Krüger, 1979; Hubel and Wiesel, 1968; Schiller, Finlay, and Volman, 1976; Tanaka, Lee, and Creutzfeldt, 1983) and cats (Heggelund, 1981b; Hubel and Wiesel, 1962; Spitzer and Hochstein, 1985). See Grossberg (1987a) for a review of relevant data and related models.

Units fulfilling the above criteria populate Level 4 of the network. Inset "D" in Figure 2 depicts the construction of Level 4 cells out of Level 3 cells. The mathematical specification is similar to the one used by Grossberg and Mingolla (1985a, 1985b) and Spitzer and Hochstein (1985). The symbol of Level 4 units expresses their sensitivity to oriented contrasts of either direction. Each Level 4 unit at a particular location is excited by two Level 3 units at the corresponding location having the same axis of orientation but opposite direction preference. For example, a 3 o'clock unit and a 9 o'clock unit in Level 3 generate a horizontal contrast detector in Level 4. Thus the twelve Level 3 networks give rise to six Level 4 networks. Interestingly, several physiological studies have found that the simple cells outnumber the complex cells in a ratio of approximately 2 to 1, and that complex cells have higher spontaneous activity levels than simple cells (Kato, Bishop, and Orban, 1978). Both of these properties are consistent with the proposed circuitry.

2.5. Level 5: Boundary Contour Units

In the simulations presented in this paper, we have used a simplified version of the Boundary Contour System. The final output of this System is located at Level 5 of the model. A unit at a given Level 5 location can be excited by any Level 4 unit located at the position corresponding to the position of the Level 5 unit. A Level 4 unit excites a Level 5 unit only if its own activity exceeds a threshold value. The pooling of signals sensitive to different orientations is sketched in inset "E" and expressed in the symbol for Level 5 in Figure 2. This pooling may, in principle, occur entirely in convergent output pathways from the Boundary Contour System to the Feature Contour System, rather than at a separate level of cells within the Boundary Contour System.

2.6. Level 6: Diffusive Filling-In within a Cell Syncytium

Network activity at Level 6 of our model corresponds to the brightness percept. Level 6 is part of the Feature Contour System, which is composed of a syncytium of cells. A syncytium of cells is a regular array of intimately connected cells such that contiguous cells can easily pass signals between each other's compartment membranes, possibly via gap junctions (Piccolino, Neyton, and Gerschenfeld, 1984). Due to the syncytial coupling of each cell with its neighbors, the activity can rapidly spread to neighboring cells, then to neighbors of the neighbors, and so on.

Because the spreading, or filling-in, of activation occurs via a process of diffusion, it tends to average the activation that is triggered by a Feature Contour input from Level 2 across the Level 6 cells that receive this spreading activity. This averaged activity spreads across the syncytium with a space constant that depends upon the electrical activities of both the cell interiors and their membranes. The electrical properties of the cell membranes can be altered by Boundary Contour signals in the following way. A Boundary Contour signal is assumed to decrease the diffusion constant of its target cell membranes within the cell syncytium. It does so by acting as an inhibitory gating signal that causes an increase in cell membrane resistance. A Boundary Contour signal hereby creates a barrier to the filling-in process at its target cells.

The inset labelled "F" in Figure 1 summarizes the three factors which influence the magnitude of activity of units at Level 6. First, each unit receives bottom-up input from Level 2, the field of concentric on-cells. Second, there are lateral connections between neighboring units at Level 6 which define the syncytium which enables within-network spread of activation, or filling-in. Third, this lateral spread is modulated by inhibition from Level 5 in the form of Boundary Contour signals capable of decreasing the magnitude of mutual influence between neighboring Level 6 units. The net effect of these interactions is that the Feature Contour signals generated by the concentric on-cells is diffused and averaged within boundaries generated by the Boundary Contour signals.

The idea of a filling-in process was invoked in various forms by several authors in discussions of different brightness phenomena (Davidson and Whiteside, 1971; Fry, 1948; Gerrits and Vendrik, 1970; Hamada, 1984; Walls, 1954). In the present model, this notion is fully formalized, related to a possible neurophysiological foundation, tied in with other mechanisms as a part of a more general vision theory, and applied in a systematic way to a variety of brightness phenomena.

3. An Example of System Dynamics and Graphical Representation: The Yin-Yang Square

Figure 3 shows an image that was used as input to the system to illustrate its functioning. It is a square version of the yin-yang symbol. The salient feature of the stimulus is the Z-shaped luminance contour, separating the top and right bright portion (yin) from the bottom and left dark portion (yang). Although the visual structure of the display is simple, it is sufficiently rich to illustrate a number of properties of our system.

The way this stimulus is represented in the system is presented in Figure 4. This representation, corresponding to Level 1 in Figure 2, has a number of features typical for our representations of two-dimensional patterns of activity at all levels of the system.

Figure 3. The Yin-Yang square. The Z-shaped luminance step separates two regions of different homogeneous luminance. This two-dimensional luminance distribution is used as an input to the model. Figures 4 through 9 present the activity profiles induced by this stimulus at various levels of the model. The equations and parameters used in the simulations are listed in the Appendix.

First, it is a square 16×16 grid of units or cells. Later we will also present 30×30 and 40×40 examples, and one-dimensional representations in cases in which the two-dimensional structure is not essential for the analysis of the image. Second, such a grid of units is only a sample from a potentially much denser and larger grid. This level of resolution and size proved, however, to represent adequately the activity patterns for the types of images we used. Third, the magnitude of activity of a unit is coded by the size of the graphical symbol representing the particular level of the system. In Figure 4, the radius of a circle is proportional to the magnitude of activity of the Level 1 unit corresponding to the grid position at the center of the circle. Since in this case the stimulus has only two intensity levels, circles of only two sizes appear in the representation. The larger circles correspond to the more luminant portion of the stimulus, the smaller ones to the less luminant portion, and their spatial arrangement corresponds to the spatial luminance structure of the stimulus.

The particular sizes of the circles on the printed page were chosen according to the following scaling procedure: the unit or units with the maximum activity are represented with circles whose radius is equal to half the distance between the centers of two neighboring units on the grid; the remaining circles are scaled proportionally. Most of the two-dimensional figures in the paper were scaled separately, meaning that each graph was scaled with respect to its own maximum. A common scale for a large set of figures was impracticable in view of many different stimulus distributions, model levels, and parameter ranges. Therefore, relative size comparisons are meaningful within a figure, but generally are not between figures. However, in some cases, which will be specifically noted, a common scale was used for several figures.

We considered other ways to represent two-dimensional activity profiles. For example, one could use three-dimensional graphs in which the x- and y-coordinate code the spatial variables, and the z-coordinate codes strength of activity. Another possibility is to use a shading representation, in which the luminance level codes magnitude of activity. There are several reasons that we have not used such more standard formats. The detailed structure of activity profiles appeared to us in most cases to be easier to grasp in the symbol-size code than in the z-coordinate or shading code. The hidden line removal technique, used in some versions of the first code, unfortunately also hides some aspects of the profile structure as well. A shading representation seemed to us particularly awkward, since our purpose was to study the more subtle and illusory aspects of brightness perception. On the other hand, since a symbol has other features in addition to size, these other features can be used to code other aspects of activity profiles. As illustrated herein, the use of different mnemonic symbols for different levels of the system enhances the clarity of presentation of its structure and function. The advantages of a symbol-size representation become apparent in the representation of the Level 2 response to the yin-yang square.

Figures 5a and 5b present computer simulations of activity profiles of Level 2 on-units and off-units, respectively, in response to the stimulus shown in Figure 3. These are 16×16 grids of units, in which symbol size codes activation strength. The shapes of these profiles are the result of two components: the structure of the stimulus and the structure of the networks. The interaction of these two factors results in field distributions in which the structure of the stimulus is recognizable, but distorted. The particular forms of these transformations will now be discussed in more detail.

In contrast to only two different magnitudes in the representation of the stimulus at Level 1, the Level 2 equilibrium activity patterns of the on-units in Figure 5a exhibit many more magnitudes. In the stimulus, differences between adjacent units exist only along the contour, and they are all of the same size. In the on-unit response fields, the largest differences are also found along the contour, but they vary systematically in size. Furthermore, the response strength gradient diminishes with increasing distance from the contour.

In addition, the extremal response values correspond to stimulus contour corners: that is, locations of abrupt change in the orientation of luminance contrast. This feature is a straightforward consequence of the structure of the stimulus transformation imposed by units with circular concentric antagonistic receptive fields. Thus the location of the most activated unit in the on-field in Figure 5a corresponds to the convex bright corner of the yin portion of the stimulus distribution. The Level 2 on-unit at this location receives in its receptive field center as much stimulation as do all other units in the bright portion of the stimulus. However, the surround of this unit contributes the least amount of inhibition, because almost three-quarters of its area lies in the concave dark corner of the yang portion of the stimulus distribution. Analogously, the minimum of the activity profile in the on-field is located in a position corresponding to the convex dark corner of the yang portion of the stimulus.

These features of the two-dimensional on-cell response profiles are consistent with well-known physiological results and theories involving reactions to one-dimensional luminance

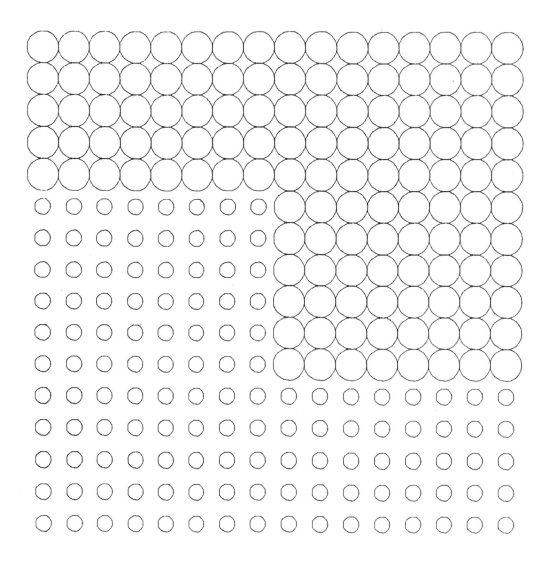

Figure 4. The representation of the Yin-Yang square at Level 1 of the model. Local luminance level is coded by the magnitude of the circle radius.

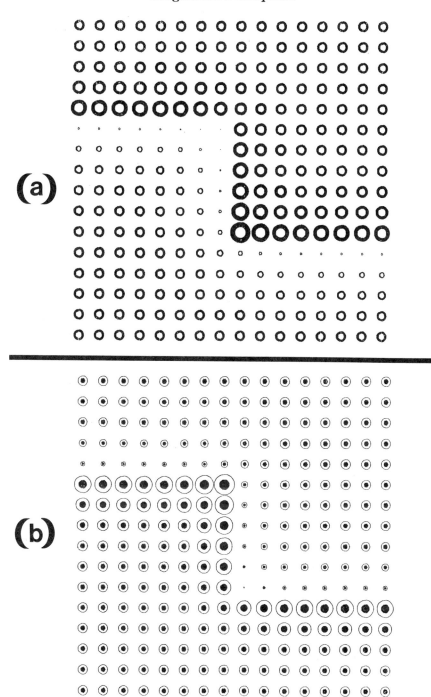

Figure 5. The Level 2 activity profiles. (a) The on-cell distribution. (b) The off-cell distribution. The extremal values in the two distributions correspond to the two corners of the Yin-Yang square. The complementarity of the two activity profiles reflects the complementary structure of the receptive fields of the on-cells and the off-cells. Neither of the two activity profiles can account for the brightness distribution. See text for details.

step-distributions in the limulus (Ratliff and Hartline, 1959) and the cat (Enroth-Cugell and Robson, 1966). The one-dimensional response profiles to such stimuli exhibit increases and decreases at the edges, resulting in cusp-shaped distributions. Such profiles can be found in many one-dimensional cross-sections of Figure 5a. For example, consider the 16 leftmost units in the on-cell field, forming the left border of Figure 5a. Starting from the top left unit, and proceeding toward the bottom left unit, the activity level increases toward the luminance edge, drops abruptly, and returns gradually to a medium level. It is widely accepted that these overshoots and undershoots in physiological activity contribute to the phenomenon of Mach bands (Ratliff, 1965).

The corner-related extrema in the Level 2 distribution profiles may contribute to the enhanced brightness phenomena involving nested sets of corners analysed by Hurvich (1981), who discovered them in paintings by Vasarely. Analogous effects were described by Todorović (1983) in some related visual situations. In analogy to Mach bands, they might be called "Mach corners". A corresponding physiological study has, to our knowledge, not been performed.

A comparison of the on-unit activity pattern in Figure 5a with the off-unit activity patterns in Figure 5b shows a symmetry or duality due to the complementary structure of the receptive fields of on-units and off-units. For example, the locus of minimum activity in Figure 5a corresponds to the locus of maximum activity in Figure 5b, and vice versa. The regions of activity overshoots and undershoots along stimulus contours have also exchanged locations. More generally, for any two units (and, in particular, for any two adjacent units) the following observation holds: If, in Figure 5a, the activity of the first unit is larger than the activity of the second one, then, for the two corresponding units in Figure 5b, the activity of the first unit will be smaller than the activity of the second one, and vice versa.

The final point with respect to the shapes of Level 2 profiles concerns the regions located at some distance from the z-shaped contour. For example, consider the bottom left and the top right unit, whose locations are most removed from the contour region. Their activity level is approximately the same, both within the on-unit field and within the off-unit field. This equality in activity level contrasts with the appearance of the corresponding image portions (Figure 3): the lower left region of the image appears darker than the upper right region. This aspect of the brightness profile cannot be accounted for by the activity profile of cells with concentric antagonistic receptive fields which are insensitive to differences of the absolute level of homogeneous stimulation. In the model, the brightness of Figure 3 is accounted for by the Level 6 distribution.

For pictorial clarity, we first present computer simulations of the Level 3 activity patterns generated across cells with a single orientational preference. (Figures 6a-f; these figures were drawn using a common scale.) Then we combine all of these results into a pictorial summary of the total Level 3 equilibrium response (Figure 8a). Figures 6a through 6d present activity profiles for four networks, containing 3 o'clock through 6 o'clock Level 3 units, respectively. There are several noteworthy points about these simulations.

The total number of activated cells in each of these Level 3 simulations is smaller than in the Level 2 simulations. While most Level 2 units show some activity, only a restricted set in each Level 3 network is active as part of the detection of a Boundary Contour. In contrast to Level 2 units, in Level 3 cells the net excitatory effect of their receptive fields balances the net inhibitory effect (see inset "C") in accord with physiological findings that cortical simple cells respond weakly if at all to homogeneous stimulation (Hubel and Wiesel, 1968).

Due to the spatial scale and orientational tuning of Level 3 cells, different units prefer

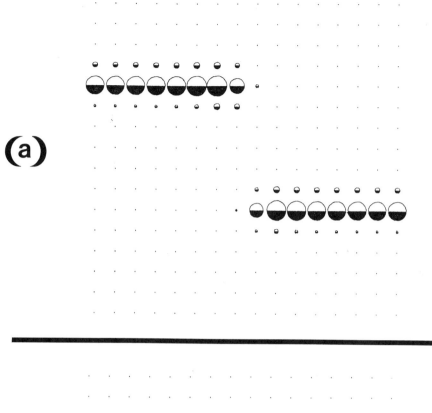

(a)

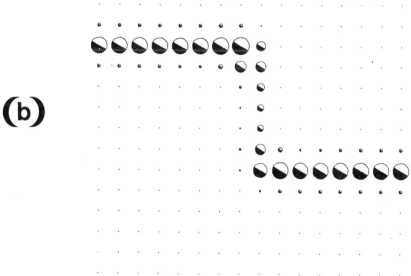

(b)

Figure 6. The activity profiles of direction-of-contrast sensitive units with different orientation preferences. (a) The 3 o'clock units. (b) The 4 o'clock units. (c) The 5 o'clock units. (d) The 6 o'clock units. (e) The 6 o'clock units with larger receptive fields than in (d). (f) The 9 o'clock units.

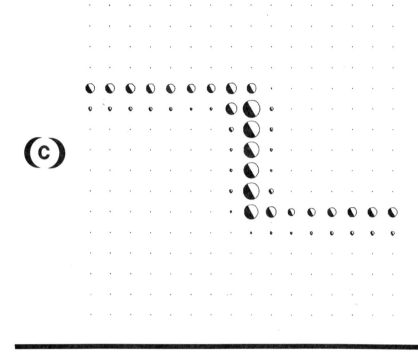

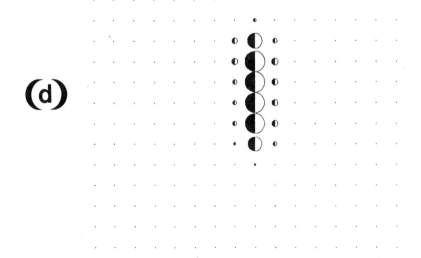

Figure 6 (continued).

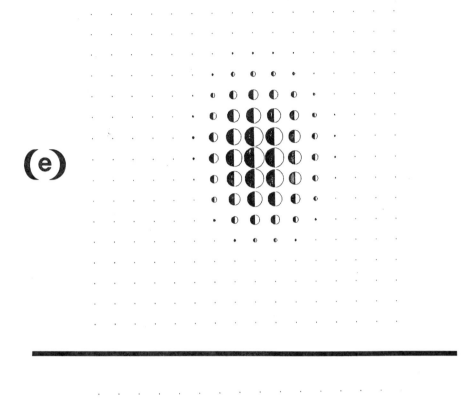

(e)

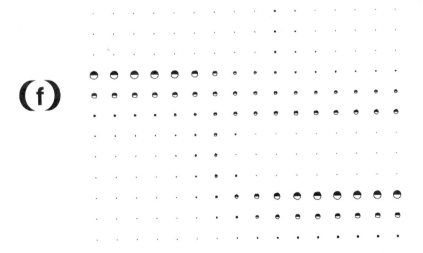

(f)

Figure 6 (continued).

different image features. As expected, the 3 o'clock cells (Figure 6a) detect the horizontal edges of appropriate contrast direction, whereas the 6 o'clock cells (Figure 6d) register the vertical edge. However, the simulations also caution against a feature-detection notion which would hold that such cells respond uniquely to particular stimulus features. As has been pointed out in various forms before (Frisby, 1979; Sekuler, 1974), the activity of a unit does not uniquely correspond to the objective presence of a feature, nor to our perception of such a feature. For example, in Figure 6d, the strongly activated column of 6 o'clock units is surrounded by a halo of weakly activated units. With larger receptive field size or, equivalently in our simulations, larger sample density, an even fuzzier swarm of vertical edge activated units emerges, as shown in Figure 6e. Such a spatially diffuse activity profile contrasts with the sharp localization of both the physical luminance edge and our percept of it.

The non-uniqueness of the relation of stimulus features to unit activity is also shown in orientation preferences. Since each cell responds to a band of orientations, sub-optimal stimuli can induce appreciable activity levels. Figures 6b and 6c show that the 4 o'clock and 5 o'clock units respond reasonably well to both horizontal and vertical stimulus features. Consequently, the overall Z-shaped structure of the stimulus contour is better reflected by the profiles of the non-optimally tuned units in Figures 6b and 6c than by the profiles of the optimally tuned units in Figures 6a and 6d. In particular, the activity patterns of the 4 o'clock and 5 o'clock cells are sensitive to the existence of stimulus corners, which are absent in the activity patterns of the 3 o'clock and 6 o'clock cells.

Figure 6f presents the activity pattern across the field of 9 o'clock units. These cells have the same preferred orientation axis as the 3 o'clock units, but an inverse direction preference. The consequence is still another type of complementary relationship between response profiles: the regions of suprathreshold activity in Figure 6a almost exactly co-incide with regions of zero activity in Figure 6f, and vice versa, although the maximal activity levels in Figure 6f are much smaller than those in Figure 6a.

The activity pattern in Figure 6f may appear counterintuitive, because the horizontally oriented luminance contrast detected by these units is opposite in direction from the one present in the stimulus. However, recall that, in accord with visual anatomy, the Level 3 units are activated by the Level 2 on-unit activity pattern (Figure 4a) rather than by the image itself (Figure 3). In particular, moving from the top left unit toward the bottom left unit in Figure 4a, the activity rises gradually. This activity gradient is picked up by 9 o'clock cells in Figure 6f. Next, there is a sharp drop, strongly activating the 3 o'clock cells in Figure 6a. Finally, the activity gradient slowly rises and is again sensed by 9 o'clock cells. Since the average magnitude of unit activity in Figure 6f is relatively small, it may *in vivo* be submerged in noise. The set of activity patterns in Figures 6a–6f provide qualitative predictions about the first few levels of the Boundary Contour computation.

Figure 7a provides a concise symbolism for the representation of all twelve Level 3 activity patterns. To construct such a total response profile, we have used a representation format in which the size of the response is coded with the length of the clock hand pointing in the direction of the hour code of a unit. Figure 7b depicts a horizontally oriented input to Level 3, with stronger activation at the top than at the bottom strip. The response to such an input would be largest for the optimally tuned 3 o'clock unit, weaker for the 2 o'clock and the 4 o'clock unit, weaker still for the 1 o'clock and the 5 o'clock unit, and zero for the other units. The cluster of lines at the center of Figure 7a concisely represents this pattern of responses at a single position. Since only 5 out of 12 units exhibit positive activity, only five clock hands are displayed. The hour to which a hand is pointing codes the

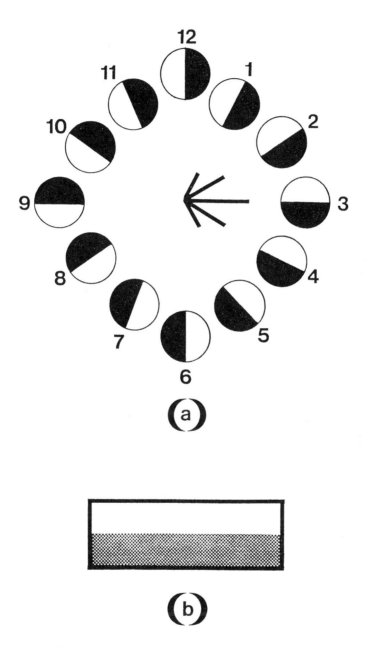

Figure 7. Units at Level 3 are symbolized by graphical mnemonics expressing their different orientation and contrast direction sensitivities. These symbols, which are used in Figure 6 to depict the activity profiles for units of a given sensitivity, are numbered according to the hour code. A different symbolism is used to to represent the activity of all Level 3 units in single graph. The activity level of a unit is coded by the length of the line pointing toward its hour code. The cluster of lines at the center of Figure 7a represents the activity of all units at a location responding to the horizontally oriented contrast depicted in Figure 7b.

orientation and direction preference of a unit, and the length of the hand codes response strength.

Figure 8a uses the representation described in Figure 7a to combine the activity patterns of all oriented Level 3 units (Figure 6) into a single representation. Each of the 16×16 locations in this representation depicts the activity of 12 units which span the full range of orientation and direction preferences.

Figure 8b depicts a representation of horizontally oriented complex cells in Level 4. These cells respond to the sum of output signals from horizontally oriented simple cells of opposite direction-of-contrast in Level 3, namely from Figures 6a and 6f. That is why Level 4 cells do not have a black hemidisk in their representation.

Figure 8c represents the total activity pattern of all Level 4 cells using a variant of the representation used in Figure 8a. In Figure 8c, the activity at a location is coded by a line centered at it. The activity magnitude is proportional to line length, and the orientation is coded by line orientation. Such a representation was called an *orientation field* by Grossberg and Mingolla (1985a, 1985b).

Figure 8d represents the activity pattern of Level 5 units, which compute a total Boundary Contour output signal from each Boundary Contour System position. Each output signal is the sum of thresholded activities from all the orientations computed at that position in Level 4. The spatial distribution of the active units traces the Z-shaped stimulus contour. The assymetrical representation of the two corners derives from the asymmetrical reaction of the on-field to these corners. A more symmetrical activity profile would have been obtained if the off-unit activity had been taken into account. In particular, the weakening of boundary activity at the upper corner of Figure 8d corresponds to the weakening of concentric on-unit activity at the corresponding location in Figure 4a. In contrast, this is a site of strong off-unit activity in Figure 4b.

Finally, Figure 9 presents the activity pattern in the field of Level 6 units. The Boundary Contour signal pattern from Level 5 divides the field into two compartments, or interaction domains: the lower left region (yang) and the upper right region (yin). Inputs from Level 2 trigger a spreading, or filling-in, of activity within each domain, but there is little communication between domains. The final activity level for points within a domain is roughly proportional to the average level of input stimulation due to the corresponding Level 2 region. Because of the increased level of on-units activity on the yin side of the Z-shaped contour, and the decreased level on the yang side, the average activity within the yang region is smaller than in the yin region. The final consequence is that, in Figure 9, the activity pattern of the Level 6 syncytium is qualitatively very similar to Figure 4, the image stimulus distribution, except for modest brightness enhancement and attenuation at the Mach corners of the percept. Since the level 6 activity profile is in our model the counterpart of the brightness percept, the prediction from the simulation is that the percept is close to being veridical.

There are two particularly noteworthy aspects of our introductory example. First, the two portions of the stimulus distributions which have homogeneous luminance levels correspond to approximately homogeneous portions in the brightness distribution. This is not a trivial result, because vision models that concentrate on edge processing generally fail to make this or any prediction about the appearance of the portions of the image located between the contours.

Second, the model correctly predicts that the more luminant portion of the stimulus (Figure 3) will be perceived as the brighter one. However, there are many examples of

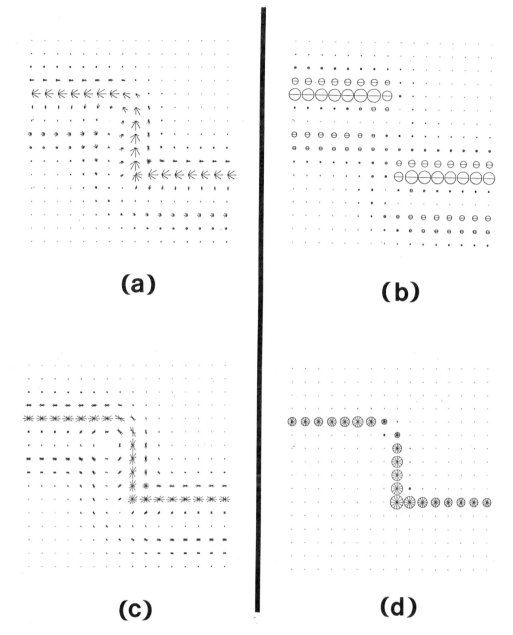

(a)

(b)

(c)

(d)

Figure 8. (a) The combined activity profile of all Level 3 units. Each cluster of lines represents the activity level of twelve units that have the same location. The representational code is described in Figure 7. (b) The activity profile of horizontally oriented direction-of-contrast insensitive Level 4 units. Each unit sums the activity of two Level 3 units with the same location and orientation but opposite direction sensitivity. (c) The combined activity profile of all Level 4 units. Each cluster of lines represents the activity level of six units that have the same location. Activity magnitude is coded by line length, and orientation preference is coded by line orientation. (d) Level 5: output of the Boundary Contour System. Each unit sums the thresholded signal of six Level 4 units with the same location. The activity profile traces the shared boundary of the two regions of the Yin-Yang square.

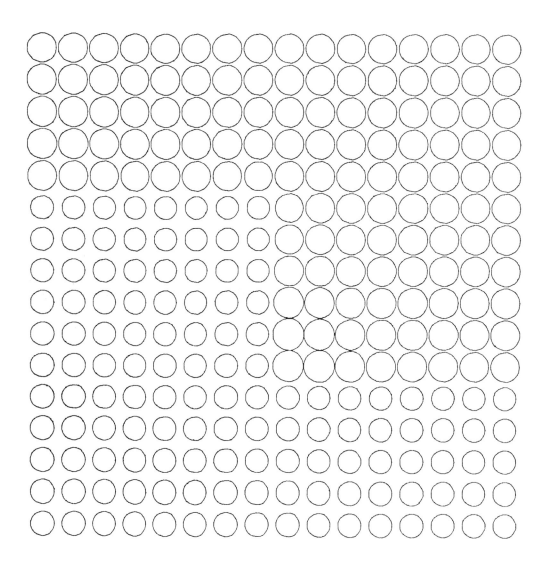

Figure 9. The final filled-in activity profile at Level 6, the Syncytium. It contains two homogeneous regions that have different activity levels. This distribution closely matches the stimulus distribution (Figure 4). The Level 6 activity profile predicts the brightness appearance of the stimulus. In this case, the percept is nearly veridical.

visual situations in which there is a mismatch between the luminance distribution and the brightness distribution. In particular, two portions of the image may have the same luminance but appear differently bright, or vice versa. An adequate model of human spatial brightness perception must be able to correctly predict these discrepancies. In the next two sections we will show how the same set of mechanisms handles in a unified way both cases of veridical perception and striking brightness illusions. In all of these examples the output of the model is in close agreement with the perceived brightness distribution.

4. 1-D Simulations

All graphical depictions of the one-dimensional simulations contain four distributions: the stimulus luminance distribution (Level 1), the on-unit distribution (Level 2), the output of the Boundary Contour system (Level 5), and the syncytium distribution (Level 6), which corresponds to the predicted brightness distribution. Cohen and Grossberg (1984) presented their simulations of various brightness phenomena in a similar format. The graphs of the four distributions were scaled separately; that is, each was normalized with respect to its own maximum.

4.1. Equally Illuminated Stimulus Patches

We begin with the simulation of a simple visual situation whose purpose is to set the context for the following simulations. The Level 1 luminance distribution, labelled Stimulus, is presented in the bottom graph of Figure 10a. It portrays the horizontal cross-section of an evenly illuminated scene containing two equally luminant homogeneous patches on a less luminant homogeneous background. The Level 2 reaction of the on-units to such a stimulation, labelled Feature, illustrates the cusp-shaped profiles corresponding to luminance discontinuities. The four boundary contours formed at Level 5 of the system are labelled Boundary. Finally, the top graph, labelled Output, presents the Level 6 filled-in activity profile embodying the prediction of a brightness distribution qualitatively isomorphic with the luminance distribution. This percept contains two homogeneous equally bright patches on a darker homogeneous background.

4.2. Unequally Illuminated Stimulus Patches: Brightness Constancy

What happens when the two-patch scene is unevenly illuminated? Figure 10b presents a luminance distribution which mimics the effect of a light source off to the right side of the scene. The luminance profile is now tilted, and the right patch has more average luminance than the left patch. One of the classical observations in perceptual psychology is that in such situations the brightness percept does not agree with the luminance distribution. Instead, brightness constancy prevails, meaning that the brightness percept is not determined by surface illumination but that it correlates with surface reflectance, a physical attribute independent of illumination.

Inspection of the Output reveals that our model exhibits brightness constancy. It predicts a percept whose structure is very similar to the preceding, evenly illuminated scene. One factor that contributes to this outcome is the ratio-processing characteristic of the Level 2 on-units. Although the absolute luminance values in the stimulus distributions in Figures 10a and 10b are different, the ratio of the lower to the higher luminance across all edges in both distributions is 1 : 3. Therefore the activity profiles of Level 2 on-units are very similar in both cases, as is the activity in all subsequent processing stages. The consequence is that the illuminant is effectively discounted.

The importance of luminance ratios for brightness perception was stressed by Wallach

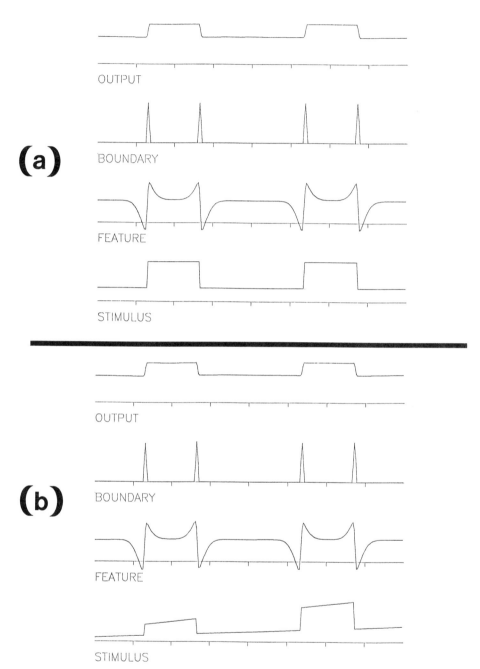

Figure 10. One-dimensional simulations of the same scene evenly and unevenly illuminated. In these and all following one-dimensional simulations the four graphs, from bottom to top respectively, refer to the Level 1 stimulus distribution (labeled "stimulus"), the Level 2 on-cell distribution (labeled "feature"), the Level 5 Boundary Contour output (labeled "boundary"), and the Level 6 filled-in Syncytium (labeled "output"). The parameters used in the simulations are listed in the Appendix. Although the two stimulus distributions in Figures 10a and 10b are different, the final output distributions are very similar. Thus the model exhibits brightness constancy.

(1948, 1976). He found that if one region is completely surrounded by another, the brightness of the inner region is predominantly influenced by the size of the ratio of its luminance to the luminance of the surrounding region. Our model provides a mechanical explanation of why the ratio principle is effective in such situations. In addition, as will be shown below, the model is applicable to more general visual situations in which multiple regions have multiple neighbors, and it provides perceptually correct predictions in situations in which the ratio principle fails.

4.3. Brightness Contrast: Narrow Patch and Wide Patch

Land (Land, 1977, 1986; Land and McCann, 1971) has devised the influential Retinex model of color perception, which includes an algorithm for discounting the illuminant. Todorović (1983) and Shapley (1986) have noted that this model cannot account for another classical perceptual effect, the phenomenon of simultaneous brightness contrast. The luminance profile characterizing the favorite textbook example of this phenomenon is depicted in Figure 11a. The luminance distribution is similar to Figure 10a in that it contains two patches of medium luminance level. However, the left patch is positioned on a lower luminant background, and the right patch on a higher luminant one. The perceptual consequence is that, despite equal luminance, the two patches look different; the patch on the dark background looks brighter than the patch on the bright background. Inspection of the Output in Figure 11a reveals that this is also the prediction of the model.

The reason that Land's model cannot account for this effect is, in part, that it is essentially geared to recover surface reflectance. However, in the phenomenon of brightness contrast, brightness constancy is violated, and two surfaces with the same reflectance look differently bright. In Land's model, the relative brightness of two regions is essentially determined by the product of ratios of luminances of locations situated along paths between the two regions. Shapley (1986) has shown that for two homogeneous regions with the same reflectance that are contained within an evenly illuminated scene composed of homogeneous regions, this ratio is 1. Consequently, according to the Land model, such regions should have the same brightness. However, the phenomenon of brightness contrast shows that this is not necessarily the case.

In the response profile of the on-units, labelled Feature in Figure 11a, the interior of the left patch contains a higher level of activity than the interior of the right patch. On the basis of a graph similar to this Figure, Cornsweet (1970, p.352) concluded that a Fourier analysis approach was able to account for brightness contrast. Such an explanation could be interpreted using the same lateral inhibitory mechanisms that are involved in generating Mach bands. In contrast, we suggest that brightness contrast depends essentially on the filling-in process (See Fry, 1948). To illustrate the role of filling-in, consider Figure 11b. The luminance distribution in Figure 11b is similar to the one in Figure 11a, but the gray patches are larger. In consequence, the central portions of the on-unit profiles corresponding to the stimulus patches in Figure 11b have the same activity magnitude. Hence, these activity profiles cannot account for the difference in appearance. However, the filled-in activity patterns within each region of the Level 6 Output in Figure 11b are different and homogeneous. This result is in accord with the study of Yund and Armington (1975), who reported that although the strength of the simultaneous brightness contrast effect is smaller for larger test regions, it persists for test regions up to ten degrees. This decrease of the effect with region size cannot be explained by the ratio principle, since it is insensitive to region size, but is predicted by our model. Due to diffusion, the brightness of a region correlates with the average amount of corresponding Level 2 activity. For a gray patch on a dark surround, this activity consists of the overshoots, corresponding to

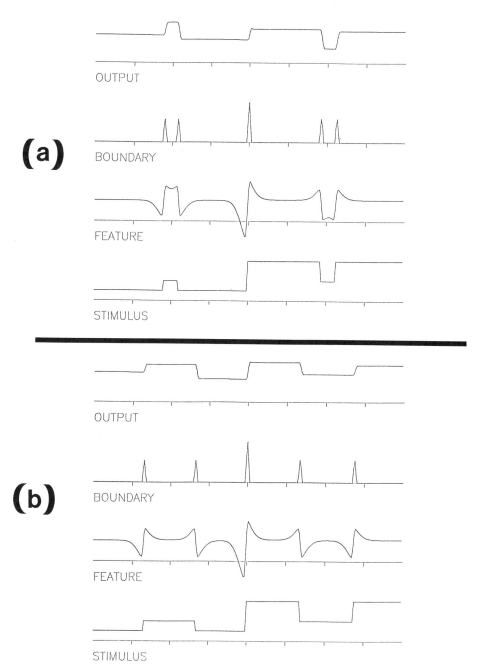

Figure 11. Simultaneous brightness contrast. The stimulus contains two medium luminance patches, the left one on a low luminant background and the right one on a high luminant background. In Figure 11a the two patches are narrow and in Figure 11b they are wide. In both cases the model output predicts the left patch to look brighter than the right patch. In contrast, in the on-unit profiles the centered activity levels corresponding to the two patches are different in Figure 11a but not in Figure 11b. These simulations demonstrate that brightness contrast cannot be explained solely by contour generated activity but that a filling-in process is also necessary.

the region's edges, and the "valley" between them. With increasing region size the relative proportion of the valley also increases (compare the portions of the Level 2 profiles corresponding to the left patches in Figure 11a and 11b). In consequence, the mean Level 2 activity corresponding to the gray patch decreases. An analogous analysis shows that for gray patches on bright surrounds the larger patch is predicted to look brighter than the smaller patch.

A more subtle quantitative difference between Figures 11a and 11b is also worth noting. In Figure 11a, the narrow luminance patches interact with the model parameters to cause filled-in brightness levels such that the middle gray patch on the left is brighter than the white background on the right, and the middle gray patch on the right is darker than the dark gray or black background on the left. In Figure 11b, the wider luminance steps cause filled-in brightness levels such that the reverse inequalities obtain, as is also the case *in vivo*. The reason for this reversal is, in part, that the boundary cusps (overshoots) in the FCS reactions to the patches form a smaller relative part of each patch in Figure 11b than in Figure 11a. Other parameters that influence this reversal are the model's baseline activity level and the relative amount of FCS contrast enhancement at image edges. To the extent that an FCS pattern such as that shown in Figure 11b always occurs *in vivo*, the explanation of brightness contrast in response to images of this type depends essentially upon filling-in.

On the other hand, informal observations suggest that, depending on the particular luminance levels and region areas, either set of brightness relationships may be perceptually realized. The characterization of the parameters which lead to one or the other set of relationships requires further psychophysical investigation.

Finally, in these simulations the two portions of the background, to the left and to the right of the gray patch, are differently bright. This is especially noticeable in the case of the dark background in Figure 11b. This outcome is an artefact of the one-dimensionality of the simulation, in which the two parts of the background are isolated from each other by the gray patch. In two dimensions, the background surrounding the patch is a topologically connected region, and the diffusional processes can freely act to homogenize it throughout.

4.4. Varieties of Brightness Contrast: Graded Backgrounds and Contrast Constancy

Shapley (1986) presented a new variant of brightness contrast that our model also explains. This luminance distribution is presented in Figure 12a. The two equiluminant patches from the classical version of the effect are retained, but the background is different. Instead of two regions of homogeneous and very different luminance, as in Figure 11a, the background now consists of a continuous gradient of luminance sloping from a high value on the right of the image to a low one on the left. The perceptual effect is similar to the classical phenomenon: the left patch looks brighter than the right one. Furthermore, the gradient itself is not very prominent in the percept. These effects are also predicted by the model Output.

Shapley (1986, p.47) pointed out a common aspect of the classical and the new version of the effect. In both cases the luminance ratio across the borders of the two patches are of opposite sign, and he suggested an explanation based upon this sign difference. However, it is not only the sign but also the size of the luminance ratio that influences brightness. Figure 12b is a luminance profile that was studied by Arend, Buehler, and Lockhead (1971). The visual situation is similar to the classical contrast profile of Figure 11a, except that now both equiluminant patches are more luminant than their backgrounds. Thus the sign of the luminance ratio is the same. Nevertheless, Arend *et al.* (1971) found,

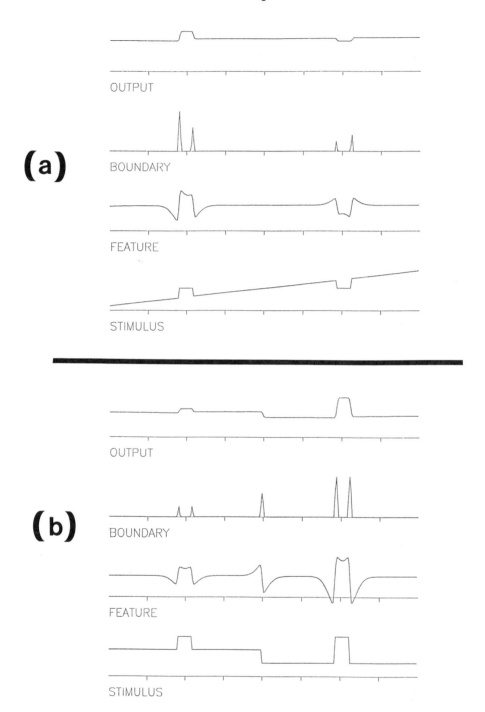

Figure 12. Varieties of brightness contrast involving non-classical background conditions. (a) The gradient background. (b) Both patches are more luminant than their backgrounds. (c) The same as (b), but with a gradient transition between the backgrounds. (d) Unevenly illuminated standard brightness contrast stimulus. "Contrast constancy" is predicted.

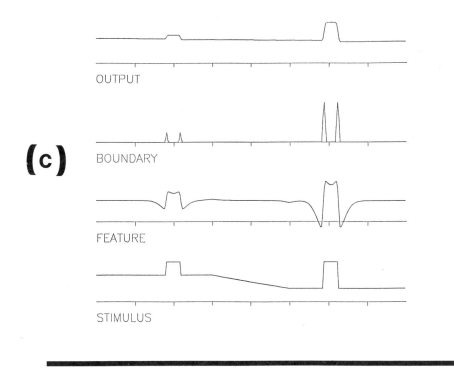

(c)

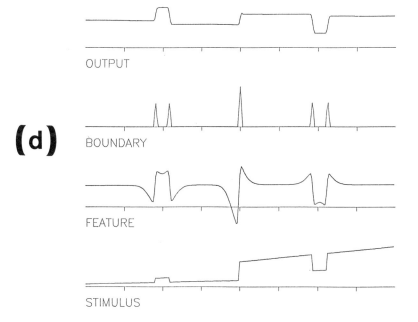

(d)

Figure 12 (continued).

and our model Output predicts, that the patch with the larger ratio is perceived as the brighter one. Arend *et al.* (1971) also studied a version of the effect similar to the Shapley (1986) gradient version. This luminance distribution is presented in Figure 12c. Again, the perceptual effect is consistent with the Output of our model in Figure 12c.

The phenomenon simulated in Figure 12c provides a useful antidote to theoretical concepts which do not sufficiently take into account effects of image context on brightness percepts. In particular, equally luminant patches are mapped into non-equally bright percepts, while a background composed of non-equally luminant regions is mapped into approximately equally bright regions. Thus the context-sensitive mapping from luminance to brightness can convert identities into differences and differences into identities.

A related version of these effects is presented in Figure 12d. It portrays an unevenly illuminated brightness contrast situation. Note that the right patch is now more luminant than the left one. However, our model predicts that the percept will be similar to classical brightness contrast. In other words, we predict an effect of "contrast constancy". Such a visual situation has, to our knowledge, not been studied yet.

A comparison of Figures 12a, 12c, and 12d calls attention to an issue concerning the choice of model parameters, and to possible influences of different parameter choices across the multiple spatial scales of a more complete model. Within these Figures, the sloping background luminance gradients are converted into approximately uniformly bright percepts. This is partly due to the relative insensitivity of the FCS to linear luminance gradients. It is also due, however, to the size of the threshold in the BCS filters relative to the size of the cusps near the patch edges in the FCS activity patterns. Had these thresholds been chosen smaller, then more BCS boundaries would have been activated in the FCS cusp regions, and the percept of background brightness would have been more nonuniform in these regions. Once this is realized, it also becomes clear that any mechanism which enhances cusp sizes or, more generally, generates a spatially nonuniform FCS activity pattern can generate a more dense spatial destribution of boundaries, or *boundary web* (Grossberg, 1987a; Grossberg and Mingolla, 1987a). Such a boundary web can trap local FCS contrasts into small boundary compartments and can thereby convert a nonuniform luminance pattern into a nonuniform brightness percept. In addition, the parameters within one spatial scale may not generate a boundary web in response to a particular nonuniform luminance pattern, whereas the parameters within a different spatial scale may generate such a boundary web. Then the total brightness percept (at a given perceived depth) would be a weighted sum of uniform and nonuniform spatial patterns.

4.5. Brightness Assimilation

Shapley and Reid (1986) have studied a more complex visual situation whose luminance profile is depicted in Figure 13. This profile can be derived from the standard brightness contrast profile (Figure 11b) by the introduction of two additional test regions. One of these regions is centered and wholly contained within one of the two original equiluminant gray patches, and the other within the other gray patch. The test regions have the same luminance level, which is higher than the luminance level of surrounding gray patches. However, the experiment showed that the left test region looks brighter than the right one. A gradient version of this distribution showed similar results.

Shapley and Reid (1986) and Shapley (1986) claimed that this effect cannot be due to brightness contrast, and that it is instead an instance of another classical brightness effect, the phenomenon of brightness assimilation (Helson, 1963). They pointed out that the ratio of the luminance of each of the innermost patches to the luminance of the immediately surrounding region is the same. If classical brightness contrast were exclusively due to the

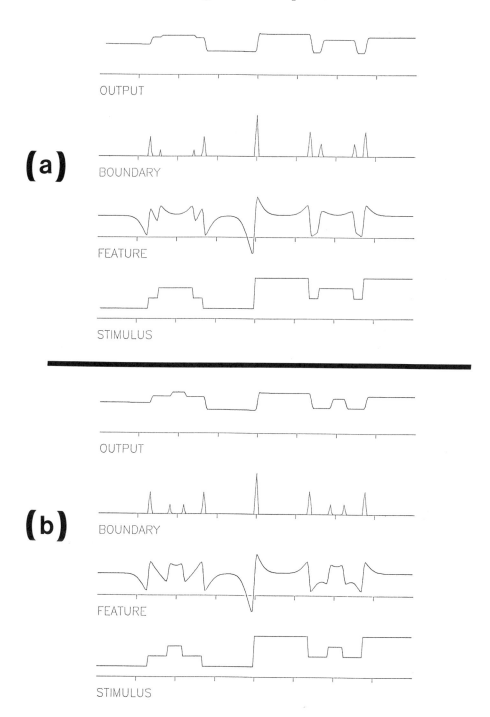

Figure 13. The Shapley and Reid (1986) assimilation stimulus. The stimulus distribution is the same as in Figure 11b, with the addition of two equiluminant test regions centered on the two gray patches. The model output correctly predicts that the left test region looks brighter than the right test region: (a) wide test regions, (b) narrow test regions.

luminance ratio, then a new explanatory principle would be needed to explain the finding. Wallach (1976) has also found that, in a series of three nested regions, the ratio principle is violated.

Inspection of the Output in Figure 13 reveals that our model correctly predicts the difference in brightness between two inner regions. Thus the model accounts for Wallach's ratio principle as well as its violation in more complex situations. In particular, the processing by on-cell units can lead to either a contrastive or assimilative brightness effect. The outcome depends upon the total configuration of Feature Contour signals that induce the filling-in within the compartments defined by the Boundary Contour signals.

In particular, two aspects of the model contribute to the brightness assimilation effect described by Shapley and Reid (1986), one at Level 2, and the other at Level 6. The first is the context-sensitive response of the Level 2 on-cells to two or more contiguous luminance steps. The amplitudes of the overshoots and the undershoots, and the exact course of the Level 2 profile corresponding to a luminance step, is influenced by the presence and polarity of nearby luminance steps. In this way the two backgrounds can differentially affect the test regions even across the surrounding gray patches. In particular, the Level 2 profile corresponding to the right test region in Figure 13a is depressed in comparison to the left test region. As reflected in Shapley and Reid (1986) data, this effect of the background should decrease with the size of the width of the surrounding gray patches.

A second way in which nearby regions can influence each other is at the diffusion stage. Although the presence of a boundary between two regions strongly attenuates the interaction between them, it may not annihilate it completely, if the strength of Boundary Contour signals can vary significantly with the amount of contrast and the spatial scale of the Feature Contour patterns, as it does in Figure 13b. If a weak boundary separates two regions with different Feature Contour activity levels, then activity from each region will, to a certain extent, diffuse across the boundary into the other region. This process will tend to increase the final filled-in activity level in the left test region of Figure 13b, and to reduce it in the right test region. This is because the left test region is surrounded by a region (corresponding to the left gray patch) whose Level 2 activity profile is, on the average, larger than the average strength of the Level 2 profile of the region (corresponding to the right gray patch) surrounding the right test region. Thus the left test path appears brighter than the right one even though their Feature Contour patterns are similar due to the combined effect of the small size of the test patches and the large size of the gray patches.

A third factor is the possible influence of multiple spatial scales (Grossberg 1987b). A small test region may generate boundary signals in one scale but not another. Featural filling-in within the latter scale will therefore cross the perceptual locations subtended by the small test region. If that region is surrounded by a darker patch, the total filled-in brightness percept, assuming that it is weighted sum of the filled-in activity levels across all scales within that region, will tend to be darker.

4.6. The Craik-O'Brien-Cornsweet and Brightness Bull's Eye Effects

One of the most attractive brightness phenomena is the Craik-O'Brien-Cornsweet Effect, or COCE (Cornsweet, 1970; see Todorović, 1987 for a review). One version of the COCE is presented in Figure 14. Readers unfamiliar with this effect might suppose that the left rectangle, being brighter than the right rectangle, is also the more luminant one. However, the luminance of the two rectangles is actually identical, except for a luminance cusp overshoot at the left flank and a luminance cusp undershoot at the right flank of the midline. The illusory nature of the phenomenon is most easily demonstrated by the

Figure 14. The COCE. The luminance distribution representing this display is shown in Figure 15a. The left rectangle looks brighter than the right rectangle although they have identical luminance, except for the cusped shaped profile of their shared vertical border.

occlusion of the contour region. Placing a pencil or a piece of wire vertically across the midline in Figure 14 causes the two rectangles to appear equally bright.

A representation of the one-dimensional luminance distribution of a horizontal cross-section of Figure 14 is given in the bottom graph, labelled Stimulus, of Figure 15a. Such a profile includes both the luminance cusps and the equally luminous dark background at the left and right side of the stimulus profile. For comparison, the bottom graph in Figure 15b displays the non-illusory counterpart of the cusp distribution. It has the form of a simple luminance step. The cusp distribution and the step distribution are examples of different stimuli causing similar percepts (Ratliff and Sirovich, 1978). This is also the prediction of our model presented in the top graphs in Figures 15a and 15b.

The similarity of the perceptual effects of the two images is already apparent in the Level 2 on-cell activity profiles (see Ratliff and Sirovich, 1978, for some related simulations). The loci of abrupt luminance changes in the stimuli induce extended cusp-shaped profiles in the on-cell activity pattern, whereas the regions of homogeneous but different

Chapter 3

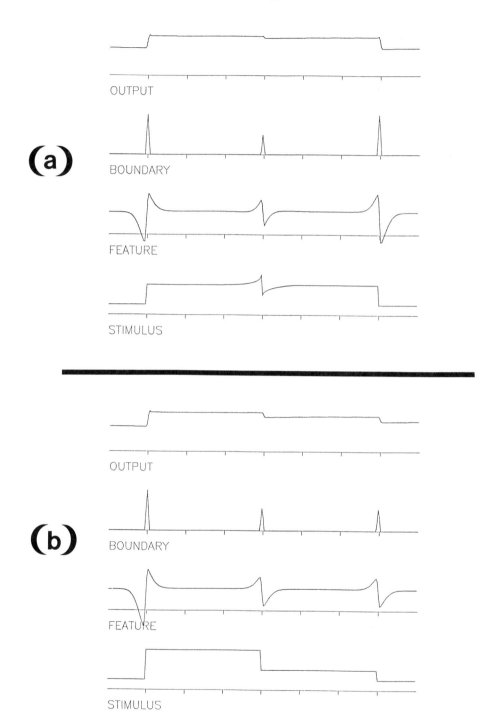

Figure 15. The one-dimensional simulations of the COCE and its non-illusory counterpart. (a) The COCE. (b) A luminance step on a less luminant background. The outputs of both simulations predict a step-shaped brightness profile.

luminance induce similar response levels. Some authors have argued that the similarity of activity patterns at this level, which is also predicted by the Fourier analysis approach, is sufficient to explain the similarity of percepts (Bridgeman, 1983; Cornsweet, 1970; Foster, 1983; Laming, 1983; Ratliff and Sirovich, 1978). Others have been critical of this idea (Arend, 1973; Arend and Goldstein, 1987; Davidson and Whiteside, 1971; Grossberg, 1983; Todorović, 1983, 1987). The obvious difficulties for such an account are that it does not explain why the left region is perceived to be brighter than the right one, nor why locations with different activities within the same region in Level 2 appear to have the same brightness in the final percept.

The model's additional processing stages enable it to explain both the similarity of the percepts and the shapes of their brightness profiles. This is achieved through the model's account of how the Boundary Contour and Feature Contour Systems interact. The output of the Boundary Contour System (Level 5) is presented in the second graph from the top in Figures 15a and 15b. Only the largest local changes in the Level 2 profiles are reflected in the Boundary Contour output pattern. The interaction of the Level 5 Boundary Contour output and the Level 2 Feature Contour output at the Level 6 syncytium, presented in the top graphs in Figures 15a and 15b, predicts the brightness percept. The difference in the activity levels between the left and the right portion, especially in the case of the COCE, is noticeable but small, but so is the perceived brightness difference.

Just as the model can handle multiple steps of different polarity, as in Figures 10–13, it can also handle complex stimuli involving several cusp or saw-tooth distributions of different polarities, as shown in Figure 16. Imagine a circularly symmetric two-dimensional luminance distribution, whose luminance cross-section along any diameter is given in the bottom graph of Figure 16a. The appearance of the central portion of such a distribution is a brightness bull's eye (Arend, 1973; Arend, Buehler, and Lockhead, 1971; Arend and Goldstein, 1987), as predicted by the top graph, labelled Output, in Figure 16a.

This filled-in bull's eye percept in Figure 16a is generated when the sawtooth luminance pattern is surrounded by a bright background. If the background is sufficiently dark, as in Figure 16b, the difference in brightness between the outermost and the middle band may disappear, as in Figure 16b. Our informal observations of small bull's eye patterns on large backgrounds are in the same direction as the model's prediction. A change of the brightness difference between the two outermost luminance bands with the change of the luminance of the surround is to be expected, because the brightness contrast effect is known to decrease with distance (Heinemann, 1972), and thus should more affect the outermost band than the middle band. However Arend (1987, personal communication) observed no strong effects of the surround luminance on the relative brightness of the bull's eye bands and, in particular, found that the outer band looks darker than the other bands even on a dark surround. His stimulus involves a relatively large bull's eye on a small surround. In such a configuration the effect of the surround may be reduced on the bull's eye percept. An additional complicating factor is the following. Suppose that a two-dimensional luminance pattern is generated by rotating a one-dimensional sawtooth pattern. Let the mean luminance of all bands in the one-dimensional sawtooth be the same, as in Figures 16a and 16b. Then the mean luminance of the two-dimensional bands decreases as a function of their distance from the center. On this ground alone, the outermost bands should look darkest, and thus could more easily counteract effects of the surround. In addition, this percept may be susceptible to effects of multiple scales. Clearly, more parametric experimental data are needed.

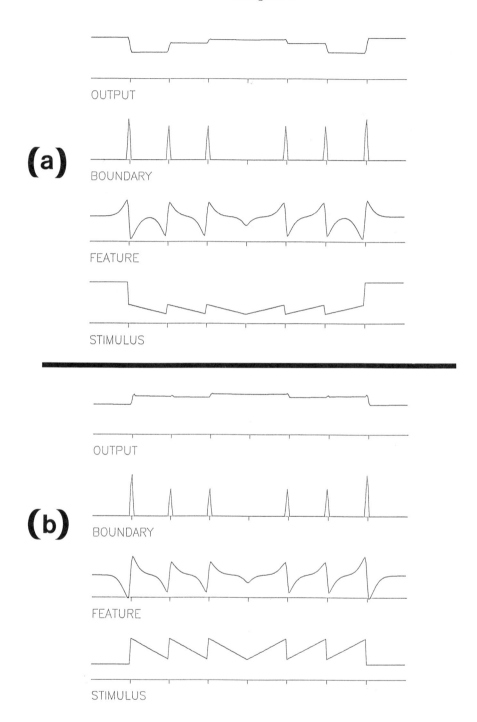

(a)

BOUNDARY

FEATURE

STIMULUS

(b)

BOUNDARY

FEATURE

STIMULUS

Figure 16. The bull's eye. The luminance distribution is a radial sawtooth (Arend and Goldstein, 1987) centered on a high luminance background (a), or a low luminance background (b). The graphs of the two luminance distributions are scaled separately. A brightness bull's eye is generated in the output of (a), but not of (b). See text for details.

4.7. Effects of Changing Model Parameters

In the above simulations, a definite choice of model parameters has necessarily been made (see the Appendix). This section illustrates how related parameter choices influence model behavior.

Figure 17 illustrates the effect of two parameter changes within the model upon the luminance profiles of Figure 15. These changes do not alter the important qualitative properties of the model's filled-in Level 6 profiles. In Figures 17a and 17b, the Boundary Contour signals to Level 6 are rendered more uniform in size by transforming the Boundary Contour patterns in Figures 15a and 15b through a sigmoid, or S-shaped, signal function. This transformation has only a minor effect on the filled-in activity pattern at Level 6 due to the strengthening of the middle Boundary Contour signal. In Figures 17c and 17d, the parameters of the syncytial diffusion at Level 6 are chosen so that the same Boundary Contour signals used in Figure 15 have a greater effect on the reduction of diffusion between boundary compartments (see Appendix for details). This manipulation strengthens Mach band-like effects corresponding to large luminance discontinuities. Both of these parametric variations may well occur across species and individuals *in vivo*.

Figure 18 depicts another robust parametric property of the Level 2 activity patterns in the model. This is the property, exploited in the previous simulations, whereby Level 2 cells maintain their sensitivity to the reflectances, or relative luminances, near luminance steps as the overall luminance level of a stimulus is parametrically varied. This reflectance-processing property is due to the fact that the Level 2 cells obey membrane, or shunting, equations (see Appendix for details). In Figure 18, each curve corresponds to a constant ratio of the luminances L_1 and L_2 on either side of a luminance step. The on-cell activity pattern generated by such a step is a cusp, as in Figure 15. Each curve plots the maximum activity of the cusp generated at a constant ratio L_2/L_1 as overall luminance is parametrically increased. Each curve increases according to a Weber law property until it asymptotes at an activity level that is characteristic of the ratio L_2/L_1 (Grossberg, 1983). Thus large luminance values do not saturate the on-cell responses. Instead, at large luminances, on-cells remain sensitive to input reflectances. The stimulus values used in all simulations fall between the dotted vertical lines, and hence within the luminance range of good ratio processing.

5. The 2-D Simulations

We now present simulations of brightness phenomena using the two-dimensional implementation of the model. A number of interesting brightness phenomena can only be defined and demonstrated in two dimensions. Arend and Goldstein (1987) have, in particular, used the curl operator of vector calculus to diagnose important properties in two-dimensional images which are not found in one-dimensional images. Our results show, however, that the curl is not needed as a model mechanism for the explanation of such brightness phenomena. In all the following simulations we present Level 1, the stimulus distribution, and Level 6, the filled-in activity distribution which predicts the brightness of the percept. In many instances we also present the intermediate activity distributions from Level 2 and Level 5.

5.1. The COCE with and without a Bounding 2-D Region

We first consider a 2-dimensional manipulation of the COCE which has no 1-dimensional analog. Figure 19, from Todorović (1983, 1987) contains a luminance cusp embedded

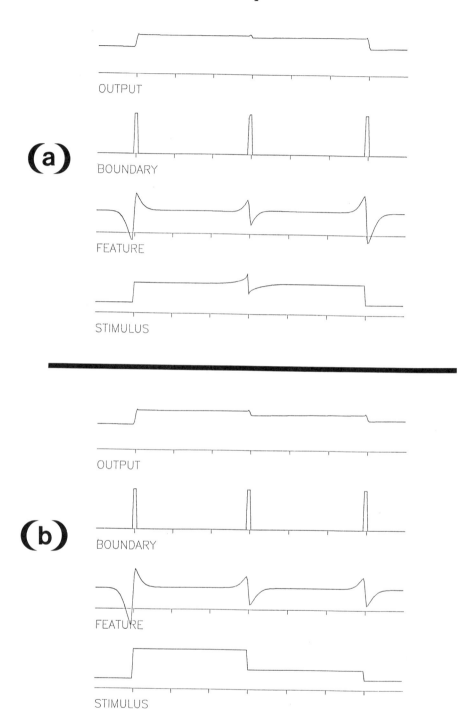

Figure 17. The effects of two parameter changes on simulations in Figure 15. (a, b) Transformation of the Boundary Contour output through a sigmoid function. (c, d) Increasing the modulation effect of the Boundary Contour signal on the filling-in process.

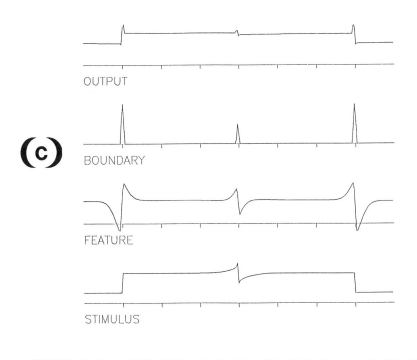

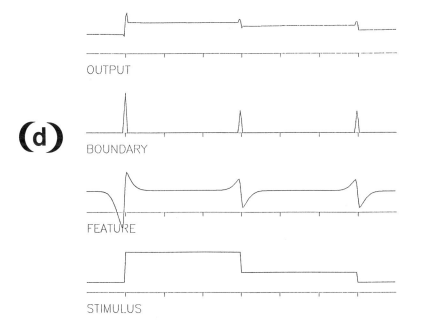

Figure 17 (continued).

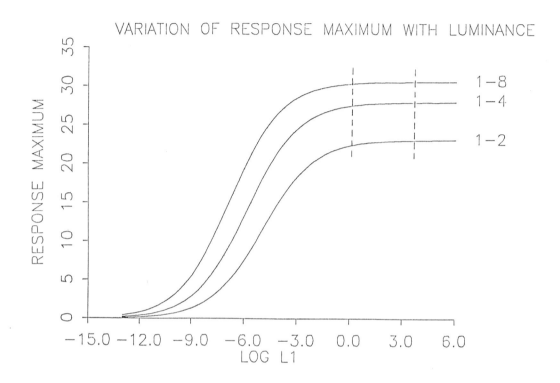

Figure 18. Luminance step processing by on-cells across a range of luminances. Stimulus distributions are luminance steps with three values of the ratio L_2/L_1 of the higher to the lower (L_1) luminance: $2/1$, $4/1$, and $8/1$. X-axis: $\log L_1$. Y-axis: maximum value of on-cell activity profile. The simulations occur in the luminance range between the vertical dashed lines, and hence exhibit good ratio processing.

into a homogeneous luminance field. The only difference between Figure 14 and Figure 19 is in the replacement of the dark bounding background in Figure 14 with a region in Figure 19 whose luminance equals the average luminance of the two central rectangles. The perceptual consequence of this change is an almost complete loss of the COCE: portions of Figure 19 at some distance from the luminance cusp have a similar homogeneous gray appearance. Related displays were studied by Arend and Goldstein (1987). The difference in appearance between Figure 14 and Figure 19 cannot be accounted for by one-dimensional approaches, nor by theories that explain the COCE by restricting their analysis to the effect of luminance cusps, which are identical in the two displays (see Todorović, 1987). In fact, Growney and Neri (1986, p.85) have recently noted concerning the percept generated by Figure 19 that alternative models have "difficulty ... in accounting for effects that are not one-dimensional" and that "the appearance of the illusion ... seems also to depend upon more global, two-dimensional characteristics of the stimulus display."

Figure 19. The two-dimensional cusp distribution without the bounding contour. This display differs from Figure 14 only with respect to the background. The dark background in Figure 14 has been replaced with a background whose luminance is equal to the average luminance of the two central rectangles. There is no illusory brightness effect in this display comparable to the COCE in Figure 14.

In our model, the cause of the difference in appearance of the two displays is due to the difference in the constraints that the Boundary Contour System imposes upon the filling-in process. Figure 20a is a two-dimensional stimulus representation (Level 1) depicting the standard case of the COCE in Figure 10. Figure 20b describes the activity pattern across the field of circular concentric on-units (Level 2). Figure 20c describes the activity pattern across the field of boundary contour units (Level 5). The activity pattern at Level 2 generates a filling-in reaction at Level 6 within the boundary compartments at Level 6 that are induced by output signals from Level 5. Figure 20d presents the final filled-in activity pattern across the field of syncytial units at Level 6. The activity in the left rectangle is higher than in the right one, in accordance with the percept. Figures 21a–21d are the analogous simulations for Figure 19. Figure 21a depicts the stimulus distribution at Level 1, Figure 21b the activity pattern at Level 2, Figure 21c the activity pattern at Level 5, and Figure 21d shows the final filled-in activity pattern at Level 6. The corresponding

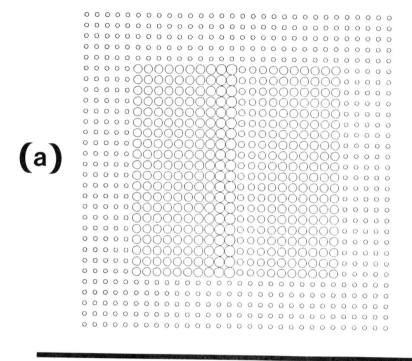

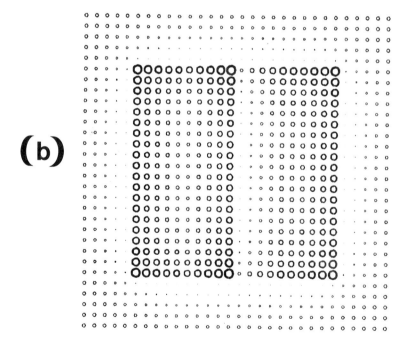

Figure 20. The simulation of the two-dimensional COCE. (a) The stimulus distribution. (b) The on-cell activity profile. (c) The output of the Boundary Contour system. (d) The filled-in syncytium, which predicts the brightness appearance of the stimulus, and should be compared with Figure 14. The parameters for this and all subsequent two-dimensional simulations are listed in the Appendix.

(c)

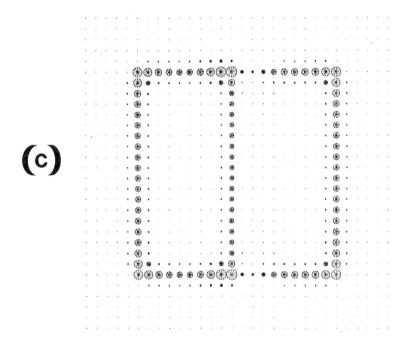

(d)

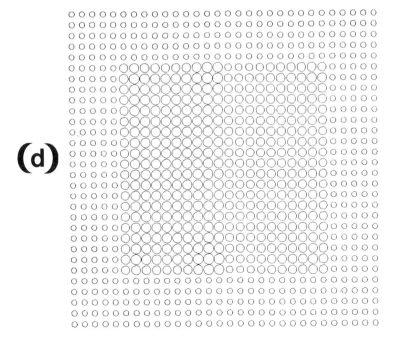

Figure 20 (continued).

activity distributions in Figures 20 and 21 were drawn on the same scale.

The stimulus distribution in the central portion of Figure 21a is identical to the one in Figure 20a. On the other hand, the background activity level of Figure 21a is higher than that of Figure 20a. As a consequence, although a boundary contour forms around the cusp region in Figure 20c, no boundary cor.tour forms around the cusp region in Figure 21c. Thus filling-in in Figure 20d occurs within a pair of rectangular compartments abutting the cusp, whereas filling-in in Figure 21d can occur around the exterior of the cusp. However, as in the percept, there still remain traces of the luminance cusp along the vertical midline in Figure 21d.

5.2. Percept of an Impossible Staircase and its Contextual Reduction to the Craik-O'Brien-Cornsweet Effect

Figure 22 presents another visual display involving luminance cusps, also from Todorović (1983); an elaborated octagonal version is displayed and discussed in Todorović (1987). The figure consists of a conjunction of four L-shaped regions on a dark background. The edges between the regions are formed by luminance cusps and their central portions all have the same luminance level.

The Level 1 representation of this luminance distribution is presented in Figure 23a. The Level 2 activity pattern across the field of on-units is shown in Figure 23b. The Level 5 activity pattern across the field of boundary contour units is illustrated in Figure 23c. This pattern delineates the compartments within which filling-in takes place in Level 6 in response to inputs from Level 2. Figure 23d presents the final filled-in activity pattern at Level 6 of the system, which is in accord with the percept.

An interesting property of the display in Figure 22 is revealed when parts of it are occluded. If the upper portion of Figure 22 is screened such that only parts of the bottom two L-shaped figures are visible, then the resulting luminance distribution is represented in Figure 24a in the case where the screening is performed with an occluder with the luminance of the background. (This is not essential.) Figure 24b displays the filled-in activity profile at Level 6 in response to the occluded luminance distribution in Figure 24a. The percept corresponding to Figure 24b is a standard case of the COCE wherein the right rectangle looks brighter than the left one. When the occluding procedure is repeated for different parts of Figure 22, the result is a paradoxical set of brightness appearances (Todorović, 1983). If the left portion of Figure 22 is occluded, the remaining top portion of the display is brighter than the bottom one. If the bottom is occluded, the remaining left portion is brighter than the right one. Finally, if the right portion is occluded, the bottom portion is brighter than the top one.

This incompatible set of relations is similar to the appearance of the "impossible staircase" by Penrose and Penrose (1958) and Escher (1961). On the other hand, observation of the whole unoccluded display does not induce stable brightness relations; the L-shaped regions partially lose their homogeneous appearance, and the brightness gradients flanking their shared edges become more prominent. These observations have been confirmed experimentally in similar displays by Arend and Goldstein (1987). Our model thus predicts in Figure 23d the inconclusive appearance of the unoccluded input pattern in Figure 23a, as well as the appearance in Figure 24b of the COCE in response to the occluded input pattern in Figure 24a. In addition, the simultaneous brightness contrast effect perceived when inspecting Figure 22, which results in reduced brightness of the inner portion of the background, is also obtained in Figure 23d.

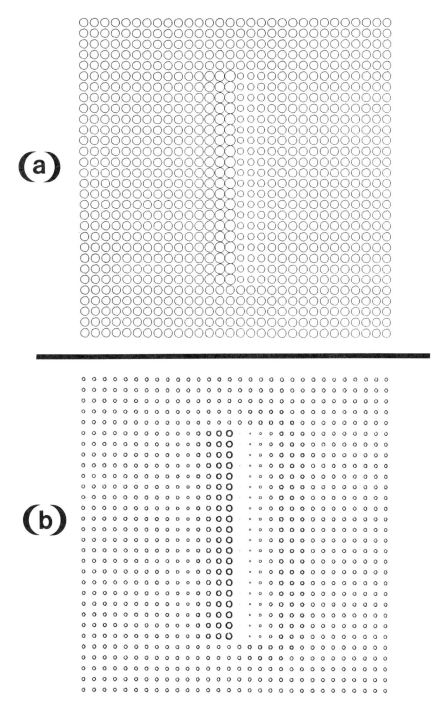

Figure 21. The simulation of the display in Figure 19. (a) The stimulus distribution. (b) The on-cell distribution. (c) The output of the Boundary Contour system. (d) The filled-in Syncytium. In contrast to Figure 20, the Boundary Contour output exhibits no closed compartments. Thus the filling-in process diffuses over the whole extent of the image and no COCE develops. The stimulus vertical cusp survives in the output.

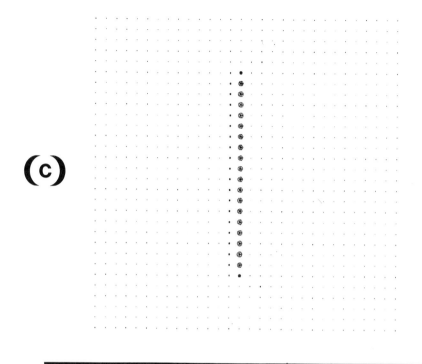

(c)

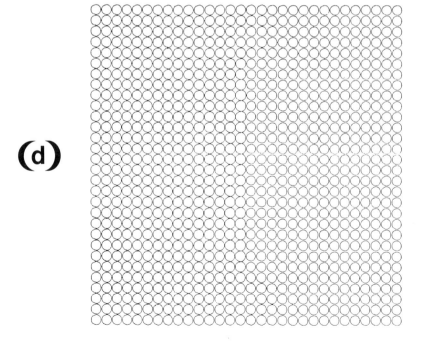

(d)

Figure 21 (continued).

Figure 22. The impossible brightness staircase. The stimulus distribution corresponding to this display is presented in Figure 23a. The display consists of four L-shaped regions whose shared borders have a cusp shaped luminance profile. When this display is occluded such that only portions of two neighboring regions are visible (see Figure 24a for an example of the resulting stimulus distribution), the result is a standard case of the COCE. If the occlusion demonstration is carried out for all four neighboring region pairs, the first member of the pair in the clockwise direction always appears brighter than the second member. In the unoccluded display no stable pattern of brightness relationships between neighboring regions emerges.

5.3. The Koffka-Benussi Ring

The interaction of Boundary Contours and the filling-in process are well illustrated through simulation of the Koffka-Benussi ring (Koffka, 1935; Berman and Leibowitz, 1965). The version that we simulate uses a rectangular annulus. The annulus has an intermediate luminance level and is superimposed upon a bipartite background of the same type as in the classical brightness contrast condition, with one half having a high luminance level and the other half a low luminance level (Figure 25a). The percept of such a stimulus is that the annulus is approximately uniform in brightness, although the right and the left halves of the annulus exhibit some brightness contrast. This percept corresponds to the Level 6 activity profile in Figure 25b.

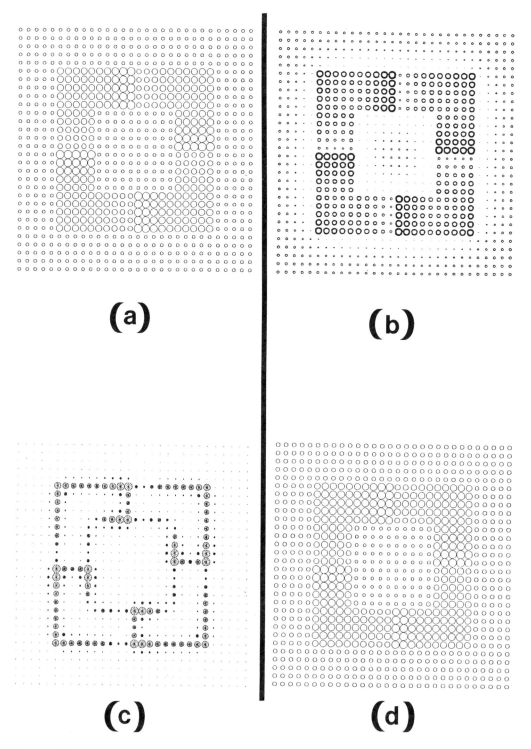

Figure 23. The simulation of the impossible staircase. (a) The stimulus distribution. (b) The on-cell activity profile. (c) The Boundary Contour output. (d) The filled-in output.

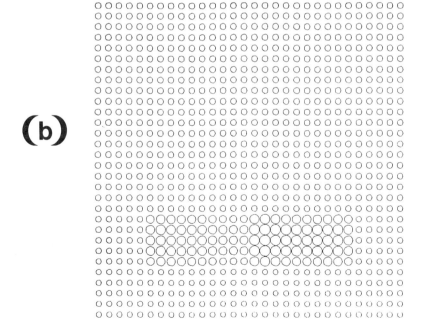

Figure 24. The occluded staircase. (a) The stimulus distribution. (b) The filled-in output. The predicted brightness profile is a standard COCE.

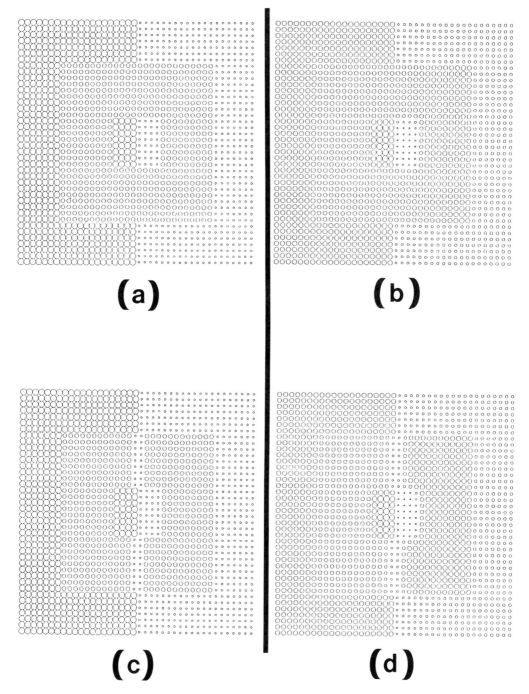

Figure 25. The Koffka-Benussi ring. (a) The stimulus distribution corresponding to the homogeneous undivided square annulus of medium luminance on a bipartite background. (b) The filled-in output corresponding to the stimulus in (a). (c) The same stimulus distribution as in (a), except that the annulus is here divided by vertical short dark lines into two equiluminant halves. (d) The filled-in output corresponding to the stimulus in (b). The two halves of the annulus are homogeneous and have different brightness levels.

The brightness distribution in the percept can be changed by the introduction of a narrow black line dividing the stimulus vertically into two halves. Figure 25c presents this new stimulus distribution. In the percept, as in the Level 6 activity profile (Figure 25d), the annulus is now divided into two regions with homogeneous but different brightnesses that are in accord with brightness contrast.

These effects depend critically upon interactions between contrast, boundaries, and filling-in in the model. In the unoccluded Koffka-Benussi ring, the annular region at Level 6 is a single connected compartment within which diffusion of activity proceeds freely. The opposite contrasts due to the two halves of the background are effectively averaged throughout the annular region, although a residual effect of opposite contrast remains. The introduction of the occluding boundary (Figure 25c) divides the annulus into two smaller compartments (Figure 25d). The different contrasts are now constrained to diffuse within these compartments, generating two homogeneous regions of different brightness.

5.4. Anomalous Brightness Differentiation

Our explanation of the Kanizsa-Minguzzi percept of anomalous brightness differentiation (Figure 1), in which the smaller region looks brighter, is consistent with the explanation of the Koffka-Benussi ring, but also illustrates finer properties of the model. The critical new property, which does not play a significant role in the percept of the Koffka-Benussi ring, is that the spokes in the luminous wheel between the black inner and outer regions induce Feature Contour signals as well as Boundary Contour signals. The Feature Contour signals are relatively small compared to those induced by the thick black inner and outer regions. Hence the perceived brightness difference is small. The Boundary Contour signals induced by the spoke divide the wheel-shaped Feature Contour System syncytium into two filling-in domains of unequal size. Due to the averaging property of the diffusive filling-in process, the smaller domain possesses a larger average activity than the larger domain. This is because its Feature Contour signals due to the spokes are averaged over a smaller region, whereas the Feature Contour signals due to the inner and outer black regions are equally well averaged within each domain. Figure 26 presents the simulation of a rectangular version of the Kanizsa-Minguzzi stimulus distribution (Figure 26a) and the filled-in Level 6 activity profile (Figure 26b).

It is instructive to contrast the model properties which give rise to the Koffka-Benussi percepts and the Kanizsa-Minguzzi percept. In the Koffka-Benussi percepts, the contrasts induced by the background (Figures 25a and 25c) are asymmetric with respect to the figure and massive due to their extent along the figure perimeter. The main effect of the thin vertical line (Figure 25c) is to induce a new Boundary Contour which divides the figure into two filling-in domains of equal size. The Feature Contours caused by this vertical line are swamped by the filled-in contrasts induced by the background within these equally large regions. In the Kanizsa-Minguzzi demonstration (Figure 26), the contrasts induced by the background are symmetric with respect to the figure. On the other hand, the additional lines divide the figure into unequal filling-in domains. Hence the influence of these lines as inducers of Feature Contour signals can cause a perceived, albeit small, brightness difference.

5.5. Mondrian Percepts under Constant and Variable Illumination

Shapley (1986) presented an achromatic Mondrian display which the Land (1977, 1986) Retinex theory cannot adequately explain. Since the Retinex theory was devised with Mondrian displays as a primary explanatory target, the Shapley (1986) demonstration represents a serious challenge to the Retinex theory of brightness perception.

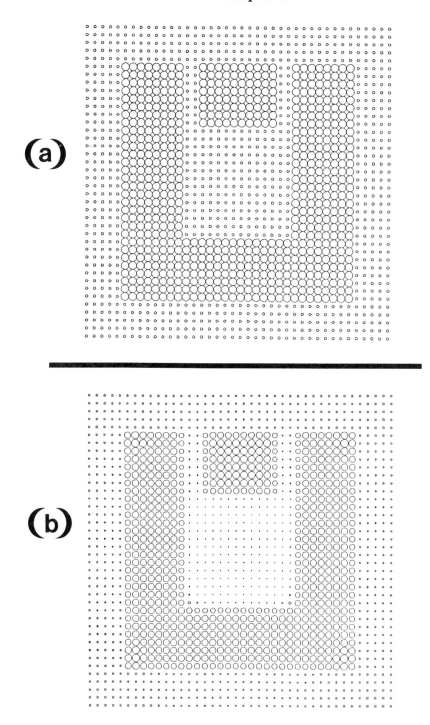

Figure 26. The simulation of the Kanizsa-Minguzzi anomalous brightness differentiation. (a) The stimulus distribution of a rectangular version of the display. (b) The filled-in output. The small segment is correctly predicted to appear brighter than the large segment.

A stimulus of this type is represented in Figure 27a. Consider the two squares in Figure 27a, the first near the top left corner and the second near the bottom right corner, which have the same size and luminance. Despite these equalities, the filled-in activity profile of the upper square is more intense than that of the lower square, corresponding to the percept that the upper square is brighter.

This brightness difference is due to the following combination of factors in our model. The luminances of the regions surrounding the two squares were chosen such that, on the average, the upper square is more luminant than its surround, and the lower square is less luminant than its surround. In consequence, as can be seen in Figure 27b, more Level 2 on-unit activity is present within the region corresponding to the upper square. The on-unit activity diffuses within the compartments delineated by the Boundary Contours (Figure 27c). Thus in the filled-in upper square of Figure 27d, a larger amount of activity is spread across the same area as in the lower square, thereby explaining the final brightness difference.

Figure 27 thus illustrates how the present model can explain a Mondrian percept which falls outside the explanatory range of Retinex theory. However, one of the important accomplishments of Retinex theory was to discount the illuminant in response to an unevenly illuminated Mondrian. The image represented by Figure 27a was evenly illuminated. A simple 1-dimensional example of how our model discounts the illuminant was shown in Figure 10b. We now show that the model can discount the illuminant in response to unevenly illuminated Mondrians, indeed in response to Mondrians whose brightness profile in even illumination is not explicable by Retinex theory.

Imagine that the Mondrian in Figure 27a is illuminated by a gradient of light which decreases linearly across space from the lower right corner of the figure. The resulting luminance distribution is depicted in Figure 28a. The upper square now receives, on the average, less luminance than the lower square. Despite this fact, the filled-in activity profile of the upper square at Level 6 is more intense than that of the lower square (Figure 28d). Figures 27b and 28b, 27c and 28c, and 27d and 28d are, in fact, virtually indistinguishable, thereby illustrating effective discounting of the illuminant in this particular situation. This successful result does not, however, imply that complete discounting will occur in response to all combinations of achromatic and chromatic images, illuminants, and bounding regions (Arend and Reeves, 1986). The systematic analysis of all these factors is a topic for future research.

5.6. The Hermann Grid: A Transitional Example

The appearance of darker spots at the intersections of bright streets in the Hermann grid is a perceptual phenomenon with a generally accepted physiological foundation related to the activity of cells with concentric antagonistic receptive fields (Baumgartner, 1960). Within our model some additional issues surrounding this phenomenon are indicated. Figure 29a is the luminance distribution of a small portion of the grid containing four streets and four intersections. Figure 29b depicts the level of activity of concentric on-units. Consistent with the standard explanation, there is a reduced level of activity associated with street intersections, compared with units located within the streets, because units in a street intersection are more inhibited than units within streets. However, in our model it is not Level 2 but Level 6 at which brightness is determined. Figure 29d presents the Level 6 distribution, showing that the difference of activities between streets and street intersections is preserved at this level.

Inspection of Figure 29c, the Boundary Contour output, reveals one reason for this effect. Since the streets are very narrow, the Boundary Contours from both sides extend

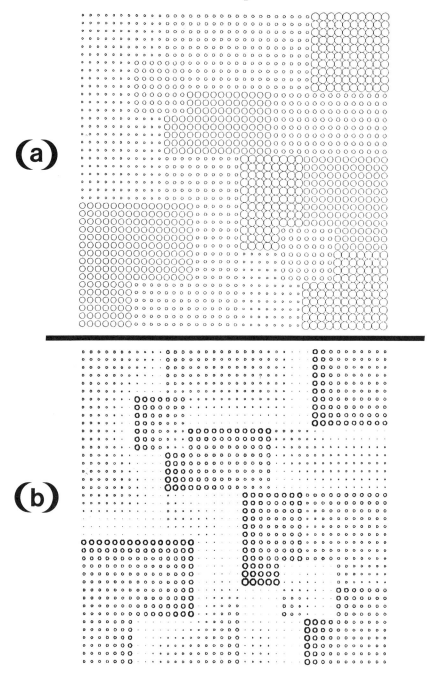

Figure 27. The evenly illuminated Mondrian. (a) The stimulus distribution consists of 13 homogeneous polygons with 4 luminance levels. Note that the square in the upper left portion of the stimulus has the same luminance as the square in the lower right portion. However, the average luminance of the regions surrounding the lower square is higher than the corresponding average luminance for the upper square. (b) The on-cell distribution. The amount of on-cell activity within the upper square is higher than within the lower square. (c) The Boundary Contour output. (d) The filled-in syncytium. The upper square is correctly predicted to look brighter than the lower square.

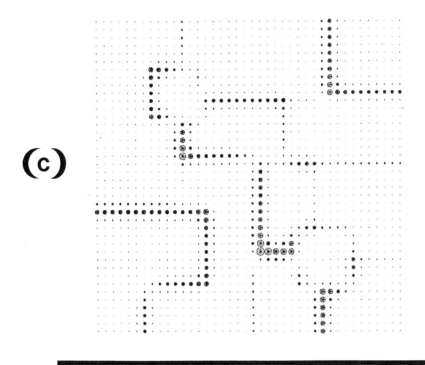

(c)

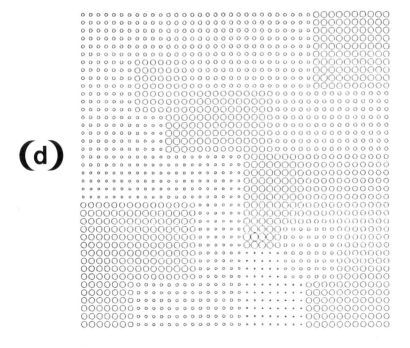

(d)

Figure 27 (continued).

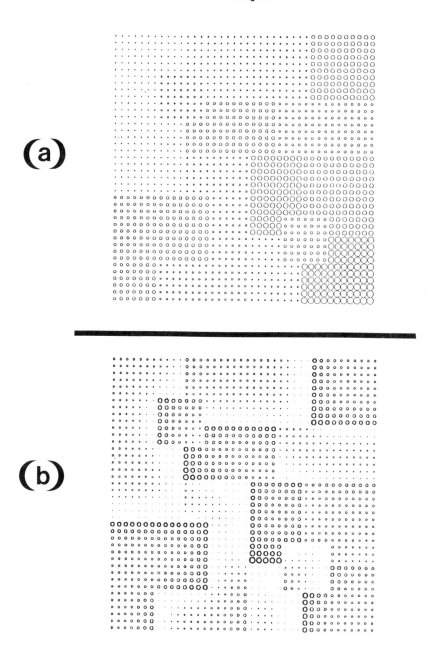

Figure 28. The unevenly illuminated Mondrian. (a) The stimulus distribution simulates the transformation of Figure 27a caused by the presence of a light source whose intensity decreases linearly from the lower right corner toward the upper left corner of the stimulus. The lower square is now more luminant than the upper square. (b) The on-cell distribution. (c) The Boundary Contour output. (d) The filled-in syncytium. Figures 28b, 28c, and 28d are very similar to the corresponding Figures for the evenly illuminated Mondrian (Figure 27). This illustrates the model's discounting of the illuminant. In addition, the upper square is still predicted to appear brighter than the lower square, which is another instance of contrast constancy (see Figure 12d).

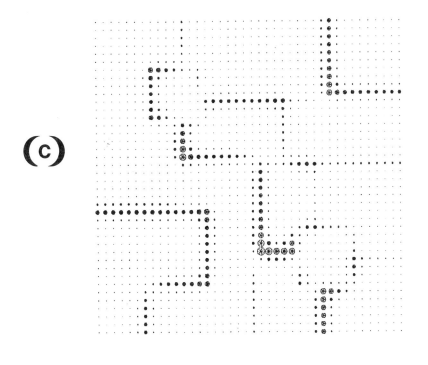

(c)

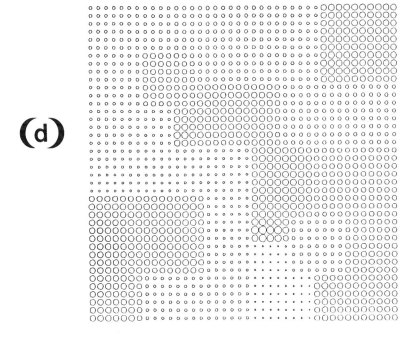

(d)

Figure 28 (continued).

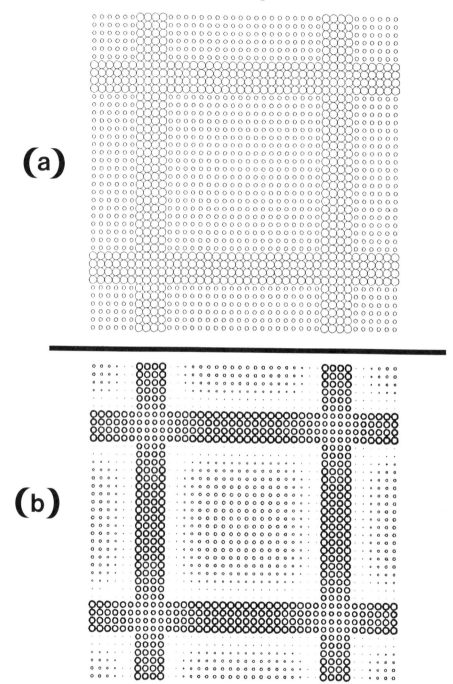

Figure 29. The Hermann Grid. (a) The stimulus distribution depicts a portion of the Hermann Grid containing four bright lines (streets) on a dark surround. (b) The on-cell distribution. The activity of units at street intersections is lower than within streets, as predicted by the standard theory of this phenomenon (Baumgartner, 1960). (c) The Boundary Contour output. Note that boundary contour activity is present along the streets but not at intersections. (d) The filled-in syncytium. The intersections are predicted to look darker than the streets. See text for details.

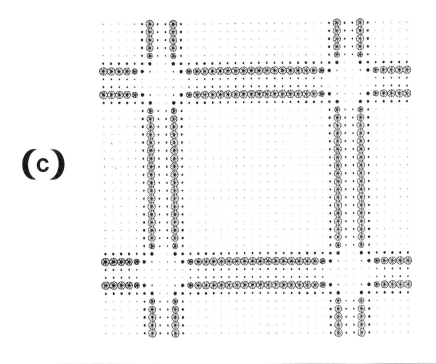

(c)

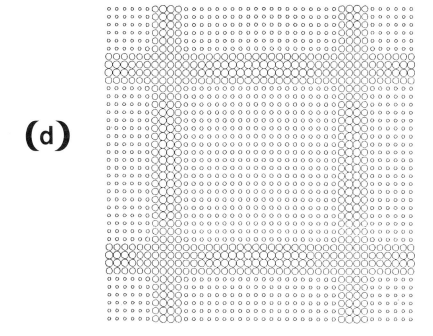

(d)

Figure 29 (continued).

into the middle of the streets, throughout their width and length, except at the intersection regions. Therefore activity at the intersections is blocked from diffusing through the streets and vice versa, and both streets and intersections retain the relative activity levels inherited from the on-unit level.

The boundaries are computed in Figure 29c using the same parameters as in all the 2-D simulations in this section (see the Appendix). Figure 29c thus illustrates that Boundary Contours may generate a plexus, or boundary web, of small compartments which prevent filling-in from spreading substantially beyond the locations of their on-cell inputs. Such boundary webs are also important, for example, in explaining aspects of 3-D surface perception (Grossberg and Mingolla, 1987a). In Figure 29c, the total thickness of each street influences whether filling-in will be trapped within that street.

The above discussion illustrates that Boundary Contours may exist at locations that do not correspond exactly to image contrasts. In order to obtain a more complete explanation of the Hermann grid, this possibility needs to include a process of emergent boundary segmentation. As noted in Section 1, the implementation of such a segmentation process lies outside the scope of this article. With emergent boundary segmentation mechanisms appended, one would also need to analyse how and when Boundary Contours colinearly cooperate from street to street across their intersections, and compete at each location across orientations, to create emergent boundary configurations in which brightness or color can flow. Grossberg and Mingolla (1985a, 1985b) have analysed a number of achromatic and chromatic percepts which are strongly influenced by such emergent boundary segmentations.

6. Discussion

The computer implementation of the model described in this paper has a limited domain of application since it deals only with monocular achromatic brightness effects. Extensions into the chromatic and binocular domains have been described in Grossberg (1987a, 1987b). Brightness can also be influenced by emergent segmentations which are not directly induced by image contrasts, as in Kanizsa's illusory triangle, the Ehrenstein illusion, and neon color spreading effects. These and related grouping and segmentation effects have been discussed by Grossberg and Mingolla (1985a, 1985b). Their implementation included a version of the Boundary Contour System in which emergent segmentations can be generated through lateral interactions between oriented channels. Such interactions may play a role in orientation-sensitive brightness effects reported by McCourt (1982), Sagi and Hochstein (1985), and White (1982). The implementation in this paper also omits possible effects of multiple scale processing, as the receptive fields of all units within a network were assumed to have a single receptive field size. Units of multiple sizes may be involved in the explanation of classical brightness assimilation (Helson, 1963). Grossberg and Mingolla (1987a) have studied the role of multiple scales in the perception of three-dimensional smoothly curved and shaded objects. A number of depth-related effects, such as in phenomena of transparency (Metelli, 1974) and proximity-luminance covariance (Dosher, Sperling, and Wurst, 1986) have been discussed by Grossberg (1987a, 1987b). The model in its current form also does not treat the temporal variations of brightness due to image motion (Cavanagh and Anstis, 1986; Todorović, 1983, 1987) or stabilization (Krauskopf, 1963; Pritchard, 1961; Yarbus, 1967). Finally, the application of the model to natural noisy images has yet to be accomplished.

In sum, the system described in this paper does not attempt to explain the complete gamut of brightness phenomena. These limitations are not, however, insurmountable obstacles but rather point to natural extensions of the model, many of which have been discussed and implemented in related work. However, even the processing of brightness in monocular, achromatic, static, noise-free images is full of surprising complexities. Only a model capable of handling these basic phenomena can be a foundation upon which still more complex effects can be explained.

Surprisingly little computationally oriented work has been devoted to these fundamental aspects of visual perception. Several contemporary algorithms were influenced by Land's seminal work (Horn, 1974; Frisby, 1979; Blake, 1985). Other computational models have provided alternative approaches to the analysis of filling-in (Arend and Goldstein, 1987; Hamada, 1984). Our model has been used to simulate a much larger set of brightness data, and includes mechanistic explanations of classical long-standing phenomena described in every review of brightness processing, recently discovered but unexplained data, and predictions of yet untested phenomena, including predictions of testable patterns of physiological activation.

The direct measurement of spatial distributions of activity in real neural networks is still hampered by considerable technical difficulties. Recently a number of procedures have been developed to enable the visualization of the spatial patterning of activation across large numbers of neurons to a given stimulus (Blasdel and Salama, 1986; Fox, Mintun, Raichle, Meizin, Allman, and van Essen, 1986; Grinvald, Leike, Frostig, Gilbert, and Wiesel, 1986; Nothdurft and Lee, 1982). These new techniques offer exciting possibilities for the study of integrating brain functions. Our computer simulations illustrate that these spatial patterns can be qualitatively different in response to the same stimulus at different levels of functional organization, and predict the types of activation patterns which should be elicited by images which are easily acquired and used in the laboratory. Of particular importance to brightness theory will be the discovery and mechanistic characterization of the cortical filling-in domains whose properties have been so essential to the success of our computer simulations of brightness percepts.

APPENDIX

The equations underlying the model are based on and are an extension of work by Grossberg (1983), Cohen and Grossberg (1984) and Grossberg and Mingolla (1985b, 1986a). The exposition follows the description of Levels in Figure 2. Only the two-dimensional versions of the equations are presented. The one-dimensional forms can be derived by straightforward simplifications. The two-dimensional simulations were performed either on a 16×16 lattice of units (the yin-yang square), a 30×30 lattice (simulations in Sections 5.1 and 5.2), or a 40×40 lattice (all other simulations). The one-dimensional simulations involve 256 units.

Level 1

We denote by I_{ij} the value of the stimulus input at position (i, j) in the lattice. In all simulations these values varied between 1 and 9. In order to compute the spatial convolutions of Level 2 cells without causing spurious edge effects at the extremities of the luminance profile, the luminance values at the extremities were continued outward as far as necessary.

Level 2

The activity x_{ij} of a Level 2 on-cell at position (i, j) of the lattice obeys a membrane equation

$$\frac{d}{dt} x_{ij} = -A x_{ij} + (B - x_{ij}) C_{ij} - (x_{ij} + D) E_{ij}, \tag{A1}$$

where C_{ij} (E_{ij}) is the total excitatory (inhibitory) input to x_{ij}. Each input C_{ij} and E_{ij} is a discrete convolution with Gaussian kernel of the inputs I_{pq}:

$$C_{ij} = \sum_{(p,q)} I_{pq} C_{pqij} \tag{A2}$$

and

$$E_{ij} = \sum_{(p,q)} I_{pq} E_{pqij}, \tag{A3}$$

where

$$C_{pqij} = C \exp\{-\alpha^{-2} \log 2[(p - i)^2 + (q - j)^2]\} \tag{A4}$$

and

$$E_{pqij} = E \exp\{-\beta^{-2} \log 2[(p - i)^2 + (q - j)^2]\}. \tag{A5}$$

Thus, the influence exerted on the Level 2 potential x_{ij} by input I_{pq} diminishes with increasing distance between the two corresponding locations. The decrease is isotropic, inducing the circular shape of the receptive fields. To achieve an on-center off-surround anatomy, coefficient C of the excitatory kernel in (A4) is chosen larger than coefficient E of the inhibitory kernel in (A5), but α, the radius of the excitatory spread at half strength in (A4), is chosen smaller than β, its inhibitory counterpart in (A5). In the simulations, this equation is solved at equilibrium. Then $\frac{d}{dt} x_{ij} = 0$, so that

$$x_{ij} = \frac{\sum_{(p,q)} (B C_{pqij} - D E_{pqij}) I_{pq}}{A + \sum_{(p,q)} (C_{pqij} + E_{pqij}) I_{pq}}. \tag{A6}$$

The denominator term normalizes the activity x_{ij}.

The off-cell potential $\overline{x}_{ij}$ at position (i, j) also obeys a membrane equation with an equilibrium value of the same form

$$\overline{x}_{ij} = \frac{\sum_{(p,q)} (B\overline{C}_{pqij} - D\overline{E}_{pqij}) I_{pq}}{A + \sum_{(p,q)} (\overline{C}_{pqij} + \overline{E}_{pqij}) I_{pq}} \qquad (A7)$$

The duality between on-cell and off-cell receptive fields was achieved by setting

$$\overline{C}_{pqij} = E_{pqij} \qquad (A8)$$

and

$$\overline{E}_{pqij} = C_{pqij}. \qquad (A9)$$

The output signal from Level 2 is the nonnegative, or rectified, part of x_{ij}:

$$X_{ij} = \max(x_{ij}, 0). \qquad (A10)$$

Level 3

The potential y_{ijk} of the cell centered at position (i, j) with orientation k on the hour code in Figure 7 obeys an additive equation

$$\frac{d}{dt} y_{ijk} = -y_{ijk} + \sum_{(p,q)} X_{pq} F^{(k)}_{pqij} \qquad (A11)$$

which is computed at equilibrium:

$$y_{ijk} = \sum_{(p,q)} X_{pq} F^{(k)}_{pqij} \qquad (A12)$$

in all our simulations. In order to generate an oriented kernel $F^{(k)}_{pqij}$ as simply as possible, let $F^{(k)}_{pqij}$ be the difference of an isotropic kernel G_{pqij} centered at (i, j) and another isotropic kernel $H^{(k)}_{pqij}$ whose center $(i + m_k, j + n_k)$ is shifted from (i, j) as follows:

$$F^{(k)}_{pqij} = G_{pqij} - H^{(k)}_{pqij} \qquad (A13)$$

where

$$G_{pqij} = \exp\{-\gamma^{-2}[(p - i)^2 + (q - j)^2]\} \qquad (A14)$$

and

$$H^{(k)}_{pqij} = \exp\{-\gamma^{-2}[(p - i - m_k)^2 + (q - j - n_k)^2]\} \qquad (A15)$$

with

$$m_k = \sin \frac{2\pi k}{K} \qquad (A16)$$

and

$$n_k = \cos \frac{2\pi k}{K}. \qquad (A17)$$

In the 2-D simulations, the number K of hour codes is 12, whereas for the 1-D simulations it is 2.

The output signal from Level 3 to Level 4 is the nonnegative, or rectified, part of y_{ijk}, namely

$$Y_{ijk} = \max(y_{ijk}, 0). \tag{A18}$$

Level 4

Each Level 4 potential z_{ijk} with position (i, j) and orientation k is made sensitive to orientation but insensitive to direction-of-contrast by summing the output signals from the appropriate pair of Level 3 units with opposite contrast sensitivities; viz.,

$$z_{ijk} = Y_{ijk} + Y_{ij(k+\frac{K}{2})} \tag{A19}$$

An output signal Z_{ijk} is generated from Level 4 to Level 5 if the activity z_{ijk} exceeds the threshold L:

$$Z_{ijk} = \max(z_{ijk} - L, 0). \tag{A20}$$

Level 5

A Level 5 signal z_{ij} at position (i, j) is the sum of output signals from all Level 4 units at that position; viz.,

$$Z_{ij} = \sum_k Z_{ijk}. \tag{A21}$$

Level 6

Each potential S_{ij} at position (i, j) of the syncytium obeys a nonlinear diffusion equation

$$\frac{d}{dt}S_{ij} = -MS_{ij} + \sum_{(p,q)\in N_{ij}} (S_{pq} - S_{ij})P_{pqij} + X_{ij} \tag{A22}$$

The diffusion coefficients that regulate the magnitude of cross influence of location (i, j) with location (p, q) depend on the Boundary Contour signals Z_{pq} and Z_{ij} as follows:

$$P_{pqij} = \frac{\delta}{1 + \epsilon(Z_{pq} + Z_{ij})} \tag{A23}$$

The set N_{ij} of locations comprises only the lattice nearest neighbors of (i, j):

$$N_{ij} = \{(i, j-1), (i-1, j), (i+1, j), (i, j+1)\}. \tag{A24}$$

At lattice edges and corners, this set is reduced to the set of existing neighbors. According to equation (A22), each potential S_{ij} is activated by the on-cell output signal X_{ij} and thereupon engages in passive decay (term $-MS_{ij}$) and diffusive filling-in with its four nearest neighbors to the degree permitted by the diffusion coefficients P_{pqij}. At equilibrium, each S_{ij} is computed as the solution of a set of simultaneous equations

$$S_{ij} = \frac{X_{ij} + \sum_{(p,q)\in N_{ij}} S_{pq}P_{pqij}}{M + \sum_{(p,q)\in N_{ij}} P_{pqij}} \tag{A25}$$

which is compared with properties of the brightness percept.

In all simulations the following parameter values were used: $A = 1, B = 90, D = 60, \gamma = 1$. Due to differences in dimensionality and scale, several parameters were given different values across sets of simulations. All two-dimensional simulations shared the following parameters: $C = 18, M = 1, \alpha = .25, \epsilon = 1$. The yin-yang square ($16 \times 16$) simulations used $E = 1, \beta = 2, \delta = 100, L = 15$. All other two-dimensional (30×30 and 40×40) simulations used $E = .5, \beta = 3, \delta = 300, L = 10$. All one-dimensional simulations used $C = 4, M = 10, \alpha = 1, \epsilon = 100, E = .5, \beta = 8, \delta = 100,000, L = 5$.

Finally, in order to illustrate the effects of parameter changes, the following values were different from the ones listed above. In Figure 6e, $\gamma = 3$. In Figures 17c and 17d, $\epsilon = 1000$. In Figures 17a and 17b the Boundary Contour signal Z_i was transformed through the sigmoid function $10Z_i^5(1 + Z_i^5)^{-1}$.

REFERENCES

Arend, L.E., Spatial differential and integral operations in human vision: Implication of stabilized retinal image fading. *Psychological Review*, 1973, **80**, 374–395.

Arend, L.E., Buehler, J.N., and Lockhead, G.R., Difference information in brightness perception. *Perception and Psychophysics*, 1971, **9**, 367–370.

Arend, L.E. and Goldstein, R.E., Lightness models, gradient illusions, and curl. *Perception and Psychophysics*, 1987, **42**, 65–80.

Arend, L.E. and Reeves, A., Simultaneous color constancy. *Journal of the Optical Society of America*, 1986, **A3**, 1743–1751.

Baumgartner, G., Indirekte Grössenbestimmung der receptiven Felder der Retina beim Menschen mittels der Hermannschen Gittertäuschung (Abstract). *Pflügers Arch. ges. Physiol.*, 1960, **272**, 21–22.

Beck, J., Perceptual grouping produced by changes in orientation and shape. *Science*, 1966, **154**, 528–540 (a).

Beck, J., Effect of orientation and of shape similarity on perceptual grouping. *Perception and Psychophysics*, 1966, **1**, 300–302 (b).

Berman, P.W. and Leibowitz, H.W., Some effects of contour on simultaneous brightness contrast. *Journal of Experimental Psychology*, 1965, **69**, 251–256.

Blake, A., Boundary conditions for lightness computation in Mondrian world. *Computer Vision, Graphics, and Image Processing*, 1985, **14**, 314–327.

Blasdel, G.G. and Salama, G., Voltage-sensitive dyes reveal a modular organization in monkey striate cortex. *Nature*, 1986, **321**, 579–585.

Braitenberg, V. and Braitenberg, C., Geometry of orientation columns in the visual cortex. *Biological Cybernetics*, 1979, **33**, 179–186.

Bridgeman, B., Isomorphism is where you find it. *Behavioral and Brain Sciences*, 1983, **6**, 658–659.

Cavanagh, P. and Anstis, S.M., Brightness shift in drifting ramp gratings isolates a transient mechanism. *Vision Research*, 1986, **26**, 899–908.

Cohen, M.A. and Grossberg, S., Neural dynamics of brightness perception: Features, boundaries, diffusion, and resonance. *Perception and Psychophysics*, 1984, **36**, 428–456.

Cornsweet, T.N., **Visual perception**. New York: Academic Press, 1970.

Davidson, M. and Whiteside, J.A., Human brightness perception near sharp contours. *Journal of the Optical Society of America*, 1971, **61**, 530–536.

DeValois, R.L., Albrecht, D.G., and Thorell, L.G., Spatial frequency selectivity of cells in macaque visual cortex. *Vision Research*, 1982, **22**, 545–559.

Dosher, B.A., Sperling, G., and Wurst, S., Tradeoffs between stereopsis and proximitiy luminance covariance as determinants of perceived 3-D structure. *Vision Research*, 1986, **26**, 973–979.

Enroth-Cugell, C. and Robson, J.G., The contrast sensitivity of retinal ganglion cells of the cat. *Journal of Physiology*, 1966, **187**, 517–552.

Enroth-Cugell, C. and Robson, J.G., Functional characteristics and diversity of cat retinal ganglion cells. *Investigative Ophthalmology and Visual Science*, 1984, **25**, 250–267.

Escher, M.C., **The graphic work of M.C. Escher**. London: Oldburne, 1961.

Fechner, G.T., **Elemente der Psychophysik** (2nd edition). Leipzig: Breitkopf und Härtel, 1889.

Foster, D.H., Experimental test of a network theory of vision. *Behavioral and Brain Sciences*, 1983, **6**, 664–665.

Fox, P.T., Mintun, M.A., Raichle, M.E., Miezin, F.M., Allman, J.M., and Van Essen, D.C., Mapping human visual cortex with positron emission tomography. *Nature*, 1986, **323**, 806–809.

Frisby, J.P., **Seeing: Illusion, brain, and mind**. Oxford: Oxford University Press, 1979.

Fry, G.A., Mechanisms subserving simultaneous brightness contrast. *American Journal of Optometry and Archives of the American Academy of Optometry*, 1948, **25**, 162–178.

Gerrits, H.J.M. and Vendrick, A.J.H., Simultaneous contrast, filling-in process and information processing in man's visual system. *Experimental Brain Research*, 1970, **11**, 411–430.

Gouras, P. and Krüger, J., Responses of cells in foveal visual cortex of the monkey to pure color contrast. *Journal of Neurophysiology*, 1979, **42**, 850–860.

Grinvald, A., Leike, E., Frostig, R.D., Gilbert, C.D., and Wiesel, T.N., Functional architecture of cortex revealed by optical imaging of intrinsic signals. *Nature*, 1986, **324**, 361–364.

Grossberg, S., The quantized geometry of visual space: The coherent computation of depth, form, and lightness. *Behavioral and Brain Sciences*, 1983, **6**, 625–692.

Grossberg, S., Cortical dynamics of three-dimensional form, color, and brightness perception, I: Monocular theory. *Perception and Psychophysics*, 1987, **41**, 87–116 (a).

Grossberg, S., Cortical dynamics of three-dimensional form, color, and brightness perception, II: Binocular theory. *Perception and Psychophysics*, 1987, **41**, 117–158 (b).

Grossberg, S. and Mingolla, E., Neural dynamics of form perception: Boundary completion, illusory figures, and neon color spreading. *Psychological Review*, 1985, **92**, 173–211 (a).

Grossberg, S. and Mingolla, E., Neural dynamics of perceptual grouping: Textures, boundaries, and emergent segmentations. *Perception and Psychophysics*, 1985, **38**, 141–171 (b).

Grossberg, S. and Mingolla, E., Neural dynamics of surface perception: Boundary webs, illuminants, and shape-from-shading. *Computer Vision, Graphics, and Image Processing*, 1987 , **37**, 116–165 (a).

Grossberg, S. and Mingolla, E., The role of illusory contours in visual segmentation. In S. Petry and G. Meyer (Eds.), **The perception of illusory contours**. New York: Springer-Verlag, 1987, 116–125 (b).

Growney, R.L. and Neri, D.F., The appearance of the Cornsweet illusion: Measures of perceived contrast and evenness of brightness. *Perception and Psychophysics*, 1986, **39**, 81–86.

Hamada, J., A multistage model for border contrast. *Biological Cybernetics*, 1984, **51**, 65–70.

Heggelund, P., Receptive field organisation of simple cells in cat striate cortex. *Experimental Brain Research*, 1981, **42**, 89–98 (a).

Heggelund, P., Receptive field organisation of complex cells in cat striate cortex. *Experimental Brain Research*, 1981, **42**, 99–107 (b).

Heggelund, P., Quantitative studies of enhancement and suppression zones in the receptive field of simple cells in cat striate cortex. *Journal of Physiology*, 1985, **373**, 293–310.

Heinemann, E.G., Simultaneous brightness induction. In D. Jameson and L.M. Hurvich (Eds.) **Handbook of Sensory Physiology, Vol. VII/4: Visual Psychophysics**, Berlin: Springer Verlag, 1972.

Helson, H., Studies of anomalous contrast and assimilation. *Journal of the Optical Society of America*, 1963, **53**, 179–184.

Hess, C. and Pretori, H., Messende Untersuchungen über die Gesetzmässigkeit des simultanen Helligkeitscontrastes. *Albrecht v. Graefes Arch. Ophthalmol.*, 1894, **40**, 1–24.

Horn, B.K.P., Determining lightness from an image. *Computer Graphics and Image Processing*, 1974, **3**, 277–299.

Hubel, D.H. and Wiesel, T.N., Receptive fields, binocular interaction and functional architecture in the cat's visual cortex. *Journal of Physiology*, 1962, **160**, 106–154.

Hubel, D.H. and Wiesel, T.N., Receptive fields and functional architecture of monkey striate cortex. *Journal of Physiology*, 1968, **195**, 215–243.

Hurvich, L.M. **Color vision**. Sunderland, MA: Sinauer Associates, 1981.

Julesz, B., **Foundations of cyclopean perception**. Chicago: University of Chicago Press, 1971.

Kanizsa, G. and Minguzzi, G.F., An anomalous brightness differentiation. *Perception*, 1986, **15**, 223–226.

Kato, H., Bishop, P.O., and Orban, G.A., Hypercomplex and simple/complex cell classifications in cat striate cortex. *Journal of Neurophysiology*, 1978, **41**, 1071–1095.

Katz, D., **The world of colour**. London: Kegan Paul, Trench, Trubner and Co. Ltd., 1935.

Koffka, K., **Principles of Gestalt psychology**. New York: Harcourt and Brace, 1935.

Krauskopf, J., Effect of retinal image stabilization on the appearance of heterochromatic targets. *Journal of the Optical Society of America*, 1963, **53**, 741–744.

Laming, D., On the need for discipline in the construction of psychological theories. *Behavioral and Brain Sciences*, 1983, **6**, 669–670.

Land, E., The Retinex theory of color vision. *Scientific American*, 1977, **237**, 108–128.

Land, E., Recent advances in Retinex theory. *Vision Research*, 1986, **26**, 7–21.

Land, E.H. and McCann, J.J., Lightness and Retinex theory. *Journal of the Optical Society of America*, 1971, **61**, 1–11.

McCourt, M.E., A spatial frequency dependent grating-induction effect. *Vision Research*, 1982, **22**, 119–134.

Metelli, F., The perception of transparency. *Scientific American*, 1974, **230**, 90–98.

Metzger, W., Optische Untersuchungen am Ganzfeld II. Zur Phänomenologie des homogenen Ganzfeldes. *Psychologische Forschung*, 1930, **13**, 6–29.

Nielsen, D.E., Retinocortical wiring of the simple cells of the visual cortex. In D. Rose and V.G. Dobson (Eds.), **Models of the visual cortex**. New York: Wiley and Sons, 1985.

Nothdurft, H.C. and Lee, B.B., Responses to colored patterns in the macaque lateral geniculate nucleus: Pattern processing in single neurons. *Experimental Brain Research*, 1982, **48**, 43–54.

Penrose, L.S. and Penrose, R., Impossible objects: A special type of visual illusion. *British Journal of Psychology*, 1958, **49**, 31–33.

Piccolino, M., Neyton, J., and Gerschenfeld, H.M., Decrease of gap junction permeability induced by dopamine and cyclic adenosine 3' : 5'-monophosphate in horizontal cells of turtle retina. *Journal of Neuroscience*, 1984, **4**, 2477–2488.

Pritchard, R.M., Stabilized images on the retina. *Scientific American*, 1961, **204**, 72–78.

Ratliff, F., **Mach bands: Quantitative studies on neural networks in the retina**. New York: Holden-Day, 1965.

Ratliff, F. and Hartline, H.U., The response of limulus optic nerve fibers to patterns of illumination on the receptor mosaic. *Journal of General Physiology*, 1959, **42**, 1241–1255.

Ratliff, F. and Sirovich, L., Equivalence classes of visual stimuli. *Vision Research*, 1978, **18**, 845–851.

Sagi, D. and Hochstein, S., Lateral inhibition between spatially adjacent spatial-frequency channels? *Perception and Psychophysics*, 1985, **37**, 315–322.

Schiller, P.H., Finlay, B.L., and Volman, S.F., Quantitative studies of single-cell properties in monkey striate cortex, I: Spatiotemporal organization of receptive fields. *Journal of Neurophysiology*, 1976, **39**, 1288–1319.

Sekuler, R., Spatial vision. In P.H. Mussen and M.R. Rosenzweig (Eds.), **Annual review of psychology**. Palo Alto: Annual Reviews, Inc., 1974.

Shapley, R., The importance of contrast for the activity of single neurons, the VEP and perception. *Vision Research*, 1986, **26**, 45–61.

Shapley, R. and Reid, R.C., Contrast and assimilation in the perception of brightness. *Proceedings of the National Academy of Sciences USA*, 1986, **82**, 5983–5986.

Sillito, A.M., Functional considerations of the operation of GABAergic inhibitory processes in the visual cortex. In A. Peters and E.G. Jones (Eds.), **Cerebral cortex**, Vol. 2A. New York: Plenum Press, 1984.

Spitzer, H. and Hochstein, S., A complex-cell receptive field model. *Journal of Neurophysiology*, 1985, **53**, 1266–1286.

Tanaka, M., Lee, B.B., and Creutzfeldt, O.D., Spectral tuning and contour representation in area 17 of the awake monkey. In J.D. Mollon and L.T. Sharpe (Eds.), **Colour vision**. New York: Academic Press, 1983.

Todorović, D., Brightness perception and the Craik-O'Brien-Cornsweet effect. Unpublished M.A. Thesis. Storrs: University of Connecticut, 1983.

Todorović, D., The Craik-O'Brien-Cornsweet effect: New varieties and their theoretical implications. *Perception and Psychophysics*, in press, 1987.

Wallach, H., Brightness constancy and the nature of achromatic colors. *Journal of Experimental Psychology*, 1948, **38**, 310–324.

Wallach, H., **On perception**. New York: Quadrangle, 1976.

Walls, G., The filling-in process. *American Journal of Optometry*, 1954, **31**, 329–340.

White, M., A new effect of pattern on perceived lightness. *Perception*, 1979, **8**, 413–416.

Yarbus, A.L., **Eye movements and vision**. New York: Plenum Press, 1967.

Yund, E.W. and Armington, J.C., Color and brightness contrast effects as a function of spatial variables. *Vision Research*, 1975, **15**, 917–930.

Behavior Research Methods, Instruments, and Computers
1986, **18** (6), 601–607
©1986 Psychonomic Society, Inc.

COMPUTER SIMULATION OF NEURAL NETWORKS
FOR PERCEPTUAL PSYCHOLOGY

Stephen Grossberg† and Ennio Mingolla‡

ABSTRACT

Computer simulations of neural network processes fill an important methodological niche, permitting the investigation of questions not resolvable by physiological, behavioral, or formal approaches alone. Two types of network simulations are considered: simulations of boundary completion and of textural segmentation. Simulations comparing properties of published models with variations of these models are presented in order to illustrate how parametric computer simulations have guided the development of neural models of visual perception.

1. The Role of Computer Simulations in Theory Development

The dynamics of large ensembles of neurons are as yet difficult to observe directly. Even if direct observation were possible, it would not explain how the interactions among neurons generate the emergent properties that subserve intelligent behavior. Additional methodologies are needed to investigate how the collective properties of a neural network are related to its components. Computer simulations of neural networks are crucial tools in the current explosion of work in brain science. While anatomical, physiological, and behavioral methods continue to be fundamental, theoretical investigations of perceptual, cognitive, and motor tasks are gaining increasing importance, thanks in part to the ability afforded by computers to implement and test formal models of distributed brain processes.

Many basic problems of skilled behavior can now be modelled in sufficiently precise terms as to permit formal mathematical investigation. Once a mathematical model of neural functioning is formulated, the investigation of its properties may culminate in the proof of theorems concerning the stability or convergence behavior of the model, as in Cohen and Grossberg (1983). Certain classes of models of neurally based processes, however, particularly those involving large and hierarchically organized systems of nonlinear ordinary differential equations, are characteristically difficult to analyse through purely formal procedures. For these systems there may be no way to determine the output of the model when given a certain input short of "running" the model in a numerical computer simulation. Thus "experiments" can be run on a model, in ways that are similar in some respects to experiments run on human or animal subjects.

---

† Supported in part by the Air Force Office of Scientific Research (AFOSR 85-0149 and AFOSR F49620-86-C-0037), the Army Research Office (ARO DAAG-29-85-K-0095), and the National Science Foundation (NSF IST-84-17756).

‡ Supported in part by the Air Force Office of Scientific Research (AFOSR 85-0149).

Models by definition do not contain all the richness of the biological process they model; their very explanatory power comes in part from their greater simplicity. Nevertheless, once the component mechanisms of a model are known to be qualitatively valid, computer simulations have certain distinct advantages over experiments on actual organisms. Simulations can be cheaper and faster, but more importantly they permit a much more precise level of control of many variables than could ever be realized in physiological or behavioral experimental paradigms. Thus, parameters in a model can be perturbed, or entire components of the model can be deleted or replaced with other mechanisms, by changing the appropriate parts of computer programs. Such systematic investigations can yield a deeper appreciation of the modeled mechanisms and their variants, both normal and abnormal; suggestions for corroborative experiments on live organisms; and even general design insights which can at times be formalized into mathematical proofs that would otherwise have been difficult to discover.

2. Simulation of a Neurally Based Model of Boundary Completion

This article presents two examples of how performing computer simulations has helped the development of a perceptual theory, whose formal equations are listed in the Appendix. These examples illustrate that each of the processing stages used in the model is essential for generating its formal perceptual properties. In this limited sense at least, the model is a *minimal* model of the properties that it sets out to explain.

The first example involves variations of simulations that were first presented in Grossberg and Mingolla (1985a), which examined certain problems in boundary detection and completion faced by mammalian visual systems. Early visual processing by orientationally tuned, contrast driven cells necessarily involves problems of positional and orientational uncertainty. For example, the very elongation of cell receptive fields (masks) necessary for preferential responses to oriented contrasts along straight luminance borders implies attenuated responses by these receptive fields at line ends and corners, as indicated in Figure 1. We summarize this property in terms of an uncertainty principle; namely, that *orientational certainty implies positional uncertainty at line ends and corners*. Figure 2 shows a computer simulation depicting this uncertainty at a line end.

Within our theory the spatial pattern of early boundary detection signals depicted in Figure 2 requires subsequent processing whereby the positional uncertainty at line ends and corners is overcome. To this end, the mask responses in Figure 2 act as an input pattern to a later processing stage which preserves the strong responses at the line's long edges, but also completes the representation of the line at its end (Grossberg and Mingolla, 1985a, 1985b). We call the emergent pattern of activity at the end of a line an *end cut*, an example of which is shown in Figure 3.

The processing stages that are hypothesized to generate end cuts are summarized in Figure 4. These processing stages have also been used to analyse a wide variety of perceptual and neural data (Grossberg, 1987a, 1987b; Grossberg and Mingolla, 1985a, 1985b, 1987). First, oriented receptive fields of like position and orientation, but opposite direction-of-contrast, cooperate at the next processing stage to activate cells whose receptive fields are sensitive to the same position and orientation as themselves, but are insensitive to direction-of-contrast. These target cells maintain their sensitivity to the *amount* of oriented contrast, but not to the *direction* of this oriented contrast. The computer simulation summarized in Figure 2 depicts the responses of cells at this processing stage. Such model cells, which play the role of complex cells in Area 17 of the visual

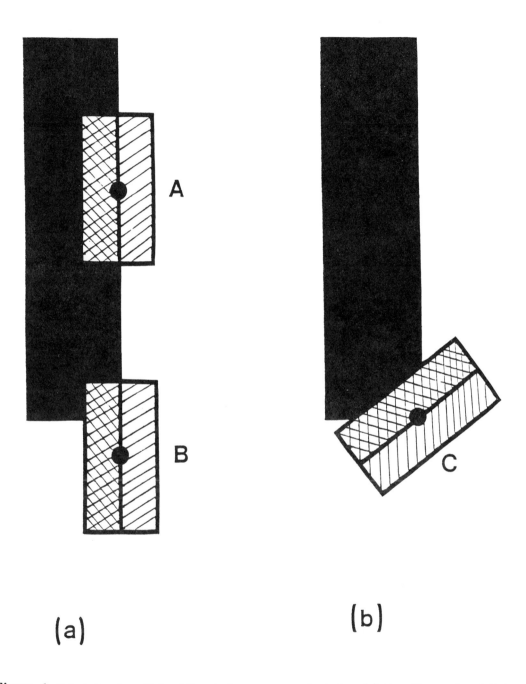

Figure 1. Orientational specificity at figural edges, corners, and exteriors. (a) At positions such as A that are along a figural edge, but not at a figural corner, the oriented mask parallel to the edge is highly favored. At positions beyond the edge, such as B, masks of the same orientation are still partially activated. This tendency can, in the absence of compensatory mechanisms, support a flow of dark featural activity down and out of the black figure. (b) A line is thin, functionally speaking, when at positions near a corner, such as C, many masks of different orientations are all weakly activated or not activated at all.

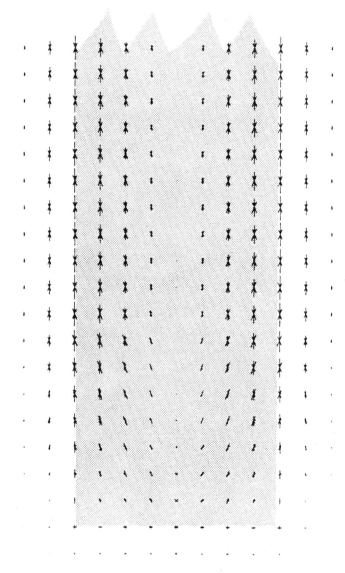

Figure 2. An orientation field: Lengths and orientations of lines encode the relative sizes of the activations and orientations of the input masks at the corresponding positions. The input pattern, which is a vertical line end as seen by the receptive fields, corresponds to the shaded area. Each mask has total exterior dimensions of 16×8 units, with a unit length being the distance between two adjacent lattice positions.

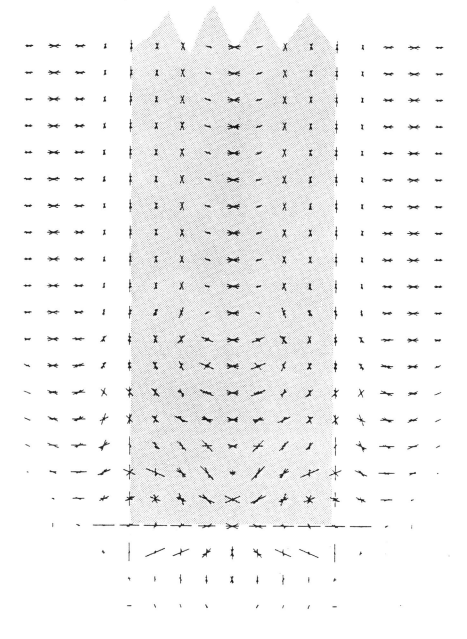

Figure 3. Responses of a network with two stages of short-range competition to the orientation field of Figure 2: A process called end cutting generates horizontal activations at line end locations that receive small and orientationally ambiguous input activations.

TO COOPERATION

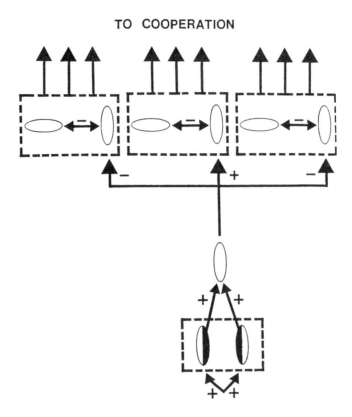

Figure 4. Early stages of Boundary Contour processing: At each position exist cells with elongated receptive fields of various sizes which are sensitive to orientation, amount-of-contrast, and direction-of-contrast. Pairs of such cells sensitive to like orientation but opposite directions-of-contrast (lower dashed box) input to cells that are sensitive to orientation and amount-of-contrast but not to direction-of-contrast (white ellipses). These cells, in turn, excite like-oriented cells corresponding to the same position and inhibit like-oriented cells corresponding to nearby positions at the first competitive stage (upper dashed boxes). At this stage, cells corresponding to the same position but different orientations inhibit each other via a push-pull competitive interaction.

cortex, pool inputs from receptive fields with opposite directions-of-contrast in order to generate boundary detectors which can detect the broadest possible range of luminance or chromatic contrasts (Grossberg, 1987a; Thorell, DeValois, and Albrecht, 1984). These two successive stages of oriented contrast-sensitive cells are called the OC Filter (Grossberg and Mingolla, 1985b).

The output from the OC Filter successively activates two types of short-range competitive interaction whose net effect is to generate end cuts. First, a cell of prescribed orientation excites like-oriented cells corresponding to its location and inhibits like-oriented cells corresponding to nearby locations at the next processing stage. In other words, an on-center off-surround organization of like-oriented cell interactions exists around each perceptual location. The outputs from this competitive mechanism interact with the second competitive mechanism. Here, cells compete that represent different orientations, notably perpendicular orientations, at the same perceptual location. This competition defines a push-pull opponent process. If a given orientation is excited, then the perpendicular orientation at its location is inhibited. If a given orientation is inhibited, then the perpendicular orientation at its location is excited via disinhibition.

These competitive rules generate end cuts as follows. The strong vertical activations along the edges of a scenic line, as in Figure 2, inhibit the weak vertical activations near the line end. These inhibited vertical activations, in turn, disinhibit horizontal activations near the line end, as in Figure 3. Thus the positional uncertainty at line ends that is caused by orientational tuning is eliminated by the interaction of two short-range competitive mechanisms.

The properties of the two stages of competition can be formally dissected through the use of simulations that omit one or the other stage. Figure 5 shows the effects of feeding signals proportional to the output of oriented masks directly to the second competitive stage; thus the first competitive stage is eliminated and the mask field pattern shown in Figure 2 is input directly to the second competitive stage. Figure 6, conversely, shows the output of the first competitive stage to the input signal pattern shown in Figure 2. Together, Figures 5 and 6 illustrate the importance of coupling the two successive competitive stages. Without the first competitive stage (Figure 5), the output pattern has a broad band of vertically oriented activity along the sides of the line, thereby failing to adequately localize the sides of the line itself. Without the second competitive stage (Figure 6), almost all signals are swamped by noise.

3. Implementation of Simulations Using Algebraic Equations

Simulations of the kind shown in Figure 2 are relatively easy to perform, both in terms of programming difficulty and computer processing time, because they involve only algebraic calculations of contrast distributions in an image. (See Appendix, Equation (A1).) In image processing terms, one performs a convolution of the image with oriented kernels (weighting functions) that express the oriented contrast sensitivity of masks. The difference between an ordinary image convolution and the simulation shown in Figure 2, is that, in the latter, only a sparse lattice of image locations is sampled in order to form the grid of mask responses over several orientations, and the larger of the two convolutions is plotted at each location and orientation to implement the insensitivity of the masks to direction-of-contrast, as defined in the numerator of equation (A1) of the Appendix.

Simulations such as shown in Figures 3, 5, and 6 are also easy to perform, since they can also be executed using only algebraic equations. The networks involved in the simulation of Figure 3 are defined by a system of equations (A1) through (A6) of the Appendix. These equations represent a feedforward flow of activation from the input masks to the competitive stages. The equilibrium states of this system can therefore be easily computed. In fact, all equations but (A4) are already computed at equilibrium. The equilibrium of (A4) can be computed by simply setting the rate of change, $\frac{d}{dt}w_{ijk}$, of w_{ijk} equal to zero. Thus, at equilibrium,

$$w_{ijk} = \frac{I + BJ_{ijk} + v_{ijk}}{1 + B\sum_{(p,q)} J_{pqk}A_{pqij}}. \tag{1}$$

For the simulations of Figures 3, 5, and 6, all v_{ijk}'s are set identically equal to zero, since no feedback is involved. The simulations shown in Figures 5 and 6 were performed by replacing equations (1) and (A6) by

$$w_{ijk} = I + BJ_{ijk} \tag{2}$$

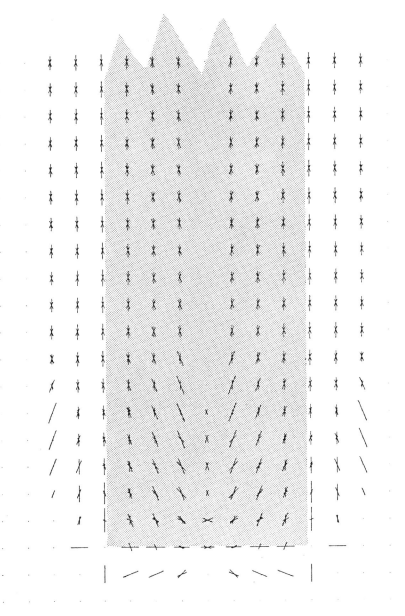

Figure 5. This simulation was performed with the second competitive stage responding directly to the inputs of the orientation field in Figure 2, without any processing by the first competitive stage. The sides of the line (indicated by the shaded region) are not well localized by the network.

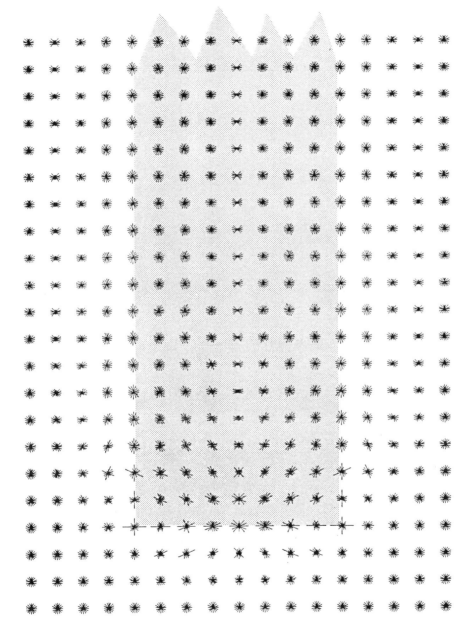

Figure 6. Responses of the first competitive stage to the input of the orientation field in Figure 2. Without processing by the second competitive stage, almost all responses to the line (indicated by the shaded region) are swamped by noise.

and

$$y_{ijk} = w_{ijk} \tag{3}$$

respectively. All other relevant equations and quantities were identical to those used for the simulation shown in Figure 3.

4. Simulation of Textural Segmentation and Perceptual Grouping

The second set of simulations concerns the role of long-range cooperative activity among oriented cells at a processing stage subsequent to the two short-range competitive stages. In our theory this cooperation is crucial to the understanding of boundary detection and completion, textural segmentation and grouping, surface perception, and the perception of illusory contours (Grossberg and Mingolla, 1985b, 1987). The cooperation is mediated by oriented cells with two separately thresholded receptive fields, as indicated in Figure 7. The alignment of the two receptive field weighting functions is such that, for example, a horizontally oriented cooperative cell tends to fire whenever it receives sufficiently strong signals from approximately horizontally oriented cells of the second competitive stage to both receptive fields simultaneously. When the cooperative cell fires, it sends excitatory signals back to the similarly oriented cells corresponding to its position at the first competitive stage, and inhibitory signals to similarly oriented cells corresponding to nearby positions. These top-down signals set up a feedback loop between the long-range cooperative process and the short-range competitive processes. This cooperative-competitive feedback process is called the CC Loop. The design constraints leading to the entire system for implementing the CC Loop are beyond the scope of this article, and can be found in Grossberg and Mingolla (1985b). The role of computer simulations in the formulation of one key functional capacity of the CC Loop is instead described in detail.

Figure 8 presents the results of two separate simulations of textural grouping. Figure 8a shows the input pattern that is presented to the CC Loop. The pattern consists of 9 clusters of 18 vertically oriented mask responses. We call each cluster a Line because it is a caricature of how a finer lattice of masks would respond to an actual line. Figure 8b displays the pattern of equilibrium activities that is generated by this input at the second competitive stage of the full model, including CC Loop feedback. This simulation is a success because, without any preassigned template or external prompting, the network has automatically regulated itself to an equilibrium state wherein each Line, besides being surrounded by its own boundary activity, is also emergently grouped with neighboring vertical and horizontal lines in a manner similar to that found in human perception. (See Beck, Prazdny, and Rosenfeld, 1983 for an excellent review.)

5. The Postulate of Spatial Impenetrability

Because the only inputs for the simulation summarized in Figure 8b were the vertical activities shown in Figure 8a, it is clear that the emergent horizontal groupings came about through horizontal cooperative activity induced by horizontal end cut signals that are generated at the ends of Lines by the second competitive stage. If such horizontal end cuts induce horizontal groupings at line ends, however, why do not the horizontal signals induced along the sides of the Lines also group, thereby flooding the entire region between Lines with activity? Precisely this event is shown in Figure 8c, which shows the results of a simulation run not on our actual model but on a variation of it.

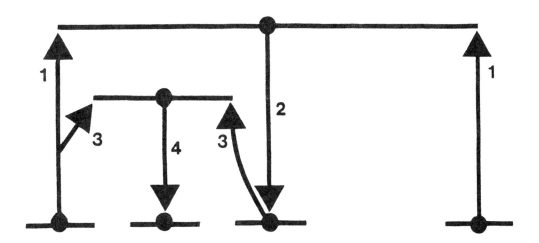

Figure 7. An overview of cooperative feedback: (a) The pair of pathways 1 activate positive boundary completion feedback along pathway 2. Then pathways such as 3 activate positive feedback along pathways such as 4. Rapid completion of a sharp boundary between the locations of pathways 1 can hereby be generated by a spatially discontinuous bisection process. (b) Circuit diagram of the Boundary Contour System: Inputs activate oriented masks which cooperate at each position and orientation before feeding into an on-center off-surround interaction. This interaction excites like-orientations at the same position and inhibits like-orientations at nearby positions. The affected cells are on-cells within a dipole field. On-cells at a fixed position compete among orientations. On-cells also inhibit off-cells which represent the same position and orientation. Off-cells at each position, in turn, compete among orientations. Both on-cells and off-cells are tonically active. Net excitation of an on-cell excites a similarly oriented cooperative receptive field at a location corresponding to that of the on-cell. Net excitation of an off-cell inhibits a similarly oriented cooperative receptive field of a bipole cell at a location corresponding to that of the off-cell. Thus, bottom-up excitation of a vertical on-cell, by inhibiting the horizontal on-cell at that position, disinhibits the horizontal off-cell at that position, which in turn inhibits (almost) horizontally oriented cooperative receptive fields that include its position. Sufficiently strong net positive activation of both receptive fields of a cooperative cell enables it to generate feedback via an on-center off-surround interaction among like-oriented cells. On-cells which receive the most favorable combination of bottom-up signals and top-down signals generate the emergent perceptual grouping. The letters in this figure are keyed to the variables in the Appendix.

Our actual CC Loop model (Figure 7b) avoids the disaster shown in Figure 8c by instantiating a computational property that implements what we have termed the *postulate of spatial impenetrability*. This postulate acknowledges the need to prevent the cooperative process from being able to leap across, and thereby penetrate, all intervening percepts. Figure 9 motivates the mechanism which we have developed to implement the postulate of spatial impenetrability. Figure 9 shows the left halves of the receptive fields of two horizontally tuned cooperative cells. In our actual model, horizontal activations at the second competitive stage which fall within such a horizontally tuned cooperative cell's receptive field generates excitatory inputs to the receptive field. Vertical activations, in contrast, generate inhibitory inputs to the receptive field. (The pairing of excitatory and inhibitory inputs at perpendicular orientations is represented by the terms $y_{pqr} - y_{pqR}$ in equation (A7).) Thus, by summing excitatory and inhibitory inputs from the second competitive stage, the lower cooperative cell of Figure 9 can have its left receptive field

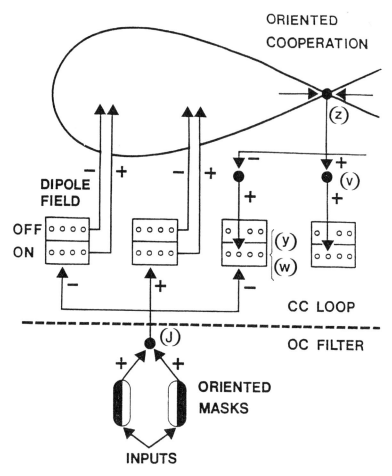

Figure 7 (continued).

excited above threshold, because of the preponderance of horizontals from the end cut. On the other hand, the upper cooperative cell's left receptive field receives net inhibition because signals from the six vertical segments overwhelm those from the four horizontals. Our neural model of how both excitatory and inhibitory signals input to a cooperative cell assumes that on-cells generate the excitatory inputs and off-cells generate the inhibitory inputs from the second competitive stage. These cells, taken together, are called a dipole field, as illustrated in Figure 7b.

The model variation whose noisy output is shown in Figure 8c was achieved by removing the inhibitory effects of signals oriented orthogonally to the cooperative cell's preferred orientation $(-y_{pqR})$, while keeping the excitatory effects of signals at the same orientation as the cooperative cell itself constant (y_{pqr}). Indeed, along with study of perceptual and physiological data and earlier theoretical results, observation of simulations such as shown in Figure 8c played a crucial role in our development of the CC Loop model in its present form.

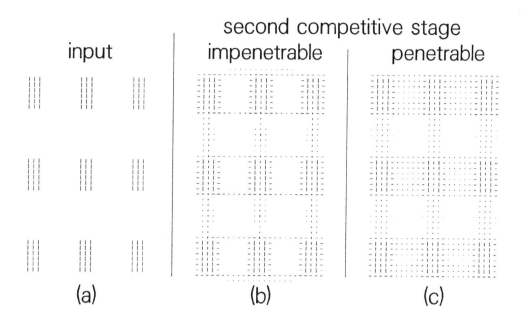

Figure 8. Computer simulations of processing underlying textural grouping. The length of each line segment is proportional to the activation of a network node responsive to one of twelve possible orientations. Part (a) displays the activity of oriented cells which input to the CC Loop. Part (b) displays the groupings sensed by our actual model network. Part (c) displays the resulting flooding of boundary activity that occurs when the model's mechanism for spatial impenetrability is removed. See the text for details of the two simulations.

6. Implementation of Perceptual Grouping Simulations

Performing the simulations of Figure 8 involves more complexity than is apparent from the output displays themselves. For example, the lattice of network nodes contains 12 orientations at each of 40 by 25 spatial locations for five network processing stages. This means that 60,000 nonlinear ordinary differential equations must be solved to perform each of the simulations in Figure 8. One factor prevents the computational demands from being completely intractable. Some of the equations can be solved algebraically, in the same manner as those for the end cut simulations (Figure 3). Because the full model involves feedback, however, the use of algebraic approximations requires making explicit assumptions about reaction rates within the model. That is, those stages whose equilibria are computed algebraically are assumed to equilibrate more rapidly than the other stages.

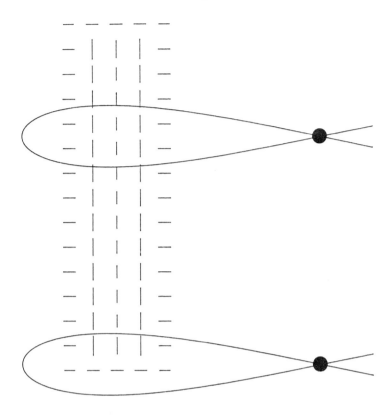

Figure 9. A mechanism to implement the postulate of spatial impenetrability: The left receptive fields of two horizontally tuned cooperative cells are crossed by a thin vertical Line. Although horizontal end-cut signals can excite the upper receptive field, these are cancelled by the greater number of inhibitory inputs due to the vertical Line inputs. Within the lower receptive field, the excitatory inputs due to end cuts prevail.

The Appendix describes which equations were solved algebraically and which were solved through numerical integration.

For the simulations of Figure 8, the numerical integration of the differential equations not solved algebraically was carried out using the DGEAR subroutine package of the IMSL Library, which is commonly available at university computational facilities. Using IMSL is not much more difficult than using the packages for statistical analysis so familiar to psychologists. Solving systems of simultaneous nonlinear differential equations, however, is notoriously slow work for general purpose digital computers. The simulations of Figure 8, for example, took hours of computer time on a large IBM mainframe.

Those of us working on neurally based network models hope than the forthcoming generation of massively parallel hardware can be used to speed up simulations for basic research. Certain prototypes of parallel processors have in fact been developed along lines suggested by theoretical research on neural models that has been performed over the past two decades. In particular, TRW's new Mark III and Mark IV computers are designed to rapidly integrate a wide range of neural models at relatively low cost. We hope that this type of cooperative feedback loop between computer simulation and hardware development will speed the attainment both of theoretical understanding of biological processes and of development of advanced parallel hardware designs.

APPENDIX

The following neural network equations represent the OC Filter and the CC Loop. All processes, except the first competitive stage, are assumed to react so quickly that they can be represented at equilibrium as algebraic equations. This approximation is merely a computational convenience to speed up the simulations, and does not influence the results. See Grossberg and Mingolla (1985b) for complete definitions of the network processes.

In all of the subsequent equations, indices (i, j) represent a cell position within a two-dimensional lattice and k represents an orientation.

OC FILTER

Complex Cell Receptive Fields

Letting S_{pq} equal the input to position (p, q),

$$J_{ijk} = \frac{[U_{ijk} - \alpha V_{ijk}]^+ + [V_{ijk} - \alpha U_{ijk}]^+}{1 + \beta(U_{ijk} + V_{ijk})}, \qquad (A1)$$

where

$$U_{ijk} = \sum_{(p,q)\in L_{ijk}} S_{pq}, \qquad (A2)$$

$$V_{ijk} = \sum_{(p,q)\in R_{ijk}} S_{pq}, \qquad (A3)$$

and the notation $[p]^+ = \max(p, 0)$. In (A1), the elongated receptive field is divided into a left half L_{ijk} and a right half R_{ijk}.

CC LOOP

First Competitive Stage

$$\frac{d}{dt} w_{ijk} = -w_{ijk} + I + B J_{ijk} + v_{ijk} - B \sum_{(p,q)} J_{pqk} A_{pqij} \qquad (A4)$$

Second Competitive Stage

$$O_{ijk} = C[w_{ijk} - w_{ijK}]^+, \qquad (A5)$$

$$y_{ijk} = \frac{E O_{ijk}}{D + O_{ij}}, \qquad (A6)$$

where K is the orientation perpendicular to k, and $O_{ij} = \sum_{k=1}^{n} O_{ijk}$.

Cooperation

$$z_{ijk} = g\left(\sum_{(p,q,r)} [y_{pqr} - y_{pqR}] F_{pqij}^{(r,k)} \right) + g\left(\sum_{(p,q,r)} [y_{pqr} - y_{pqR}] G_{pqij}^{(r,k)} \right), \qquad (A7)$$

where

$$g(s) = \frac{H[s]^+}{K + [s]^+} \qquad (A8)$$

and kernels $F_{pqij}^{(r,k)}$ and $G_{pqij}^{(r,k)}$ define the cell's two receptive fields.

Cooperative Feedback to First Competitive Stage

$$v_{ijk} = \frac{h(z_{ijk})}{1 + \sum_{(p,q)} h(z_{pqk})W_{pqij}}, \tag{A9}$$

where

$$h(s) = L[s - M]^{+}. \tag{A10}$$

REFERENCES

Beck, J., Prazdny, K., and Rosenfeld, A., A theory of textural segmentation. In J. Beck, B. Hope, and A. Rosenfeld (Eds.), **Human and machine vision**. New York: Academic Press, 1983.

Cohen, M.A. and Grossberg, S., Absolute stability of global pattern formation and parallel memory storage by competitive neural networks. *Transactions IEEE*, 1983, **SMC-13**, 815–826.

Grossberg, S., Cortical dynamics of three-dimensional form, color, and brightness perception, I: Monocular theory. *Perception and Psychophysics*, 1987, **41**, 87–116 (a).

Grossberg, S., Cortical dynamics of three-dimensional form, color, and brightness perception, II: Binocular theory. *Perception and Psychophysics*, 1987, **41**, 117–158 (b).

Grossberg, S. and Mingolla, E., Neural dynamics of form perception: Boundary completion, illusory figures, and neon color spreading. *Psychological Review*, 1985, **92**, 173–211 (a).

Grossberg, S. and Mingolla, E., Neural dynamics of perceptual grouping: Textures, boundaries, and emergent segmentations. *Perception and Psychophysics*, 1985, **38**, 141–171 (b).

Grossberg, S. and Mingolla, E., Neural dynamics of surface perception: Boundary webs, illuminants, and shape-from-shading. *Computer Vision, Graphics, and Image Processing*, 1987, **37**, 116–165.

Thorell, L.G., DeValois, R.L., and Albrecht, D.G., Spatial mapping of monkey V1 cells with pure color and luminance stimuli. *Vision Research*, 1984, **24**, 751–769.

Cognitive Science
1987, **11**, 23–63
©1987 Cognitive Science Society

COMPETITIVE LEARNING:
FROM INTERACTIVE ACTIVATION TO ADAPTIVE RESONANCE

Stephen Grossberg†

ABSTRACT

Functional and mechanistic comparisons are made between several network models of cognitive processing: competitive learning, interactive activation, adaptive resonance, and back propagation. The starting point of this comparison is the article of Rumelhart and Zipser (1985) on feature discovery through competitive learning. All of the models which Rumelhart and Zipser (1985) have described were shown in Grossberg (1976b) to exhibit a type of learning which is temporally unstable. Competitive learning mechanisms can be stabilized in response to an arbitrary input environment by being supplemented with mechanisms for learning top-down expectancies, or templates; for matching bottom-up input patterns with the top-down expectancies; and for releasing orienting reactions in a mismatch situation, thereby updating short term memory and searching for another internal representation. Network architectures which embody all of these mechanisms were called adaptive resonance models by Grossberg (1976c). Self-stabilizing learning models are candidates for use in real-world applications where unpredictable changes can occur in complex input environments. Competitive learning postulates are inconsistent with the postulates of the interactive activation model of McClelland and Rumelhart (1981), and suggest different levels of processing and interaction rules for the analysis of word recognition. Adaptive resonance models use these alternative levels and interaction rules. The self-organizing learning of an adaptive resonance model is compared and contrasted with the teacher-directed learning of a back propagation model. A number of criteria for evaluating real-time network models of cognitive processing are described and applied.

1. Introduction

Many cognitive scientists are now rapidly translating their intuitions about human intelligence into real-time network models. As each research group injects a stream of new models into this sprawling literature, it becomes ever more essential to penetrate behind the many ephemeral differences between models to the deeper architectural level on which a formal model lives. What are the key issues, principles, properties, mechanisms, and data that may be used to distinguish one model from another? How may we decide whether two seemingly different models are really formally equivalent, or are probing profoundly different aspects of cognitive processing?

This article outlines a comparative analysis of network models within a focused conceptual domain. Its starting point is the recent article by Rumelhart and Zipser (1985) on

† Supported in part by the Air Force Office of Scientific Research (AFOSR 85-0149 and AFOSR F49620-86-C-0037) and the National Science Foundation (NSF IRI-84-17756).

competitive learning models that was published in this journal as part of a special issue on connectionist models. The discussions raised by this article lead naturally to a comparison of several distinct models, notably competitive learning, interactive activation, adaptive resonance, and back propagation models. Before considering these models, I briefly discuss why real-time network models are so important, and why their very promise makes them difficult to understand.

2. Emergent Properties of Network Interactions: Function versus Mechanism

A key issue leading to network models concerns how the behavior of individuals adapts successfully in real-time to constraints imposed by their environments. In order to analyse this issue, one needs to identify the functional level on which an individual's behavioral success is defined. Much theoretical and experimental evidence suggests that this is the level of neural networks, rather than the level of individual nerve cells. Key behavioral properties are often emergent properties due to interactions among many cells in a neural network. Thus the study of real-time networks is important because behavior can best be understood on the level of a network analysis.

Often a network's emergent properties are much more complex than the network components from which they arise. In a good network model, the whole is far greater than the sum of its parts. In addition, the formal relationships among those emergent properties may be quite subtle, and may reflect the delicate interplay of behavioral properties that are characteristic of living organisms. Thus network models can excite our interest by showing us how subtle and complex functional properties can emerge from interactions among simple components.

The very fact, however, that simple network laws can generate complex behaviors makes network models difficult to understand. In order to effectively analyse a network model, one needs powerful analytic and computational methods to derive the complex emergent properties of the network from a description of its simple components. A network model cannot, in principle, be understood merely as a list of processing rules or as a computer program. In order to adequately describe the dynamism of such a network, it is necessary to use a mathematical formalism that can naturally analyse interactions which may occur in a nonlinear fashion across thousands or even millions of components. The need for such a formal analysis is especially great when the network can learn, since the same laws define the network at all times, but its functional properties may be radically different before and after learning occurs.

The distinction between a network's emergent functional properties and its simple mechanistic laws also clarifies why the controversy surrounding the relationship of an intelligent system's abstract properties to its mechanistic instantiation has been so enduring. Without a linkage to mechanism, a network's functional properties cannot be formally or physically explained. On the other hand, how do we decide which mechanisms are crucial for generating desirable functional properties and which mechanisms are adventitious? Two seemingly different models can be equivalent from a functional viewpoint if they both generate similar sets of emergent properties. An analysis which proves such a functional equivalence between models does not, however, minimize the importance of their mechanistic descriptions. Rather, such an analysis identifies mechanistic variations which are not likely to be differentiated by evolutionary pressures which select for these functional properties on the basis of behavioral success.

Another side of such an evolutionary analysis concerns the identification of the fundamental network modules which are specialized by the evolutionary process for use in a variety of behavioral tasks. How do evolutionary variations of a single network module, or blueprint, generate behavioral properties which, on the level of raw experience, seem to be phenomenally different and even functionally unrelated? Although each specialized network may generate a characteristic bundle of emergent properties, parametric changes of these specialized networks within the framework of a single network design may generate bundles of emergent properties that are qualitatively different. In order to identify the mechanistic unity behind this phenomenal diversity, appropriate analytic methods are once again indispensable.

In summary, the relationship between the emergent functional properties that govern behavioral success and the mechanisms that generate these properties is far from obvious. A single network module may generate qualitatively different functional properties when its parameters are changed. Conversely, two mechanisms which are mechanistically different may generate formally homologous functional properties. The intellectual difficulties caused by these possibilities are only compounded by the fact that we are designed by evolution to be serenely ignorant of our own mechanistic substrates. The very cognitive and learning mechanisms which enable us to group, or chunk, ever more complex information into phenomenally simple unitized representations act to hide from us the myriad interactions that subserve these representations during every moment of experience. Thus we cannot turn to our daily intuitions or to our lay language for secure guidance in discovering or analysing network models. The simple lesson that the whole is greater than the sum of its parts forces us to use an abstract mathematical language that is capable of analysing interactive emergence and functional equivalence.

3. Processing Levels and Interactions: Models or Metaphors?

A network model is usually easy to define using just a few equations. These equations specify the dynamical laws governing the model's nodes, or cells, including the processing *levels* in which these nodes are embedded. The equations also specify the *interactions* between these nodes, including which nodes are connected by pathways and the types of signals or other processes that go on in these pathways. Inputs to the network, outputs from the network, parameter choices within the network, and initial values of network variables often complete the model description. Such components are common to essentially all real-time network models. Thus, to merely say that a model has such components is scientifically vacuous.

How, then, can we decide when a network model is wrong? Such a task is deceptively simple. If the model's levels are incorrectly chosen, then it is wrong. If its interactions are incorrectly chosen, then it is wrong. And so on. The only escape from such a critique would be to demonstrate that a different set of levels and interactions can be correctly chosen, and shares similar functional properties with the original model. The new choice of levels and interactions would, however, constitute a new model. The old model would still be wrong. Such an analysis would show that the shared model properties are essentially model-independent, yet that there exist finer tests to distinguish between models. I will describe several such tests below.

In the absence of such a literal process of model selection and rejection, it would soon become impossible to criticize a model at all, since its authors could claim that they really did not intend their model to be literally interpreted. To avoid criticism or disconfirmation, the model could be turned into a metaphor of itself, or even into a vaguely outlined framework that could be broadly enough defined to include all future modeling possibilities, including possibilities that flatly contradicted the original model.

McClelland (1985, p.144) essentially advocated this position when he wrote "we would not view the interactive activation model as a description of a mechanism at all ... it allows us to study interactive activation models of a wide range of phenomena at a psychological or functional level without necessarily worrying about the plausibility of assuming that they provide an adequate description of the actual implementation." As noted above, dissociation of a functional description from a mechanistic description is impossible in a network model. The possibility that a particular mechanistic instantiation may be functionally equivalent to a different instantiation does not in the least free us from committing ourselves to particular classes of mechanisms. McClelland's usage would become acceptable only if we agreed to use the term "interactive activation" model to mean any real-time network model. Such a usage would, however, make the term scientifically vacuous. In addition, the interactive activation model is a relatively recent member of the family of real-time network models in psychology. It has added no new qualitative concepts to this class of models *as a framework*, hence it needs to be analysed *as a model* in order to appreciate its contribution to the network modeling literature. All models discussed in this article will be treated literally as models, rather than as metaphors or frameworks of models.

4. Feature Discovery by Competitive Learning

I will use the Rumelhart and Zipser (1985) article to motivate my analysis of a number of issues which promise to play a central role in evaluating the strengths and weaknesses of various network models. Rumelhart and Zipser (1985) analyse a type of learning model which is called a *competitive learning* model. They acknowledge that competitive learning models have been intensively studied for some time and thus conclude that "it seems reasonable to put the whole issue into historical perspective " (p.76). They also note that "It is a common practice to handcraft networks to carry out particular tasks. Whenever one creates such a network that performs a task rather successfully, the question arises as to how such a network might have evolved. The word perception model developed in McClelland and Rumelhart (1981) and Rumelhart and McClelland (1982) is one such case in point. That model offers rather detailed accounts of a variety of word perception experiments, but it was crafted to do its job. How could it have evolved naturally? Could a competitive learning mechanism create such a network?" (p.98). Thus these authors ask how a competitive learning network can be joined to an interactive activation network in order to endow the latter type of network with a learning capability.

Their discussion does not, however, acknowledge that both the levels and the interactions of a competitive learning model are incompatible with those of an interactive activation model (Grossberg, 1984). The authors likewise do not state that the particular competitive learning model which they have primarily analysed is identical to the model introduced and analysed in Grossberg (1976a, 1976b), nor that this model was consistently embedded into an adaptive resonance model in Grossberg (1976c) and later developed in Grossberg (1978) to articulate the key functional properties which McClelland and Rumelhart described when they introduced the interactive activation model in McClelland and Rumelhart (1981). In summary, the stated goal of Rumelhart and Zipser (1985)—to join a competitive learning model with a model capable of generating functional properties that are shared with the interactive activation model—was carried out using an adaptive resonance model in Grossberg (1978). In addition, the interactive activation model *as a model* is incapable of participating in such a synthesis.

The Rumelhart and Zipser (1985) article thus raises a number of the issues which make real-time network models so difficult to understand and to differentiate. How can an adaptive resonance model share functional properties with an interactive activation model, yet be mechanistically consistent with a competitive learning model with which the interactive activation model is mechanistically inconsistent? What design principles are realized by an adaptive resonance model but not by an interactive activation model which can be used to distinguish these models on a deep computational level? The analysis of Rumelhart and Zipser (1985) provides no light into these matters. Indeed, these authors also stated that "our analyses differ from many of these [former analyses] in that we focus on the development of feature detectors rather than pattern classification" (p.76). A glance at such titles as Malsburg (1973) and Grossberg (1976a, 1976b) shows that this observation is also inaccurate.

5. The Problem of Temporally Unstable Learning

Analysis of the competitive learning model revealed a fundamental problem which is shared by most other learning models that are now being developed and which was overcome by the adaptive resonance theory. I will now illustrate this general problem using a competitive learning model, before indicating that adaptive variants of the interactive activation model cannot solve it.

The particular competitive learning models described in Grossberg (1976b) and in Rumelhart and Zipser (1985) were used to show how a stream of input patterns to a network level F_1 can adaptively tune the weights, or long term memory (LTM) traces, in the pathways from F_1 to a coding level F_2. Although these LTM traces may initially be randomly chosen, the presentation of inputs at F_1 can alter the LTM traces through learning in such a way that F_2 eventually parses the input patterns into sets which activate distinct recognition categories. Appendix 1 describes this competitive learning scheme as well as the formal identity of the Grossberg (1976b) model with the model studied by Rumelhart and Zipser (1985).

In Grossberg (1976b), a theorem was proved which described input environments to which the model responds by learning a temporally stable recognition code. This theorem is described in Appendix 2. The theorem proved that, if not too many input patterns are presented to F_1, relative to the number of coding nodes in F_2, or if the input patterns form not too many clusters, then learning of the recognition code eventually stabilizes. In addition, the learning process elicits the best distribution of LTM traces that is consistent with the structure of the input environment. The computer simulations of Rumelhart and Zipser (1985) essentially confirm this theorem.

Despite the demonstration of input environments that can be stably coded, it was also shown, through explicit counterexamples, that a competitive learning model cannot learn a temporally stable code in response to arbitrary input environments. Moreover, these counterexamples included input environments that could easily occur in many important applications. In these counterexamples, as a list of input patterns perturbed level F_1 through time, the response of level F_2 to the *same* input pattern could be different on each successive presentation of that input pattern. Moreover, the F_2 response to a given input pattern might never settle down as learning proceeded.

Such unstable learning in response to a prescribed input is due to the learning that occurs in response to the other, intervening, inputs. In other words, the network's adaptability, or plasticity, enables prior learning to be washed away by more recent learning in response to a wide variety of input environments. Carpenter and Grossberg (1987a, 1987b) have extended this instability analysis by describing infinitely many input environments in which periodic presentation of just four input patterns can cause temporally unstable learning. This instability problem is not, moreover, peculiar to competitive learning models. As I shall indicate below, it is a problem of almost all learning models that are now being developed.

6. The Stability-Plasticity Dilemma: Self-Stabilized Learning in a Complex and Changing Environment

This instability problem was too fundamental to be ignored. In addition to showing that learning could become unstable in response to a complex input environment, the analysis also showed that learning could all too easily become unstable due to simple changes in an input environment. Changes in the probabilities of inputs, or in the deterministic sequencing of inputs, could readily wash away prior learning.

The seriousness of this problem can be dramatized by imagining that you have grown up in Boston before moving to Los Angeles, but periodically return to Boston to visit your parents. Although you may need to learn many new things to enjoy life in Los Angeles, these new learning experiences do not prevent you from knowing how to find your parent's house or otherwise remembering Boston. A multitude of similar examples illustrate that we are designed to successfully adapt to environments whose rules may change—without necessarily forgetting our old skills. Moreover, we are designed to successfully adapt to environments whose rules may change *unpredictably*, and can do so even if no one tells us that the environment has changed. We can adapt, in short, without a teacher, and through a direct confrontation with our experiences. Such adaptation is called *self-organization* in the network modeling literature.

The instability of the competitive learning model thus emphasized the fundamental nature of the *stability-plasticity dilemma* (Grossberg, 1980, 1982a, 1982b): How can a learning system be designed to remain plastic in response to significant new events, yet also remain stable in response to irrelevant events? How does the system know how to switch between its stable and its plastic modes in order to prevent the relentless degradation of its learned codes by the "blooming buzzing confusion" of irrelevant experience? How can it do so without using a teacher? The problem addresses one of the key capabilities that makes a human cognitive system so remarkable: its ability to learn internal representations of awesome amounts of the widest possible variety of environmental stimuli in real-time and without a teacher. The stability-plasticity dilemma articulates one sense in which a cognitive system is *universal*. Unlike the individual senses, which are specialized to deal with particular classes of inputs, a cognitive system is designed to integrate unanticipated combinations of events from all the senses into coherent moments of resonant recognition.

Rumelhart and Zipser (1985) were able to ignore this fundamental issue by considering simple input environments whose probabilistic rules do not change through time. Other modelers, for example Kohonen (1984), have stabilized learning in their applications of the competitive learning model by externally shutting off plasticity before the learned code can be erased. This approach creates the danger of shutting off plasticity too soon, in which case important information is not learned, or too late, in which case important learned information can be erased. The only way to overcome instability using this approach in an unpredictable input environment is to assume that the observer, or teacher, who shuts off plasticity is omniscient. If a model of an omniscient teacher is available, however, then you will not also need a model of a potentially unstable learning process.

Yet other modelers, such as Ackley, Hinton, and Sejnowski (1985), Hopfield (1982), Knapp and Anderson (1984), McClelland and Rumelhart (1985), Rumelhart, Hinton, and Williams (1986), and Sejnowski and Rosenberg (1986), have stabilized their models by externally restricting the input environment. They thereby recaste the problem of model instability into one about model capacity: What sorts of restricted input environments can these models handle before their learned codes are washed away by the flux of input experience? None of these learning models has yet addressed the general instability problem that was articulated a decade ago.

7. The Incompatibility of the Competitive Learning and Interactive Activation Models: Letter and Word Levels Do Not Exist

Before outlining a solution of the stability-plasticity dilemma, I indicate the nature of the inconsistency between the competitive learning model and the interactive activation model. Both the levels and the interactions of the two models are incompatible.

In a competitive learning model, *all* interactions between levels are excitatory. The only inhibitory interactions occur within each level. By contrast, in the Rumelhart and McClelland (1982, p.61) model "Each letter node is assumed to activate all of those word nodes consistent with it and inhibit all other words nodes." Thus the two models postulate different types of interlevel interactions. The selective activations and inhibitions that are hypothesized to exist between consistent and inconsistent letter nodes and word nodes must obviously be learned. In Grossberg (1984), it was shown that such connections cannot be learned using competitive learning mechanisms. Thus the postulated connections from letter nodes to word nodes are inconsistent, in a fundamental way, with competitive learning mechanisms.

An equally serious issue concerns the fact that the letter level and the word level which are postulated in the interactive activation model do not exist either in a language learning model that is based upon competitive learning mechanisms or, I would claim, *in vivo*. Instead, these levels code what I have called *items* and *lists*, respectively (Cohen and Grossberg, 1986; Grossberg, 1978, 1982a, 1984, 1987b; Grossberg and Stone, 1986). This insight is hinted at in the simulations which Rumelhart and Zipser (1985) have performed on lists of letters. These simulations are inconsistent with the existence of a letter level and a word level because both letters and words can have representations on both levels F_1 and F_2.

The difference between levels built up from letters and words and levels built up from items and lists can begin to be appreciated through the following observations (Grossberg, 1984). McClelland and Rumelhart (1981) postulated that a stage of letter nodes precedes a stage of word nodes. They used these stages to discuss the processing of letters in 4-letter words. The hypothesis of separate stages for letter and word processing implies that letters are not also represented on the level of words of length four. In order to be of general applicability, these concepts should certainly be generalizable to words of length less than four, notably to 1-letter words such as A and I. A consistent extension of the McClelland and Rumelhart stages would require that those letters which are also words, such as A and I, are represented on both the letter level and the word level, whereas those letters which are not words, such as E and F, are represented only on the letter level. How this distinction could be learned by an unsupervised learning model remains unclear.

This problem of processing units is symptomatic of a more general difficulty. The letter and word levels contain only nodes that represent letters and words. What did these nodes represent before their respective letters and words were learned? Where will the nodes come from to represent the letters and words that the model individual has not yet learned? Are these nodes to be created *de novo*? They certainly cannot be created *de novo* within the five or six trials that enable a pseudoword to acquire many of the recognition characteristics of a word (Salasso, Shiffrin, and Feustel, 1984)? These concerns clarify the need to define a processing substrate that can represent the learned units of a subject's internal lexicon before, during, or after they are learned.

The assumption of separate letter and word levels also requires special assumptions to deal with various data, such as the data of Wheeler (1970) and Samuel, van Santen, and Johnston (1982, 1983) concerning the word superiority effect. If separate letter and word levels exist, then letters such as A and I which are also words should, as words, be able to prime their letter representations. In contrast, letters such as D and E which are not words should receive no significant priming from the word level. One might therefore expect easier recognition of A and I than of D and E. Wheeler (1970) showed that this is not the case.

The assumptions of separate letter and word levels could escape this contradiction by assuming that *all* letters can be recognized so much more quickly than words of length at least two that no priming whatsoever can be received from the word level before letter recognition is complete. This assumption seems to be incompatible with the word length data of Samuel, van Santen, and Johnston (1982, 1983). These authors showed that recognition improves if a letter is embedded in words of greater length. Thus a letter that is presented alone for a fixed time before a mask appears is recognized less well than a letter presented for the same amount of time in a word of length 2, 3, or 4. These data cast doubt on any explanation based on speed of processing alone, since they suggest that priming of letters due to multiletter words is effective.

In contrast, within a model which uses an item level and a list level, *all* familiar letters possess both item and list representations, not just letters such as A and I that are also words. Thus a model which uses an item level and a list level can readily explain the Wheeler (1970) data. An analysis of how item and list representations are built up led, in fact, to the prediction of a word length effect for words of lengths 1, 2, 3, and 4 (Grossberg, 1978, Section 41; reprinted in Grossberg, 1982a). Cohen and Grossberg (1986, 1987) describe computer simulations of how item and list levels interact.

8. Adaptive Resonance Theory: Self-Stabilization of Code Learning in an Arbitrary Input Environment

A formal analysis of how to overcome the learning instability experienced by a competitive learning model led to the introduction of an expanded theory, called adaptive resonance theory (ART), in Grossberg (1976c). This formal analysis showed that a certain type of top-down learned feedback and matching mechanism could significantly overcome the instability problem. It was also realized that top-down attentional mechanisms, which had earlier been discovered through an analysis of interactions between cognitive and reinforcement mechanisms (Grossberg, 1975), had the same properties as these code-stabilizing mechanisms. In other words, once it was recognized how to formally solve the instability problem, it also became clear that one did not need to invent any qualitatively new mechanisms to do so. One only needed to remember to include previously discovered attentional mechanisms! These additional mechanisms enable code learning to self-stabilize in response to an essentially arbitrary input environment. For a recent mathematical proof of this type of stability, see Carpenter and Grossberg (1987b).

The types of top-down effects, such as the "rich-get-richer" and "gang" effects, which McClelland and Rumelhart (1981) experimentally reported were predicted formal properties of the ART theory as developed in Grossberg (1978). Such properties are shared by many networks which undergo reciprocal bottom-up and top-down feedback exchanges. They arose in ART as predictions about the emergent properties of network architectures that were designed to guarantee self-stabilizing self-organization of cognitive recognition codes—the very properties that are absent from the interactive activation model. In addition to such properties, ART has by now been used to analyse and predict data about speech perception, word recognition and recall, visual perception, olfactory coding, classical and instrumental conditioning, decision making under risk, event related potentials, neural substrates of learning and memory, critical period termination, and amnesias (Banquet and Grossberg, 1987; Carpenter and Grossberg, 1987a, 1987b, 1987c; Cohen and Grossberg, 1986, 1987; Grossberg, 1982b, 1984, 1987a, 1987b; Grossberg and Gutowski, 1987; Grossberg and Levine, 1987; Grossberg and Stone, 1986a, 1986b). Thus ART has already demonstrated an explanatory and predictive competence as an interdisciplinary physical theory. It is now being developed both to expand its predictive range and to implement it in real-time hardware. In Sections 9–15, some properties of ART are outlined as a basis for comparisons with other learning models in the literature, such as the back propagation model. These comparisons delineate issues that could just as easily be raised in the evaluation of any network learning model.

9. Solving the Stability-Plasticity Dilemma Using Interacting Attentional and Orienting Systems

In addition to the bottom-up mechanisms of a competitive learning model, an ART system includes processes for learning of top-down expectancies, or templates; for matching bottom-up input patterns with top-down expectancies; and for releasing orienting reactions in a mismatch situation, thereby leading to rapid updating, or reset, of short term memory as the network carries out a hypothesis testing scheme that searches for and, if necessary, leads to learning of a better representation of the input pattern (Figure 1).

Using these mechanisms, an ART system can generate recognition codes adaptively, and without a teacher, in response to a series of environmental inputs. As learning procceeds, interactions between the inputs and the system generate new steady states, or equilibrium points. The steady states are formed as the system discovers and learns *critical feature patterns*, or prototypes, that represent invariants of the set of all experienced input patterns. These learned codes are dynamically buffered, or stabilized, against relentless recoding by irrelevant inputs. The formation of steady states is internally controlled using mechanisms that suppress possible sources of system instability.

An ART system can adaptively switch between its stable and plastic modes. It is capable of plasticity in order to learn about significant new events, yet it can also remain stable in response to irrelevant events. In order to make this distinction, an ART system is sensitive to *novelty*. It is capable, without a teacher, of distinguishing between familiar and unfamiliar events, as well as between expected and unexpected events.

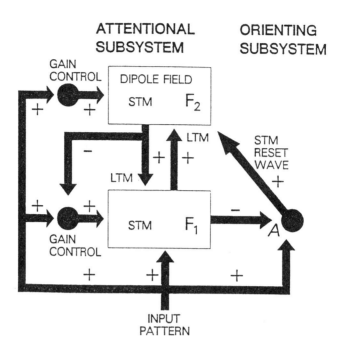

Figure 1. Anatomy of the attentional-orienting system: Two successive stages, F_1 and F_2, of the attentional subsystem encode patterns of activation in short term memory (STM). Bottom-up and top-down pathways between F_1 and F_2 contain adaptive long term memory (LTM) traces which multiply the signals in these pathways. The remainder of the circuit modulates these STM and LTM processes. Modulation by gain control enables F_1 to distinguish between bottom-up input patterns and top-down priming, or template, patterns, as well as to match these bottom-up and top-down patterns. Gain control signals also enable F_2 to react supraliminally to signals from F_1 while an input pattern is on. The orienting subsystem generates a reset wave to F_2 when mismatches between bottom-up and top-down patterns occur at F_1. This reset wave selectively and enduringly inhibits active F_2 cells until the input is shut off. (Reprinted with permission from Carpenter and Grossberg, 1987b.)

Multiple interacting memory systems are needed to monitor and adaptively react to the novelty of events without an external teacher. Within ART, interactions between two functionally complementary subsystems are used to process familiar and unfamiliar events. Familiar events are processed within an attentional subsystem, which is built up from a competitive learning network. The attentional subsystem establishes ever more precise internal representations of and responses to familiar events. It also learns the top-down expectations that help to stabilize the learned bottom-up codes of familiar events. As described above, however, the attentional subsystem is unable simultaneously to maintain stable representations of familiar categories and to create new categories for unfamiliar patterns in certain input environments. An isolated attentional subsystem can become either too rigid and incapable of creating new categories for unfamiliar patterns, or too unstable and capable of ceaselessly recoding the categories of familiar patterns as the statistics of the input environment change.

The second subsystem is an orienting subsystem that resets the attentional subsystem when an unfamiliar event occurs. Interactions between the attentional subsystem and the orienting subsystem help to express whether a novel pattern is familiar and well represented by an existing recognition code, or unfamiliar and in need of a new recognition code (Figure 1). Within an ART system, attentional mechanisms play a major role in self-stabilizing the learning of an emergent recognition code. A mechanistic analysis of the role of attention in learning has led Carpenter and Grossberg (1987a, 1987b) to distinguish between four types of attentional mechanism: attentional priming, attentional gain control, attentional vigilance, and intermodality competition (see Figure 4).

10. Self-Scaling Computational Units, Self-Adjusting Memory Search, Direct Access, and Attentional Vigilance

Four properties are basic to the workings of an ART network. Violating any one of these properties prevents the network from learning well in certain input environments. Essentially all other learning models violate one or more of these properties.

A. Self-Scaling Computational Units: Critical Feature Patterns

Properly defining signal and noise in a self-organizing system raises a number of subtle issues. Pattern context must enter the definition so that input features which are treated as irrelevant noise when they are embedded in a given input pattern may be treated as informative signals when they are embedded in a different input pattern. The system's unique learning history must also enter the definition so that portions of an input pattern which are treated as noise when they perturb a system at one stage of its self-organization may be treated as signals when they perturb the same system at a different stage of its self-organization. The present systems automatically self-scale their computational units to embody context- and learning-dependent definitions of signal and noise.

One property of these self-scaling computational units is illustrated in Figure 2. In Figure 2a, each of the two input patterns is composed of three features. The patterns agree at two of the three features, but disagree at the third feature. A mismatch of one out of three features may be designated as informative by the system. When this occurs, these mismatched features are treated as signals which can elicit learning of distinct recognition codes for the two patterns. Moreover, the mismatched features, being informative, are incorporated into these distinct recognition codes through the learning process.

In Figure 2b, each of the two input patterns is composed of thirty-one features. The patterns are constructed by adding identical subpatterns to the two patterns in Figure 2a. Thus the input patterns in Figure 2b disagree at the same features as the input patterns in Figure 2a. In the patterns of Figure 2b, however, this mismatch is less important, other things being equal, than in the patterns of Figure 2a. Consequently, the system may treat the mismatched features as noise. A single recognition code may be learned to represent both of the input patterns in Figure 2b. The mismatched features would not be learned as part of this recognition code because they are treated as noise.

The assertion that *critical feature patterns* are the computational units of the code learning process summarizes this self-scaling property. The term *critical feature* indicates that not all features are treated as signals by the system. The learned units are *patterns* of critical features because the perceptual context in which the features are embedded influences which features will be processed as signals and which features will be processed as noise. Thus a feature may be a critical feature in one pattern (Figure 2a) and an irrelevant noise element in a different pattern (Figure 2b).

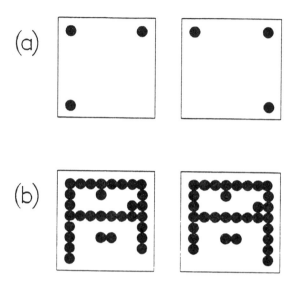

Figure 2. Self-scaling property discovers critical features in a context-sensitive way: (a) Two input patterns of 3 features mismatch at 1 feature. When this mismatch is sufficient to generate distinct recognition codes for the two patterns, the mismatched features are encoded in LTM as part of the critical feature patterns of these recognition codes. (b) Identical subpatterns are added to the two input patterns in (a). Although the new input patterns mismatch at the same one feature, this mismatch may be treated as noise due to the additional complexity of the two new patterns. Both patterns may thus learn to activate the same recognition code. When this occurs, the mismatched feature is deleted from LTM in the critical feature pattern of the code.

B. Self-Adjusting Memory Search

No pre-wired search algorithm, such as a search tree, can maintain its efficiency as a knowledge structure evolves due to learning in a unique input environment. A search order that may be optimal in one knowledge domain may become extremely inefficient as that knowledge domain becomes more complex due to learning.

An ART system is capable of a parallel memory search that adaptively updates its search order to maintain efficiency as its recognition code becomes arbitrarily complex due to learning. This self-adjusting search mechanism is part of the network design whereby the learning process self-stabilizes by engaging the orienting subsystem.

None of these mechanisms is akin to the rules of a serial computer program. Instead, the circuit architecture as a whole generates a self-adjusting search order and self-stabilization as emergent properties that arise through sy stem interactions. Once the ART architecture is in place, a little randomness in the initial values of its memory traces, rather than a carefully wired search tree, enables the search to carry on until the recognition code self-stabilizes.

C. Direct Access to Learned Codes

A hallmark of human recognition performance is the remarkable rapidity with which familiar objects can be recognized. The existence of many learned recognition codes for alternative experiences does not necessarily interfere with rapid recognition of an unambiguous familiar event. This type of rapid recognition is very difficult to understand using models wherein trees or other serial algorithms need to be searched for longer and longer periods as a learned recognition code becomes larger and larger.

In an ART model, as the learned code becomes globally self-consistent and predictively accurate, the search mechanism is automatically disengaged. Subsequently, no matter how large and complex the learned code may become, familiar input patterns *directly access*, or activate, their learned code, or category. Unfamiliar patterns can also directly access a learned category if they share invariant properties with the critical feature pattern of the category. In this sense, the critical feature pattern acts as a prototype for the entire category. As in human pattern recognition experiments, a "prototype" input pattern that perfectly matches a learned critical feature pattern may be better recognized than any of the "exemplar" input patterns that gave rise to the critical feature pattern (Posner, 1973; Posner and Keele, 1968, 1970). Grossberg and Stone (1986a) have shown, moreover, that these direct access properties can be used to explain RT and error data from lexical decision and word familiarity experiments.

Unfamiliar input patterns which cannot stably access a learned category engage the self-adjusting search process in order to discover a network substrate for a new recognition category. After this new code is learned, the search process is automatically disengaged and direct access ensues.

We use the term critical feature pattern, rather than prototype, because critical feature patterns are learned, matched, and regulate future learning in a manner different from classical prototype models. Estes (1986) compared several types of category learning models in the light of recent data and showed that exemplar models, prototype models, and exemplar similarity models all have their merits. An ART model can also be sensitive to exemplars, prototypes, or similarity between exemplars, depending upon the experimental conditions. One factor that mediates between these alternatives is now summarized.

D. Environment as a Teacher: Modulation of Attentional Vigilance

Although an ART system self-organizes its recognition code, the environment can also modulate the learning process and thereby carry out a teaching role. This teaching role allows a system with a fixed set of feature detectors to function successfully in an environment which imposes variable performance demands. Different environments may demand either coarse discriminations or fine discriminations to be made among the same set of objects.

In an ART system, if an erroneous recognition is followed by an environmental disconfirmation, such as a punishment, then the system becomes more *vigilant*. This change in vigilance may be interpreted as a change in the system's attentional state which increases its sensitivity to mismatches between bottom-up input patterns and active top-down critical feature patterns. A vigilance change alters the size of a single parameter in the network. The interactions within the network respond to this parameter change by learning recognition codes that make finer distinctions. In other words, if the network erroneously groups together some input patterns, then negative reinforcement can help the network to learn the desired distinction by making the system more vigilant. The system then behaves *as if* it has a better set of feature detectors. Thus at a level of very high vigilance, a category may emerge that accepts only one exemplar. At lower levels of vigilance, similarity relationships among the accepted exemplars help to mold the category's emergent critical feature pattern. Different vigilance levels may, moreover, be imposed by environmental feedback in response to easy or difficult discriminations during the course of a single experiment or experience.

The ability of a vigilance change to alter the course of pattern recognition illustrates a theme that is common to a variety of neural processes: a one-dimensional parameter change that modulates a simple nonspecific neural process can have complex specific effects upon high-dimensional neural information processing.

11. Bottom-Up Adaptive Filtering and Contrast-Enhancement in Short Term Memory

The typical network reactions to a single input pattern I within a temporal stream of input patterns are now briefly summarized. Each input pattern may be the output pattern of a preprocessing stage. Different preprocessing is given, for example, to speech signals and to visual signals before the outcome of such modality-specific preprocessing ever reaches the attentional subsystem. The preprocessed input pattern I is received at the stage F_1 of an attentional subsystem. Pattern I is transformed into a pattern X of activation across the nodes, or abstract "feature detectors", of F_1 (Figure 3). The transformed pattern X is said to represent I in short term memory (STM). In F_1 each node whose activity is sufficiently large generates excitatory signals along pathways to target nodes at the next processing stage F_2. A pattern X of STM activities across F_1 hereby elicits a pattern S of output signals from F_1. When a signal from a node in F_1 is carried along a pathway to F_2, the signal is multiplied, or *gated*, by the pathway's long term memory (LTM) trace. The LTM gated signal (i.e., signal times LTM trace), not the signal alone, reaches the target node. Each target node sums up all of its LTM gated signals. In this way, pattern S generates a pattern T of LTM-gated and summed input signals to F_2 (Figure 4a). The transformation from S to T is called an *adaptive filter*.

The input pattern T to F_2 is quickly transformed by interactions among the nodes of F_2. These interactions contrast-enhance the input pattern T. The resulting pattern of activation across F_2 is a new pattern Y. The contrast-enhanced pattern Y, rather than the input pattern T, is stored in STM by F_2. These interactions also occur in a competitive learning model.

12. Top-Down Template Matching and Stabilization of Code Learning

As soon as the bottom-up STM transformation $X \rightarrow Y$ takes place, the STM activities Y in F_2 elicit a top-down excitatory signal pattern U back to F_1 (Figure 4b). Only sufficiently large STM activities in Y elicit signals in U along the feedback pathways $F_2 \rightarrow F_1$. As in the bottom-up adaptive filter, the top-down signals U are also gated by LTM traces and the LTM-gated signals are summed at F_1 nodes. The pattern U of output signals from F_2 hereby generates a pattern V of LTM-gated and summed input signals to F_1. The transformation from U to V is thus also an adaptive filter. The pattern V is called a *top-down template*, or *learned expectation*.

Two sources of input now perturb F_1: the bottom-up input pattern I which gave rise to the original activity pattern X, and the top-down template pattern V that resulted from activating X. The activity pattern X^* across F_1 that is induced by I and V taken together is typically different from the activity pattern X that was previously induced by I alone. In particular, F_1 acts to *match* V against I. The result of this matching process determines the future course of learning and recognition by the network.

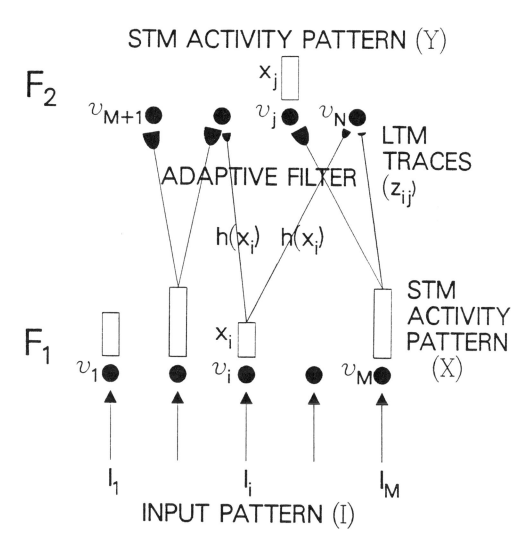

Figure 3. Stages of bottom-up activation: The input pattern I generates a pattern of STM activation X across F_1. Sufficiently active F_1 nodes emit bottom-up signals to F_2. This signal pattern S is gated by long term memory (LTM) traces within the $F_1 \rightarrow F_2$ pathways. The LTM gated signals are summed before activating their target nodes in F_2. This LTM-gated and summed signal pattern T generates a pattern of activation Y across F_2. The nodes in F_1 are denoted by $v_1, v_2, \ldots, v_M$. The nodes in F_2 are denoted by $v_{M+1}, v_{M+2}, \ldots v_N$. The input to node v_i is denoted by I_i. The STM activity of node v_i is denoted by x_i. The LTM trace of the pathway from v_i to v_j is denoted by z_{ij}.

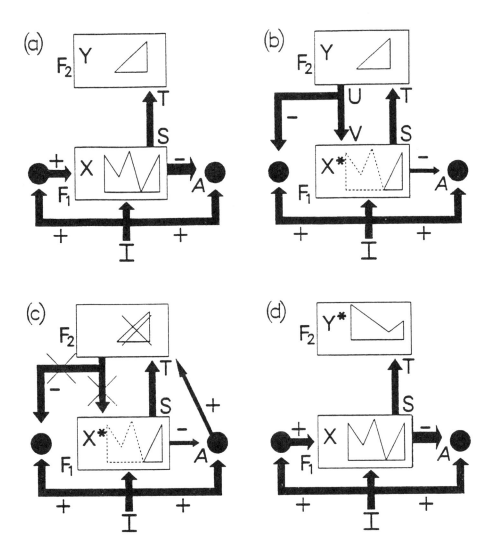

Figure 4. Search for a correct F_2 code: (a) The input pattern I generates the specific STM activity pattern X at F_1 as it nonspecifically activates A. Pattern X both inhibits A and generates the output signal pattern S. Signal pattern S is transformed into the input pattern T, which activates the STM pattern Y across F_2. (b) Pattern Y generates the top-down signal pattern U which is transformed into the template pattern V. If V mismatches I at F_1, then a new STM activity pattern X^* is generated at F_1. The reduction in total STM activity which occurs when X is transformed into X^* causes a decrease in the total inhibition from F_1 to A. (c) Then the input-driven activation of A can release a nonspecific arousal wave to F_2, which resets the STM pattern Y at F_2. (d) After Y is inhibited, its top-down template is eliminated, and X can be reinstated at F_1. Now X once again generates input pattern T to F_2, but since Y remains inhibited T can activate a different STM pattern Y^* at F_2. If the top-down template due to Y^* also mismatches I at F_1, then the rapid search for an appropriate F_2 code continues.

The entire activation sequence

$$I \to X \to S \to T \to Y \to U \to V \to X^* \tag{1}$$

takes place very quickly relative to the rate with which the LTM traces in either the bottom-up adaptive filter $S \to T$ or the top-down adaptive filter $U \to V$ can change. Even though none of the LTM traces changes during such a short time, their prior learning strongly influences the STM patterns Y and X* that evolve within the network by determining the transformations $S \to T$ and $U \to V$. I now sketch how a match or mismatch of I and V at F_1 regulates the course of learning in response to the pattern I, and in particular solves the stability-plasticity dilemma.

13. Interactions between Attentional and Orienting Subsystems: STM Reset and Search

In Figure 4a, an input pattern I generates an STM activity pattern X across F_1. The input pattern I also excites the orienting subsystem A, but pattern X at F_1 inhibits A before it can generate an output signal. Activity pattern X also elicits an output pattern S which, via the bottom-up adaptive filter, instates an STM activity pattern Y across F_2. In Figure 4b, pattern Y reads a top-down template pattern V into F_1. Template V mismatches input I, thereby significantly inhibiting STM activity across F_1. The amount by which activity in X is attenuated to generate X* depends upon how much of the input pattern I is encoded within the template pattern V.

When a mismatch attenuates STM activity across F_1, the total size of the inhibitory signal from F_1 to A is also attenuated. If the attenuation is sufficiently great, inhibition from F_1 to A can no longer prevent the arousal source A from firing. Figure 4c depicts how disinhibition of A releases an arousal burst to F_2 which equally, or nonspecifically, excites all the F_2 cells. The cell populations of F_2 react to such an arousal signal in a state-dependent fashion. In the special case that F_2 chooses a single population for STM storage, the arousal burst selectively inhibits, or resets, the active population in F_2. This inhibition is long-lasting. One physiological design for F_2 processing which has these properties is a *gated dipole field* (Grossberg, 1982a, 1987a). A gated dipole field consists of opponent processing channels which are gated by habituating chemical transmitters. A nonspecific arousal burst induces selective and enduring inhibition of active populations within a gated dipole field.

In Figure 4c, inhibition of Y leads to removal of the top-down template V, and thereby terminates the mismatch between I and V. Input pattern I can thus reinstate the original activity pattern X across F_1, which again generates the output pattern S from F_1 and the input pattern T to F_2. Due to the enduring inhibition at F_2, the input pattern T can no longer activate the original pattern Y at F_2. A new pattern Y* is thus generated at F_2 by I (Figure 4d).

The new activity pattern Y* reads-out a new top-down template pattern V*. If a mismatch again occurs at F_1, the orienting subsystem is again engaged, thereby leading to another arousal-mediated reset of STM at F_2. In this way, a rapid series of STM matching and reset events may occur. Such an STM matching and reset series controls the system's hypothesis testing and search of LTM by sequentially engaging the novelty-sensitive orienting subsystem. Although STM is reset sequentially in time via this mismatch-mediated, self-terminating LTM search process, the mechanisms which control the LTM search are all parallel network interactions, rather than serial algorithms. Such a parallel search scheme continuously adjusts itself to the system's evolving LTM codes. The LTM code depends upon both the system's initial configuration and its unique learning history, and hence cannot be predicted *a priori* by a pre-wired search algorithm. Instead, the mismatch-mediated engagement of the orienting subsystem realizes the type of self-adjusting search that was described in Section 10B.

The mismatch-mediated search of LTM ends when an STM pattern across F_2 reads-out a top-down template which matches I, to the degree of accuracy required by the level of attentional vigilance (Section 10D), or which has not yet undergone any prior learning. In the latter case, a new recognition category is then established as a bottom-up code and top-down template are learned.

14. Attentional Gain Control and Pattern Matching: The 2/3 Rule

The STM reset and search process described in Section 13 makes a paradoxical demand upon the processing dynamics of F_1: the *addition* of new excitatory top-down signals in the pattern V to the bottom-up signals in the pattern I causes a *decrease* in overall F_1 activity (Figures 4a and 4b). Some auxiliary mechanism must exist to distinguish between bottom-up and top-down inputs. This auxiliary mechanism is called *attentional gain control* to distinguish it from *attentional priming* by the top-down template V. While F_2 is active, the attentional priming mechanism delivers *excitatory specific learned* template patterns to F_1. Top-down attentional gain control has an *inhibitory nonspecific unlearned* effect on the sensitivity with which F_1 responds to the template pattern, as well as to other patterns received by F_1. The attentional gain control process enables F_1 to tell the difference between bottom-up and top-down signals.

In Figure 4a, during bottom-up processing, a suprathreshold node in F_1 is one which receives both a specific input from the input pattern I and a nonspecific attentional gain control input. In Figure 4b, during the matching of simultaneous bottom-up and top-down patterns, attentional gain control signals to F_1 are inhibited by the top-down channel. Nodes of F_1 must then receive sufficiently large inputs from both the bottom-up and the top-down signal patterns to generate suprathreshold activities. Nodes which receive a bottom-up input or a top-down input, but not both, cannot become suprathreshold: mismatched inputs cannot generate suprathreshold activities. Attentional gain control thus leads to a matching process whereby the addition of top-down excitatory inputs to F_1 can lead to an overall decrease in F_1's STM activity. Since, in each case, an F_1 node becomes active only if it receives large signals from two of the three input sources, we call this matching process the 2/3 Rule (Figure 5).

15. Stable Code Learning in an Arbitrary Input Environment

If an ART system violates the 2/3 Rule, there are infinitely many input sequences, each containing only four distinct patterns, that cannot be stably encoded (Carpenter and Grossberg, 1987b). It has also been mathematically proved that, when the 2/3 Rule is reinstated, the ART architecture self-organizes, self-stabilizes, and self-scales its learning of a recognition code in response to an arbitrary ordering of arbitrarily many, arbitrarily chosen binary input patterns (Carpenter and Grossberg, 1987b). Moreover, each of the LTM traces oscillates at most once through time as learning proceeds in response to any such environment. Thus learning in an ART architecture is remarkably stable. Figure 6

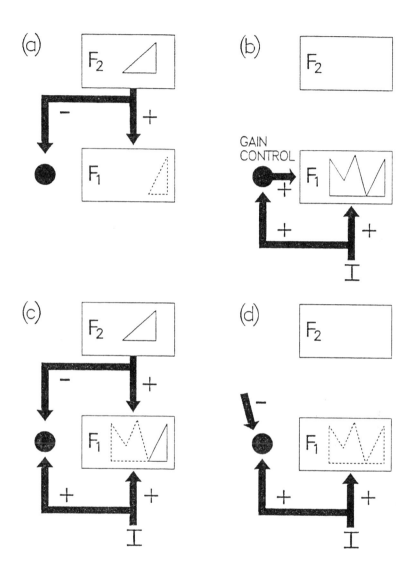

Figure 5. Matching by the 2/3 Rule: (a) A top-down template from F_2 inhibits the attentional gain control source as it subliminally primes target F_1 cells. (b) Only F_1 cells that receive bottom-up inputs and gain control signals can become supraliminally active. (c) When a bottom-up input pattern and a top-down template are simultaneously active, only those F_1 cells that receive inputs from both sources can become supraliminally active. (d) Intermodality inhibition can shut off the F_1 gain control source and thereby prevent a bottom-up input from supraliminally activating F_1. Similarly, disinhibition of the F_1 gain control source may cause a top-down prime to become supraliminal.

illustrates computer simulations of alphabet learning by an ART circuit. At two difference values of the vigilance parameter ρ, different numbers of recognition categories are learned. In both cases, code learning is complete and self-stabilizes in response to the 26 letters after only 3 trials.

Computer simulations of code learning using a coding level F_2 which carries out a multiple scale, distributed decomposition of its input patterns have also been carried out (Cohen and Grossberg, 1986, 1987). Such a design for F_2, and by extension for the higher coding levels $F_3, F_4, \ldots$ fed by F_2, is called a *masking field*. A masking field instantiates the *list level* that was described in Section 7. Such a network can simultaneously detect multiple groupings within its input patterns and assigns weights to the codes for these groupings which are predictive with respect to the contextual information embedded within the patterns and the prior learning of the system. A masking field automatically rescales its sensitivity as the overall size of an input pattern changes, yet also remains sensitive to the microstructure within each input pattern. In this way, such a network distinguishes between codes for pattern wholes and for pattern parts, yet amplifies the code for a pattern part when it becomes a pattern whole in a new input context. This capability is useful in speech recognition, visual object recognition, and cognitive information processing.

To achieve these properties, a masking field F_2 performs a new type of multiple scale analysis in which unpredictive list codes are competitively masked, or inhibited, and predictive codes are amplified in direct response to trainable signals from an adaptive filter $F_1 \rightarrow F_2$ that is activated by an input source F_1. An adaptive sharpening property obtains whereby a familiar input pattern causes a more focal spatial activation of its recognition code than an unfamiliar input pattern. The recognition code also becomes less distributed when an input pattern contains more information on which to base an unambiguous prediction of which input pattern is being processed. Thus a masking field suggests a solution of the credit assignment problem by embodying a real-time code for the predictive evidence contained within its input patterns. Such a network processing level can be used to build up an ART system $F_1 \leftrightarrow F_2 \leftrightarrow F_3 \leftrightarrow \ldots$ with any number of processing levels.

16. The Back Propagation and NETtalk Models

The ART architecture may be usefully compared with the back propagation (BP) model of Rumelhart, Hinton, and Williams (1986). The similarities and differences of these models highlight many of the types of formal comparisons that can help to evaluate other network learning models.

The BP model is a steepest descent algorithm in which each LTM trace, or weight, in the network is adjusted to minimize its contribution to the total mean square error between the desired and actual system outputs. Although steepest descent algorithms have a long history in technology and the neural modelling literature, the BP model has attracted widespread interest, partly because of the demonstration of Sejnowski and Rosenberg (1986), in which the BP algorithm is part of a system that learns to convert printed text into spoken language. Despite the appeal of this demonstration, the BP model does not model a brain process, as will be shown below. This shortcoming does not limit the model's possible value in technological applications, which can benefit from a steepest descent algorithm, but it undermines the model's usefulness in explaining behavioral or neural data.

The BP model is usually described as a three level model, with levels F_1, F_2, F_3, such that level F_2 is a level of "hidden units" between F_1 and F_3. The purpose of the model

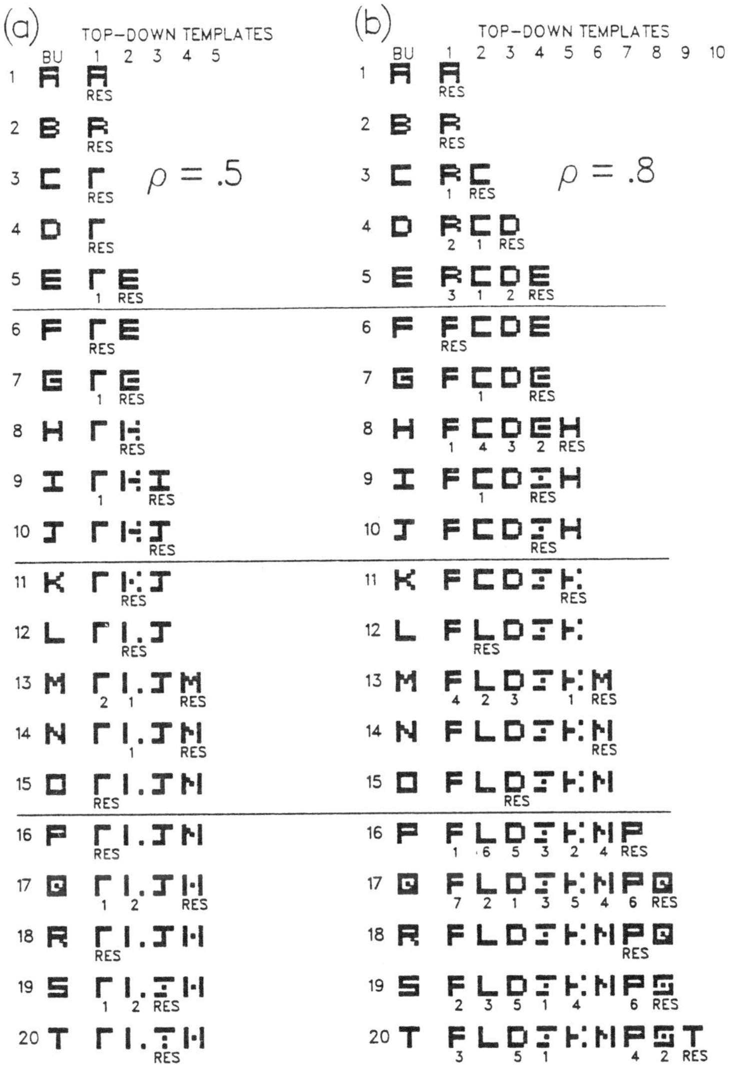

Figure 6. Alphabet learning: Code learning in response to the first presentation of the first 20 letters of the alphabet is shown. Two different vigilance levels were used, $\rho = .5$ and $\rho = .8$. Each row represents the total code that is learned after the letter at the left-hand column of the row is presented at F_1. Each column represents the critical feature pattern that is learned through time by the F_2 node listed at the top of the column. The critical feature patterns do not, in general, equal the pattern exemplars which change them through learning. Instead, each critical feature pattern acts like a prototype for the entire set of these exemplars, as well as for unfamiliar exemplars which share invariant properties with familiar exemplars. The simulation illustrates the "fast learning" case, in which the altered LTM traces reach a new equilibrium in response to each new stimulus. Slow learning is more gradual than this. (Reprinted with permission from Carpenter and Grossberg, 1987b.)

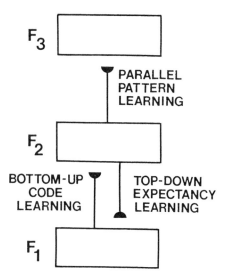

Figure 7. Self-organization of an associative map can be accomplished using a network with three levels F_1, F_2, and F_3. Levels F_1 and F_2 regulate learning within bottom-up pathways $F_1 \to F_2$ and top-down pathways $F_2 \to F_1$. This learning process discovers compressed recognition codes with invariant properties for the set of input patterns processed at F_1. Activation of these recognition codes at F_2 enables the activated sampling cells to learn output patterns at F_3. The total transformation $F_1 \to F_3$ defines the associative mapping.

is to learn an associative map between the input level F_1 and the output level F_3. The map is designed to be sufficiently distributed to allow alterations in the inputs at F_1 to generate appropriate alterations in the outputs at F_3. Such a possibility depends upon general projection properties of distributed associative maps (Kohonen, 1984). The key property demonstrated by computer simulations of the BP model is that it can learn a distributed associative map.

Some of the claims for the BP model have been based on comparisons with the early Perceptron model (Rosenblatt, 1962). Sejnowski and Rosenfeld (1986) have written that "until recently, learning in multilayered networks was an unsolved problem and considered by some impossible ... In a multilayered machine the internal, or hidden, units can be used as feature detectors which perform a mapping between input units and output units, and the difficult problem is to discover proper features." Carpenter and Grossberg (1986) note, in contrast, that learning an associative map using hidden units is an old problem with definite solutions in the neural modelling literature subsequent to the introduction of the Perceptron. Indeed, ART was developed in part to develop a theory of how learning of an associative map could proceed in a self-stabilizing fashion (Figure 7). A basic difference does, however, exist between models of associative map learning, such as ART and the BP model. The former model is self-organizing, whereas the BP model requires an external teacher.

The way in which this teacher works is what distinguishes the BP model from other types of steepest descent learning algorithms, such as the classical Adaline model (Widrow,

1962). The teaching algorithm is also what makes the BP model impossible as a model of a brain process. In addition to the levels F_1, F_2, and F_3 and the pathways $F_1 \to F_2 \to F_3$, the BP model also requires levels F_4, F_5, F_6, and F_7 as well as a complicated set of highly specific interactions between these levels and the rest of the network (Figure 8). These levels and interactions will now be described.

Inputs delivered to F_1 propagate forward through F_2 to F_3, where they generate the actual outputs of the network. The desired, or expected, outputs are independently delivered to level F_4 by an external teacher on every learning trial. The actual outputs are subtracted from the expected outputs at F_4 to generate error signals. These error signals propagate from F_4 to the $F_2 \to F_3$ pathways, where they change the weights in the $F_2 \to F_3$ pathways.

Back propagation proceeds as follows. The weights computed in the bottom-up $F_2 \to F_3$ pathways are *transported* to the top-down $F_4 \to F_5$ pathways. Once in these pathways, the differences between expected and real outputs at F_4 are multiplied by the transported weights within the $F_4 \to F_5$ pathways to generate weighted error signals that determine the inputs to F_5. These inputs activate F_5, which in turn generates output signals to the $F_1 \to F_2$ pathways. These output signals act as error signals which change the weights in the $F_1 \to F_2$ pathways.

Such a physical transport of weights has no plausible physical interpretation. The weights in the $F_2 \to F_3$ pathways must be computed *within* these pathways in order to multiply signals from F_2 to F_3. These weights cannot also exist *within* the pathways from F_4 to F_5 in order to multiply signals from F_4 to F_5 without being physically transported from $(F_2 \to F_3)$ to $(F_4 \to F_5)$ pathways, thereby violating basic properties of locality. Moreover, the levels F_3 and F_4 cannot be lumped together, because F_3 must record actual outputs, whereas F_4 must record differences between expected and actual outputs. The BP model is thus not a model of a brain process.

The computation of the error signal has an additional complexity. In addition to subtracting each actual output at F_3 from each expected output at F_4, the *derivative* of each actual output is also computed. The difference between each expected and actual output is multiplied by the corresponding derivative in addition to being multiplied by the corresponding transported weight. Thus there exist additional levels F_6 and F_7 at each layer for converting outputs into derivatives of outputs before signalling these derivatives, with great positional specificity, to the correct transported weights (Figure 8). This complex interaction scheme must be replicated at every stage of hidden units that is used in a BP model.

17. Comparing Adaptive Resonance and Back Propagation Models

Some BP mechanisms are evocative of ART mechanisms. The BP mechanisms do not, however, possess the key properties which endow an ART model with its computational power.

A. Stability

The learned code of the BP model is unstable in a complex environment. It keeps tracking whatever expected outputs are imposed from outside. An omniscient teacher would be needed to decide if the model had learned enough in response to an unpredictable input environment. The learned code of an ART model is self-stabilizing in an arbitrary input environment.

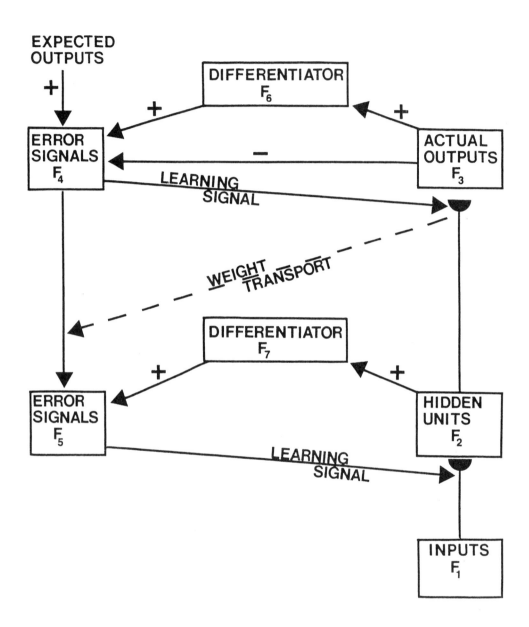

Figure 8. Circuit diagram of the back propagation model: In addition to the processing levels F_1, F_2, F_3, there are also levels F_4, F_5, F_6, and F_7 to carry out the computations which control the learning process. The transport of learned weights from the $F_2 \rightarrow F_3$ pathways to the $F_4 \rightarrow F_5$ pathways shows that this algorithm cannot represent a learning process in the brain.

B. Expectations as Exemplars or as Prototypes

Within a BP model, an expected or template pattern is imposed on every trial by an external teacher. Errors are computed by comparing each component of the expected output pattern with the corresponding component of the actual output pattern. There is no self-scaling property to alter the importance of each expected component when it is embedded in expected outputs of variable complexity. There is no concept of a critical feature pattern, or prototype. Instead, the expected pattern in a BP model is a particular exemplar at every stage of learning, rather than a prototype that gradually discovers invariant properties of all the exemplars that are ever experienced.

In contrast, an ART model learns its own expectations without a teacher. Because an ART model is self-scaling, it can learn critical feature patterns, or expected prototypes, by evaluating the predictive importance of particular features in input patterns of variable complexity at each stage of learning.

C. Weight Transport or Top-Down Template Learning

In both a BP model and an ART model, both bottom-up and top-down LTM traces exist. In a BP model (Figure 8), the top-down LTM traces in $F_4 \rightarrow F_5$ pathways are formal transports of the learned $F_2 \rightarrow F_3$ LTM traces. In an ART model (Figure 1), the top-down LTM traces in $F_2 \rightarrow F_1$ pathways are directly learned by a real-time associative process. These top-down LTM weights are not transports of the learned LTM traces in the $F_1 \rightarrow F_2$ pathways, and they need not equal these bottom-up LTM traces. Thus an ART model is designed so that both bottom-up learning and top-down learning are part of a single information processing hierarchy, which can be realized by a locally computable real-time process.

D. Matching to Alter Information Processing and/or to Regulate Learning

In both the BP model and an ART model, there exists a concept of matching. Within an ART model, matching both alters information processing and regulates the learning process. In particular, the 2/3 Rule (Section 14) enables a top-down expectation to sub-liminally sensitize the network in preparation for any exemplar of an expected class of input patterns, and to coherently deform such an exemplar, when it occurs, towards the prototype of the class. This STM transformation, also helps to regulate any learning that may be necessary to generate a globally self-consistent recognition code.

In contrast, matching within the BP model only changes LTM weights. It does not have any effects on the fast information processing that occurs within each input trial.

E. Learning an Associative Mapping

BP and ART provide different descriptions of how associative maps between seen language and spoken language are learned. Figure 9 describes a macrocircuit that schematizes our conception of this process (Cohen and Grossberg, 1986; Grossberg, 1978, 1986, 1987b; Grossberg and Stone, 1986a). The associative map $V^* \rightarrow \{A_4, A_5\}$ in Figure 9 joins seen language to spoken language. Unlike a BP model, all the learning of recognition codes that is triggered by auditory, visual, or motor patterns in Figure 9 is regulated by self-organizing mechanisms in reciprocal bottom-up and top-down adaptive filters. Once these codes self-stabilize their invariant recognition properties, the learning of associative maps between these code invariants can also proceed in a self-organizing fashion.

F. Speech Invariants, Coherence, and Perception

The NETtalk application of the back propagation algorithm (Sejnowski and Rosenberg, 1986) uses a familiar associative learning device: the number of nodes in F_1 and F_3 is chosen

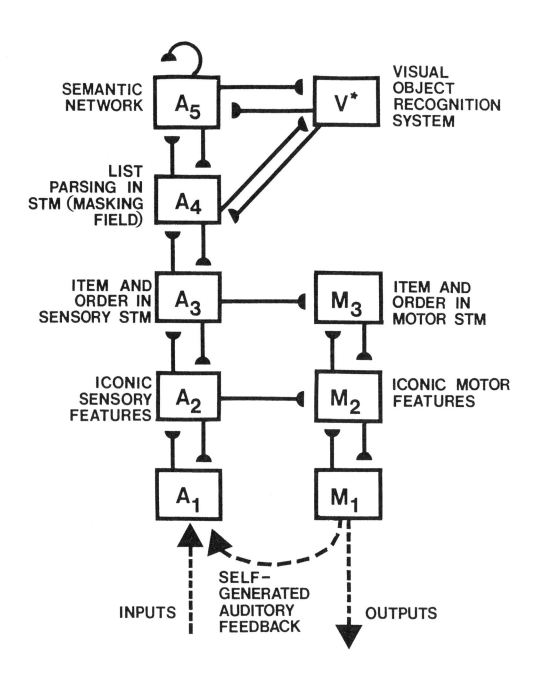

Figure 9. A macrocircuit governing self-organization of recognition and recall processes: Auditorily mediated language processes (the A_i), visual recognition processes (V^*), and motor control processes (the M_j) interact internally via conditionable pathways (black lines) and externally via environmental feedback (dotted lines) to self-organize the various processes which occur at the different network stages.

to be large enough to separate features of the inputs and outputs, thereby avoiding too much cross-talk in the associative map, but small enough to enable some generalization to occur among the distributed $F_1 \rightarrow F_3$ projections. In particular, the time between letter scans is represented in NETtalk by leaving some coding slots in F_1 empty. This mechanism does not generalize to a model capable of computing the temporal invariances of reading or speech perception.

The NETtalk model also makes the strong assumptions that exactly seven letter slots in F_1 correspond to a single, isolated phoneme slot in F_3, and that this isolated phoneme slot corresponds to the entry in the middle letter slot. These assumptions prevent the model from attempting to solve the fundamental problem of how speech sounds are coherently grouped in real-time. Furthermore, it is not clear how a phoneme-by-phoneme match between actual output and expected output could be realized during a learning episode *in vivo*.

In addition to assuming the automatic isolation, scaling, and centering of information, NETtalk also postulates that each phoneme slot in F_3 contains 23 separate nodes. These nodes provide enough spatial dimensions to represent a large number of articulatory features, such as point of articulation, voicing, vowel height, etc. Extra nodes are introduced to encode stress and syllable boundaries. The model builds in the transformations from visual input to F_1 nodal representation and from F_3 nodal representation to phoneme sound. Because the model automates all of its F_1 and F_3 representations, all questions about visual and speech perception, as such, lie outside its scope.

The ART speech model in Figure 9 was derived from postulates concerning real-time constraints on speech learning and perception. In particular, the model includes mechanisms capable of learning some speech invariants (Grossberg, 1986, 1987b), and the top-down expectancies between its processing levels have coherent grouping properties. One of the primary functions of such templates is to define and complete resonant contexts of features, no less than to generate error signals for self-regulating changes in associative weights.

In summary, the BP model suggests a new way to use steepest descent to learn associative maps between input and output environments which are statistically stationary and not too complex. Desirable properties of associative map learning are, however, shared by many associative learning models. Real-time network models must do more than learn an associative map or to store distributed codes for carefully controlled environments. Moreover, the use of an unphysical process such as weight transport in a model casts an unanswerable doubt over all empirical applications of the model.

18. Concluding Remarks

I conclude this essay with two general observations. The architectures of many popular learning and information processing models are often inadequate because they have not been constrained by the use of design principles whereby they could stably self-organize. Many models are actually incompatible with such constraints and some models utilize physically unrealizable formal mechanisms. Learning models which cannot adaptively cope with unpredictable changes in a complex environment have an unpromising future as models of mind and brain, and provide little hope of solving the outstanding cognitive problems which are not alredy well-handled by traditional methods of artificial intelligence and engineering.

Models which do embody self-organization constraints in a fundamental way have frequently been shown to have a broader explanatory and predictive range than models which do not. Thus an analysis of learning, in particular of the mechanisms capable of self-stabilizing competitive learning, can lead psychology from metaphorical models to integrative theories which functionally and mechanistically express both a psychological and a neural reality.

APPENDIX 1

Competitive Learning Models

Rumelhart and Zipser (1985, pp.86–87) summarize competitive learning models as follows.

"1. The units in a given layer are broken into a set of nonoverlapping clusters. Each unit within a cluster inhibits every other unit within a cluster. The clusters are winner-take-all, such that the unit receiving the largest input achieves its maximum value while all other units in the cluster are pushed to the minimum value. We have arbitrarily set the maximum value to 1 and the minimum value to 0.

2. Every element in every cluster receives inputs from the same lines.

3. A unit learns if and only if it wins the competition with other units in its cluster.

4. A stimulus pattern S_j consists of a binary pattern in which each element of the pattern is either *active* or *inactive*. An active element is assigned the value 1 and an inactive element is assigned the value 0.

5. Each unit has a fixed amount of weight (all weights are positive) which is distributed among its input lines. The weight on the line connecting unit i on the lower (or input) layer to unit j on the upper layer, is designated ω_{ij}. The fixed total amount of weight for unit j is designated $\sum_i \omega_{ij} = 1$. A unit learns by shifting weight from its inactive to its active input lines. If a unit does not respond to a particular pattern no learning takes place in that unit. If a unit wins the competition, then each of its input lines gives up some proportion g of its weight and that weight is then distributed equally among the active input lines. More formally, the learning rule we have studied is:

$$\Delta\omega_{ij} = \begin{cases} 0 & \text{if unit } j \text{ loses on stimulus } k \\ g\frac{c_{ik}}{n_k} - g\omega_{ij} & \text{if unit } j \text{ wins on stimulus } k \end{cases} \qquad (A1)$$

where c_{ik} is equal to 1 if in stimulus pattern S_k unit i on the lower layer is active and zero otherwise, and n_k is the number of active units in pattern S_k (thus

$$n_k = \sum_i c_{ik}).'' \qquad (A2)$$

Rumelhart and Zipser (1985, p.87) go on to say that "This learning rule was proposed by Von der Malsburg (1973). As Grossberg (1976) points out, renormalization of the weights is not necessary." Actually, this learning rule was proposed by Grossberg (1976a, 1976b), and is not the one used in the important article of Malsburg (1973), as I will show below.

A simple change of notation shows that the Rumelhart and Zipser (1985) model is identical with the Grossberg (1976a, 1976b) model. Equation (6) in Grossberg (1976b) is the learning equation

$$\frac{d}{dt}z_{ij} = (-z_{ij} + \theta_i)x_{2j}, \qquad (A3)$$

for the long term memory (LTM) trace z_{ij}. In (A3), x_{2j} is the activity of the jth unit. Activity $x_{2j} = 1$ if unit j wins the competition and $x_{2j} = 0$ if unit j loses the competition, as in equation (A1). In (A3),

$$\theta_i = \frac{I_i}{\sum_m I_m} \qquad (A4)$$

where I_i is the ith element of the input pattern. Function θ_i in (A4) is the same as function $c_{ik}n_k^{-1}$ in (A1) and (A2). Function θ_i is just the normalized input weight. The LTM trace z_{ij} in (A3) is identical with the weight ω_{ij} in (A1). The factor g in (A1) just rescales the time variable, and thus adds no generality to the model.

By contrast, the learning rule used by Malsburg (1973) is (in my notation)

$$\frac{d}{dt}z_{ij} = I_i x_{2j} \tag{A5}$$

subject to the constraint

$$\sum_m z_{mj} = \text{constant.} \tag{A6}$$

Thus Malsburg (1973) normalized the LTM traces z_{mj} which abut each unit j, not the input weights. The normalization constraint (A6) is, in fact, inconsistent with (A5) unless

$$\sum_m I_m = 0. \tag{A7}$$

Thus a rigorous application of Malsburg's 1973 learning rule forces the choice of both positive and negative inputs, unlike the Grossberg (1976b) model that was used by Rumelhart and Zipser (1985). In his computer simulations, Malsburg implemented equations (A5) and (A6) in alternating time slices. The implication shown in (A7) is then not forced because neither (A5) nor (A6) is true at all times.

Malsburg (1973) needed condition (A6) because he simplified the learning law

$$\frac{d}{dt}z_{ij} = -Az_{ij} + I_i x_{2j} \tag{A8}$$

which was used in the competitive learning model of Grossberg (1972). In fact, the equations used by Malsburg (1973) are identical to the equations used by Grossberg (1972) with this one exception. As Malsburg (1973, p.88) noted: "To answer these questions we have to write down the equations which govern the evolution of the system. They are summarized in Table 1 (compare Grossberg, 1972)." Term $-Az_{ij}$ in (A8) describes the decay of LTM. Malsburg's equation (A5) eliminates LTM decay. Since term $I_i x_{2j}$ is non-negative in these applications, the LTM trace in Malsburg's equation (A5) can only increase. Without additional constraints, all LTM traces could therefore explode to infinity. Malsburg (1973) partially overcame this problem with his constraint (A6). The solution in equation (A3) was to preserve LTM decay (term $-Az_{ij}$) while normalizing the inputs I_i to be learned. Then non-negative inputs I_i could freely be used, instead of inputs constrained by (A7).

Rumelhart and Zipser (1985) also mentioned and studied two related models. Equivalent models were introduced in Grossberg (1976b). These alternative models were designed to show that both of them also exhibit temporally unstable learning. Analysis of these variations of the simplest coding model confirmed that its unstable behavior was not an artifact of its simplicity.

Rumelhart and Zipser (1985) attributed one of these modified models to Bienenstock, Cooper, and Munro (1982). They noted that in such a model "a unit modulates its own sensitivity so that when it is not receiving enough inputs, it becomes increasingly sensitive. When it is receiving too many inputs, it decreases its sensitivity. This mechanism can be implemented in the present context by assuming that there is a threshold and that the relevant activation is the degree to which the unit exceeds its threshold. If, whenever a unit fails to win it decreases its threshold, and whenever it does win it increases its threshold, then this method will also make all of the units eventually respond, thereby engaging the mechanism of competitive learning" (Rumelhart and Zipser, 1985, p.100). In equations (23)–(24) of Grossberg (1976b), such a variable-threshold model was introduced without changing the basic learning equation

$$\frac{d}{dt}z_{ij} = (-z_{ij} + \theta_i)x_{2j}. \tag{A3}$$

The sensitivity of x_{2j} to its inputs was modified as follows:

$$x_{2j}(t) = \begin{cases} G_j(t) & \text{if } S_j(t)G_j(t) > \max\{S_k(t)G_k(t) : k \neq j\} \\ 0 & \text{if } S_j(t)G_j(t) < \max\{S_k(t)G_k(t) : k \neq j\} \end{cases} \tag{A9}$$

where

$$G_j(t) = g(1 - \int_0^t x_{2j}(v)K(t-v)dv), \tag{A10}$$

$S_j(t)$ is the total input to unit j, $g(w)$ is an increasing function such that $g(0) = 0$ and $g(1) = 1$, and $K(w)$ is a decreasing function such that $K(0) = 1$ and $K(\infty) = 0$; for example, $K(w) = e^{-w}$.

The history-dependent threshold is the term

$$\int_0^t x_{2j}(v)K(t-v)dv \tag{A11}$$

in equation (A10). If unit j wins the competition then, by (A9), its activity x_{2j} becomes positive. Consequently, its threshold (A11) increases. If unit j loses the competition then, by (A9), its activity x_{2j} equals zero. Consequently, its threshold (A11) decreases. Thus, "a unit modulates its own sensitivity so that when it is not receiving enough inputs, it becomes increasingly sensitive." By (A9) and (A10), when a unit wins the competition, its activation level $G_j(t)$ "is the degree to which the unit exceeds its threshold." Moreover, by (A3), the learning rate covaries with the activation $G_j(t)$ of unit j. Thus if unit j is active for a long time, then its threshold (A11) becomes large, so its learning rate (A10) becomes small. The converse is also true: inactivity increases sensitivity and learning rate.

In the limiting case where the threshold in (A11) equals zero for all time because $K \equiv 0$, this learning model reduces to the simplest competitive learning model. This can be seen as follows. If the threshold is set equal to zero, then $G_j(t) \equiv 1$ in (A10). Hence, by (A9),

$$x_{2j}(t) = \begin{cases} 1 & \text{if } S_j(t) > \max\{S_k : k \neq j\} \\ 0 & \text{if } S_j(t) < \max\{S_k : k \neq j\} \end{cases}. \tag{A12}$$

In other words $x_{2j}(t) = 1$ if unit j wins the competition, and $x_{2j}(t) = 0$ if unit j loses the competition, as in equation (A1).

Thus the model summarized by equations (A3), (A9), and (A10) has all the properties described by Rumelhart and Zipser (1985) for a variable-threshold model and includes the simplest competitive learning model as a special case. In Grossberg (1976b, p.132), it was noted that "Such a mechanism is inadequate if the training schedule allows v_{2j} [unit j] to recover its maximal strength." I illustrated this inadequacy by displaying "an ordering of patterns that permits recoding of essentially all populations."

Bienenstock, Cooper, and Munro (1982) studied a formally analogous model with a history-dependent threshold. However, they restricted their analysis to coding by a *single* unit j. Grossberg (1982c, p.332), assumed the viewpoint of competitive learning and considered how that model behaves—in their coding application—when more than one coding unit j exists and the units compete with each other for activation. It was shown that persistent presentation of even a *single* input pattern could cause temporally unstable coding in this competitive learning situation. This crippling form of instability seems to rule out the use of history-dependent thresholds as a viable learning rule, at least if the thresholds can recover from unit inactivity, which is the main property cited in their favor by Rumelhart and Zipser (1985, p.100).

Rumelhart and Zipser (1985) call the third model variant that they study the *leaky learning* model. This model is a special case of the *partial contrast* model that was introduced in Grossberg (1976b, p.132), where it was pointed out that, using such a model, "There can...be a shift in the locus of maximal responsiveness even to a single pattern—that is, recoding." Rumelhart and Zipser (1985, p.100) consider this a good property, rather than a bad one: "This change has the property that it slowly moves the losing units into the region where the actual stimuli lie, at which point they begin to capture some units and the ordinary dynamics of competitive learning take over." These authors are willing to accept this instability property in order to avoid the even worse problem that "one of the units would have most of its weight on input lines that were never active, whereas another unit may have had most of its weight on lines common to all of the stimulus patterns. Since a unit never learns unless it wins, it is possible that one of the units will never win, and therefore never learn. This, of course, takes the competition out of competitive learning" (pp.98–99).

This scheme cannot, however, be fully effective without having catastrophic results on code stability. If the recoding is minor, then many nodes may remain unused and too many input patterns may be lumped together. In this case, the scheme cannot solve the problem for which it was introduced. Alternatively, major recoding may be allowed, but this property is just another way to describe a temporally unstable code.

The formal relationship between the leaky learning model and the partial contrast model is now summarized. In the leaky learning model, equation (A1) is replaced by

$$\Delta\omega_{ij} = \begin{cases} g_l \frac{c_{ik}}{n_k} - g_\omega \omega_{ij} & \text{if } j \text{ loses on stimulus } k \\ g_\omega \frac{c_{ik}}{n_k} - g_\omega \omega_{ij} & \text{if } j \text{ wins on stimulus } k \end{cases} \qquad (A13)$$

where

$$g_l \ll g_\omega. \qquad (A14)$$

In other words, slower learning occurs at losing units than at winning units. The leaky learning model is a variant of the partial contrast model. The partial contrast model continues to use the basic learning equation

$$\frac{d}{dt}z_{ij} = (-z_{ij} + \theta_i)x_{2j}. \qquad (A3)$$

However, x_{2j} is now defined by a partial contrast rule

$$x_{2j} = \begin{cases} \frac{f(S_j)}{\sum_{S_m > \epsilon} f(S_m)} & \text{if } S_j > \epsilon \\ 0 & \text{if } S_j < \epsilon \end{cases} \qquad (A15)$$

where $f(w)$ is an increasing function of the total input S_j to unit j, and ϵ is a non-negative threshold. By (A15), the learning rate is fastest at the node x_{2j} which receives the largest input S_j and is slower at other nodes, as in the leaky learning model. In summary, all of the types of models described by Rumelhart and Zipser (1985) were shown in Grossberg (1976b) to exhibit a basic problem of learning instability.

APPENDIX 2

Stable Code Learning for Sparse Input Patterns

To simplify notation, the simplest competitive learning model is defined again below: Let the input patterns $I_i(t)$ across nodes v_i in F_1 be immediately and perfectly normalized; that is, input $I_i(t) = \theta_i I(t)$ generates activity $x_i(t) = \theta_i$ at v_i. The signals from a node v_i in F_1 to nodes v_j in F_2 is chosen to be a linear function of the activity x_i. For simplicity, let the signal emitted by v_i equal θ_i. The competition across nodes v_j in F_2 normalizes the total activity to the value 1 for definiteness and rapidly chooses that node v_j for STM storage which receives the largest input; e.g., design F_2 as a cooperative-competitive feedback network with faster-than-linear or (properly chosen) sigmoid signal functions. These properties can be approximated by the simple rule that

$$x_j = \begin{cases} 1 & \text{if } T_j > \max\{\epsilon, T_k : k \neq j\} \\ 0 & \text{if } T_j < \max\{\epsilon, T_k : k \neq j\} \end{cases} \qquad (A16)$$

where the total input T_j to v_j is the inner product

$$T_j = \sum_{k \epsilon I} \theta_k z_{kj}. \qquad (A17)$$

The LTM traces in the $F_1 \to F_2$ pathways sample the pattern $\theta = (\theta_1, \theta_2, \ldots, \theta_n)$ of input signals only when their sampling cell is active. Thus

$$\frac{d}{dt} z_{ij} = \epsilon x_j (-z_{ij} + \theta_i). \qquad (A18)$$

This non-Hebbian associative law was introduced into the neural network literature in Grossberg (1969).

If a single pattern θ is practiced, it maximizes the input T_j to its coding cell v_j. Input T_j increases as the classifying vector $z_j = (z_{ij} : i\epsilon I)$ become parallel to θ and the length $\|z_j\|$ of z_j become normalized. Grossberg (1976b) also described circumstances under which a list of input patterns to F_1 could generate temporally stable learning capable of parsing these patterns into distinct recognition categories at F_2. It was proved that, if not too many input patterns are presented, relative to the number of coding nodes in F_2, or if the input patterns are grouped into not too many clusters, then the recognition code stabilizes and the classifying vectors approach the convex hull of the patterns which they code. The latter property shows that the classifying nodes ultimately receive maximal inputs consistent with the fact that the classifying vectors z_j can fluctuate in response to all the input patterns that they code.

To state this theorem, the following notation is convenient. A *partition* $\oplus_{j=1}^J P_j$ of a finite set P is a subdivision of P into nonoverlapping and exhaustive subsets P_j. The *convex hull* $H(P)$ of P is the set of all convex combinations of elements of P. Given a set $Q \subset P$, let $R = P - Q$ denote the elements of P that are not in Q. The distance between a vector p and a set of vectors Q, denoted by $\| p - Q \|$, is defined by $\| p - Q \| = \inf(\| p - Q \| : q \in Q)$.

Suppose that, at time t, the classifying vector $z_j(t) = (z_{ij}(t) : i \in I)$ codes the set of patterns $P_j(t)$; that is, node v_j in F_2 would be chosen if any pattern in $P_j(t)$ were presented at that time. Define $P_j^*(t) = P_j(t) \cup z_j(t)$ and $P^*(t) = U_{j=1}^J P_j^*(t)$.

Theorem (Stable Code Learning of Sparse Patterns)

Let the network practice any finite set $P = (\theta^{(l)} : l = 1, 2, \ldots, L)$ of input patterns. Suppose that at some time $t = T$, the partition $\oplus_{j=1}^{J} P_j(T)$ of P has the property that

$$\min(u \cdot v : u \in P_j(T), v \in P_j^*(T)) > \max(u \cdot v : u \in P_j(T), v \in P^*(T) - P_j^*(T)) \quad (A19)$$

for all $j = 1, 2, \ldots, J$. Then the network partitions the patterns P into the stable categories $P_j(T)$; that is,

$$P_j(t) = P_j(T) \quad (A20)$$

for all $j = 1, 2, \ldots, J$ and all $t \geq T$. In addition, learning maximizes the input to the classifying nodes; that is, the functions

$$D_j(t) = \| z_j(t) - H(P_j(t)) \| \quad (A21)$$

are monotone decreasing for all $j = 1, 2, \ldots, J$ and $t \geq T$. If, moreover, the patterns $P_j(T)$ are practiced in time intervals $[U_{jk}, V_{jk}]$, $k = 1, 2, \ldots$, such that

$$\sum_{k=1}^{\infty} (V_{jk} - U_{jk}) = \infty, \quad (A22)$$

then

$$\lim_{t \to \infty} D_j(t) = 0. \quad (A23)$$

Thus the theorem describes circumstances under which practice of input patterns in P can cause the classifying vectors z_j, which may have any initial distribution $z_j(0)$, to be separated well enough, as in (A19), to enable their later tuning to proceed, as in (A23), without disrupting the emergent partition $\oplus_{j=1}^{J} P_j(T)$ of the patterns P into recognition categories.

REFERENCES

Banquet, J.-P. and Grossberg, S., Probing cognitive processes through the structure of event-related potentials during learning: An experimental and theoretical analysis. *Applied Optics*, in press, 1987.

Bienenstock, E.L., Cooper, L.N., and Munro, P.W., Theory for the development of neuron selectivity: Orientation specificity and binocular interaction in visual cortex. *Journal of Neuroscience*, 1982, **2**, 32–48.

Carpenter, G.A. and Grossberg, S., Associative learning, adaptive pattern recognition, and cooperative-competitive decision making by neural networks. In H. Szu (Ed.), **Hybrid and optical computing**. SPIE Proceedings, 1986.

Carpenter, G.A. and Grossberg, S., Neural dynamics of category learning and recognition: Attention, memory consolidation, and amnesia. In J. Davis, R. Newburgh, and E. Wegman (Eds.), **Brain structure, learning, and memory**. AAAS Symposium Series, 1987 (a).

Carpenter, G.A. and Grossberg, S., A massively parallel architecture for a self-organizing neural pattern recognition machine. *Computer Vision, Graphics, and Image Processing*, 1987, **37**, 54–115 (b).

Carpenter, G.A. and Grossberg, S., Neural dynamics of category learning and recognition: Structural invariants, reinforcement, and evoked potentials. In M.L. Commons, S.M. Kosslyn, and R.J. Herrnstein (Eds.), **Pattern recognition and concepts in animals, people, and machines**, 1987 (c).

Cohen, M.A. and Grossberg, S., Neural dynamics of speech and language coding: Developmental programs, perceptual grouping, and competition for short term memory. *Human Neurobiology*, 1986, **5**, 1–22.

Cohen, M.A. and Grossberg, S., Masking fields: A massively parallel neural architecture for learning, recognizing, and predicting multiple groupings of patterned data. *Applied Optics*, 1987, **26**, 1866–1891.

Estes, W.K., Memory storage and retrieval processes in category learning. *Journal of Experimental Psychology: General*, 1986, **115**, 155–174.

Grossberg, S., On learning and energy-entropy dependence in recurrent and nonrecurrent signed networks. *Journal of Statistical Physics*, 1969, **1**, 319–350.

Grossberg, S., Neural expectation: Cerebellar and retinal analogs of cells fired by learnable or unlearned pattern classes. *Kybernetik*, 1972, **10**, 49–57.

Grossberg, S., A neural model of attention, reinforcement, and discrimination learning. *International Review of Neurobiology*, 1975, **18**, 263–327.

Grossberg, S., On the development of feature detectors in the visual cortex with applications to learning and reaction-diffusion systems. *Biological Cybernetics*, 1976, **21**, 145–159 (a).

Grossberg, S., Adaptive pattern classification and universal recoding, I: Parallel development and coding of neural feature detectors. *Biological Cybernetics*, 1976, **23**, 121–134 (b).

Grossberg, S., Adaptive pattern classification and universal recoding, II: Feedback, expectation, olfaction, and illusions. *Biological Cybernetics*, 1976, **23**, 187–202 (c).

Grossberg, S., A theory of human memory: Self-organization and performance of sensory-motor codes, maps, and plans. In R. Rosen and F. Snell (Eds.), **Progress in theoretical biology, Vol. 5**. New York: Academic Press, 1978, pp.233-374.

Grossberg, S., How does a brain build a cognitive code? *Psychological Review*, 1980, **87**, 1-51.

Grossberg, S., **Studies of mind and brain: Neural principles of learning, perception, development, cognition, and motor control**. Boston: Reidel Press, 1982 (a).

Grossberg, S., Processing of expected and unexpected events during conditioning and attention: A psychophysiological theory. *Psychological Review*, 1982, **89**, 529-572 (b).

Grossberg, S., Associative and competitive principles of learning and development: The temporal unfolding and stability of STM and LTM patterns. In S.I. Amari and M. Arbib (Eds.), **Competition and cooperation in neural networks**. New York: Springer-Verlag, 1982 (c). Reprinted in Grossberg (1987a).

Grossberg, S., Unitization, automaticity, temporal order, and word recognition. *Cognition and Brain Theory*, 1984, **7**, 263-283.

Grossberg, S., The adaptive self-organization of serial order in behavior: Speech, language, and motor control. In E.C. Schwab and H.C. Nusbaum (Eds.), **Pattern recognition by humans and machines, Vol. 1: Speech perception**. New York: Academic Press, 1986.

Grossberg, S., **The adaptive brain, I: Cognition, learning, reinforcement, and rhythm**. Amsterdam: North-Holland, 1987 (a).

Grossberg, S., **The adaptive brain, II: Vision, speech, language, and motor control**. Amsterdam: North-Holland, 1987 (b).

Grossberg, S. and Gutowski, W., Neural dynamics of decision making under risk: Affective balance and cognitive-emotional interactions. *Psychological Review*, 1987, **94**, 300-318.

Grossberg, S. and Levine, D.S., Neural dynamics of attentionally modulated Pavlovian conditioning: Blocking, inter-stimulus interval, and secondary reinforcement. *Applied Optics*, in press, 1987.

Grossberg, S. and Stone, G.O., Neural dynamics of word recognition and recall: Attentional priming, learning, and resonance. *Psychological Review*, 1986, **93**, 46-74 (a).

Grossberg, S. and Stone, G.O., Neural dynamics of attention switching and temporal order information in short-term memory. *Memory and Cognition*, 1986, **14**, 451-468 (b).

Hopfield, J.J., Neural networks and physical systems with emergent collective computational abilities. *Proceedings of the National Academy of Sciences*, 1982, **79**, 2554-2558.

Knapp, A.G. and Anderson, J.A., Theory of categorization based on distributed memory storage. *Journal of Experimental Psychology: Learning, Memory, and Cognition*, 1984, **10**, 616-637.

Kohonen, T., **Self-organization and associative memory**. New York: Springer-Verlag, 1984.

Malsburg, C. von der, Self-organization of orientation sensitive cells in the striate cortex. *Kybernetik*, 1973, **14**, 85-100.

McClelland, J.L., Putting knowledge in its place: A scheme for programming parallel processing structures on the fly. *Cognitive Science*, 1985, **9**, 113–146.

McClelland, J.L. and Rumelhart, D.E., An interactive activation model of context effects in letter perception, Part I: An account of basic findings. *Psychological Review*, 1981, **88**, 375–407.

McClelland, J.L. and Rumelhart, D.E., Distributed memory and the representation of general and specific information. *Journal of Experimental Psychology: General*, 1985, **114**, 159–188.

Posner, M.I., **Cognition: An introduction**. Glenview, IL: Scott, Foresman, and Company, 1973.

Posner, M.I. and Keele, S.W., On the genesis of abstract ideas. *Journal of Experimental Psychology*, 1968, **77**, 353–363.

Posner, M.I. and Keele, S.W., Retention of abstract ideas. *Journal of Experimental Psychology*, 1970, **83**, 304–308.

Rosenblatt, F., **Principles of neurodynamics**. Washington, DC: Spartan Books, 1962.

Rumelhart, D.E., Hinton, G.E., and Williams, R.J., Learning internal representations by error propagation. **Institute for Cognitive Science Report 8506, UCSD**, September, 1985.

Rumelhart, D.E. and McClelland, J.L., An interactive activation model of context effects in letter perception, Part 2: The contextual enhancement effect and some tests and extensions of the model. *Psychological Review*, 1982, **89**, 60–94.

Rumelhart, D.E. and Zipser, D., Feature discovery by competitive learning. *Cognitive Science*, 1985, **9**, 75–112.

Salasoo, A., Shiffrin, R.M., and Feustal, T.C., Building permanent memory codes: Codification and repetition effects in word identification. *Journal of Experimental Psychology: General*, 1985, **114**, 50–77.

Samuel, A.G., van Santen, J.P.H., and Johnston, J.C., Length effects in word perception: We is better than I but worse than you or them. *Journal of Experimental Psychology: Human Perception and Performance*, 1982, **8**, 91–105.

Samuel, A.G., van Santen, J.P.H., and Johnston, J.C., Reply to Matthei: We really is worse than you or them, and so are ma and pa. *Journal of Experimental Psychology: Human Perception and Performance*, 1983, **9**, 321–322.

Sejnowski, T.J. and Rosenberg, C.R., NETtalk: A parallel-network that learns to read aloud. Johns Hopkins University, January, 1986.

Wheeler, D.D., Processes in word recognition. *Cognitive Psychology*, 1970, **1**, 59–85.

Widrow, B., Generalization and information storage in networks of Adaline neurons. In M.C. Yovits, G.T. Jacobi, and G.D. Goldstein (Eds.), **Self-organizing systems**. Washington, DC: Spartan Books, 1962.

Computer Vision, Graphics, and Image Processing
1987, **37**, 54–115
©1987 Academic Press, Inc.

A MASSIVELY PARALLEL ARCHITECTURE
FOR A SELF-ORGANIZING NEURAL PATTERN
RECOGNITION MACHINE

Gail A. Carpenter† and Stephen Grossberg‡

ABSTRACT

A neural network architecture for the learning of recognition categories is derived. Real-time network dynamics are completely characterized through mathematical analysis and computer simulations. The architecture self-organizes and self-stabilizes its recognition codes in response to arbitrary orderings of arbitrarily many and arbitrarily complex binary input patterns. Top-down attentional and matching mechanisms are critical in self-stabilizing the code learning process. The architecture embodies a parallel search scheme which updates itself adaptively as the learning process unfolds. After learning self-stabilizes, the search process is automatically disengaged. Thereafter input patterns directly access their recognition codes without any search. Thus recognition time does not grow as a function of code complexity. A novel input pattern can directly access a category if it shares invariant properties with the set of familiar exemplars of that category. These invariant properties emerge in the form of learned critical feature patterns, or prototypes. The architecture possesses a context-sensitive self-scaling property which enables its emergent critical feature patterns to form. They detect and remember statistically predictive configurations of featural elements which are derived from the set of all input patterns that are ever experienced. Four types of attentional process—priming, gain control, vigilance, and intermodal competition—are mechanistically characterized. Top-down priming and gain control are needed for code matching and self-stabilization. Attentional vigilance determines how fine the learned categories will be. If vigilance increases due to an environmental disconfirmation, then the system automatically searches for and learns finer recognition categories. A new nonlinear matching law (the 2/3 Rule) and new nonlinear associative laws (the Weber Law Rule, the Associative Decay Rule, and the Template Learning Rule) are needed to achieve these properties. All the rules describe emergent properties of parallel network interactions. The architecture circumvents the noise, saturation, capacity, orthogonality, and linear predictability constraints that limit the codes which can be stably learned by alternative recognition models.

---

† Supported in part by the Air Force Office of Scientific Research (AFOSR 85-0149 and AFOSR F49620-86-C-0037), the Army Research Office (ARO DAAG-29-85-K-0095), and the National Science Foundation (NSF DMS-84-13119).

‡ Supported in part by the Air Force Office of Scientific Research (AFOSR 85-0149 and AFOSR F49620-86-C-0037) and the Army Research Office (ARO DAAG-29-85-K0095).

1. Introduction: Self-Organization of Neural Recognition Codes

A fundamental problem of perception and cognition concerns the characterization of how humans discover, learn, and recognize invariant properties of the environments to which they are exposed. When such recognition codes spontaneously emerge through an individual's interaction with an environment, the processes are said to undergo *self-organization* (Basar, Flohr, Haken, and Mandell, 1983). This article develops a theory of how recognition codes are self-organized by a class of neural networks whose qualitative features have been used to analyse data about speech perception, word recognition and recall, visual perception, olfactory coding, evoked potentials, thalamocortical interactions, attentional modulation of critical period termination, and amnesias (Banquet and Grossberg, 1987; Carpenter and Grossberg, 1985a, 1985b, 1987a, 1987b; Grossberg, 1976a, 1976b, 1978a, 1980, 1986; Grossberg and Stone, 1986a, 1986b). These networks comprise the *adaptive resonance theory* (ART) which was introduced in Grossberg (1976b).

This article describes a system of differential equations which completely characterizes one class of ART networks. The network model is capable of self-organizing, self-stabilizing, and self-scaling its recognition codes in response to arbitrary temporal sequences of arbitrarily many input patterns of variable complexity. These formal properties, which are mathematically proven herein, provide a secure foundation for designing a real-time hardware implementation of this class of massively parallel ART circuits.

Before proceeding to a description of this class of ART systems, we summarize some of their major properties and some scientific problems for which they provide a solution.

A. Plasticity

Each system generates recognition codes adaptively in response to a series of environmental inputs. As learning procceeds, interactions between the inputs and the system generate new steady states and basins of attraction. These steady states are formed as the system discovers and learns *critical feature patterns*, or prototypes, that represent invariants of the set of all experienced input patterns.

B. Stability

The learned codes are dynamically buffered against relentless recoding by irrelevant inputs. The formation of steady states is internally controlled using mechanisms that suppress possible sources of system instability.

C. Stability-Plasticity Dilemma: Multiple Interacting Memory Systems

The properties of plasticity and stability are intimately related. An adequate system must be able to adaptively switch between its stable and plastic modes. It must be capable of plasticity in order to learn about significant new events, yet it must also remain stable in response to irrelevant or often repeated events. In order to prevent the relentless degradation of its learned codes by the "blooming, buzzing confusion" of irrelevant experience, an ART system is sensitive to *novelty*. It is capable of distinguishing between familiar and unfamiliar events, as well as between expected and unexpected events.

Multiple interacting memory systems are needed to monitor and adaptively react to the novelty of events. Within ART, interactions between two functionally complementary subsystems are needed to process familiar and unfamiliar events. Familiar events are processed within an attentional subsystem. This subsystem establishes ever more precise internal representations of and responses to familiar events. It also builds up the learned top-down expectations that help to stabilize the learned bottom-up codes of familiar events. By itself, however, the attentional subsystem is unable simultaneously to maintain stable representations of familiar categories and to create new categories for unfamiliar patterns.

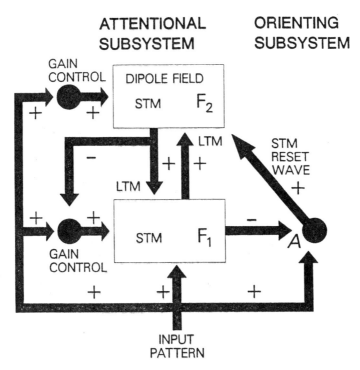

Figure 1. Anatomy of the attentional-orienting system: Two successive stages, F_1 and F_2, of the attentional subsystem encode patterns of activation in short term memory (STM). Bottom-up and top-down pathways between F_1 and F_2 contain adaptive long term memory (LTM) traces which multiply the signals in these pathways. The remainder of the circuit modulates these STM and LTM processes. Modulation by gain control enables F_1 to distinguish between bottom-up input patterns and top-down priming, or template, patterns, as well as to match these bottom-up and top-down patterns. Gain control signals also enable F_2 to react supraliminally to signals from F_1 while an input pattern is on. The orienting subsystem generates a reset wave to F_2 when mismatches between bottom-up and top-down patterns occur at F_1. This reset wave selectively and enduringly inhibits active F_2 cells until the input is shut off. Variations of this architecture are depicted in Figure 14.

An isolated attentional subsystem is either rigid and incapable of creating new categories for unfamiliar patterns, or unstable and capable of ceaselessly recoding the categories of familiar patterns in response to certain input environments.

The second subsystem is an orienting subsystem that resets the attentional subsystem when an unfamiliar event occurs. The orienting subsystem is essential for expressing whether a novel pattern is familiar and well represented by an existing recognition code, or unfamiliar and in need of a new recognition code. Figure 1 schematizes the architecture that is analysed herein.

D. Role of Attention in Learning

Within an ART system, attentional mechanisms play a major role in self-stabilizing the learning of an emergent recognition code. Our mechanistic analysis of the role of attention in learning leads us to distinguish between four types of attentional mechanism: attentional priming, attentional gain control, attentional vigilance, and intermodality competition. These mechanisms are characterized below.

E. Complexity

An ART system dynamically reorganizes its recognition codes to preserve its stability-plasticity balance as its internal representations become increasingly complex and differentiated through learning. By contrast, many classical adaptive pattern recognition systems become unstable when they are confronted by complex input environments. The instabilities of a number of these models are identified in Grossberg (1976a, 1978b, 1986). Models which become unstable in response to nontrivial input environments are not viable either as brain models or as designs for adaptive machines.

Unlike many alternative models (e.g., Anderson, Silverstein, Ritz, and Jones, 1977; Fukushima, 1980; Hopfield, 1982; Kohonen, 1977; McClelland and Rumelhart, 1985), the present model constraints arbitrary combinations of binary input patterns. In particular, it places no orthogonality or linear predictability constraints upon its input patterns. The model computations remain sensitive no matter how many input patterns are processed. The model does not require that very small, and thus noise-degradable, increments in memory be made in order to avoid saturation of its cumulative memory. The model can store arbitrarily many recognition categories in response to input patterns that are defined on arbitrarily many input channels. Its memory matrices need not be square, so that no restrictions on memory capacity are imposed by the number of input channels. Finally, all the memory of the system can be devoted to stable recognition learning. It is not he case that the number of stable classifications is bounded by some fraction of the number of input channels or patterns.

Thus a primary goal of the present article is to characterize neural networks capable of self-stabilizing the self-organization of their recognition codes in response to an arbitrarily complex environment of input patterns in a way that parsimoniously reconciles the requirements of plasticity, stability, and complexity.

2. Self-Scaling Computational Units, Self-Adjusting Memory Search, Direct Access, and Attentional Vigilance

Four properties are basic to the workings of the networks that we characterize herein.

A. Self-Scaling Computational Units: Critical Feature Patterns

Properly defining signal and noise in a self-organizing system raises a number of subtle issues. Pattern context must enter the definition so that input features which are treated as irrelevant noise when they are embedded in a given input pattern may be treated as informative signals when they are embedded in a different input pattern. The system's unique learning history must also enter the definition so that portions of an input pattern which are treated as noise when they perturb a system at one stage of its self-organization may be treated as signals when they perturb the same system at a different stage of its self-organization. The present systems automatically self-scale their computational units to embody context- and learning-dependent definitions of signal and noise.

One property of these self-scaling computational units is schematized in Figure 2. In Figure 2a, each of the two input patterns is composed of three features. The patterns agree at two of the three features, but disagree at the third feature. A mismatch of one out of three features may be designated as informative by the system. When this occurs, these mismatched features are treated as signals which can elicit learning of distinct recognition codes for the two patterns. Moreover, the mismatched features, being informative, are incorporated into these distinct recognition codes.

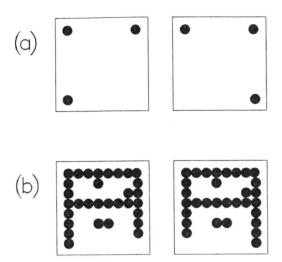

Figure 2. Self-scaling property discovers critical features in a context-sensitive way: (a) Two input patterns of 3 features mismatch at 1 feature. When this mismatch is sufficient to generate distinct recognition codes for the two patterns, the mismatched features are encoded in LTM as part of the critical feature patterns of these recognition codes. (b) Identical subpatterns are added to the two input patterns in (a). Although the new input patterns mismatch at the same one feature, this mismatch may be treated as noise due to the additional complexity of the two new patterns. Both patterns may thus learn to activate the same recognition code. When this occurs, the mismatched feature is deleted from LTM in the critical feature pattern of the code.

In Figure 2b, each of the two input patterns is composed of thirty-one features. The patterns are constructed by adding identical subpatterns to the two patterns in Figure 2a. Thus the input patterns in Figure 2b disagree at the same features as the input patterns in Figure 2a. In the patterns of Figure 2b, however, this mismatch is less important, other things being equal, than in the patterns of Figure 2a. Consequently, the system may treat the mismatched features as noise. A single recognition code may be learned to represent both of the input patterns in Figure 2b. The mismatched features would not be learned as part of this recognition code because they are treated as noise.

The assertion that *critical feature patterns* are the computational units of the code learning process summarizes this self-scaling property. The term *critical feature* indicates that not all features are treated as signals by the system. The learned units are *patterns* of critical features because the perceptual context in which the features are embedded influences which features will be processed as signals and which features will be processed as noise. Thus a feature may be a critical feature in one pattern (Figure 2a) and an irrelevant noise element in a different pattern (Figure 2b).

The need to overcome the limitations of featural processing with some type of contextually sensitive pattern processing has long been a central concern in the human pattern recognition literature. Experimental studies have led to the general conclusions that "The trace system which underlies the recognition of patterns can be characterized by a central tendency and a boundary" (Posner, 1973, p.54), and that "just listing features does not go far enough in specifying the knowledge represented in a concept. People also know something about the relations between the features of a concept, and about the variability that is permissible on any feature" (Smith and Medin, 1981, p.83). We illustrate herein how these properties may be achieved using self-scaling computational units such as critical feature patterns.

B. Self-Adjusting Memory Search

No pre-wired search algorithm, such as a search tree, can maintain its efficiency as a knowledge structure evolves due to learning in a unique input environment. A search order that may be optimal in one knowledge domain may become extremely inefficient as that knowledge domain becomes more complex due to learning.

The ART system considered herein is capable of a parallel memory search that adaptively updates its search order to maintain efficiency as its recognition code becomes arbitrarily complex due to learning. This self-adjusting search mechanism is part of the network design whereby the learning process self-stabilizes by engaging the orienting subsystem (Section 1C).

None of these mechanisms is akin to the rules of a serial computer program. Instead, the circuit architecture as a whole generates a self-adjusting search order and self-stabilization as emergent properties that arise through system interactions. Once the ART architecture is in place, a little randomness in the initial values of its memory traces, rather than a carefully wired search tree, enables the search to carry on until the recognition code self-stabilizes.

C. Direct Access to Learned Codes

A hallmark of human recognition performance is the remarkable rapidity with which familiar objects can be recognized. The existence of many learned recognition codes for alternative experiences does not necessarily interfere with rapid recognition of an unambiguous familiar event. This type of rapid recognition is very difficult to understand using models wherein trees or other serial algorithms need to be searched for longer and longer periods as a learned recognition code becomes larger and larger.

In an ART model, as the learned code becomes globally self-consistent and predictively accurate, the search mechanism is automatically disengaged. Subsequently, no matter how large and complex the learned code may become, familiar input patterns *directly access*, or activate, their learned code, or category. Unfamiliar patterns can also directly access a learned category if they share invariant properties with the critical feature pattern of the category. In this sense, the critical feature pattern acts as a prototype for the entire category. As in human pattern recognition experiments, an input pattern that matches a learned critical feature pattern may be better recognized than any of the input patterns that gave rise to the critical feature pattern (Posner, 1973; Posner and Keele, 1968, 1970).

Unfamiliar input patterns which cannot stably access a learned category engage the self-adjusting search process in order to discover a network substrate for a new recognition category. After this new code is learned, the search process is automatically disengaged and direct access ensues.

D. Environment as a Teacher: Modulation of Attentional Vigilance

Although an ART system self-organizes its recognition code, the environment can also modulate the learning process and thereby carry out a teaching role. This teaching role allows a system with a fixed set of feature detectors to function successfully in an environment which imposes variable performance demands. Different environments may demand either coarse discriminations or fine discriminations to be made among the same set of objects. As Posner (1973, pp.53–54) has noted:

> "If subjects are taught a tight concept, they tend to be very careful about classifying any particular pattern as an instance of that concept. They tend to reject a relatively small distortion of the prototype as an instance, and they rarely classify a pattern as a member of the concept when it is not. On the other hand, subjects learning high-variability concepts often falsely classify patterns as members of the concept, but rarely reject a member of the concept incorrectly...The situation largely determines which type of learning will be superior."

In an ART system, if an erroneous recognition is followed by negative reinforcement, then the system becomes more *vigilant*. This change in vigilance may be interpreted as a change in the system's attentional state which increases its sensitivity to mismatches between bottom-up input patterns and active top-down critical feature patterns. A vigilance change alters the size of a single parameter in the network. The *interactions* within the network respond to this parameter change by learning recognition codes that make finer distinctions. In other words, if the network erroneously groups together some input patterns, then negative reinforcement can help the network to learn the desired distinction by making the system more vigilant. The system then behaves *as if* it has a better set of feature detectors.

The ability of a vigilance change to alter the course of pattern recognition illustrates a theme that is common to a variety of neural processes: a one-dimensional parameter change that modulates a simple nonspecific neural process can have complex specific effects upon high-dimensional neural information processing.

Sections 3–7 outline qualitatively the main operations of the model. Sections 8–11 describe computer simulations which illustrate the model's ability to learn categories. Section 12 defines the model mathematically. The remaining sections characterize the model's properties using mathematical analysis and more computer simulations, with the model hypotheses summarized in Section 18.

3. Bottom-Up Adaptive Filtering and Contrast-Enhancement in Short Term Memory

We begin by considering the typical network reactions to a single input pattern I within a temporal stream of input patterns. Each input pattern may be the output pattern of a preprocessing stage. Different preprocessing is given, for example, to speech signals and to visual signals before the outcome of such modality-specific preprocessing ever reaches the attentional subsystem. The preprocessed input pattern I is received at the stage F_1 of an attentional subsystem. Pattern I is transformed into a pattern X of activation across the nodes, or abstract "feature detectors", of F_1 (Figure 3). The transformed pattern X represents a pattern in short term memory (STM). In F_1 each node whose activity is sufficiently large generates excitatory signals along pathways to target nodes at the next processing stage F_2. A pattern X of STM activities across F_1 hereby elicits a pattern S of output signals from F_1. When a signal from a node in F_1 is carried along a pathway to F_2, the signal is multiplied, or *gated*, by the pathway's long term memory (LTM) trace. The LTM-gated signal (i.e., signal times LTM trace), not the signal alone, reaches the target node. Each target node sums up all of its LTM-gated signals. In this way, pattern S generates a pattern T of LTM-gated and summed input signals to F_2 (Figure 4a). The transformation from S to T is called an *adaptive filter*.

The input pattern T to F_2 is quickly transformed by interactions among the nodes of F_2. These interactions contrast-enhance the input pattern T. The resulting pattern of activation across F_2 is a new pattern Y. The contrast-enhanced pattern Y, rather than the input pattern T, is stored in STM by F_2.

A special case of this contrast-enhancement process is one in which F_2 chooses the node which receives the largest input. The chosen node is the only one that can store activity in STM. In general, the contrast enhancing transformation from T to Y enables more than one node at a time to be active in STM. Such transformations are designed to simultaneously represent in STM several groupings, or chunks, of an input pattern (Cohen and Grossberg, 1986, 1987a, 1987b; Grossberg, 1978a, 1986). When F_2 is designed to make a choice in STM, it selects that global grouping of the input pattern which is preferred by the adaptive filter. This process automatically enables the network to partition all the input patterns which are received by F_1 into disjoint sets of recognition categories, each corresponding to a particular node (or "pointer," or "index") in F_2. Such a categorical mechanism is both interesting in itself and a necessary prelude to the analysis of recognition codes in which multiple groupings of X are simultaneously represented by Y. In the example that is characterized in this article, level F_2 is designed to make a choice.

All the LTM traces in the adaptive filter, and thus all learned past experiences of the network, are used to determine the recognition code Y via the transformation $I \to X \to S \to T \to Y$. However, only those nodes of F_2 which maintain stored activity in the STM pattern Y can elicit new learning at contiguous LTM traces. Because the recognition code Y is a more contrast-enhanced pattern than T, many F_2 nodes which receive positive inputs ($I \to X \to S \to T$) may not store any STM activity ($T \to Y$). The LTM traces in pathways leading to these nodes thus influence the recognition event but are not altered by the recognition event. Some memories which influence the focus of attention are not themselves attended.

4. Top-Down Template Matching and Stabilization of Code Learning

As soon as the bottom-up STM transformation $X \to Y$ takes place, the STM activities Y in F_2 elicit a top-down excitatory signal pattern U back to F_1 (Figure 4b). Only sufficiently large STM activities in Y elicit signals in U along the feedback pathways $F_2 \to F_1$. As in the bottom-up adaptive filter, the top-down signals U are also gated by LTM traces and the LTM-gated signals are summed at F_1 nodes. The pattern U of output signals from F_2 hereby generates a pattern V of LTM-gated and summed input signals to F_1. The transformation from U to V is thus also an adaptive filter. The pattern V is called a *top-down template*, or *learned expectation*.

Two sources of input now perturb F_1: the bottom-up input pattern I which gave rise to the original activity pattern X, and the top-down template pattern V that resulted from activating X. The activity pattern X^* across F_1 that is induced by I and V taken together is typically different from the activity pattern X that was previously induced by I alone. In particular, F_1 acts to match V against I. The result of this matching process determines the future course of learning and recognition by the network.

The entire activation sequence

$$I \to X \to S \to T \to Y \to U \to V \to X^* \tag{1}$$

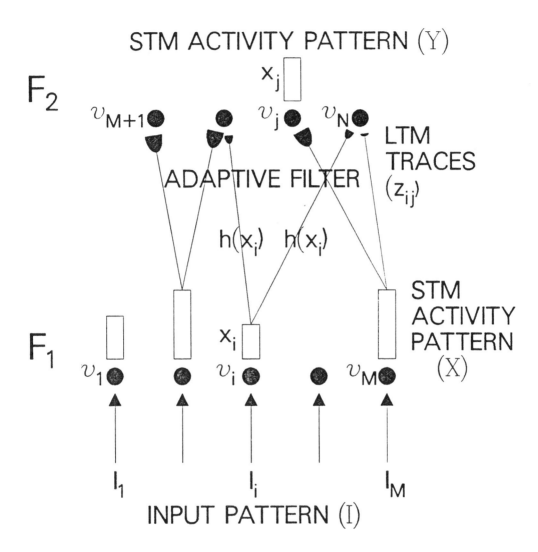

Figure 3. Stages of bottom-up activation: The input pattern I generates a pattern of STM activation X across F_1. Sufficiently active F_1 nodes emit bottom-up signals to F_2. This signal pattern S is gated by long term memory (LTM) traces within the $F_1 \rightarrow F_2$ pathways. The LTM gated signals are summed before activating their target nodes in F_2. This LTM-gated and summed signal pattern T generates a pattern of activation Y across F_2. The nodes in F_1 are denoted by $v_1, v_2, \ldots, v_M$. The nodes in F_2 are denoted by $v_{M+1}, v_{M+2}, \ldots v_N$. The input to node v_i is denoted by I_i. The STM activity of node v_i is denoted by x_i. The LTM trace of the pathway from v_i to v_j is denoted by z_{ij}.

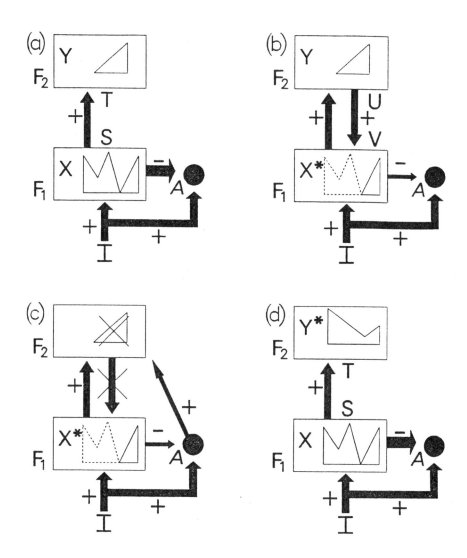

Figure 4. Search for a correct F_2 code: (a) The input pattern I generates the specific STM activity pattern X at F_1 as it nonspecifically activates A. Pattern X both inhibits A and generates the output signal pattern S. Signal pattern S is transformed into the input pattern T, which activates the STM pattern Y across F_2. (b) Pattern Y generates the top-down signal pattern U which is transformed into the template pattern V. If V mismatches I at F_1, then a new STM activity pattern X^* is generated at F_1. The reduction in total STM activity which occurs when X is transformed into X^* causes a decrease in the total inhibition from F_1 to A. (c) Then the input-driven activation of A can release a nonspecific arousal wave to F_2, which resets the STM pattern Y at F_2. (d) After Y is inhibited, its top-down template is eliminated, and X can be reinstated at F_1. Now X once again generates input pattern T to F_2, but since Y remains inhibited T can activate a different STM pattern Y^* at F_2. If the top-down template due to Y^* also mismatches I at F_1, then the rapid search for an appropriate F_2 code continues.

takes place very quickly relative to the rate with which the LTM traces in either the bottom-up adaptive filter $S \to T$ or the top-down adaptive filter $U \to V$ can change. Even though none of the LTM traces changes during such a short time, their prior learning strongly influences the STM patterns Y and X^* that evolve within the network by determining the transformations $S \to T$ and $U \to V$. We now discuss how a match or mismatch of I and V at F_1 regulates the course of learning in response to the pattern I, and in particular solves the stability-plasticity dilemma (Section 1C).

5. Interactions between Attentional and Orienting Subsystems: STM Reset and Search

In Figure 4a, an input pattern I generates an STM activity pattern X across F_1. The input pattern I also excites the orienting subsystem A, but pattern X at F_1 inhibits A before it can generate an output signal. Activity pattern X also elicits an output pattern S which, via the bottom-up adaptive filter, instates an STM activity pattern Y across F_2. In Figure 4b, pattern Y reads a top-down template pattern V into F_1. Template V mismatches input I, thereby significantly inhibiting STM activity across F_1. The amount by which activity in X is attenuated to generate X^* depends upon how much of the input pattern I is encoded within the template pattern V.

When a mismatch attenuates STM activity across F_1, the total size of the inhibitory signal from F_1 to A is also attenuated. If the attenuation is sufficiently great, inhibition from F_1 to A can no longer prevent the arousal source A from firing. Figure 4c depicts how disinhibition of A releases an arousal burst to F_2 which equally, or nonspecifically, excites all the F_2 cells. The cell populations of F_2 react to such an arousal signal in a state-dependent fashion. In the special case that F_2 chooses a single population for STM storage, the arousal burst selectively inhibits, or resets, the active population in F_2. This inhibition is long-lasting. One physiological design for F_2 processing which has these properties is a *gated dipole field* (Grossberg, 1980, 1984a). A gated dipole field consists of opponent processing channels which are gated by habituating chemical transmitters. A nonspecific arousal burst induces selective and enduring inhibition of active populations within a gated dipole field.

In Figure 4c, inhibition of Y leads to removal of the top-down template V, and thereby terminates the mismatch between I and V. Input pattern I can thus reinstate the original activity pattern X across F_1, which again generates the output pattern S from F_1 and the input pattern T to F_2. Due to the enduring inhibition at F_2, the input pattern T can no longer activate the original pattern Y at F_2. A new pattern Y^* is thus generated at F_2 by I (Figure 4d). Despite the fact that some F_2 nodes may remain inhibited by the STM reset property, the new pattern Y^* may encode large STM activities. This is because level F_2 is designed so that its total suprathreshold activity remains approximately constant, or normalized, despite the fact that some of its nodes may remain inhibited by the STM reset mechanism. This property is related to the limited capacity of STM. A physiological process capable of achieving the STM normalization property is based upon on-center off-surround feedback interactions among cells obeying membrane equations (Grossberg, 1980, 1983).

The new activity pattern Y^* reads-out a new top-down template pattern V^*. If a mismatch again occurs at F_1, the orienting subsystem is again engaged, thereby leading to another arousal-mediated reset of STM at F_2. In this way, a rapid series of STM matching and reset events may occur. Such an STM matching and reset series controls the system's search of LTM by sequentially engaging the novelty-sensitive orienting subsystem. Although STM is reset sequentially in time via this mismatch-mediated, self-terminating LTM search process, the mechanisms which control the LTM search are all parallel network interactions, rather than serial algorithms. Such a parallel search scheme continuously adjusts itself to the system's evolving LTM codes. In general, the spatial configuration of LTM codes depends upon both the system's initial configuration and its unique learning history, and hence cannot be predicted *a priori* by a pre-wired search algorithm. Instead, the mismatch-mediated engagement of the orienting subsystem realizes the type of self-adjusting search that was described in Section 2B.

The mismatch-mediated search of LTM ends when an STM pattern across F_2 reads-out a top-down template which matches I, to the degree of accuracy required by the level of attentional vigilance (Section 2D), or which has not yet undergone any prior learning. In the latter case, a new recognition category is then established as a bottom-up code and top-down template are learned.

6. Attentional Gain Control and Attentional Priming

Further properties of the top-down template matching process can be derived by considering its role in the regulation of attentional priming. Consider, for example, a situation in which F_2 is activated by a level other than F_1 before F_1 can be activated by a bottom-up input (Figure 5a). In such a situation, F_2 can generate a top-down template V to F_1. The level F_1 is then primed, or sensitized, to receive a bottom-up input that may or may not match the active expectancy. As depicted in Figure 5a, level F_1 can be primed to receive a bottom-up input without necessarily eliciting suprathreshold output signals in response to the priming expectancy.

On the other hand, an input pattern I must be able to generate a suprathreshold activity pattern X even if no top-down expectancy is active across F_1 (Figures 4a and 5b). How does F_1 know that it should generate a suprathreshold reaction to a bottom-up input pattern but not to a top-down input pattern? In both cases, excitatory input signals stimulate F_1 cells. Some auxiliary mechanism must exist to distinguish between bottom-up and top-down inputs. This auxiliary mechanism is called *attentional gain control* to distinguish it from *attentional priming* by the top-down template itself (Figure 5a). While F_2 is active, the attentional priming mechanism delivers *excitatory specific learned* template patterns to F_1. The attentional gain control mechanism has an *inhibitory nonspecific unlearned* effect on the sensitivity with which F_1 responds to the template pattern, as well as to other patterns received by F_1. The attentional gain control process enables F_1 to tell the difference between bottom-up and top-down signals.

7. Matching: The 2/3 Rule

A rule for pattern matching at F_1, called the 2/3 Rule, follows naturally from the distinction between attentional gain control and attentional priming. It says that two out of three signal sources must activate an F_1 node in order for that node to generate suprathreshold output signals. In Figure 5a, during top-down processing, or priming, the nodes of F_1 receive inputs from at most one of their three possible input sources. Hence no cells in F_1 are supraliminally activated by the top-down template. In Figure 5b, during bottom-up processing, a suprathreshold node in F_1 is one which receives both a specific input from the input pattern I and a nonspecific excitatory signal from the gain control channel. In

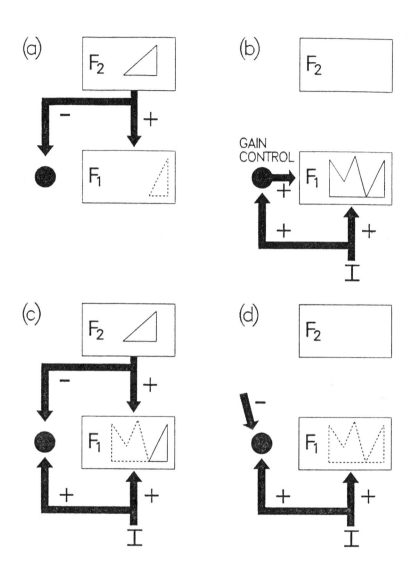

Figure 5. Matching by the 2/3 Rule: (a) A top-down template from F_2 inhibits the attentional gain control source as it subliminally primes target F_1 cells. (b) Only F_1 cells that receive bottom-up inputs and gain control signals can become supraliminally active. (c) When a bottom-up input pattern and a top-down template are simultaneously active, only those F_1 cells that receive inputs from both sources can become supraliminally active. (d) Intermodality inhibition can shut off the F_1 gain control source and thereby prevent a bottom-up input from supraliminally activating F_1. Similarly, disinhibition of the F_1 gain control source may cause a top-down prime to become supraliminal.

Figure 5c, during the matching of simultaneous bottom-up and top-down patterns, the nonspecific gain control signal to F_1 is inhibited by the top-down channel. Nodes of F_1 which receive sufficiently large inputs from both the bottom-up and the top-down signal patterns generate suprathreshold activities. Nodes which receive a bottom-up input or a top-down input, but not both, cannot become suprathreshold: mismatched inputs cannot generate suprathreshold activities. Attentional gain control thus leads to a matching process whereby the addition of top-down excitatory inputs to F_1 can lead to an overall decrease in F_1's STM activity (Figures 4a and 4b). Figure 5d shows how competitive interactions across modalities can prevent F_1 from generating a supraliminal reaction to bottom-up signals when attention shifts from one modality to another.

8. Code Instability and Code Stability

The importance of using the 2/3 Rule for matching is now illustrated by describing how its absence can lead to a temporally unstable code (Figure 6a). The system becomes unstable when the inhibitory top-down attentional gain control signals (Figure 5c) are too small for the 2/3 Rule to hold at F_1. Larger attentional gain control signals restore code stability by reinstating the 2/3 Rule (Figure 6b). Figure 6b also illustrates how a novel exemplar can directly access a previously established category; how the category in which a given exemplar is coded can be influenced by the categories which form to encode very different exemplars; and how the network responds to exemplars as coherent groupings of features, rather than to isolated feature matches or mismatches.

Code Instability Example

In Figure 6, four input patterns, A, B, C, and D, are periodically presented in the order ABCAD. Patterns B, C, and D are all subsets of A. The relationships among the inputs that make the simulation work are as follows: $D \subset C \subset A$; $B \subset A$; $B \cap C = \phi$; and $|D| < |B| < |C|$, where $|I|$ denotes the number of features in input pattern I. The choice of input patterns in Figure 6 is thus one of infinitely many examples in which, without the 2/3 Rule, an alphabet of four input patterns cannot be stably coded.

The numbers $1, 2, 3, \ldots$ listed at the left in Figure 6 itemize the presentation order. The next column, labeled BU for Bottom-Up, describes the input pattern that was presented on each trial. Each Top-Down Template column corresponds to a different node in F_2. If M nodes $v_1, v_2, \ldots, v_M$ exist in F_1, then the F_2 nodes are denoted by $v_{M+1}, v_{M+2}, \ldots v_N$. Column 1 corresponds to node v_{M+1}, column 2 corresponds to node v_{M+2}, and so on. Each row summarizes the network response to its input pattern. The symbol RES, which stands for *resonance*, designates the node in F_2 which codes the input pattern on that trial. For example, v_{M+2} codes pattern C on trial 3, and v_{M+1} codes pattern B on trial 7. The patterns in a given row describe the templates after learning has equilibrated on that trial.

In Figure 6a, input pattern A is periodically recoded. On trial 1, it is coded by v_{M+1}; on trial 4, it is coded by v_{M+2}; on trial 6, it is coded by v_{M+1}; on trial 9, it is coded by v_{M+2}. This alternation in the nodes v_{M+1} and v_{M+2} which code pattern A repeats indefinitely.

Violation of the 2/3 Rule occurs on trials 4, 6, 8, 9, and so on. This violation is illustrated by comparing the template of v_{M+2} on trials 3 and 4. On trial 3, the template of v_{M+2} is coded by pattern C, which is a subset of pattern A. On trial 4, pattern A is presented and directly activates node v_{M+2}. Since the inhibitory top-down gain control is

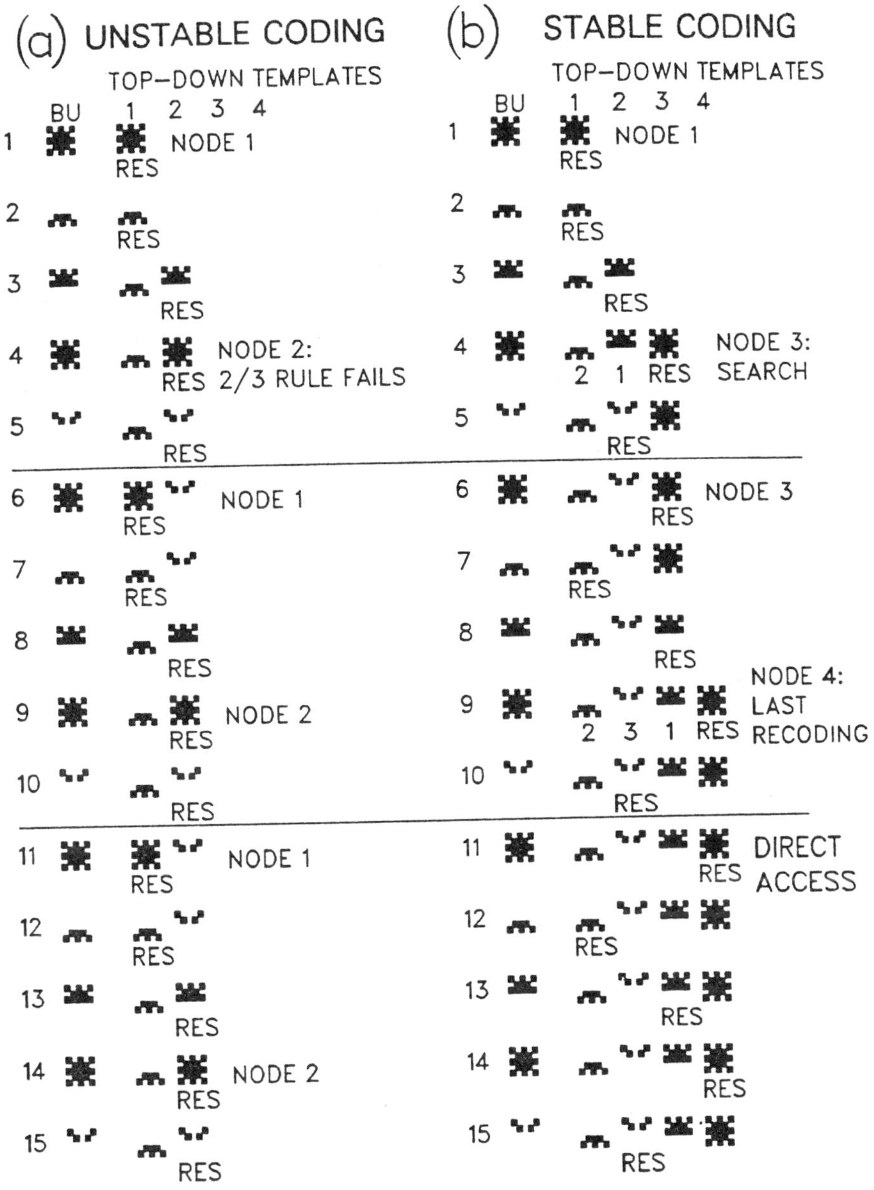

Figure 6. Stabilization of categorical learning by the 2/3 Rule: In both (a) and (b), four input patterns A, B, C, and D are presented repeatedly in the list order ABCAD. In (a), the 2/3 Rule is violated because the top-down inhibitory gain control mechanism is weak (Figure 5c). Pattern A is periodically coded by v_{M+1} and v_{M+2}. It is never coded by a single stable category. In (b), the 2/3 Rule is restored by strengthening the top-down inhibitory gain control mechanism. After some initial recoding during the first two presentations of ABCAD, all patterns directly access distinct stable categories. A black square in a template pattern designates that the corresponding top-down LTM trace is large. A blank square designates that the LTM trace is small.

too weak to quench the mismatched portion of the input, pattern A remains supraliminal in F_1 even after the template C is read-out from v_{M+2}. No search is elicited by the mismatch of pattern A and its subset template C. Consequently the template of v_{M+2} is recoded from pattern C to its superset pattern A.

Code Stability Example

In Figure 6b, the 2/3 Rule does hold because the inhibitory top-down attentional gain control channel is strengthened. Thus the network experiences a sequence of recodings that ultimately stabilizes. In particular, on trial 4, node v_{M+2} reads-out the template C, which mismatches the input pattern A. Here, a search is initiated, as indicated by the numbers beneath the template symbols in row 4. First, v_{M+2}'s template C mismatches A. Then v_{M+1}'s template B mismatches A. Finally A activates the uncommitted node v_{M+3}, which resonates with F_1 as it learns the template A.

In Figure 6b, pattern A is coded by v_{M+1} on trial 1; by v_{M+3} on trials 4 and 6; and by v_{M+4} on trial 9. Note that the self-adjusting search order in response to A is different on trials 4 and 9 (Section 2B). On all future trials, input pattern A is coded by v_{M+4}. Moreover, all the input patterns A, B, C, and D have learned a stable code by trial 9. Thus the code self-stabilizes by the second run through the input list ABCAD. On trials 11 through 15, and on all future trials, each input pattern chooses a different code $(A \rightarrow v_{M+4}; B \rightarrow v_{M+1}; C \rightarrow v_{M+3}; D \rightarrow v_{M+2})$. Each pattern belongs to a separate category because the vigilance parameter (Section 2D) was chosen to be large in this example. Moreover, after code learning stabilizes, each input pattern directly activates its node in F_2 without undergoing any additional search (Section 2C). Thus after trial 9, only the "RES" symbol appears under the top-down templates. The patterns shown in any row between 9 and 15 provide a complete description of the learned code.

Examples of how a novel exemplar can activate a previously learned category are found on trials 2 and 5 in Figures 6a and 6b. On trial 2 pattern B is presented for the first time and directly accesses the category coded by v_{M+1}, which was previously learned by pattern A on trial 1. In other words, B activates the same categorical "pointer," or "marker," or "index" as A. In so doing, B may change the categorical template, which determines which input patterns will also be coded by this index on future trials. The category does not change, but its invariants may change.

9. Using Context to Distinguish Signal from Noise in Patterns of Variable Complexity

The simulation in Figure 7 illustrates how, at a fixed vigilance level, the network automatically rescales its matching criterion in response to inputs of variable complexity (Section 2A). On the first four trials, the patterns are presented in the order ABAB. By trial 2, coding is complete. Pattern A directly accesses node v_{M+1} on trial 3, and pattern B directly accesses node v_{M+2} on trial 4. Thus patterns A and B are coded by different categories. On trials 5–8, patterns C and D are presented in the order CDCD. Patterns C and D are constructed from patterns A and B, respectively, by adding identical upper halves to A and B. Thus, pattern C differs from pattern D at the same locations where pattern A differs from pattern B. Due to the addition of these upper halves, the network does not code C in the category v_{M+1} of A and does not code D in the category v_{M+2} of B. Moreover, because patterns C and D represent many more features than patterns A and B, the difference between C and D is treated as noise, whereas the identical difference between A and B is considered significant. In particular, both patterns C and D are coded within

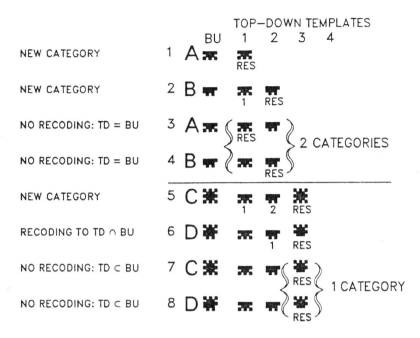

Figure 7. Distinguishing noise from patterns for inputs of variable complexity: Input patterns A and B are coded by the distinct category nodes v_{M+1} and v_{M+2}, respectively. Input patterns C and D include A and B as subsets, but also possess identical subpatterns of additional features. Due to this additional pattern complexity, C and D are coded by the same category node v_{M+3}. At this vigilance level ($\rho = .8$), the network treats the difference between C and D as noise, and suppresses the discordant elements in the v_{M+3} template. By contrast, it treats the difference between A and B as informative, and codes the difference in the v_{M+1} and v_{M+2} templates, respectively.

the same category v_{M+3} on trials 7 and 8, and the critical feature pattern which forms the template of v_{M+3} does not contain the subpatterns at which C and D are mismatched. In contrast, these subpatterns are contained within the templates of v_{M+1} and v_{M+2} to enable these nodes to differentially classify A and B.

Figure 7 illustrates that the matching process compares whole activity patterns across a field of feature-selective cells, rather than activations of individual feature detectors, and that the properties of this matching process which enable it to stabilize network learning also automatically rescale the matching criterion. Thus the network can both differentiate finer details of simple input patterns and tolerate larger mismatches of complex input patterns. This rescaling property also defines the difference between irrelevant features and significant pattern mismatches.

If a mismatch within the attentional subsystem does not activate the orienting subsystem, then no further search for a different code occurs. Thus on trial 6 in Figure 7, mismatched features between the template of v_{M+3} and input pattern D are treated as noise in the sense that they are rapidly suppressed in short term memory (STM) at F_1, and are eliminated from the critical feature pattern learned by the v_{M+3} template. If the mismatch does generate a search, then the mismatched features may be included in the critical feature pattern of the category to which the search leads. Thus on trial 2 of Figure 6, the input pattern B mismatches the template of node v_{M+1}, which causes the search to select node v_{M+2}. As a result, A and B are coded by the distinct categories v_{M+1} and v_{M+2}, respectively. If a template mismatches a simple input pattern at just a few features, a search may be elicited, thereby enabling the network to learn fine discriminations among patterns composed of few features, such as A and B. On the other hand, if a template mismatches the same number of features within a complex input pattern, then a search may not be elicited and the mismatched features may be suppressed as noise, as in the template of v_{M+3}. Thus the pattern matching process of the model automatically exhibits properties that are akin to attentional focussing, or "zooming in."

10. Vigilance Level Tunes Categorical Coarseness: Disconfirming Feedback

The previous section showed how, given each fixed vigilance level, the network automatically rescales its sensitivity to patterns of variable complexity. The present section shows that changes in the vigilance level can regulate the coarseness of the categories that are learned in response to a fixed sequence of input patterns. First we need to define the vigilance parameter ρ.

Let $| I |$ denote the number of input pathways which receive positive inputs when I is presented. Assume that each such input pathway sends an excitatory signal of fixed size P to A whenever I is presented, so that the total excitatory input to A is $P | I |$. Assume also that each F_1 node whose activity becomes positive due to I generates an inhibitory signal of fixed size Q to A, and denote by $| X |$ the number of active pathways from F_1 to A that are activated by the F_1 activity pattern X. Then the total inhibitory input from F_1 to A is $Q | X |$. When

$$P | I |> Q | X |, \tag{2}$$

the orienting subsystem A receives a net excitatory signal and generates a nonspecific reset signal to F_2 (Figure 4c). The quantity

$$\rho \equiv \frac{P}{Q} \tag{3}$$

is called the *vigilance parameter* of A. By (2) and (3), STM reset is initiated when

$$\rho > \frac{| X |}{| I |}. \tag{4}$$

STM reset is prevented when

$$\rho \leq \frac{| X |}{| I |}. \tag{5}$$

In other words, the proportion $| X | / | I |$ of the input pattern I which is matched by the top-down template to generate X must exceed ρ in order to prevent STM reset at F_2.

While F_2 is inactive (Figure 5b), $| X |=| I |$. Activation of A is always forbidden in this case to prevent an input I from resetting its correct F_2 code. By (5), this constraint is achieved if

$$\rho \leq 1; \tag{6}$$

that is, if $P \leq Q$.

In summary, due to the 2/3 Rule, a bad mismatch at F_1 causes a large collapse of total F_1 activity, which leads to activation of A. In order for this to happen, the system maintains a measure of the original level of total F_1 activity and compares this criterion level with the collapsed level of total F_1 activity. The criterion level is computed by summing bottom-up inputs from I to A. This sum provides a stable criterion because it is proportional to the initial activation of F_1 by the bottom-up input, and it remains unchanged as the matching process unfolds in real-time.

We now illustrate how a low vigilance level leads to learning of coarse categories, whereas a high vigilance level leads to learning of fine categories. Suppose, for example, that a low vigilance level has led to a learned grouping of inputs which need to be distinguished for successful adaptation to a prescribed input environment, but that a punishing event occurs as a consequence of this erroneous grouping (Section 2D). Suppose that, in addition to its negative reinforcing effects, the punishing event also has the cognitive effect of increasing sensitivity to pattern mismatches. Such an increase in sensitivity is modelled within the network by an increase in the vigilance parameter, ρ, defined by (3). Increasing this single parameter enables the network to discriminate patterns which previously were lumped together. Once these patterns are coded by different categories in F_2, the different categories can be associated with different behavioral responses. In this way, environmental feedback can enable the network to parse more finely whatever input patterns happen to occur without altering the feature detection process *per se*. The vigilance parameter is increased if a punishing event amplifies all the signals from the input pattern to A so that parameter P increases. Alternatively, ρ may be increased either by a nonspecific decrease in the size Q of signals from F_1 to A, or by direct input signals to A.

Figure 8 describes a series of simulations in which four input patterns—A, B, C, D—are coded. In these simulations, $A \subset B \subset C \subset D$. The different parts of the figure show how categorical learning changes with changes of ρ. When $\rho = .8$ (Figure 8a), 4 categories are learned: (A)(B)(C)(D). When $\rho = .7$ (Figure 8b), 3 categories are learned: (A)(B)(C,D). When $\rho = .6$ (Figure 8c), 3 different categories are learned: (A)(B,C)(D). When $\rho = .5$ (Figure 8d), 2 categories are learned: (A,B)(C,D). When $\rho = .3$ (Figure 8e), 2 different categories are learned: (A,B,C)(D). When $\rho = .2$ (Figure 8f), all the patterns are lumped together into a single category.

11. Rapid Classification of an Arbitrary Type Font

In order to illustrate how an ART network codifies a more complex series of patterns, we show in Figure 9 the first 20 trials of a simulation using alphabet letters as input patterns. In Figure 9a, the vigilance parameter $\rho = .5$. In Figure 9b, $\rho = .8$. Three properties are notable in these simulations. First, choosing a different vigilance parameter can determine different coding histories, such that higher vigilance induces coding into finer categories. Second, the network modifies its search order on each trial to reflect the cumulative effects of prior learning, and bypasses the orienting subsystem to directly access categories after learning has taken place. Third, the templates of coarser categories tend to be more abstract because they must approximately match a larger number of input pattern exemplars.

Given $\rho = .5$, the network groups the 26 letter patterns into 8 stable categories within 3 presentations. In this simulation, F_2 contains 15 nodes. Thus 7 nodes remain uncoded because the network self-stabilizes its learning after satisfying criteria of vigilance and

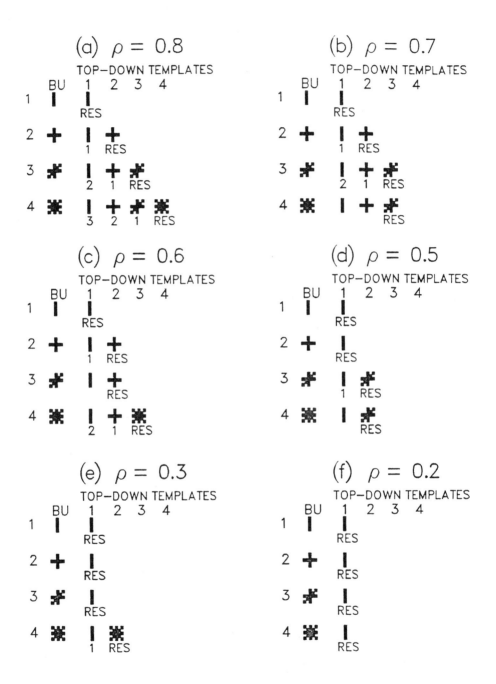

Figure 8. Influence of vigilance level on categorical groupings: As the vigilance parameter ρ decreases, the number of categories progressively decreases.

global self-consistency. Given $\rho = .8$ and 15 F_2 nodes, the network groups 25 of the 26 letters into 15 stable categories within 3 presentations. The 26th letter is rejected by the network in order to self-stabilize its learning while satisfying its criteria of vigilance and global self-consistency. Given a choice of ρ closer to 1, the network classifies 15 letters into 15 distinct categories within 2 presentations. In general, if an ART network is endowed with sufficiently many nodes in F_1 and F_2, it is capable of self-organizing an arbitrary ordering of arbitrarily many and arbitrarily complex input patterns into self-stabilizing recognition categories subject to the constraints of vigilance and global code self-consistency.

We now turn to a mathematical analysis of the properties which control learning and recognition by an ART network.

12. Network Equations: Interactions between Short Term Memory and Long Term Memory Patterns

The STM and LTM equations are described below in dimensionless form (Lin and Segal, 1974), where the number of parameters is reduced to a minimum.

A. STM Equations

The STM activity x_k of any node v_k in F_1 or F_2 obeys a membrane equation of the form

$$\epsilon \frac{d}{dt} x_k = -x_k + (1 - A x_k) J_k^+ - (B + C x_k) J_k^-, \tag{7}$$

where J_k^+ is the total excitatory input to v_k, J_k^- is the total inhibitory input to v_k, and all the parameters are nonnegative. If $A > 0$ and $C > 0$, then the STM activity $x_k(t)$ remains within the finite interval $[-BC^{-1}, A^{-1}]$ no matter how large the nonnegative inputs J_k^+ and J_k^- become.

We denote nodes in F_1 by v_i, where $i = 1, 2, \ldots, M$. We denote nodes in F_2 by v_j, where $j = M + 1, M + 2, \ldots, N$. Thus by (7),

$$\epsilon \frac{d}{dt} x_i = -x_i + (1 - A_1 x_i) J_i^+ - (B_1 + C_1 x_i) J_i^- \tag{8}$$

and

$$\epsilon \frac{d}{dt} x_j = -x_j + (1 - A_2 x_j) J_j^+ - (B_2 + C_2 x_j) J_j^-. \tag{9}$$

In the notation of (1) and Figure 4a, the F_1 activity pattern $X = (x_1, x_2, \ldots, x_M)$ and the F_2 activity pattern $Y = (x_{M+1}, x_{M+2}, \ldots, x_N)$.

The input J_i^+ to the ith node v_i of F_1 is a sum of the bottom-up input I_i and the top-down template input V_i:

$$V_i = D_1 \sum_j f(x_j) z_{ji}; \tag{10}$$

that is,

$$J_i^+ = I_i + V_i, \tag{11}$$

where $f(x_j)$ is the signal generated by activity x_j of v_j, and z_{ji} is the LTM trace in the top-down pathway from v_j to v_i. In the notation of Figure 4b, the input pattern $I = (I_1, I_2, \ldots, I_M)$, the signal pattern $U = (f(x_{M+1}), f(x_{M+2}), \ldots, f(x_N))$, and the template pattern $V = (V_1, V_2, \ldots, V_M)$.

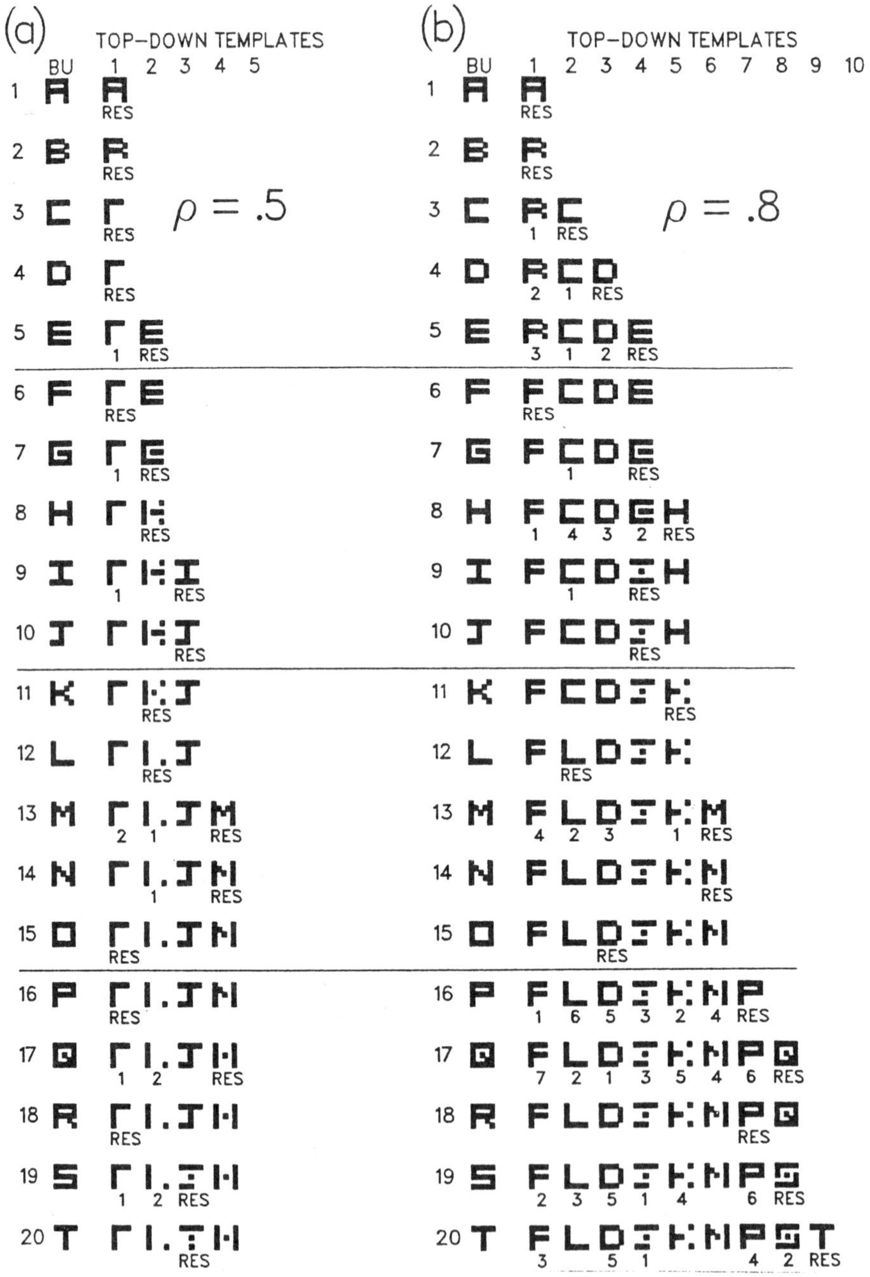

Figure 9. Alphabet learning: Different vigilance levels cause different numbers of letter categories and different critical feature patterns, or templates, to form.

The inhibitory input J_i^- governs the attentional gain control signal:

$$J_i^- = \sum_j f(x_j). \tag{12}$$

Thus $J_i^- = 0$ if and only if F_2 is inactive. When F_2 is active, $J_i^- > 0$ and hence term J_i^- in (8) has a nonspecific inhibitory effect on all the STM activities x_i of F_1. In Figure 5c, this nonspecific inhibitory effect is mediated by inhibition of an active excitatory gain control channel. Such a mechanism is formally described by (12). The attentional gain control signal can be implemented in any of several formally equivalent ways. See the Appendix for some alternative systems.

The inputs and parameters of STM activities in F_2 are chosen so that the F_2 node which receives the largest input from F_1 wins the competition for STM activity. Theorems in Ellias and Grossberg (1975), Grossberg (1973), and Grossberg and Levine (1975) provide a basis for choosing these parameters. The inputs J_j^+ and J_j^- to the F_2 node v_j have the following form.

Input J_j^+ adds a positive feedback signal $g(x_j)$ from v_j to itself to the bottom-up adaptive filter input T_j, where

$$T_j = D_2 \sum_i h(x_i) z_{ij}. \tag{13}$$

That is,

$$J_j^+ = g(x_j) + T_j, \tag{14}$$

where $h(x_i)$ is the signal emitted by the F_1 node v_i and z_{ij} is the LTM trace in the pathway from v_i to v_j. Input J_j^- adds up negative feedback signals $g(x_k)$ from all the other nodes in F_2:

$$J_j^- = \sum_{k \neq j} g(x_k). \tag{15}$$

In the notation of (1) and Figure 4a, the output pattern $S = (h(x_1), h(x_2), \ldots, h(x_M))$ and the input pattern $T = (T_{M+1}, T_{M+2}, \ldots, T_N)$.

Taken together, the positive feedback signal $g(x_j)$ in (14) and the negative feedback signal J_j^- in (15) define an on-center off-surround feedback interaction which contrast-enhances the STM activity pattern Y of F_2 in response to the input pattern T. When F_2's parameters are chosen properly, this contrast-enhancement process enables F_2 to choose for STM activation only the node v_j which receives the largest input T_j. In particular, when parameter ϵ is small in equation (9), F_2 behaves approximately like a binary switching, or choice, circuit:

$$f(x_j) = \begin{cases} 1 & \text{if } T_j = \max\{T_k\} \\ 0 & \text{otherwise.} \end{cases} \tag{16}$$

In the choice case, the top-down template in (10) obeys

$$V_i = \begin{cases} D_1 z_{ji} & \text{if the } F_2 \text{ node } v_j \text{ is active} \\ 0 & \text{if } F_2 \text{ is inactive.} \end{cases} \tag{17}$$

Since V_i is proportional to the LTM trace z_{ji} of the active F_2 node v_j, we can define the template pattern that is read-out by each active F_2 node v_j to be $V^{(j)} \equiv D_1(z_{j1}, z_{j2}, \ldots, z_{jM})$.

B. LTM Equations

The equations for the bottom-up LTM traces z_{ij} and the top-down LTM traces z_{ji} between pairs of nodes v_i in F_1 and v_j in F_2 are formally summarized in this section to facilitate the description of how these equations help to generate useful learning and recognition properties.

The LTM trace of the bottom-up pathway from v_i to v_j obeys a learning equation of the form

$$\frac{d}{dt}z_{ij} = K_1 f(x_j)[-E_{ij}z_{ij} + h(x_i)]. \tag{18}$$

In (18), term $f(x_j)$ is a postsynaptic sampling, or learning, signal because $f(x_j) = 0$ implies $\frac{d}{dt}z_{ij} = 0$. Term $f(x_j)$ is also the output signal of v_j to pathways from v_j to F_1, as in (10).

The LTM trace of the top-down pathway from v_j to v_i also obeys a learning equation of the form

$$\frac{d}{dt}z_{ji} = K_2 f(x_j)[-E_{ji}z_{ji} + h(x_i)]. \tag{19}$$

In the present model, the simplest choice of K_2 and E_{ji} was made for the top-down LTM traces:

$$K_2 = E_{ji} = 1. \tag{20}$$

A more complex choice of E_{ij} was made for the bottom-up LTM traces in order to generate the Weber Law Rule of Section 14. The Weber Law Rule requires that the positive bottom-up LTM traces learned during the encoding of an F_1 pattern X with a smaller number $|X|$ of active nodes be larger than the LTM traces learned during the encoding of an F_1 pattern with a larger number of active nodes, other things being equal. This inverse relationship between pattern complexity and bottom-up LTM trace strength can be realized by allowing the bottom-up LTM traces at each node v_j to compete among themselves for synaptic sites. The Weber Law Rule can also be generated by the STM dynamics of F_1 when competitive interactions are assumed to occur among the nodes of F_1. Generating the Weber Law Rule at F_1 rather than at the bottom-up LTM traces enjoys several advantages, and this model will be developed elsewhere (Carpenter and Grossberg, 1986). In particular, implementing the Weber Law Rule at F_1 enables us to choose $E_{ij} = 1$.

Competition among the LTM traces which abut the node v_j is modelled herein by defining

$$E_{ij} = h(x_i) + L^{-1}\sum_{k \neq i} h(x_k) \tag{21}$$

and letting $K_1 =$ constant. It is convenient to write K_1 in the form $K_1 = KL$. A physical interpretation of this choice can be seen by rewriting (18) in the form

$$\frac{d}{dt}z_{ij} = Kf(x_j)[(1 - z_{ij})Lh(x_i) - z_{ij}\sum_{k \neq i} h(x_k)]. \tag{22}$$

By (22), when a postsynaptic signal $f(x_j)$ is positive, a positive presynaptic signal from the F_1 node v_i can commit receptor sites to the LTM process z_{ij} at a rate $(1 - z_{ij})Lh(x_i)K f(x_j)$. In other words, uncommitted sites—which number $(1 - z_{ij})$ out of the total population size 1—are committed by the joint action of signals $Lh(x_i)$ and $Kf(x_j)$. Simultaneously signals $h(x_k)$, $k \neq i$, which reach v_j at different patches of the v_j membrane, compete for the sites which are already committed to z_{ij} via the mass action competitive terms $-z_{ij}h(x_k)Kf(x_j)$. In other words, sites which are committed to z_{ij} lose their commitment at a rate $-z_{ij}\sum_{k\neq i}h(x_k)Kf(x_j)$ which is proportional to the number of committed sites z_{ij}, the total competitive input $-\sum_{k\neq i}h(x_k)$, and the postsynaptic gating signal $Kf(x_j)$.

Malsburg and Willshaw (1981) have used a different type of competition among LTM traces in their model of retinotectal development. Translated to the present notation, Malsburg and Willshaw postulate that for each fixed F_1 node v_i, competition occurs among all the bottom-up LTM traces z_{ij} in pathways emanating from v_i in such a way as to keep the total synaptic strength $\sum_j z_{ij}$ constant through time. This model does not generate the Weber Law Rule. We show in Section 14 that the Weber Law Rule is essential for achieving direct access to learned categories of arbitrary input patterns in the present model.

C. STM Reset System

A simple type of mismatch-mediated activation of A and STM reset of F_2 by A were implemented in the simulations. As outlined in Section 10, each active input pathway sends an excitatory signal of size P to the orienting subsystem A. Potentials x_i of F_1 which exceed zero generate an inhibitory signal of size Q to A. These constraints lead to the following Reset Rule.

Reset Rule:

Population A generates a nonspecific reset wave to F_2 whenever

$$\frac{|X|}{|I|} < \rho = \frac{P}{Q} \tag{23}$$

where I is the current input pattern and $|X|$ is the number of nodes across F_1 such that $x_i > 0$. The nonspecific reset wave successively shuts off active F_2 nodes until the search ends or the input pattern I shuts off. Thus (16) must be modified as follows to maintain inhibition of all F_2 nodes which have been reset by A during the presentation of I:

F_2 Choice and Search

$$f(x_j) = \begin{cases} 1 & \text{if } T_j = \max\{T_k : k \in \mathbf{J}\} \\ 0 & \text{otherwise} \end{cases} \tag{24}$$

where $\mathbf{J}$ is the set of indices of F_2 nodes which have not yet been reset on the present learning trial. At the beginning of each new learning trial, $\mathbf{J}$ is reset at $\{M+1\dots N\}$. (See Figure 1.) As a learning trial proceeds, $\mathbf{J}$ loses one index at a time until the mismatch-mediated search for F_2 nodes terminates.

13. Direct Access to Subset and Superset Patterns

The need for a Weber Law Rule can be motivated as follows. Suppose that a bottom-up input pattern $I^{(1)}$ activates a network in which pattern $I^{(1)}$ is perfectly coded by the adaptive filter from F_1 to F_2. Suppose that another pattern $I^{(2)}$ is also perfectly coded and that $I^{(2)}$ contains $I^{(1)}$ as a subset; that is, $I^{(2)}$ equals $I^{(1)}$ at all the nodes where $I^{(1)}$ is positive. If $I^{(1)}$ and $I^{(2)}$ are sufficiently different, they should have access to distinct categories at F_2. However, since $I^{(2)}$ equals $I^{(1)}$ at their intersection, and since all the F_1 nodes where $I^{(2)}$ does not equal $I^{(1)}$ are inactive when $I^{(1)}$ is presented, how does the network decide between the two categories when $I^{(1)}$ is presented?

To accomplish this, the node $v^{(1)}$ in F_2 which codes $I^{(1)}$ should receive a bigger signal from the adaptive filter than the node $v^{(2)}$ in F_2 which codes a superset $I^{(2)}$ of $I^{(1)}$. In order to realize this constraint, the LTM traces at $v^{(2)}$ which filter $I^{(1)}$ should be smaller than the LTM traces at $v^{(1)}$ which filter $I^{(1)}$. Since the LTM traces at $v^{(2)}$ were coded by the superset pattern $I^{(2)}$, this constraint suggests that larger patterns are encoded by smaller LTM traces. Thus the absolute sizes of the LTM traces projecting to the different nodes $v^{(1)}$ and $v^{(2)}$ reflect the overall scale of the patterns $I^{(1)}$ and $I^{(2)}$ coded by the nodes. The quantitative realization of this inverse relationship between LTM size and input pattern scale is called the Weber Law Rule.

This inverse relationship suggests how a subset $I^{(1)}$ may selectively activate its node $v^{(1)}$ rather than the node $v^{(2)}$ corresponding to a superset $I^{(2)}$. On the other hand, the superset $I^{(2)}$ must also be able to directly activate its node $v^{(2)}$ rather than the node $v^{(1)}$ of a subset $I^{(1)}$. To achieve subset access, the positive LTM traces of $v^{(1)}$ become larger than the positive LTM traces of $v^{(2)}$. Since presentation of $I^{(2)}$ activates the entire subset pattern $I^{(1)}$, a further property is needed to understand why the subset node $v^{(1)}$ is not activated by the superset $I^{(2)}$. This property—which we call the Associative Decay Rule— implies that some LTM traces decay toward zero during learning. Thus the associative learning laws considered herein violate Hebb's (1949) learning postulate.

In particular, the relative sizes of the LTM traces projecting to an F_2 node reflect the internal structuring of the input patterns coded by that node. During learning of $I^{(1)}$, the LTM traces decay toward zero in pathways which project to $v^{(1)}$ from F_1 cells where $I^{(1)}$ equals zero (Figure 10a). Simultaneously, the LTM traces become large in the pathways which project to $v^{(1)}$ from F_1 cells where $I^{(1)}$ is positive (Figure 10a). In contrast, during learning of $I^{(2)}$, the LTM traces become large in all the pathways which project to $v^{(2)}$ from F_1 cells where $I^{(2)}$ is positive (Figure 10b), including those cells where $I^{(1)}$ equals zero. Since $I^{(2)}$ is a superset of $I^{(1)}$, the Weber Law Rule implies that LTM traces in pathways to $v^{(2)}$ (Figure 10b) do not grow as large as LTM traces in pathways to $v^{(1)}$ (Figure 10a). On the other hand, after learning occurs, more positive LTM traces exist in pathways to $v^{(2)}$ than to $v^{(1)}$. Thus a trade-off exists between the individual sizes of LTM traces and the number of positive LTM traces which lead to each F_2 node. This trade-off enables $I^{(1)}$ to access $v^{(1)}$ (Figure 10c) and $I^{(2)}$ to access $v^{(2)}$ (Figure 10d).

14. Weber Law Rule and Associative Decay Rule for Bottom-Up LTM Traces

We now describe more precisely how the conjoint action of a Weber Law Rule and an Associative Decay Rule allow direct access to both subset and superset F_2 codes. To fix ideas, suppose that each input pattern I to F_1 is a pattern of 0's and 1's. Let $| I |$ denote the number of 1's in the input pattern I. The two rules can be summarized as follows.

Associative Decay Rule:

As learning of I takes place, LTM traces in the bottom-up coding pathways and the top-down template pathways between an inactive F_1 node and an active F_2 node approach 0. Associative learning within the LTM traces can thus cause decreases as well as increases in the sizes of the traces. This is a non-Hebbian form of associative learning.

Weber Law Rule:

As learning of I takes place, LTM traces in the bottom-up coding pathways which join

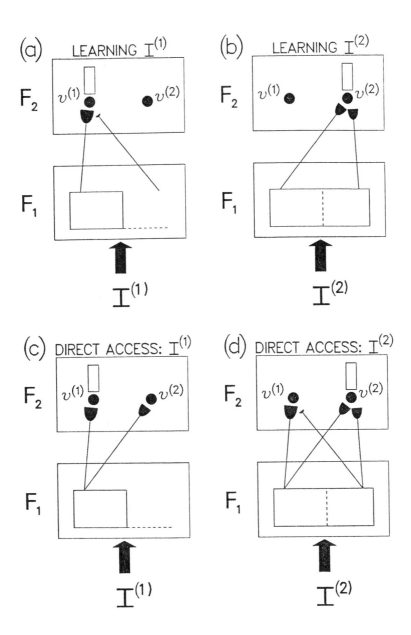

Figure 10. The Weber Law Rule and the Associative Decay Rule enable both subset and superset input patterns to directly access distinct F_2 nodes: (a) and (b) schematize the learning induced by presentation of $I^{(1)}$ (a subset pattern) and $I^{(2)}$ (a superset pattern). Larger path endings designate larger learned LTM traces. (c) and (d) schematize how $I^{(1)}$ and $I^{(2)}$ directly access the F_2 nodes $v^{(1)}$ and $v^{(2)}$, respectively. This property illustrates how distinct, but otherwise arbitrary, input patterns can directly access different categories. No restrictions on input orthogonality or linear predictability are needed.

active F_1 and F_2 nodes approach an asymptote of the form

$$\frac{\alpha}{\beta + \mid I \mid}, \tag{25}$$

where α and β are positive constants. By (25), larger $\mid I \mid$ values imply smaller positive LTM traces in the pathways encoding I.

Direct access by the subset $I^{(1)}$ and the superset $I^{(2)}$ can now be understood as follows. By (25), the positive LTM traces which code $I^{(1)}$ have size

$$\frac{\alpha}{\beta + \mid I^{(1)} \mid} \tag{26}$$

and the positive LTM traces which code $I^{(2)}$ have size

$$\frac{\alpha}{\beta + \mid I^{(2)} \mid}, \tag{27}$$

where $\mid I^{(1)} \mid < \mid I^{(2)} \mid$. When $I^{(1)}$ is presented at F_1, $\mid I^{(1)} \mid$ nodes in F_1 are suprathreshold. Thus the *total* input to $v^{(1)}$ is proportional to

$$T_{11} = \frac{\alpha \mid I^{(1)} \mid}{\beta + \mid I^{(1)} \mid} \tag{28}$$

and the *total* input to $v^{(2)}$ is proportional to

$$T_{12} = \frac{\alpha \mid I^{(1)} \mid}{\beta + \mid I^{(2)} \mid}. \tag{29}$$

Because (25) defines a *decreasing* function of $\mid I \mid$ and because $\mid I^{(1)} \mid < \mid I^{(2)} \mid$, it follows that $T_{11} > T_{12}$. Thus $I^{(1)}$ activates $v^{(1)}$ instead of $v^{(2)}$.

When $I^{(2)}$ is presented at F_1, $\mid I^{(2)} \mid$ nodes in F_1 are suprathreshold. Thus the *total* input to $v^{(2)}$ is proportional to

$$T_{22} = \frac{\alpha \mid I^{(2)} \mid}{\beta + \mid I^{(2)} \mid}. \tag{30}$$

We now invoke the Associative Decay Rule. Because $I^{(2)}$ is a superset of $I^{(1)}$, only those F_1 nodes in $I^{(2)}$ that are also activated by $I^{(1)}$ project to positive LTM traces at $v^{(1)}$. Thus the *total* input to $v^{(1)}$ is proportional to

$$T_{21} = \frac{\alpha \mid I^{(1)} \mid}{\beta + \mid I^{(1)} \mid}. \tag{31}$$

Both T_{22} and T_{21} are expressed in terms of the Weber function

$$W(\mid I \mid) = \frac{\alpha \mid I \mid}{\beta + \mid I \mid}, \tag{32}$$

which is an *increasing* function of $\mid I \mid$. Since $\mid I^{(1)} \mid < \mid I^{(2)} \mid$, $T_{22} > T_{21}$. Thus the superset $I^{(2)}$ activates its node $v^{(2)}$ rather than the subset node $v^{(1)}$. In summary, direct access to subsets and supersets can be traced to the opposite monotonic behavior of the functions (25) and (32).

It remains to show how the Associative Decay Rule and the Weber Law Rule are generated by the STM and LTM laws (8)–(22). The Associative Decay Rule for bottom-up LTM traces follows from (22). When the F_1 node v_i is inactive, $h(x_i) = 0$. When the F_2 node v_j is active, $f(x_j) = 1$. Thus if z_{ij} is the LTM trace in a bottom-up pathway from an inactive F_1 node v_i to an active F_2 node v_j, (22) reduces to

$$\frac{d}{dt} z_{ij} = -K z_{ij} \sum_{k \neq i} h(x_k). \tag{33}$$

The signal function $h(x_k)$ is scaled to rise steeply from 0 to the constant 1 when x_k exceeds zero. For simplicity, suppose that

$$h(x_k) = \begin{cases} 1 & \text{if } x_k > 0 \\ 0 & \text{otherwise.} \end{cases} \tag{34}$$

Thus during a learning trial when v_i is inactive,

$$\sum_{k \neq i} h(x_k) = | X | \tag{35}$$

where $| X |$ is the number of positive activities in the F_1 activity pattern X. By (33) and (35), when v_i is inactive and v_j is active,

$$\frac{d}{dt} z_{ij} = -K z_{ij} | X | \tag{36}$$

which shows that z_{ij} decays exponentially toward zero.

The Weber Law Rule for bottom-up LTM traces z_{ij} follows from (22), (24), and (34). Consider an input pattern I of 0's and 1's that activates $| I |$ nodes in F_1 and node v_j in F_2. Then, by (34),

$$\sum_{k=1}^{M} h(x_k) = | I | . \tag{37}$$

For each z_{ij} in a bottom-up pathway from an active F_1 node v_i to an active F_2 node $v_j, f(x_j) = 1$ and $h(x_i) = 1$, so

$$\frac{d}{dt} z_{ij} = K[(1 - z_{ij})L - z_{ij}(| I | -1)]. \tag{38}$$

At equilibrium, $dz_{ij}/dt = 0$. It then follows from (38) that at equilibrium

$$z_{ij} = \frac{\alpha}{\beta + | I |} \tag{39}$$

as in (25), with $\alpha = L$ and $\beta = L - 1$. Both α and β must be positive, which is the case if $L > 1$. By (22), this means that each lateral inhibitory signal $-h(x_k)$, $k \neq i$, is weaker than the direct excitatory signal $Lh(x_i)$, other things being equal.

When top-down signals from F_2 to F_1 supplement a bottom-up input pattern I to F_1, the number $| X |$ of positive activities in X may become smaller than $| I |$ due to the 2/3 Rule. If v_i remains active after the F_2 node v_j becomes active, (38) generalizes to

$$\frac{d}{dt} z_{ij} = K[(1 - z_{ij})L - z_{ij}(| X | -1)]. \tag{40}$$

By combining (36) and (40), both the Associative Decay Rule and the Weber Law Rule for bottom-up LTM traces may be understood as consequences of the LTM equation

$$\frac{d}{dt} z_{ij} = \begin{cases} K[(1 - z_{ij})L - z_{ij}(| X | -1)] & \text{if } v_i \text{ and } v_j \text{ are active} \\ -K | X | z_{ij} & \text{if } v_i \text{ is inactive and } v_j \text{ is active} \\ 0 & \text{if } v_j \text{ is inactive} \end{cases} \tag{41}$$

Evaluation of term $| X |$ in (41) depends upon whether or not a top-down template perturbs F_1 when a bottom-up input pattern I is active.

15. Template Learning Rule and Associative Decay Rule for Top-Down LTM Traces

The Template Learning Rule and the Associative Decay Rule together imply that the top-down LTM traces in all the pathways from an F_2 node v_j encode the critical feature pattern of all input patterns which have activated v_j without triggering F_2 reset. To see this, as in Section 14, suppose that an input pattern I of 0's and 1's is being learned.

Template Learning Rule:

As learning of I takes place, LTM traces in the top-down pathways from an active F_2 node to an active F_1 node approach 1.

The Template Learning Rule and the Associative Decay Rule for top-down LTM traces z_{ji} follow by combining (19) and (20) to obtain:

$$\frac{d}{dt} z_{ji} = f(x_j)[-z_{ji} + h(x_i)]. \tag{42}$$

If the F_2 node v_j is active and the F_1 node v_i is inactive, then $h(x_i) = 0$ and $f(x_j) = 1$, so (42) reduces to

$$\frac{d}{dt} z_{ji} = -z_{ji}. \tag{43}$$

Thus z_{ji} decays exponentially toward zero and the Associative Decay Rule holds. On the other hand, if both v_i and v_j are active, then $f(x_j) = h(x_i) = 1$, so (42) reduces to

$$\frac{d}{dt} z_{ji} = -z_{ji} + 1. \tag{44}$$

Thus z_{ji} increases exponentially toward 1 and the Template Learning Rule holds.

Combining equations (42)-(44) leads to the learning rule governing the LTM traces z_{ji} in a top-down template:

$$\frac{d}{dt} z_{ji} = \begin{cases} -z_{ji} + 1 & \text{if } v_i \text{ and } v_j \text{ are active} \\ -z_{ji} & \text{if } v_i \text{ is inactive and } v_j \text{ is active} \\ 0 & \text{if } v_j \text{ is inactive} \end{cases} \tag{45}$$

Equation (45) says that the template of v_j tries to learn the activity pattern across F_1 when v_j is active.

The 2/3 Rule controls which nodes v_i in (45) remain active in response to an input pattern I. The 2/3 Rule implies that if the F_2 node v_j becomes active while the F_1 node v_i is receiving a large bottom-up input I_i, then v_i will remain active only if z_{ji} is sufficiently large. Hence there is some critical strength of the top-down LTM traces such that if z_{ji} falls below that strength, then v_i will never again be active when v_j is active, even if I_i is large. As long as z_{ji} remains above the critical LTM strength, it will increase when I_i is large and v_j is active, and decrease when I_i is small and v_j is active. Once z_{ji} falls below the critical LTM strength, it will decay toward 0 whenever v_j is active; that is, the feature represented by v_i drops out of the critical feature pattern encoded by v_j.

These and related properties of the network can be summarized compactly using the following notation.

Let I denote the set of indices of nodes v_i which receive a positive input from the pattern I. When I is a pattern of 0's and 1's, then

$$I_i = \begin{cases} 1 & \text{if } i \in \mathbf{I} \\ 0 & \text{otherwise} \end{cases}, \tag{46}$$

where I is a subset of the F_1 index set $\{1 \dots M\}$. As in Section 12, let $V^{(j)} = D_1(z_{j1} \dots z_{ji} \dots z_{jM})$ denote the template pattern of top-down LTM traces in pathways leading from the F_2 node v_j. The index set $\mathbf{V}^{(j)} = \mathbf{V}^{(j)}(t)$ is defined as follows: $i \in \mathbf{V}^{(j)}$ iff z_{ji} is larger than the critical LTM strength required for v_i to be active when v_j is active and $i \in \mathbf{I}$. For fixed t, let X denote the subset of indices $\{1 \dots M\}$ such that $i \in \mathbf{X}$ iff the F_1 node v_i is active at time t.

With this notation, the 2/3 Rule can be summarized by stating that when a pattern I is presented,

$$\mathbf{X} = \begin{cases} \mathbf{I} & \text{if } F_2 \text{ is inactive} \\ \mathbf{I} \cap \mathbf{V}^{(j)} & \text{if the } F_2 \text{ node } v_j \text{ is active.} \end{cases} \tag{47}$$

The link between STM dynamics at F_1 and F_2 and LTM dynamics between F_1 and F_2 can now be succinctly expressed in terms of (47),

$$\frac{d}{dt} z_{ij} = \begin{cases} K[(1 - z_{ij})L - z_{ij}(|\mathbf{X}| - 1)] & \text{if } i \in \mathbf{X} \text{ and } f(x_j) = 1 \\ -K |\mathbf{X}| z_{ij} & \text{if } i \notin \mathbf{X} \text{ and } f(x_j) = 1 \\ 0 & \text{if } f(x_j) = 0 \end{cases} \tag{48}$$

and

$$\frac{d}{dt} z_{ji} = \begin{cases} -z_{ji} + 1 & \text{if } i \in \mathbf{X} \text{ and } f(x_j) = 1 \\ -z_{ji} & \text{if } i \notin \mathbf{X} \text{ and } f(x_j) = 1 \\ 0 & \text{if } f(x_j) = 0 \end{cases}. \tag{49}$$

A number of definitions that were made intuitively in Sections 3–9 can now be summarized as follows.

Definitions

Coding: An active F_2 node v_J is said to *code* an input I on a given trial if no reset of v_J occurs after the template $V^{(J)}$ is read out at F_1.

Reset could, in principle, occur due to three different factors. The read-out of the template $V^{(J)}$ can change the activity pattern X across F_1. The new pattern X could conceivably generate a maximal input via the $F_1 \rightarrow F_2$ adaptive filter to an F_2 node other than v_J. The theorems below show how the 2/3 Rule and the learning rules prevent template read-out from undermining the choice of v_J via the $F_1 \rightarrow F_2$ adaptive filter. Reset of v_J could also, in principle, occur due to the learning induced in the LTM traces z_{iJ} and z_{Ji} by the choice of v_J. In a real-time learning system whose choices are determined by a continuous flow of bottom-up and top-down signals, one cannot take for granted that the learning process, which alters the sizes of these signals, will maintain a choice within a single learning trial. The theorems in the next sections state conditions which prevent either template readout or learning from resetting the F_2 choice via the adaptive filter from F_1 to F_2.

Only the third possible reset mechanism—activation of the orienting subsystem A by a mismatch at F_1—is allowed to reset the F_2 choice. Equations (5) and (47) imply that if v_J becomes active during the presentation of I, then inequality

$$| \, \mathbf{I} \cap \mathbf{V}^{(J)} \, | \geq \rho \, | \, \mathbf{I} \, | \tag{50}$$

is a necessary condition to prevent reset of v_J by activation of A. Sufficient conditions are stated in the theorems below.

Direct Access: Pattern I is said to have *direct access* to an F_2 node v_J if presentation of I leads at once to activation of v_J and v_J codes I on that trial.

By equations (13) and (34), input I chooses node v_J first if, for all $j \neq J$,

$$\sum_{i \in \mathbf{I}} z_{iJ} > \sum_{i \in \mathbf{I}} z_{ij}. \tag{51}$$

The conditions under which v_J then codes I are characterized in the theorems below.

Fast Learning: For the remainder of this article we consider the *fast learning case* in which learning rates enable LTM traces to approximately reach the asymptotes determined by the STM patterns on each trial. Given the fast learning assumption, at the end of a trial during which v_J was active, (48) implies that

$$z_{iJ} \cong \begin{cases} \frac{L}{L-1+|\mathbf{x}|} & \text{if } i \in \mathbf{X} \\ 0 & \text{if } i \notin \mathbf{X} \end{cases} \tag{52}$$

and (49) implies that

$$z_{Ji} \cong \begin{cases} 1 & \text{if } i \in \mathbf{X} \\ 0 & \text{if } i \notin \mathbf{X} \end{cases}. \tag{53}$$

Thus although $z_{ij} \neq z_{ji}$ in (52) and (53), z_{ij} is large iff z_{ji} is large and $z_{ij} = 0$ iff $z_{ji} = 0$. We can therefore introduce the following definition.

Asymptotic Learning: An F_2 node v_j has *asymptotically learned* the STM pattern X if its LTM traces z_{ij} and z_{ji} satisfy (52) and (53).

By (47), X in (52) and (53) equals either I or $\mathbf{I} \cap \mathbf{V}^{(j)}$. This observation motivates the following definition.

Perfect Learning: An F_2 node v_j has *perfectly learned* an input pattern I iff v_j has asymptotically learned the STM pattern X = I.

16. Direct Access to Nodes Coding Perfectly Learned Patterns

We can now prove the following generalization of the fact that subset and superset nodes can be directly accessed (Section 13).

Theorem 1 (Direct Access by Perfectly Learned Patterns): An input pattern I has direct access to a node v_J which has perfectly learned I if $L > 1$ and all initial bottom-up LTM traces satisfy the

Direct Access Inequality

$$0 < z_{ij}(0) < \frac{L}{L-1+M}, \tag{54}$$

where M is the number of nodes in F_1.

Proof:

In order to prove that I has direct access to v_J we need to show that: (i) v_J is the first F_2 node to be chosen; (ii) v_J remains the chosen node after its template $V^{(J)}$ is read-out at F_1; (iii) read-out of $V^{(J)}$ does not lead to F_2 reset by the orienting subsystem; and (iv) v_J remains active as fast learning occurs.

To prove property (i), we must establish that, at the start of the trial, $T_J > T_j$ for all $j \neq J$. When I is presented, $|\,\mathbf{I}\,|$ active pathways project to each F_2 node. In particular, by (13) and (34),

$$T_J = D_2 \sum_{i \in \mathbf{I}} z_{iJ} \tag{55}$$

and

$$T_j = D_2 \sum_{i \in \mathbf{I}} z_{ij}. \tag{56}$$

Because node v_J perfectly codes I at the start of the trial, it follows from (52) that

$$z_{iJ} = \begin{cases} \frac{L}{L-1+|\mathbf{I}|} & \text{if } i \in \mathbf{I} \\ 0 & \text{if } i \notin \mathbf{I}. \end{cases} \tag{57}$$

By (55) and (57),

$$T_J = \frac{D_2 L \,|\,\mathbf{I}\,|}{L-1+|\,\mathbf{I}\,|}. \tag{58}$$

In order to evaluate T_j in (56), we need to consider nodes v_j which have asymptotically learned a different pattern than I, as well as nodes v_j which are as yet uncommitted. Suppose that v_j, $j \neq J$, has asymptotically learned a pattern $V^{(j)} \neq I$. Then by (52),

$$z_{ij} = \begin{cases} \frac{L}{L-1+|\mathbf{v}^{(j)}|} & \text{if } i \in \mathbf{V}^{(j)} \\ 0 & \text{if } i \notin \mathbf{V}^{(j)}. \end{cases} \tag{59}$$

By (59), the only positive LTM traces in the sum $\sum_{i \in \mathbf{I}} z_{ij}$ in (56) are the traces with indices $i \in \mathbf{I} \cap \mathbf{V}^{(j)}$. Moreover, all of these positive LTM traces have the same value. Thus (59) implies that

$$T_j = \frac{D_2 L \,|\,\mathbf{I} \cap \mathbf{V}^{(j)}\,|}{L-1+|\,\mathbf{V}^{(j)}\,|}. \tag{60}$$

We now prove that T_J in (58) is larger than T_j in (60) if $L > 1$; that is,

$$\frac{|\mathbf{I}|}{L-1+|\mathbf{I}|} > \frac{|\mathbf{I} \cap \mathbf{V}^{(j)}|}{L-1+|\mathbf{V}^{(j)}|}. \tag{61}$$

Suppose first that $|\mathbf{V}^{(j)}| > |\mathbf{I}|$. Then $|\mathbf{I}| \geq |\mathbf{I} \cap \mathbf{V}^{(j)}|$ and $(L-1+|\mathbf{I}|) < (L-1+|\mathbf{V}^{(j)}|)$, which together imply (61).

Suppose next that $|\mathbf{V}^{(j)}| \leq |\mathbf{I}|$. Then, since $\mathbf{V}^{(j)} \neq \mathbf{I}$, it follows that $|\mathbf{I}| > |\mathbf{I} \cap \mathbf{V}^{(j)}|$. Thus, since the function $w/(L-1+w)$ is an increasing function of w,

$$\frac{|\mathbf{I}|}{L-1+|\mathbf{I}|} > \frac{|\mathbf{I} \cap \mathbf{V}^{(j)}|}{L-1+|\mathbf{I} \cap \mathbf{V}^{(j)}|}. \tag{62}$$

Finally, since $|\mathbf{V}^{(j)}| \geq |\mathbf{I} \cap \mathbf{V}^{(j)}|$,

$$\frac{|\mathbf{I} \cap \mathbf{V}^{(j)}|}{L-1+|\mathbf{I} \cap \mathbf{V}^{(j)}|} \geq \frac{|\mathbf{I} \cap \mathbf{V}^{(j)}|}{L-1+|\mathbf{V}^{(j)}|}. \tag{63}$$

Inequalities (62) and (63) together imply (61). This completes the proof that I first activates v_J rather than any other previously coded node v_j.

It remains to prove that I activates v_J rather than an uncommitted node v_j which has not yet been chosen to learn any category. The LTM traces of each uncommitted node v_j obey the Direct Access Inequality (54), which along with $|\mathbf{I}| \leq M$ implies that

$$T_J = \frac{D_2 L |\mathbf{I}|}{L-1+|\mathbf{I}|} \geq \frac{D_2 L |\mathbf{I}|}{L-1+M} > D_2 \sum_{i \in \mathbf{I}} z_{ij} = T_j. \tag{64}$$

This completes the proof of property (i).

The proof of property (ii), that v_J remains the chosen node after its template $V^{(J)}$ is read-out, follows immediately from the fact that $\mathbf{V}^{(J)} = \mathbf{I}$. By (47), the set $\mathbf{X}$ of active nodes remains equal to $\mathbf{I}$ after $V^{(J)}$ is read-out. Thus T_J and T_j are unchanged by read-out of $V^{(J)}$, which completes the proof of property (ii).

Property (iii) also follows immediately from the fact that $\mathbf{I} \cap \mathbf{V}^{(J)} = \mathbf{I}$ in the inequality

$$|\mathbf{I} \cap \mathbf{V}^{(J)}| \geq \rho |\mathbf{I}|. \tag{50}$$

Property (iv) follows from the fact that, while v_J is active, no new learning occurs, since v_J had already perfectly learned input pattern I before the trial began. This completes the proof of Theorem 1.

17. Initial Strengths of LTM Traces

A. Direct Access Inequality: Initial Bottom-Up LTM Traces are Small

Theorem 1 shows that the Direct Access Inequality (54) is needed to prevent uncommitted nodes from interfering with the direct activation of perfectly coded nodes. We now show that violation of the Direct Access Inequality may force all uncommitted nodes to code a single input pattern, and thus to drastically reduce the coding capacity of F_2.

To see this, suppose that for all v_j in F_2 and all $i \in \mathbf{I}$,

$$z_{ij}(0) > \frac{L}{L - 1 + |\mathbf{I}|}. \tag{65}$$

Suppose that on the first trial, v_{j_1} is the first F_2 node to be activated by input I. Thus $T_{j_1} > T_j$, where $j \neq j_1$, at the start of the trial. While activation of v_{j_1} persists, T_{j_1} decreases towards the value $D_2 L |\mathbf{I}| (L - 1 + |\mathbf{I}|)^{-1}$ due to learning. However, for all $j \neq j_1$,

$$T_j = D_2 \sum_{i \in \mathbf{I}} z_{ij}(0) > \frac{D_2 L |\mathbf{I}|}{L - 1 + |\mathbf{I}|}. \tag{66}$$

By (66), T_{j_1} eventually decreases so much that $T_{j_1} = T_{j_2}$ for some other node v_{j_2} in F_2. Thereafter, T_{j_1} and T_{j_2} both approach $D_2 L |\mathbf{I}| (L - 1 + |\mathbf{I}|)^{-1}$ as activation alternates between v_{j_1} and v_{j_2}. Due to inequality (65), all F_2 nodes v_j eventually are activated and their T_j values decrease towards $D_2 L |\mathbf{I}| (L - 1 + |\mathbf{I}|)^{-1}$. Thus *all* the F_2 nodes asymptotically learn the same input pattern I. The Direct Access Inequality (54) prevents these anomalies from occurring. It makes precise the idea that the initial values of the bottom-up LTM traces $z_{ij}(0)$ must not be too large.

B. Template Learning Inequality: Initial Top-Down Traces are Large

In contrast, the initial top-down LTM traces $z_{ji}(0)$ must not be too small. The 2/3 Rule implies that if the initial top-down LTM traces $z_{ji}(0)$ were too small, then no uncommitted F_2 node could ever learn any input pattern, since all F_1 activity would be quenched as soon as F_2 became active.

To understand this issue more precisely, suppose that an input I is presented. While F_2 is inactive, $\mathbf{X} = \mathbf{I}$. Suppose that, with or without a search, the uncommitted F_2 node v_J becomes active on that trial. In order for v_J to be able to encode I given an arbitrary value of the vigilance parameter ρ, it is necessary that $\mathbf{X}$ remain equal to $\mathbf{I}$ after the template $V^{(J)}$ has been read out; that is,

$$\mathbf{I} \cap \mathbf{V}^{(J)}(0) = \mathbf{I} \quad \text{for any I.} \tag{67}$$

Because I is arbitrary, the 2/3 Rule requires that $\mathbf{V}^{(J)}$ initially be the entire set $\{1, \ldots, M\}$. In other words, the initial strengths of all the top-down LTM traces $z_{J1} \ldots z_{JM}$ must be greater than the critical LTM strength, denoted by $\bar{z}$, that is required to maintain suprathreshold STM activity in each F_1 node v_i such that $i \in \mathbf{I}$. Equation (49) and the 2/3 Rule then imply that, as long as I persists and v_J remains active, $z_{Ji} \to 1$ for $i \in \mathbf{I}$ and $z_{Ji} \to 0$ for $i \notin \mathbf{I}$. Thus $\mathbf{V}^{(J)}$ contracts from $\{1, \ldots, M\}$ to I as the node v_J encodes the pattern I.

It is shown in the Appendix that the following inequalities imply the 2/3 Rule:

2/3 Rule Inequalities

$$\max\{1, D_1\} < B_1 < 1 + D_1; \tag{68}$$

and that the critical top-down LTM strength is

$$\bar{z} \equiv \frac{B_1 - 1}{D_1}. \tag{69}$$

Then the

Template Learning Inequality

$$1 \geq z_{ji}(0) > \bar{z} \tag{70}$$

implies that $\mathbf{V}^{(j)}(0) = \{1 \ldots M\}$ for all j, so (67) holds.

C. Activity-Dependent Nonspecific Tuning of Initial LTM Values

Equations (52) and (53) suggest a simple developmental process by which the opposing constraints on $z_{ij}(0)$ and $z_{ji}(0)$ of Sections 17A and 17B can be achieved. Suppose that at a developmental stage prior to the category learning stage, all F_1 and F_2 nodes become endogenously active. Let this activity nonspecifically influence F_1 and F_2 nodes for a sufficiently long time interval to allow their LTM traces to approach their asymptotic values. The presence of noise in the system implies that the initial z_{ij} and z_{ji} values are randomly distributed close to these asymptotic values. At the end of this stage, then,

$$z_{ij}(0) \cong \frac{L}{L - 1 + M} \tag{71}$$

and

$$z_{ji}(0) \cong 1 \tag{72}$$

for all $i = 1 \ldots M$ and $j = M + 1 \ldots N$. The bottom-up LTM traces $z_{ij}(0)$ and the top-down LTM traces $z_{ji}(0)$ are then as large as possible, and still satisfy the Direct Access Inequality (54) and the Template Learning Inequality (70). Switching from this early developmental stage to the category learning stage could then be viewed as a switch from an endogenous source of broadly-distributed activity to an exogenous source of patterned activity.

18. Summary of the Model

Below, we summarize the hypotheses that define the model. All subsequent theorems in the article assume that these hypotheses hold.

Binary Input Patterns

$$I_i = \begin{cases} 1 & \text{if } i \in \mathbf{I} \\ 0 & \text{otherwise} \end{cases} \tag{46}$$

Automatic Bottom-Up Activation and 2/3 Rule

$$\mathbf{X} = \begin{cases} \mathbf{I} & \text{if } F_2 \text{ is inactive} \\ \mathbf{I} \cap \mathbf{V}^{(j)} & \text{if the } F_2 \text{ node } v_j \text{ is active} \end{cases} \tag{47}$$

Weber Law Rule and Bottom-Up Associative Decay Rule

$$\frac{d}{dt} z_{ij} = \begin{cases} K[(1 - z_{ij})L - z_{ij}(|\mathbf{X}| - 1)] & \text{if } i \in \mathbf{X} \text{ and } f(x_j) = 1 \\ -K|\mathbf{X}| z_{ij} & \text{if } i \notin \mathbf{X} \text{ and } f(x_j) = 1 \\ 0 & \text{if } f(x_j) = 0 \end{cases} \tag{48}$$

Template Learning Rule and Top-Down Associative Decay Rule

$$\frac{d}{dt} z_{ji} = \begin{cases} -z_{ji} + 1 & \text{if } i \in \mathbf{X} \text{ and } f(x_j) = 1 \\ -z_{ji} & \text{if } i \notin \mathbf{X} \text{ and } f(x_j) = 1 \\ 0 & \text{if } f(x_j) = 0 \end{cases} \tag{49}$$

Reset Rule

An active F_2 node v_j is reset if

$$\frac{|\,\mathbf{I} \cap \mathbf{V}^{(j)}\,|}{|\,\mathbf{I}\,|} < \rho \equiv \frac{P}{Q}. \tag{73}$$

Once a node is reset, it remains inactive for the duration of the trial.

F_2 Choice and Search

If $\mathbf{J}$ is the index set of F_2 nodes which have not yet been reset on the present learning trial, then

$$f(x_j) = \begin{cases} 1 & \text{if } T_j = \max\{T_k : k \in \mathbf{J}\} \\ 0 & \text{otherwise} \end{cases} \tag{24}$$

where

$$T_j = D_2 \sum_{i \in \mathbf{x}} z_{ij}. \tag{74}$$

In addition, all STM activities x_i and x_j are reset to zero after each learning trial. The initial bottom-up LTM traces $z_{ij}(0)$ are chosen to satisfy the

Direct Access Inequality

$$0 < z_{ij}(0) < \frac{L}{L - 1 + M}. \tag{54}$$

The initial top-down LTM traces are chosen to satisfy the

Template Learning Inequality

$$1 \ge z_{ji}(0) > \overline{z} \equiv \frac{B_1 - 1}{D_1}. \tag{75}$$

Fast Learning

It is assumed that fast learning occurs so that, when v_j in F_2 is active, all LTM traces approach the asymptotes,

$$z_{ij} \cong \begin{cases} \frac{L}{L - 1 + |\mathbf{x}|} & \text{if } i \in \mathbf{X} \\ 0 & \text{if } i \in \mathbf{X} \end{cases} \tag{52}$$

and

$$z_{ji} \cong \begin{cases} 1 & \text{if } i \in \mathbf{X} \\ 0 & \text{if } i \notin \mathbf{X} \end{cases} \tag{53}$$

on each learning trial. A complete listing of parameter constraints is provided in Table 1 of the Appendix.

19. Order of Search and Stable Choices in Short-Term Memory

We will now analyze further properties of the class of ART systems which satisfy the hypotheses in Section 18. We will begin by characterizing the order of search. This analysis provides a basis for proving that learning self-stabilizes and leads to recognition by direct access.

This discussion of search order does not analyse where the search ends. Other things being equal, a network with a higher level of vigilance will require better F_1 matches, and hence will search more deeply, in response to each input pattern. The set of learned filters and templates thus depends upon the prior levels of vigilance, and the same ordering of input patterns may generate different LTM encodings due to the settings of the nonspecific vigilance parameter. The present discussion considers the order in which search will occur in response to a single input pattern which is presented after an arbitrary set of prior inputs has been asymptotically learned.

We will prove that the values of the F_2 input functions T_j at the start of each trial determine the order in which F_2 nodes are searched, assuming that no F_2 nodes are active before the trial begins. To distinguish these initial T_j values from subsequent T_j values, let O_j denote the value of T_j at the start of a trial. We will show that, if these values are ordered by decreasing size, as in

$$O_{j_1} > O_{j_2} > O_{j_3} > \ldots, \tag{76}$$

then F_2 nodes are searched in the order $v_{j_1}, v_{j_2}, v_{j_3}, \ldots$ on that trial. To prove this result, we first derive a formula for O_j.

When an input I is first presented on a trial,

$$O_j = D_2 \sum_{i \in I} z_{ij}, \tag{77}$$

where the z_{ij}'s are evaluated at the start of the trial. By the Associative Decay Rule, z_{ij} in (77) is positive only if $i \in \mathbf{V}^{(j)}$, where $\mathbf{V}^{(j)}$ is also evaluated at the start of the trial. Thus by (77),

$$O_j = D_2 \sum_{i \in I \cap \mathbf{v}^{(j)}} z_{ij}. \tag{78}$$

If the LTM traces z_{ij} have undergone learning on a previous trial, then (52) implies

$$z_{ij} = \frac{L}{L - 1 + \mid \mathbf{V}^{(j)} \mid} \tag{79}$$

for all $i \in \mathbf{V}^{(j)}$. If v_j is an uncommitted node, then the Template Learning Inequality implies that $I \cap \mathbf{V}^{(j)} = I$. Combining these facts leads to the following formula for O_j.

Order Function

$$O_j = \begin{cases} \frac{D_2 L \mid I \cap \mathbf{v}^{(j)} \mid}{L - 1 + \mid \mathbf{v}^{(j)} \mid} & \text{if } v_j \text{ has been chosen on a previous trial} \\ D_2 \sum_{i \in I} z_{ij}(0) & \text{if } v_j \text{ is an uncommitted node.} \end{cases} \tag{80}$$

In response to input pattern I, (76) implies that node v_{j_1} is initially chosen by F_2. After v_{j_1} is chosen, it reads-out template $V^{(j_1)}$ to F_1. When $V^{(j_1)}$ and I both perturb F_1, a new activity pattern X is registered at F_1, as in Figure 4b. By the 2/3 Rule, $\mathbf{X} = \mathbf{I} \cap \mathbf{V}^{(j_1)}$. Consequently, a new bottom-up signal pattern from F_1 to F_2 will then be registered at F_2. How can we be sure that v_{j_1} will continue to receive the largest input from F_1 after its template is processed by F_1? In other words, does read-out of the top-down template $V^{(j_1)}$ confirm the choice due to the ordering of bottom-up signals O_j in (76)? Theorem 2 provides this guarantee. Then Theorem 3 shows that the ordering of initial T_j values determines the order of search on each trial despite the fact that the T_j values can fluctuate dramatically as different F_2 nodes get activated.

Theorem 2 (Stable Choices in STM)

Assume the model hypotheses of Section 18. Suppose that an F_2 node v_J is chosen for STM storage instead of another node v_j because $O_J > O_j$. Then read-out of the top-down template $V^{(J)}$ preserves the inequality $T_J > T_j$ and thus confirms the choice of v_J by the bottom-up filter.

Proof: Suppose that a node v_J is activated due to the input pattern I, and that v_J is not an uncommitted node. When v_J reads out the template $V^{(J)}$ to F_1, $\mathbf{X} = \mathbf{I} \cap \mathbf{V}^{(J)}$ by the 2/3 Rule. Then

$$T_j = D_2 \sum_{i \in \mathrm{I} \cap \mathbf{v}^{(J)}} z_{ij}. \tag{81}$$

Since $z_{ij} > 0$ only if $i \in \mathbf{V}^{(j)}$,

$$T_j = D_2 \sum_{i \in \mathrm{I} \cap \mathbf{v}^{(J)} \cap \mathbf{v}^{(j)}} z_{ij}. \tag{82}$$

By (79), if T_j is not an uncommitted node,

$$T_j = \frac{D_2 L \,|\, \mathbf{I} \cap \mathbf{V}^{(J)} \cap \mathbf{V}^{(j)} \,|}{L - 1 + |\, \mathbf{V}^{(j)} \,|}. \tag{83}$$

By (80) and (83),

$$T_j \leq O_j. \tag{84}$$

Similarly, if v_j is an uncommitted node, the sum T_j in (82) is less than or equal to the sum O_j in (80). Thus read-out of template $V^{(J)}$ can only cause the bottom-up signals T_j, other than T_J, to decrease. Signal T_J, on the other hand, remains unchanged after read-out of $V^{(J)}$. This can be seen by replacing $V^{(j)}$ in (83) by $V^{(J)}$. Then

$$T_J = \frac{D_2 L \,|\, \mathbf{I} \cap \mathbf{V}^{(J)} \,|}{L - 1 + |\, \mathbf{V}^{(J)} \,|}. \tag{85}$$

Hence, after $V^{(J)}$ is read-out

$$T_J = O_J. \tag{86}$$

Combining (84) and (86) shows that inequality $T_J > T_j$ continues to hold after $V^{(J)}$ is read-out, thereby proving that top-down template read-out confirms the F_2 choice of the bottom-up filter.

The same is true if v_J is an uncommitted node. Here, the Template Learning Inequality shows that $\mathbf{X} = \mathbf{I}$ even after $v^{(J)}$ is read-out. Thus *all* bottom-up signals T_j remain unchanged after template read-out in this case. This completes the proof of Theorem 2.

Were the 2/3 Rule not operative, read-out of the template $V^{(j_1)}$ might activate many F_1 nodes that had not previously been activated by the input I alone. For example, a top-down template could, in principle, activate all the nodes of F_1, thereby preventing the input pattern, as a pattern, from being coded. Alternatively, disjoint input patterns could be coded by a single node, despite the fact that these two patterns do not share any features. The 2/3 Rule prevents such coding anomalies from occurring.

Theorem 3 (Initial Filter Values Determine Search Order)

The Order Function O_j determines the order of search no matter how many times F_2 is reset during a trial.

Proof: Since $O_{j_1} > O_{j_2} > \ldots$, node v_{j_1} is the first node to be activated on a given trial. After template $V^{(j_1)}$ is read-out, Theorem 2 implies that

$$T_{j_1} = O_{j_1} > \max\{O_j : j \neq j_1\} \geq \max\{T_j : j \neq j_1\}, \tag{87}$$

even though the full ordering of the T_j's may be different from that defined by the O_j's. If v_{j_1} is reset by the orienting subsystem, then template $V^{(j_1)}$ is shut off for the remainder of the trial and subsequent values of T_{j_1} do not influence which F_2 nodes will be chosen.

As soon as v_{j_1} and $V^{(j_1)}$ are shut off, $T_j = O_j$ for all $j \neq j_1$. Since $O_{j_2} > O_{j_3} > \ldots$, node v_{j_2} is chosen next and template $V^{(j_2)}$ is read-out. Theorem 2 implies that

$$T_{j_2} = O_{j_2} > \max\{O_j : j \neq j_1, j_2\} \geq \max\{T_j : j \neq j_1, j_2\}. \tag{88}$$

Thus $V^{(j_2)}$ confirms the F_2 choice due to O_{j_2} even though the ordering of T_j values may differ both from the ordering of O_j values and from the ordering of T_j values when $V^{(j_1)}$ was active.

This argument can now be iterated to show that the values $O_{j_1} > O_{j_2} > \ldots$ of the Order Function determine the order of search. This completes the proof of Theorem 3.

20. Stable Category Learning

Theorems 2 and 3 describe choice and search properties which occur on such a fast time scale that no new learning can occur. We now analyse properties of learning throughout an entire trial, and use these properties to show that code learning self-stabilizes across trials in response to an arbitrary list of binary input patterns. In Theorem 2, we proved that read-out of a top-down template confirms the F_2 choice made by the bottom-up filter. In Theorem 4, we will prove that learning also confirms the F_2 choice and does not trigger reset by the orienting subsystem. In addition, learning on a single trial causes monotonic changes in the LTM traces.

Theorem 4 (Learning on a Single Trial)

Assume the model hypotheses of Section 18. Suppose that an F_2 node v_J is chosen for STM storage and that read-out of the template $V^{(J)}$ does not immediately lead to reset of node v_J by the orienting subsystem. Then the LTM traces z_{iJ} and z_{Ji} change monotonically in such a way that T_J increases and all other T_j remain constant, thereby confirming the choice of v_J by the adaptive filter. In addition, the set $\mathbf{I} \cap \mathbf{V}^{(J)}$ remains constant during learning, so that learning does not trigger reset of v_J by the orienting subsystem.

Proof: We first show that the LTM traces $z_{Ji}(t)$ can only change monotonically and that the set $\mathbf{X}(t)$ does not change as long as v_J remains active. These conclusions follow from the learning rules for the top-down LTM traces z_{Ji}. Using these facts, we then show that the $z_{iJ}(t)$ change monotonically, that $T_J(t)$ can only increase, and that all other $T_j(t)$ must be constant while v_J remains active. These conclusions follow from the learning rules for the bottom-up LTM traces z_{iJ}. Together, these properties imply that learning confirms the choice of v_J and does not trigger reset of v_J by the orienting subsystem.

Suppose that read-out of $V^{(J)}$ is first registered by F_1 at time $t = t_0$. By the 2/3 Rule, $\mathbf{X}(t_0) = \mathbf{I} \cap \mathbf{V}^{(J)}(t_0)$. By (49), $z_{Ji}(t)$ begins to increase towards 1 if $i \in \mathbf{X}(t_0)$, and begins to decrease towards 0 if $i \notin \mathbf{X}(t_0)$. The Appendix shows that when v_J is active at F_2, each activity x_i in F_2 obeys the equation

$$\epsilon \frac{dx_i}{dt} = -x_i + (1 - A_1 x_i)(I_i + D_1 z_{Ji}) - (B_1 + C_1 x_i). \tag{89}$$

By (89), $x_i(t)$ increases if $z_{Ji}(t)$ increases, and $x_i(t)$ decreases if $z_{Ji}(t)$ decreases. Activities x_i which start out positive hereby become even larger, whereas activities x_i which start out non-positive become even smaller. In particular, $\mathbf{X}(t) = \mathbf{X}(t_0) = \mathbf{I} \cap \mathbf{V}^{(J)}(t_0)$ for all times $t \geq t_0$ at which v_J remains active.

We next prove that $T_J(t)$ increases, whereas all other $T_j(t)$ remain constant, while v_J is active. We suppose first that v_J is not an uncommitted node before considering the case in which v_J is an uncommitted node. While v_J remains active, the set $\mathbf{X}(t) = \mathbf{I} \cap \mathbf{V}^{(J)}(t_0)$. Thus

$$T_J(t) = D_2 \sum_{i \in \mathbf{I} \cap \mathbf{V}^{(J)}(t_0)} z_{iJ}(t). \tag{90}$$

At time $t = t_0$, each LTM trace in (90) satisfies

$$z_{iJ}(t_0) \cong \frac{L}{L - 1 + |\mathbf{V}^{(J)}(t_0)|} \tag{91}$$

due to (79). While v_J remains active, each of these LTM traces responds to the fact that $\mathbf{X}(t) = \mathbf{I} \cap \mathbf{V}^{(J)}(t_0)$. By (47) and (52), each $z_{iJ}(t)$ with $i \in \mathbf{I} \cap \mathbf{V}^{(J)}(t_0)$ increases towards

$$\frac{L}{L - 1 + |\mathbf{I} \cap \mathbf{V}^{(J)}(t_0)|}, \tag{92}$$

each $z_{iJ}(t)$ with $i \notin \mathbf{I} \cap \mathbf{V}^{(J)}(t_0)$ decreases towards 0, and all other bottom-up LTM traces $z_{ij}(t)$ remain constant. A comparison of (91) with (92) shows that $T_J(t)$ in (90) can only increase while v_J remains active. In contrast, all other $T_j(t)$ are constant while v_J remains active.

If v_J is an uncommitted node, then no LTM trace $z_{iJ}(t)$ changes before time $t = t_0$. Thus

$$z_{iJ}(t_0) = z_{iJ}(0), \quad i = 1, 2, \ldots, M. \tag{93}$$

By the Template Learning Inequality (75), $\mathbf{I} \cap \mathbf{V}^{(J)}(t_0) = \mathbf{I}$, so that (90) can be written as

$$T_J(t) = D_2 \sum_{i \in \mathbf{I}} z_{iJ}(t). \tag{94}$$

By (93) and the Direct Access Inequality (54),

$$z_{iJ}(t_0) < \frac{L}{L - 1 + M}, \quad i = 1, 2, \ldots, M. \tag{95}$$

While v_J remains active, $\mathbf{X}(t) = \mathbf{I} \cap \mathbf{V}^{(J)}(t_0) = \mathbf{I}$, so that each $z_{iJ}(t)$ in (94) approaches the value

$$\frac{L}{L - 1 + |\mathbf{I}|}. \tag{96}$$

Since $|\mathbf{I}| \leq M$ for any input pattern I, a comparison of (95) and (96) shows that each $z_{iJ}(t)$ with $i \in \mathbf{I}$ increases while v_J remains active. In contrast, each $z_{iJ}(t)$ with $i \notin \mathbf{I}$ decreases towards zero and all other $z_{ij}(t)$ remain constant. Consequently, by (94), $T_J(t)$ increases and all other $T_j(t)$ are constant while v_J remains active. Thus learning confirms the choice of v_J. Hence the set $\mathbf{X}(t)$ remains constant and equal to $\mathbf{I} \cap \mathbf{V}^{(J)}(t_0)$ while learning proceeds.

This last fact, along with the hypothesis that read-out of $V^{(J)}$ does not immediately cause reset of v_J, implies that learning cannot trigger reset of v_J. By the Reset Rule (73), the hypothesis that read-out of $V^{(J)}$ does not immediately cause reset of v_J implies that

$$| \mathbf{I} \cap \mathbf{V}^{(J)}(t_0) | = | \mathbf{X}(t_0) | \geq \rho | \mathbf{I} | . \tag{97}$$

The fact that $\mathbf{X}(t)$ does not change while v_J remains active implies that

$$| \mathbf{X}(t) | = | \mathbf{X}(t_0) | \geq \rho | \mathbf{I} | \tag{98}$$

and hence that learning does not trigger reset of v_J. Thus v_J remains active and learning in its LTM traces $z_{iJ}(t)$ and $z_{Ji}(t)$ can continue until the trial is ended. This completes the proof of Theorem 4.

Theorems 2-4 immediately imply the following important corollary, which illustrates how 2/3 Rule matching, the learning laws, and the Reset Rule work together to prevent spurious reset events.

Corollary 1 (Reset by Mismatch)

An active F_2 node v_J can be reset only by the orienting subsystem. Reset occurs when the template $V^{(J)}$ causes an F_1 mismatch such that

$$| \mathbf{I} \cap \mathbf{V}^{(J)} | < \rho | \mathbf{I} | . \tag{99}$$

Reset cannot be caused within the attentional subsystem due to reordering of adaptive filter signals T_j by template read-out or due to learning.

Theorem 4 implies another important corollary which characterizes how a template changes due to learning on a given trial.

Corollary 2 (Subset Recoding)

If an F_2 node v_J is activated due to an input I and if read-out of $V^{(J)}$ at time $t = t_0$ implies that

$$| \mathbf{I} \cap \mathbf{V}^{(J)}(t_0) | \geq \rho | \mathbf{I} | , \tag{100}$$

then v_J remains active until I shuts off, and the template set $\mathbf{V}^{(J)}(t)$ contracts from $\mathbf{V}^{(J)}(t_0)$ to $\mathbf{I} \cap \mathbf{V}^{(J)}(t_0)$.

With these results in hand, we can now prove that the learning process self-stabilizes in response to an arbitrary list of binary input patterns.

Theorem 5 (Stable Category Learning)

Assume the model hypotheses of Section 18. Then in response to an arbitrary list of binary input patterns, all LTM traces $z_{ij}(t)$ and $z_{ji}(t)$ approach limits after a finite number of learning trials. Each template set $\mathbf{V}^{(j)}$ remains constant except for at most $M-1$ times $t_1^{(j)} < t_2^{(j)} < \ldots < t_{r_j}^{(j)}$ at which it progressively loses elements, leading to the

Subset Recoding Property

$$\mathbf{V}^{(j)}(t_1^{(j)}) \supset \mathbf{V}^{(j)}(t_2^{(j)}) \supset \ldots \supset \mathbf{V}^{(j)}(t_{r_j}^{(j)}). \tag{101}$$

All LTM traces oscillate at most once due to learning. The LTM traces $z_{ij}(t)$ and $z_{ji}(t)$ such that $i \notin \mathbf{V}^{(j)}(t_1^{(j)})$ decrease monotonically to zero. The LTM traces $z_{ij}(t)$ and $z_{ji}(t)$ such that $i \in \mathbf{V}^{(j)}(t_{r_j}^{(j)})$ are monotone increasing functions. The LTM traces $z_{ij}(t)$ and $z_{ji}(t)$ such that $i \in \mathbf{V}^{(j)}(t_k^{(j)})$ but $i \notin \mathbf{V}^{(j)}(t_{k+1}^{(j)})$ can increase at times $t \leq t_{k+1}^{(j)}$ but can only decrease towards zero at times $t > t_{k+1}^{(j)}$.

Proof:

Suppose that an input pattern I is presented on a given trial and the Order Function satisfies

$$O_{j_1} > O_{j_2} > O_{j_3} > \ldots. \tag{76}$$

Then no learning occurs while F_2 nodes are searched in the order $v_{j_1}, v_{j_2}, \ldots$, by Theorem 3. If all F_2 nodes are reset by the search, then no learning occurs on that trial. If a node exists such that

$$| \mathbf{I} \cap \mathbf{V}^{(j)} | \geq \rho | \mathbf{I} |, \tag{102}$$

then search terminates at the first such node, v_{j_k}. Only the LTM traces z_{ij_k} and $z_{j_k i}$ can undergo learning on that trial, by Theorem 4. In particular, if an uncommitted node v_{j_k} is reached by the search, then the Template Learning Inequality implies

$$| \mathbf{I} \cap \mathbf{V}^{(j_k)} | = | \mathbf{I} \cap \mathbf{V}^{(j_k)}(0) | = | \mathbf{I} | \geq \rho | \mathbf{I} | \tag{103}$$

so that its LTM traces undergo learning on that trial. In summary, learning on a given trial can change only the LTM traces of the F_2 node v_{j_k} at which the search ends.

Corollary 2 shows that the template set $\mathbf{V}^{(j_k)}$ of the node v_{j_k} is either constant or contracts due to learning. A contraction can occur on only a finite number of trials, because there are only finitely many nodes in F_1. In addition, there are only finitely many nodes in F_2, hence only finitely many template sets $\mathbf{V}^{(j)}$ can contract. The Subset Recoding Property is hereby proved.

The monotonicity properties of the LTM traces follow from the Subset Recoding Property and Theorem 4. Suppose for definiteness that the search on a given trial terminates at a node v_J in response to an input pattern I. Suppose moreover that the template set $\mathbf{V}^{(J)}(t)$ contracts from $\mathbf{V}^{(J)}(t_k^{(J)})$ to $\mathbf{V}^{(J)}(t_{k+1}^{(J)}) = \mathbf{I} \cap \mathbf{V}^{(J)}(t_k^{(J)})$ due to read-out of the template $V^{(J)}(t_k^{(J)})$ on that trial. A comparison of (91) and (92) shows that each $z_{iJ}(t)$ with $i \in \mathbf{V}^{(J)}(t_{k+1}^{(J)})$ increases from

$$\frac{L}{L - 1 + | \mathbf{V}^{(J)}(t_k^{(J)}) |} \tag{104}$$

to

$$\frac{L}{L - 1 + | \mathbf{V}^{(J)}(t_{k+1}^{(J)}) |}, \tag{105}$$

that each $z_{iJ}(t)$ with $i \notin \mathbf{V}^{(J)}(t_{k+1}^{(J)})$ decreases towards zero, and that all other bottom-up LTM traces $z_{ij}(t)$ remain constant. In a similar fashion, each $z_{Ji}(t)$ with $i \in \mathbf{V}^{(J)}(t_{k+1}^{(J)})$

remains approximately equal to one, each $z_{Ji}(t)$ with $i \notin \mathbf{V}^{(J)}(t_{k+1}^{(J)})$ decreases towards zero, and all other top-down LTM traces $z_{ji}(t)$ remain constant.

Due to the Subset Recoding Property (101),

$$\mid \mathbf{V}^{(J)}(t_1^{(J)}) \mid > \mid \mathbf{V}^{(J)}(t_2^{(J)}) \mid > \ldots > \mid \mathbf{V}^{(J)}(t_{r_J}^{(J)}) \mid . \tag{106}$$

Thus each LTM trace $z_{iJ}(t)$ with $i \in \mathbf{V}^{(J)}(t_{r_J}^{(J)})$ increases monotonically, as from (104) to (105), on the r_J trials where search ends at v_J and the template set $\mathbf{V}^{(J)}(t)$ contracts. On all other trials, these LTM traces remain constant. The other monotonicity properties are now also easily proved by combining the Subset Recoding Property (101) with the learning properties on a single trial. In particular, by the Subset Recoding Property, no LTM traces change after time

$$t = \max \{t_{r_j}^{(j)} : j = M+1, M+2, \ldots, N\}. \tag{107}$$

Thus all LTM traces approach their limits after a finite number of learning trials. This completes the proof of Theorem 5.

21. Critical Feature Patterns and Prototypes

The property of stable category learning can be intuitively summarized using the following definitions.

The *critical feature pattern* at time t of a node v_j is the template $V^{(j)}(t)$. Theorem 5 shows that the critical feature pattern of each node v_j is progressively refined as the learning process discovers the set of features that can match all the input patterns which v_j codes. Theorem 5 also says that the network discovers a set of *self-stabilizing* critical feature patterns as learning proceeds. At any stage of learning, the set of all critical feature patterns determines the order in which previously coded nodes will be activated, via the Order Function

$$O_j = \frac{D_2 L \mid \mathbf{I} \cap \mathbf{V}^{(j)} \mid}{L - 1 + \mid \mathbf{V}^{(j)} \mid}. \tag{108}$$

The *Reset Function*

$$R_j = \frac{\mid \mathbf{I} \cap \mathbf{V}^{(j)} \mid}{\mid \mathbf{I} \mid} \tag{109}$$

determines how many of these nodes will actually be searched, and thus which node may be recoded on each trial. In particular, an unfamiliar input pattern which has never before been experienced by the network will directly access a node v_{j_1} if the

Direct Access Conditions

$$O_{j_1} > \max(O_j : j \neq j_1) \text{ and } R_{j_1} \geq \rho. \tag{110}$$

are satisfied.

An important example of direct access occurs when the input pattern I^* satisfies $I^* = \mathbf{V}^{(j)}$, for some $j = M+1, M+2, \ldots, N$. Such an input pattern is called a *prototype*. Due to the Subset Recoding Property (101), at any given time a prototype pattern includes all the features common to the input patterns which have previously been coded by node v_j. Such a prototype pattern may never have been experienced itself. When an unfamiliar prototype pattern is presented for the first time, it will directly access its category v_j and is thus recognized. This property follows from Theorem 1, since v_j has perfectly learned I^*. Moreover, because $\mathbf{I}^* = \mathbf{V}^{(j)}$, a prototype is optimally matched by read-out of the template $V^{(j)}$.

A prototype generates an optimal match in the bottom-up filter, in the top-down template, and at F_1, even though it is unfamiliar. This is also true in human recognition data (Posner, 1973; Posner and Keele, 1968, 1970). Theorem 5 thus implies that an ART system can discover, learn, and recognize stable prototypes of an arbitrary list of input patterns. An ART system also supports direct access by unfamiliar input patterns which are not prototypes, but which share invariant properties with learned prototypes, in the sense that they satisfy the Direct Access Conditions.

22. Direct Access After Learning Self-Stabilizes

We can now prove that all patterns directly access their categories after the recognition learning process self-stablizes. In order to discuss this property precisely, we define three types of learned templates with respect to an input pattern I: subset templates, superset templates, and mixed templates. The LTM traces of a subset template V satisfy $\mathbf{V} \subseteq \mathbf{I}$: they are large only at a subset of the F_1 nodes which are activated by the input pattern I (Figure 11a). The LTM traces of a superset template V satisfy $\mathbf{V} \supset \mathbf{I}$: they are large at all the F_1 nodes which are activated by the input pattern I, as well as at some F_1 nodes which are not activated by I (Figure 11b). The LTM traces of a mixed template V are large at some, but not all, the F_1 nodes which are activated by the input pattern I, as well as at some F_1 nodes which are not activated by I: the set $\mathbf{I}$ is neither a subset nor a superset of $\mathbf{V}$ (Figure 11c).

Theorem 6 (Direct Access After Learning Self-Stabilizes)

Assume the model hypotheses of Section 18. After recognition learning has self-stabilized in response to an arbitrary list of binary input patterns, each input pattern I either has direct access to the node v_j which possesses the largest subset template with respect to I, or I cannot be coded by any node of F_2. In the latter case, F_2 contains no uncommitted nodes.

Remark: The possibility that an input pattern cannot be coded by any node of F_2 is a consequence of the fact that an ART network self-stabilizes its learning in response to a list containing arbitrarily many input patterns no matter how many coding nodes exist in F_2. If a list contains many input patterns and F_2 contains only a few nodes, one does not expect F_2 to code all the inputs if the vigilance parameter ρ is close to 1.

Proof:

Since learning has already stabilized, I can be coded only by a node v_j whose template $V^{(j)}$ is a subset template with respect to I. Otherwise, after template $V^{(j)} = V$ was read-out, the set $\mathbf{V}^{(j)}$ would contract from $\mathbf{V}$ to $\mathbf{I} \cap \mathbf{V}$ by Corollary 2 (Section 20), thereby contradicting the hypothesis that learning has already stabilized. In particular, input I cannot be coded by a node whose template is a superset template or a mixed template with respect to I. Nor can I be coded by an uncommitted node. Thus if I activates any node other than one with a subset template, that node must be reset by the orienting subsystem.

For the remainder of the proof, let v_J be the first F_2 node activated by I. We show that if $V^{(J)}$ is a subset template, then it is the subset template with the largest index

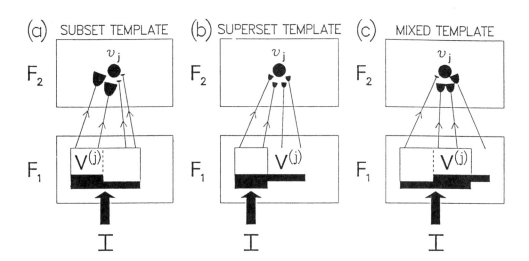

Figure 11. Subset, superset, and mixed templates $V^{(j)}$ with respect to an input pattern I: In (a), (b), and (c), the lower black bar designates the set of F_1 nodes that receive positive bottom-up inputs due to I. The upper black bar designates the set of F_1 nodes that receive positive top-down inputs due to the template $V^{(j)}$. (a) denotes a subset template $V^{(j)}$ with respect to I. (b) denotes a superset template $V^{(j)}$ with respect to I. (c) denotes a mixed template $V^{(j)}$ with respect to I. When node v_j in F_2 is not an uncommitted node, the top-down LTM traces in the template $V^{(j)}$ are large if and only if the LTM traces in the corresponding bottom-up pathways are large (Section 15). The absolute bottom-up LTM trace size depends inversely upon the size $\mid V^{(j)} \mid$ of $V^{(j)}$, due to the Weber Law Rule (Section 14). Larger LTM traces are drawn as larger endings on the bottom-up pathways. The arrow heads denote the pathways that are activated by I before any top-down template influences F_1.

set; and that if the orienting subsystem resets v_J, then it also resets all nodes with subset templates which get activated on that trial. Thus either the node with maximal subset template is directly accessed, or all nodes in F_2 that are activated by I are quickly reset by the orienting subsystem because learning has already self-stabilized.

If v_j is any node with a subset template $V^{(j)}$ with respect to I, then the Order Function

$$O_j = \frac{D_2 L \mid \mathbf{V}^{(j)} \mid}{L - 1 + \mid \mathbf{V}^{(j)} \mid}, \tag{111}$$

by (108). Function O_j in (111) is an increasing function of $\mid \mathbf{V}^{(j)} \mid$. Thus if the first chosen node v_J has a subset template, then $V^{(J)}$ is the subset template with the largest index set.

If v_j is any node with a subset template $V^{(j)}$ with respect to I, then the Reset Function

$$R_j = \frac{\mid \mathbf{I} \cap \mathbf{V}^{(j)} \mid}{\mid \mathbf{I} \mid} = \frac{\mid \mathbf{V}^{(j)} \mid}{\mid \mathbf{I} \mid}, \tag{112}$$

by (109). Once activated, such a node v_j will be reset if

$$R_j < \rho. \tag{113}$$

Thus if the node with the largest index set $\mathbf{V}^{(j)}$ is reset, (112) and (113) imply that all other nodes with subset templates will be reset.

Finally, suppose that v_J, the first node activated, does not have a subset template, but that some node v_j with a subset template is activated in the course of search. We need to show that $|\mathbf{I} \cap \mathbf{V}^{(j)}| = |\mathbf{V}^{(j)}| < \rho |\mathbf{I}|$, so that v_j is reset. Since v_j has a subset template,

$$O_j = \frac{D_2 L |\mathbf{V}^{(j)}|}{L - 1 + |\mathbf{V}^{(j)}|}. \tag{111}$$

Since $|\mathbf{I} \cap \mathbf{V}^{(J)}| \leq |\mathbf{V}^{(J)}|$,

$$O_J = \frac{D_2 L |\mathbf{I} \cap \mathbf{V}^{(J)}|}{L - 1 + |\mathbf{V}^{(J)}|} \leq \frac{D_2 L |\mathbf{V}^{(J)}|}{L - 1 + |\mathbf{V}^{(J)}|}. \tag{114}$$

Since v_J was chosen first, $O_J > O_j$. Comparison of (111) and (114) thus implies that $|\mathbf{V}^{(J)}| > |\mathbf{V}^{(j)}|$. Using the properties $O_j < O_J, |\mathbf{I} \cap \mathbf{V}^{(J)}| < \rho |\mathbf{I}|$, and $|\mathbf{V}^{(J)}| > |\mathbf{V}^{(j)}|$ in turn, we find

$$\frac{|\mathbf{V}^{(j)}|}{L - 1 + |\mathbf{V}^{(j)}|} < \frac{|\mathbf{I} \cap \mathbf{V}^{(J)}|}{L - 1 + |\mathbf{V}^{(J)}|} < \frac{\rho |\mathbf{I}|}{L - 1 + |\mathbf{V}^{(J)}|} < \frac{\rho |\mathbf{I}|}{L - 1 + |\mathbf{V}^{(j)}|}, \tag{115}$$

which implies that

$$|\mathbf{I} \cap \mathbf{V}^{(j)}| = |\mathbf{V}^{(j)}| < \rho |\mathbf{I}|. \tag{116}$$

Therefore all F_2 nodes are reset if v_J is reset. This completes the proof of Theorem 6.

Theorem 6 shows that, in response to any familiar input pattern I, the network knows how to directly access the node v_j whose template $V^{(j)}$ corresponds to the prototype $I^* = V^{(j)}$ which is closest to I among all prototypes learned by the network. Because direct access obviates the need for search, recognition of familiar input patterns and of unfamiliar patterns that share categorical invariants with familiar patterns is very rapid no matter how large or complex the learned recognition code may have become. Grossberg and Stone (1986a) have, moreover, shown that the variations in reaction times and error rates which occur during direct access due to prior priming events are consistent with data collected from human subjects in lexical decision experiments and word familiarity and recall experiments.

Theorems 5 and 6 do not specify how many list presentations and F_2 nodes are needed to learn and recognize an arbitrary list through direct access. We make the following conjecture: in the fast learning case, if F_2 has at least n nodes, then each member of a list of n input patterns which is presented cyclically will have direct access to an F_2 node after at most n list presentations.

Given arbitrary lists of input patterns, this is the best possible result. If the vigilance parameter ρ is close to 1 and if a nested set of n binary patterns is presented in order of decreasing size, then exactly n list presentations are required for the final code to be learned. On the other hand, if a nested set of n patterns is presented in order of increasing size, then only one list presentation is required for the final code to be learned. Thus the number of trials needed to stabilize learning in the fast learning case depends upon both the ordering and the internal structure of the input patterns, as well as upon the vigilance level.

23. Order of Search: Mathematical Analysis

The Order Function

$$O_j = \frac{D_2 L \mid \mathbf{I} \cap \mathbf{V}^{(j)} \mid}{L - 1 + \mid \mathbf{V}^{(j)} \mid} \tag{108}$$

for previously coded nodes v_j shows that search order is determined by two opposing tendencies. A node v_j will be searched early if $\mid \mathbf{I} \cap \mathbf{V}^{(j)} \mid$ is large and if $\mid \mathbf{V}^{(j)} \mid$ is small. Term $\mid \mathbf{I} \cap \mathbf{V}^{(j)} \mid$ is maximized if $V^{(j)}$ is a superset template of I. Term $\mid \mathbf{V}^{(j)} \mid$ is small if $V^{(j)}$ codes only a few features. The relative importance of the template intersection $\mid \mathbf{I} \cap \mathbf{V}^{(j)} \mid$ and the template size $\mid \mathbf{V}^{(j)} \mid$ is determined by the size of $L - 1$ in (108). If $L - 1$ is small, both factors are important. If $L - 1$ is large, the template intersection term dominates search order. The next theorem completely characterizes the search order in the case that $L - 1$ is small.

Theorem 7 (Search Order)

Assume the model hypotheses of Section 18. Suppose that input pattern I satisfies

$$L - 1 \leq \frac{1}{\mid \mathbf{I} \mid} \tag{117}$$

and

$$\mid \mathbf{I} \mid \leq M - 1. \tag{118}$$

Then F_2 nodes are searched in the following order, if they are reached at all.

Subset templates with respect to I are searched first, in order of decreasing size. If the largest subset template is reset, then all subset templates are reset. If all subset templates have been reset and if no other learned templates exist, then the first uncommitted node to be activated will code I. If all subset templates are searched and if there exist learned superset templates but no mixed templates, then the node with the smallest superset template will be activated next and will code I. If all subset templates are searched and if both superset templates $V^{(J)}$ and mixed templates $V^{(j)}$ exist, then v_j will be searched before v_J if and only if

$$\mid \mathbf{V}^{(j)} \mid < \mid \mathbf{V}^{(J)} \mid \quad \text{and} \quad \frac{\mid \mathbf{I} \mid}{\mid \mathbf{V}^{(J)} \mid} < \frac{\mid \mathbf{I} \cap \mathbf{V}^{(j)} \mid}{\mid \mathbf{V}^{(j)} \mid}. \tag{119}$$

If all subset templates are searched and if there exist mixed templates but no superset templates, then a node v_j with a mixed template will be searched before an uncommitted node v_J if and only if

$$\frac{L \mid \mathbf{I} \cap \mathbf{V}^{(j)} \mid}{L - 1 + \mid \mathbf{V}^{(j)} \mid} > \sum_{i \in \mathbf{I}} z_{iJ}(0). \tag{120}$$

The proof is based upon the following lemma.

Lemma 1: If (117) holds, then for any pair of F_2 nodes v_J and v_j with learned templates, $O_J > O_j$ if either

$$\frac{|\mathbf{I} \cap \mathbf{V}^{(J)}|}{|\mathbf{V}^{(J)}|} > \frac{|\mathbf{I} \cap \mathbf{V}^{(j)}|}{|\mathbf{V}^{(j)}|} \tag{121}$$

or

$$\frac{|\mathbf{I} \cap \mathbf{V}^{(J)}|}{|\mathbf{V}^{(J)}|} = \frac{|\mathbf{I} \cap \mathbf{V}^{(j)}|}{|\mathbf{V}^{(j)}|} \quad \text{and} \quad |\mathbf{V}^{(J)}| > |\mathbf{V}^{(j)}|. \tag{122}$$

Proof of Lemma 1: We need to show that if either (121) or (122) holds, then $O_J > O_j$. By (108), $O_J > O_j$ is equivalent to

$$\begin{aligned} |\mathbf{I} \cap \mathbf{V}^{(J)}| \cdot |\mathbf{V}^{(j)}| - |\mathbf{I} \cap \mathbf{V}^{(j)}| \cdot |\mathbf{V}^{(J)}| \\ + (L-1)[|\mathbf{I} \cap \mathbf{V}^{(J)}| - |\mathbf{I} \cap \mathbf{V}^{(j)}|] > 0. \end{aligned} \tag{123}$$

Suppose that (121) holds. Then:

$$|\mathbf{I} \cap \mathbf{V}^{(J)}| \cdot |\mathbf{V}^{(j)}| - |\mathbf{I} \cap \mathbf{V}^{(j)}| \cdot |\mathbf{V}^{(J)}| > 0. \tag{124}$$

Since $L > 1$, inequality (123) then follows at once if $[|\mathbf{I} \cap \mathbf{V}^{(J)}| - |\mathbf{I} \cap \mathbf{V}^{(j)}|] \geq 0$.

Suppose that $|\mathbf{I} \cap \mathbf{V}^{(j)}| > |\mathbf{I} \cap \mathbf{V}^{(J)}|$. Each term in (124) is an integer. The entire left-hand side of (124) is consequently a positive integer, so

$$|\mathbf{I} \cap \mathbf{V}^{(J)}| \cdot |\mathbf{V}^{(j)}| - |\mathbf{I} \cap \mathbf{V}^{(j)}| \cdot |\mathbf{V}^{(J)}| \geq 1 > \frac{|\mathbf{I}| - 1}{|\mathbf{I}|}. \tag{125}$$

Inequality (124) also implies that $|\mathbf{I} \cap \mathbf{V}^{(J)}| \geq 1$, and in general $|\mathbf{I}| \geq |\mathbf{I} \cap \mathbf{V}^{(j)}|$. Thus by (117) and (125),

$$\begin{aligned} |\mathbf{I} \cap \mathbf{V}^{(J)}| \cdot |\mathbf{V}^{(j)}| - |\mathbf{I} \cap \mathbf{V}^{(j)}| \cdot |\mathbf{V}^{(J)}| > (L-1)(|\mathbf{I}| - 1) \\ \geq (L-1)[|\mathbf{I} \cap \mathbf{V}^{(j)}| - |\mathbf{I} \cap \mathbf{V}^{(J)}|] \end{aligned} \tag{126}$$

Inequality (126) implies (123), and hence $O_J > O_j$.

Suppose next that (122) holds. Then

$$|\mathbf{I} \cap \mathbf{V}^{(J)}| \cdot |\mathbf{V}^{(j)}| - |\mathbf{I} \cap \mathbf{V}^{(j)}| \cdot |\mathbf{V}^{(J)}| = 0. \tag{127}$$

Also, $|\mathbf{V}^{(J)}| > |\mathbf{V}^{(j)}|$, so

$$\frac{|\mathbf{I} \cap \mathbf{V}^{(J)}|}{|\mathbf{I} \cap \mathbf{V}^{(j)}|} = \frac{|\mathbf{V}^{(J)}|}{|\mathbf{V}^{(j)}|} > 1. \tag{128}$$

Equations (127) and (128) imply (123), thereby completing the proof of Lemma 1.

We can now prove the theorem.

Proof of Theorem 7: First we show that a node v_J with a subset template is searched before any node v_j with a mixed or superset template. Since $\mathbf{I} \cap \mathbf{V}^{(J)} = \mathbf{V}^{(J)}$ but $\mathbf{I} \cap \mathbf{V}^{(j)}$ is a proper subset of $\mathbf{V}^{(j)}$,

$$\frac{|\mathbf{I} \cap \mathbf{V}^{(J)}|}{|\mathbf{V}^{(J)}|} = \frac{|\mathbf{V}^{(J)}|}{|\mathbf{V}^{(J)}|} = 1 > \frac{|\mathbf{I} \cap \mathbf{V}^{(j)}|}{|\mathbf{V}^{(j)}|}. \tag{129}$$

By (121) in Lemma 1, $O_J > O_j$. Thus all subset templates are searched before mixed templates or learned superset templates.

We next show that a node v_J with a subset template is also searched before any uncommitted node v_j. Since

$$O_j = D_2 \sum_{i \in \mathbf{I}} z_{ij}, \tag{130}$$

the Direct Access Inequality (54) implies that

$$O_j < \frac{D_2 L \, | \, \mathbf{I} \, |}{L - 1 + M}. \tag{131}$$

The right-hand side of (131) is an increasing function of L. Thus by (117),

$$\frac{D_2 L \, | \, \mathbf{I} \, |}{L - 1 + M} \leq \frac{D_2 (| \, \mathbf{I} \, |^{-1} + 1) \, | \, \mathbf{I} \, |}{| \, \mathbf{I} \, |^{-1} + M} = \frac{D_2 (1 + | \, \mathbf{I} \, |)}{| \, \mathbf{I} \, |^{-1} + M}. \tag{132}$$

Inequality (118) implies that

$$\frac{D_2 (1 + | \, \mathbf{I} \, |)}{| \, \mathbf{I} \, |^{-1} + M} \leq \frac{D_2 M}{| \, \mathbf{I} \, |^{-1} + M} < D_2. \tag{133}$$

On the other hand, since $| \, \mathbf{V}^{(J)} \, | \geq 1$,

$$O_J = \frac{D_2 L \, | \, \mathbf{V}^{(J)} \, |}{L - 1 + | \, \mathbf{V}^{(J)} \, |} \geq \frac{D_2 L \cdot 1}{L - 1 + 1} = D_2. \tag{134}$$

Inequalities (131)–(134) together imply $O_J > O_j$.

If v_J has a subset template, then $| \, \mathbf{I} \cap \mathbf{V}^{(J)} \, | = | \, \mathbf{V}^{(J)} \, |$. Thus all nodes with subset templates have the same ratio $| \, \mathbf{I} \cap \mathbf{V}^{(J)} \, | \, \| \, \mathbf{V}^{(J)} \, |^{-1} = 1$. By (122) in Lemma 1, nodes with subset templates are searched in the order of decreasing template size.

If all subset templates are searched and if no other learned templates exist, then an uncommitted node will be activated. This node codes I because it possesses an unlearned superset template that does not lead to $\mathbf{F}_2$ reset.

Suppose all subset templates have been searched and that there exist learned superset templates but no mixed templates. If node v_J has a superset template $V^{(J)}$, then

$$O_J = \frac{D_2 L \, | \, \mathbf{I} \, |}{L - 1 + | \, \mathbf{V}^{(J)} \, |}. \tag{135}$$

By (135), the first superset node to be activated is the node v_J whose template is smallest. Node v_J is chosen before any uncommitted node v_j because, by (54),

$$O_J \geq \frac{D_2 L \, | \, \mathbf{I} \, |}{L - 1 + M} > D_2 \sum_{i \in \mathbf{I}} z_{ij}(0) = O_j. \tag{136}$$

If v_J is activated, it codes I because its template satisfies

$$| \, \mathbf{I} \cap \mathbf{V}^{(J)} \, | = | \, \mathbf{I} \, | \geq \rho \, | \, \mathbf{I} \, |. \tag{137}$$

Suppose that all subset templates are searched and that a superset template $V^{(J)}$ and a mixed template $V^{(j)}$ exist. We prove that $O_j > O_J$ if and only if (119) holds. Suppose that (119) holds. Then also

$$\frac{|\mathbf{I} \cap \mathbf{V}^{(J)}|}{|\mathbf{V}^{(J)}|} = \frac{|\mathbf{I}|}{|\mathbf{V}^{(J)}|} < \frac{|\mathbf{I} \cap \mathbf{V}^{(j)}|}{|\mathbf{V}^{(j)}|}. \tag{138}$$

By condition (121) of Lemma 1, $O_j > O_J$. Conversely, suppose that $O_j > O_J$. Then

$$\frac{|\mathbf{I} \cap \mathbf{V}^{(j)}|}{L - 1 + |\mathbf{V}^{(j)}|} > \frac{|\mathbf{I} \cap \mathbf{V}^{(J)}|}{L - 1 + |\mathbf{V}^{(J)}|} = \frac{|\mathbf{I}|}{L - 1 + |\mathbf{V}^{(J)}|}. \tag{139}$$

Since $V^{(j)}$ is a mixed template with respect to I, $|\mathbf{I} \cap \mathbf{V}^{(j)}| < |\mathbf{I}|$. Thus (139) implies that $|\mathbf{V}^{(j)}| < |\mathbf{V}^{(J)}|$ as well as

$$|\mathbf{I} \cap \mathbf{V}^{(j)}| \cdot |\mathbf{V}^{(J)}| - |\mathbf{I}| \cdot |\mathbf{V}^{(j)}| > (L - 1)[|\mathbf{I}| - |\mathbf{I} \cap \mathbf{V}^{(j)}|] > 0, \tag{140}$$

from which (119) follows. This completes the proof of Theorem 7.

Note that Lemma 1 also specifies the order of search among mixed templates. If all the activated mixed template nodes are reset, then the node v_J with the minimal superset template will code I. Unless (120) holds, it is possible for an uncommitted node v_J to code I before a node with a mixed template v_j is activated. Inequality (120) does not automatically follow from the Direct Access Inequality (54) because $|\mathbf{I} \cap \mathbf{V}^{(j)}|$ may be much smaller than $|\mathbf{I}|$ when $V^{(j)}$ is a mixed template.

24. Order of Search: Computer Simulations

Figures 12 and 13 depict coding sequences that illustrate the order of search specified by Theorem 7 when $(L - 1)$ is small and when the vigilance parameter ρ is close to 1. In Figure 12, each of nine input patterns was presented once. Consider the order of search that occurred in response to the final input pattern I that was presented on trial 9. By trial 8, nodes v_{M+1} and v_{M+2} had already encoded subset templates of this input pattern. On trial 9, these nodes were therefore searched in order of decreasing template size. Nodes v_{M+3}, v_{M+4}, v_{M+5}, and v_{M+6} had encoded mixed templates of the input pattern. These nodes were searched in the order $v_{M+3} \to v_{M+5} \to v_{M+4}$. This search order was not determined by template size per se, but was rather governed by the ratio $|\mathbf{I} \cap \mathbf{V}^{(j)}| \, |\mathbf{V}^{(j)}|^{-1}$ in (121) and (122). These ratios for nodes v_{M+3}, v_{M+5}, and v_{M+4} were 9/10, 14/16, and 7/8, respectively. Since $14/16 = 7/8$, node v_{M+5} was searched before node v_{M+4} because $|\mathbf{V}^{(M+5)}| = 16 > 8 = |\mathbf{V}^{(M+4)}|$. The mixed template node v_{M+6} was not searched. After searching v_{M+5}, the network activated the node v_{M+7} which possessed the smallest superset template. A comparison of rows 8 and 9 in column 7 shows how the superset template of v_{M+7} was recoded to match the input pattern. By (119), the superset template node v_{M+7} was searched before the mixed template node v_{M+6} because the ratio $|\mathbf{I}| \, |\mathbf{V}^{(M+7)}|^{-1} = 17/21$ was larger than $|\mathbf{I} \cap \mathbf{V}^{(M+6)}| \, |\mathbf{V}^{(M+6)}|^{-1} = 14/18$.

The eight input patterns of Figure 13 illustrate a search followed by coding of an uncommitted node. The last input pattern I in Figure 13 is the same as the last input pattern in Figure 12. In Figure 13, however, there are no superset templates corresponding

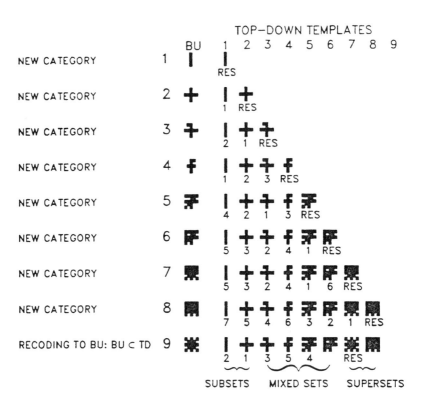

Figure 12. Computer simulation to illustrate order of search: On trial 9, the system first searches subset templates, next searches some, but not all, mixed templates, and finally recodes the smallest superset template. A smaller choice of vigilance parameter could have terminated the search at a subset template or mixed template node.

to input pattern I. Consequently I was coded by a previously uncommitted node v_{M+8} on trial 8. On trial 8 the network searched nodes with subset templates in the order $v_{M+2} \to v_{M+1}$ and the mixed template nodes in the order $v_{M+4} \to v_{M+6} \to v_{M+5} \to v_{M+7}$. The mixed template node v_{M+3} was not searched because its template badly mismatched the input pattern I and thus did not satisfy (120). Instead, the uncommitted node v_{M+8} was activated and learned a template that matched the input pattern. If $(L-1)$ is not small enough to satisfy inequality (117), then mixed templates or superset templates may be searched before subset templates. For all $L > 1$, however, Theorem 6 implies that all input patterns have direct access to their coding nodes after the learning process equilibrates.

25. Biasing the Network towards Uncommitted Nodes

Another effect of choosing L large is to bias the network to choose uncommitted nodes in response to unfamiliar input patterns I. To understand this effect, suppose that for all i

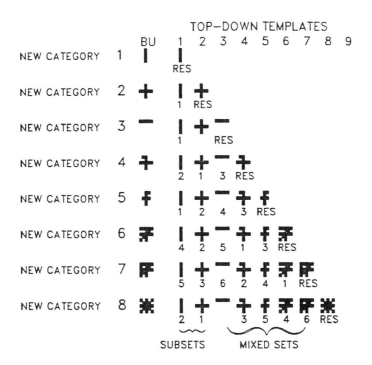

Figure 13. Computer simulation to illustrate order of search: Unlike the search described in Figure 12, no learned superset template exists when the search begins on trial 8. Consequently, the system first searches subset templates, next searches mixed templates, and finally terminates the search by coding a previously uncommitted node.

and j,

$$z_{ij}(0) \cong \frac{L}{L-1+M}. \tag{71}$$

Then when I is presented, an uncommitted node is chosen before a coded node v_j if

$$\frac{|\,\mathbf{I} \cap \mathbf{V}^{(j)}\,|}{L-1+|\,\mathbf{V}^{(j)}\,|} < \frac{|\,\mathbf{I}\,|}{L-1+M}. \tag{141}$$

This inequality is equivalent to

$$\frac{|\,\mathbf{I} \cap \mathbf{V}^{(j)}\,|}{|\,\mathbf{I}\,|} < \frac{L-1+|\,\mathbf{V}^{(j)}\,|}{L-1+M}. \tag{142}$$

As L increases, the ratio

$$\frac{L-1+|\,\mathbf{V}^{(j)}\,|}{L-1+M} \to 1, \tag{143}$$

whereas the left-hand side of (142) is always less than or equal to 1. Thus for large values of L, the network tends to code unfamiliar input patterns into new categories, even if the vigilance parameter ρ is small. As L increases, the automatic scaling property (Section 2A) of the network also becomes weaker, as does the tendency to search subset templates first.

Recall that parameter L describes the relative strength of the bottom-up competition among LTM traces which gives rise to the Weber Law Rule (Section 12B), with smaller L corresponding to stronger LTM competition. Thus the structural process of LTM competition works with the state-dependent process of attentional vigilance to control how coarse the learned categories will be.

26. Computer Simulation of Self-Scaling Computational Units: Weighing The Evidence

We can now understand quantitatively how the network automatically rescales its matching and signal-to-noise criteria in the computer simulations of Figure 7. On the first four presentations, the input patterns are presented in the order ABAB. By trial 2, learning is complete. Pattern A directly accesses node v_{M+1} on trial 3, and pattern B directly accesses node v_{M+2} on trial 4. Thus patterns A and B are coded within different categories. On trials 5–8, patterns C and D are presented in the order CDCD. Patterns C and D are constructed from patterns A and B, respectively, by adding identical upper halves to A and B. Thus, pattern C differs from pattern D at the same locations where pattern A differs from pattern B. However, because patterns C and D represent many more active features than patterns A and B, the difference between C and D is treated as noise and is deleted from the critical feature pattern of v_{M+3} which codes both C and D, whereas the difference between A and B is considered significant and is included within the critical feature patterns of v_{M+1} and v_{M+2}.

The core issue in the network's different categorization of patterns A and B vs. patterns C and D is the following: Why on trial 2 does B reject the node v_{M+1} which has coded A, whereas D on trial 6 accepts the node v_{M+3} which has coded C? This occurs despite the fact that the mismatch between B and $V^{(M+1)}$ equals the mismatch between D and $V^{(M+3)}$:

$$| \mathbf{B} | - | \mathbf{B} \cap \mathbf{V}^{(M+1)} | = 3 = | \mathbf{D} | - | \mathbf{D} \cap \mathbf{V}^{(M+3)} | . \tag{144}$$

The reason is that

$$\frac{| \mathbf{B} \cap \mathbf{V}^{(M+1)} |}{| \mathbf{B} |} = \frac{8}{11} \tag{145}$$

whereas

$$\frac{| \mathbf{D} \cap \mathbf{V}^{(M+3)} |}{| \mathbf{D} |} = \frac{14}{17}. \tag{146}$$

In this simulation, the vigilance parameter $\rho = .8$. Thus

$$\frac{| \mathbf{B} \cap \mathbf{V}^{(M+1)} |}{| \mathbf{B} |} < \rho < \frac{| \mathbf{D} \cap \mathbf{V}^{(M+3)} |}{| \mathbf{D} |}. \tag{147}$$

By (73), pattern B resets v_{M+1} on trial 2 but D does not reset v_{M+3} on trial 6. Consequently, B is coded by a different category than A, whereas D is coded by the same category as C.

27. Concluding Remarks: Self-Stabilization and Unitization within Associative Networks

Two main conclusions of our work are especially salient. First, the code learning process is one of progressive refinement of distinctions. The distinctions that emerge are the resultant of all the input patterns which the network ever experiences, rather than of some preassigned features. Second, the matching process compares whole patterns, not just separate features. It may happen that two different input patterns to F_1 overlap a template at the same set of feature detectors, yet the network will reset the F_2 node in response to one input but not the other. The degree of mismatch of template pattern and input pattern *as a whole* determines whether coding or reset will occur. Thus the learning of categorical invariants resolves two opposing tendencies. As categories grow larger, and hence code increasingly global invariants, the templates which define them become smaller, as they discover and base the code on sets of critical feature patterns, or prototypes, rather than upon familiar pattern exemplars. This article shows how these two opposing tendencies can be resolved within a self-organizing system, leading to dynamic equilibration, or self-stabilization, of recognition categories in response to an arbitrary list of arbitrarily many binary input patterns. This self-stabilization property is of major importance for the further development of associative networks and the analysis of cognitive recognition processes.

Now that properties of self-organization, self-stabilization, and self-scaling are completely understood within the class of ART networks described herein, a number of generalizations also need to be studied. Within this article, an input pattern to level F_1 is globally grouped at F_2 when the F_2 population which receives the maximal input from the $F_1 \rightarrow F_2$ adaptive filter is chosen for short term memory (STM) storage. Within the total architecture of an ART system, even this simple type of F_2 reaction to the $F_1 \rightarrow F_2$ adaptive filter leads to powerful coding properties. On the other hand, a level F_2 which makes global choices must be viewed as a special case of a more general design for F_2.

If the second processing stage F_2 makes a choice, then later processing stages which are activated by F_2 alone could not further analyse the input pattern across F_1. The coding hierarchy for individual input patterns would end at the choice, or global grouping, stage. By contrast, a coding scheme wherein F_2 generates a spatially distributed representation of the F_1 activity pattern, rather than a choice, could support subsequent levels F_3, F_4, ..., F_n for coding multiple groupings, or chunks, and thus more abstract invariants of an input pattern. This possibility raises many issues concerning the properties of these configurations and their invariants, and of the architectural constraints which enable a multi-level coding hierarchy to learn and recognize distributed invariants in a stable and globally self-consistent fashion.

A parallel neural architecture, called a *masking field* (Cohen and Grossberg, 1986, 1987a, 1987b; Grossberg, 1978a, 1984b, 1986; Grossberg and Stone, 1986a) is a type of circuit design from which F_2—and by extension higher levels F_3, F_4, ..., F_n—may be fashioned to generate distributed representations of filtered input patterns. Masking field properties are of value for visual object recognition, speech recognition, and higher cognitive processes. Indeed, the same circuit design can be used for the development of general spatially distributed self-organizing recognition codes. The purpose of a masking field is to detect simultaneously, and weight properly in STM, all salient parts, or groupings, of an input pattern. The pattern as a whole is but one such grouping. A masking field generates a spatially distributed, yet unitized, representation of the input pattern in STM. Computer simulations of how a masking field can detect and learn unitized distributed representations of an input are found in Cohen and Grossberg (1986, 1987a, 1987b). Much further work needs to be done to understand the design of ART systems all of whose levels F_i are masking fields.

Other useful generalizations of the ART system analysed herein include systems whose learning rate is slow relative to the time scale of a single trial; systems in which forgetting of LTM values can occur; systems which process continuous as well as binary input and output patterns; and systems in which Weber Law processing is realized through competitive STM interactions among F_1 nodes rather than competitive LTM interactions among bottom-up LTM traces (Section 12B). All of these generalizations will be considered in our future articles of this series.

Preprocessing of the input patterns to an ART system is no less important than choosing levels F_i capable of supporting a hierarchy of unitized codes of parts and wholes. In applications to visual object recognition, neural circuits which generate pre-attentively completed segmentations of a visual image before these completed segmentations generate inputs to an ART network have recently been constructed. (Grossberg, 1987; Grossberg and Mingolla, 1985a, 1985b, 1987). In applications to adaptive speech recognition, inputs are encoded as STM patterns of temporal order information across item representations before these STM patterns generate inputs to an ART network (Grossberg, 1978a, 1984b, 1986; Grossberg and Stone, 1986a, 1986b). Further work needs to be done to characterize these preprocessing stages and how they are joined to their ART coding networks. Although a great deal of work remains to be done, results such as those in the present article amply illustrate that the whole is much greater than the sum of its parts both in human experience and in self-organizing models thereof.

APPENDIX

Table 1 lists the constraints on the dimensionless model parameters for the system summarized in Section 18. We will now show that the 2/3 Rule holds when these constraints are satisfied. Then we describe four alternative, but dynamically equivalent, systems for realizing the 2/3 Rule and attentional gain control.

TABLE 1

Parameter Constraints

$$A_1 \geq 0$$

$$C_1 \geq 0$$

$$\max\{1, D_1\} < B_1 < 1 + D_1$$

$$0 < \epsilon << 1$$

$$K = O(1)$$

$$L > 1$$

$$0 < \rho \leq 1$$

$$0 < z_{ij}(0) < \frac{L}{L-1+M}$$

$$1 > z_{ji}(0) > \overline{z} \equiv \frac{B_1 - 1}{D_1}$$

$$0 \leq I_i, f, g, h \leq 1$$

Recall that x_i ($i = 1 \ldots M$) denotes the STM activity of an F_1 node v_i; that x_j ($j = M+1 \ldots N$) denotes the STM activity of an F_2 node v_j; that z_{ij} denotes the strength of the LTM trace in the bottom-up pathway from v_i to v_j; that z_{ji} denotes the strength of the LTM trace in the top-down pathway from v_j to v_i; that I_i denotes the bottom-up input to x_i; that $\mathbf{I}$ denotes the set of indices $i \in \{1 \ldots M\}$ such that $I_i > 0$; that $\mathbf{X} = \mathbf{X}(t)$ denotes the set of indices i such that $x_i(t) > 0$; and that $\mathbf{V}^{(j)} = \mathbf{V}^{(j)}(t)$ denotes the set of indices i such that $z_{ji}(t) > \overline{z}$.

Combining equations (8), (10), (11), and (12), we find the following equation for the ith STM trace of F_1:

$$\epsilon \frac{dx_i}{dt} = -x_i + (1 - A_1 x_i)(I_i + D_1 \sum_j f(x_j) z_{ji}) - (B_1 + C_1 x_i) \sum_j f(x_j). \quad (A1)$$

When F_2 is inactive, all top-down signals $f(x_j) = 0$. Hence by (A1),

$$\epsilon \frac{dx_i}{dt} = -x_i + (1 - A_1 x_i) I_i. \quad (A2)$$

When the F_2 node v_J is active, only the top-down signal $f(x_J)$ is non-zero. Since $f(x_J) = 1$,

$$\epsilon \frac{dx_i}{dt} = -x_i + (1 - A_1 x_i)(I_i + D_1 z_{Ji}) - (B_1 + C_1 x_i). \quad (A3)$$

Since each x_i variable changes rapidly relative to the rate of change of the LTM trace z_{Ji} (since $0 < \epsilon << 1$), then x_i is always close to its steady state, $\frac{dx_i}{dt} = 0$. By (A2), then

$$x_i \cong \frac{I_i}{1 + A_1 I_i} \quad \text{if } F_2 \text{ is inactive} \quad (A4)$$

and, by (A3),

$$x_i \cong \frac{I_i + D_1 z_{Ji} - B_1}{1 + A_1(I_i + D_1 z_{Ji}) + C_1} \quad \text{if the } F_2 \text{ node } v_J \text{ is active.} \tag{A5}$$

The 2/3 Rule, as defined by:

$$\mathbf{X} = \begin{cases} \mathbf{I} & \text{if } F_2 \text{ is inactive} \\ \mathbf{I} \cap \mathbf{V}^{(J)} & \text{if the } F_2 \text{ node } v_J \text{ is active} \end{cases}, \tag{47}$$

can be derived as follows. Note first that (A4) implies that, when F_2 is inactive, $x_i > 0$ iff $I_i > 0$; i.e., $\mathbf{X} = \mathbf{I}$. On the other hand, if v_J is active, (A5) implies that :

$$x_i > 0 \text{ iff } z_{Ji} > \frac{B_1 - I_i}{D_1}. \tag{A6}$$

The 2/3 Rule requires that x_i be positive when the F_1 node v_i is receiving large inputs, both top-down and bottom-up. Thus setting $z_{Ji} = 1$ and $I_i = 1$ (their maximal values) in (A6) implies the constraint:

$$1 > \frac{B_1 - 1}{D_1}. \tag{A7}$$

The 2/3 Rule also requires that x_i be negative if v_i receives no top-down input, even if the bottom-up input is large. Thus setting $z_{Ji} = 0$ and $I_i = 1$ in (A6) implies the constraint:

$$0 < \frac{B_1 - 1}{D_1}. \tag{A8}$$

Finally, the 2/3 Rule requires that x_i be negative if v_i receives no bottom-up input, even if the top-down input is large. Thus setting $I_i = 0$ and $z_{Ji} = 1$ in (A6) implies the constraint:

$$1 < \frac{B_1}{D_1}. \tag{A9}$$

Inequalities (A7), (A8), and (A9) are summarized by the
2/3 Rule Inequalities:

$$\max\{1, D_1\} < B_1 < 1 + D_1. \tag{68}$$

Since $0 \leq I_i \leq 1$, (A6) also shows that if v_J is active and if

$$z_{Ji}(t) \leq \frac{B_1 - 1}{D_1}, \tag{A10}$$

then $x_i(t) \leq 0$; i.e., $i \notin \mathbf{X}$. However if $i \notin \mathbf{X}$, z_{Ji} decays toward 0 whenever v_J is active. Thus if (A10) is true at some time $t = t_0$, it remains true for all $t \geq t_0$. Therefore

$$\bar{z} \equiv \frac{B_1 - 1}{D_1} \tag{69}$$

is the critical top-down LTM strength such that if $z_{Ji}(t_0) \leq \bar{z}$, then $z_{Ji}(t) \leq \bar{z}$ for all $t \geq t_0$. Whenever v_J is active and $t \geq t_0$, the F_1 node v_i will be inactive.

Figure 14 depicts four ways in which attentional gain control can distinguish bottom-up and top-down processing to implement the 2/3 Rule. All of these systems generate the same asymptote (A5) when F_2 is active, and the same asymptotes, up to a minor change in parameters, when F_2 is inactive. The parameters in all four systems are defined to satisfy the constraints in Table 1.

In Figure 14a, F_2 can phasically excite the gain control channel, which thereupon nonspecifically inhibits the cells of F_1. Thus

$$\epsilon \frac{dx_i}{dt} = -x_i + (1 - A_1 x_i)(I_i + D_1 \sum_j f(x_j) z_{ji}) - (B_1 + C_1 x_i)G_1 \qquad (A11)$$

where

$$G_1 = \begin{cases} 0 & \text{if } I \text{ is active and } F_2 \text{ is inactive} \\ 1 & \text{if } I \text{ is inactive and } F_2 \text{ is active} \\ 1 & \text{if } I \text{ is active and } F_2 \text{ is active} \\ 0 & \text{if } I \text{ is inactive and } F_2 \text{ is inactive.} \end{cases} \qquad (A12)$$

In other words $G_1 = \sum_j f(x_j)$. Thus (A11) is just (A1) in a slightly different notation.

In Figure 14b, the plus sign within an open circle in the gain control channel designates that the gain control cells, in the absence of any bottom-up or top-down signals, are endogenously maintained at an equilibrium potential which exceeds their output threshold. Output signals from the gain control cells nonspecifically inhibit the cells of F_1. In short, the gain control channel tonically, or persistently, inhibits F_1 cells in the absence of bottom-up or top-down signals. Bottom-up and top-down signals phasically modulate the level of nonspecific inhibition. In particular, a bottom-up input alone totally inhibits the gain control channel, thereby disinhibiting the cells of F_1. A top-down signal alone maintains the inhibition from the gain control channel, because the inhibition is either on or off, and is thus not further increased by F_2. When both a bottom-up input and a top-down signal are active, their inputs to the gain control channel cancel, thereby again maintaining the same level of inhibition to F_1. The STM equations at F_1 are

$$\epsilon \frac{dx_i}{dt} = -x_i + (1 - A_1 x_i)(I_i + D_1 \sum_j f(x_j) z_{ji}) - (B_1 + C_1 x_i)G_2, \qquad (A13)$$

where

$$G_2 = \begin{cases} 0 & \text{if } I \text{ is active and } F_2 \text{ is inactive} \\ 1 & \text{if } I \text{ is inactive and } F_2 \text{ is active} \\ 1 & \text{if } I \text{ is active and } F_2 \text{ is active} \\ 1 & \text{if } I \text{ is inactive and } F_2 \text{ is inactive.} \end{cases} \qquad (A14)$$

The equilibrium activities of x_i are as follows. If I is active and F_2 is inactive, then (A4) again holds. If I is inactive and F_2 is active, then (A5) again holds. Equation (A5) also holds if I is active and F_2 is active. If I is inactive and F_2 is inactive, then

$$x_i \cong \frac{-B_1}{1 + C_1}, \qquad (A15)$$

which is negative; hence no output signals are generated.

In Figure 14c, as in Figure 14b, the gain control cells are tonically active (plus sign in open circle). In Figure 14c, however, these cells nonspecifically excite the cells of F_1. In the absence of any external signals, F_1 cells are maintained in a state of tonic hyperpolarization, or negative activity (denoted by the minus sign in the open circle). The tonic excitation

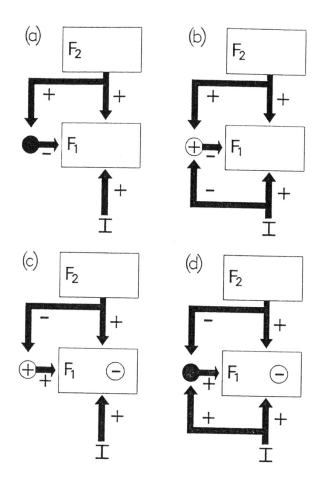

Figure 14. Design variations for realizing 2/3 Rule matching properties at F_1: In (a) and (b), F_2 excites the gain control channel, whereas in (c) and (d), F_2 inhibits the gain control channel. In (b), the input pattern I inhibits the gain control channel, whereas in (d), I excites the gain control channel. In (a) and (d), the gain control channel phasically reacts to its inputs (closed circles). Activation of the gain control channel in (a) nonspecifically inhibits F_1, and in (d) nonspecifically excites F_1. In (b) and (c), the gain control channel is tonically, or persistently, active in the absence of inputs (open circles surrounding plus signs). Activation of the gain control channel in (b) nonspecifically inhibits F_1, and in (c) nonspecifically excites F_1. In (c) and (d), the F_1 cells are maintained in a state of tonic hyperpolarization, or inhibition, in the absence of external inputs (open circles surrounding minus signs). All four cases lead to equivalent dynamics.

from the gain control cells balances the tonic inhibition due to hyperpolarization and thereby maintains the activity of F_2 cells near their output threshold of zero. A bottom-up input can thereby excite F_1 cells enough for them to generate output signals. When top-down signals are active, they inhibit the gain control cells. Consequently those F_1 cells which do not receive bottom-up or top-down signals become hyperpolarized. Due to tonic hyperpolarization, F_1 cells which receive a bottom-up signal or a top-down signal, but not both, cannot exeed their output threshold. Only F_1 cells at which large top-down and bottom-up signals converge can generate an output signal.

The STM equations at F_1 are

$$\epsilon \frac{dx_i}{dt} = -x_i + (1 - A_1 x_i)(I_i + D_1 \sum_j f(x_j) z_{ji} + B_1 G_3) - (B_1 + C_1 x_i), \qquad (A16)$$

where

$$G_3 = \begin{cases} 1 & \text{if } I \text{ is active and } F_2 \text{ is inactive} \\ 0 & \text{if } I \text{ is inactive and } F_2 \text{ is active} \\ 0 & \text{if } I \text{ is active and } F_2 \text{ is active} \\ 1 & \text{if } I \text{ is inactive and } F_2 \text{ is inactive} \end{cases} . \qquad (A17)$$

The equilibrium activities of x_i are as follows. If I is active and F_2 is inactive, then

$$x_i \cong \frac{I_i}{1 + A_1 I_i + A_1 B_1 + C_1}. \qquad (A18)$$

Thus $x_i > 0$ iff $I_i > 0$. If I is inactive and F_2 is active, then (A5) holds. If I is active and F_2 is active, then (A5) holds. If I is inactive and F_2 is inactive, then

$$x_i \cong \frac{B_1 - B_1}{1 + A_1 B_1 + C_1} = 0. \qquad (A19)$$

Hence no output signals are generated from F_1. The coefficient B_1 in term $B_1 G_3$ of (A16) may be decreased somewhat without changing system dynamics.

In Figure 14d, the gain control cells are phasically excited by bottom-up signals and inhibited by top-down signals. Once active, they nonspecifically excite F_1 cells. In the absence of any external signals, F_1 cells are maintained in a state of tonic hyperpolarization, or negativity. In response to a bottom-up input, the gain control channel balances the tonic hyperpolarization of F_1 cells, thereby allowing those cells which receive bottom-up inputs to fire. When a top-down signal is active, no gain control outputs occur. Hence top-down signals alone cannot overcome the tonic hyperpolarization enough to generate output signals from F_1. Simultaneous convergence of an excitatory bottom-up signal and an inhibitory top-down signal at the gain control cells prevents these cells from generating output signals to F_1. Consequently, only those F_1 cells at which a bottom-up input and top-down template signal converge can overcome the tonic hyperpolarization to generate output signals.

The STM equations of F_1 are

$$\epsilon \frac{dx_i}{dt} = -x_i + (1 - A_1 x_i)(I_i + D_1 \sum_j f(x_j) z_{ji} + B_1 G_4) - (B_1 + C_1 x_i), \qquad (A20)$$

where

$$G_4 = \begin{cases} 1 & \text{if } I \text{ is active and } F_2 \text{ is inactive} \\ 0 & \text{if } I \text{ is inactive and } F_2 \text{ is active} \\ 0 & \text{if } I \text{ is active and } F_2 \text{ is active} \\ 0 & \text{if } I \text{ is inactive and } F_2 \text{ is inactive} \end{cases} . \qquad (A21)$$

The equilibrium activities of x_i are as follows. If I is active and F_2 is inactive, then (A18) holds. If I is inactive and F_2 is active, then (A5) holds. Equation (A5) also holds if I is active and F_2 is active. If I is inactive and F_2 is inactive, then (A15) holds.

In all four cases, an F_1 cell fires only if the number of active excitatory pathways which converge upon the cell exceeds the number of active inhibitory pathways which converge upon the cell, where we count a source of tonic hyperpolarization as one input pathway. A similar rule governs the firing of the gain control channel in all cases.

REFERENCES

Anderson, J.A., Silverstein, J.W., Ritz, S.R., and Jones, R.S., Distinctive features, categorical perception, and probability learning: some applications of a neural model. *Psychological Review*, 1977, **84**, 413–451.

Banquet, J.P. and Grossberg, S., Probing cognitive processes through the structure of event-related potentials during learning: An experimental and theoretical analysis. *Applied Optics*, in press, 1987.

Basar, E., Flohr, H., Haken, H., and Mandell, A.J. (Eds.), **Synergetics of the brain.** New York: Springer-Verlag, 1983.

Carpenter, G.A. and Grossberg, S., Category learning and adaptive pattern recognition: A neural network model. *Proceedings of the Third Army Conference on Applied Mathematics and Computing*, 1985, ARO Report 86-1, 37–56 (a).

Carpenter, G.A. and Grossberg, S., Neural dynamics of adaptive pattern recognition: Priming, search, attention, and category formation. *Society for Neuroscience Abstracts*, 1985, **11**, 1110 (b).

Carpenter, G.A. and Grossberg, S., Self-organization of neural recognition codes: Nonlinear Weber Law modulation of associative learning. In preparation, 1986.

Carpenter, G.A. and Grossberg, S., Neural dynamics of category learning and recognition: Attention, memory consolidation, and amnesia. In J. Davis, R. Newburgh, and E. Wegman (Eds.), **Brain structure, learning, and memory.** AAAS Symposium Series, 1987 (a).

Carpenter, G.A. and Grossberg, S., Neural dynamics of category learning and recognition: Structural invariants, reinforcement, and evoked potentials. In M.L. Commons, S.M. Kosslyn, and R.J. Herrnstein (Eds.), **Pattern recognition and concepts in animals, people, and machines.** Hillsdale, NJ: Erlbaum, 1987 (b).

Cohen, M.A. and Grossberg, S., Neural dynamics of speech and language coding: Developmental programs, perceptual grouping, and competition for short term memory. *Human Neurobiology*, 1986, **5**, 1–22.

Cohen, M.A. and Grossberg, S., Unitized recognition codes for parts and wholes: The unique cue in configural discriminations. In M.L. Commons, S.M. Kosslyn, and R.J. Herrnstein (Eds.), **Pattern recognition and concepts in animals, people, and machines.** Hillsdale, NJ: Erlbaum, 1987 (a).

Cohen, M.A. and Grossberg, S., Masking fields: A massively parallel architecture for discovering learning, and recognizing multiple groupings of patterned data. *Applied Optics*, 1987, **26**, 1866–1891 (b).

Ellias, S. and Grossberg, S., Pattern formation, contrast control, and oscillations in the short term memory of shunting on-center off-surround networks. *Biological Cybernetics*, 1975, **20**, 69–98.

Fukushima, K., Neocognitron: A self-organizing neural network model for a mechanism of pattern recognition unaffected by shift in position. *Biological Cybernetics*, 1980, **36**, 193–202.

Grossberg, S., Contour enhancement, short-term memory, and constancies in reverberating neural networks. *Studies in Applied Mathematics*, 1973, **52**, 217–257.

Grossberg, S., Adaptive pattern classification and universal recoding, I: Parallel development and coding of neural feature detectors. *Biological Cybernetics*, 1976, **23**, 121–134 (a).

Grossberg, S., Adaptive pattern classification and universal recoding, II: Feedback, expectation, olfaction, and illusions. *Biological Cybernetics*, 1976, **23**, 187–202 (b).

Grossberg, S., A theory of human memory: Self-organization and performance of sensory-motor codes, maps, and plans. In R. Rosen and F. Snell (Eds.), **Progress in theoretical biology**, Vol.5, pp.233–374. New York: Academic Press, 1978 (a).

Grossberg, S., Do all neural networks really look alike? A comment on Anderson, Silverstein, Ritz, and Jones. *Psychological Review*, 1978, **85**, 592–596 (b).

Grossberg, S., How does a brain build a cognitive code? *Psychological Review*, 1980, **87**, 1–51.

Grossberg, S., The quantized geometry of visual space: The coherent computation of depth, form, and lightness. *Behavioral Brain Sciences*, 1983, **6**, 625–692.

Grossberg, S., Some psychophysiological and pharmacological correlates of a developmental, cognitive and motivational theory. In R. Karrer, J. Cohen, and P. Tueting (Eds.), **Brain and information: Event related potentials**, pp.58-151. New York: New York Academy of Sciences, 1984 (a).

Grossberg, S., Unitization, automaticity, temporal order, and word recognition. *Cognition and Brain Theory*, 1984, **7**, 263–283 (b).

Grossberg, S., The adaptive self-organization of serial order in behavior: Speech, language, and motor control. In E.C. Schwab and H.C. Nusbaum (Eds.), **Pattern recognition by humans and machines**, Vol.1. New York: Academic Press, 1986.

Grossberg, S., Cortical dynamics of three-dimensional form, color, and brightness perception: Parts I and II. *Perception and Psychophysics*, 1987, **41**, 87–158.

Grossberg, S. and Levine, D., Some developmental and attentional biases in the contrast enhancement and short term memory of recurrent neural networks. *Journal of Theoretical Biology*, 1975, **53**, 341–380.

Grossberg, S. and Mingolla, E., Neural dynamics of form perception: Boundary completion, illusory figures, and neon color spreading. *Psychological Review*, 1985, **92**, 173–211 (a).

Grossberg, S. and Mingolla, E., Neural dynamics of perceptual grouping: Textures, boundaries, and emergent segmentations. *Perception and Psychophysics*, 1985, **38**, 141–171 (b).

Grossberg, S. and Mingolla, E., Neural dynamics of surface perception: Boundary webs, illuminants, and shape-from-shading. *Computer Vision, Graphics, and Image Processing*, 1987, **37**, 116–165.

Grossberg, S. and Stone, G.O., Neural dynamics of word recognition and recall: Attentional priming, learning, and resonance. *Psychological Review*, 1986, **93**, 46–74 (a).

Grossberg, S. and Stone, G.O., Neural dynamics of attention switching and temporal order information in short term memory. *Memory and Cognition*, 1986, **14**, 451–468 (b).

Hebb, D.O., **The organization of behavior**. New York: Wiley, 1949.

Hopfield, J.J., Neural networks and physical systems with emergent collective computational abilities. *Proceedings of The National Academy of Sciences USA*, 1982, **79**, 2554–2558.

Kohonen, T., **Associative memory: A system-theoretical approach.** New York: Springer-Verlag, 1977.

Lin, C.C. and Segal, L.A., **Mathematics applied to deterministic problems in the natural sciences.** New York: Macmillan, 1974.

Malsburg, C. von der and Willshaw, D.J., Differential equations for the development of topological nerve fibre projections. In S. Grossberg (Ed.), **Mathematical psychology and psychophysiology.** Providence, RI: American Mathematical Society, 1981, pp.39–47.

McClelland, J.I. and Rumelhart, D.E., Distributed memory and the representation of general and specific information. *Journal of Experimental Psychology: General*, 1985, **114**, 159–188.

Posner, M.I., **Cognition: An introduction.** Glenview, IL: Scott, Foresman, and Company, 1973.

Posner, M.I. and Keele, S.W., On the genesis of abstract ideas. *Journal of Experimental Psychology*, 1968, **77**, 353–363.

Posner, M.I. and Keele, S.W., Retention of abstract ideas. *Journal of Experimental Psychology*, 1970, **83**, 304–308.

Smith, E.E. and Medin, D.L., **Categories and concepts.** Cambridge, MA: Harvard University Press, 1981.

Applied Optics
1987, **26** (10), 1866–1891
©1987 The Optical Society of America

MASKING FIELDS: A MASSIVELY PARALLEL NEURAL ARCHITECTURE FOR LEARNING, RECOGNIZING, AND PREDICTING MULTIPLE GROUPINGS OF PATTERNED DATA

Michael A. Cohen† and Stephen Grossberg‡

ABSTRACT

A massively parallel neural network architecture, called a *masking field*, is characterized through systematic computer simulations. A masking field is a multiple scale, self-similar, automatically gain-controlled cooperative-competitive feedback network F_2. Network F_2 receives input patterns from an adaptive filter $F_1 \rightarrow F_2$ that is activated by a prior processing level F_1. Such a network F_2 behaves like a content-addressable memory. It activates compressed recognition codes that are predictive with respect to the activation patterns flickering across the feature detectors of F_1, and competitively inhibits, or masks, codes which are unpredictive with respect to the F_1 patterns. In particular, a masking field can simultaneously detect multiple groupings within its input patterns and assign activation weights to the codes for these groupings which are predictive with respect to the contextual information embedded within the patterns and the prior learning of the system. A masking field automatically rescales its sensitivity as the overall size of an input pattern changes, yet also remains sensitive to the microstructure within each input pattern. In this way, a masking field can more strongly activate a code for the whole F_1 pattern than for its salient parts, yet amplifies the code for a pattern part when it becomes a pattern whole in a new input context. A masking field can also be primed by inputs from F_1: it can activate codes which represent predictions of how the F_1 pattern may evolve in the subsequent time interval. Network F_2 can also exhibit an adaptive sharpening property: repetition of a familiar F_1 pattern can tune the adaptive filter to elicit a more focal spatial activation of its F_2 recognition code than does an unfamiliar input pattern. The F_2 recognition code also becomes less distributed when an input pattern contains more contextual information on which to base an unambiguous prediction of which F_1 pattern is being processed. Thus a masking field suggests a solution of the credit assignment problem by embodying a real-time code for the predictive evidence contained within its input patterns. Such capabilities are useful in speech recognition, visual object recognition, and cognitive information processing. An absolutely stable design for a masking field is disclosed through an analysis of the computer simulations. This design suggests how associative mechanisms, cooperative-competitive interactions, and modulatory gating signals can be joined together to regulate

† Supported in part by the Air Force Office of Scientific Research (AFOSR F49620-86-C-0037) and the National Science Foundation (NSF IRI-84-17756).

‡ Supported in part by the Air Force Office of Scientific Research (AFOSR F49620-86-C-0037), the Army Research Office (ARO DAAG-29-85-K-0095), and the National Science Foundation (NSF IRI-84-17756).

the learning of compressed recognition codes. Data about the neural substrates of learning and memory are compared with these mechanisms.

1. Introduction: Context-Sensitive Grouping in Recognition Processes

One of the fundamental problem areas in perception, cognition, and artificial intelligence concerns the characterization of the functional units into which perceptual and cognitive mechanisms group the patterned information that they process. A core issue concerns the context-sensitivity of these functional units, or the manner in which a grouping into functional units can depend upon the spatiotemporal patterning of all the signals being processed. Another core issue concerns the adaptive tuning of recognition mechanisms, and the manner in which such tuning can alter the groupings which emerge within a context containing familiar elements. Adaptive tuning of recognition processes is one of the mechanisms whereby representations become *compressed*, *chunked*, or *unitized* into coherent recognition codes through experience.

The present article describes the further development of a real-time neural network model, called a *masking field*, which was introduced in Grossberg (1978). A masking field is a multiple-scale, self-similar, automatically gain-controlled cooperative-competitive feedback network. This type of network acts like a content-addressable memory whose properties are useful for understanding how a large class of compressed recognition codes are established during real-time speech recognition, visual object recognition, and cognitive information processing. The analyses of cooperative-competitive content-addressable memories which led to the masking field concept are found in Grossberg (1973) and Grossberg and Levine (1975). Since its introduction in 1978, the masking field model has played an important role in the development of the *adaptive resonance theory* which was introduced in Grossberg (1976a, 1976b) and which has since undergone extensive development and application (Banquet and Grossberg, 1987; Carpenter and Grossberg, 1987a, 1987b, 1987c, 1987d; Cohen and Grossberg, 1986, 1987; Grossberg, 1982, 1987a, 1987b; Grossberg and Gutowski, 1987; Grossberg and Kuperstein, 1986; Grossberg and Levine, 1987; Grossberg and Schmajuk, 1987; Grossberg and Stone, 1986a, 1986b).

A related family of cooperative-competitive content-addressable networks, which also grew out of the Grossberg (1973) analysis, was identified through the discovery of a global Liapunov function in Cohen and Grossberg (1983). The Liapunov function described in Hopfield (1984) is a special case of the Cohen-Grossberg function, a case that was explicitly noted in Cohen and Grossberg (1983, p.819). The Cohen-Grossberg Liapunov function requires symmetry of connections between pairs of network nodes. Symmetry of connections is strongly violated in a masking field. This symmetry violation is a consequence of the network's self-similar design. In particular, the masking fields analysed herein obey the differential equations

$$\frac{d}{dt}x_i^{(J)} = -Ax_i^{(J)} + (B - x_i^{(J)})\Big\{\sum_{j \in J} I_j[\frac{1}{|J|}(1 - p_{|J|}) + r_{ji}^{(J)}p_{|J|}]z_{ji}^{(J)} + D \mid J \mid f(x_i^{(J)})\Big\}$$

$$- F(x_i^{(J)} + C)\frac{\sum_{m,K} g(x_m^{(K)}) \mid K \mid (1 + \mid K \cap J \mid)}{\sum_{m,K} \mid K \mid (1 + \mid K \cap J \mid)}$$

(1)

and

$$\frac{d}{dt}z_{ji}^{(J)} = \epsilon f(x_i^{(J)})(-z_{ji}^{(J)} + LI_j) \tag{2}$$

where the variables $x_i^{(J)}$ are activations, or short term memory (STM) traces, of F_2 nodes and the variables $z_{ji}^{(J)}$ are adaptive weights, or long term memory (LTM) traces, of the pathways within the $F_1 \to F_2$ adaptive filter. These equations are derived in the Appendix. The competitive interaction coefficients in (1) from an F_2 node $v_m^{(K)}$ to an F_2 node $v_i^{(J)}$, namely

$$\frac{|K|(1+|K \cap J|)}{\sum_{m,L}|L|(1+|L \cap J|)}, \tag{3}$$

are asymmetric functions of K and J.

Despite the asymmetry of the coefficients in (3), the masking field equation (1) can be written in Cohen-Grossberg form using a simple change of variables. This fact clarifies why the networks considered herein always approach an equilibrium point. Grossberg (1987c) describes how (1) as well as a number of other well-studied content-addressable network memory models can be written in this form.

In order to achieve a parametric understanding of masking fields, we have developed these networks through the use of systematic computer simulations. The present article reports computer simulations carried out to design masking fields capable of robustly solving the following type of adaptive coding problem.

2. Detecting and Encoding Multiple Groupings in Short Term Memory using a Masking Field

A masking field is capable of simultaneously detecting multiple groupings within its input patterns and automatically assigning activation weights to the codes for these groupings which are predictive with respect to the context of the patterns and the prior learning of the system.

For example, a word such as Myself is used by a fluent speaker as a unitized verbal chunk. In different verbal contexts, however, the components My, Self, and Elf of Myself are all words in their own right. Moreover, although an utterance which ended at My generates one grouping of the speech flow, an utterance which goes on to include the entire word Myself supplants this encoding with one appropriate to the longer word. Thus in order to understand how context-sensitive content-addressable language units are perceived by a fluent speaker, one must analyse how all possible groupings of the speech flow are analysed through time, and how certain groupings can be chosen in one context without preventing other groupings from being chosen in a different context.

The same considerations hold when words such as Myself are presented visually, rather than auditorily. Then the problem becomes one of visual object recognition and of figure-ground segmentation. The problem exists also on a finer level of visual or auditory processing, since letters such as E contain, as parts, letters such as L and F. The masking field design is capable of sensing multiple pattern groupings, which subtend multiple spatial scales, and assigns each of these groupings a proper activation weight in its short term memory (STM) representation of these groupings.

3. Developmental Rules Imply Cognitive Rules as Emergent Properties of Neural Network Interactions

It has been shown how a masking field network F_2 can arise through simple rules of neuronal growth (Cohen and Grossberg, 1986; Grossberg, 1978, 1982, 1987b) for the connections from its input source F_1 and among its own cells, or nodes. These rules include random growth of connections along spatial gradients from F_1 to F_2, activity-dependent self-similar cell growth within F_2, and intercellular interactions among F_2 cells which compete for conserved synaptic sites (Figure 1a). Although these growth rules are of interest at the present time primarily in applications of masking fields to cognitive psychology and developmental neurobiology, they may at a future time suggest procedures for realizing a masking field in hardware. In addition, these growth processes illustrate how simple rules of neuronal development can give rise to a system whose parallel interactions act *as if* it obeys complex rules of context-sensitive cognitive coding. Because these growth rules can be obeyed by any number of network levels, masking fields can be linked into a coding hierarchy $F_1 \rightarrow F_2 \rightarrow F_3 \rightarrow \ldots F_n$ whose successive levels are able to detect and manipulate ever more abstract recognition codes and hypotheses about the input patterns received by F_1.

A masking field network F_2 selects its compressed representations by performing a new type of multiple scale analysis of the activity patterns which reach it from its input level F_1. This analysis enhances correct groupings and competitively inhibits, or masks, unappropriate groupings in STM. Otherwise expressed, the masking field network does not confuse "wholes" with their "parts," yet—despite this fact—it enables familiar "parts" to emerge as "wholes" in their own right in an appropriate input context, just as the words My and Self may be processed as "wholes" if they are presented separately or as "parts" within Myself when presented together (Section 1).

The spatial pattern of enhanced STM activities across F_2 embodies a hypothesis, or compressed content-addressable code, which represents the input stream. As will be described in greater detail below, this code can predict, or anticipate, subsequent events by assigning activities to groupings which have not yet fully occurred, based on the available evidence. Thus the network acts like a real-time prediction, or evidence gathering, machine. No serial programs, cognitive rule structures, or teachers exist within the masking field network to accomplish these properties. Instead, the model nodes, or neurons, obey membrane equations undergoing shunting (mass action) on-center off-surround (cooperative-competitive) recurrent (feedback) interactions (Figure 1b). The STM activation code of a masking field is an automatic emergent property of these interactions.

4. Sensitivity to Multiple Pattern Scales and to Intrascale Microstructure

The multiple scale analysis that is performed by a masking field is sensitive to two different types of pattern changes.

A. Sensitivity to Multiple Pattern Scales

As a word like Myself is processed, a subword such as My occurs before the entire word Myself is experienced. Figure 2a schematizes this type of informational change. As the word is presented, it activates an increasing number of F_1 nodes, or feature detectors, through time. As increasing numbers of F_1 nodes are activated, earlier STM activations within F_1 may be modified as they are supplemented by later STM activations. After Myself is fully stored within F_1, parts such as My, Self, and Elf are still present within

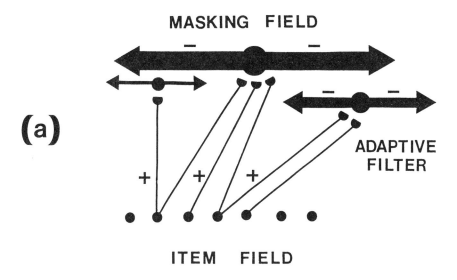

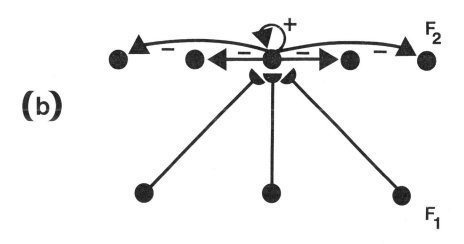

Figure 1. Masking field interactions: (a) Cells from an item field F_1 grow randomly to a masking field F_2 along positionally sensitive gradients. The nodes in the masking field grow so that larger item groupings, up to some optimal size, can activate nodes with broader and stronger inhibitory interactions. Thus the $F_1 \rightarrow F_2$ connections and the $F_2 \leftrightarrow F_2$ interactions exhibit properties of self-similarity. (b) The interactions within a masking field F_2 include positive feedback from a node to itself and negative feedback from a node to its neighbors. Long term memory (LTM) traces at the ends of $F_1 \rightarrow F_2$ pathways (designated by hemidisks) adaptively tune the filter defined by these pathways to amplify the F_2 reaction to item groupings which have previously succeeded in activating their target F_2 nodes.

EXPANDING ACTIVATION
PATTERNS ACROSS F$_1$

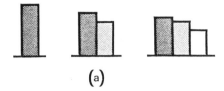

(a)

DIFFERENT ACTIVATION PATTERNS
ACROSS THE SAME SET
OF F$_1$ NODES

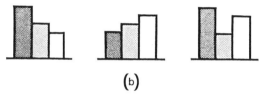

(b)

Figure 2. Two types of masking field sensitivity: (a) A masking field F_2 can automatically rescale its sensitivity to differentially react as the F_1 activity pattern expands through time to activate more F_1 cells. It hereby acts like a "multiple spatial frequency filter." (b) A masking field can differentially react to different F_1 activity patterns which activate the same set of F_1 cells. By (a) and (b), F_2 acts like a spatial pattern discriminator which can compensate for changes in overall spatial scale without losing its sensitivity to pattern changes at the finest spatial scale.

the whole. However, the masking field F_2 can automatically rescale its initial response to My as the remainder of Myself is presented. In this way, the masking field can favor the whole word Myself rather than its parts, such as My, Self, or Elf, even though My may have been favored before Self also occurred.

A masking field's ability to favor a representation of a whole word rather than its parts derives from its sensitivity to the overall scale of each of the groupings which it can detect. The subtlety of this automatic scaling property is revealed through the following issue. If a masking field favors a whole pattern rather than its parts, then why does not the field continue to favor the *same* whole pattern code when only a part of the pattern is presented? How does the field sensitively respond to the part as a *new* content-addressable whole in its own right? Otherwise expressed, if larger pattern codes are favored when the larger patterns actually occur, then how can smaller pattern codes be favored when smaller patterns occur?

B. *Sensitivity to Internal Pattern Microstructure*

The second type of masking field sensitivity is illustrated by the two words Left and Felt. This comparison is merely illustrative. It does not attempt to characterize the many subtle context-sensitive alterations that occur in evolving sound patterns or visually detected reading patterns. The words Left and Felt illustrate the issue that the same *set* of item representations within F_1 may be activated by different item *orderings*. To distinguish two such activity patterns across F_1, sensitivity within F_2 to different spatial scales of F_1 is insufficient because both lists may activate the same spatial scale of F_1. Instead, sensitivity to different STM patterns which excite the same set of items is required (Figure 2b).

The automatic rescaling and microstructure detection properties follow from the manner in which *nonlinear feedback* interactions among F_2 nodes automatically reorganize the sizes of the inputs received at F_2 by F_1. This type of nonlinear feedback is absent from many alternative grouping algorithms, such as the Hough transform (Duda and Hart, 1972; Hough, 1962). In recent contributions to developing the Hough transform, a central problem is to discover how to use "negative votes" to cancel "off-peak positive votes in parameter space" (Brown, 1983). A related type of problem is solved by a masking field. However, a masking field replaces algorithms for positive and negative "voting" with a real-time network undergoing positive and negative feedback interactions. The key insights of the present article concern how to combine the design of nonlinear feedback within F_2 with the proper type of nonlinear learning in the $F_1 \rightarrow F_2$ adaptive filter to generate stable learning of unitized groupings with environmenally predictive properties.

5. Hypothesis Formation, Anticipation, Evidence, and Prediction

The dynamics of a masking field express in an abstract language a number of important properties of cognitive information processing, no less than of perceptual grouping. Consider for definiteness a masking field F_2 that is capable of simultaneously discriminating more than one grouping within a list of events that activates F_1. For example, a masking field F_2 might respond to the F_1 representation of the word Myself by strongly activating an F_2 population that is sensitive to the whole word and weakly activating F_2 populations that are sensitive to the word's most salient parts. More generally, it might react to a pair of events A and B by representing the events singly and as a unitized configuration. In such a representation, the total STM pattern across F_2 represents the F_1 STM pattern. The relative sizes of F_2's STM activities weight the relative importance of the unitized groupings which are coded by the respective F_2 cell populations.

The suprathreshold STM activities across F_2 are approximately normalized, or conserved, due to the fact that its feedback interactions obey a type of *shunting* cooperative-competitive law which is capable of automatic gain control (Figure 1b). The STM activities across F_2 thus function like a type of real-time probabilistic logic, or hypothesis-testing algorithm, or model of the evidence which F_2 has about the pattern across F_1. The self-normalizing properties of such cooperative-competitive feedback networks also invite comparisons with the classical formalisms of statistical mechanics and quantum mechanics (Grossberg, 1978, 1982).

A masking field also possesses a predictive, anticipatory, or priming capability. In response to a single item across F_1, the F_2 population which is most vigorously activated may code that item. In addition, less vigorous activations may arise at those F_2 populations which represent the most salient larger groupings of which the item forms a part. Such a masking field can predictively prime the masking field to anticipate the larger groupings of which the item may form a part during the next time interval. As more items are stored by F_1 through time, F_2's uncertainty concerning the information represented at F_1 may decrease due to the emergence of a more predictive overall F_1 pattern. As F_2's uncertainty decreases, the spatial distribution of STM activity across F_2 becomes more focussed, or spatially localized, and includes fewer predictive groupings. This type of spatial sharpening measures the degree of informational uncertainty within the F_2 code about the activation pattern at F_1.

6. Computer Simulations of Global Choices and Multiple Groupings without Learning

The masking field design is described mathematically in the Appendix. This description is self-contained and may be read at any point during the subsequent exposition. The grouping properties of a masking field are illustrated in Sections 6–10 through computer simulations. These simulations are then used to motivate a refinement of masking field design in Sections 11–14. This refined design leads to a number of predictions about mechanisms of neural learning.

Figures 3–5 depict the simplest type of grouping by a masking field. In this example, each distinct STM activity pattern across F_1 activates a unique node, or population, for STM storage within F_2. In other words, such a masking field globally groups an activity pattern across F_1 into an STM choice within F_2. Distinct choices are made in response to F_1 patterns which vary in overall scale as well as in their microstructure, thereby demonstrating the properties summarized in Section 4. The same numerical parameters were used in all these simulations to demonstrate that a single masking field can generate all the properties being claimed. Sensitivity analyses were also carried out to determine the robustness of the design, but these will not be reported here. In this series of simulations, no learning was allowed to occur within the long term memory (LTM) traces, or adaptive weights, that multiply the signals in the $F_1 \rightarrow F_2$ pathways (see Appendix).

In Figures 6 and 7, a fixed but different set of parameters was used to illustrate how a masking field can generate STM representations which encode multiple groupings, including predictive groupings, of activity patterns across F_1. In these STM representations, the masking field is maximally sensitive to the total STM pattern across F_1, but it also generates partial activations to salient subpatterns ("parts") and superpatterns ("predictions") of this pattern. As in Figures 3–5, the simulations described in Figures 6 and 7 do not allow the LTM traces in the $F_1 \rightarrow F_2$ pathways to change due to learning. The computer simulation results in Figures 3–7 provide the foundation for analysing how learning within $F_1 \rightarrow F_2$ pathways interacts with the cooperative-competitive interactions within F_2. Before proceeding to this analysis, we summarize the results due to the cooperative-competitive interactions in the absence of learning.

In these simulations, the level F_1 is called the *item level*, and the level F_2 is called the *list level*. These abstract terms are consistent with the dynamical properties of the two levels F_1 and F_2, and avoid pitfalls of alternative nomenclatures—such as "letter level" and "word level"—which do not adequately deal with the context-sensitivity of code reorganizations that occur during perceptual and cognitive processing. These nomenclature issues are discussed more fully in Grossberg (1984b, 1986a, 1986c) and Grossberg and Stone (1986).

In Figure 3, a single item in F_1 is active. This item broadcasts positive inputs to a large number of nodes in F_2. The input sizes over the target F_2 nodes are depicted by the heights of the bars in the three rows labelled Input Pattern. Each row lists all F_2 nodes which receive the same number of pathways from F_1. The first row consists of F_2 nodes which receive one pathway, the second row consists of F_2 nodes which receive two pathways, and the third row consists of F_2 nodes which receive three pathways. In row 1, each F_2 node in the set labelled $\{i\}$ receives a pathway from the F_1 item node labelled $\{i\}$, $i = 0, 1, 2, \ldots, 4$. Note that four F_2 nodes receive inputs from the $\{0\}$ F_1 node. In row 2, all F_2 nodes labelled $\{0, 1\}$ receive pathways from the F_1 nodes $\{0\}$ and $\{1\}$. In row 3, all F_2 nodes labelled $\{0, 1, 2\}$ receive pathways from the F_1 nodes $\{0\}$, $\{1\}$, and $\{2\}$. The mathematical rules whereby these connections and input sizes are established are described in the Appendix.

ITEM FIELD (F1)

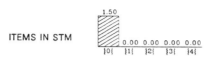

ITEMS IN STM

MASKING FIELD (F2)

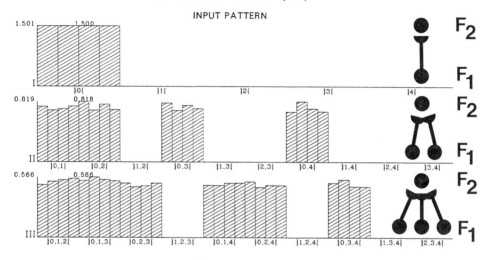

LIST CODE IN STM

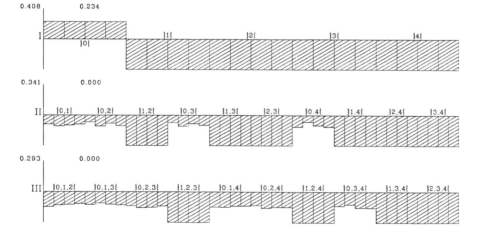

Figure 3. List coding of a single item: Network F_1 encodes in short term memory (STM) a spatial pattern of activation over item representations. In this figure, the single item $\{0\}$ is activated. Network F_2 encodes in STM the pattern of sublist chunks that are activated by F_1. The first three rows depict the inputs from F_1 to F_2. They are broadly distributed across F_2. The List Code in STM depicts the STM response to these inputs. Only the $\{0\}$ cells in F_2 are stored in STM, despite the broad distribution of inputs.

The inputs to *all* the F_2 nodes which receive pathways from the F_1 node $\{0\}$ are positive. There are 44 such nodes in Figure 3. Despite this fact, the only F_2 nodes capable of becoming persistently active in STM are the nodes which receive pathways *only* from the active item node $\{0\}$. These are the F_2 nodes labelled $\{0\}$. The STM activities of all other F_2 nodes are quickly inhibited by the competitive feedback interactions within F_2 (Figure 1b), despite the fact that many of these F_2 nodes also receive large excitatory inputs from F_1. The equilibrium STM activities of the F_2 nodes are listed in three rows under the heading List Code in STM. These are the activities which the nodes store in STM after the network equilibrates to the entire input pattern. Figure 3 thus illustrates how F_2 can transform a widespread input pattern into a focal, and appropriate, STM activation.

Figures 4 and 5 further illustrate this property. Each panel in these Figures represents the network response to a different input pattern. The panels are reduced relative to the scale of Figure 3 in order to present a larger number of simulations. In Figures 4a and 4b, a different item at F_1 is activated. Each item generates a widespread input pattern to F_2. Each input pattern is contrast-enhanced into a focal STM activation. This STM activation is restricted to the F_2 nodes which receive pathways from only the active item node.

A comparison of Figures 3, 4a, and 4c illustrates the self-scaling property of masking field dynamics. Suppose that the list of items $\{0\}$, $\{1\}$ is successively received by F_1. The list as a whole generates a different spatial pattern across F_1 (Figure 4c) than does its first item (Figure 3) or its second item (Figure 4a) taken in isolation. The list as a whole also activates even more nodes than does either item taken separately: 82 nodes in all. Despite this fact, only a single F_2 node's activity is stored in STM. This F_2 node is, moreover, an appropriate node because it is one of the $\{0,1\}$ nodes that receive pathways only from the F_1 items $\{0\}$ and $\{1\}$. This comparison thus illustrates the ability of F_2 nodes which are activated by larger numbers of F_1 nodes to mask the activity of F_2 nodes which are activated by smaller subsets of F_1 nodes. This is a key property in F_2's functioning as a content-addressable memory.

A comparison of Figures 4c and 4d illustrates the ability of F_2 to distinguish item patterns with different microstructures. In both of these Figures, the same set of F_1 items—$\{0\}$ and $\{1\}$—is activated, but a different spatial pattern of activity exists across the items. The spatial pattern in Figure 4c may represent the list of items $\{0,1\}$, whereas the spatial pattern in Figure 4d may represent the list of items $\{1,0\}$. The simulations show that F_2 is sensitive to the item pattern *as a whole*, because F_2 can generate different STM responses to these patterns even though they activate the same unordered set of F_1 nodes. In particular, in Figures 4c and 4d, different F_2 nodes become active within the set of F_2 nodes which receives pathways only from items $\{0\}$ and $\{1\}$.

A comparison of Figures 3, 4, and 5a illustrates a more demanding variant of these F_2 properties. As an ordered list of items $\{0\}$, $\{1\}$, $\{2\}$ is successively stored by F_1, all the items become active at F_1 as the spatial patterns in Figures 3, 4c, and 5a evolve through time. The stored STM pattern in Figure 5a is, however, restricted to a single F_2 node, which is one of the nodes receiving pathways only from items $\{0\}$, $\{1\}$, and $\{2\}$. Thus F_2 selects a content-addressable representation of the whole pattern at F_1, rather than of its constituent items.

A comparison of Figures 5a–5c makes the same point as the comparison of Figures 4c and 4d, but in a more demanding variation. In each of the panels in Figure 5, the same unordered set of items—$\{0\}$, $\{1\}$, and $\{2\}$—is active across F_1. The different spatial

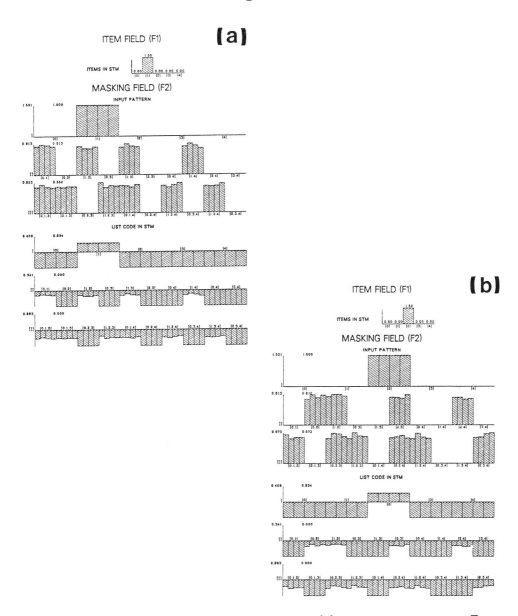

Figure 4. (a) List coding of a single item: In response to item $\{1\}$ in F_1, the masking field in F_2 chooses the $\{1\}$ cells in response to a broad distribution of inputs. Thus the List Code in STM responds selectively to individual items in F_1. The same thing is true in the next figure. (b) Here item $\{2\}$ chooses the subset of list nodes $\{2\}$ for storage in STM. (c) List coding of an STM primacy gradient across two items: A primacy gradient in STM across two items of F_1 generates a broader input pattern to F_2. The List Code in STM no longer responds at either the $\{0\}$ cells or the $\{1\}$ cells. Instead, a choice occurs among the set of possible $\{0, 1\}$ cells. Comparison with Figure 3 shows that F_2 can update its internal representation in a context-sensitive way. (d) List coding of an STM recency gradient across two items: A recency gradient in STM occurs across the same two items of F_2, rather than a primacy gradient. Again, the $\{0\}$ cells and the $\{1\}$ cells are suppressed. A different choice among the $\{0, 1\}$ cells occurs than in response to the primacy gradient of the preceding figure. Thus F_2 can distinguish different temporal orderings of the same items.

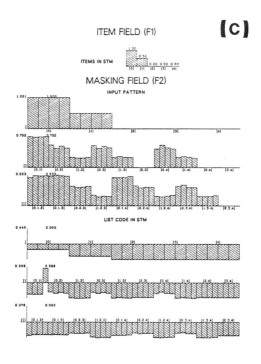

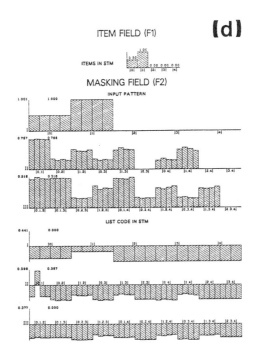

Figure 4 (continued).

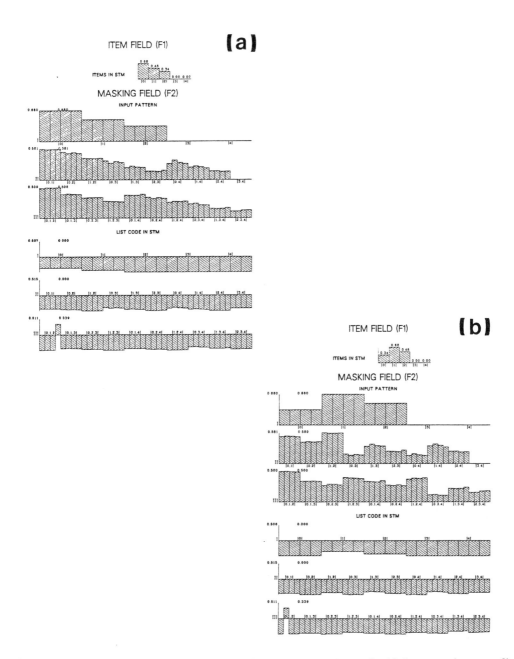

Figure 5. (a) List coding of an STM primacy gradient across three items: In this figure, a primacy gradient in STM occurs across three items of F_1. The input pattern to F_2 is even broader than before. However, the STM response of F_2 retains its selectivity. Network F_2 suppresses all $\{0\}$, $\{1\}$, $\{2\}$, $\{0,1\}$, $\{0,2\}$, ... cells and chooses for STM storage a population from among the $\{0,1,2\}$ cells. (b) List codings of different temporal orderings across three items: In this and the next figure, different temporal orderings of the same three items generate selective STM responses among the $\{0,1,2\}$ cells. Thus as future items activate an updated STM item code across F_1, the STM list coding within F_2 is also updated in a context-sensitive way. (c) See legend to Figure 5b.

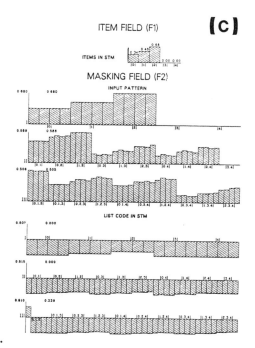

Figure 5 (continued).

patterns across F_1 represent different orderings of these items: $\{0, 1, 2\}$, $\{1, 2, 0\}$, and $\{2, 1, 0\}$, respectively. In each Figure, a different F_2 node is activated. The active F_2 node is, moreover, one of the nodes that receives pathways only from the item nodes $\{0\}$, $\{1\}$, and $\{2\}$. Thus the content-addressable F_2 code is sensitive to the microstructure of the F_1 activity patterns.

Figure 6 and 7 describe the reactions of a masking field whose parameters are chosen to enable multiple groupings of F_1 patterns to be coded in STM at F_2. Multiple groupings can emerge when the competitive interactions across F_2 are uniformly weakened. The same input patterns were used as in Figures 3–5. Comparison of Figures 6a, 6d, and 7b shows how the automatic scaling property enables F_2 to update its STM representations based upon all the groupings which it can detect as the F_1 activity pattern expands. In Figure 6a, item $\{0\}$ most strongly activates the $\{0\}$ nodes of F_2, but also weakly activates predictive F_2 nodes that represents groupings which include $\{0\}$. The F_2 nodes which receive an item pathway only from $\{0\}$ have a maximal activity of .163. The F_2 nodes which receive two item pathways, including a pathway from $\{0\}$, have a maximal activity of .07. The F_2 nodes which receive three item pathways, including a pathway from $\{0\}$, have a maximal activity of .007. These activity weights characterize the degree of "predictive evidence" which the masking field possesses that each grouping is reflected in the input pattern.

In Figure 6d, the $\{0, 1\}$ spatial pattern across F_1 most strongly activates a node within the $\{0, 1\}$ subfield of F_2, but also weakly activates other nodes of F_2 which receive inputs from $\{0\}$. The activity levels are .246 and .04, respectively. Thus the multiple-scale self-similar interactions cause a reversal in activation strength when item $\{1\}$ follows item $\{0\}$ at F_1: whereas the F_2 code for $\{0\}$ is strong and for $\{0, 1\}$ is weak in response to item $\{0\}$ at F_1, the F_2 code for $\{0\}$ is weak and for $\{0, 1\}$ is strong in response to the list $\{0\}$, $\{1\}$ of items at F_1. In Figure 7b, the $\{0, 1, 2\}$ spatial pattern across F_1 most strongly activates a node within the $\{0, 1, 2\}$ subfield of F_2 (with activity .184) but also weakly activates the

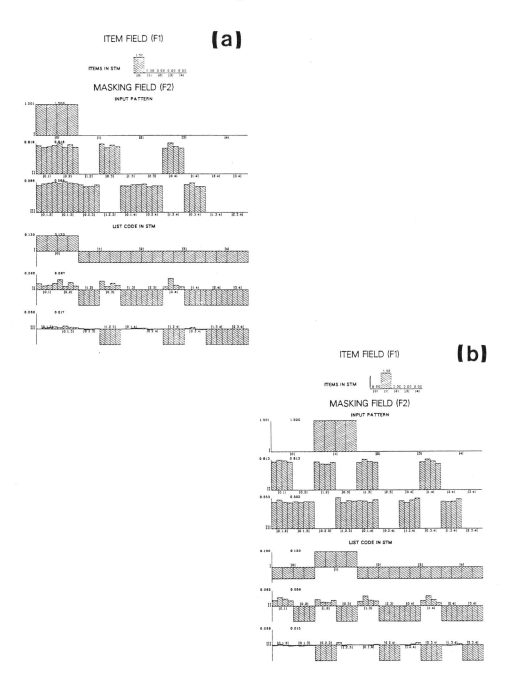

Figure 6. (a) The correct list code $\{0\}$ is preferred in STM, but predictive list codes which include $\{0\}$ as a part are also activated with lesser STM weights. The prediction gets less activation if $\{0\}$ forms a smaller part of it. (b) The correct list code $\{1\}$ is preferred in STM, but the predictive list codes which include $\{1\}$ as a part are also activated with lesser STM weights. (c) The list code in response to item $\{1\}$ also generates an appropriate reaction. (d) A list code of type $\{0, 1\}$ is maximally activated, but part codes $\{0\}$ and predictive codes which include $\{0, 1\}$ as a part are also activated with lesser STM weights.

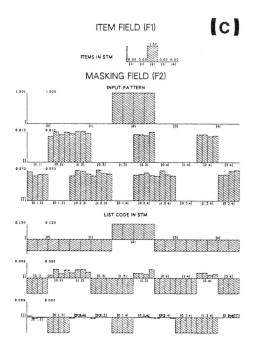

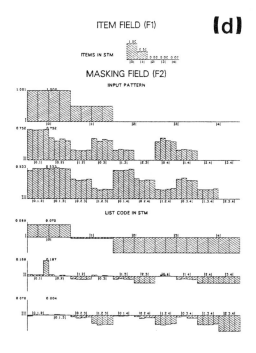

Figure 6 (continued).

{0} subfield of F_2 (with activity .004). The STM activity pattern across F_2 becomes more focussed from Figure 6a to 6d to 7b as increasing contextual information across F_1 reduces F_2's predictive uncertainty.

7. Adaptive Discovery of Segmentation Rules: The Adaptive Sharpening Property

The following criterion was applied to test the adequacy of associative learning laws for adaptive tuning of STM groupings across F_2:

Adaptive Sharpening Property

Suppose that an arbitrary unfamiliar input pattern to F_1 generates an STM representation across F_2. The LTM law for the adaptive weights within the $F_1 \to F_2$ pathways must learn from this $F_1 - F_2$ pairing in such a way that, after learning occurs, the same input pattern to F_1 generates a spatially sharpened, or contrast-enhanced, STM pattern across F_2.

In particular, if F_2 makes a choice in STM, as in Figures 3–5, then learning which satisfies the adaptive sharpening property acts to confirm this choice. More generally, the adaptive sharpening property prevents learning in the pathways which adaptively filter signals between F_1 and F_2 from destroying the good pre-wired properties of the masking field. Learning can accentuate the initial decisions due to interactions of the adaptive filter with the masking field, but cannot upset this balance due *merely* to repeated presentations of the same F_1 pattern.

The adaptive sharpening property is not trivially satisfied by all the associative learning laws that one might reasonably wish to consider. This is because F_2 automatically reorganizes its STM reactions based upon the *global* patterning of the inputs received by all of its nodes (Section 4). A *single* LTM law, used in all the $F_1 \to F_2$ pathways, must be able to react to *all possible* combinations of activity patterns across F_1 and F_2 with adaptive sharpening, and not a destruction of the global balance between $F_1 \to F_2$ inputs and $F_2 \leftrightarrow F_2$ interactions.

After such a LTM law is characterized, the adaptive sharpening property which it guarantees provides a foundation for studying how segmentation of an F_1 pattern into multiple groupings can be influenced by learning. For example, if a prescribed pattern across F_1 is repeatedly presented, then this pattern becomes "familiar" by tuning the adaptive filter to preferentially code its most salient groupings in STM at F_2. If a novel superset pattern at F_1 is then presented—that is, a pattern which includes the familiar pattern as a subpattern—then the subset pattern groupings of the familiar pattern can coherently "break away" from the complementary superset groupings. The superset pattern can consequently be represented by an STM pattern of resonant "parts," or "structural groupings," across F_2. In other words, prior adaptive tuning can enable a novel F_1 pattern to generate a directly accessed STM reaction across F_2 which *segments* the F_1 pattern into a distributed code of familiar groupings.

A related implication of the adaptive sharpening property is that repeated presentation of a superset grouping may gradually mask otherwise possible subset groupings, unless the subset patterns are also frequently presented, in their own right, to F_1. In intuitive terminology, a coherent set of familiar parts may come to represent the whole, or a more global segmentation may come to represent the whole, depending upon the statistics of the input time series. Interactions between an adaptive filter and a masking field can

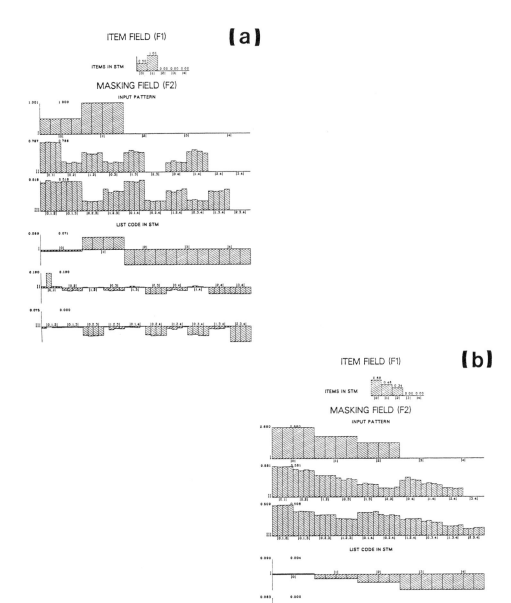

Figure 7. (a) A different list code of type $\{0, 1\}$ is maximally activated, but part codes $\{1\}$ are also activated with lesser STM weight. Due to the random growth of $F_1 \rightarrow F_2$ pathways, no predictive list codes are activated (to 3 significant digits). (b)–(d) When the STM pattern across F_1 includes three items, the list code in STM strongly activates an appropriate list code. Part groupings are suppressed due to the high level of predictiveness of this list code. Comparison of Figures 6a, 6d, and 7b shows that as the item code across F_1 becomes more constraining, the list code representation becomes less distributed across F_2.

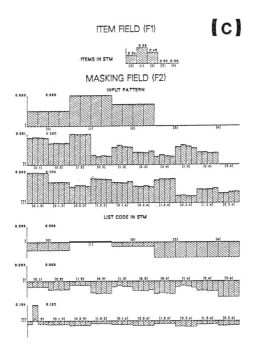

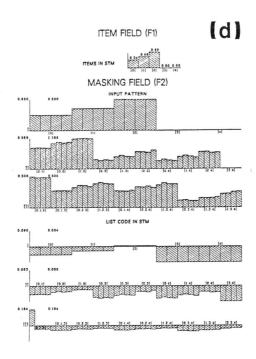

Figure 7 (continued).

hereby *dynamically* organize incoming input patterns into structural relationships which are learned from the statistics of a unique input environment, rather than trying to out-guess the environment using pre-wired segmentation rules that are bound to fail in most environments.

8. The Functional Unit of Associative Learning is a Spatial Pattern: A Nonlinear Non-Hebbian Learning Law

In our computer simulations, we demand a strict version of the adaptive sharpening property in order to direct our investigation of STM and LTM interactions. Given all the STM groupings in Figures 3–7, we demanded that adaptive sharpening transform these groupings into STM choices at F_2 in response to releated presentation of individual activation patterns at F_1. In particular, we demanded that adaptive sharpening choose that F_2 population which was maximally favored by F_2 in response to that F_1 pattern before learning began.

As in (2), an LTM law which satisfies this property has the form

$$\frac{d}{dt}z_{ji} = \epsilon f(x_i)[-z_{ji} + LI_j]. \tag{4}$$

In (4), z_{ji} is the LTM trace in the pathway from the jth node v_j in F_1 to the ith node v_i in F_2; I_j is the input from v_j; x_i is the STM activity of v_i; $f(x_i)$ is a nonlinear sampling signal that is activated by sufficiently large values of x_i; and ϵ and L are constants. Such a law was introduced into the associative learning literature in Grossberg (1968, 1969a) and has since been used in many models (Amari, 1982; Amari and Takeuchi, 1978; Kohonen, 1982, 1983; Rumelhart and Zipser, 1985). In particular, it was the associative law that was chosen to introduce the adaptive resonance theory (Grossberg, 1976a, 1976b), and it has played an important role in the complete numerical and mathematical characterization of an adaptive resonance circuit (Carpenter and Grossberg, 1987a). Recent neurophysiological experiments about cortical and hippocampal processing have, moreover, supported this associative rule both qualitatively and quantitatively (Levy, 1985; Levy, Brassel, and Moore, 1983; Levy and Desmond, 1985; Rauchecker and Singer, 1979; Singer, 1983).

One reason why such a law cannot be taken for granted is that it violates the Hebbian associative postulate (Hebb, 1949) that is the basis for many current learning models. On p.64 of his classic book, Hebb proposed his famous *Hebb Postulate*: "When the axon of cell A is near enough to excite a cell B and repeatedly or persistently takes part in firing it, some growth process takes place in one or both cells such that A's efficiency, as one of the cells firing B is increased." The development of neural network models of conditioning since Hebb's work is discussed in detail by Levine (1983). The learning rule in (4) is called an *associative rule*, whereby LTM efficacy changes as a function of a time average of correlated presynaptic and postsynaptic cell activities. Associative rules are often called "Hebbian" rules to honor the pioneering work of Hebb (1949). This convention has, we believe, caused a great deal of confusion in the conditioning literature because different associative rules can support qualitatively different types of learning properties.

The Hebb Postulate seems plausible if one assumes that the unit of associative learning is a single cell's activity whose correlation with another cell's activity can increase the LTM strength of a pathway between the cells. A different associative rule is needed, however, if one agrees that the unit of associative learning is a spatial pattern of activity across a network of cells, as is required by Figures 3–7. Then the correlation of a spatial pattern

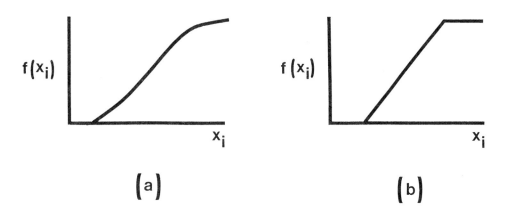

Figure 8. Sampling functions: (a) A faster-than-linear increase of $f(x_i)$ with x_i over a large domain of x_1 activities, or (b) a threshold-linear increase of $f(x_i)$ over a large domain of x_i activities illustrate two possible types of sampling functions.

across F_1 with a cell's activity in F_2 enables the LTM traces in the set of pathways from F_1 to the active F_2 cell to encode the entire spatial pattern of activity into LTM. In this situation, an associative rule is needed which can encode both increases *and* decreases of LTM strength as a function of the pairing of cell activities, because an inactive cell v_j at F_1 should cause z_{ji} to approach zero when correlated with an active cell v_i at F_2. Thus a change in the functional unit of learning from a single cell to a spatial pattern across a network of cells necessitates an associative rule that violates the Hebb Postulate.

Another nonclassical property of the learning law (1) is that the sampling signal $f(x_i)$ is a nonlinear function of x_j; in particular, $f(x_i)$ is a nonnegative function which grows faster-than-linearly, for example quadratically or in a threshold-linear fashion (Figure 8), as x_i increases above zero. In (4), the sampling signal $f(x_i)$ multiplies the constant ϵ to determine a state-dependent learning rate $\epsilon f(x_i)$. Due to the faster-than-linear growth of $f(x_i)$ with x_i, small values of x_i determine a much slower learning rate in z_{ji} than do large values of x_i. Consequently, F_2 cells which acquire an initial STM advantage can greatly amplify that advantage by speeding up the learning of their contiguous LTM traces. In contrast, F_2 cells whose activities remain below zero cannot trigger any learning in their contiguous LTM traces because $f(x_i) = 0$ if $x_i \leq 0$. This property justifies calling $f(x_i)$ a *sampling signal*.

Speaking intuitively, the state-dependent learning rate $\epsilon f(x_i)$ in (4) says that learning can occur only at LTM traces z_{ji} whose target activities x_i are chosen by the cooperative-competitive decision-making machinery of F_2. All LTM traces z_{ji} whose F_1 items receive positive inputs I_j can influence F_2's decision-making by multiplying these inputs on their way to F_2. In contrast, a much smaller number of LTM traces can learn from the decision-making process due to the property that F_2 chooses a *compressed* recognition code which is much less distributed than the input patterns which it receives. In this sense, LTM *read-out* through the adaptive $F_1 \rightarrow F_2$ filter and LTM *read-in* by the associative law (4) are at least partly dissociated due to intervention of the cooperative-competitive interactions within F_2. Such dissociation of signalling and learning by code compression mechanisms is not easily accomplished using an autoassociator. It was, in part, to avoid the attendant limitations, notably the instabilities, of learning by an autoassociator that hierarchical neural networks, with multiple network levels, began to be designed in the late 1960's. These developments included the introduction of hierarchies of nonlinear avalanche-type circuits for spatio-temporal pattern learning; of prewired and adaptive pattern recognition circuits, including competitive learning and adaptive resonance circuits; and of circuits for the active regulation of information processing by reinforcement and homeostatic mechanisms to attentively direct information processing towards the realization of desired goals. Several of these early contributions are described in Grossberg (1982). More recent contributions built upon this foundation are brought together in Grossberg (1987a, 1987b).

9. Computer Simulations: Adaptive Sharpening of Multiple Groupings

In this section, we illustrate the adaptive sharpening property by showing how the multiple groupings depicted in Figures 6 and 7 are adaptively transformed into STM choices when the learning law (1) is used in the $F_1 \rightarrow F_2$ adaptive filter. We have demonstrated, in addition, that the learning law (1) confirms all the STM choices described in Figures 3–5. These simulations are not, however, displayed herein.

All the Figures in this section describe the equilibrium STM choice that is generated by F_2 when the learning process approaches a limit in response to sustained presentation of each input pattern. The fact that the system always does approach equilibrium STM and LTM values is, in itself, a fundamental property, since feedback interactions between STM (fast) and LTM (slow) processes can easily lead to sustained oscillations, such as travelling waves, bursts, or even chaotic oscillations (Carpenter, 1979, 1981; Carpenter and Grossberg, 1983, 1984, 1985). In some physical systems, complex oscillations are functionally desirable. In the present applications, they are not. Theorems which guarantee global approach to equilibrium in related cooperative-competitive feedback networks are found in Cohen and Grossberg (1983), Ellias and Grossberg (1975), Grossberg and Levine (1975), and Grossberg (1982).

In the absence of global theorems about masking fields, we have studied the approach within F_2 to STM and LTM limits using a variety of techniques. The simplest technique uses a *singular approximation* to the full dynamical system. In the full dynamical system, STM reacts to an input pattern more quickly than does the slower LTM learning process. In a singular approximation, it is assumed that LTM does not change at all until the STM activities have almost reached an equilibrium value. Then the LTM learning process is switched on and both STM and LTM interact until they conjointly approach equilibrium. Using such a singular approximation, a much faster LTM learning rate (viz., a larger ϵ in (4)) can be used without significantly changing the equilibrium STM and LTM patterns that are found using the full system. A computer simulation of a singular system can thus be done much more quickly than a simulation in which the full system is integrated with a small ϵ until it reaches equilibrium. Carpenter (1977a, 1977b, 1979) and Fenichel (1979) have proved theorems which describe conditions under which solutions of a nonlinear dynamical system with fast and slow processes lie close to solutions of a singular approximation to the full dynamical system.

Once we confirmed the adaptive sharpening property using a singular approximation, we then did simulations with the full system using several different choices of the learning rate parameter ϵ in equation (4). Our goal was to understand how fast the learning rate could be before it might disrupt the adaptive sharpening process. More generally, we wanted to understand whether LTM changes must necessarily occur more slowly than STM changes in order to achieve basic functional properties such as adaptive sharpening.

Figures 9 and 10 describe the equilibrium patterns in a singular system all of whose parameters, except the learning rate ϵ, are the same as in the simulations of Figures 6 and 7. In Figures 6 and 7, the learning rate $\epsilon = 0$. In Figures 9 and 10, ϵ was set equal to zero until the STM traces across F_2 were close to equilibrium. Then we switched ϵ to equal 1 to allow the full system to approach equilibrium.

Comparison of Figures 9 and 10 with Figures 6 and 7 shows that the adaptive sharpening property is obtained. Comparison of the input patterns to F_2 nodes without learning and after learning shows how LTM changes in the $F_1 \rightarrow F_2$ pathways alters the total inputs to the F_2 nodes, and thereby biases the competitive feedback process within F_2 to make global choices in STM.

Having achieved the adaptive sharpening property in a singular system, we then demonstrated the property, without a change of parameters other than ϵ, in the full system. In one successful series of full system simulations, the choice $\epsilon = .01$ was made. In all of these simulations, the decay rate of STM activities across F_2, in the absence of internal feedback signals, was chosen equal to 1. Thus the adaptive sharpening property was confirmed in the full system using plausible relative rates of STM and LTM change. Figure 11 depicts a computer simulation of how the LTM values in a subset of $F_1 \rightarrow F_2$ pathways changed through time due to learning. The simulations show that the present masking field and associative learning laws are sufficient to generate all the properties that we have claimed.

Despite these successful results, a finer study of the transient behavior of the full system, before equilibrium was reached, raised a number of issues which have led us to propose a refinement of masking field design which promises to generate even stronger properties.

10. Transient STM Surge Precedes Competitive Contrast Enhancement

Three major phases in F_2's reaction to an input pattern at F_1 can be identified. In Phase 1, the input pattern starts to deliver signals to F_2 nodes via the $F_1 \rightarrow F_2$ pathways and many F_2 nodes thereby start to become activated. As these nodes become activated, they begin to generate feedback signals, notably competitive signals, to other F_2 nodes (Figure 1b). The balance between excitatory and inhibitory signals to each node quickly contrast enhances the input pattern from F_1 and generates the more focal STM reactions at F_2 which are depicted in Figures 3–7. In the absence of additional learning, reset, or habituative mechanisms. these focal STM reactions are stored by the balance of inputs and feedback signals within F_2. Phase 2 consists in the contrast enhancement and storage of these STM patterns. In the language of the Hough transform, the positive and negative "votes" cast by the masking field cancel both "off-peaks" and "false peaks" caused by the adaptive filter.

Figure 12 summarizes a computer simulation of the transition from Phase 1 to Phase 2. The parameters are the same as those in Figure 4c. Each successive picture depicts the STM activities of F_2 nodes at a later time after the onset of the input pattern to F_1.

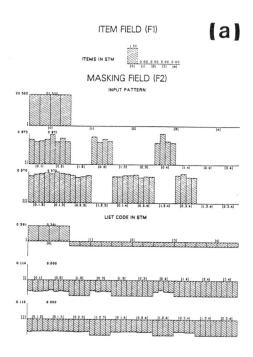

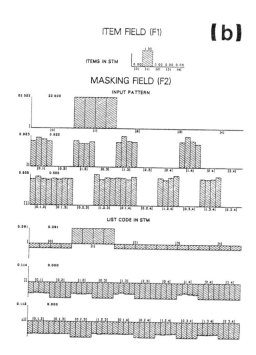

Figure 9. Adaptive sharpening in response to the input patterns of Figure 6. Comparison of input patterns here with those in Figure 6 shows how learning biases the adaptive filter $F_1 \rightarrow F_2$ to choose the preferred list code at F_2.

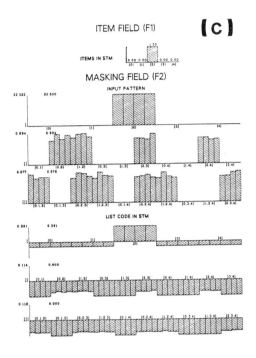

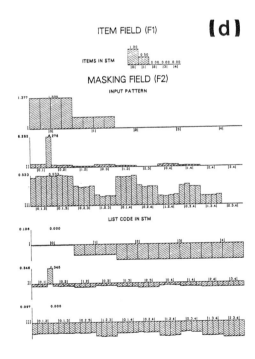

Figure 9 (continued).

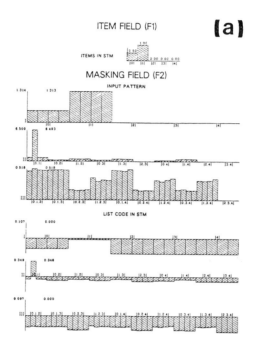

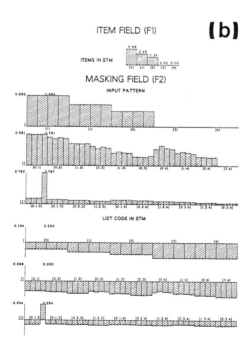

Figure 10. Adaptive sharpening in response to the input patterns of Figure 7.

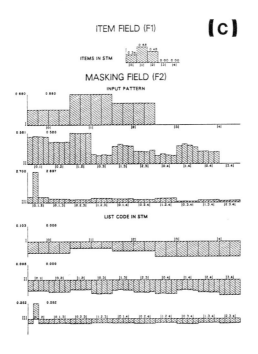

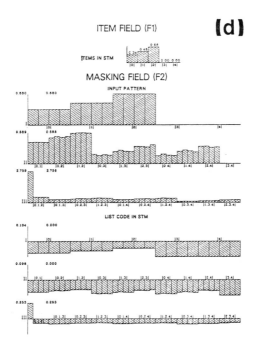

Figure 10 (continued).

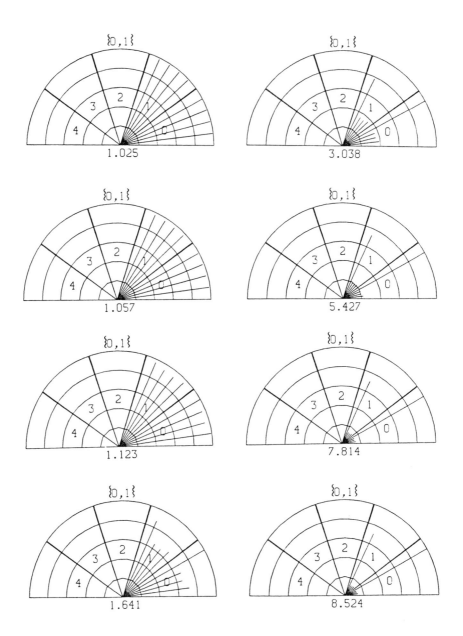

Figure 11. Changes in LTM strength through time due to learning. Lengths of the spokes are proportional to the sizes of the corresponding LTM traces. LTM traces at increasing times are plotted down column 1 and then column 2. The numbers under each figure designate the size of the maximal LTM trace in that figure.

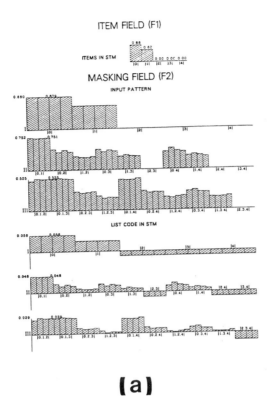

(a)

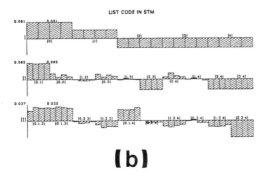

(b)

Figure 12. Transition through time from a widespread Phase 1 burst of activation across F_2 to a more focal Phase 2 activation that is under inhibitory control. Successive List Codes in column 1 and column 2 are evaluated at logarithmically increasing times.

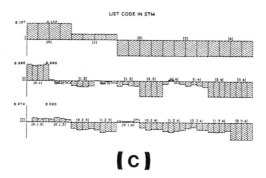

(c)

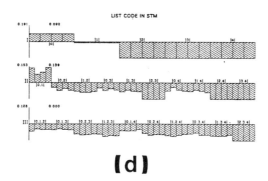

(d)

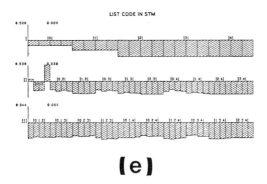

(e)

Figure 12 (continued).

In summary, after an input pattern activates F_1, there is a massive but transient activity burst across F_2 which is quickly sculpted by F_2's feedback interactions. The key question is: *How* quickly, relative to the learning rate?

11. Spurious Learning of the Transient Surge

The following problem can arise if the learning rate is too fast. Suppose that ϵ in (4) is chosen so large that significant learning can occur during Phase 1. Then many F_2 nodes v_j can sample the F_1 activity pattern because their learning rates $\epsilon f(x_i)$ are large during Phase 1. In contrast, if ϵ is small, then insignificant learning occurs during Phase 1 because the duration of Phase 1 is not long enough to integrate a large LTM change at rate $\epsilon f(x_i)$. During Phase 2, only those F_2 nodes which are selected by the internal feedback interactions within F_2 can sample the input pattern, and thereby tune their LTM traces, because $f(x_i) = 0$ at all other F_2 nodes.

In summary, if the learning rate is fast relative to the duration of Phase 1, then learning is not controlled by the masking field's grouping process. Moreover, such spurious learning can interfere with the masking field's ability to select a predictive grouping during Phase 2.

Figure 13 describes computer simulations which illustrate how a change in the learning parameter ϵ can alter the equilibrium grouping that is finally learned. Choosing ϵ too large can also cause violations of the adaptive sharpening property. Figure 13a repeats Figure 4c to facilitate comparison of the no-learning case with several learned groupings. In Figures 13b–d, ϵ was chosen equal to 1, .1, and .01, respectively. When $\epsilon = 1$, F_2 chose the $\{0\}$ nodes. When $\epsilon = .1$, F_2 selected both $\{0\}$ and $\{0,1\}$ nodes. When $\epsilon = .01$, F_2 chose the correct $\{0,1\}$ node. In all cases, the learned F_2 grouping exhibited a form of adaptive sharpening. In Figure 13b, however, the chosen F_2 nodes do not code information about item $\{1\}$ at all.

The reason for this bias towards $\{0\}$ nodes at fast learning rates can be traced to properties of the Phase 1 surge. In Figure 11, an initial advantage of $\{0\}$ nodes above $\{0,1\}$ nodes can be seen before the self-scaling feedback interactions within F_2 reverse this advantage.

These results illustrate that, in the masking field heretofore described, there exists a trade-off between the rate of cooperative-competitive decision-making by F_2 and the rate of learning by the $F_1 \rightarrow F_2$ adaptive filter. Learning must be sufficiently slow relative to the decision-making process to avoid spurious learning of transient decisions. The results also show, however, that a proper scaling of rates, with LTM approximately 100 times slower than STM, can avoid this sampling problem. On the other hand, these simulations also call attention to the following design problem, should one with to be freed from concerns about the proper scaling of slow LTM rates against fast STM rates.

12. Structurally Stabilized Learning

The design problem that is raised by the simulations in Figures 12 and 13 can be stated as follows:

Structurally Stabilized Masking Field

Does there exist a modification of masking field design which overcomes the Phase 1 surge (Figure 12) and the fast learning (Figure 13) problems, given essentially *any* choice

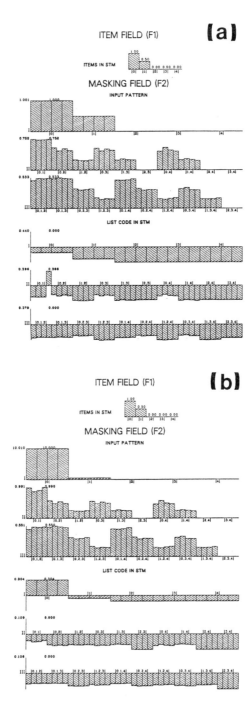

Figure 13. Comparison of the list code stored in STM at F_2 in a no-learning case (a) with the list code that is stored after learning with (b) $\epsilon = 1$, (c) $\epsilon = .1$, and (d) $\epsilon = .01$. The learning rates $\epsilon = 1$ and $\epsilon = .1$ are both too fast to achieve the adaptive sharpening property because the LTM traces can learn significantly during the Phase 1 burst.

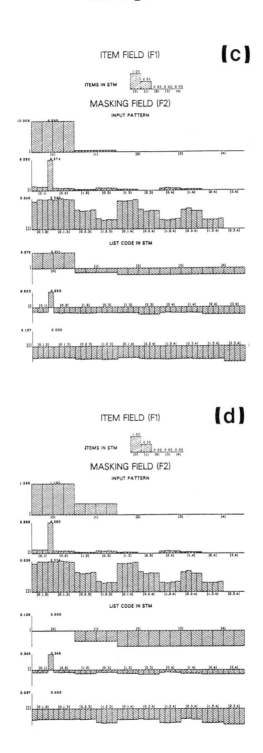

Figure 13 (continued).

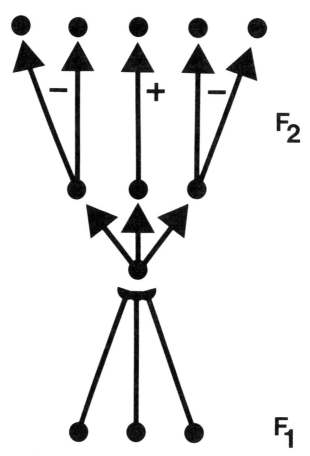

Figure 14. The Phase 1 burst can be partially eliminated by causing each $F_1 \to F_2$ input to activate both excitatory and inhibitory pathways leading to target F_2 nodes.

of STM and LTM rate parameters?

We now suggest a modification of a masking field's internal connections which can substantially reduce the Phase 1 surge. We also suggest a modification of a masking field's internal connections which enables it to learn in a way that is insensitive to whatever residual surge may still occur. We hereby overcome a problem that may arise due to improperly chosen *rates* by modifying the system's interactive *structure* to work well given a more careless choice of rates. Otherwise expressed, a structurally stabilized masking field is more fault-tolerant of a poor choice of processing rates.

13. Feedforward and Feedback Sharing of Internal Feedback Pathways

The Phase 1 surge is due to the fact that all $F_1 \to F_2$ inputs are excitatory. We propose that, before these inputs can influence their target cells in F_2, they activate internal feedback pathways within F_2 which balance the excitatory signals with inhibitory signals (Figure 14). Inhibitory signals will therefore be registered at the same moment that excitatory signals are registered. There does not exist a time interval during which excitatory inputs can activate a Phase 1 burst that is not controlled by inhibitory signals.

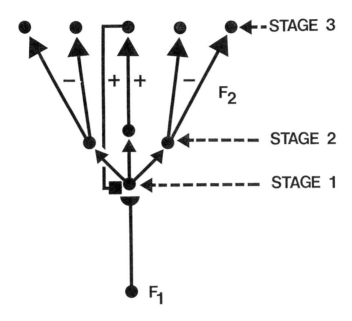

Figure 15. The excitatory and inhibitory pathways which eliminate the Phase 1 burst are the internal feedback pathways of F_2. These pathways connect Stage 2 with Stage 3 of F_2. Stage 3 cells receive mixtures of excitatory and inhibitory inputs from their first moments of activation by F_1 inputs registered at Stage 1. Only those Stage 3 cells which receive a net excitatory input can generate feedback signals to Stage 1. The positive feedback signal from Stage 3 to Stage 1 acts both to amplify activation of Stage 1 cells and also as the sampling signal that triggers learning by LTM traces within contiguous $F_1 \rightarrow F_2$ pathways. The square at the end of the feedback pathway designates the specialized role which signals within this pathway play in the learned tuning of the $F_1 \rightarrow F_2$ adaptive filter.

How should these excitatory and inhibitory signals be chosen? In particular, how can they be chosen so that they do not upset the feedback interactions that are the basis of a masking field's grouping properties? A simple answer is available: Let the feedforward inputs from the adaptive filter use the *same* interneurons, or internal feedback cells, that are used to define the masking field (Figure 15). Such a design was first described by Grossberg (1976b). Then the uncontrolled Phase 1 burst is prevented bv a structural mechanism which immediately begins the grouping process when it receives an input burst.

As Figure 15 shows, the masking field is now broken into three internal stages. Stage 1 receives the excitatory inputs from F_1. Stage 2 contains the internal pathways which distribute excitatory and inhibitory signals across the masking field. Stage 3 contains the target cells of these internal pathways. These target cells always receive a mixture of excitatory and inhibitory signals. They are never exposed to an uncontrolled Phase 1 burst. The Stage 3 cells give rise to topographic, positive feedback pathways to their Stage 1 source cells. These positive feedback pathways close the feedback loops within the masking field. Using these stages, the internal feedback interactions of the masking field remain unchanged, yet the F_1 inputs engage these interactions before they ever influence Stage 3 cells.

The architecture in Figure 15 prevents a totally uncontrolled Phase 1 burst from occurring. On the other hand, the internal feedback within the masking field does not
instantaneously select an equilibrium grouping. Rapidly cycling feedback signals within
the masking field select such a grouping. It remains to say how the LTM traces within
the $F_1 \rightarrow F_2$ pathways can be buffered against learning activity patterns that are far from
equilibrium.

14. Internal Feedback as a Sampling Signal

The main problem to be overcome is clearly illustrated in Figure 15. Although the Stage
3 cells receive a mixture of excitatory and inhibitory signals, the Stage 1 cells receive only
excitatory signals. Moreover, the $F_1 \rightarrow F_2$ pathways abut the Stage 1 cells. What prevents
the LTM traces within the endings of these pathways from being activated by sampling
signals from the Stage 1 cells?

We hypothesize that the sampling signal which activates an LTM trace is not derived
from a Stage 1 cell. Rather, the sampling signal is activated by feedback from a Stage 3
cell (Figure 15). Many Stage 3 cells will be immediately inhibited by Stage 2 interneurons
when an input pattern turns on. Use of Stage 3 cells as a source of sampling signals enables
masking field interactions to restrict learning from its very first moments of interaction,
because many Stage 1 cells which are initially activated by F_1 inputs correspond to Stage 3
cells which are never activated during the ensuing grouping process. In order to instantiate
this constraint, we simply replace equation (4) by equation

$$\frac{d}{dt}z_{ji} = \epsilon f(x_i^{(3)})(-z_{ji} + LI_j), \tag{5}$$

where $x_i^{(3)}$ is the activity of the ith cell population in Stage 3 of the masking field.

The concept that internal feedback signals generate LTM sampling signals was introduced in Grossberg (1975). We now believe that it may be a design principle which is
widely used in the brain, whether the feedback signal is intercellularly generated, as in
Figure 15, or intracellularly generated by a network of biochemical feedback interactions.
Computer simulations which illustrate how such a feedback signal regulates learning are
described in a related type of circuit for combining cooperative-competitive and associative
mechanisms in Grossberg and Schmajuk (1987). Some of the properties which can be used
to experimentally test for this design are now summarized.

15. Dissociation of LTM Read-In and Read-Out: Feedback as a Neural Modu-
lator

Read-out of LTM occurs when an LTM trace multiplicatively gates a signal on its way
from F_1 to F_2 (Appendix). In the masking fields which we have simulated, LTM is read-
out into the same F_2 cells which enable the LTM traces to sample, or read-in, new LTM
values (Figure 1b). The design in Figure 15 structurally dissociates the processes of LTM
read-out and LTM read-in by enabling some Stage 1 cells to become activated without
triggering any learning, no matter how fast the learning rate is chosen.

The feedback signals from Stage 3 to Stage 1 do not, however, act only as sampling
signals. They must also activate their target Stage 1 cells in order to close the internal
nonlinear feedback loops which enable the masking field to select its compressed recognition

code for storage in STM. If the feedback signals can activate Stage 1 cells, then how can the LTM traces which abut Stage 1 cells tell the difference between the activation of Stage 1 cells by inputs from F_1 and activation of Stage 1 cells by feedback signals from Stage 3? If such a distinction cannot be made, then a functional dissociation of LTM read-out and LTM read-in cannot be achieved.

There exist two types of solution to the dissociation problem: a dynamical solution and a structural solution, which can be instantiated either chemically or electrically. In the dynamical solution, the LTM traces continue to use Stage 1 cells as sampling signals, but the threshold for activating the sampling signal $f(x_j)$ is chosen high. It is assumed that Stage 1 cells can only be activated enough to exceed the sampling threshold when their direct activation by inputs from F_1 is supplemented by large positive feedback signals from Stage 3 cells. Although such a mechanism may be adequate to solve simple learning problems, it is inadequate in a complex learning system. For example, in a masking field, if the sampling threshold is chosen too small, then the Phase 1 surge can be learned. If the sampling threshold is chosen too large, then many groupings which should induce adaptive tuning will fail to do so. We have performed many computer simulations which support our contention that such a design is not robust.

In contrast, a structural solution to the problem is manifestly robust. In one such structural solution, the feedback signal is delivered via a different chemical transmitter than the chemical transmitter which gates signals from F_1 to F_2 and regulates learned LTM changes in $F_1 \rightarrow F_2$ pathways. Term $f(x_j^{(3)})$ in equation (5) can then be realized by a modulatory action of the feedback transmitter upon the feedforward transmitter. A modulatory action of catecholaminergic transmitters upon learning by cholinergic transmitters has been reported in neural data (e.g., Friedhoff, 1975a, 1975b) and has also been postulated in neural models of classical and instrumental conditioning (Grossberg, 1982, 1987a).

The use of two transmitters enables both transmitter systems to electrically activate Stage 1 cells, yet also enables LTM traces abutting Stage 1 cells to distinguish between feedback signals from Stage 3 and their aggregate effects upon Stage 1 cells. In one microscopic realization of such a dual transmitter system, either transmitter can cause macromolecular changes in the cell membranes of Stage 1 cells which enable electrical activation to occur, but only their conjoint action can cause those macromolecular changes which enable the learning process to unfold. Data concerning associative learning in invertebrates implicates a Ca^{++}-dependent membrane current which is activated only when pairs of critical events occur together (Alkon, 1979, 1984a, 1984b). A catecholaminergic transmitter may, moreover, participate in the activation of this Ca^{++} current (Alkon, 1984b). The feedback signal from Stage 3 to Stage 1 plays an analogous formal role in the circuit depicted in Figure 15. The suggestion that associative learning may depend upon a Ca^{++} current was made in Grossberg (1968, 1969b), based upon the fragmentary biochemical evidence then available, to explain how a learning equation such as (4) could be physically realized.

Another structural solution of the problem can also be envisaged. In this solution, each $F_1 \rightarrow F_2$ pathway causes a local change in its target cell membranes at Stage 1 (Figure 16). These local membrane channels cause local changes in potential which are summated by the Stage 1 cells before these cells activate Stage 2 cells. Feedback signals from Stage 3 cells cause global action potentials throughout the Stage 1 cells. These global action potentials activate membrane channels which cannot be activated merely by local signals from F_1. These membrane channels enable learning to occur within the abutting LTM traces. This possibility was used in Grossberg (1975) to discuss classical conditioning

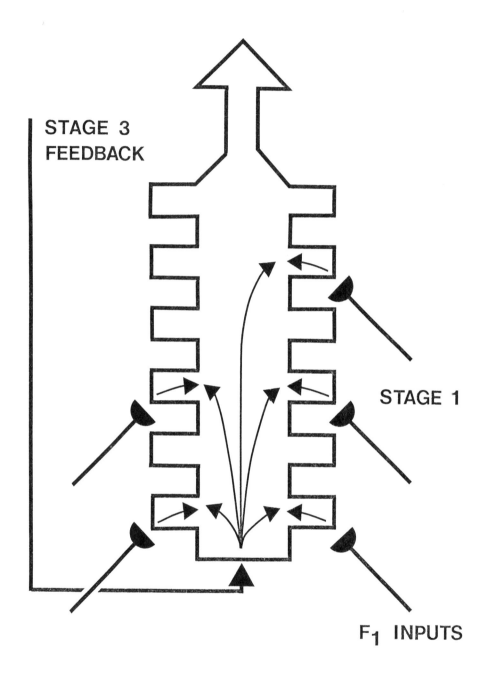

Figure 16. Stage 1 cells receive inputs from F_1 on branches, or dendrites, whose local activations summate to generate the total output signal to Stage 2 cells. Stage 3 feedback signals cause a massive global activation of Stage 1 cells which triggers the biophysical events that enable LTM traces (hemidisks) in active F_1 pathways to learn.

within the hippocampus and in Grossberg (1978) to discuss possible sites of neocortical conditioning. It is a structural, rather than a dynamical, scheme because *all* feedback signals are assumed to trigger the global change which enables learning to occur, not only feedback signals which can summate sufficiently with feedforward signals. Such a structural scheme could also be used to trigger a Ca^{++}-dependent current when the cell is globally activated. This type of structural scheme is used to interpret the systems simulated by Grossberg and Schmajuk (1987).

16. Concluding Remarks: Self-Stabilization of Learning within ART Circuits

Subsequent work on masking fields will proceed in several directions. In addition to quantitative analyses of the structurally stabilized masking field architecture summarized in Figure 15, each masking field design will be embedded within the total architecture which defines an adaptive resonance theory (ART) module (Figure 17). Such as ART architecture is capable of self-organizing and *self-stabilizing* its recognition codes in response to arbitrary orderings of arbitrarily many and arbitrarily complex input patterns. Carpenter and Grossberg (1987a, 1987b, 1987c, 1987d) have numerically and mathematically characterized ART architectures which use a masking field F_2 that always makes a global choice. In this special case, they have rigorously proved that the learned recognition code self-stabilizes in response to arbitrary orderings of arbitrarily many arbitrarily chosen binary input patterns (Carpenter and Grossberg, 1987a). Using masking fields capable of coding multiple groupings, the design of masking field hierarchies $F_1 \leftrightarrow F_2 \leftrightarrow \cdots \leftrightarrow F_n$ becomes possible. Such hierarchies show promise of being able to self-organize highly abstract grouping, hypothesis testing, and logical operations. The design of masking field hierarchies can now be pursued by combining the results of Carpenter and Grossberg with the results described herein.

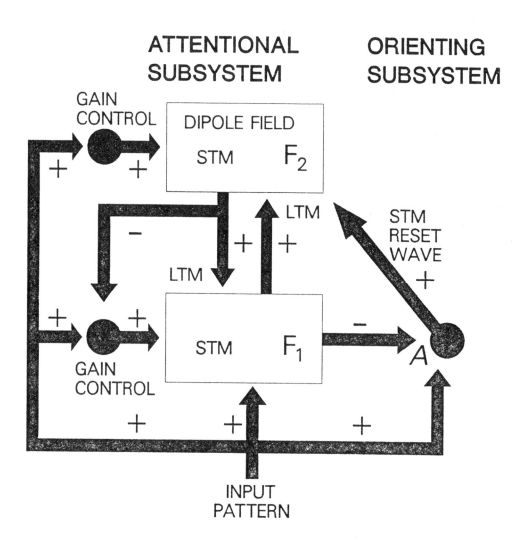

Figure 17. An adaptive resonance theory (ART) architecture: Two successive stages F_1 and F_2 of the code learning, or attentional, subsystem are depicted. In addition to a bottom-up adaptive filter $F_1 \rightarrow F_2$, a top-down adaptive filter $F_2 \rightarrow F_1$ learns templates, or critical feature patterns, which are matched against input patterns at F_1. This matching process protects already learned codes against unstable recoding by activating the orienting subsystem A. A reset wave from A quickly resets the list code at F_2 before it can be erroneously associated with the current activity pattern at F_1, and initiates a self-adjusting search for a better list code. The gain control channels enable F_1 to distinguish between bottom-up input patterns and top-down templates during the matching process, and enable stored STM activity to decay when gain control is shut off.

APPENDIX

Mathematical Description of a Masking Field

A. Shunting On-Center Off-Surround Networks

The cell populations v_i of a masking field have potentials $x_i(t)$, or STM activities, which obey the membrane equations of neurophysiology; namely,

$$C\frac{\partial V}{\partial t} = (V^+ - V)g^+ + (V^- - V)g^- + (V^p - V)g^p. \qquad (A1)$$

In (A1), $V(t)$ is a variable voltage; C is a constant capacitance; the constants V^+, V^-, and V^p are excitatory, inhibitory, and passive saturation points, respectively; and the terms g^+, g^-, and g^p are conductances which can vary through time as a function of input signals. Due to the multiplicative relationship between conductances and voltages in (A1), a membrane equation is also said to describe a *shunting* interaction.

In a masking field, the cells are linked together via recurrent, or feedback, on-center off-surround interactions (Figure 1b). The properties of a masking field are thus part of the general theory of shunting recurrent on-center off-surround networks. Grossberg (1981, 1983) reviews general properties of this class of networks.

The masking field equations are most simply built up in stages. Rewrite equation (A1) for the potential $x_i(t)$ in the form

$$\frac{d}{dt}x_i = -Ax_i + (B - x_i)P_i - (x_i + C)Q_i, \qquad (A2)$$

where 0 is the passive equilibrium point, $B(> 0)$ is the excitatory saturation point, and $-C(\le 0)$ is the inhibitory saturation point. Term P_i is the total excitatory input and term Q_i is the total inhibitory input to v_i. Potential $x_i(t)$ can vary between B and $-C$ in equation (A2) as the inputs P_i and Q_i fluctuate through time. The multiplication of P_i and Q_i by terms which include x_i endow the circuit with properties of automatic gain control.

The excitatory input P_i is a sum of two components: the total input from the item field plus a positive feedback signal from v_i to itself (Figure 1b). Thus P_i can be written in the form

$$P_i = \sum_{j \in J} I_j p_{ji} z_{ji} + Df(x_i). \qquad (A3)$$

In (A3), term I_j is the output from the item node $\{j\}$, p_{ji} is the connection strength of the pathway from v_j in F_1 to v_i in F_2, and z_{ji} is the LTM trace, or adaptive weight, within this pathway. Term $Df(x_i)$ describes the positive feedback signal from v_i to itself. This feedback signal enables v_i to store activities in STM after the inputs I_j terminate.

The inhibitory input Q_i in (A2) is a sum of feedback signals $g(x_m)$ from other populations v_m in the masking field. Thus Q_i can be written as

$$Q_i = \sum_{m \in I} g(x_m)E_{mi}. \qquad (A4)$$

B. Mass Action Interaction Rules

The notation in equations (A2)–(A4) is now refined to express the fact that the cells in different subfields of a masking field possess different parameters. To express the fact that an F_2 population receives F_1 pathways only from a prescribed (unordered) set J of items, let $x_i^{(J)}$ denote the STM activity of an F_2 population $v_i^{(J)}$ which receives input pathways only from the set J of F_1 items. Any number of different populations $v_i^{(J)}$ in F_2 may correspond to each fixed set J of F_1 items. Equation (A2) is replaced by the equation

$$\frac{d}{dt}x_i^{(J)} = -Ax_i^{(J)} + (B - x_i^{(J)})P_i^{(J)} - (x_i^{(J)} + C)Q_i^{(J)}, \tag{A5}$$

which holds for all unordered sets J of F_1 items that can selectively send pathways to nodes in F_2.

Equation (A3) for the excitatory input P_i is replaced by

$$P_i^{(J)} = \sum_{j \in J} I_j p_{ji}^{(J)} z_{ji}^{(J)} + D_{|J|} f(x_i^{(J)}). \tag{A6}$$

In term $D_{|J|}$, notation $|J|$ denotes the size of set J. Thus $D_{|J|}$ depends upon the size of set J, but not upon the items in set J. Thus the excitatory feedback coefficient $D_{|J|}$ is sensitive to the spatial scale of the population $v_i^{(J)}$.

Equation (A4) for the inhibitory input Q_i is refined in several stages. Function $Q_i^{(J)}$ obeys an equation of the form

$$Q_i^{(J)} = \sum_{m,K} g(x_m^{(K)})E_{KJ}, \tag{A7}$$

where coefficient E_{KJ} determines the strength of the inhibitory feedback pathway from $v_m^{(K)}$ to $v_i^{(J)}$. This path strength depends only upon the unordered sets K and J of items to which $v_m^{(K)}$ and $v_i^{(J)}$ respond. Coefficient E_{KJ} expresses the randomness of the self-similar growth process between populations in F_2 (Cohen and Grossberg, 1986a) as follows.

Mass Action Interactions

$$E_{KJ} = F_{|J|}G_{|K|}H_{|K \cap J|}. \tag{A8}$$

By (A8), E_{KJ} is a product of three factors. Each factor depends only upon the size of an unordered set of items. These unordered sets are set K, set J, and their intersection $K \cap J$. Equation (A8) can be explained by assuming that the inhibitory interaction strength from $v_m^{(K)}$ to $v_i^{(J)}$ is the result of an interaction of three independent random factors. The net strength E_{KJ} can thus arise from a statistically independent interaction between growth factors that depend on the sizes of K, J, and their overlap. By putting together all of these contraints, we find the following:

Masking Field Equations

$$\begin{aligned}
\frac{d}{dt}x_i^{(J)} = &-Ax_i^{(J)} + (B - x_i^{(J)})[\sum_{j \in J} I_j p_{ji}^{(J)} z_{ji}^{(J)} + D_{|J|} f(x_i^{(J)})] \\
&- (x_i^{(J)} + C)\sum_{m,K} g(x_m^{(K)})F_{|J|}G_{|K|}H_{|K \cap J|}.
\end{aligned} \tag{A9}$$

We now define how the coefficients $D_{|J|}$, $F_{|J|}$, $G_{|K|}$, and $H_{|K \cap J|}$ depend upon the unordered sets K and J; how the positive and negative feedback functions $f(w)$ and $g(w)$

depend upon their activities w; how the path strengths $p_{ji}^{(J)}$ from F_1 to F_2 express a random growth rule; and how numerical parameters were chosen.

C. Self-Similar Growth within List Nodes

The coefficient $D_{|J|}$ determines how the positive feedback from a node to itself varies with the node's self-similar scale. We assume that $D_{|J|}$ increases with scale, thereby enabling nodes corresponding to longer sublists to gain a competitive advantage in STM, other things being equal. The simplest choice is made in our simulations, namely

$$D_{|J|} = D \, | \, J \, |, \tag{A10}$$

where D is a positive constant. This rule is consistent with the possibility that, as an F_2 cell (population) grows in response to high levels of F_1 input, it also produces more excitatory synaptic sites for its own axon collaterals.

D. Conservation of Synaptic Sites

The dependence of the intermodal connection strengths $p_{ji}^{(J)}$, $F_{|J|}$, $G_{|K|}$, and $H_{|K \cap J|}$ on the sets K and J will now be described. The *total* connection strength to each population $v_i^{(J)}$ from all cells in F_1 and the *total* inhibitory connection strength to each population $v_i^{(J)}$ from all cells in F_2 are both chosen to be independent of K and J. This property is compatible with the interpretation that the size of each cell (population) is scaled to the total strength of its input pathways. If more pathways input to such a cell, then each input's effect is diluted more due to the larger size of the cell. The property of matching cell (population) volume to the total number of input pathways is called *conservation of synaptic sites*.

Conservation of synaptic sites enables the network to overcome the following problem. Due to the randomness of the growth rules, there may exist different numbers of cells in each of F_2's masking subfields. As these F_2 cells compete for STM activity, the competitive balance could be biased by accidents of random growth. A mechanism is needed to control the proliferation of random connections. Conservation of synaptic sites is one effective mechanism. A masking field embodies a new functional role for such a growth rule. Thus we impose the following constraints:

Synaptic Conservation Rule:

Let

$$\sum_{j \in J} p_{ji}^{(J)} = \text{constant} = 1 \tag{A11}$$

and

$$\sum_{m,K} F_{|J|} G_{|K|} H_{|K \cap J|} = \text{constant} = F. \tag{A12}$$

By (A12),

$$F_{|J|} = \frac{F}{\sum_{m,K} G_{|K|} H_{|K \cap J|}} \tag{A13}$$

We also did simulations in which the coefficients $p_{ji}^{(J)}$ are replaced by coefficients $p_{ji}^{(J)}[1 + \alpha \sum_k p_{jk}^{(J)}]^{-1}$ which obey a Weber Law Rule, and found similar results within a reasonable parameter range.

E. Random Growth from Item Nodes to List Nodes

The connections $p_{ji}^{(J)}$ from F_1 to F_2 are chosen to satisfy the conservation law (A11) as well as a random growth law.

<u>Random Normalized Growth Rule:</u>

Let

$$p_{ji}^{(J)} = \frac{1}{|J|}(1 - p_{|J|}) + r_{ji}^{(J)} p_{|J|}. \tag{A14}$$

The *fluctuation coefficient* $p_{|J|}$ in (A14) determines how random the growth is from F_1 to F_2. If $p_{|J|} = 0$, then growth is deterministic (but spatially distributed) because $p_{ji}^{(J)} = \frac{1}{|J|}$. In this limiting case, all connection strengths from item nodes in F_1 to a *fixed* list node in F_2 are equal, and vary inversely with the number $|J|$ of item nodes that contact the list node. If $0 < p_{|J|} \leq 1$, then the coefficients $r_{ji}^{(J)}$ in (A14) influence the connection strengths $p_{ji}^{(J)}$. The numbers $\{r_{ji}^{(J)} : j \in J\}$ are chosen pseudo-randomly: They are uniformly distributed between 0 and 1 such that

$$\sum_{j \in J} r_{ji}^{(J)} = 1 \tag{A15}$$

Equations (A14) and (A15) together imply the conservation rule (11).

It remains to say how the fluctuation coefficients $p_{|J|}$ depend upon the set size $|J|$. We choose these coefficients to keep the statistical variability of the connection strengths independent of $|J|$. In other words, we choose $p_{|J|}$ so that the standard deviation of $\{p_{ji}^{(J)} : j \in J\}$ divided by the mean of $\{p_{ji}^{(J)} : j \in J\}$ is independent of $|J|$. This is accomplished as follows.

To produce a pseudorandom sequence of numbers $\{r_{ji}^{(J)} : j \in J\}$ distributed uniformly over the simplex

$$S_n = \{(y_1, y_2, \ldots, y_{n+1}) : y_i \geq 0, \sum_{j=1}^{n+1} y_j = 1\}, \tag{A16}$$

we proceed as follows. By a standard algorithm (Knuth, 1981), we obtain a vector of numbers $w = (w_1, w_2, \ldots, w_n)$ uniformly distributed over the n-cube $I_n = \times_{j=1}^{n}[0,1]$. Rearrange the numbers in w in order of increasing size to produce a new vector $w' = (w_1', w_2', \ldots, w_n')$ such that $w_1' \leq w_2' \leq \ldots \leq w_n'$. The map $w \to w'$ from I_n into itself is determined by a permutation σ of the indices $\{1, 2, \ldots, n\}$ such that $w_i' = w_{\sigma(i)}$. Each permutation σ can transform a different subset of I_n into vectors with increasing entries. Thus I_n can be decomposed into sets D_σ such that a single permutation σ can map *all* $w \in D_\sigma$ into $w' \in I_n$. Hence the map $w \to w'$ transforms uniformly distributed vectors in I_n onto uniformly distributed vectors in I_n with elements in increasing order.

We next map vectors w' in I_n with elements in increasing order onto vectors y in S_{n+1} via the one-to-one linear transformation $y_1 = w_1'$, $y_2 = w_2' - w_1'$, ..., $y_n = w_n' - w_{n-1}'$, and $y_{n+1} = 1 - w_n$. Since this linear transformation maps equal volumes onto equal surface areas, the vectors y are uniformly distributed on the simplex S_{n+1}.

The coefficient of variation of $\{p_{ji}^{(J)} : j \in J\}$ is made independent of $|J|$ (> 1) as follows. By the above construction, the marginal distribution $r_{ji}^{(J)}$ in (A14) is distributed with density function $(|J| - 1)(1 - x)^{|J|-2}$. The mean of this distribution is $\frac{1}{|J|}$, and its standard deviation is $\frac{1}{|J|}\sqrt{\frac{|J|-1}{|J|+1}}$. Thus the mean of $p_{ji}^{(J)}$ is also $\frac{1}{|J|}$ and its standard deviation is

$$p_{|J|}\frac{1}{|J|}\sqrt{\frac{|J|-1}{|J|+1}}. \tag{A17}$$

The coefficient of variation of $p_{ji}^{(J)}$ is its standard deviation divided by its mean, which we set equal to a constant p independent of $|J|$. Thus we chose

$$p_{|J|} = p\sqrt{\frac{|J|+1}{|J|-1}}. \tag{A18}$$

In the simulations reported herein, $p = \frac{1}{10\sqrt{3}}$.

F. Self-Similar Competitive Growth between List Nodes

Coefficient $F_{|J|}$ in (A9) describes the total number of inhibitory synaptic sites within a population $v_i^{(J)}$. By (A13), this quantity is chosen to keep the number of synaptic sites constant across all the cells. Small random variations could also be allowed, but we have absorbed all of the effects of randomness into the coefficients $p_{ji}^{(J)}$ in (A14) for simplicity.

Coefficient $G_{|K|}$ in (A9) measures the total number of inhibitory connections, or axons, emitted by each population $v_m^{(K)}$ to all other F_2 populations. Due to self-similar growth, $G_{|K|}$ increases with $|K|$. In our simulations, we make the simplest choice.

Self − Similar Axon Generation:

Let

$$G_{|K|} = |K|. \tag{A19}$$

Thus $G_{|K|} = 0$ if $|K| = 0$.

Coefficient $H_{|K \cap J|}$ in (A9) describes how well growing axons from a population $v_m^{(K)}$ can compete for synaptic sites at a population $v_i^{(J)}$. In particular, coefficient $G_{|K|}$ describes the number of emitted axons, whereas coefficient $H_{|K \cap J|}$ measures the fraction of these axons that can reach $v_i^{(J)}$ and compete for synaptic space there. Due to self-similar growth (Cohen and Grossberg, 1986), $H_{|K \cap J|}$ increases with $|K \cap J|$. Consequently, if either set K or J increases, then $H_{|K \cap J|}$ also increases, other things being equal. Given fixed sizes of K and J, then $H_{|K \cap J|}$ increases as the overlap, or intersection, of the sets increases. In other words, list nodes *become* list nodes due to random growth of connections from item nodes. Two list nodes therefore tend to be closer in F_2 if they receive more input pathways from the same item nodes in F_1. If a pair of list nodes in F_2 is closer, then their axons can more easily contact each other, other things being equal. In the simulations, we choose $H_{|K \cap J|}$ as follows. Let

$$H_{|K \cap J|} = 1 + |K \cap J|. \tag{A20}$$

By (A20), $H_{|K \cap J|}$ increases linearly with $|K \cap J|$. Because $H_{|K \cap J|}$ is always positive, when $H_{|K \cap J|}$ multiplies $G_{|K|}$ in (A9), every population $v_m^{(K)}$ can send weak long-range inhibitory pathways across the whole of F_2, but these pathways tend to arborize with greater density at populations $v_i^{(J)}$ which receive inputs from the same F_1 nodes. Equations (A13), (A19), and (A20) imply that

$$F_{|J|} = \frac{F}{\sum_{m,K} |K| (1 + |K \cap J|)}. \tag{A21}$$

G. Contrast Enhancement by Sigmoid Signal Functions

The positive and negative feedback signals $f(x_i^{(J)})$ and $g(x_m^{(K)})$ in (A9) enable the network to contrast enhance its input patterns before storing them in STM. To achieve this property, we choose both $f(w)$ and $g(w)$ to be sigmoid, or S-shaped, functions of the activity level w (Grossberg, 1981, 1982). In particular, we let

$$f(w) = \frac{([w]^+)^2}{f_0 + ([w]^+)^2} \tag{A22}$$

and

$$g(w) = \frac{([w]^+)^2}{g_0 + ([w]^+)^2}. \tag{A23}$$

The notation $[w]^+$ in (A22) and (A23) stands for $\max(w, 0)$. Thus $f(w)$ and $g(w)$ do not generate feedback signals if w is smaller than the signal threshold zero. As w increases above zero, both $f(w)$ and $g(w)$ grow quadratically with w until they begin to saturate at their maximum value 1.

H. Associative Learning

The associative law that we have used is the one described in equation (1).

Associative Learning Law

$$\frac{d}{dt} z_{ji}^{(J)} = \epsilon f(x_i^{(J)})(-z_{ji}^{(J)} + L I_j). \tag{A24}$$

In (A24), the sampling signal $f(x_i^{(J)})$ is assumed to equal the positive feedback signal in (A9), and is thus a sigmoid function (A22) of activity $x_i^{(J)}$. The parameter ϵ determines the learning rate and the parameter L is a constant that multiplies the input I_j from node v_j in F_1.

The learning law contains term I_j, rather than term $I_j p_{ji}^{(J)}$ as in (A9), due to the following interpretation. Term $z_{ji}^{(J)}$ in (A9) is the LTM density, or LTM strength per unit cross-sectional area, in the pathways from v_j in F_1 to v_i in F_2. Term $p_{ji}^{(J)}$ describes the total cross-sectional area of these pathways. The input term I_j is broadcast along all these pathways, where it influences the LTM densities as in (A24). The total signal that is read out from these pathways into v_i equals the read-out of all the LTM densities $z_{ji}^{(J)}$ by I_j, summed across all the pathways. This sum equals $I_j p_{ji}^{(J)} z_{ji}^{(J)}$, as in (A9).

All of the above constraints can be summarized in the following system of equations.

Adaptively Filtered Masking Field

$$\frac{d}{dt}x_i^{(J)} = -Ax_i^{(J)} + (B - x_i^{(J)})\{\sum_{j \in J} I_j\Big[\frac{1}{|J|}(1 - p_{|J|}) + r_{ji}^{(J)}p_{|J|}\Big]z_{ji}^{(J)} + D\,|\,J\,|\,f(x_i^{(J)})\}$$

$$- F(x_i^{(J)} + C)\frac{\sum_{m,K} g(x_m^{(K)})\,|\,K\,|\,(1+\,|\,K \cap J\,|)}{\sum_{m,K}\,|\,K\,|\,(1+\,|\,K \cap J\,|)}$$

$$\tag{A25}$$

and

$$\frac{d}{dt}z_{ji}^{(J)} = \epsilon f(x_i^{(J)})(-z_{ji}^{(J)} + LI_j) \tag{A24}$$

where f and g are sigmoid signal functions. All of the "intelligence" of a masking field is embodied in the emergent properties which arise from the parallel interactions defined by these equations.

I. Parameters

The following parameter choices were made: $A = 1$, $B = 1$, $D = 4$, $L = 10$, $f_0 = 1$, $g_0 = 16$. In all runs $CF = 1088$. Additional parameters are listed by figure. Unless otherwise noted, the system has run to near equilibrium value.

Figure 3: $\epsilon = 0$, $C = 1$, $F = 1088$, $I_0 = 1.5$.

Figure 4a: same as Figure 3 except $I_1 = 1.5$; Figure 4b: $I_2 = 1.5$; Figure 4c: $I_0 = 1$, $I_1 = .5$; Figure 4d: $I_0 = .5$, $I_1 = 1$.

Figure 5a: $I_0 = .68$, $I_1 = .48$, $I_2 = .34$; Figure 5b: $I_0 = .34$, $I_1 = .68$, $I_2 = .48$; Figure 5c: $I_0 = .34$, $I_1 = .48$, $I_2 = .68$.

Figure 6: $\epsilon = 0$, $C = .125$, $F = 8704$.

Figure 6a: $I_0 = 1.5$; Figure 6b: $I_1 = 1.5$, Figure 6c: $I_2 = 1.5$, Figure 6d: $I_0 = 1.0$, $I_1 = .5$.

Figure 7a: $I_0 = .5$, $I_1 = 1.0$; Figure 7b: $I_0 = .68$, $I_3 = .48$, $I_2 = .34$; Figure 7c: $I_0 = .34$, $I_3 = .68$, $I_2 = .48$; Figure 7d: $I_0 = .34$, $I_1 = .48$, $I_2 = .68$.

Figure 9: Simulation is run at $\epsilon = 0$ until no single step nor the size of any component of the derivative is greater than 1.0×10^{-4}. ϵ is then set equal to 1 and simulation proceeds to equilibrium parameters; $C = .125$, $F = 8704$.

Figure 9a: $I_0 = 1.5$; Figure 9b: $I_1 = 1.5$; Figure 9c: $I_2 = 1.5$; Figure 9d: $I_0 = 1.0$, $I_1 = .5$.

Figure 10: Same parameters and conditions as in Figure 9 except where noted.

Figure 10a: $I_0 = .5$, $I_1 = 1.0$; Figure 10b: $I_0 = .68$, $I_1 = .48$, $I_2 = .34$; Figure 10c: $I_0 = .34$, $I_1 = .68$, $I_2 = .48$; Figure 10d: $I_0 = .34$, $I_1 = .48$, $I_2 = .68$.

Figure 11: $\epsilon = .1$, $C = .125$, $F = 8704$. Figures are output of $\{0, 1\}$ long term memory traces at times 1, 2, 4, 8, 16, 32, 64, 96.

Figure 12: $\epsilon = 0$, $C = 1$, $F = 1088$, $t = .1$, $t = .2$, $t = .4$, $t = .8$, $t = 1.6$.

Figure 13a: $\epsilon = 0$, $C = .125$, $F = 8704$, $I_0 = 1$, $I_1 = .5$; Figure 13b: $\epsilon = 1$; Figure 13c: $\epsilon = .1$; Figure 13d: $\epsilon = .01$.

REFERENCES

Alkon, D.L., Voltage-dependent calcium and potassium ion conductances: A contingency mechanism for an associative learning model. *Science*, 1979, **205**, 810–816.

Alkon, D.L., Calcium-mediated reduction of ionic currents: A biophysical memory trace. *Science*, 1984, **226**, 1037–1045 (a).

Alkon, D.L., Changes of membrane currents during learning. *Journal of Experimental Biology*, 1984, **112**, 95–112 (b).

Amari, S., Competitive and cooperative aspects in dynamics of neural excitation and self-organization. In S. Amari and M. Arbib (Eds.), **Competition and cooperation in neural networks**. New York: Springer-Verlag, 1982.

Amari, S. and Takeuchi, A., Mathematical theory on formation of category detecting nerve cells. *Biological Cybernetics*, 1978, **29**, 127–136.

Banquet, J.-P. and Grossberg, S., Probing cognitive processes through the structure of event-related potentials during learning: An experimental and theoretical analysis. *Applied Optics*, in press, 1987.

Brown, C.M., Inherent bias and noise in the Hough transform. *IEEE Transactions on Pattern Analysis and Machine Intelligence*, 1983, **PAMI-5**, 493–505.

Carpenter, G.A., A geometric approach to singular perturbation problems with applications to nerve impulse equations. *Journal of Differential Equations*, 1977, **23**, 335–367 (a).

Carpenter, G.A., Periodic solutions of nerve impulse equations. *Journal of Mathematical Analysis and Applications*, 1977, **58**, 152–173 (b).

Carpenter, G.A., Bursting phenomena in excitable membranes. *SIAM Journal on Applied Mathematics*, 1979, **36**, 334–372.

Carpenter, G.A., Normal and abnormal signal patterns in nerve cells. In S. Grossberg (Ed.), **Mathematical psychology and psychophysiology**, SIAM-AMS Proceedings, **13**, 1981, 49–90.

Carpenter, G.A. and Grossberg, S., A neural theory of circadian rhythms: The gated pacemaker. *Biological Cybernetics*, 1983, **48**, 35–59.

Carpenter, G.A. and Grossberg, S., A neural theory of circadian rhythms: Aschoff's rule in diurnal and nocturnal mammals. *American Journal of Physiology*, 1984, **247**, R1067–R1082.

Carpenter, G.A. and Grossberg, S., A neural theory of circadian rhythms: Split rhythms, after-effects, and motivational interactions. *Journal of Theoretical Biology*, 1985, **113**, 163–223.

Carpenter, G.A. and Grossberg, S., A massively parallel architecture for a self-organizing neural pattern recognition machine. *Computer Vision, Graphics, and Image Processing*, 1987, **37**, 54–115 (a).

Carpenter, G.A. and Grossberg, S., Neural dynamics of category learning and recognition: Attention, memory consolidation, and amnesia. In J. Davis, R. Newburgh, and E. Wegman (Eds.), **Brain structure, learning, and memory**. AAAS Symposium Series, 1987 (b).

Carpenter, G.A. and Grossberg, S., Neural dynamics of category learning and recognition: Structural invariants, reinforcement, and evoked potentials. In M.L. Commons, S.M. Kosslyn, and R.J. Herrnstein (Eds.), **Pattern recognition and concepts in animals, people, and machines**. Hillsdale, NJ: Erlbaum, 1987 (c).

Carpenter, G.A. and Grossberg, S., ART 2: Self-organization of stable category recognition codes for analog input patterns. *Applied Optics*, in press, 1987 (d).

Cohen, M.A. and Grossberg, S., Absolute stability of global pattern formation and parallel memory storage by competitive neural networks. *IEEE Transactions on Systems, Man, and Cybernetics*, 1983, **SMC-13**, 815–826.

Cohen, M.A. and Grossberg, S. Neural dynamics of speech and language coding: Developmental programs, perceptual grouping, and competition for short term memory. *Human Neurobiology*, 1986, **5**, 1–22.

Cohen, M.A. and Grossberg, S., Unitized recognition codes for parts and wholes: The unique cue in configural discriminations. In M.L. Commons, S.M. Kosslyn, and R.J. Herrnstein (Eds.), **Pattern recognition and concepts in animals, people, and machines**. Hillsdale, NJ: Erlbaum, 1987.

Duda, R.O. and Hart, P.E., Use of the Hough transform to detect lines and curves in pictures. *Commun. Ass. Comput. Mach.*, 1972, **15**, 11–15.

Ellias, S.A. and Grossberg, S., Pattern formation, contrast control, and oscillations in the short term memory of shunting on-center off-surround networks. *Biological Cybernetics*, 1975, **20**, 69–98.

Fenichel, N., Geometric singular perturbation theory for ordinary differential equations. *Journal of Differential Equations*, 1979, **31**, 53–98.

Grossberg, S., Some physiological and biochemical consequences of psychological postulates. *Proceedings of the National Academy of Sciences*, 1968, **60**, 758–765.

Grossberg, S., On learning and energy-entropy dependence in recurrent and nonrecurrent signed networks. *Journal of Statistical Physics*, 1969, **1**, 319–350 (a).

Grossberg, S., On the production and release of chemical transmitters and related topics in cellular control. *Journal of Theoretical Biology*, 1969, **22**, 325–364 (b).

Grossberg, S., A neural model of attention, reinforcement, and discrimination learning. *International Review of Neurobiology*, 1975, **18**, 263–327.

Grossberg, S., Adaptive pattern classification and universal recoding, I: Parallel development and coding of neural feature detectors. *Biological Cybernetics*, 1976, **23**, 121–134 (a).

Grossberg, S., Adaptive pattern classification and universal recoding, II: Feedback, expectation, olfaction, and illusions. *Biological Cybernetics*, 1976, **23**, 187–202 (b).

Grossberg, S., A theory of human memory: Self-organization and performance of sensory-motor codes, maps, and plans. In R. Rosen and F. Snell (Eds.), **Progress in theoretical biology**, Vol. 5. New York: Academic Press, 1978.

Grossberg, S., (Ed.), Adaptive resonance in development, perception, and cognition. In **Mathematical psychology and psychophysiology**. Providence, RI: American Mathematical Society, 1981.

Grossberg, S., **Studies of mind and brain: Neural principles of learning, perception, development, cognition, and motor control**. Boston: Reidel Press, 1982.

Grossberg, S. (Ed.), **The adaptive brain, I: Cognition, learning, reinforcement, and rhythm**. Amsterdam: Elsevier/North-Holland, 1987 (a).

Grossberg, S. (Ed.), **The adaptive brain, II: Vision, speech, language, and motor control**. Amsterdam: Elsevier/North-Holland, 1987 (b).

Grossberg, S., Nonlinear neural networks: Principles, mechanisms, and architectures. *Neural Networks*, in press, 1987 (c).

Grossberg, S. and Gutowski, W., Neural dynamics of decision making under risk: Affective balance and cognitive-emotional interactions. *Psychological Review*, 1987, **94**, 300–318.

Grossberg, S. and Kuperstein, M., **Neural dynamics of adaptive sensory-motor control: Ballistic eye movements**. Amsterdam: Elsevier/North-Holland, 1986.

Grossberg, S. and Levine, D.S., Some developmental and attentional biases in the contrast enhancement and short term memory of recurrent neural networks. *Journal of Theoretical Biology*, 1975, **53**, 341–380.

Grossberg, S. and Levine, D.S., Neural dynamics of attentionally modulated Pavlovian conditioning: Blocking, inter-stimulus interval, and secondary reinforcement. *Applied Optics*, in press, 1987.

Grossberg, S. and Schmajuk, N.A., Neural dynamics of attentionally modulated Pavlovian conditioning: Conditioned reinforcement, inhibition, and opponent processing. *Psychobiology*, 1987, **15**, 195–240.

Grossberg, S. and Stone, G.O., Neural dynamics of word recognition and recall: Attentional priming, learning, and resonance. *Psychological Review*, 1986, **93**, 46–74 (a).

Grossberg, S. and Stone, G.O., Neural dynamics of attention switching and temporal order information in short term memory. *Memory and Cognition*, 1986, **14**, 451–468 (b).

Hebb, D.O., **The organization of behavior**. New York: Wiley, 1949.

Hopfield, J.J., Neurons with graded response have collective computational properties like those of two-state neurons. *Proceedings of the National Academy of Sciences*, 1984, **81**, 3088–3092.

Hough, P.V.C., Method and means for recognizing complex patterns. United States Patent #3069654, 1962.

Knuth, D.E., **Seminumerical algorithms: The art of computer programming**, Vol. 2. Reading, MA: Addison-Wesley, 1981.

Kohonen, T., A simple paradigm for the self-organized formation of structural feature maps. In S. Amari and M. Arbib (Eds.), **Competition and cooperation in neural networks**. New York: Springer-Verlag, 1982.

Kohonen, T., Representation of information in spatial maps which are produced by self-organization. In E. Basar, H. Flohr, H. Haken, and A.J. Mandell (Eds.), **Synergetics of the brain**. New York: Springer-Verlag, 1983.

Levine, D.S., Neural population modeling and psychology: A review. *Mathematical Biosciences*, 1983, **66**, 1–86.

Levy, W.B., Associative changes at the synapse: LTP in the hippocampus. In W.B. Levy, J. Anderson, and S. Lehmkuhle (Eds.), **Synaptic modification, neuron selectivity and nervous system organization**. Hillsdale, NJ: Erlbaum, 1985, 5–33.

Levy, W.B., Brassel, S.E., and Moore, S.D., Partial quantification of the associative synaptic learning rule of the dentate gyrus. *Neuroscience*, 1983, **8**, 799–808.

Levy, W.B. and Desmond, N.L., The rules of elemental synaptic plasticity. In W.B. Levy, J. Anderson, and S. Lehmkuhle (Eds.), **Synaptic modification, neuron selectivity and nervous system organization**. Hillsdale, NJ: Erlbaum, 1985, 105–121.

Rauschecker, J.P. and Singer, W., Changes in the circuitry of the kitten's visual cortex are gated by postsynaptic activity. *Nature*, 1979, **280**, 58–60.

Rumelhart, D.E. and Zipser, D., Feature discovery by competitive learning. *Cognitive Science*, 1985, **9**, 75–112.

Singer, W., Neuronal activity as a shaping factor in the self-organization of neuron assemblies. In E. Basar, H. Flohr, H. Haken, and A.J. Mandell (Eds.), **Synergetics of the brain**. New York: Springer-Verlag, 1983.

Memory and Cognition
1986, **14** (6), 451–468
©1986 Psychonomic Society, Inc.

NEURAL DYNAMICS OF ATTENTION SWITCHING AND
TEMPORAL ORDER INFORMATION IN SHORT TERM MEMORY

Stephen Grossberg† and Gregory Stone‡

ABSTRACT

Reeves and Sperling have developed an experimental paradigm and a model for how attention switching influences the storage of temporal order information in short term memory (STM), or working memory. The present article suggests that attention switching influences initial storage of items in STM, but that competitive interactions among the STM representations of stored items control the further evolution of temporal order information as new items are processed. The laws governing these competitive interactions, called the long term memory (LTM) invariance principle and the STM normalization rule, were originally derived from postulates which ensure that STM is updated in a way that enables temporally stable list learning in LTM to occur. Despite these adaptive constraints, and often because of them, temporal order information is not always stored veridically. Both feedforward and feedback STM processes, with different invariant properties, are identified in the storage of temporal order information.

1. Introduction

The critical importance of temporary storage in perception has long been recognized (James, 1890) and has been the subject of extensive experimental and theoretical work (Atkinson and Shiffrin, 1971; Baddeley, 1976; Healy, 1975; Lee and Estes, 1977, 1981; Rundus, 1971; Sperling and Melchner, 1976; Tulving, 1983). Such temporary storage occurs at multiple levels of processing, from low-level sensory buffers to conceptually based, cross-modal representations. While the various forms of temporary storage differ in many details—depending upon the nature of processing at the level in question—the fundamental role of such storage and the problems which must be solved in devising real-time mechanisms for its instantiation have led to the recognition of several general principles governing the short term storage process (Grossberg, 1978a; 1978b). Within the framework provided by these principles, it is possible to investigate and specify in greater detail specific short term storage phenomena. In particular, this paper will use data on the effect of a shift of visual attention on temporal order information over item representations in short term memory (Reeves, 1977; Reeves and Sperling, 1986; Sperling and Reeves, 1980) to elucidate the dynamics of short term memory at a central stage of processing.

† Supported in part by the Air Force Office of Scientific Research (AFOSR 85-0149), the National Science Foundation (NSF IRI-84-17756), and the Office of Naval Research (ONR N00014-83-K0337).

‡ Supported in part by the Office of Naval Research (ONR N00014-83-K0337).

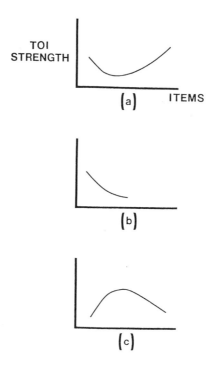

Figure 1. Possible patterns of temporal order information in STM: The abscissa represents presentation order of items in a list. The ordinate represents the precedence strength of the items, which determines mean report order. (a) Classic bow with primacy for early items and recency for later items; (b) pure primacy giving correct temporal order; (c) inverted bow found by Reeves and Sperling (1986).

2. Temporal Order Information in Short Term Memory

A number of paradigms have been used to probe the mechanisms by which subjects can store temporal order information about a list of items in short term memory (STM). The present model provides a principled explanation of several of the patterns that have been reported in the literature.

In free recall tests of short term memory, items from the beginning and the end of a sufficiently long list are reported earlier than are items from the middle of the list (Murdock, 1962; Atkinson and Shiffrin, 1971). Although, in general, this bowed serial position effect reflects both long term memory (LTM) and STM effects, immediate free recall by amnesic subjects with long term memory deficits also produces a bowed serial position effect (Baddeley and Warrington, 1970). This suggests that bowing can occur in STM with little or no LTM contribution (Figure 1a). This conclusion is also supported by free recall data for normal subjects. Hogan and Hogan (1975) theoretically disentangle STM and LTM contributions in their free recall data, and found an STM bow in addition to the expected LTM primacy gradient. Lee and Estes (1981) and Ratcliff (1978) also present evidence for a primacy effect in STM.

When shorter lists are presented (e.g., a telephone number), they can be recalled immediately in the correct order but are subject to forgetting if a distraction is introduced before recall, suggesting that the correct temporal order is maintained in STM. Correct temporal order information can be encoded by a primacy gradient in STM (Figure 1b).

Reeves and Sperling (Reeves, 1977; Reeves and Sperling, 1986) found that when a list is presented rapidly and subjects must shift visual attention to the list, items in the middle of the list are reported first. Thus, under these conditions, the serial position curve in STM is an inverted bow (Figure 1c).

The type of model that we will develop here has already been used to suggest an explanation of primacy gradients and bows in STM (Grossberg, 1978a, 1978b). In this article, we further develop the model to quantitatively analyse the Reeves and Sperling data. In particular, we consider how attention switching interacts with the processing of temporal order information in STM during conditions of rapid item presentation. In order to emphasize the critical role which temporal order information in short term memory plays in our account of the Reeves-Sperling data, we refer to the model developed in this article as the *Temporal Order Model* (TOM). Before presenting the TOM model, we will describe the data of Reeves and Sperling, the empirical model which they developed to fit them, and systematic deviations of their model from the data which suggest separate effects of attentional gate opening and internal STM dynamics on report order.

3. The Reeves-Sperling Paradigm

Reeves and Sperling had subjects monitor a sequence of letters which appeared successively at a position to the left of a fixation point. The presentation rate of the letters was fixed for each subject such that accuracy in reporting the letters was nearly perfect (about 98% correct), but required the subjects' full attention. When a predesignated target symbol was detected, subjects shifted their attention, without moving their eyes, to a stream of numerals which appeared sequentially to the right of the fixation point. Subjects responded by reporting, in order, the first four numerals they were able to detect.

There were two within subjects variables: target symbol and presentation rate for the numerals. For each of the three subjects, the target symbol was either a C, a U, or a square. The choice of target symbol on each trial was randomized and was not known to the subject before the trial began. Two of the subjects (AR and GL), who were experienced in the task, ran in four numeral presentation rate conditions (4.6, 6.9, 9.2, and 13.4 numerals per sec). The third subject (AK), who was naive, ran in three numeral presentation rate conditions (5.6, 6.9, and 9.2 per sec). These presentation rates were selected to avoid both "blurring" (about 20 per sec) and implicit naming of each numeral as it appeared (about 3 per sec: cf. Landauer, 1962; Sperling, 1963). For each subject and presentation rate, the "critical set" was defined as the seven consecutive numerals most likely to be reported, based on pilot studies. Numeral positions were numbered such that the numeral occurring simultaneously with the target symbol was assigned to position 0. For AR and GL the critical set began at positions -1, 0, 1, and 2 for the slowest to the fastest conditions. For AK, the critical set began at positions -1, 1, and 2 for the slowest to the fastest conditions. Feedback indicating the first six numerals in the critical set was provided after each trial.

Reeves and Sperling (1986) evaluated the data using several performance measures, which can be grouped into item scores and order scores. The item score P_i describes the proportion of trials in which the subject reports a numeral from position i in the critical set, irregardless of its position in the response. Figure 2 shows P_i as a function of the onset asynchrony between the target letter and the numeral in position i, for each subject in each condition. The bell shaped curves indicate that subjects most often reported numerals clustered around 400 msec after target onset. Also computed were the numbers $P_i(r)$, the proportion of trials in which the numeral in stimulus position i is reported in

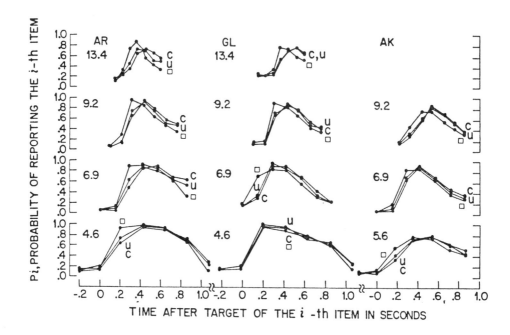

Figure 2. The item score P_i for all conditions in the Reeves and Sperling experiment: P_i describes the proportion of trials in which the subject reports a numeral from position i in the critical set. The abscissa gives the onset asynchrony between the target letter and the numeral in position i. Data for a given subject appear in the same column, as indicated. Each panel within a column presents the data for the given presentation rate. Each curve within a panel represents a different target condition, as indicated. (Reprinted from Reeves and Sperling (1986) with permission.)

response to position r.

The order score P_{iBj} describes the proportion of trials on which the numeral in position i is reported before the numeral in position j. Typical values of P_{iBj} (subject AR, target U) are presented in Figure 3.

When the P_{iBj} curves do not cross each other, they are said to display laminarity. For example, in the upper left panel of Figure 3 (presentation rate = 13.4 numerals per sec), stimulus position 6 tends to be reported before all other positions. To the extent that laminarity holds, responses show an order of precedence. In other words, the top curve gives the stimulus position which tends to be reported first, the second to the top the stimulus position which tends to be reported second, etc. Thus, the data for AR, target U, rate 13.4/sec shows a precedence order of (6,5,7,8,4,3,2). This pattern of precedence, in which a central position has the greatest precedence and the nearest pre-central and post-central positions are reported next, is referred to as folding. The central position

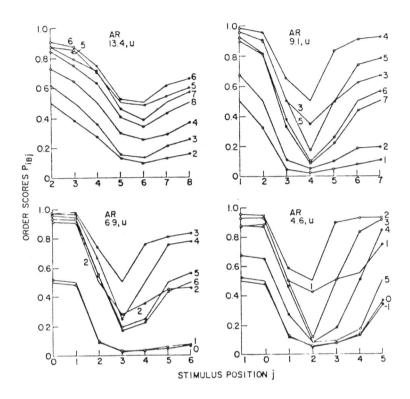

Figure 3. The order score P_{iBj} for subject AR, target U: Quantity P_{iBj} describes the proportion of trials on which the numeral in position i is reported before the numeral in position j. The abscissa represents list position j. The curve for each value of i is labelled with that value of i. The four panels are for the four different presentation rates, as indicated. (Reprinted from Reeves and Sperling (1986) with permission.)

(6 in the preceeding example) is called the "folding point". At faster presentation rates, precedence orders showed strong folding. At slower presentation rates, folding was present, but tempered by a tendency to report correct temporal order.

Another aspect of Reeves and Sperling's (1986) results is worth noting. Subjects reported that they actually "saw" the numerals in the reported order and were surprised to find that the reported order was not veridical. This phenomenology was compelling enough that the first author, who also served as a subject, initially assumed that the discrepancy between report order and the order indicated by the feedback was due to a programming error (Reeves, personal communication, 1985). These introspections lead to several conclusions. The re-ordering of numerals in short term memory occurs prior to conscious awareness. Despite the fact that all list items activate the same retinal region, later items can appear to occur before earlier items without masking recognition of these earlier items. Thus, the later items do not "catch up" to the earlier items to inhibit them.

Rather, items are successively transformed from retinal coordinates into a space which can simultaneously store several item representations in short term, or working, memory. Under certain conditions, later items can encode earlier temporal order properties than can earlier items. In the TOM model, one such temporal order factor is the relative activation levels of the different item representations in short term memory (Figure 1). When these item representations are stored in short term memory, later items can be activated more than earlier items, even though later items began to enter STM after earlier items.

4. The Reeves-Sperling Analysis

After presenting evidence which discounts both an item guessing and an order forgetting account of these results, Reeves and Sperling (1986) established the viability of a one-dimensional scale of precedence for order information in STM for their data. In addition, they assumed that P_{iBj} depends upon the difference in precedences according to the equation:

$$P_{iBj} = H[V(i) - V(j)] \tag{1}$$

where $V(i)$ is the precedence strength for stimulus position i, and H is some monotone increasing function mapping the reals into the interval $[0, 1]$. Reeves and Sperling tested these assumptions using a "quadruple" condition on the P_{iBj} probabilities (Block and Marschak, 1960):

$$P_{iBj} < P_{kBl} <=> P_{iBk} < P_{jBl}. \tag{2}$$

This condition should hold for all i, j, k, and l for any choice of the $V(i)$ and H satisfying the constraints previously given. The mean proportion of quadruple violations ranged from 4% at the fastest rates to 7% at the slowest rates. Assuming that response order reflects both the precedence strengths $V(i)$ and an equal-variance normally distributed noise component, Reeves and Sperling estimated the seven $V(i)$ for each cell of the subject × experimental condition design (Figure 4). The $V(i)$ were derived from equation (1) by assuming that H was a cumulative normal distribution and then performing a Monte Carlo simulation.

The inverted-U shapes of the $V(i)$, based on relative order scores, are quite similar to the P_i scores based on the probability of a single item appearing in the response. In fact, the predicted item scores, using the $V(i)$, accounted for 98% of the overall variance in the data. For the order scores P_{iBj}, the fit was very close at the fast rates but was not as good at slower rates (overall, the $V(i)$ accounted for 94% of the variance). Finally, Reeves and Sperling argued that the violations of laminarity could reflect averaging of trials with different precedence scales and noted that simulations in which trials with the same V functions but different folding points were averaged produced violations of laminarity typical of the data.

5. The Attention Gating Model (AGM)

Having demonstrated the utility of the strength model of precedence in accounting for the P_i and P_{iBj} scores, Reeves and Sperling (1986) proposed a parsimonious description of precedence strengths using an Attention Gating Model (AGM). The AGM assumes that all stimulus items are represented peripherally and that the strength of temporal order information in central storage is determined by two factors: the attention gating function

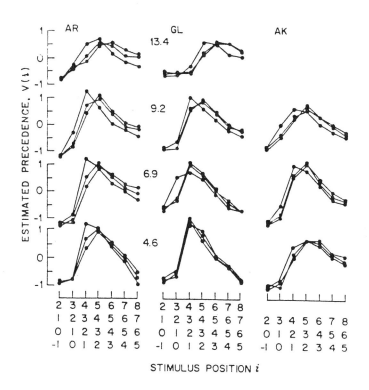

Figure 4. The estimated precedence strengths $V(i)$ for all experimental conditions: $V(i)$ was obtained by least squares fit to the P_{iBj} and $P_i(1)$ scores. The abscissa represents position in the critical set. The abscissa labels under the critical set positions give the absolute list positions, with the top row describing the fastest rate and the bottom row the slowest rate. Data for each subject are presented in the same column, as indicated. Each panel within a column presents data for the presentation rate indicated. Each curve in a panel represents a different target condition. (Reprinted from Reeves and Sperling (1986) with permission.)

$a(t)$, and a peripheral availability—or persistence—function, $b_i(t)$, for each stimulus position. The STM activity s_i for the ith item r_i at its time of storage is thus the cumulative central availability of the item's peripheral persistence:

$$s_i = \int_{-\infty}^{\infty} a(w)b_i(w)dw. \tag{3}$$

These s_i serve the same function in the AGM model that the estimated precedences $V(i)$, as defined in (1), serve for the empirical characterization of Reeves and Sperling's results. Reeves and Sperling assumed that $b_i(t) = 1$ from the onset of item r_i at time t_i to the onset of item r_{i+1} at time t_{i+1} and $b_i(t) = 0$ at all other times. Thus, by (3),

$$s_i = \int_{t_i}^{t_{i+1}} a(w)\,dw. \tag{4}$$

By (4), an item's STM activity depends entirely upon the degree to which the attention gate is open while the item is being presented. The AGM model assumes that there is no spontaneous STM decay nor interactions between the STM activities of different item representations. The STM activity of an item at the time of recall is assumed to equal its strength upon completion of central storage.

It is convenient to rewrite (4) in a form which emphasizes that s_i is a constant portion of a total integrated STM activity. After j items have been stored in STM, the total STM activity is

$$T(t_{j+1}) = \sum_{k=1}^{j} s_k = \int_{t_1}^{t_{j+1}} a(w)\,dw. \tag{5}$$

Using this expression, (4) can be written in the form

$$s_i = T(t_{i+1}) - T(t_i). \tag{6}$$

In order to compare the s_i values with the analogous quantities in the TOM model, we define the normalized precedences

$$Y_i = \frac{T(t_{i+1}) - T(t_i)}{T(\infty)}. \tag{7}$$

Equations (3)-(7) are true within the AGM model for any choice of the attention gate $a(t)$. Reeves and Sperling were able to fit their data by defining $a(t)$ to be a gamma function:

$$a(t) = \begin{cases} \frac{t^*}{\sigma^2} e^{-t^*} & \text{if } t^* \geq 0 \\ 0 & \text{if } t^* < 0 \end{cases} \tag{8}$$

where

$$t^* = (t - \tau)/\alpha. \tag{9}$$

In (9), the attentional reaction time, τ, is the time at which the attention gate begins to open; α is a time scale constant; and σ scales $a(t)$ relative to the noise distribution. For each subject, α and σ were chosen constant across conditions, and a τ_{targ} was set for each target letter. For subject AR, the attentional reaction time, τ in (8), was dependent only on the choice of target letter, so that $\tau = \tau_{targ}$. For subjects GL and AK, the attentional reaction time τ was assumed to depend upon both the target and the presentation rate. These two factors were assumed to have an independent influence on the attentional reaction time τ. Thus, for these subjects, the τ in (8) was chosen to satisfy $\tau = \tau_{targ} + \tau_{rate}$, subject to the constraint that $\sum \tau_{rate} = 0$ for each subject. The model of the data for subject GL included 3 τ_{rate} parameters and that for subject AK included 2 τ_{rate} parameters. For each subject, a least squares fit to the P_{iBj} and the $P_i(1)$ scores was obtained, where $P_i(1)$ is the probability of the numeral in stimulus position i being reported in response position 1. The fits were quite good for the small number of parameters chosen. The percent of variance accounted for by subject was: 83% for AR, 86% for GL, and 89% for AK. Thus, 13,200 experimental data points were first reduced to 198 precedence strength parameters, which in turn were replaced by 20 AGM parameters capable of accounting for at least 83%

of the variance in the P_{iBj} and $P_i(1)$ performance measures. Clearly, the AGM provides an elegant and parsimonious descriptive model of the experimental results.

However, it is worth noting that comparison of the AGM model's predicted precedences, the Y_i in (7), with the empirical estimates of precedence, the $V(i)$ in (1), shows distinct trends across presentation order (Figure 5). In particular, the Y_i tend to underestimate the $V(i)$ for early items and overestimate them for later items. This difference also tends to become more negative as presentation order approaches the folding point and then becomes more positive as presentation order increases beyond the folding point. In other words, the AGM model tends to underestimate the rate of change in precedence scores for early items and overestimate the rate of change for later items. In the AGM model, a single parameter α is used to account for the rate of gate opening and the rate of gate closing; thus, the best fit estimate of α must compromise between the faster rate of change for early items and the slower rate of change for later items.

We will use the descriptive AGM model as the basis for an alternative quantitative explanation of the Reeves and Sperling data. This will be done using the TOM model, in which STM dynamics between the time of central storage and recall plays a critical role. The principles from which the TOM model was derived illustrate some of the reasons we believe it provides a deeper explanation of the Reeves and Sperling data than does the AGM model. In particular, the TOM model acounts for the decreasing precedence scores for later items in terms of STM dynamics and the increasing precedence of early items as also reflecting the influence of a fast-opening attention gate. This account is consistent with the apparent difference in rate of change of precedence strengths for early and later items, which is not captured by the AGM model. In addition, the TOM model generalizes to a number of other experimental paradigms in which temporal order information in STM is critical, whereas the AGM model does not. For example, the TOM formulation of STM dynamics has been used to analyse data concerning speech and language recognition (Cohen and Grossberg, 1986, 1987a; Grossberg, 1978a, 1987b; Grossberg and Stone, 1986), free recall (Grossberg, 1978b), serial verbal learning (Grossberg, 1978a), and predictive sequences of motor acts (Grossberg, 1978a, 1986, 1987b; Grossberg and Kuperstein, 1986).

6. The LTM Invariance Principle: Deriving STM Laws from an LTM Stability Principle

We now characterize laws whereby a list of items can be stored in STM. We relate the laws which store individual items in STM to the LTM laws which group, or chunk, these items into unitized lists. We require that individual items be stored in STM in a manner which enables LTM to form unitized lists in a temporally stable way. Such laws show how to alter the STM activities of previous items in response to the presentation of new items so that the repatterning of STM activities that is caused by the new items does not inadvertently obliterate the LTM codes for old item groupings.

Consider from this perspective learning of the new word MYSELF, supposing that the words MY, SELF, and ELF are already familiar. We would not wish the LTM codes for the words MY, SELF, and ELF to be distorted or suppressed just because we are learning the new word MYSELF. On the other hand, the predictive importance of the groupings MY, SELF, and ELF may be reduced by their temporal embedding within the list MYSELF. Thus, the laws whereby STM activities over item representations are updated as new items are processed must enable the new items to alter the STM activities of previously processed item groupings without destroying the LTM codes for these groupings. This constraint on

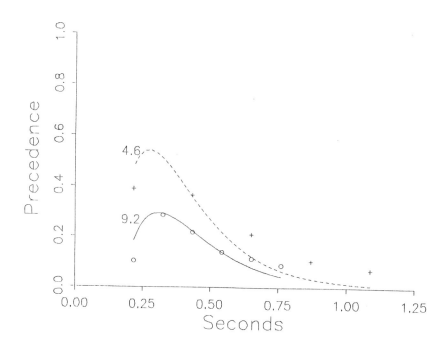

Figure 5. Best fit of normalized AGM precedence scores, Y_i, to empirically derived precedence scores, $V(i)$: Data are for subject GL, target C, rates 9.2 and 4.6 items/second. The abscissa represents each item's presentation order. The curves represent the Y_i function and the symbols represent the $V(i)$ scores. Precedence scores for 9.2 items/second are given by the solid curve and the o symbols. Precedence scores for the 4.6 items/second condition are given by the dashed curve and the + symbols. Because the Y_i and $V(i)$ were scaled differently, a least squares fit of the Y_i to the $V(i)$ was performed separately for each condition and used to rescale the $V(i)$.

STM coding is therefore called the LTM Invariance Principle (Grossberg, 1978a, 1978b). A remarkable consequence of this principle is that it shows how breakdowns in the encoding of temporal order information in STM can be derived from mechanisms which enable LTM chunks to be learned in a temporally stable way.

The theoretical macrocircuit depicted in Figure 6 (Cohen and Grossberg, 1986; Grossberg, 1978a, 1986, 1987b; Grossberg and Stone, 1986) provides a vantage point from which to review briefly how the LTM Invariance Principle is computationally implemented. In Figure 6, the processing stage A_3 stores an STM activity pattern which encodes both item information and temporal order information. Item information is coded in terms of which representations are activated, whereas temporal order information is coded in terms of the spatial patterning of activation across representations. In this way, a single spatial pattern of STM activity across A_3 encodes both the set of items that has been stored (i.e., item information), as well as a measure—perhaps inaccurate—of the order in which the items were stored (i.e., temporal order information). As a new item representation in A_3 is activated by external events, this STM activity pattern is updated to include the new item in a way that satisfies the LTM Invariance Principle.

Stage A_4 encodes in STM the sublists, or groupings, of items across A_3 to which the network is sensitive. In the simplest realization of this idea, a single A_4 population is activated by an STM pattern across A_3, and different STM patterns across A_3 activate different A_4 populations. In other words, individual A_4 populations encode whole lists of items. In more general versions of the idea, an STM pattern across A_3 activates several A_4 populations. Each A_4 population encodes a particular sublist of the A_3 encoding. The spatial patterning of STM activity across these A_4 populations encodes which sublist groupings of the whole list are salient to A_4; in particular, the list as a whole, its most salient parts, and the predictive wholes of which it forms a salient part. A network A_4 whose STM patterns are capable of representing salient parts and wholes of the A_3 pattern is called a *masking field* (Cohen and Grossberg, 1986, 1987a, 1987b).

Both prewired featural biases and subsequent learning experiences help to determine the sublist groupings to which A_4 is sensitive (Carpenter and Grossberg, 1987a, 1987c; Cohen and Grossberg, 1987b; Grossberg, 1987b). In particular, the pathways from A_3 to A_4 contain modifiable LTM traces which change as a function of the STM patterns that A_3 experiences. These LTM traces enable A_4 to react preferentially to familiar sublist groupings. The laws for storing individual items in STM at A_3 are chosen to guarantee the temporal stability of LTM encoding within the $A_3 \rightarrow A_4$ pathways. We can now state more precisely how the design of A_3 is constrained by the need to stabilize LTM within the $A_3 \rightarrow A_4$ pathways.

LTM Invariance Principle: The spatial patterns of STM activity across A_3 are instated and reset by a sequentially presented list in such a way as to leave the $A_3 \rightarrow A_4$ LTM codes of past event groupings invariant.

In order to understand how to implement this rule, it is necessary to know how the $A_3 \rightarrow A_4$ LTM traces help to transform STM activity patterns across A_3 into STM activity patterns across A_4. The conditionable pathways from A_3 to A_4 define an *adaptive filter*. In other words, if node v_i in A_3 generates a signal S_i in the pathway to node v_j in A_4, this signal is multiplied, or *gated*, by an LTM trace z_{ij} before the gated signal $S_i z_{ij}$ can activate v_j. The sum $T_j = \sum_i S_i z_{ij}$ of all gated signals is the total input from A_3 to v_j. The input pattern $(T_1, T_2, \ldots)$ determines which sublist groupings will be stored in STM by A_4. The relative sizes of the signals S_i determine the relative sizes of the inputs T_j. Accordingly, in order to prevent new items at A_3 from disturbing the LTM coding of past item groupings, we assume that a new item entering A_3 may alter the absolute sizes of S_i for previously active nodes, but does not alter their relative sizes. In other words, each new item can multiply, or *shunt*, the previous STM activities across A_3 by a common multiplicative factor as a new item is stored in STM at A_3. Grossberg (1978a, 1978b) noted that such a rule could be implemented by designing A_3 as an on-center (cooperative) off-surround (competitive) recurrent (feedback) network undergoing shunting (mass action) interactions.

In order to implement the LTM Invariance Principle within the TOM model, we consider a sequence of items $r_1, r_2, \ldots, r_n$ presented at times $t_1, t_2, \ldots, t_n$, respectively. We work with the STM activities $x_i(t_{j+1})$ for the representation of item i that obtain just

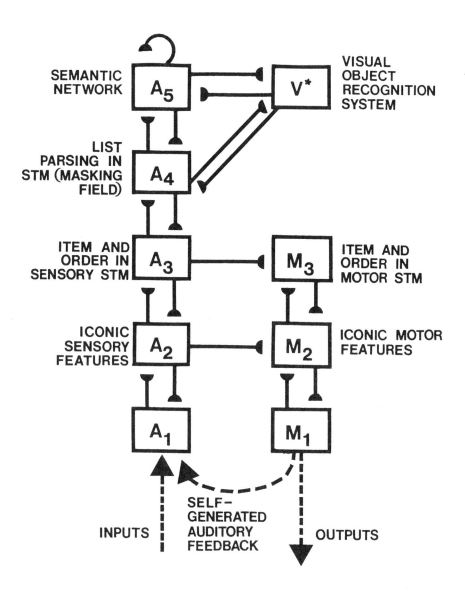

Figure 6. Theoretical macrocircuit involved in processing list items: Stage A_3 encodes both the identity of items (item information) and a measure of the order in which they were stored (order information). Stage A_4 encodes unitized sublists of items represented at A_3 and is called a masking field. (Reprinted from Grossberg and Stone (1986) with permission.)

before the r_{j+1} item begins to take effect. The LTM Invariance Principle constrains the development, during the course of list presentation, of these STM activities. The STM activities at time t_{j+1} (the instant that item $j+1$ begins to take effect) provide the best estimate of the equilibrated pattern of STM activity in response to the jth item in the list. We introduce the notation $\mu_i = x_i(t_{i+1})$ for the STM activity of the ith item at the time its STM memory trace is first activated. Quantity μ_i covaries with the amount of attention payed to the ith item in the list at the time it is presented, with smaller μ_i reflecting less attention. The theory sharply distinguishes between the vigilance devoted by a subject to a stimulus and the amount of attention received by that stimulus in STM. See Carpenter and Grossberg (1987a, 1987b) and Grossberg and Stone (1986) for discussions of this distinction. We also introduce the notation ω_j for the STM reset parameter, which multiplies, or shunts, the STM traces of all previous items upon entry of the jth item into STM. These relationships are expressed mathematically by the equation

$$x_i(t_{j+1}) = \begin{cases} 0 & \text{if } i > j \\ \mu_i & \text{if } i = j \\ \omega_j x_i(t_j) & \text{if } i < j. \end{cases} \tag{10}$$

Thus, the activity of each item's STM representation is the product of a term μ_i reflecting the attention paid to each item as it is presented and of shunting parameters ω_j which reset STM when each subsequent item is presented. Recursive solution of (10) leads to an equation for $x_i(t_{j+1})$ expressed entirely in terms of these factors:

$$x_i(t_{j+1}) = \mu_i \Pi_{k=i+1}^{j} \omega_k, \quad i \leq j. \tag{11}$$

While the μ_i reflect attentional factors and will vary according to the task, we can specify the STM reset parameters ω_j in terms of the attentional parameters μ_i.

7. The Normalization Rule: Limited Capacity of STM

Expression of the STM reset parameters, ω_j, in terms of the attentional weights, μ_i, is achieved by implementing the STM Normalization Rule. The STM Normalization Rule refers to the fact that total STM strength grows towards a finite maximum level of activity which is independent of the number of items being processed. In other words, STM at the item level A_3 is of limited capacity. This rule is not an independent assumption within the theory. Rather, it is a property of the competitive STM interactions among the item representations which also give rise to the LTM Invariance Principle (Grossberg, 1978a, 1978b). In order to impose the Normalization Rule, we first derive a convenient equation for the total STM activity $S(t_{j+1})$ after the item field has equilibrated in response to storage of the jth item.

By definition,

$$S(t_{j+1}) = \sum_{i=1}^{j} x_i(t_{j+1}). \tag{12}$$

Using the expression (10) of the LTM Invariance Principle, (12) implies that

$$S(t_{j+1}) = \omega_j S(t_j) + \mu_j. \tag{13}$$

Equation (13) suggests a functional relationship between the STM reset parameters ω_j and the attentional parameters μ_i. This relationship must satisfy three requirements:

a) If $\mu_j = 0$ then $\omega_j = 1$: If the attentional weight μ_j for item j equals zero (i.e., item j receives no attention and so produces no STM activity), the total STM activity should not change due to that item.

b) ω_j is a decreasing function of μ_j: As the attentional weight μ_j is parametrically increased, the STM reset weight ω_j is parametrically decreased. In other words, the greater the attentional weight μ_j given to the item currently being stored, the greater its ability to competitively reset the STM traces of previous items. This implies that as μ_j increases, previous item codes will be more strongly inhibited.

c) Given constant vigilance across experimental trials, ω_j covaries with μ_j in such a way that $S(t_{j+1})$ increases monotonically to a finite limit as successive items are stored.

8. Relating STM Reset to Attentional Processing

Our computations herein have implemented the simplest function which satisfies these constraints:

$$\omega_j = 1 - \mu_j \tag{14}$$

where $0 \leq \mu_j \leq 1$. This choice allows us to derive explicit attentional weights μ_j from the precedence scores predicted by the AGM model.

Before implementing these computations, it is necessary to verify that (14) implies the Normalization Rule. By (13) and (14),

$$S(t_{j+1}) = (1 - \mu_j)S(t_j) + \mu_j \tag{15}$$

from which it follows that

$$S(t_{j+1}) \leq 1, \quad j \geq 0. \tag{16}$$

By rewriting (15) as

$$1 - S(t_{j+1}) = (1 - \mu_j)(1 - S(t_j)) \tag{17}$$

it is also readily seen that $S(t_{j+1})$ increases with j so long as $0 \leq \mu_j \leq 1$ for all $j = 1, 2, \ldots$. By (13) and (17),

$$\frac{1 - S(t_{j+1})}{1 - S(t_j)} = \omega_j. \tag{18}$$

By (18), the rate ω_j with which previously active representations are reset, as in (13), equals the rate with which previously uncommitted STM capacity becomes committed. Thus the linear relationship (14) describes the important special case in which a balance exists between the processes of STM resource utilization and STM reset.

Equations (11) and (14) allow us to express the activity of each item in STM as a function of the attentional weights assigned to the items as they were presented:

$$x_i(t_{j+1}) = \mu_i \Pi_{k=i+1}^{j}(1 - \mu_k). \tag{19}$$

In the preceeding analysis, we have considered two fundamental constraints on STM processing—the LTM Invariance Principle and the STM Normalization Rule—which result from an analysis of how a processing system can learn in a stable fashion in response to a temporal list of events. These principles allow us to convert a given sequence of attentional weights, which characterize each item's strength upon storage in STM, into an expanding spatial pattern of STM activities which define the precedence scores reponsible for report order at the time of response. In the following section, we consider the reverse problem: how to convert estimated precedences based on observed responses into estimated sequences of attentional weights. Further analysis of these empirically derived attentional weight sequences will then reveal theoretically interesting characteristics of the interaction between STM dynamics and attentional gating processes. In particular, conversion of the AGM model precedence scores into our formulation reveals an unanticipated interaction between feedforward and feedback processes in the storage of temporal order information in STM.

9. Derivation of Attention Weights from the AGM Model

Equation (19) converts a sequence of attentional weights (the μ_i) into a set of temporal order precedence scores (the $x_i(t_{j+1})$). The analysis of experimental results requires conversion of observed response orders into unobserved attentional weights. The model as developed thus far can be used for this analysis without additional assumptions.

We begin by relating the normalized precedence values Y_i of the AGM, which are defined in (7), to the analogous quantities within the TOM model. If n is the number of items in the list, then $x_i(t_{n+1})$ is the STM activity of item r_i at the time of read-out from STM, assuming that spontaneous STM decay is not appreciable. We therefore let

$$x_i(t_{n+1}) = Y_i \tag{20}$$

as a basis for deriving further information about the TOM from the AGM. First, we compute the attention weights as a function of AGM parameters.

The attention weights μ_i are a function of the onset asynchrony δ between successive items, the time τ at which the attention gate begins to open, and the rate parameter α in (8):

$$\mu_i = \frac{(1+t_i^*)e^{-t_i^*} - (1+t_{i+1}^*)e^{-t_{i+1}^*}}{1 - [(1+t_{i+1}^*)e^{-t_{i+1}^*} - (1+t_{n+1}^*)e^{-t_{n+1}^*}]} \tag{21}$$

where

$$t_i^* = \begin{cases} \frac{\delta i - \tau}{\alpha} & \text{if } \delta i > \tau \\ 0 & \text{if } \delta i \le \tau \end{cases}. \tag{22}$$

The proof is given in Appendix 1.

Figure 7 compares the sequence of these μ_i values with the Y_i at each presentation rate, using the data for subject GL, target C.

Unlike the pattern of precedences Y_i, the pattern of attention weights μ_i does not exhibit significant bowing. In other words, bowing is not a major effect within the TOM model at the times when items are first stored in STM. The TOM model is thus consistent with the existence of an attentional gate that opens more rapidly than does the gate hypothesized in the AGM model. Since $x_i(t_{n+1}) = Y_i$, the TOM model suggests that much of the bowing effect evolves due to competitive interactions which reset the STM activites of item representations when later items are presented. Competitive interactions also account for the decrement in the attention weights μ_i for later items r_i.

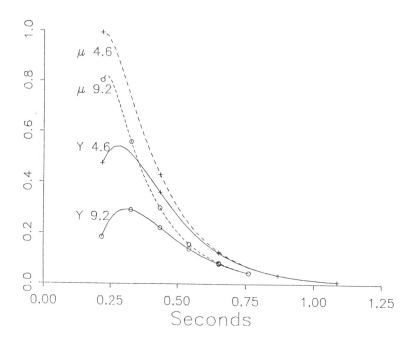

Figure 7. Comparison of TOM attention weights μ_i and normalized AGM precedence scores Y_i: Data shown are for subject GL, target C, rates 9.2 and 4.6 items/second. In the TOM model, each item's strength at storage is given by the μ_i; however, due to STM reset its strength on retrieval from STM is given by the Y_i. In the AGM model, each item's strength does not change after storage and is given by the Y_i. The abscissa represents presentation order. The solid curves represent the Y_i scores and the dashed curves represent the μ_i scores. The 4.6 items/second condition is indicated by the $+$ symbols. The 9.2 items/second condition is indicated by the o symbols.

10. STM Onset and STM Reset

The distinct effects of attention switching and of STM interactions on temporal order information can be better seen through the following pair of equations:

STM Onset Equation

$$x_i(t_j) = \gamma \nu_i x_{i-1}(t_j), \quad j > i \tag{23}$$

where

$$\gamma = e^{\frac{-\delta}{\alpha}}. \tag{24}$$

STM Reset Equation

$$x_i(t_{j+1}) = \omega_j x_i(t_j), \quad j > i. \tag{25}$$

The STM Onset Equation describes the relative activities $x_i(t_j)/x_{i-1}(t_j)$ of the STM representations corresponding to successive items r_{i-1} and r_i at all times t_j after the items are stored in STM. The equation says that these relative activities equal a quantity $\gamma\nu_i$ which is independent of t_j. In other words, the relative advantage or disadvantage of items r_{i-1} and r_i in STM is determined by the time r_i is stored, and does not change thereafter.

The STM Reset Equation describes the relative sizes $x_i(t_{j+1})/x_i(t_j)$ of the STM activities corresponding to a single item r_i at successive times t_j and t_{j+1} after the item is stored in STM. The equation says that these relative activities equal a quantity ω_j which is independent of the item r_i. In other words, after items are stored in STM, a new item resets all their stored activities by a constant multiple ω_j. The STM Reset Equation realizes the LTM Invariance Principle, as in (10).

The meaning of equations (23) and (25) resides within the two *gain functions* $\gamma\nu_i$ and ω_i, whose form is derived by fitting equations (23) and (25) to the AGM model. Such a fit discloses some remarkable and unexpected properties. Before describing these properties, we introduce a physical interpretation of equations (23) and (25) which the properties are used to support and refine.

Function $\gamma\nu_i$ is called the *feedforward gain function* and ω_i is called the *feedback gain function*. Function $\gamma\nu_i$ determines a property of STM activities as items begin to be stored. We suggest that this function reflects, among other processes, the opening of an attentional gate. Function ω_i, in contrast, determines a property of STM activities after they are stored. We suggest that this function reflects interactions between STM activities that are already stored. The following properties of these functions support these interpretations:

Function ν_i is (A) a decreasing function of i; (B) greater than 1; and (C) shift invariant in item time.

Function ω_i is (A) an increasing function of i; (B) less than 1; and (C) shift invariant in real time.

Examples of the functions ν_i and ω_i, as derived from fitting (23) and (25) to the TOM model's fit to the data of subject AR, target U, are plotted in Figure 8. Figure 8 also plots each function in real time (t) and in item time (i) to demonstrate the shift invariance described by property (3).

Equations (23) and (25) can be better understood by writing them in a notation that more explicitly exhibits their dependent variables. Since $t_j = \delta j$, where δ is the onset asynchrony, (22) can be rewritten as

$$x_i(\delta j) = e^{\frac{-\delta}{\alpha}} N(i, \tau, \alpha, \delta) x_{i-1}(\delta j), \tag{26}$$

where

$$\nu_i \equiv N(i, \tau, \alpha, \delta); \tag{27}$$

and

$$x_i(\delta(j+1)) = \Omega(j, \tau, \alpha, \delta) x_i(\delta j), \tag{28}$$

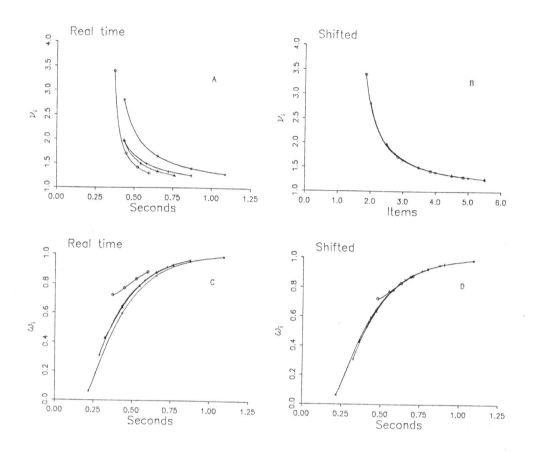

Figure 8. The feedforward gain, ν_i, feedback gain, ω_i, and their shift invariance properties: All data are for subject AR, target U. The four curves in each graph represent the four presentation rate conditions. (a) The feedforward gain function, ν_i, is plotted against the onset asynchrony measured in seconds. (b) The ν_i functions are plotted against onset asynchrony measured in number of items elapsed (item time) and have been shifted onto the curve for 4.6 items/second. (c) The feedback gain function, ω_i, is plotted against the onset asynchrony measured in seconds. (d) The ω_i have been shifted in real time onto the curve for 4.6 items/second.

where

$$\omega_j \equiv \Omega(j, \tau, \alpha, \delta). \tag{29}$$

11. Opening of the Attention Gate

Figure 9 schematizes how the shift-invariance in item time of $N(i, \tau, \alpha, \delta,)$ interacts with $e^{\frac{-\delta}{\alpha}}$ to control whether correct temporal order information or folding will occur. By equa-

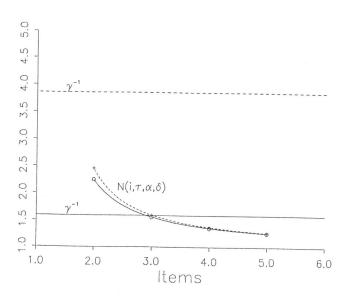

Figure 9. Illustration of the interaction of N and γ^{-1} to determine folding versus correct temporal order: When N is greater than γ^{-1}, a recency effect obtains. When N is less than γ^{-1}, a primacy effect obtains. Thus, the intersection of N and γ^{-1} indicates the point at which folding occurs. For slow presentation rates (dashed curves), γ^{-1} is large and passes over the N curve without intersecting it. This implies no folding and correct report of temporal order. For fast presentation rates (solid curves), γ^{-1} is smaller and intersects the N curve, so that folding occurs with the item immediately preceding the intersection (in this case the second item) as the folding point.

tion (26), correct temporal order information (an STM primacy gradient) occurs for items r_{i-1} and r_i such that

$$e^{\frac{-\delta}{\alpha}} N(i, \tau, \alpha, \delta) < 1. \tag{30}$$

Reversed temporal order information (an STM recency gradient) occurs for items r_{i-1} and r_i such that

$$e^{\frac{-\delta}{\alpha}} N(i, \tau, \alpha, \delta) > 1. \tag{31}$$

Folding occurs if the feedforward gain function $e^{\frac{-\delta}{\alpha}} N(i, \tau, \alpha, \delta)$ passes through the value 1 at an index $i > 1$.

As presentation rate decreases, the onset asynchrony δ increases. Consequently, N shifts to the left and $e^{\frac{\delta}{\alpha}}$ increases, yielding curves such as those in Figure 9. By (30), primacy occurs if $N < e^{\frac{\delta}{\alpha}}$; by (31), recency occurs if $N > e^{\frac{\delta}{\alpha}}$. Figure 9 indicates that the folding point moves towards the beginning of the list as δ increases. When it is smaller than the first item to be processed, correct temporal order information prevails.

The shift invariance of N in item time implies that processing of items is attenuated until a later list position when δ is small. The term $\gamma = e^{\frac{-\delta}{\alpha}}$ describes the effect of an integration process which takes place in real-time within the duration δ between successive items. More items can be crowded in a constant duration when δ is small than when δ is large. Correspondingly, $\gamma^{-1} = e^{\frac{\delta}{\alpha}}$ in Figure 9 decreases as δ decreases, with the effect that brief presentation of many items in a fixed duration tends to cause folding. In effect, the STM activities of early items relative to later items are weakened if they are presented very quickly.

This effect may be related to the opening of an attention gate by considering the limiting case in which $N \cong 1$ for all items. In other words, choose δ so large that $N \cong 1$ before even the first item's STM storage equilibrates. Then (23) reduces to

$$x_i(t_j) \cong \gamma x_{i-1}(t_j) \tag{32}$$

for all items, which shows that correct temporal order information obtains if gate opening does not prevent full storage of all the items. The proof that ν_i is shift invariant in item time is provided in Appendix 2. Function $\nu_i \equiv N(i, \tau, \alpha, \delta)$ is a function of i and the variables α/δ and τ/δ, which are the parameters α and τ scaled in item time:

$$N(i, \tau, \alpha, \delta) = \frac{i - 1 - P(\frac{\tau}{\delta}, \frac{\alpha}{\delta})}{i - P(\frac{\tau}{\delta}, \frac{\alpha}{\delta})} \tag{33}$$

where

$$P(u, v) = u - v - \frac{1}{1 - e^{-\frac{1}{v}}}. \tag{34}$$

12. STM Reset Mediated by Inter-Item Feedback Interactions

Equation (25), and its more precise counterpart (28), describe the reset of STM that is driven by new items competing for limited capacity STM resources. This conclusion can be supported in several ways:

The gain Ω in (28) increases towards 1 as the item j increases. The explicit equation for Ω is derived in Appendix 1. When $j \gg 1$, STM is hardly reset by a new item, because the limited capacity of STM is almost fully utilized. The approximate shift-invariance of $\Omega(j, \tau, \alpha, \delta)$ in real-time (Figure 8) also clarifies the STM reset interpretation. Shift-invariance implies that, for every pair δ_1 and δ_2 of onset asynchronies, there exists a shift λ such that

$$\Omega_{\delta_1}(t - \lambda) \cong \Omega_{\delta_2}(t) \tag{35}$$

for all times t at which both functions are defined. Consider a time T which can be written in the form $T = j_1\delta_1 = j_2\delta_2$ for appropriate choices of indices j_1 and j_2. In particular, suppose $\delta_1 < \delta_2$ and $j_1 > j_2$. Then we can define

$$\Omega \equiv \Omega_{\delta_1}(T - \lambda) \cong \Omega_{\delta_2}(T). \tag{36}$$

Hence, by (28),

$$x_i(\delta_1(j_1 + 1) - \lambda) = \Omega x_i(\delta_1 j_1 - \lambda) \tag{37}$$

and

$$x_i(\delta_2(j_2 + 1)) = \Omega x_i(\delta_2 j_2). \tag{38}$$

Equations (37) and (38) say that, up to a shift in time scale, a fixed amount Ω of STM reset is determined by continuous STM integration for the duration T, whether this processing has been divided among many items, each integrated for a brief time as in (37), or few items, each integrated a longer time, as in (38). When many items are presented quickly, each item can reset previous items less, but the cumulative effect of storing a fixed total STM activity is to generate a fixed amount of reset. Thus the STM Reset Equation embodies a type of Bloch's Law trade-off between number of items and processing time to describe how cumulative STM activity regulates subsequent STM storage and reset.

This interpretation is strengthened by consideration of the hypothesis

$$\mu_j = 1 - \omega_j \tag{39}$$

that was made in (14). As ω_j increases towards 1, less STM reset can occur. Correspondingly, by (39), new items cannot be well stored in STM.

A more detailed interpretation of (39) can be given by noting a remarkable property of the μ_j functions which was empirically derived from the data. We believe that this property provides additional evidence for the neural existence of the μ_j process, and thus for the STM reset process which converts μ_j values into x_j values.

In particular, the following significant linear trend was found for later items in the critical set:

$$ln\ \mu_j = -m_\delta j + b_\delta. \tag{40}$$

The slopes m_δ and intercepts b_δ can themselves be fit as linear functions of the onset asynchrony δ:

$$m_\delta = m\delta - c \tag{41}$$

$$b_\delta = b\delta - d \tag{42}$$

where $c \simeq 0$. Setting $c = 0$, we find that

$$ln\ \mu_j \simeq -m\delta j + b\delta - d. \tag{43}$$

Illustrative plots of estimated $ln\ \mu_j$ values against j are shown in Figure 10. A detailed description of the regressions is provided in Appendix 3. Deviations from this log linear function are more pronounced for early items and faster rates, and so are consistent with the opening of an attentional gate. Note that, at larger values of δ, the first significantly attended item whose μ_j is stored in STM tends to be larger. In other words, this item has more time in which its activity can be integrated in STM. On the other hand, the slope $-m\delta$ of $ln\ \mu_j$ as a function of j tends to be steeper at larger values of δ. Thus a fixed number of items can interfere more with subsequent STM storage of the next item if each of these items has had more time to be stored in STM.

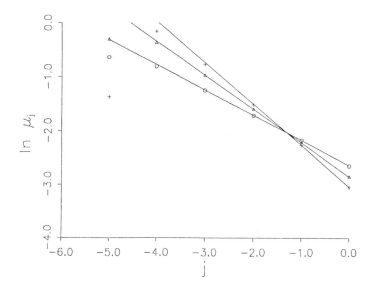

Figure 10. $ln\ \mu_j$ as a function of j (presentation order): Data are for subject AK, target square. Best fit regression lines, based on the final three items in each presentation rate condition are compared with the actual $ln\ \mu_j$ values, represented by the symbols. Each regression line is labelled with the presentation rate, in items/second, of the condition it represents. The symbols representing the $ln\ \mu_j$ are assigned to presentation rate as follows: 0, 5.6 items/second; Δ, 8.9 items/second; $+$, 9.2 items/second. A detailed description of the regression analysis for these conditions is given in Table C3.

13. STM Onset and STM Reset Interact to Determine Temporal Order Information

The nature of the interaction between STM onset and reset factors in determining temporal order information may be seen by combining equations (10), (23), and (25) to show that

$$\mu_i = \gamma\nu_i\omega_i\mu_{i-1}. \tag{44}$$

Equation (44) follows by letting $j = i + 1$ in (23):

$$x_i(t_{i+1}) = \gamma\nu_i x_{i-1}(t_{i+1}); \tag{45}$$

rewriting (25) as

$$x_{i-1}(t_{i+1}) = \omega_i x_{i-1}(t_i); \tag{46}$$

combining (45) and (46) to find

$$x_i(t_{i+1}) = \gamma\nu_i\omega_i x_{i-1}(t_i); \tag{47}$$

and using (10) to rewrite (47) as (44).

Equation (44) shows that the processes which cause successive items r_{i-1} and r_i to generate different activities μ_{i-1} and μ_i when they are first stored in STM include both STM onset factors $\gamma\nu_i$ (notably attention gating) and STM reset factors ω_i (notably competitive feedback interactions among active STM representations). The STM reset mechanism synchronizes the STM activities of successive items by transforming μ_{i-1} into the STM activity $x_{i-1}(t_{i+1}) = \omega_i\mu_{i-1}$ one time step later. The STM onset mechanism in (45) shows how attention gating when μ_i is being stored can cause further differences in the STM activities of successive items.

14. Concluding Remarks: Comparison with the GAGM Model

This article suggests how attentional processes can modulate the temporal unfolding of competitive interactions among active STM representations. The combined effects of both processes give rise to temporal order information in STM that may not veridically encode the external order of item presentation.

In our analysis of the Reeves and Sperling (1986) data, we have fit TOM model parameters to the AGM model in order to analyse whether, indeed, opening of an attention gate combined with competitive shunting interactions among active STM representations can provide a conceptually better explanation of these data than the AGM model. Several analytic results strongly support this conclusion. These include the unexpected discovery of the feedforward gain function $\gamma\nu_i$ and the feedback gain function ω_i, the unexpected discovery of the shift invariant properties of these functions, the confirmation of the expected property that the attention function μ_i is monotone decreasing rather than bowed, and the unexpected discovery of the Bloch's Law trade-off between number of items and processing time that is shown by the form of μ_i in (40) as a function of experimental parameters.

In addition to their analysis of the AGM model, Reeves and Sperling (1986) also sketched a Generalized Attention Gate Model (GAGM) that is closer in spirit to the TOM model. As in the TOM model, the GAGM postulated that order information is regulated by a shunting competitive interaction. Using the notation introduced herein, the GAGM model mixes item and order information via the equation

$$x_i = \mu_i(1 - \beta \sum_{k=1}^{i-1} \mu_k),\tag{48}$$

rather than the TOM equation

$$x_i(t_{j+1}) = \mu_i \Pi_{k=i+1}^{j} \omega_k.\tag{11}$$

Thus the GAGM model supplements the item measure μ_i with the competitive order measure $\beta\mu_i \sum_{k=1}^{i-1} \mu_k$. Unlike the TOM model, in the GAGM model, once the activity level x_i of item i is established, it is not updated as additional items are stored in STM. Thus the GAGM model assumes that each of the activities μ_i is independently stored in STM, after which all stored items compete in a *feedforward* fashion to determine the activities x_i at the next processing stage. In contrast, the TOM model posits that item representations are activated at a previous processing stage before interacting with each other at the next processing stage via a *feedback* competitive interaction. This feedback process enables both previously stored activities and newly presented items to update their STM activities by struggling for a limited capacity total STM resource.

One major difference between the models is that a recency gradient in STM, as in a free recall paradigm, can only be generated by the GAGM model if successive activities μ_i increase to offset the growing effect of the accumulating inhibition $\beta\mu_i \sum_{k=1}^{i-1} \mu_k$. This would seem to require that increasing attention be paid to later list items to generate a recency gradient in a free recall study, which seems not to be the case. In contrast, a feedback competitive interaction can generate a recency gradient in STM without making this assumption (Grossberg, 1978a, 1982). The invariance properties and the Bloch's Law properties derived from the TOM model also seem to argue for a feedback competitive process in the control of temporal order information. In any case, both models point to the importance of shunting competitive processes in the regulation of temporal order information, and future analyses will doubtless disclose finer details than either model has yet articulated within this general class of competitive mechanisms.

As indicated above, in other applications of the TOM model, where the form and time scale of attention switching are not themselves the processes under analysis, the hypothesis that constant attention is paid to stimulus materials does not lead to the folding of temporal order information through time. Instead, Grossberg (1978a, 1978b, 1982) analysed situations in which a recency gradient in STM, a bow in STM (Figure 1a), or a primacy gradient in STM (Figure 1b) are the only outcomes that can occur. Moreover, under these circumstances, the list position at which the STM activity pattern begins to bow does not change as more list items are presented. This strong property is a consequence of the LTM Invariance Principle (Section 10). Thus one can define the *transient memory span* of a list to be the list position at which an STM bow begins to develop in a given experimental setup. Measurement of the transient memory span is to be desired in paradigms that provide relatively pure measures of STM processing. In general, measurement of the transient memory span is complicated by the fact that STM and LTM processes often interact, as in generating the bowed curve observed in free recall experiments (Atkinson and Shiffrin, 1971; Baddeley and Warrington, 1970; Hogan and Hogan, 1975). Circumstances have been characterized during which the transient memory span is shorter than the more familiar immediate memory span. A model of STM and LTM interactions has also been developed wherein the contribution of both types of factors to the observed temporal order information can, in principle, be disentangled.

In the present article, we have assumed that each item code is represented by a single population activity $x_i(t)$ through time, since the data do not probe the internal organization of an item's STM representation. Concepts such as the LTM Invariance Principle easily generalize to consideration of item representations that are distributed among several unequally activated populations. In this general case, each new item again shunts the STM activity of all previously activated populations at level A_3 without regard to which combinations of these populations possesses unitized list codes at the next processing level A_4 (Section 6).

Breakdowns of temporal order information in STM are traced in all these cases to biological processes that possess a manifest adaptive value. The competitive STM interactions are designed to enable stored STM patterns to be stably encoded in LTM. Factors such as attention gating have also been related to stabilization of LTM encoding (Carpenter and Grossberg, 1987a, 1987b, 1987c; Grossberg, 1980, 1984). The TOM thus suggests that even experimental paradigms which provide relatively pure measures of STM processing, such as the remarkably flexible and informative Reeves and Sperling paradigm, indirectly probe brain mechanisms which are designed to enable us to learn about the world in a stable fashion. This insight suggests the value of developing new experimental paradigms in which relatively pure measures of STM processing can be taken before and after subjects are trained to achieve different stages or types of learning. Such direct manipulations of STM and LTM interactions may provide important new information concerning the adaptive principles which govern brain design.

APPENDIX 1

Computation of Attention Weights and STM Reset Weights

Theorem 1 (equations (21) and (22)) expresses the attention weights, μ_i, as a function of the AGM parameters δ, α, τ:

$$\mu_i = \frac{(1 + t_i^*)e^{-t_i^*} - (1 + t_{i+1}^*)e^{-t_{i+1}^*}}{1 - [(1 + t_{i+1}^*)e^{-t_{i+1}^*} - (1 + t_{n+1}^*)e^{-t_{n+1}^*}]} \tag{A1}$$

where

$$t_i^* = \begin{cases} \frac{\delta i - \tau}{\alpha} & \delta i > \tau \\ 0 & \delta i \leq \tau \end{cases}. \tag{A2}$$

The proof of Theorem 1 begins by equating the precedence scores in the two models at the time of STM readout (20):

$$x_i(t_{n+1}) = Y_i. \tag{A3}$$

We next observe that, due to the LTM Invariance Principle, the ratio of successive item strengths is unaffected by STM reset, so that

$$\frac{Y_i}{Y_{i+1}} = \frac{x_i(t_{n+1})}{x_{i+1}(t_{n+1})} = \frac{x_i(t_{i+2})}{x_{i+1}(t_{i+2})} = \frac{\omega_{i+1}\mu_i}{\mu_{i+1}}, \tag{A4}$$

where the final equality derives from the formal statement of the LTM Invariance Principle (10). By introducing the assumed relationship

$$\omega_i = 1 - \mu_i \tag{A5}$$

from (14), equation (A4) provides a recursive relationship between the μ_i, using the Y_i:

$$\mu_i = \frac{Y_i}{Y_{i+1}} \frac{\mu_{i+1}}{(1 - \mu_{i+1})}. \tag{A6}$$

To convert this recursive relationship into a direct expression for the μ_i in terms of the Y_j alone, we exploit the fact that the final item in the list is not reset by subsequent item storage, so that:

$$Y_n = x_n(t_{n+1}) = \mu_n. \tag{A7}$$

With $i = n - 1$ in (A6), we can derive the expression for μ_{n-1} using (A6):

$$\mu_{n-1} = \frac{Y_{n-1}}{Y_n} \cdot \frac{Y_n}{(1 - Y_n)} = \frac{Y_{n-1}}{1 - Y_n}. \tag{A8}$$

The general expression for μ_i in terms of the Y_i begins to emerge when the expression for μ_{n-1} (A8) is substituted into (A6) to give

$$\mu_{n-2} = \left(\frac{Y_{n-2}}{Y_{n-1}}\right)\left(\frac{Y_{n-1}}{1 - Y_n}\right)\left(\frac{1}{1 - \frac{Y_{n-1}}{1 - Y_n}}\right). \tag{A9}$$

Multiplying the third term by $\frac{1-Y_n}{1-Y_n}$, then cancelling the $1 - Y_n$ and Y_{n-1} terms which appear in the numerator and denominator reduces (A9) to

$$\mu_{n-2} = \frac{Y_{n-2}}{1 - Y_{n-1} - Y_n}. \tag{A10}$$

We now prove by induction that

$$\mu_i = \frac{Y_i}{1 - \sum_{j=i+1}^n Y_j}. \tag{A11}$$

By (A10) this is true for the initial condition $i = n - 2$. Using (A6), we now show that the case for μ_{i-1} follows from the case of μ_i:

$$\mu_{i-1} = \left(\frac{Y_{i-1}}{Y_i}\right)\left(\frac{Y_i}{1 - \sum_{j=i+1}^n Y_j}\right)\left(\frac{1}{1 - \frac{Y_i}{1-\sum_{j=i+1}^n Y_j}}\right). \tag{A12}$$

Multiplying the third term by $\frac{1-\sum_{j=i+1}^n Y_j}{1-\sum_{j=i+1}^n Y_j}$ and cancelling the Y_i and $1 - \sum_{j=i+1}^n Y_j$ terms which appear in the numerator and denominator, we obtain

$$\mu_{i-1} = \frac{Y_{i-1}}{1 - \sum_{j=i+1}^n Y_j - Y_i} = \frac{Y_{i-1}}{1 - \sum_{j=i+1}^n Y_j}, \tag{A13}$$

which is (A11) for the case μ_{i-1}.

Note that the relationship between μ_i and the Y_j given in (A11) derives from the LTM Invariance Principle and the relationship between μ_i and ω_i given by (A5). Equation (A11) will hold for *any* arbitrary set of Y_j. In other words, (A11) does not compute the pattern of temporal order information in STM at the time of readout. Rather, it provides a method for converting an arbitrary set of observed precedence scores into a sequence of attentional weights, μ_i.

To finish the proof of Theorem 1, we need only substitute the precedence scores Y_j derived from the AGM model into (A11). Setting the attention gate function, $a(\omega)$, in (5) equal to the gamma function assumed by Reeves and Sperling (8, 9) gives Y_i as

$$Y_i = \int_{t_i^*}^{t_{i+1}^*} \omega e^{-\omega} d\omega = -(1 + \omega)e^{-\omega} \big|_{t_i^*}^{t_{i+1}^*} \tag{A14}$$

so that

$$Y_i = (1 + t_i^*)e^{-t_i^*} - (1 + t_{i+1}^*)e^{-t_{i+1}^*} \tag{A15}$$

with t_i^* defined as in (A2). Likewise,

$$\sum_{j=i+1}^n Y_j = (1 + t_{i+1}^*)e^{-t_{i+1}^*} - (1 - t_{n+1}^*)e^{-t_{n+1}^*}. \tag{A16}$$

Theorem 1 (A1) follows from substitution of (A15) and (A16) into (A11).

Using (A5), ω_i can also be expressed in terms of the AGM parameters as a corollary of Theorem 1. By (A1) and (A5),

$$\omega_i = 1 - \frac{(1 + t_i^*)e^{-t_i^*} - (1 + t_{i+1}^*)e^{-t_{i+1}^*}}{1 - [(1 + t_{i+1}^*)e^{-t_{i+1}^*} - (1 + t_{i+1}^*)e^{-t_{n+1}^*}]} \tag{A17}$$

which implies

$$\omega_i = \frac{1 - [(1 + t_i^*)e^{-t_i^*} - (1 + t_{n+1}^*)e^{-t_{n+1}^*}]}{1 - [(1 + t_{i+1}^*)e^{-t_{i+1}^*} - (1 + t_{n+1}^*)e^{-t_{n+1}^*}]}. \tag{A18}$$

APPENDIX 2

Shift Invariance in Item Time

In order to prove the shift invariance in item time of $\nu_i = N(i, \tau, \alpha, \delta)$, we will derive the inverse function of ν_i, namely

$$i = \frac{1}{\nu_i - 1} + P(\xi, \eta) \qquad (B1)$$

where

$$P(\xi, \eta) = \xi - \eta - \frac{1}{1 - e^{-\frac{1}{\eta}}} \qquad (B2)$$

and

$$\xi = \frac{\tau}{\delta}, \qquad (B3)$$

$$\eta = \frac{\alpha}{\delta}. \qquad (B4)$$

Shift invariance follows from (B1) as follows. Let one or more of the parameters τ, α, δ (especially δ) be changed to new values $\tau^*, \alpha^*, \delta^*$, so that $P(\xi, \eta)$ is replaced by $P(\xi^*, \eta^*)$ in (B1). Then given any *fixed* value $\nu_i = \nu$, the indices

$$i = \frac{1}{\nu - 1} + P(\xi, \eta) \qquad (B5)$$

and

$$i^* = \frac{1}{\nu - 1} + P(\xi^*, \eta^*) \qquad (B6)$$

corresponding to the different parameter choices shift by an amount

$$i - i^* = P(\xi, \eta) - P(\xi^*, \eta^*) \qquad (B7)$$

that is independent of ν. In other words, a change in the parameters τ, α, δ shifts the entire curve in item time by the predicted amount $P(\xi, \eta) - P(\xi^*, \eta^*)$. From (B1) the equation

$$\nu_i = N(i, \tau, \alpha, \delta) = \frac{i + 1 - P(\frac{\tau}{\delta}, \frac{\alpha}{\delta})}{i - P(\frac{\tau}{\delta}, \frac{\alpha}{\delta})} \qquad (B8)$$

in (33) follows immediately.

The inverse function (B1) is derived from the definition (22) of ν_i:

$$\gamma \nu_i = \frac{x_i(t_j)}{x_{i-1}(t_j)}, \quad j > i, \qquad (B9)$$

where

$$\gamma = e^{-\frac{\delta}{\alpha}}. \qquad (B10)$$

Letting $j = n + 1$ in (B5) and using (20) to convert into the AGM precedences Y_i, we obtain:

$$\gamma \nu_i = \frac{Y_i}{Y_{i-1}}. \qquad (B11)$$

By equation (A15) of Appendix 1,

$$\gamma \nu_i = \frac{(1+t_i^*)e^{-t_i^*} - (1+t_{i+1}^*)e^{-t_{i+1}^*}}{(1+t_{i-1}^*)e^{-t_{i-1}^*} - (1+t_i^*)e^{-t_i^*}}. \tag{B12}$$

The definition of t_i^* in (22) implies that

$$t_{i+1}^* = \frac{\delta}{\alpha} + t_i^* \tag{B13}$$

and thus that

$$e^{-t_{i+1}^*} = e^{-\frac{\delta}{\alpha}}e^{-t_i^*} = \gamma e^{-t_i^*}. \tag{B14}$$

Using (B13) and (B14), all terms t_{i+1}^* and t_{i-1}^* in (B12) can be expressed in terms of t_i^*. Then cancelling the $e^{-t_i^*}$ terms from the numerator and denominator leads to

$$\gamma \nu_i = \frac{(1+t_i^*) - (1+t_i^* + \frac{\delta}{\alpha})\gamma}{(1+t_i^* - \frac{\delta}{\alpha})\gamma^{-1} - (1+t_i^*)}. \tag{B15}$$

Further simplification is achieved by combining the $1+t_i^*$ terms on the right and dividing the left and right side of (B15) by γ:

$$\nu_i = \frac{(1+t_i^*)(1-\gamma) - \frac{\delta\gamma}{\alpha}}{(1+t_i^*)(1-\gamma) - \frac{\delta}{\alpha}}. \tag{B16}$$

Rearranging (B16) to get all t_i^* terms on the left-hand side leads to

$$(1+t_i^*)(1-\gamma)(\nu_i - 1) = \frac{\delta}{\alpha}(\nu_i - \gamma). \tag{B17}$$

Dividing both sides of (B17) by $(1-\gamma)(\nu_i - 1)$, rewriting the term $\nu_i - \gamma$ as $\nu_i - 1 + 1 - \gamma$, and dividing wherever possible, we obtain

$$t_i^* = \frac{\delta}{\alpha}\left(\frac{1}{\nu_i - 1} - \frac{1}{1-\gamma}\right) - 1. \tag{B18}$$

Finally, we substitute for t_i^* using (22) and move all terms on the left except i to the right:

$$i = \frac{1}{\nu_i - 1} + \frac{\tau}{\alpha} - \frac{\alpha}{\delta} - \frac{1}{1-\gamma}, \tag{B19}$$

which is the same as the inverse function in (B1).

APPENDIX 3

Computation of ln μ_j Regressions

Because the attention gate introduces deviation from the log linear μ functions, regressions were performed for the final 3 items in each condition, where attention gating has the least impact.

The index j is based on an item's position relative to the final item in the list. This indexing method has several advantages. First, indexing from the first item to receive attention is complicated by the possibility that this first item can receive so little attention that it has essentially no impact on subsequent item storage and is virtually undetectable in noise (cf. condition AR, square, rate 13.2 in Table C1). In other words, indices anchored at the first attended item are sensitive to decisions about how much attention constitutes "significant" activation of an item's code. Second, when the indices are anchored at the final item in the list, a significant linear trend of the intercept, b_δ, as a function of onset asynchrony, δ, emerges. This is not the case when the indices are anchored at the first attended item.

Tables C1–C3 present the regression analyses for subjects AR, GL, and AK, respectively. For each (target)×(presentation rate) condition, μ, $ln\ \mu$ and the best fit to $ln\ \mu$, denoted by $ln\ \hat{\mu}$, are given for each item. The regression equation, correlation coefficient, and significance level are given for each condition. The regressions of m_δ and b_δ as a function of onset asynchrony are given for each target condition.

TABLE C1

AR, U

4.6 items/sec ($\delta = .2174$ sec/item)

j	$ln\ \mu$	$ln\ \hat{\mu}$
-4	-0.0150	1.0123
-3	-0.4853	-0.3119
-2	-1.6487	-1.6361
-1	-2.9352	-2.9603
0	-4.2971	-4.2845

$ln\ \hat{\mu} = -1.3242j - 4.2845$
$\gamma = -0.99986\ \ p < .05$

6.9 items/sec ($\delta = .1449$ sec/item)

j	$ln\ \mu$	$ln\ \hat{\mu}$
-4	-0.0950	0.2671
-3	-0.6450	-0.5920
-2	-1.4559	-1.4511
-1	-2.3007	-2.3102
0	-3.1741	-3.1693

$ln\ \hat{\mu} = -0.8591j - 3.1693$
$\gamma = -0.99995\ \ p < .01$

9.2 items/sec ($\delta = .1087$ sec/item)

j	$ln\ \mu$	$ln\ \hat{\mu}$
-5	-1.3438	0.4668
-4	-0.3109	-0.1745
-3	-0.8336	-0.8158
-2	-1.4588	-1.4571
-1	-2.0951	-2.0984
0	-2.7414	-2.7397

$ln\ \hat{\mu} = -0.6413j - 2.7393$
$\gamma = -0.99999\ \ p < .01$

13.4 items/sec ($\delta = .0746$ sec/item)

j	$ln\ \mu$	$ln\ \hat{\mu}$
-5	-5.9933	-0.0851
-4	-1.0578	-0.5064
-3	-0.9982	-0.9278
-2	-1.3516	-1.3491
-1	-1.7655	-1.7705
0	-2.1943	-2.1918

$ln\ \hat{\mu} = -0.4213j - 2.1918$
$\gamma = -0.99995\ \ p < .01$

slopes (m) versus δ

δ	.0746	.1087	.1449	.2174
m	-0.4213	-0.6413	-0.8591	-1.3242

$\hat{m} = -6.3069\delta + 0.0488$
$r = -.99993\ \ p < .01$

intercepts (b) versus δ

δ	.0746	.1087	.1449	.2174
b	-2.191	-2.7393	-3.1693	-4.2845

$\hat{b} = -14.4969\delta - 1.1189$
$r = -.99899\ \ p < .01$

TABLE C2

GL, C

4.6 items/sec $(\delta = .2174)$

j	$\ln \mu$	$\ln \hat{\mu}$
-5	-0.3061	1.3795
-4	-0.0619	0.2843
-3	-0.9012	-0.8110
-2	-1.9141	-1.9062
-1	-2.9857	-3.0015
0	-4.1046	-4.0967

$\ln \hat{\mu} = -1.0953j - 4.0967$
$r = -.99992 \quad p < .01$

9.2 items/sec $(\delta = .1087)$

j	$\ln \mu$	$\ln \hat{\mu}$
-5	-1.0283	0.0621
-4	-0.5549	-0.4675
-3	-1.0076	-0.9971
-2	-1.5275	-1.5267
-1	-2.0548	-2.0563
0	-2.5867	-2.5859

$\ln \hat{\mu} = -0.5296j - 2.5859$
$r < -.99999 \quad p < .01$

6.9 items/sec $(\delta = .1449)$

j	$\ln \mu$	$\ln \hat{\mu}$
-5	-0.3167	0.4174
-4	-0.3704	-0.2971
-3	-1.0331	-1.0115
-2	-1.7285	-1.7260
-1	-2.4353	-2.4404
0	-3.1574	-3.1549

$\ln \hat{\mu} = -0.7145j - 3.1549$
$r = -.99998 \quad p < .01$

13.4 items/sec $(\delta = .0746)$

j	$\ln \mu$	$\ln \hat{\mu}$
-4	-1.7117	-0.8236
-3	-1.2780	-1.1434
-2	-1.4686	-1.4631
-1	-1.7719	-1.7829
0	-2.1081	-2.1026

$\ln \hat{\mu} = -0.3197j - 2.1026$
$r = -.99956 \quad p < .05$

slope (m) versus δ

δ	.0746	.1087	.1449	.2174
m	-0.3197	-0.5296	-0.7145	-1.0953

$\hat{m} = -5.3802\delta + 0.0691$
$r = -.99939 \quad p < .01$

intercept (b) versus δ

δ	.0746	.1087	.1449	.2174
b	-2.102	-2.5859	-3.1549	-4.0967

$\hat{b} = -14.0002\delta - 1.0754$
$r = -.99920 \quad p < .01$

TABLE C3

AK, Square

5.6 items/sec $(\delta = .1786)$

j	$ln\ \mu$	$ln\ \hat{\mu}$
-5	-1.3653	0.8012
-4	-0.1573	0.0320
-3	-0.7703	-0.7371
-2	-1.5096	-1.5063
-1	-2.2688	-2.2754
0	-3,0479	-3.0446

$ln\ \hat{\mu} = -0.7692j - 3.0446$
$r = -.99997\ \ p < .01$

6.9 items/sec $(\delta = .1449)$

j	$ln\ \mu$	$ln\ \hat{\mu}$
-5	-0.3016	0.2858
-4	-0.3686	-0.3425
-3	-0.9760	-0.9707
-2	-1.6001	-1.5990
-1	-2.2249	-2.2272
0	-2.8566	-2.8555

$ln\ \hat{\mu} = -0.6283j - 2.8555$
$r = -.99999\ \ p < .01$

9.2 items/sec $(\delta = .1087)$

j	$ln\ \mu$	$ln\ \hat{\mu}$
-5	-0.6321	-0.3055
-4	-0.8060	-0.7739
-3	-1.2464	-1.2423
-2	-1.7111	-1.7107
-1	-2.1784	-2.1791
0	-2.6479	-2.6475

$ln\ \hat{\mu} = -0.4684j - 2.6475$
$r < -.99999\ \ p < .01$

slope (m) versus δ

δ	.1087	.1449	.1786
m	-0.4684	-0.6283	-0.7692

$\hat{m} = -4.3047\delta - .0018$
$r = -.99988\ \ p < .05$

intercept (b) versus δ

δ	.1087	.1449	.1786
b	-2.6475	-2.8555	-3.0446

$\hat{b} = -5.6818\delta - 2.03065$
$r = -.99998\ \ p < .01$

REFERENCES

Atkinson, R.C. and Shiffrin, R.M., The control of short term memory. *Scientific American*, August, 1971.

Baddeley, A.D., **The psychology of memory**. New York: Basic Books, 1976.

Baddeley, A.D. and Warrington, E.K., Amnesia and the distinction between long- and short-term memory. *Journal of Verbal Learning and Verbal Behavior*, 1970, **9**, 176–189.

Block, H.D. and Marschak, J., Random orderings and stochastic theories of response. In I. Olkin, S. Gharye, W. Hoeffding, W. Madow, and H. Mann (Eds.), **Contributions to probability and statistics**. Stanford: Stanford University Press, 1960.

Carpenter, G.A. and Grossberg, S., Neural dynamics of adaptive pattern recognition: Priming, search, attention, and category formation. *Society for Neuroscience Abstracts*, 1985, **11**.

Carpenter, G.A. and Grossberg, S., Neural dynamics of category learning and recognition: Attention, memory consolidation, and amnesia. In J. Davis, R. Newburgh, and E. Wegman (Eds.) **Brain structure, learning, and memory**. AAAS Symposium Series, in press, 1987 (a).

Carpenter, G.A. and Grossberg, S., Neural dynamics of category learning and recognition: Structural invariants, reinforcement, and evoked potentials. In M.L. Commons, S.M. Kosslyn, and R.J. Herrnstein (Eds.), **Pattern recognition and concepts in animals, people, and machines**. Hillsdale, NJ: Erlbaum, 1987 (b).

Carpenter, G.A. and Grossberg, S., A massively parallel architecture for a self-organizing neural pattern recognition machine. *Computer Vision, Graphics, and Image Processing*, 1987, **37**, 54–115 (c).

Cohen, M.A. and Grossberg, S., Neural dynamics of speech and language coding: Developmental programs, perceptual grouping, and competition for short term memory. *Human Neurobiology*, 1986, **5**, 1–22.

Cohen, M.A. and Grossberg, S., Unitized recognition codes for parts and wholes: The unique cue in configural discriminations. In M.L. Commons, S.M. Kosslyn, and R.J. Herrnstein (Eds.), **Pattern recognition and concepts in animals, people, and machines**. Hillsdale, NJ: Erlbaum, 1987 (a).

Cohen, M.A. and Grossberg, S., Masking fields: A massively parallel neural architecture for learning, recognizing, and predicting multiple groupings of patterned data. *Applied Optics*, 1987, **26**, 1866–1891 (b).

Grossberg, S., Behavioral contrast in short-term memory: Serial binary memory models or parallel continuous memory models? *Journal of Mathematical Psychology*, 1978, **17**, 199–219 (a).

Grossberg, S., A theory of human memory: Self-organization and performance of sensory-motor codes, maps, and plans. In R. Rosen and F. Snell (Eds.), **Progress in theoretical biology**, Vol. 5, pp.233–374. New York: Academic Press, 1978 (b).

Grossberg, S., How does a brain build a cognitive code? *Psychological Review*, 1980, **87**, 1–51.

Grossberg, S., **Studies of mind and brain: Neural principles of learning, perception, development, cognition, and motor control**. Boston: Reidel Press, 1982.

Grossberg, S., Some psychophysiological and pharmacological correlates of a developmental, cognitive, and motivational theory. In R. Karrer, J. Cohen, and P. Tueting (Eds.), **Brain and information: Event related potentials**. New York: New York Academy of Sciences, 1984, pp.58–151.

Grossberg, S., The adaptive self-organization of serial order in behavior: Speech, language, and motor control. In E.C. Schwab and H.C. Nusbaum (Eds.), **Pattern recognition by humans and machines, Vol. 1: Speech perception**. New York: Academic Press, 1986, pp.187–294.

Grossberg, S. **The adaptive brain I: Cognition, learning, reinforcement, and rhythm**. Amsterdam: Elsevier/North-Holland, 1987 (a).

Grossberg, S. **The adaptive brain II: Vision, speech, language, and motor control**. Amsterdam: Elsevier/North-Holland, 1987 (b).

Grossberg, S. and Kuperstein, M., **Neural dynamics of adaptive sensory-motor control: Ballistic eye movements**. Amsterdam: Elsevier/North-Holland, 1986.

Grossberg, S. and Stone, G.O., Neural dynamics of word recognition and recall: Attentional priming, learning, and resonance. *Psychological Review*, 1986, **93**, 46–74.

Healy, A.F., Separating item from order information in short-term memory. *Journal of Verbal Learning and Verbal Behavior*, 1975, **13**, 644–655.

Memory and Cognition, 1975, **3**, 210–215.

James, W., **The principles of psychology**. New York: Holt, 1890.

Landauer, T.K., Rate of implicit speech. *Perception and Motor Skills*, 1962, **15**, 646.

Lee, C. and Estes, W.K., Order and position in primary memory for letter strings. *Journal of Verbal Learning and Verbal Behavior*, 1977, **16**, 395–418.

Lee, C. and Estes, W.K., Item and order information in short-term memory: Evidence for multilevel perturbation processes. *Journal of Experimental Psychology: Human Learning and Memory*, 1981, **7**, 149–169.

Murdock, B.B. Jr., The serial position effect in free recall. *Journal of Experimental Psychology*, 1962, **64**, 482–488.

Ratcliff, R., A theory of memory retrieval. *Psychological Review*, 1978, **85**, 59–108.

Reeves, A., The identification and recall of rapidly displayed letters and digits. Unpublished doctoral dissertation, City University of New York, 1977.

Reeves, A. and Sperling, G., Attentional theory of order information in short-term visual memory. *Psychological Review*, 1986, **93**, 180–206.

Rundus, D., Analysis of rehearsal processes in free recall. *Journal of Experimental Psychology*, 1971, **89**, 63–77.

Sperling, G., A model for visual memory tasks. *Human Factors*, 1963, **51**, 19–31.

Sperling, G. and Melchner, M.J., Estimating item and order information. *Journal of Mathematical Psychology*, 1976, **13**, 192–213.

Sperling, G. and Reeves, A., Measuring the reaction time of a shift of visual attention. In R. Nickerson (Ed.), **Attention and performance VIII**. Hillsdale, NJ: Erlbaum, 1980.

Tulving, E., **Elements of episodic memory**. Oxford: Clarendon Press, 1983.

Applied Optics
1987, **26**, 5015–5030

NEURAL DYNAMICS OF ATTENTIONALLY MODULATED PAVLOVIAN CONDITIONING: BLOCKING, INTER-STIMULUS INTERVAL, AND SECONDARY REINFORCEMENT

Stephen Grossberg† and Daniel S. Levine

ABSTRACT

Selective information processing in neural networks is studied through computer simulations of Pavlovian conditioning data. The model reproduces properties of blocking, inverted-U in learning as a function of interstimulus interval, anticipatory conditioned responses, secondary reinforcement, attentional focussing by conditioned motivational feedback, and limited capacity short-term memory processing. Conditioning occurs from sensory to drive representations ("conditioned reinforcer" learning), from drive to sensory representations ("incentive motivational" learning), and from sensory to motor representations ("habit" learning). The conditionable pathways contain long-term memory traces that obey a non-Hebbian associative law. The neural model embodies a solution to two key design problems of conditioning, the synchronization and persistence problems. This model of vertebrate learning is compared with data and models of invertebrate learning. Predictions derived from models of vertebrate learning are compared with data about invertebrate learning, including data from *Aplysia* about facilitator neurons and data from *Hermissenda* about voltage-dependent Ca^{++} currents. A prediction is stated about classical conditioning in all species, called the Secondary Conditioning Alternative, and if confirmed would constitute an evolutionary invariant of learning.

1. Introduction: The Problem of Selective Information Processing

An important problem for any information processing system, whether biological or artificial, is that of limited capacity. Amid the "buzzing blooming confusion of experience", it is necessary to be able to process some events (the most "significant") and ignore others, perhaps unmasking ignored events at a later time when their significance changes with context. Hence we must ask: How can a limited-capacity information processing system that receives a constant stream of diverse inputs be designed to selectively process those inputs that are most significant to the objectives of the system?

Classical, or Pavlovian, conditioning provides a good simplified system for studying the selective information processing problem. For this reason, it has been an increasingly active area of recent study both by neural modellers (Blazis *et al.*, 1986; Grossberg, 1971, 1975, 1982a, 1982b; Grossberg and Schmajuk, 1987; Hebb, 1949; Sutton and Barto, 1981) and neurophysiologists (Hawkins *et al.*, 1983; Kelso and Brown, 1986; Levy, 1985; Levy, Brassel, and Moore, 1983).

† Supported in part by the Air Force Office of Scientific Research (AFOSR 85-0149 and AFOSR F49620-86-C-0037), the Army Research Office (ARO DAAG-29-85-K-0095), and the National Science Foundation (NSF IRI 84-17756).

1. CS_1 —— US

CS_1 —→ CR

2. $CS_1 + CS_2$ —— US

CS_2 ⇸ CR

Figure 1. A blocking paradigm: The two stages of the experiment are discussed in the text.

In particular, classical conditioning is subject to numerous attentional modulations. An example is the blocking paradigm (Figure 1). The basic blocking paradigm (Kamin, 1968, 1969; see also Mackintosh, 1974 and Staddon, 1983 for many variants) is as follows. First, a neutral stimulus (CS_1), such as a tone, is presented followed at a given time interval by an unconditioned stimulus (US), such as electric shock. The CS_1-US pairing occurs several times until a conditioned response (CR) is established to the CS_1. Then a series of trials is given in which CS_1 and another neutral stimulus (CS_2), such as a light, are presented simultaneously, followed at the same time interval by the US. Finally, the CS_2 is presented alone but not reinforced. On these recall trials, no CR occurs in response to the CS_2. (Kamin found that blocking may not occur the CS_1-CS_2 combination is associated with a different level of shock from that associated with CS_1 alone—a point to which we will return in Section 13.

In the blocking paradigm, the CS_1 which is selectively attended has more motivational significance than the CS_2 which is blocked. In this article, we use computer simulations to show that the same kind of selective attention can explain some data on temporal order effects in Pavlovian conditioning. For example, the strength of a conditioned response typically depends in an inverted-U manner on the time interval, or interstimulus interval (ISI), between conditioned stimulus (CS) and unconditioned stimulus, as shown in the curve of Figure 2. This curve is a composite of data on the nictitating membrane response of the rabbit (Smith, Coleman, and Gormenzano, 1969; Schneiderman and Gormenzano, 1964), where a conditioned eyeblink develops to a tone that has been paired with a puff of air to the cornea. The relationship between learning and ISI has also been studied in many other classical conditioning paradigms, such as salivation (Ost and Lauer, 1965) and shock avoidance (Bitterman, 1965). The length of the optimal interstimulus interval varies from one paradigm to another, and different measures are used for the strength of the response,

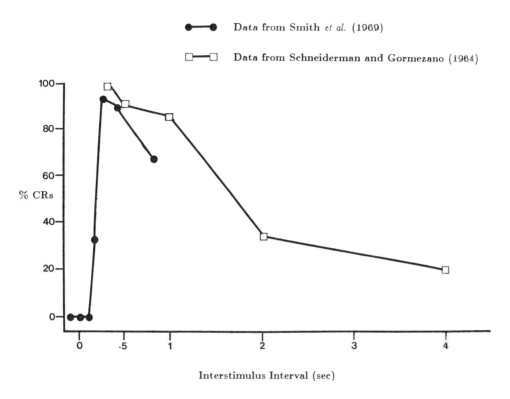

Figure 2. Experimental relationship between conditioned response strength (measured by percentage of trials on which response occurs) and inter-stimulus interval in the rabbit nictitating membrane response. (From Sutton and Barto, 1981. Reprinted with permission.)

but the qualitative relationship described in Figure 2 holds in a variety of cases.

Our explanation of the curve of Figure 2 is as follows. For interstimulus intervals (ISI's) that are too short, the CS and the US are processed nearly simultaneously. Since the US already has motivational significance for the organism and the CS does not, the organism selectively attends to the US and its processing of the CS is inhibited. For ISI's that are of intermediate length, this inhibition of CS processing by the US has less effect because the strength of the CS's neural representation can increase via a mechanism of short-term memory reverberation before the US is presented. For ISI's that are too long, the CS neural representation has decayed before the US is presented, because of competition from other incoming stimuli or passive decay.

In both blocking and the ISI effect, the stimulus of the pair which is selectively attended is the one that has more motivational significance. In the blocking paradigm, a CS_2 is blocked by a simultaneous CS_1 that has previously acquired reinforcing properties. In the ISI paradigm, a CS is blocked by a US. The US may be either a conditioned reinforcer, as is CS_1 in the blocking paradigm, or an unconditioned reinforcer, such as shock or the taste of food.

Thus the ISI effect can be regarded as a variant of blocking if one can understand how four types of processes work: How does the pairing of CS_1 with US in the first phase of the blocking experiment endow the CS_1 cue with properties of a conditioned, or secondary, reinforcer? How do the reinforcing properties of a cue, whether primary (US) or secondary (CS_1), shift the focus of attention toward its own processing? How does the limited capacity of attentional resources arise, so that a shift of attention towards one set of cues (CS_1 or US) can prevent other cues (CS_2 or CS) from being attended? How does withdrawal of attention from a cue prevent that cue from entering into new conditioned relationships?

The present article provides a unified model, and computer simulations, of the ISI inverted-U and attentional blocking which is based upon neural model of how reinforcement, motivation, and limited capacity attention interact during classical conditioning. The model is a component of a conditioning theory that was originally developed to analyze classical and instrumental conditioning data other than the ISI curve, many of which are summarized by Grossberg (1982a, 1982b, 1984b). The present article and that of Grossberg and Schmajuk (1987) initiate a systematic program using quantitative computer simulations of conditioning phenomena to further develop this theory. The neural network architectures of these two articles combine four fundamental design principles: associative synaptic modification; competition between sensory representations; resonant feedback between two or more network levels; and opponent processing. The first three of these principles, and their implementation for the present application, will now be discussed. The fourth will be discussed at the end of this article in the context of related research.

2. Associative Synaptic Modification

Much attention has been paid recently by neural modellers, machine learning theorists, and neurophysiologists, to rules for modifying connection strengths (or synaptic weights). The nodes in our neural network (and many others in the literature) may correspond either to populations of neurons or to individual neurons. In the former cases a connection between nodes represents the average connection strength of a population of pathways. In the latter case it describes the strength of an individual synapse between neurons.

The modern era for analyzing neurophysiological correlates of Pavlovian conditioning can be dated to the well-known book of Hebb (1949). On p.62, Hebb proposed the famous *Hebb Postulate:* "When the axon of cell A is near enough to excite a cell B and repeatedly or persistently takes part in firing it, some growth process takes place in one or both cells such that A's efficiency, as one of the cells firing B, is increased." The development of neural network models of conditioning since Hebb's work is discussed in detail by Levine (1983). Briefly, the hypothesis of an actual cellular growth process has largely been supplanted by other neurophysiological processes which could also alter synaptic efficacy. Mechanisms proposed have included, for example, correlated changes in the amounts of usable presynaptic transmitter substance and of postsynaptic protein synthesis (Grossberg, 1969); changes in postsynaptic membrane receptor protein (Stent, 1973); and changes in postsynaptic membrane resistance (Woody *et al.*, 1976). In this article we shall discuss the computational properties of a particular synaptic modification rule, without attempting to specify the biochemical mechanism leading to that rule. All of the above biochemical mechanisms could generate such a formal conditioning rule.

Many learning theorists, such as Pavlov, Guthrie, Hull, and Hebb, have noted the importance of changes in a contiguity trace, habit strength, or path connection as a function of learning. The book of Hebb (1949) has been an enduring source of qualitative inspiration for such an *associative rule*, whereby synaptic efficacy changes as a function of the correlation between presynaptic and postsynaptic activities. Such conditioning rules are often called "Hebbian" rules, but we do not use this term because Hebb's postulate alone provides insufficient guidance for developing a quantitative model. Hebb's pioneering contribution did not, for example, suggest a quantitative framework or equation for specifying his postulate and his qualitative postulate, as stated above, leads to serious difficulties when implemented formally. Indeed during the two decades subsequent to Hebb's book, modellers often used information theoretic algebraic operations to define an associative learning postulate. Grossberg (1968, 1969, 1974, 1976) pioneered the development of a quantitative theory of associative pattern learning within a real-time neural network. In such a network, pairing of presynaptic and, postsynaptic signals occurs, but is counteracted by other network effects so that Hebb's postulate is not obeyed. These non-Hebbian associative rules have been used by other neural modellers (Amari, 1982; Amari and Takeuchi, 1978; Kohonen, 1982, 1983; Rumelhart and Zipser, 1985) and verified by recent mammalian neural data (Levy, 1985; Levy, Brassel, and Moore, 1983; Levy and Desmond, 1985; Rauschecker and Singer, 1979; Singer, 1983).

The distinction between Hebbian and non-Hebbian associative rules is illustrated in Figure 3. The Hebb Postulate seems plausible if one assumes that the unit of associative learning is a single cell's activity whose correlation with another cell's activity can increase the synaptic strength of a pathway between the cells (Figure 3a). A different conditioning rule is needed, however, if one agrees that the unit of associative learning is a spatial pattern of activity across network of cells (Figure 3b). Then the correlation of this spatial pattern with another cell's activity enables the set of pathways from the network to the active cell to encode the entire spatial pattern of activity into long-term memory (LTM). In this situation, a conditioning rule is needed that can enclode both increases *and* decreases of LTM strength as a function of the pairing of cell activities. The Hebb rule, in contrast, requires that only increases in strength be caused by associative pairing.

In the simplest non-Hebbian associative rules, a model synapse as in Figure 3b has a synaptic efficacy z that obeys a differential equation of the form

$$dz/dt = -Az + f_1(x)f_2(y) \tag{1}$$

or of the form

$$dz/dt = [-Az + f_2(y)]f_1(x) \tag{2}$$

where dz/dt denotes the time rate of change of the associative strength z, while x and y are the correlated cell activities, parameter A is a (slow) decay rate, and f_1 and f_2 are monotone nondecreasing, non-negative signal function. Our equation therefore includes a "Hebbian" term $f_1(x)f_2(y)$ that increases with correlated cell activities, but Hebb's postulate is not obeyed because of the counteracting memory decay term and because of network interactions.

In the present simulations, we use equation (1), although similar properties derive from equation (2) using our numerical parameters. If time is divided into discrete intervals, the difference equation form of (1) is

$$z(t+1) = (1 - A)z(t) + f_1(x(t))f_2(y(t)) \tag{3}$$

.

The signal functions f_1 and f_2 can, for example, be chosen linear above a threshold and zero below it (a "threshold-linear" signal function) or linear within a range but flat above

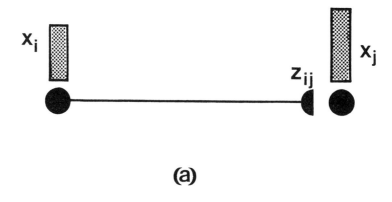

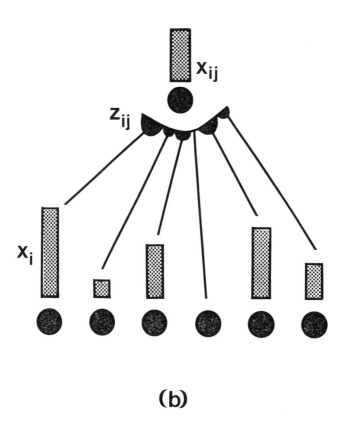

Figure 3. Hebbian vs non-Hebbian associative rule: (a) In a Hebbian associative rule, correlation of the cell activities x_i and x_j always increases the long term memory (LTM) trace, or synaptic strength, z_{ij} of the intervening pathway. (b) In our non-Hebbian associative rule, correlation of a spatial pattern of cell activities x_i with a cell activity x_j enables the LTM traces z_{ij} in the intervening pathways to either increase or decrease to match the spatial pattern.

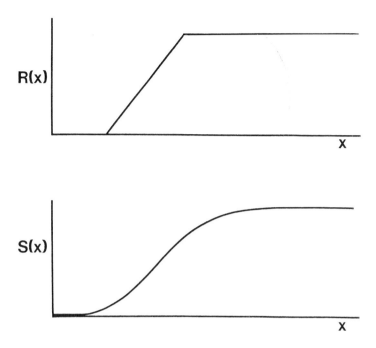

Figure 4. Two signal functions: Either a ramp function $R(x)$ or a sigmoid function $S(x)$ enables the network to suppress noise and contrast enhance the input pattern before storing it in short term memory (STM).

and below it (a "ramp" or "sigmoid" signal function). The effects of different choices of signal functions on sensory pattern processing have been classified mathematically, including the important contrast enhancement and noise suppression properties of sigmoid signal functions (Ellias and Grossberg, 1975; Grossberg, 1973; Grossberg and Levine, 1975). The "ramp" function of Figure 4 was used in our simulations because it has similar mathematical properties to the sigmoid but is simpler to compute.

3. Alternative Explanations of the ISI Effect: The Critical Role of the Conditioning Rule

Barto and Sutton (1982) and Sutton and Barto (1981) have argued that associative rules such as (1) and (2) cannot account for the conditioning data of Figure 2. They contended that a network with associative synapses should, to a first approximation, have an optimal ISI of zero, because cross-correlation between two stimulus traces is strongest when the two stimuli occur simultaneously. To avoid this difficulty, other modellers (Burke, 1966; Uttley, 1979) introduced a delay in the CS pathway that was equal to that of the optimal ISI. Hence, if the ISI between CS and US occurrences equaled the delay in the CS pathway, then the CS and US signals would actually arrive simultaneously at the associative synapse between their representations. Such a delay, however, has other implications which are not easy to support. For one, delays within individual neural pathways, or axons, are typically very brief, and cannot easily account for optimal ISI's that are hundreds of milliseconds long. More seriously, such a delay would also delay the conditioned response (CR) elicited in response to the CS by an equal amount, and hence is incompatible with the fact that a well-trained CR normally occurs earlier than the onset time of the US (the so-called anticipatory CR).

The alternative model simulated here reproduces both the ISI data and the anticipatory CR without invoking a long delay in the CS pathway. Such a delay is not needed to account for the ISI data, and moreover it violates symmetry properties between CS and US which are necessary for secondary conditioning to be possible. The need for such CS-US symmetry, or "path equivalence", is discussed more fully in Grossberg (1971, 1975, 1982b).

The argument of Barto and Sutton was incomplete because their model did not incorporate certain network factors that are crucial to the model described here. These factors include the role of attention in regulating the conditioning rate, the role of reinforcing signals in shifting the focus of attention towards motivationally salient cues, and the role of inhibition between sensory representations in carrying out attention shifts by reallocating limited capacity short-term memory resources. Indeed, Barto and Sutton themselves stated (1982, p.232): "The model clearly does not address higher order modulatory influences such as those produced by attentional or stimulus salience factors."

Because the Sutton-Barto model—and the more recent, related model of Blazis *et al* (1986)—did not incorporate attentional factors, their explanation of ISI effects and blocking relied on a particular law of synaptic modification that differs from ours. In their conditioning law, presynaptic activity is correlated with change in postsynaptic activity, rather than with postsynaptic activity itself. Other neural and psychological models which utilize some variant of this law are frequent (Frey and Sears, 1978; Klopf, 1982; Mackintosh, 1975; Pearce and Hall, 1980; Rescorla and Wagner, 1972; Stone, 1986). Grossberg (1982b) reviews a variety of context-sensitive conditioning data that such models have so far been unable to explain, primarily because of their lack of network mechanisms such as limited capacity competition and modulation of attention by motivational feedback. For example, Mackintosh (1975) has stated that his own model cannot account for the fact that a more salient stimulus can block a less salient one but not vice versa, a fact that is easily explained by our model (see Section 7).

To understand our model, let us review the qualitative development (Grossberg, 1971, 1975, 1982a, 1982b) of the type of network shown schematically in Figure 5. In addition to using conditionable synapses to encode associations in long-term memory (LTM), such a network uses modulatory mechanisms that were derived from three simple postulates: that CS-US associations can develop without catastrophic cross-talk even if the time lag separating the two stimuli is variable across trials; that the more we practice a task, the better we can learn it ("practice makes perfect"), other things being equal; and that freely attended inspection of multiple cues with different reinforcing properties does not, in itself, extinguish the reinforcing properties of these cues. Our review will provide just enough detail to define the model and explain the computer simulations. Extensive discussions of model derivations and of the large interdisciplinary data base clarfied by the model are found in the original articles.

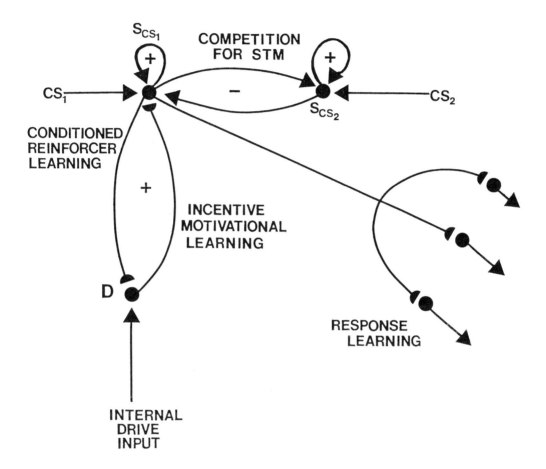

Figure 5. Schematic conditioning circuit: Conditioned stimuli (CS$_i$) activate sensory representations (S$_{CS_i}$) which compete among themselves for limited capacity short term memory activation and storage. The activated S$_{CS_i}$ ellicit conditionable signals to drive representations and motor command representations. Learning from a S$_{CS_i}$ to a drive representation D is called conditioned reinforcer learning. Learning from D to a S$_{CS_i}$ is called incentive motivational learning. Signals from D to S$_{CS_i}$ are elicited when the combination of external sensory plus internal drive inputs is sufficiently large. In the simulations reported herein, the drive level is assumed to be large and constant.

4. Review: The Synchronization and Persistence Problems of Classical Conditioning

Grossberg (1971, pp.227–237) posed the problem, called the *synchronization problem*, of how CS-US associations can develop in a stable fashion in spite of the variability of time lag between CS and US on successive learning trials. In previous work (Grossberg, 1969b, 1970), each elementary sensory representation or motor command was interpreted mathematically as a spatial pattern of activation across a network of cell populations. If activity at a population coding a CS was followed repeatedly by the same US, the LTM traces activated by the CS population could cumulatively learn the spatial pattern corresponding to that US. However, if the CS was followed at different time intervals by two or more events, among which only a single US occurred, the CS-activated LTM traces would not learn the spatial pattern corresponding to the US. Instead, they would learn a mixture of the spatial patterns corresponding to all the events which occurred when the CS was active, whether meaningful to the organism or not. Such a mixture would typically encode little useful information about the environment and would certainly not resemble the US pattern.

Thus the synchronization problem brought into focus two related problems of fundamental importance: How does an organism know how to distinguish significant events for encoding in LTM among all the irrelevant environmental fluctuations that never cease to occur? How are conditioning systems designed to be capable of stably operating in continuous, or real, time, despite the fact that meaningful events, such as novel events or US's, occur at irregular and discrete time intervals?

Analysis of the synchronization problem led to the proposal that populations of cells, called D for drive representations, exist that are separate from the sensory representations of particular stimuli but are related to particular drives and emotions. Later workers have called such a drive represenation an "emotion node" (Bower, 1981; Bower, Gilligan, and Monteiro, 1981) or an "adaptive critical element" (Barto, Sutton, and Anderson, 1983). These drive nodes are not "drive reduction" areas but are areas analogous to loci in "emotional" regions of the brain, such as the hypothalamus, where mechanisms of conditioning, reinforcement, homeostastis, and competition interact to select pathways for conditioned reinforcer learning and attentional feedback. (See Grossberg (1982a, 1982b) for further discussion of this concept.) A food US, for example, unconditionally activates the D population corresponding to the hunger drive if the hunger drive level is sufficiently high. Repeated pairing of a CS with a food US thus causes pairing of stimulation of the CS sensory representation, which we denote by S_{CS}, with that of the D representation for the hunger drive, which we denote by D_H. If the $S_{CS} \to D_H$ synapses are assumed to be modifiable according to an associative rule, then the pairing $S_{CS} \to D_H$ can become strengthened, so that eventually the CS by itself will be able to activate the drive representation D_H and thereby becomes a conditioned, or secondary, reinforcer for food. Once a neutral CS (call it CS_1) has been conditioned, it can be used as a US to reinforce responses to another CS (call it CS_2) in a later experiment. Thus, after the $S_{CS_1} \to D_H$ synapses have been strengthened, repeated presentation of CS_2 followed by CS_1 can, in turn, strengthen the associative $S_{CS_2} \to D_H$ synapses.

Further study revealed that $S \to D$ conditioning must be supplemented by $D \to S$ conditioning. This became apparent through the definition and analysis of the *persistence problem* of classical conditioning (Grossberg, 1975).

In Figure 6b, the cues CS_1 and CS_2 have previously been conditioned to responses CR_1 and CR_2. Responses CR_1 and CR_2 are assumed to be motivationally incompatible, such

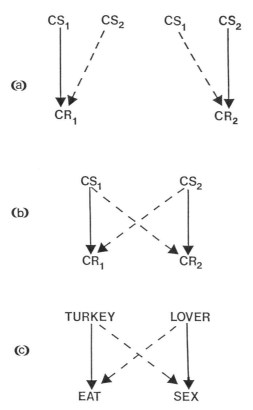

Figure 6. The persistence problem of classical conditioning: (a) A CS_j can be quickly associated with the CR_i of a distinct CS_i; (b) When each of the conditioned stimuli CS_1 and CS_2 is already conditioned to a distinct conditioned response CR_1 and CR_2, respectively, at the beginning of an experiment, alternative scanning of CS_1 and CS_2 does not always cause rapid cross conditioning of CS_1 to CR_2 and CS_2 to CR_1, as is clear by consideration of the absurd consequence depicted in (c) that would arise after dining with one's lover.

as eating and sex. A catastrophic problem could occur in an improperly designed learning circuit if CS_1 and CS_2 were then alternately scanned in rapid succession. If only one of the cues had previously been conditioned to a response, then no difficulty would occur (Figure 6a). However, if both cues were already conditioned and if classical conditioning were merely a feedforward process which associatively links cues with simultaneously active responses, then rapid cross-conditioning from CS_1 to CR_2 and CS_2 to CR_1 could occur. This example identifies the core issue: When many cues are processed in parallel, and some of the cues are already conditioned to motivationally incompatible responses, then why are not these associations quickly degraded by cross-conditioning? How can the ubiquity of parallel cue processing be reconciled with the persistence of learned meanings?

The above paradigm identifies the persistence problem, which is also occasionally called the *turkey–love fiasco* to dramatize the absurd world to which it would lead if not actively prevented. During an otherwise uneventful turkey dinner with one's lover, suppose that one alternately looks at lover and turkey, where lover is associated with sexual responses (among others!) and turkey is associated with eating responses. Why do we not come away from dinner wanting to eat our lover and have sex with turkeys? The fact that we do not illustrate that the persistence of learned meanings can endure despite the fact that sensory cues which are processed in parallel often control motivationally incompatible responses. Further discussion of the persistence problem is provided in Grossberg and Schmajuk (1987).

The solution of the persistence problem offered in Grossberg (1975) led to explanations of a wide variety of difficult conditioning data, including blocking, unblocking, latent inhibition, overshadowing on a single trial, and the enhanced short-term memory (STM) encoding of novel cues (Grossberg, 1975, 1982b, 1984b). More generally, this solution suggested how incentive motivational feedback due to conditionable $D \rightarrow S$ pathways could shift an organism's sensory attentional focus to process preferentially reinforcing cues and other motivationally salient cues. That is, conditioning in $S \rightarrow D$ pathways endows a sensory cue with *conditioned reinforcer*, or secondary reinforcing, properties. Conditioning in $D \rightarrow S$ pathways endows a sensory cue with *incentive motivational* properties. A sensory cue which possesses a large conditioned $S \rightarrow D \rightarrow S$ feedback pathway can quickly augment the STM activity of its sensory representation (Figure 7). In other words, reinforcing cues can draw attention to themselves via self-generated incentive motivational feedback signals.

5. Competition between Sensory Representations: Limited Capacity Short-Term Memory Activity

The sensory representations which emit conditioned reinforcer signals and receive incentive motivational signals also compete among themselves for a limited capacity STM resource. The ubiquitous occurrence of limited capacity STM was traced (Grossberg, 1973, 1975, 1980) to a more basic processing requirement: the ability of cell networks to process spatially distributed input patterns without irreparably distorting these input patterns due to either internal noise or saturation effects. This *noise-saturation dilemma* can be prevented by an on-center off-surround anatomy through which the cells interact via mass action (or shunting) laws (Figure 8). Within a robust parameter range, the off-surround competition of such a network interaction implies that the total suprathreshold activation of the network tends to be conserved, and thus that the network has a limited capacity.

When a shunting on-center off-surround network is also designed to accomplish STM storage, its on-center off-surround interactions are recurrent, or feedback, interactions in which the nodes excite themselves and inhibit other nodes via feedback pathways (Figure 8b). In addition to its noise-saturation and limited capacity properties, such a recurrent on-center off-surround network contrast enhances an input pattern before storing the contrast-enhanced activation pattern which emerges across the cells in STM (also called working memory). Thus one must distinguish between the input pattern and the more focal STM activity pattern that it generates. "Attention is paid" to those sensory representations whose cells receive a positive level of *stored* STM activity.

When incentive motivational feedback signals form part of the total input pattern to the sensory representations (Figure 7), these signals can bias the competition for STM activity towards motivationally salient cues. Due to the limited capacity of STM, primary and secondary reinforcers can draw attention to themselves via their strong conditioned $S \rightarrow D \rightarrow S$ feedback loops. In order to initiate such an attention shift, such cues must first start to be processed due to their sensory properties. After sensory processing is initiated, it can activate the learned reinforcing $S \rightarrow D$ and motivating $D \rightarrow S$ pathways of the cues, and can thereby help to direct the ultimate allocation of sensory and attentional resources.

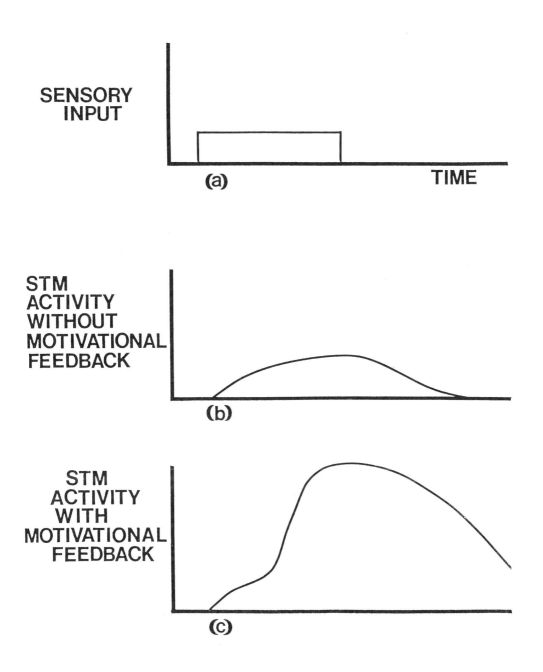

Figure 7. Augmentation of STM activation at a sensory representation S_{CS} by feedback signalling through the pathway $S_{CS} \to D \to S_{CS}$: In response to the sensory input (a) received by S_{CS}, the STM activation profile before learning is schematized in (b). After learning within the $S_{CS} \to D \to S_{CS}$ pathway takes place, the initial activation remains as in (b). However, as the feedback signals are registered, the STM activation of S_{CS} can be greatly amplified and prolonged, as schematized in (c).

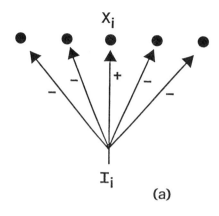

(a)

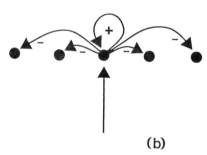

(b)

Figure 8. The noise-saturation dilemma is solved by mass action on-center off-surround networks: (a) A feedforward, or nonrecurrent, network with inputs I_i activating and inhibiting STM activities x_j. (b) In a feedback, or recurrent, network excitatory and inhibitory signals are distributed among the network cells.

Once attention shifts away from a sensory represenation, its activity can become subthreshold. In both equations (1) and (2), a subthreshold activity x or y prevents new growth of associative strength. In particular, if $f_1(x) = 0$ in equation (2), then $dz/dt = 0$, so that no associative change whatsoever can occur. If $f_2(y) = 0$ in equation (1) or (2), then $dz/dt \leq 0$, so that no increase of associative strength can occur.

6. Effects of ISI on Conditioning: Inverted U

These mechanisms are sufficient to describe the relationship which we claim to exist between attentional blocking and the ISI effect. To explain the inverted-U as a function of ISI, consider first a CS and a US that are simultaneously presented. Each of these sensory cues will initially receive less STM activity than either one presented separately, due to the competition that they elicit for limited capacity STM resources. The US can nonetheless quickly activate a strong $S_{US} \to D \to S_{US}$ feedback pathway. Delivery of this large positive feedback signal to S_{US} signifies that the US is a motivationally important cue. Due to this large feedback signal, the STM activity of the sensory representation S_{US} is amplified as attention is drawn to S_{US} (Figure 9). As a result of competition for STM resources (Figure 8b), the sensory representation S_{CS} of the CS is quickly inhibited before it can elicit significant conditioning in the $S_{CS} \to D$ conditioned reinforcer pathway or the

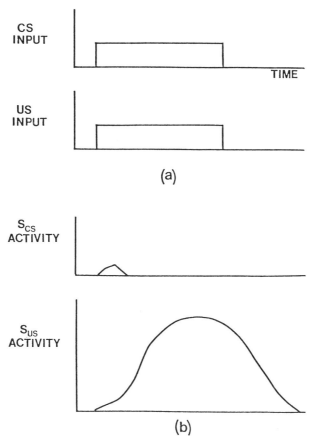

Figure 9. Schematic of STM activation at zero ISI: (a) Simultaneous onset of CS and US. (b) Rapid amplification of S_{US} by $S_{US} \rightarrow D \rightarrow S_{US}$ feedback signals enables S_{US} to quickly inhibit the S_{CS} representation.

$D \rightarrow S_{CS}$ incentive motivational pathway (Figure 9).

In contrast, suppose that CS onset precedes US onset by a duration sufficient to enable the CS to generate, in the absence of US competition, a fully developed STM activation of its sensory representation S_{CS} (Figure 10). When the US then does occur, it must from the outset compete for STM activity with an active S_{CS} representation. The initial activation of S_{US} therefore proceeds less vigorously than during simultaneous CS-US presentation. Consequently, the activation of the feedback loop $S_{US} \rightarrow D \rightarrow S_{US}$ also builds up more slowly. Throughout the time interval when the S_{US} is activating the $S_{US} \rightarrow D \rightarrow S_{US}$ feedback pathway, growing competition from S_{US} to S_{CS} begins to develop. However, the S_{CS} is also sending the S_{US} large competitive signals during this interval due to its large STM activity when the US is presented. All of these factors conspire to enable the S_{CS} to remain intensely active for a time interval after US onset. Throughout this time interval, large sampling signals in the $S_{CS} \rightarrow D$ pathway and the $D \rightarrow S_{CS}$ pathway enable the LTM traces in these pathways to grow.

Finally, suppose that the CS occurs so long before the US that S_{CS} is already inactive before the drive representation D gets activated by the US. Then no conditioning can occur

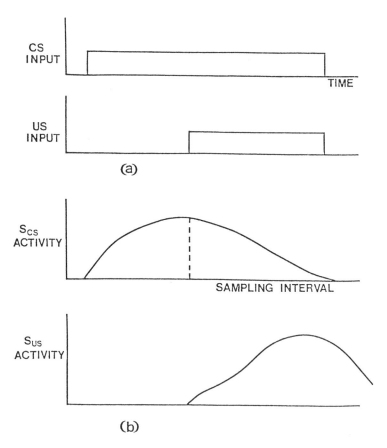

Figure 10. Schematic of STM activation at positive ISI: (a) CS is presented before US onset. (b) Large S_{CS} activation prior to US onset enables the S_{CS} to drive learning during the sampling interval after US onset before the S_{US} can inhibit the S_{CS}.

within the $S_{CS} \rightarrow D$ pathway and the $D \rightarrow S_{CS}$ pathway, so that the CS does not acquire reinforcing or motivating properties.

These considerations suggest how incentive motivational feedback from a drive representation D can give rise to the ISI inverted-U. In other words, the ISI effect is a consequence of the feedback mechanisms which identify a US sensory cue as a motivationally salient, and therefore differentially attended, event. The argument above can now be readily applied to stimulus-response, or S-R, conditioning (Figure 5). An inverted-U in S-R conditioning is also explained if the conditioning rate is a function of S_{CS} activity, as it is in the associative equations (1) and (2).

7. Effects of ISI on Conditioning: Blocking, Secondary Conditioning, Anticipatory CR's, Overshadowing

One remark now suffices to relate our explanation of the ISI inverted-U to phenomena of attentional blocking and secondary conditioning. In the above explanation, simply replace CS by CS_2 and US by CS_1. In a typical blocking experiment, CS_1 is paired with a US until conditioning enables CS_1 to control a strong feedback pathway $S_{CS_1} \to D \to S_{CS_1}$. Such conditioning operationally defines CS_1 as a secondary, or conditioned, reinforcer that can draw attention to itself. Later simultaneous presenation of CS_1 and CS_2 can now be seen to be mechanistically similar to simultaneous presentation of a CS and a US. Simultaneous CS–US presentation in an ISI paradigm prevents conditioning to the CS due to a combination of large $S_{US} \to D \to S_{US}$ feedback and $S_{US} \to S_{CS}$ competition which quickly drives the activity of S_{CS} below threshold. After CS_1 becomes a conditioned reinforcer in a blocking paradigm, simultaneous presentation of CS_1 and CS_2 prevents conditioning to CS_2 due to a combination of large $S_{CS_1} \to D \to S_{CS_1}$ feedback and $S_{CS_1} \to S_{CS_2}$ competition which quickly drives the activity of S_{CS_2} below threshold.

In summary, our explanation of secondary conditioning enables us to show how suppression of CS conditioning during zero ISI and the blocking of a CS by a US can both be caused by the same mechanisms. The existence of anticipatory CR's is also easily explained within the network of Figure 5. The pathways $S \to D, D \to S$, and $S \to R$ do not create significant delays in the network. The times needed for STM activities to grow, for the competition between sensory representations to take effect, and for the firing thresholds in $D \to S$ pathways to be exceeded by $S \to D$ reinforcing inputs are the rate-limiting times within the network. As the LTM traces within the $S \to D, D \to S, S \to R$ pathways grow larger, the STM activity of S_{CS} can grow more quickly and can more quickly and strongly read out a CR via the $S \to R$ pathway, thereby leading to an anticipatory CR.

The unified explanation of ISI, blocking, and anticipatory CR's depends critically upon the manner in which attention can be shifted by conditioned $S \to D \to S$ feedback. Attentional factors are particularly important for a thorough understanding of blocking. Mackintosh (1975) has, for example, stated that his own model cannot account for the fact that a more salient stimulus can block a less salient one, but not vice versa. Since our model of blocking is based on a limited capacity competitive interaction between stimulus representations, it can easily account for this fact. A similar argument suggests how overshadowing occurs (Staddon, 1983); that is, how a more intense stimulus can dominate learning when it is presented with a less intense stimulus. Any factor which enables the sensory representation of a cue to better compete for limited capacity STM resources increases its chance to emit effective learning signals to the drive and motor representations of the network.

8. Quantitative Model

The networks that we have simulated are depicted in Figure 11. The network of Figure 11 includes on-center off-surround competition between sensory representations for two CS's (with activities x_{11} and x_{21}) and a single US (with activity x_{31}), all projecting to the same drive representation D with activity y via conditioned reinforcer pathways with LTM strengths z_{11}, z_{21}, and z_{31}, respectively. In Figure 5, the drive representation D projects back to the same sensory representations via incentive motivational pathways that possess their own LTM strengths. The sensory representations also project via conditionable sensory-motor pathways to representations of motor commands. Figure 11 describes a variant of Figure 5 (Grossberg, 1975, 1982b) in which the sensory representations are divided into two successive stages. The activity x_{i1} of the ith first stage can activate conditioned reinforcer pathways, whereas the activity x_{i2} of the ith second stage receives conditioned incentive motivational pathways from D. The x_{i2} loci, in turn, project back to the x_{i1}, thereby closing the $S \to D \to S$ feedback loop, and also project forward to the motor

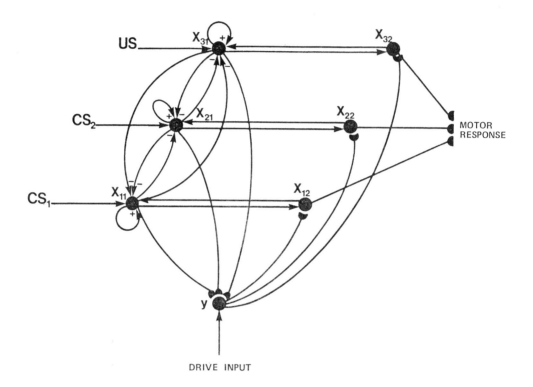

Figure 11. Simulated network: Each sensory representation possesses two stages with STM activities x_{i1} and x_{i2}, respectively. A CS or US input activates its corresponding x_{i1}. Activation of x_{i1} generates unconditionable signals to x_{i2} and conditioned reinforcer signals to D, whose activity is denoted by y. Conditionable incentive motivational feedback signals from D activate the second stage potentials x_{i2}, which then deliver feedback signals to x_{i1}. Motor learning is elicited by sensory-motor signals from the x_{i2} to the motor command representations. Long term memory traces are designated by semi-disks at the ends of conditionable pathways.

representations.

An additional mechanism was used to regulate STM decay of the sensory representations of CS's and US's. Short-term memory can be weakened through time due to habituation, competition from other incoming stimuli, and nonspecific gain changes that occur, for example, when attention shifts to a different modality. (See Carpenter and Grossberg, 1987a, 1987b; Grossberg, 1972; Grossberg and Schmajuk (1987); and Grossberg and Stone, 1986 for theories and simulations incorporating some of these effects.) These multiple influences on STM decay are replaced here by a simple rule which suffices for our present purposes. We assume that the self-excitatory feedback term that maintains STM storage is multiplied by a factor that equals 1 for a short time after the initiation of STM activa-

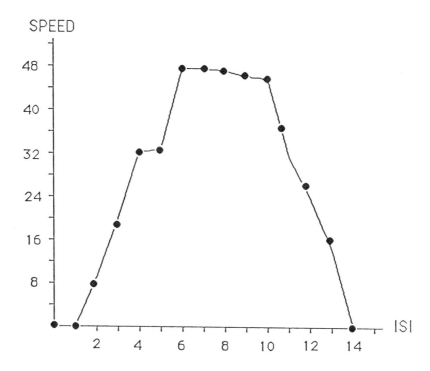

Figure 12. Plot of CR acquisition speed as a function of ISI. This speed was computed by the formula 100 x (number of time units per trial)/(number of time units to first CR).

tion and decays exponentially thereafter. The self-excitation term is also supplemented by feedback due to x_{i2}, so that STM decay is slower for motivationally significant stimuli.

9. Computer Simulation Results

Figures 12–14 show some representative computer simulations of the ISI effects using the network in Figure 11. Various measures of the strength of conditioning were plotted against the ISI, all other parameters being equal. The first measure is the speed of CR acquisition, as indicated by the reciprocal of the number of trials to the first conditioned response. To generate this figure, a conditioned response was said to occur if the STM trace y of D was activated by the CS representation x_{11} in the absence of the US.

The curve of Figure 12 shows that the speed of CR acquisition relates to ISI in a manner that is qualitatively compatible with the experimental data of Gormezano and his coworkers (Smith, Coleman, and Gormezano, 1969; Schneiderman and Gormezano, 1964) on the nictitating membrane response. For ISI's of 1 time unit or less, the competition from the US representation x_{31} prevented the CS activity x_{11} from staying above the threshold in the $S_{CS} \to D$ pathway long enough while y at D was being activated by the US for the associative strength z_{11} to increase appreciably. At long ISI's, the decay of the

STM trace x_{11} prevented z_{11} from sensing the later large values of y at D.

In Figure 13, the STM activites of S_{CS}, S_{US}, and D (x_{11}, x_{31}, and y) and the LTM trace z_{11} of the $S_{CS} \rightarrow D$ pathway are plotted in real-time given a choice of ISI=6 that led to good learning in Figure 12. Although the US (Figure 13b) suppressed the x_{11} variable (Figure 13a) after activating the y variable (Figure 13c), the LTM trace z_{11} correlated positive x_{11} and y values well enough to achieve an S-shaped cumulative learning curve across trials (Figure 13d). As the LTM trace z_{11} grew, the CS elicited a progressively larger STM reaction x_{11} across trials due to the increasing size of the positive feedback signal which it generated in the $S_{CS} \rightarrow D \rightarrow S_{CS}$ pathway (Figure 13a). This reduced the STM activity x_{31} of the US (Figure 13b) due to competition between CS and US sensory representations. Such a small decrement in the sensory activity of S_{US} during conditioning is an, as yet, untested prediction of the model. Figure 14 plots the asymptotic, or maximal, value of z_{11} as a function of ISI. An inverted-U function obtained even after many learning trials.

Figure 15 illustrates a computer simulation of a blocking experiment using the same parameters. The STM activities of the CS_1 and CS_2 representations (x_{11} and x_{21}) and the LTM traces of the $S_{CS} \rightarrow D$ pathway (z_{11} and z_{21}) were plotted in real-time. Pairing of CS_1 with a delayed US enabled the LTM trace z_{11} to achieve a classical S-shaped learning curve (Figure 15c). After CS_1 became a conditioned reinforcer, it enhanced its own STM storage via x_{11} by generating a large $S_{CS_1} \rightarrow D \rightarrow S_{CS_1}$ feedback signal (Figure 15a). As a result, when CS_1 and CS_2 were simultaneously presented, the STM activity x_{21} of S_{CS_2} (Figure 15b) was suppressed by competition from x_{11}. Consequently, the LTM trace z_{21} (Figure 15d) could not grow, and the CS_2 could not learn to elicit a CR.

10. Comparison with Invertebrate Learning: An Evolutionary Invariant of Associative Learning?

Much discussion has recently focussed upon the relationships which may exist between vertebrate and invertebrate learning circuits in order to identify possible evolutionary invariants of associative learning. Hawkins and Kandel (1984) have described neural data and a conditioning model based upon studies of the invertebrate *Aplysia*. We compare their model with the model that we have here used to simulate mammalian learning data.

The Hawkins and Kandel (1984) model was described from data reported in Hawkins *et al.* (1983) and Walters and Byrne (1983). These data suggested that each US activates a *facilitator neuron* that influences each pathway activated by a CS. Only when a CS and a US can simultaneously activate a CS pathway and a facilitator neuron can the LTM trace in the CS pathway grow.

The functional similarity between a facilitator neuron and a $D \rightarrow S$ incentive motivational pathway (Figure 5) was used in Hawkins and Kandel (1984) to suggest a possible explanation of secondary conditioning and blocking much like our own (Grossberg, 1971, 1975, 1982b). The existence of a conditionable pathway from the CS to the facilitator neuron was postulated that is analogous to the $S \rightarrow D$ conditioned reinforcer pathway. This scheme was suggested as a possible model of secondary conditioning and blocking in *Aplysia* as well as higher organisms.

Despite these qualitative similarities between the two models, the model suggested in Hawkins and Kandel (1984) cannot explain either secondary conditioning or blocking, and is inconsistent with the data reported in Hawkins *et al.* (1983). The analysis leading

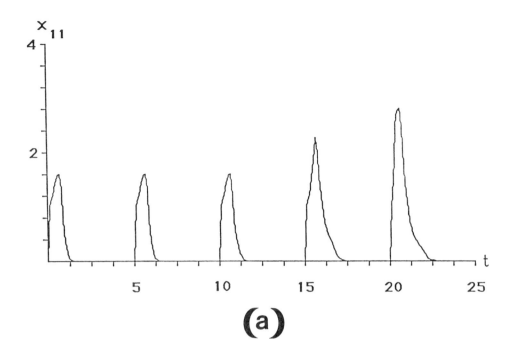

(a)

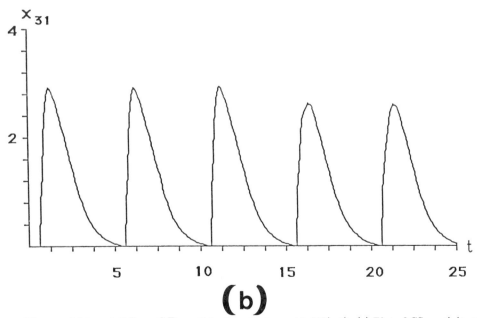

(b)

Figure 13. Acquisition of $CS_1 - CR$ conditioning at a favorable ISI(=6): (a) Plot of CS_1 activity x_{11} through time over 5 trials during which CS_1 is paired with US; (b) Plot of US activity x_{31} through time over 5 trials; (c) Plot of D activity y through time over 5 trials. As CS_1 becomes a conditioned reinforcer, it activates y before the US occurs; (d) Plot of $CS_1 \rightarrow D$ LTM trace z_{11} over 20 trials during which CS_1 is paired with US.

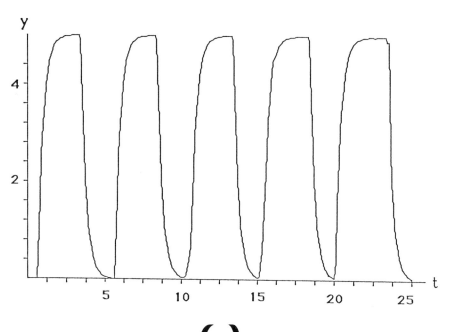

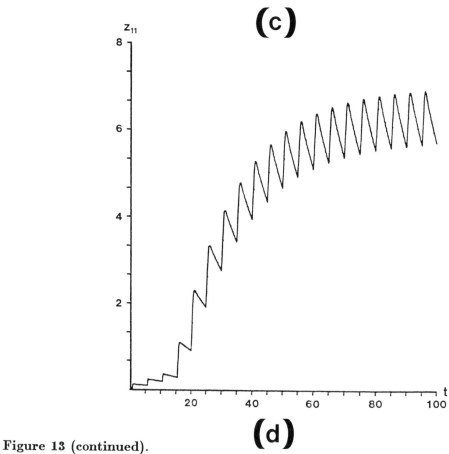

Figure 13 (continued).

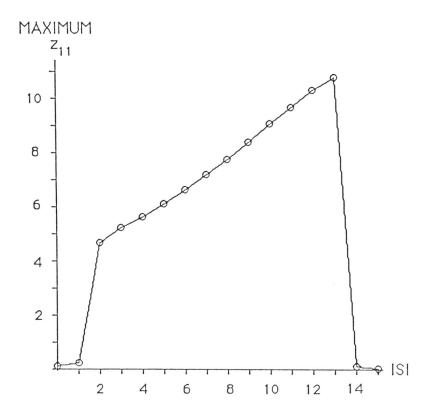

Figure 14. Plot of maximal z_{11} over 20 paired trials as a function of ISI.

to these conclusions is provided below. In addition, we state an organizational principle, called the Secondary Conditioning Alternative, that is consistent with these data, and that is predicted to hold across all species, both vertebrate and invertebrate (Grossberg, 1984a). If confirmed, the Alternative would constitute an evolutionary invariant of associative learning.

The hypothesis that a facilitator neuron mediates conditioning in *Aplysia* was based upon data which showed that "the US produces substantially more facilitation of the synaptic potential from the sensory neuron to a motor neuron than if the US is not paired with activity in the sensory neuron" (Hawkins and Kandel, 1984, p.379). However, Hawkins *et al.* (1983, p.403) reported that "paired presentation of the CS and the US produced no more total activation of the facilitators than did unpaired presentation." These *Aplysia* data are inconsistent with the existence of a conditionable pathway from the CS to the facilitator neuron, and the circuits derived directly from the data in Hawkins *et al.* (1983) and Walters and Byrne (1983) did not contain such a pathway.

To reconcile these *Aplysia* experiments with data about vertebrate conditioning, it was suggested in Grossberg (1982a) that an anatomical difference may exist between the con-

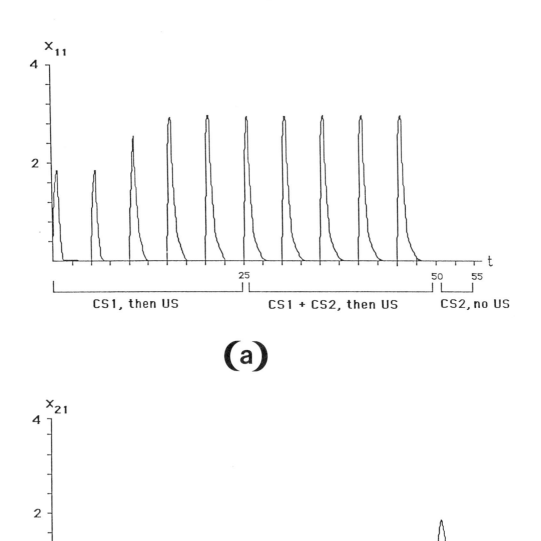

Figure 15. Blocking simulation: In (a)–(d), the ISI=6 between CS_1 and US onset. Five trials of $CS_1 - US$ pairing are followed by five trials of $(CS_1 + CS_2) - US$ pairing. Then CS_2 is presented alone for one trial: (a) Activity x_{11} of S_{CS_1} through time; (b) Activity x_{21} of S_{CS_2} through time; (c) LTM trace z_{11} from S_{CS_1} to D through time; (d) LTM trace z_{21} from S_{CS_2} to D through time. Conditioning of z_{21} is blocked by prior conditioning of z_{11}.

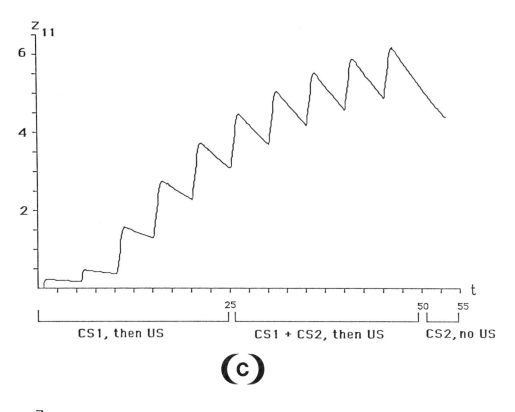

(c)

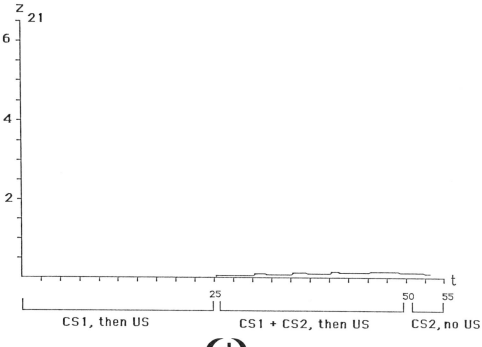

Figure 15 (continued).

(d)

ditioning circuits of certain invertebrates and vertebrates, and that this difference would influence the ability of different species to undergo secondary conditioning and to experience motivationally-biased attention shifts. The following statement summarizes this possible difference in circuitry in a way that can be tested across all species.

The Secondary Conditioning Alternative

Either a neural system is incapable of secondary conditioning, or a CS will cause increased total firing of its facilitator neuron (read $D \rightarrow S$ pathway) as CS-US pairing continues.

The Secondary Conditioning Alternative suggests that a modest modification of an invertebrate conditioning circuit, namely adding on a conditionable $S \rightarrow D$ pathway, can permit the circuit to undergo secondary conditioning.

11. Properties of an Invertebrate Conditioning Model

Hawkins and Kandel (1984, p.385) suggested that blocking is due to the postulated property that "the output of the facilitator neurons decreases when they are stimulated continuously." Thus after a CS_1 is paired with a US on a number of trials, subsequent presentation of a compound stimulus $CS_1 + CS_2$ with a US would not condition CS_2 because the facilitator neuron could not fire adequately. Unfortunately, this explanation is incompatible with the phenomenon of unblocking, which is the counterpoint to blocking in vertebrates, as well as with the phenomenon of secondary conditioning.

This hypothesis cannot explain unblocking for the following reason. Blocking of a CS_2 occurs if a compound stimulus $CS_1 + CS_2$ occurs prior to the same US that was paired with CS_1. However, unblocking of CS_2 is observed if a compound cue $CS_1 + CS_2$ occurs prior to either a less or more intense US than did the previous CS_1 (Kamin, 1968, 1969); that is, under these conditions, the CS_2 can become conditioned to the subsequent US. If the facilitator neuron is fatigued by the previous US, it cannot enable a CS_2 which occurs prior to a different US to become conditioned for the same reason that is cannot allow such a CS_2 to become conditioned if it occurs prior to the same US.

Secondary conditioning cannot be explained for a similar reason. After a CS_1 becomes well enough conditioned to act as a US, it cannot activate the facilitator neuron during a subsequent time interval because the facilitator neuron has become depressed due to previous activation by the US. Consequently, pairing a CS_2 with the conditioned reinforcer CS_1 does not enable the CS_2 to become conditioned, and secondary conditioning does not occur.

12. Modulation of Conditioning by a Ca^{++} Current

Confirmation of the Secondary Conditioning Alternative would provide an example of an evolutionary invariant of associative learning, while clarifying the role that variations and specializations of anatomical circuitry may play in endowing some species with a more sophisticated repertoire of conditionable skills than others. Evolutionary invariants of associative learning have also been identified on the more microscopic level of biochemical learning mechanisms. For example, Alkon and his colleagues have studied the anatomy, physiology, and biochemistry of an associative learning circuit in the nudibranch mollusc *Hermissenda crassicornis* (Alkon, 1974, 1976, 1979, 1980, 1984a, 1984b, 1984c; Farley and

Alkon, 1982). These experiments have identified postsynaptic membrane channels that mediate an association which is learned by *Hermissenda* when light (the CS) and rotation (the US) are paired (Alkon, 1984). The *Hermissenda* data thus support the existence of an associative rule, such as (1) or (2), wherein both presynaptic and postsynaptic influences are required during the learning process. In this learning situation, a sustained voltage-dependent inward Ca^{++} current inactivates an outward K^+ current, thereby causing enhanced depolarization of the cell membrane and further inward flow of Ca^{++}. In addition, the level of Ca^{++}-dependent phosphorylation of specific cell proteins changes only in the cells of conditioned animals. Vertebrate conditioning studies are reviewed in (Alkon, 1984c) in which a voltage-dependent inward Ca^{++} current is again implicated as a mediator of more long-lasting cellular changes due to learning.

These experiments support and significantly refine a prediction (Grossberg, 1968, 1969a; see also Grossberg, 1982c, Chapter 3) whose goal was to biochemically interpret the associative rules (1) and (2). The prediction was based on a comparison of these associative rules, which were derived from mammalian conditioning data, with the fragmentary biochemical evidence that was available in the 1960's. The prediction suggested that an inward Ca^{++} current is synergetic with an inward Na^+ current during associative learning. This prediction was based upon an analysis which suggested that an inward ionic current, other than Na^+, was needed which could act synergetically with the inward Na^+ current and the outward K^+ current that were well-known to occur during cell depolarization. A functional analysis suggested that this extra ionic current should be able to accumulate intracellularly and thereby trigger more permanent associative changes. Based upon what was known in the 1960's about biochemical regulation by synergetic ionic currents, an inward Ca^{++} current was selected as the most likely candidate for the predicted current, and an increase in an inward Na^+ current was identified as likely synergist. A decrease in an outward K^+ current can also augment cell depolarization, however, and that possibility is the one which conditioning models, recent data have supported.

This early prediction illustrates a convergence of models for vertebrate and invertebrate associative learning that has recently emerged, and highlights the way in which conditioning models, vertebrate behavioral studies, and invertebrate biochemical studies can complement and strengthen each other during their shared search for evolutionary invariants.

Not all studies of invertebrate conditioning have identified a postsynaptic influence on the site of adaptive biochemical change. Aplysia data (Hawkins *et al.*, 1983; Walters and Byrne, 1983) suggest that a US uses its facilitator neuron to activate a Ca^{++} current which acts directly upon the presynaptic terminals of a CS-activated pathway without postsynaptic mediation. A special feature of the relatively simple circuitry *Aplysia* may clarify the absence of a postsynaptic influence on presynaptic conditioning in this organism. In this *Aplysia* circuit, direct prewired pathways exist between sensory and motor neurons. Only a modest number of sensory pathways converge upon each motor neuron. A postsynaptic influence on presynaptic conditioning is not functionally mandated in this type of simple circuit. A postsynaptic influence becomes more useful if a very large number of neurons converge upon each target cell. In such a circuit, a $D \to S$ pathway which acted presynaptically would have to send a separate signal to every sensory pathway which converge upon a target cell. It seems to be much simpler, other things being equal, to send a single $D \to S$ pathway to the target cell and to let the target cell communicate a postsynaptic learning signal—possibly in the form of a Ca^{++} current—to all the synaptic terminals which converge upon it.

In some learning situations it is, in principle, impossible to use exclusively presynaptic conditioning mechanisms. For example, in order to self-organize a spatial map from one sensory field to another, postsynaptic competition mediates the learning at interfield synapses (Carpenter and Grossberg, 1987a, 1987b; Cohen and Grossberg, 1986, 1987; Grossberg, 1976, 1982c; Kohonen, 1982, 1983; Malsburg, 1973). A number of model circuits for mammalian adaptive sensory-motor control have also been proposed in which a presynaptic modulatory signal, such as a Ca^{++} current, regulates a postsynaptic-to-presynaptic learning signal (Grossberg and Kuperstein, 1986). Thus the anatomies of specialized learning circuits may vary widely across neural systems and species, but the associative rules, such as (1) and (2), and their biochemical substrates may be much more universal.

13. Gated Dipole Opponent Processing and Adaptive Resonance Cognitive Processing

The qualitative arguments and quantitative computer simulations reported herein show how blocking, overshadowing, non-zero optimal ISI, anticipatory conditioned responses, secondary reinforcement, attentional focussing by conditioned motivational feedback, and limited capacity short term memory processing can be explained as emergent properties of a neural network model of Pavlovian conditioning. This model uses a type of associative learning law for which neurophysiological data have recently been reported (Kelso and Brown, 1986; Levy, 1985; Levy, Brassel, and Moore, 1983; Levy and Desmond, 1985; Rauschecker and Singer, 1979; Singer, 1983), thereby providing direct support for an early prediction of neural network theory (Grossberg, 1968, 1969b, 1970, 1976).

The interactive circuitry of the model, as in Figures 5 and 11, is just as important as its microscopic cellular laws for explaining these data and their mutual relationships. In particular, the nonlinear positive feedback interactions between the model's distinct network levels–the sensory representations S and drive representations D–and the competitive interactions within each level S and D, respectively, constitute the first adaptive resonance theory (ART) circuit to have been modelled (Grossberg, 1975). For simplicity, the present article has omitted a number of circuit interactions that are not necessary to treat the data simulated herein, but that play a major role in the modelling of other conditioning phenomena.

This article does not, for example, analyse opponent positive and negative drive representations. A model of positive and negative opponent interactions, called a *gated dipole* model (Grossberg, 1972, 1975, 1982b, 1984b), was developed to explain how termination of a negative or aversive stimulus, such as an electric shock, can be positively reinforcing. The property that the sudden termination of a negative input can generate an internal positive reaction is called a *temporal contrast* or *antagonistic rebound* effect.

Many conditioning theorists (Barto and Sutton, 1982; Mackintosh, 1975; Pearce and Hall, 1980; Rescorla and Wagner, 1972; Sutton and Barto, 1981) have modeled such contrast phenomena in terms of single synapse whose associative strength is a function of the change in the activity of that synapse's postsynaptic cell. Such a learning rule cannot, however, account for several important sets of data; for example, the amount of positive reinforcement associated with shock termination depends on the shock's duration; cutting shock level in half can be less reinforcing than shutting off a shock of half the size; a sudden increase in shock can be more punishing than a gradual increase; and reinforcement is an inverted-U function of arousal. All of these phenomena can be explained in terms of emergent properties of a gated dipole circuit (Grossberg, 1972, 1984b).

Although the use of a gated dipole circuit to build up a drive representation expands the explanatory range of a conditioning theory, many conditioning data cannot be explained without the inclusion of cognitive mechanisms, notably the attentional and orienting mechanisms that regulate the learning of sensory and cognitive codes and expectations (Banquet and Grossberg, 1987; Carpenter and Grossberg, 1987b). Conditioning data were in fact, a primary source of design constraints leading to the discovery of adaptive resonance theory (Grossberg, 1982b, 1984b). Such an expanded conditioning theory can be viewed as an adaptive resonance theory in which two specialized types of ART circuits interact: a sensory-cognitive circuit and a cognitive-reinforcement circuit. In this expanded theory, which represents a computational synthesis of sensory, cognitive, learning, reinforcement, and homeostatic mechanisms, a very large body of conditioning data—including such subtle phenomena as unblocking and dishabituation due to novel cues—has been analysed and predicted (Grossberg, 1982b, 1984b, 1984c, 1987; Grossberg and Schmajuk, 1987). The present article and that of Grossberg and Schmajuk (1987) together begin a new phase in the development of this conditioning theory by initiating a systematic program of parametric computer simulations whose goal is to explain finer quantitative details of behavioral conditioning data and of the functional anatomy and dynamics of their generative brain regions.

APPENDIX

Simulated Equations and Parameters

The computer simulations reported in this article are based upon the network depicted in Figure 11. The STM variables (x_{i1}, x_{i2}, and y) and LTM variables (z_{i1}) are intuitively described in Section 8.

The equations for x_{i1} describe an on-center off-surround network undergoing mass action, or shunting, feedback interactions. In particular, x_{i1} obeys an equation of the form.

$$\frac{d}{dt}x_{i1} = -Ax_{i1} + (B - x_{i1})I_{i1} - x_{i1}J_{i1}, \qquad (A1)$$

$i = 1, 2, 3$. In (A1), term $-Ax_{i1}$ represents passive decay of STM. The constant B is the maximum possible activity of each variable x_{i1}. If B is interpreted as the number of sites (cells or membrane patches) capable of being excited, then $B - x_{i1}$ represents the number of inactive sites that can be excited, whereas x_{i1} represents the number of active sites that can be inhibited. Terms I_{i1} and J_{i1} are the total excitatory and inhibitory inputs, respectively, that influence x_{i1}. Term $(B - x_{i1})I_{i1}$ says that inactive sites are activated by I_{i1} via mass action. Term $-x_{i1}J_{i1}$ says that active sites are activated by J_{i1} via mass action.

The total excitatory input is a sum of an external CS or UCS activated signal, plus a positive feedback signal from x_{i1} to itself, plus a positive feedback signal from x_{i2} to x_{i1}. All feedback signal functions in the simulations are ramp functions (Figure 4), which are the simplest type of sigmoid signal functions. A ramp function is defined in terms of parameters α and β by

$$R(x; \alpha, \beta) = \begin{cases} 0, & x \leq \alpha \\ x - \alpha, & \alpha < x \leq \beta \\ \beta - \alpha, & \beta < x \end{cases} \qquad (A2)$$

Parameter α is the threshold and parameter β is the saturation point of the signal function. When possibly distinct sets α_i, β_i of parameters are used, we write

$$R_i(x) = R(x; \alpha_i, \beta_i) \qquad (A3)$$

for simplicity.

We assume, in addition, that the positive feedback signal from x_{i1} to itself triggers a process of habituation that steadily attenuates the net size of the feedback signal. For simplicity, we model this habituative process as an exponentially decaying function of time, rather than as a habituating transmitter gate. Thus

$$I_{i1} = I_i + C(R_1(x_{i1}) + R_2(x_{i2}))e^{-D[t-T_i-E]^+} \qquad (A4)$$

where $C, D, E, \alpha_i, \beta_i$ are positive constants, I_i is the ith externally activated input, T_i is the onset time of I_i after each input presentation, and $[w]^+ = \max(w, 0)$.

The total inhibitory input J_{i1} is a sum of inhibitory feedback signals activated by the other activities x_{j1}. Thus

$$J_{i1} = F \sum_{j \neq i} R_1(x_{j1}). \qquad (A5)$$

In all

$$\frac{d}{dt}x_{i1} = -Ax_{i1} + (B - x_{i1})[I_i + C(R_1(x_{i1}) + R_2(x_{i2}))e^{-D[t-T_i-E]^+}] - Fx_{i1} \sum_{j \neq \iota} R_1(x_{j1}), \qquad (A6)$$

$i = 1, 2, 3.$

We assume that each activity x_{i1} reads-out a signal $GR_1(x_{i1})$ towards the drive representation D, where G is a positive constant. This signal is gated by the LTM trace z_{i1} before the net LTM-gated signal influences D. The drive representation D is activated only if the total input due to all x_{i1} exceeds a threshold α_3. Thus we let

$$\frac{d}{dt}y = -Hy + KR_3(\sum_{j=1}^{3} GR_1(x_{j1})z_{j1}). \qquad (A7)$$

Simultaneous signals from x_{i1} and y are needed to activate x_{i2}. The signal from x_{i2} is gated by an LTM trace, which is assumed for simplicity to equal z_{i1} due to the fact that x_{i1} and x_{i2} are both activated at similar times during the conditioning process. We also assume, for simplicity, that these inputs do not drive x_{i2} into its saturation range. In all, we let

$$\frac{d}{dt}x_{i2} = -Lx_{i2} + MR_4(x_{i1})R_5(y)z_{i1}, \qquad (A8)$$

$i = 1, 2, 3.$

Finally, each LTM trace corresponding to a CS is assumed to obey a law such as equation (1):

$$\frac{d}{dt}z_{i1} = -Nz_{i1} + PR_1(x_{i1})R_6(y), \qquad (A9)$$

$i = 1, 2.$ The LTM trace corresponding to the UCS was assumed to be constant:

$$z_{31} = Q. \qquad (A10)$$

The following numerical parameters were used in the reported simulations. Several other sets of parameters were identified which are capable of generating the same qualitative results. $A = 2, B = 4, C = 2, D = 1.5, E = .4, F = 4, G = 4, H = 3, K = 10, L = 3, M = 10, N = .05, P = 1.25, Q = 10; \alpha_1 = .5, \beta_1 = 2, \alpha_2 = .2, \beta_2 = 2, \alpha_3 = .5, \beta_3 = 2, \alpha_4 = .25, \beta_4 = 2, \alpha_5 = .05, \beta_5 = 1, \alpha_6 = .5, \beta_6 = 1.5.$

REFERENCES

Alkon, D.L., Associative training of *Hermissenda*. *The Journal of General Physiology*, 1974, **64**, 70–84.

Alkon, D.L., Neural modification by paired sensory stimuli. *The Journal of General Physiology*, 1976, **68**, 341–358.

Alkon, D.L., Voltage-dependent calcium and potassium ion conductances: A contingency mechanism for an associative learning model. *Science*, 1979, **205**, 810–816.

Alkon, D.L., Cellular analysis of a gastropod *(Hermissenda Crassicornis)* model of associative learning. *The Biological Bulletin*, 1980, **159**, 505–560.

Alkon, D.L., Calcium-mediated reduction of ionic currents: A biophysical memory trace. *Science*, 1984, **226**, 1037–1045 (a).

Alkon, D.L., Changes of membrane currents during learning. *Journal of Experimental Biology*, 1984, **112**, 95–112 (b).

Alkon, D.L., Persistent calcium-mediated changes of identified membrane currents as a cause of associative learning. In D.L. Alkon and J. Farley (Eds.), **Primary neural substrates of learning and behavioral change**. Cambridge, England: Cambridge University Press, 1984 (c).

Amari, S., Competitive and cooperative aspects in dnamics of neural excitation and self-organization. In S. Amari and M.A. Arbib (Eds.), **Competition and cooperation in neural networks**. New York: Springer-Verlag, 1982.

Amari, S. and Takeuchi, A., Mathematical theory on formation of category detecting nerve cells. *Biological Cybernetics*, 1978, **29**, 127–136.

Banquet, J.-P. and Grossberg, S., Probing cognitive processes through the structure of event-related potentials during learning: An experimental and theoretical analysis. *Applied Optics*, in press, 1987.

Barto, A.G. and Sutton, R.S., Simulation of anticipatory responses in classical conditioning by a neuron-like adaptive element. *Behavioral Brain Research*, 1982, **4**, 221–235.

Barto, A.G., Sutton, R.S., and Anderson, C.W., Neuron-like adaptive elements that can solve difficult learning control problems. *IEEE Transactions*, 1983, **SMC-13**, 834–846.

Bitterman, M.E., The CS-US interval in classical and avoidance conditioning. In W.F. Prokasy (Ed.), **Classical conditioning: A symposium**. New York: Appleton-Century-Crofts, 1965, pp.1–19.

Blazis, D.E.J., Desmond, J., Moore, J.W., and Berthier, N.E., Simulation of the classically conditioned nictitating membrane response by a neuron-like adaptive element: A real-time variant of the Sutton-Barto model. In **Proceedings of the eighth annual conference of the Cognitive Science Society**. Hillsdale, NJ: Erlbaum, 1986, 176–186.

Bower, G.H., Mood and memory. *American Psychologist*, 1981, **36**, 129–148.

Bower, G.H., Gilligan, S.G., and Monteiro, K.P., Selectivity of learning caused by adaptive states. *Journal of Experimental Psychology: General*, 1981, **110**, 451–473.

Burke, W., Neuronal models for conditioned reflexes. *Nature*, 1966, **210**, 269–271.

Carpenter, G.A. and Grossberg, S., A massively parallel architecture for a self-organizing neural pattern recognition machine. *Computer Vision, Graphics, and Image Processing*, 1987, **37**, 54–115 (a).

Carpenter, G.A. and Grossberg, S., ART 2: Self-organization of stable recognition categories for analog input patterns. *Applied Optics*, in press, 1987 (b).

Cohen, M.A. and Grossberg, S., Neural dynamics of speech and language coding: Developmental programs, perceptual grouping, and competition for short term memory. *Human Neurobiology*, 1986, **5**, 1–22.

Cohen, M.A. and Grossberg, S., Masking fields: A massively parallel architecture for learning, recognizing, and predicting multiple groupings of patterned data. *Applied Optics*, 1987, **26**, 1866–1881.

Ellias, S.A. and Grossberg, S., Pattern formation, contrast control, and oscillations in the short term memory of shunting on-center off-surround networks. *Biological Cybernetics*, 1975, **20**, 69–98.

Farley, J. and Alkon, D.L., Associative neural and behavioral change in *Hermissenda*: Consequences of nervous system orientation for light and pairing specificity. *Journal of Neurophysiology*, 1982, **48**, 785–807.

Frey, P.W. and Sears, R.J., Model of conditioning incorporating the Rescorla-Wagner associative axiom, a dynamic attention rule and a catastrophe rule. *Psychological Review*, 1978, **85**, 321–340.

Grossberg, S., Some physiological and biochemical consequences of psychological postulates. *Proceedings of the National Academy of Sciences*, 1968, **60**, 758–765.

Grossberg, S., On the production and release of chemical transmitters and related topics in cellular control. *Journal of Theoretical Biology*, 1969, **22**, 325–364 (a).

Grossberg, S., On learning and energy-entropy dependence in recurrent and nonrecurrent signed networks. *Journal of Statistical Physics*, 1969, **1**, 319–350 (b).

Grossberg, S., Some networks that can learn, remember, and reproduce any number of complicated space-time patterns, II. *Studies in Applied Mathematics*, 1970, **49**, 135–166.

Grossberg, S., On the dynamics of operant conditioning. *Journal of Theoretical Biology*, 1971, **33**, 225–255.

Grossberg, S., A neural theory of punishment and avoidance, II. Quantitative theory. *Mathematical Biosciences*, 1972, **15**, 253–285.

Grossberg, S., Contour enhancement, short-term memory, and constancies in reverberating neural networks. *Studies in Applied Mathematics*, 1973, **52**, 217–257.

Grossberg, S., Classical and instrumental learning by neural networks. In R. Rosen and F. Snell (Eds.), **Progress in theoretical biology, Vol. 3**. New York: Academic Press, 1974.

Grossberg, S., A neural model of attention, reinforcement, and discrimination learning. *International Review of Neurobiology*, 1975, **18**, 263–327.

Grossberg, S., Adaptive pattern classification and universal recoding, I: Parallel development and coding of neural feature detectors. *Biological Cybernetics*, 1976, **23**, 121–134.

Grossberg, S., How does a brain build a cognitive code? *Psychological Review*, 1980, **87**, 1–51.

Grossberg, S., A psychophysiological theory of reinforcement drive, motivation, and attention. *Journal of Theoretical Neurobiology*, 1982, **1**, 286–369 (a).

Grossberg, S., Processing of expected and unexpected events during conditioning and attention: A psychophysiological theory. *Psychological Review*, 1982, **89**, 529–572 (b).

Grossberg, S., Studies of mind and brain: Neural principles of learning, perception, development, cognition, and motor control. Boston: Reidel Press, 1982 (c).

Grossberg, S., Neuroethology and theoretical neurobiology. *The Behavioral and Brain Sciences*, 1984, **7**, 388–390 (a).

Grossberg, S., Some psychophysiological and pharmacological correlates of a developmental, cognitive, and motivational theory. In R. Karrer, J. Cohen, and P. Tueting (Eds.), **Brain and information: Event related potentials.** New York: New York Academy of Sciences, 1984 (b).

Grossberg, S., Some normal and abnormal behavioral syndromes due to transmitter gating of opponent processes. *Biological Psychiatry*, 1984, **19**, 1075–1118 (c).

Grossberg, S. (Ed.), **The adaptive brain, I: Cognition, learning, reinforcement, and rhythm.** Amsterdam: Elsevier/North-Holland, 1987.

Grossberg, S. and Kuperstein, M., **Neural dynamics of adaptive sensory-motor control: Ballistic eye movements.** Amsterdam: Elsevier/North-Holland, 1986.

Grossberg, S. and Levine, D.S., Some developmental and attentional biases in the contrast enhancement and short term memory of recurrent neural networks. *Journal of Theoretical Biology*, 1975, **53**, 341–380.

Grossberg, S. and Schmajuk, N.A., Neural dynamics of attentionally-modulated Pavlovian conditioning: Conditioned reinforcement, inhibition, and opponent processing. *Psychobiology*, 1987, **15**, 195–240.

Grossberg, S. and Stone, G.O., Neural dynamics of word recognition and recall: Attentional priming, learning, and resonance. *Psychological Review*, 1986, **93**, 46–74.

Hawkins, R.D. and Kandel, E.R., Is there a cell-biological alphabet for simple forms of learning? *Psychological Review*, 1984, **91**, 375–391.

Hawkins, R.D., Abrams, T.W., Carew, T.J., and Kandel, E.R., A cellular mechanism of classical conditioning in *Aplysia*: Activity-dependent amplification of presynaptic facilitation. *Science*, 1983, **219**, 400–405.

Hebb, D.O., **The organization of behavior.** New York: Wiley, 1949.

Kamin, L.J., "Attention-like" processes in classical conditioning. In M.R. Jones (Ed.), **Miami symposium on the prediction of behavior: Aversive stimulation.** Miami: University of Miami, 1968.

Kamin, L.J., Predictability, surprise, attention, and conditioning. In B.A. Campbell and R.M. Church (Eds.), **Punishment and aversive behavior.** New York: Appleton-Century-Crofts, 1969.

Kelso, S.R. and Brown, T.H., Differential conditioning of associative synaptic enhancement in hippocampal brain slices. *Science*, 1986, **232**, 85–87.

Klopf, A.H., **The hedonistic neuron.** Washington, DC: Hemisphere, 1982.

Kohonen, T., A simple paradigm for the self-organized formation of structured feature maps. In S. Amari and M.A. Arbib (Eds.), **Competition and cooperation in neural networks.** New York: Springer Verlag, 1982.

Kohonen, T., Representation of information in spatial maps which are produced by self-organization. In E. Basar, H. Flohr, H. Haken, and A.J. Mandell (Eds.), **Synergetics of the brain.** New York: Springer-Verlag, 1983.

Levine, D.S., Neural population modeling and psychology: A review. *Mathematical Biosciences*, 1983, **66**, 1–86.

Levy, W.B., Associative changes at the synapse: LTP in the hippocampus. In W.B. Levy, J. Anderson, and S. Lehmkuhle (Eds.), **Synaptic modification, neuron selectivity and nervous system organization**. Hillsdale, NJ: Erlbaum, 1985, pp. 5–33.

Levy, W.B., Brassel, S.E., and Moore, S.D., Partial quantification of the associative synaptic learning rule of the dentate gyrus. *Neuroscience*, 1983, **8**, 799–808.

Levy, W.B. and Desmond, N.L., The rules of elemental synaptic plasticity. In W.B. Levy, J. Anderson, and S. Lehmkuhle (Eds.), **Synaptic modification, neuron selectivity and nervous system organization**. Hillsdale, NJ: Erlbaum, 1985, pp. 105–121.

Mackintosh, N.J., **The psychology of animal learning**. London: Academic Press, 1974.

Mackintosh, N.J., A theory of attention: Variations in the associability of stimuli with reinforcement. *Psychological Reveiw*, 1975, **82**, 276–295.

Malsburg, C. von der, Self-organization of orientation sensitive cells in the striate cortex. *Kybernetik*, 1973, **14**, 85–100.

Ost, J.W.P. and Lauer, D.W., Some investigations of classical salivary conditioning in the dog. In W.R. Prokasy (Ed.), **Classical conditioning: A symposium**. New York: Appleton-Century-Crofts, 1965, pp. 192–207.

Pearce, J.M. and Hall, G., A model of Pavlovian learning: Variations in the effectiveness of conditioned but not unconditioned stimulus. *Psychological Review*, 1980, **87**, 532–552.

Rauschecker, J.P. and Singer, W., Changes in the circuitry of the kitten's visual cortex are gated by postsynaptic activity. *Nature*, 1979, **280**, 58–60.

Rescorla, R.A. and Wagner, A.R., A theory of Pavlovian conditioning: Variations in the effectiveness of reinforcement and nonreinforcement. In A.H. Black and W.F. Prokasy (Eds), **Classical conditioning, II: Current research and theory**. New York: Appleton-Century-Crofts, 1972.

Rumelhart, D.E. and Zipser, D., Feature discovery by competitive learning. *Cognitive Science*, 1985, **9**, 75–112.

Schneiderman, N. and Gormezano, I., Conditioning of the nictitating membrane response of the rabbit as a function of the CS-US interval. *Journal of Comparative and Physiological Psychology*, 1964, **57**, 188–195.

Singer, W., Neuronal activity as a shaping factor in the self-organization of neuron assemblies. In E. Basar, H. Flohr, H. Haken, and A.J. Mandell (Eds.), **Synergetics of the brain**. New York: Springer-Verlag, 1983.

Smith, M.C., Coleman, S.R., and Gormezano, I., Classical conditioning of the rabbit's nictitating membrane response at backward, simultaneous, and forward CS-US intervals. *Journal of Comparative and Physiological Psychology*, 1969, **69**, 226–231.

Staddon, J.E.R., **Adaptive behavior and learning**. Cambridge, England: Cambridge University Press, 1983.

Stent, G.S., A physiological mechanism for Hebb's postulate of learning. *Proceedings of the National Academy of Sciences*, 1973, **70**, 997–1001.

Stone, G.O., An analysis of the delta rule and the learning of statistical associations. In D. Rumelhart and J.L. McClelland (Eds.), **Parallel distributed processing.** Cambridge, MA: MIT Press, 1986, pp. 444–459.

Sutton, R.S. and Barto, A.G., Toward a modern theory of adaptive networks: Expectation and prediction. *Psychological Review*, 1981, **88**, 135–170.

Uttley, A.M., **Information transmission in the nervous system.** London: Academic Press, 1979.

Walters, E.T. and Byrne, J.H., Associative conditioning of single sensory neurons suggests a cellular mechanism for learning. *Science*, 1983, **219**, 405–408.

Woody, C.D., Buerger, A.A., Unger, R.A., and Levine, D.S., Modeling aspects of learning by altering biophysical properties of a simulated neuron. *Biological Cybernetics*, 1976, **23**, 73–82.

Psychobiology
1987, **15**, 195–240
©1987 Psychonomic Society, Inc.

NEURAL DYNAMICS OF ATTENTIONALLY MODULATED PAVLOVIAN CONDITIONING: CONDITIONED REINFORCEMENT, INHIBITION, AND OPPONENT PROCESSING

Stephen Grossberg† and Nestor A. Schmajuk‡

ABSTRACT

A real-time neural network model is developed to explain data about the acquisition and extinction of conditioned excitors and inhibitors. Systematic computer simulations are described of a READ circuit, which joins together a mechanism of associative learning with an opponent processing circuit, called a *recurrent gated dipole*. READ circuit properties clarify how positive and negative reinforcers are learned and extinguished during primary and secondary conditioning. Habituating chemical transmitters within a gated dipole determine an affective adaptation level, or context, against which later events are evaluated. Neutral CS's can become reinforcers by being associated either with direct activations or with antagonistic rebounds within a previously habituated dipole. Neural mechanisms are characterized whereby conditioning can be actively extinguished, and associative saturation prevented, by a process called *opponent extinction*, even if no passive memory decay occurs. Opponent extinction exploits a functional dissociation between read-in and read-out of associative memory, which may be achieved by locating the associative mechanism at dendritic spines. READ circuit mechanisms are joined to cognitive-emotional mechanisms for associative learning of conditioned reinforcers and of incentive motivation; and to cognitive, in particular adaptive resonance theory, mechanisms for activating and storing internal representations of sensory cues in a limited capacity short term memory (STM); for learning, matching, and mismatching sensory expectancies, leading to the enhancement or updating of STM; and for shifting the focus of attention towards sensory representations whose reinforcement history is consistent with momentary appetitive requirements. This total neural architecture is used to explain conditioning and extinction of a conditioned excitor; conditioning and non-extinction of a conditioned inhibitor; properties of conditioned inhibition as a "slave" process and as a "comparator" process, including effects of pretest deflation or inflation of the conditioning context, of familiar or novel training or test contexts, of weak or strong shocks, and of preconditioning US-alone exposures. The same mechanisms have elsewhere been used to explain phenomena such as blocking, unblocking, overshadowing, latent inhibition, superconditioning, inverted U in conditioning as a function of interstimulus interval, anticipatory conditioned responses, partial reinforcement acquisition effect, learned helplessness, and vicious-circle behavior. The theory clarifies why alternative models have been unable to explain an equally large data base.

† Supported in part by the Air Force Office of Scientific Research (AFOSR 85-0149 and AFOSR F49620-86-C-0037), the Army Research Office (ARO DAAG-29-85-K-0095), and the National Science Foundation (NSF IRI-84-17756).

‡ Supported in part by the National Science Foundation (NSF IRI-84-17756).

1. Introduction: The Analysis of Distributed Neural Architectures

A key problem in biological theories of intelligence concerns the manner in which external events interact with internal organismic requirements to focus attention upon motivationally desired goals. The present work further develops a theory that involves sensory-cognitive and cognitive-reinforcement circuits. The theory is applied to the explanation of data about the acquisition and extinction of classically conditioned excitors and inhibitors.

The neural architectures which are engaged during classical conditioning are distributed across several brain regions. Even the relatively simple architecture which controls the rabbit's nictitating membrane response includes such widely separated regions as cerebellum (McCormick and Thompson, 1984) and hippocampus (Berger and Thompson, 1978). In order to understand the workings of such a distributed neural architecture, one needs to simultaneously analyse both the whole and its parts, both the macroscopic and the microscopic description of the architecture. On the macroscopic level, one needs to understand the functional and computational relationships which clarify how the architecture controls a particular class of behaviors, and why it is composed of particular types of circuits. On the microscopic level, one needs to attain a detailed analytic understanding of how each circuit is designed, of how it works, and of what types of mechanistic variations can be expected to occur as evolutionary variations across species. These macroscopic functional analyses and microscopic mechanistic analyses are, moreover, not independent, because the behavioral properties controlled by a neural architecture are typically emergent properties that arise from interactions among its component circuits.

A thoroughly characterized neural architecture provides an explicit *real-time* description of how behaviorally observable stimuli influence the internal neural transformations which regulate behaviorally observable responses. Although a number of extremely useful phenomenological and formal conditioning models have been described during the past two decades, most of these models do not provide an explicit description of the real-time mechanisms that would be required to instantiate their concepts and equations. In particular, although the classical Rescorla and Wagner (1972) model is formulated in terms of difference equations whose variables change through time, these equations do not provide an explicit characterization of real-time mechanisms that might be able to instantiate the model's properties. Such an attempt at explication shows, moreover, that the Rescorla-Wagner model cannot be consistently embedded into an explicit real-time model (Grossberg, 1982a).

The demand for a real-time processing description has been shown to impose important design constraints upon the formulation of conditioning processes. The advantage of a real-time theory can be appreciated through examples of how such a theory has articulated the coordinated neural events that are triggered by unexpected changes in external environmental contingencies, notably by the unexpected nonoccurrence of a primary or conditioned reinforcer, or by unexpected changes in contingent or noncontingent probabilities of CS or US in a given experimental context.

At least two types of neural network macrocircuits are needed to provide a real-time explanation of a broad range of data about the acquisition and extinction of conditioned excitors and inhibitors.

Sensory-Cognitive Circuit

Sensory-cognitive interactions in the theory are carried out by an Adaptive Resonance Theory (ART) circuit (Carpenter and Grossberg, 1985, 1987; Grossberg, 1976b, 1987a).

The ART architecture suggests how internal representations of sensory events, including conditioned stimuli (CS) and unconditioned stimuli (US), can be learned in stable fashion (Figure 1). Among the mechanisms used for stable self-organization of sensory recognition codes are the top-down expectations which are matched against bottom-up sensory signals. When a mismatch occurs, an orienting arousal burst acts to reset the sensory representation of all cues that are currently being stored in STM. In particular, representations with high STM activation tend to become less active, representations with low STM activation tend to become more active, and the novel event wich caused the mismatch tends to be more actively stored than it would have been had it been expected.

Cognitive-Reinforcement Circuit

Cognitive-reinforcer interactions in the theory are carried out in the circuit described in Figure 2. In this circuit, there exist cell populations that are separate from sensory representations and related to particular drives and motivational variables (Grossberg, 1972a, 1987a). Repeated pairing of a CS sensory representation, S_{cs}, with activation of a drive representation, D, by a reinforcer causes the modifiable synapses connecting S_{cs} with D to become strengthened. Incentive motivational pathways from the drive representations to the sensory representations are also assumed to be conditionable. These conditioned $S \rightarrow D \rightarrow S$ feedback pathways shift the attentional focus to the set of previously reinforced, motivationally compatible cues (Figure 2). This shift of attention occurs because the sensory representations, which emit conditioned reinforcer signals and receive conditioned incentive motivation signals, compete among themselves for a limited capacity short-term memory (STM) via on-center off-surround interactions. When incentive motivational feedback signals are received at the sensory representational field, these signals can bias the competition for STM activity towards motivationally salient cues.

In order to explain the moment-by-moment dynamics of conditioning, an additional microcircuit needs to be embedded in the drive representations of the macrocircuit depicted in Figure 2. This microcircuit, called a *gated dipole* (Grossberg, 1972a, 1972b), instantiates a neurophysiological theory of opponent processing. The need for a certain type of opponent processing for conditioning circuits can be seen from the following considerations.

The Gated Dipole Opponent Process

In the cognitive-reinforcement circuit, CS's are conditioned to either the onset or the offset of a reinforcer. For example, a CS that is conditioned to the onset of a shock can become a source of conditioned fear (excitor). A CS that is conditioned to the offset of a shock can become a source of conditioned relief (inhibitor). A gated dipole opponent process explains how the offset of a reinforcer can generate an off-response, or antagonistic rebound, to which a simultaneous CS can be conditioned. A gated dipole is a minimal neural network opponent process which is capable of generating a sustained, but habituative, on-response (e.g., a fear reaction) to onset of a cue (e.g., a shock), as well as a transient off-response (e.g., a relief reaction), or antagonistic rebound, to offset of the cue.

The READ Circuit: A Synthesis of Opponent Processing and Associative Learning Mechanisms

A specialized gated dipole circuit is needed to explain phenomena such as secondary inhibitory conditioning. Secondary inhibitory conditioning consists of two phases. In phase one, CS_1 becomes an excitatory conditioned reinforcer (e.g., source of conditioned fear) by being paired with a US (e.g., a shock). In phase two, the offset of CS_1 can generate an off-response which can condition a subsequent CS_2 to become an inhibitory conditioned reinforcer (e.g., source of conditioned relief). In order to explain secondary inhibitory

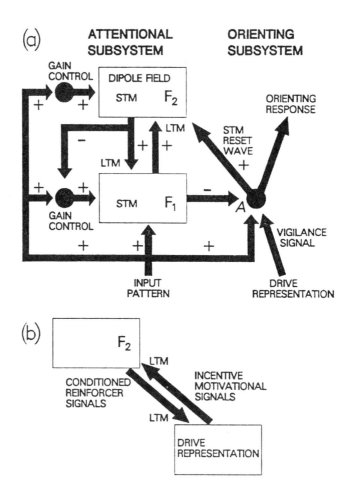

Figure 1. Anatomy of an adaptive resonance theory (ART) circuit: (a) Interactions between the attentional and orienting subsystems: Code learning takes place at the long term memory (LTM) traces within the bottom-up and top-down pathways between levels F_1 and F_2. The top-down pathways can read-out learned expectations, or templates, that are matched against bottom-up input patterns at F_1. Mismatches activate the orienting subsystem A, thereby resetting short term memory (STM) at F_2 and initiating search for another recognition code. Subsystem A can also activate an orienting response. Sensitivity to mismatch at F_1 is modulated by vigilance signals from drive representations. (b) Trainable pathways exist between level F_2 and the drive representations. Learning from F_2 to a drive representation endows a recognition category with conditioned reinforcer properties. Learning from a drive representation to F_2 associates the drive representation with a set of motivationally compatible categories. (Reprinted with permission from Carpenter and Grossberg, 1987c.)

conditioning, a gated dipole circuit must also contain internal feedback pathways, i.e., it should be recurrent. In addition, such a recurrent gated dipole must be joined to a mechanism of associative learning, whereby CS's may become conditioned excitors or inhibitors. A circuit design that realizes all these properties is called a READ circuit, as a mnemonic for REcurrent Associative gated Dipole (Figure 3).

The design of the READ circuit clarifies many properties of conditioning data; for

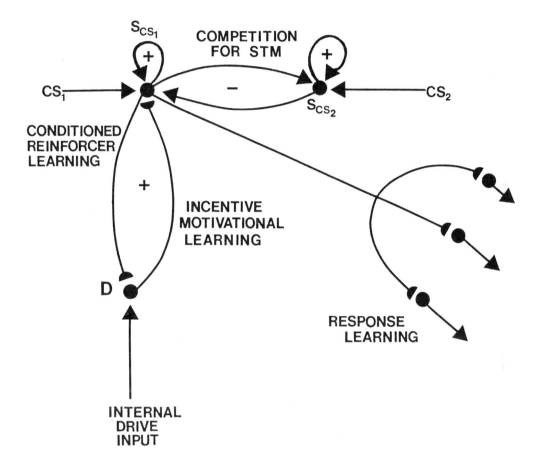

Figure 2. Schematic conditioning circuit: Conditioned stimuli (CS_i) activate sensory representations (S_{CS_i}) which compete among themselves for limited capacity short term memory activation and storage. The activated S_{CS_i} elicit conditionable signals to drive representations and motor command representations. Learning from a S_{CS_i} to a drive representation D is called conditioned reinforcer learning. Learning from D to a S_{CS_i} is called incentive motivational learning. Signals from D to S_{CS_i} are elicited when the combination of external sensory plus internal drive inputs is sufficiently large. In the simulations reported herein, the drive level is assumed to be large and constant.

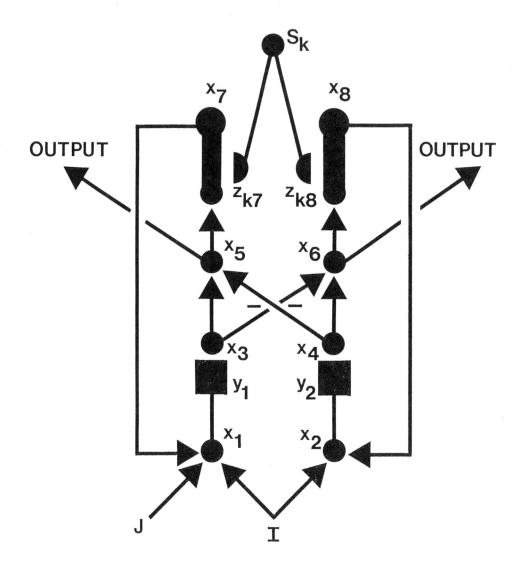

Figure 3. A READ I circuit: This circuit joins together a recurrent gated dipole with an associative learning mechanism. Learning is driven by signals S_k from sensory representations S_k which activate long term memory (LTM) traces z_{k7} and z_{k8} that sample activation levels at the on-channel and off-channel, respectively, of the gate dipole. See text for details.

example, how the extinction of conditioned excitors and the non-extinction of conditioned inhibitors may be explained by a single neural circuit (Part II). Our analysis links these data properties to the functional property that opponent interactions may actively cause extinction even in cases wherein passive extinction does not occur. In the absence of passive extinction, an associative memory could easily saturate. Opponent extinction shows how saturation is prevented and active extinction obtained even if no passive memory decay occurs. These functional properties of opponent extinction can be achieved using a mechanistic property which dissociates the read-in and read-out of associative memory. Such a mechanistic property can, in turn, be realized by locating associative synapses on dendritic spines.

Thus, the present article describes two related types of results. Part I of the article provides a quantitative computational analysis of several variants of a READ circuit design that forms part of the total neural architecture for the control of classically and operantly conditionable behaviors that is schematized in Figures 1–3. Based upon the mathematical theory of classical conditioning and associative learning that was provided in Grossberg (1969a, 1969b, 1970), the development of this architecture began in Grossberg (1971). Since that time, the component circuits of the architecture have been progressively elaborated in a series of articles aimed at explaining and predicting an ever larger behavioral, psychophysiological, neurophysiological, anatomical, and neuropharmacological data base about conditioning and its control mechanisms. Key accomplishments of this theory during its first decade of existence are reviewed and further development provided in Grossberg (1982a, 1982b, 1984a). These recent articles are gathered together in Grossberg (1987a).

The READ circuit design which is analysed in Part I is one of several specialized gated dipole circuits that have been identified through the parametric analysis of behavioral and brain data. Specialized gated dipole circuits have also played a key role in helping to explain and predict a wide variety of other data bases (see Note 1). Thus a gated dipole circuit may at this time be said with some confidence to instantiate a basic principle of neural design.

Involvement of a gated dipole circuit can be inferred from behavioral data through its characteristic constellation, or bundle, of emergent properties. These include mutually dependent properties of habituation, antagonistic rebound, adaptation level processing, and an inverted U in sensitivity. The habituative, antagonistic rebound, and adaptation level properties play an important role in the applications described herein. Antagonistic rebound properties are particularly important for understanding how a real-time theory can fill conceptual gaps which are left by a merely formal theory. This is because antagonistic rebound reactions often occur subsequent to the offset of an external cue or subsequent to the nonoccurrence of an expected cue. Such antagonistic rebounds thus occur during time intervals when no experimentally controlled external cues are active. Only in a real-time theory can such reactions be explained without invoking *ad hoc* hypotheses. Indeed, the very existence, no less than the size, of an antagonistic rebound can depend upon a host of contextual and learning-dependent factors, whose properties can be conveniently analysed in a real-time theory but not a merely formal theory. Since such rebounds influence key observable properties of behavioral conditioning and extinction, formal theories are fundamentally limited in their ability to explain data in which the spatiotemporal organization of CS's and US's mixes together learnable direct reactions and antagonistic rebounds to these cues.

Part II of the article joins the results of Part I to the other real-time circuits of the neural architecture schematized in Figures 1 and 2 to explain conditioning data. These include mechanisms of activating and storing internal representations of sensory cues in a limited capacity working memory, or short term memory (STM); mechanisms for learning, matching, and mismatching of sensory expectancies, leading to the enhancement or updating of STM processing; and mechanisms for shifting the focus of attention towards sensory representations whose reinforcement history is consistent with momentary appetitive requirements. This total architecture is then used to qualitatively explain the important data concerning acquisition and extinction of conditioned excitation and inhibition, of Lysle and Fowler (1985) and Miller and Schachtman (1985), as well as the results of many other related studies. Along the way, the qualitative explanatory concepts of these authors are explicated, refined, and generalized, and related data about such phenomena as blocking are also analysed in a unified fashion.

PART I

2. Simulating the Mechanism of Conditioned Reinforcement

In Part I, computer simulations are used to characterize the behavior of a circuit in which a gated dipole is joined to a mechanism of Pavlovian conditioning. Multiple neural circuits are conditioned during a typical conditioning experiment. The conditioning events described in Part I constitute the type of learning whereby a conditioned stimulus, or CS, becomes a conditioned reinforcer by being paired with an unconditioned stimulus, or US. Both primary conditioning and secondary conditioning, as well as excitatory conditioning and inhibitory conditioning, are demonstrated.

In the simulations of primary excitatory conditioning, a conditioned stimulus (CS_1) precedes onset of an unconditioned stimulus (US), as in Figure 4a. As a result of conditioning, the CS_1 becomes a conditioned reinforcer with the same motivational sign as the US. In the simulations of secondary conditioning, another conditioned stimulus (CS_2) precedes a conditioned reinforcer (the conditioned CS_1 of a primary conditioning experiment), as in Figure 4b. As a result of conditioning, the CS_2 also becomes a conditioned reinforcer with the same motivational sign as the CS_1. In primary inhibitory conditioning, a CS_1 occurs subsequent to offset of a US, as in Figure 4c. As a result of conditioning, the CS_1 becomes a conditioned reinforcer with the *opposite* motivational sign than the US. In secondary inhibitory conditioning, a CS_2 occurs subsequent to offset of a conditioned reinforcer CS_1, as in Figure 4d. As a result of conditioning, the CS_2 becomes a conditioned reinforcer with the *opposite* motivational sign than the CS_1. In addition, we investigate how these several types of conditioned reinforcer learning can extinguish if the CS's are presented without reinforcement on subsequent trials.

Many variations of the temporal sequencing of the events CS_1, CS_2 and US can be better understood through an analysis of these four types of conditioning events. Sections 3–5 describe qualitatively the mechanisms which comprise a gated dipole opponent process and contrast them with the opponent process model of Solomon and Corbit (1974). Sections 6–16 mathematically describe the neural circuits which we have developed to carry out conditioned reinforcer learning. Sections 17 and 18 display real-time computer simulations of the several types of conditioned reinforcer learning. Then Sections 19–31 in Part II use these quantitative results as a basis for providing qualitative explanations of conditioning experiments in which conditioned reinforcer learning plays a part. The gated dipole mechanisms described herein characterize only one of several types of model circuits that comprise the total neural architecture which we use to explain these data about conditioning. Mechanisms of attention, expectation, orienting, sensory and cognitive chunking,

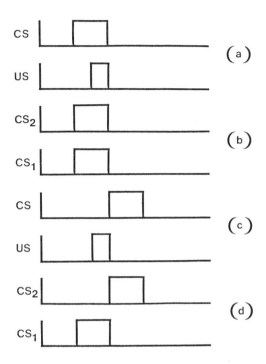

Figure 4. Some simulated combinations of conditioned stimulus (CS) and unconditioned stimulus (US) on individual trials: (a) primary excitatory conditioning; (b) secondary excitatory conditioning; (c) primary inhibitory conditioning; (d) secondary inhibitory conditioning. Because a READ circuit does not, in itself, cause blocking of simultaneously presented CS's, CS onset times in (b) were chosen synchronous. When blocking mechanisms are added, as in Part II, staggered CS_1–CS_2 onset times would be necessary.

motor learning, and sensory-motor planning are no less important than gated dipole mechanisms Mathematical analyses and extensive computer simulations of these other types of mechanisms have been reported elsewhere (Bullock and Grossberg, 1987; Carpenter and Grossberg, 1987a, 1987b; Cohen and Grossberg, 1986, 1987; Grossberg, 1987a; Grossberg and Kuperstein, 1986; Grossberg and Levine, 1987).

3. The READ Circuit: A Synthesis of Opponent Processing and Associative Learning Mechanisms

A gated dipole opponent process is a minimal neural network which is capable of generating a sustained, but habituative, on-response to onset of a cue, as well as a transient off-response, or antagonistic rebound, to offset of the cue (Figure 5). Properties of the on-response are used to explain excitatory conditioning, whereas properties of the off-response are used to explain inhibitory conditioning.

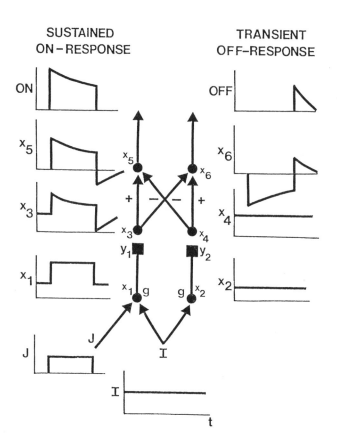

Figure 5. Example of a feedforward gated dipole: A sustained habituating on-response (top left) and a transient off-rebound (top right) are elicited in response to onset and offset, respectively, of a phasic input J (bottom left) when tonic arousal I (bottom center) and opponent processing (diagonal pathways) supplement the slow gating actions (square synapses). See text for details.

In order to explain secondary conditioning, a gated dipole circuit must also contain internal feedback pathways (Grossberg, 1972b, 1982b). Then a single CS_1 can engage in two types of events: The CS_1 can learn to become an excitatory conditioned reinforcer by being paired with a subsequent US. After conditioning occurs, offset of CS_1 can generate an antagonistic rebound which can condition a subsequent CS_2 to become an inhibitory secondary reinforcer. When a neural network contains internal feedback pathways, it is said to be *recurrent*.

In order to explain these several types of conditioned reinforcer learning, such a recurrent gated dipole must be joined to a mechanism of associative learning. Thus the total circuit which we have analysed is called a READ circuit, as a mnemonic for REcurrent Associative gated Dipole.

A number of design constraints must be simultaneously satisfied by a READ circuit. The opponent processing laws and the associative learning laws must fit together in such a way that *all* the desired properties of conditioned reinforcer learning obtain with a *single* choice of parameters. Moreover, the range of parameters for which this is true must be robust. A READ circuit contains processes which fluctuate on three different time scales—a fast activation time scale, a slower habituation time scale, and a yet slower conditioning time scale. As noted above, these processes are linked together by nonlinear feedback interactions, due to the recurrent anatomy of the circuit. The design of nonlinear feedback circuits which possess three distinct time scales is a difficult task in any scientific discipline. That a READ circuit forms only one of the several circuits that are engaged during conditioning, and that all of these circuits interact via nonlinear feedback signals, highlights the difficulty of building a rigorous real-time conditioning theory. On the other hand, many additional design constraints become evident when one actually attempts to build such a theory. The simultaneous satisfaction of these stringent design requirements have led us to some neurophysiologically testable predictions about how associative learning is regulated by gated dipole opponent processing.

4. Qualitative Properties of a Gated Dipole

Four main ingredients go into the design of a gated dipole: slowly habituating and recovering chemical transmitters; opponent, or competitive, interactions between an on-channel and an off-channel; phasic inputs, such as a CS or US, which perturb the on-channel or the off-channel through time; and a sustained, or tonic, arousal input which equally perturbs both channels, thereby setting the sensitivity of dipole outputs to phasic input fluctuations, and providing the energy to generate an antagonistic rebound in response to offset of an input.

Figure 5 describes the simplest type of feedforward, or nonrecurrent, gated dipole. Figure 5 also schematizes how a gated dipole can generate a sustained, but habituative, on-response to input onset, and a transient off-response, or antagonistic rebound, to input offset. These reactions can be qualitatively explained as follows. (See Grossberg (1972b, 1984b, 1987a) for quantitative mathematical analyses.)

A. Transmitter Gating: Signals in both the on-channel and the off-channel are multiplied, or *gated*, by a chemical transmitter (square synapses) before the gated signals are further transformed by opponent processing. Each transmitter $y(t)$ multiplies its input signal $S(t)$ to form such a gated output signal $T(t)$; viz,

$$T = Sy. \tag{1}$$

B. Slow Transmitter Habituation and Recovery: The transmitter y habituates and recovers according to the law (Grossberg, 1968, 1972b):

$$\frac{d}{dt}y = B(1-y) - CSy \tag{2}$$

where B and C are positive constants. In (2), the notation $\frac{d}{dt}y$ denotes the net rate of change of y. Term $B(1-y)$ says that transmitter y recovers at a rate B until it reaches the target level 1. Term $-CSy$ says that transmitter y habituates at a rate proportional to its gating action in (1).

Many refinements of the laws (1)–(2) have been described, including equations for transmitter mobilization, post-tetanic potentiation, enzymatic activation, and autoreceptive competition (Carpenter and Grossberg, 1981; Grossberg, 1969c, 1987a, 1987b). These refinements, albeit important for some purposes, do not play a major role in explaining qualitative properties of conditioned reinforcer learning.

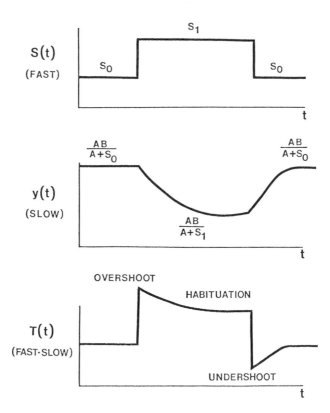

Figure 6. Reaction of output signal T and transmitter gate y to changes in input S: The output T is the product of a fast process S and a slow process y. Overshoots and undershoots in T are caused by y's slow habituation to fast changes in S.

C. Overshoot and Undershoot: A critical property for explaining conditioned reinforcer data is that the input signal S can fluctuate more quickly than the transmitter y can react. This property leads to an overshoot in the output T in response to onset of the input S and an undershoot in T in response to offset of S (Figure 6). To see how this happens, note that in response to a constant input of size S, (2) implies that the transmitter y approaches the equilibrium value

$$y = \frac{B}{B + CS}.\tag{3}$$

In other words, larger signals S cause more transmitter habituation. On the other hand, the output signal that is generated by an input S does not equal y. The output signal is equal to $T = Sy$, due to (1).

Figure 6 describes how the output T reacts to changes in the size of the input S. A rapid increase in S from S_0 to S_1 elicits a slow decrease in y, due to (3). Multiplication of the graphs of $S(t)$ and $y(t)$ shows that a rapid increase in S generates a rapid increase in T followed by a slow decrease, or habituation, of T to an intermediate level. In a similar way, a rapid decrease in S from S_1 to S_0 generates a rapid decrease in T followed by a slow increase, or habituation, to an intermediate level. In all, rapid increases and decreases in the input S generate overshoots and undershoots in the output T due to the slow rate of reaction, or habituation, of the transmitter. These habituative reactions are fundamental to many basic properties of gated dipoles and, by extension, of conditioned reinforcer learning.

D. Tonically Aroused Transmitter Gates in Opponent Processes: We can now explain the properties depicted in Figure 5. In such an opponent process, a phasic input (J) can elicit a sustained on-response, whereas offset of the input can elicit a transient off-rebound, or temporal contrast effect. These properties are explained as follows.

The left-hand series of stages in Figure 5 represents the on-channel, and the right-hand series of stages represents the off-channel. Both channels receive an equal arousal input, denoted by I, that is constant through time. The arousal input provides the tonic internal activity which triggers the antagonistic rebound that occurs after the on-input shuts off. The on-input, denoted by J, is delivered only to the on-channel. Input J is switched from zero to a positive level and held at that level long enough for transmitter habituation to occur. Then J is shut off.

Inputs I and J are added by the activity (or potential) $x_1(t)$. Activity $x_1(t)$ responds quickly to input fluctuations, relative to the reaction rate of the network's slow transmitter gates. The graph of $x_1(t)$ has the same form as the top graph in Figure 6: a rapid switch from a lower positive activity to a higher positive activity, followed by a rapid return to the lower level. The activity $x_1(t)$ generates an output signal $g(x_1(t))$ in its pathway that again has the form of a double-switch between two positive values. The output signal $g(x_1(t))$ is gated by a slow transmitter $y_1(t)$ that accumulates and habituates within the square synapse in the on-channel. Figure 6 describes the effect of this slow gate on the input to the next stage. Consequently, activity $x_3(t)$ follows an overshoot-habituation-undershoot-habituation sequence through time. Then $x_3(t)$ relays an output signal of the same form to $x_5(t)$. Activity $x_5(t)$ also receives an inhibitory signal from $x_4(t)$. To determine what happens next, we consider the dynamics of the off-channel.

The off-channel receives only the constant tonic input I. Hence $x_2(t)$ and the slow gate $y_2(t)$ in the off-channel square synapses are constant through time. The activity $x_4(t)$ is therefore also constant through time. For definiteness, we make the simplest assumption that corresponding stages in the on-channel and the off-channel possess the same parameters. Since the arousal input I to both channels is also equal, the size of x_4 equals the baseline activity level of $x_3(t)$. This is not always true, but its violation is easy to analyse after the symmetric case is understood (Grossberg, 1984a).

We can now determine the reactions of activity $x_5(t)$ through time. Since the signals from $x_3(t)$ and $x_4(t)$ subtract before perturbing $x_5(t)$, and their baseline activities are the same, the baseline activity of $x_5(t)$ equals zero. Activity $x_5(t)$ thus overshoots and undershoots a zero baseline when the input J is turned on and off. By contrast, activity $x_6(t)$ responds in an opposite way from $x_5(t)$ because x_3 excites x_5 and inhibits x_6, whereas x_4 inhibits x_5 and excites x_6.

The final assumption is that the output signals caused by activities $x_5(t)$ and $x_6(t)$ are rectified: outputs are generated only if these activities exceed a nonnegative threshold. As a result, the on-channel generates a sustained output signal while the input J is on. This output signal habituates as the gate $y_1(t)$ slowly equilibrates to the input. By contrast, the off-channel generates a transient off-response, or antagonistic rebound, after the input J shuts off.

5. Comparison with the Solomon and Corbit Opponent Process Model

The antagonistic rebound in the off-channel of a gated dipole is energized by an undershoot of the dipole's on-activity function x_3 (Figure 5). In a gated dipole, such an undershoot is due to habituation of the transmitter gate within the on-channel. Overshoots and undershoots have also been hypothesized to exist in alternative models of opponent processing, but the properties have not been traced to the action of a slowly habituating transmitter gate. For example, Solomon and Corbit (1974) and Solomon (1980, 1982) describe a model of opponent processing in which overshoots and undershoots occur. These authors ascribe the overshoots and undershoots to the subtraction of two opponent processes that both evolve according to similar time scales (Figure 7). Neither process, in itself, undergoes an overshoot or an undershoot. Instead, overshoots and undershoots are derived from the assumption that the off-process begins to build up only after the on-process is initiated. The model assumes, in addition, that "the second component, the b process, is aroused via the arousal of a" (Solomon and Corbit, 1974, p.126). Neither assumption is made in a gated dipole opponent process, wherein the slow habituation of the transmitter gate within the on-channel generates an overshoot and an undershoot within that channel. Consequently, in a gated dipole, opponent processing *per se* between the on-channel and the off-channel generates the antagonistic rebound within the off-channel without necessitating the hypothesis that on-channel activation triggers a delayed off-channel activation.

Solomon and Corbit's (1974) opponent process is not defined by a dynamical model, such as the gated dipole architecture. Thus the Solomon and Corbit model does not explain why the maximum size of the a process should sometimes, but not always, exceed the maximum size of the b process, or why the b process is delayed in time relative to the a process by just the right amount to produce an overshoot and an undershoot. The hypothesis that slowly habituating, tonically aroused, transmitter gates exist in an opponent anatomy provides simple answers to all of these questions, and implies other properties which enable the gated dipole model to explain data about conditioned reinforcer learning.

6. Laws for a READ Circuit

Dynamical equations for a READ circuit are described and explained in this section. Our analysis has revealed that several variations on the same basic network design have the properties that we desire. Which variation may exist in particular species is testable by neurophysiological and anatomical techniques. The simplest network variation is depicted in Figure 3. This circuit will be defined first. Then the functional significance of its equations will be explained. After that, the equations corresponding to the other circuits will be explained.

As in the nonrecurrent gated dipole described in Section 4, the variables x_i describe cell potentials, or activations, and the variables y_i describe slowly habituating transmitter gates. In addition, the variables z_{kl} describe long-term memory (LTM) traces, or associative weights, that exist at the ends of the pathways from the sensory representations of CS and US cues to the on-channel and the off-channel of the gated dipole. The equations for the READ I circuit are as follows:

READ I EQUATIONS

Arousal + US + Feedback On-Activation

$$\frac{d}{dt}x_1 = -Ax_1 + I + J + f(x_7) \tag{4}$$

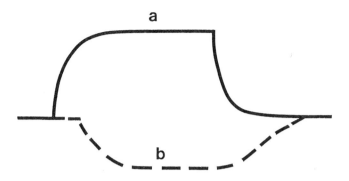

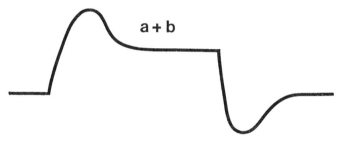

Figure 7. In the opponent process model of Solomon (1982), overshoots and undershoots are caused by an excitatory process (a) and an inhibitory process (b) that both change at a similar rate such that (b) lags behind (a) and neither (a) nor (b) separately exhibits overshoots or undershoots.

Arousal + Feedback Off-Activation

$$\frac{d}{dt}x_2 = -Ax_2 + I + f(x_8) \tag{5}$$

On-Transmitter

$$\frac{d}{dt}y_1 = B(1 - y_1) - Cg(x_1)y_1 \tag{6}$$

Off-Transmitter

$$\frac{d}{dt}y_2 = B(1 - y_2) - Cg(x_2)y_2 \tag{7}$$

Gated On-Activation

$$\frac{d}{dt}x_3 = -Ax_3 + Dg(x_1)y_1 \tag{8}$$

Gated Off-Activation

$$\frac{d}{dt}x_4 = -Ax_4 + Dg(x_2)y_2 \tag{9}$$

Normalized Opponent On-Activation

$$\frac{d}{dt}x_5 = -Ax_5 + (E - x_5)x_3 - (x_5 + F)x_4 \qquad (10)$$

Normalized Opponent Off-Activation

$$\frac{d}{dt}x_6 = -Ax_6 + (E - x_6)x_4 - (x_6 + F)x_3 \qquad (11)$$

On-Activation by CS Inputs

$$\frac{d}{dt}x_7 = -Ax_7 + G[x_5]^+ + L\sum_k S_k z_{k7}, \qquad (12)$$

where $[w]^+ = \max(w, 0)$.

Off-Activation by CS Inputs

$$\frac{d}{dt}x_8 = -Ax_8 + G[x_6]^+ + H\sum_k S_k z_{k8} \qquad (13)$$

On-Conditioned Reinforcer Learning

$$\frac{d}{dt}z_{k7} = S_k(-Kz_{k7} + L[x_5]^+) \qquad (14)$$

Off-Conditioned Reinforcer Learning

$$\frac{d}{dt}z_{k8} = S_k(-Kz_{k8} + L[x_6]^+) \qquad (15)$$

On-Output Signal
$$O_1 = [x_5]^+ \qquad (16)$$

Off-Output Signal
$$O_2 = [x_6]^+ \qquad (17)$$

7. Tonic Arousal, Phasic US Input, and Feedback Signaling

In equations (4) and (5), term I denotes the tonically active arousal level which sets the baseline sensitivity of the READ circuit and energizes its antagonistic rebounds. Term J in equation (4) denotes the US input. This US input corresponds to a primary US, not to a conditioned reinforcer which acquires US properties through conditioning.

Term $f(x_7)$ in equation (4) describe the nonnegative signal which converts the on-channel into a positive feedback loop. In a similar fashion, term $f(x_8)$ in equation (5) describes the nonnegative signal which converts the off-channel into a positive feedback loop. Terms $-Ax_1$ and $-Ax_2$ in equations (4) and (5), respectively, describe the passive decay terms whereby the potentials x_1 and x_2 return to the equilibrium value 0. The equations governing all the potentials x_i contain such passive decay terms $-Ax_i$. For simplicity, the same parameter A was chosen in all of these equations.

8. Gating Fast Signals with Slowly Habituating Transmitters

Equations (6) and (7) describe the dynamics of the habituating transmitters y_1 and y_2 in the on-channel and the off-channel, respectively. These equations are the same as equation (2). In (6), the nonnegative input signal $S = g(x_1)$, whereas in (7), the nonnegative input signal $S = g(x_2)$.

Equation (8) describes the effect of the gated on-channel signal $Dg(x_1)y_1$ on the next on-potential x_3. Potential x_3 averages these gated signals through time at rate $-A$. In a similar fashion, equation (9) describes the effect of the gated off-channel signal $Dg(x_2)y_2$ on the next off-potential x_4.

9. Normalized Opponent Interactions

Equations (10) and (11) describe the effects of opponent, or competitive, signals from x_3 and x_4 on the next on-potential x_5 and off-potential x_6. Equation (10) is a membrane, or shunting, equation of the form

$$C\frac{dV}{dt} = (V^p - V)g^p + (V^+ - V)g^+ + (V^- - V)g^-, \tag{18}$$

where C is a capacitance (scaled to equal 1 for convenience); V^p, V^+, and V^- are saturation potentials; g^p, g^+, and g^- are conductances; and V is a variable potential. See the books Grossberg (1982c, 1987a, 1987b) and Grossberg and Kuperstein (1986) for many applications of this equation. The additive equations (4), (5), (7), and (8) may be interpreted as approximations to (18) whose inputs are not large enough to drive their potentials close to their saturation potentials V^+ and V^-.

The crucial properties of a shunting equation can be appreciated by studying its equilibrium values. At equilibrium, $\frac{d}{dt}x_5 = 0$. Then (10) implies

$$x_5 = \frac{(E + F)(x_3 + x_4)}{A + x_3 + x_4}\left[\frac{x_3}{x_3 + x_4} - \frac{F}{E + F}\right] \tag{19}$$

(Grossberg, 1970, 1976b, 1983). In (19), if $x_3 + x_4 \gg A$, then term $(E + F)(x_3 + x_4)(A + x_3 + x_4)^{-1}$ is approximately constant. Then (19) implies that x_5 is sensitive to the *ratio* $x_3(x_3+x_4)^{-1}$ relative to the *adaptation level* $F(E+F)^{-1}$. Thus equation (10) automatically regulates the overall operating range of the circuit. In addition, $x_5 > 0$ in (19) only if

$$\frac{x_3}{x_3 + x_4} > \frac{F}{E + F}. \tag{20}$$

Since the output signal due to x_5 is $[x_5]^+$ in equations (12), (14), and (16), all subsequent processing by the on-channel is controlled by whether or not the *relative* size of x_3 to x_4 enables ratio $x_3(x_3 + x_4)^{-1}$ to exceed the constant adaptation level $F(E + F)^{-1}$. Thus equation (10) evaluates whether the total balance of all factors influencing the network favors the on-channel over the off-channel enough to cause inequality (20) to hold.

In the circuit depicted in Figure 3, we chose $E = F$ in equation (10). Then (19) may be more simply written as

$$x_5 = \frac{E(x_3 - x_4)}{A + x_3 + x_4}. \tag{21}$$

In this special case, $x_5 > 0$ only if $x_3 > x_4$. Thus $[x_5]^+ > 0$ only if the balance of all network factors favors the on-channel over the off-channel. In addition, the denominator

$A + x_3 + x_4$ in (21) assures that x_5, and likewise x_6, computes a ratio scale, in addition to an opponent scale, from x_3 and x_4.

Equation (11) for x_6 is the same as equation (10) for x_5 with the opponent input terms x_3 and x_4 reversed. Thus at equilibrium, when $E = F$ in (11),

$$x_6 = \frac{E(x_4 - x_3)}{A + x_3 + x_4}. \tag{22}$$

By (21) and (22),

$$\mathrm{sgn}(x_5) = -\mathrm{sgn}(x_6) \tag{23}$$

where

$$\mathrm{sgn}(w) = \begin{cases} +1 & \text{if } w > 0 \\ 0 & \text{if } w = 0 \\ -1 & \text{if } w < 0. \end{cases} \tag{24}$$

In summary, if $E = F$, then x_5 and x_6 compute a *normalized opponent process*.

10. Positive and Negative Conditioned Reinforcer Inputs: Total Context versus Individual Cue

Equation (12) registers the normalized opponent signal $[x_5]^+$ from the on-channel, as well as a sum $L \sum_k S_k z_{k7}$ of signals due to all CS's and conditioned US's. Term S_k is the output signal from the kth sensory representation. This signal is multiplied, or gated, by the LTM trace z_{k7} at the end of the pathway from the kth sensory representation to the on-channel of the READ circuit. The sum $L \sum_k S_k z_{k7}$ is called the *total positive conditioned reinforcer signal*.

In a similar fashion, equation (13) registers the normalized opponent signal $[x_6]^+$ from the off-channel, as well as the *total negative conditioned reinforcer signal* $L \sum_k S_k z_{k8}$. Thus the output signal S_k from the kth sensory representation is gated by an LTM trace z_{k7} abutting the READ on-channel *and* an LTM trace z_{k8} abutting the READ off-channel. Due to the opponent organization of the READ circuit, the kth sensory representation is a positive conditioned reinforcer if

$$z_{k7} > z_{k8} \tag{25}$$

and a negative conditioned reinforcer if

$$z_{k7} < z_{k8}. \tag{26}$$

These inequalities determine the conditioned reinforcer properties of a single sensory event. In general, many active sensory events may simultaneously input to the READ circuit. Then the total behavioral environment behaves like a *positive conditioned reinforcer context* if

$$\sum_k S_k z_{k7} > \sum_k S_k z_{k8} \tag{27}$$

and like a *negative conditioned reinforcer context* if

$$\sum_k S_k z_{k7} < \sum_k S_k z_{k8} \tag{28}$$

(Grossberg, 1972a, 1972b). Clearly, a positive conditioned reinforcer context can obtain even if it contains active negative reinforcers, and vice versa.

11. Context-Dependent Adaptation Level and Associative Averaging

The total positive and negative conditioned reinforcer signals interact within a gated dipole circuit to cause context-dependent, and hence learning-dependent, shifts in the circuit's *adaptation level* (Grossberg, 1972b, 1987a). The adaptation level is the baseline level of tonic activation that is maintained across both the on-channel and the off-channel of the circuit during a time interval which is long enough to modulate the circuit's habituation, rebound, or conditioning properties. Changes in the total configuration of conditioned reinforcing cues, including contextual cues, can dramatically alter READ circuit dynamics by changing its adaptation level. This fact will be critical in explaining the data summarized in Part II. The main factors that control the circuit's adaptation level are now summarized.

In the absence of any inputs to the gated dipole, both its on-channel and the off-channel become equally active; thus $x_1 = x_2, y_1 = y_2, x_3 = x_4, x_5 = x_6$, and $x_7 = x_8$. In the READ I circuit, the choice $E = F$ implies, in addition, that $x_5 = x_6 = 0$ by (21) and (22), and thus that $x_7 = x_8 = 0$, by (12) and (13). Consequently, in the no-input case, the adaptation level equals the tonic arousal level I that is defined by (4) and (5).

In contrast, when conditioned reinforcers are active, the terms $f(x_7)$ in (4) and $f(x_8)$ in (5) can cause an increase in the adaptation level. To understand this property more precisely, consider the following facts. The potentials x_7 and x_8 react quickly to their input signals. Hence during a time interval when the conditioned reinforcer signals S_k are maintained, x_7 and x_8 can achieve an approximate equilibrium with respect to these signals. Then $\frac{d}{dt}x_7 \cong 0$ and $\frac{d}{dt}x_8 \cong 0$ in (12) and (13), respectively, whence

$$x_7 \cong \frac{G}{A}[x_5]^+ + \frac{L}{A}\sum_k S_k z_{k7} \tag{29}$$

and

$$x_8 \cong \frac{G}{A}[x_6]^+ + \frac{L}{A}\sum_k S_k z_{k8}. \tag{30}$$

In equations (4) and (5), we chose $f(x_7) = Mx_7$ and $f(x_8) = Mx_8$ in our computer simulations. Hence by (29) and (30),

$$\frac{d}{dt}x_1 \cong -Ax_1 + I + J + \frac{MG}{A}[x_5]^+ + \frac{ML}{A}\sum_k S_k z_{k7} \tag{31}$$

and

$$\frac{d}{dt}x_2 \cong -Ax_1 + I + \frac{MG}{A}[x_6]^+ + \frac{ML}{A}\sum_k S_k z_{k8}. \tag{32}$$

Guided by equations (31) and (32), we define the circuit's adaptation level $\hat{I}$ by the minimum of $I + J + \frac{ML}{A}\sum_k S_k z_{k7}$ in (31) and of $I + \frac{ML}{A}\sum_k S_k z_{k8}$ in (32); that is,

$$\hat{I} = \min[I + J + \frac{ML}{A}\sum_k S_k z_{k7}, I + \frac{ML}{A}\sum_k S_k z_{k8}] \tag{33}$$

(Figure 8). In other words, $\hat{I}$ describes the tonic baseline due to the totality of internally generated tonic arousal signals and externally generated primary and secondary reinforcer signals. Variables x_1 and x_2 in (4) and (5) activate x_3 and x_4, which compete to generate

x_5 and x_6 before these net activations regulate the READ circuit's antagonistic rebounds and conditioning signals. Thus the net input signal which determines whether rebounds or conditioning will occur is the *difference*

$$\Delta = J + \frac{ML}{A} \sum_k S_k(z_{k7} - z_{k8}) \tag{34}$$

of the *total* arousal and reinforcing signals $I + J + \frac{ML}{A} \sum_k S_k z_{k7}$ and $I + \frac{ML}{A} \sum_k S_k z_{k8}$ which define the adaptation level. If all primary reinforcers and conditioned reinforcers balance out so that $\Delta = 0$, then their only effect on the gated dipole is to cause a shift in adaptation level. No new conditioning occurs under these circumstances because equal total inputs to x_1 and x_2 cause $x_5 = x_6 = 0$ after the transmitter gates y_1 and y_2 habituate to these equal total inputs. If $\widehat{I}$ is very large but Δ is very small (Figure 8b), then any conditioning which does occur is weak, because x_5 and x_6 in (21) and (22) would both be close to zero due to the normalization property. If $\Delta > 0$, then conditioning of positive conditioned reinforcers occurs, due to (21) and (14). If $\Delta < 0$, then conditioning of negative conditioned reinforcers occurs, due to (22) and (15). Thus a contextual cue which is a potent positive reinforcer can interfere with conditioning of a discrete CS as a negative reinforcer, and vice versa.

An important constraint on the terms $\widehat{I}$ and Δ (see Part II for details) follows from the property that the total STM activation which reads-out the signals S_k also tends to be normalized, or conserved, at each time (Grossberg, 1972a, 1975, 1982c). This normalization property explicates the concept of a limited capacity STM, or working memory, that is operative during Pavlovian conditioning. In its simplest form, the normalization property may be realized by the constraint that

$$\sum_k S_k = S \equiv \text{ constant.} \tag{35}$$

It then follows from (33) and (34) that both $\widehat{I}$ and Δ are determined by a type of associative *averaging*, rather than by *summation*. In particular, term

$$\sum_k S_k(z_{k7} - z_{k8}) \tag{36}$$

in (34) is a weighted average, with weights equal to the net LTM strengths $z_{k7} - z_{k8}$, of the signals S_k. By (36), any mechanism which increases a signal S_k that generate a net positive conditioned reinforcer input ($z_{k7} > z_{k8}$) to the gated dipole *a fortiori* weakens the total net negative conditioned reinforcer input to the gated dipole. On the other hand, such an increase may or may not increase the total net positive conditioned reinforcer input to the dipole because the increase in one positive input may be balanced by a decrease in a different positive net input. Thus there exists an asymmetry in the net effect which an attention shift among the sensory representations may cause on the overall performance of a READ circuit.

12. Associative Learning: Learned LTM Increases or Decreases Gated by CS Read-Out

Equation (14) describes the associative learning law whereby the positive conditioned reinforcer LTM trace is trained. This associative learning law was introduced into the

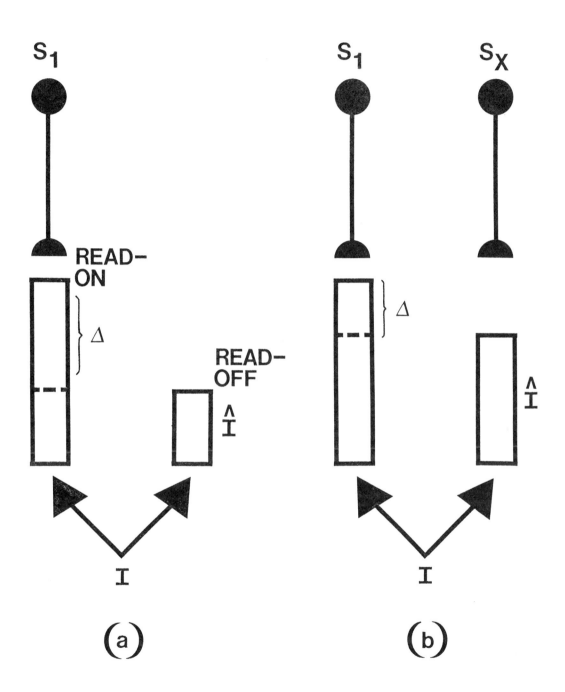

Figure 8. (a) If the total input to the ON-channel of the READ circuit is large, whereas the total input to the OFF-channel is small, then $\widehat{I}$ is small and Δ is large and positive. (b) If the total inputs to both channels are large, then $\widehat{I}$ is large and Δ is small.

associative learning literature in Grossberg (1969a) and has played a central role in the development of neural architectures in a variety of applications (Carpenter and Grossberg, 1987a, 1987b; Cohen and Grossberg, 1987; Grossberg, 1982c, 1987a, 1987b; Grossberg and Levine, 1987; Grossberg and Stone, 1986b). Recently, direct neurophysiological evidence for this associative learning law has been reported (Levy, 1985; Levy, Brassel, and Moore, 1983; Levy and Desmond, 1985; Rauschecker and Singer, 1979; Singer, 1983). In (14), the signal S_k from the kth sensory representation turns learning of the LTM trace z_{k7} on and off. When $S_k = 0$, learning turns off because $\frac{d}{dt}z_{k7} = 0$. When $S_k > 0$, learning turns on. Thus activation of a sensory representation both *reads-out* a conditioned reinforcer signal, via term $S_k z_{k7}$ in (12), and *reads-in* new learned information, via (14). When $S_k > 0$, the LTM trace performs a time-average at rate $-KS_k$, of the learning signal $LS_k[x_5]^+$. As a result, the LTM trace z_{k7} attempts to track the normalized opponent signal $[x_5]^+$ through time. In particular, during a time interval $t_0 \leq t \leq t$, when $S_k(t)$ equals a positive constant S_k, (14) may be integrated to yield

$$z_{k7}(t) = z_{k7}(t_0)e^{-KS_k(t-t_0)} + L\int_{t_0}^t [x_5(v)]^+ e^{-KS_k(t-v)}dv. \tag{38}$$

In other words, z_{k7} performs a time-average of $[x_5]^+$ at a rate proportional to S_k. Due to this property, z_{k7} can either decrease (when $[x_5]^+$ becomes small for a time) or increase (when $[x_5]^+$ becomes large for a time). This learning property is critical in our work.

13. Dissociation of LTM Read-In and Read-Out: A Possible Role for Dendritic Spines

A key property of the READ circuit may be understood by comparing equations (12), (14), and (16). This property is the basis for the opponent extinction property (Section 24) that is used to explain extinction of a conditioned excitor (Section 27) and non-extinction of a conditioned inhibitor (Section 28).

By equation (12), prior conditioned reinforcer learning is *read-out* via term $L\sum_k S_k z_{k7}$ to activate the potential x_7. In contrast, x_7 does not appear in the learning equation (14). Instead, $[x_5]^+$ appears in (14). Thus LTM *read-out* and LTM *read-in* are *dissociated* in equations (12) and (14). In addition, the term $[x_5]^+$ which is read into LTM by (14) is the on-channel output signal, as in (16). Thus the READ circuit embodies the intuition that the signals which drive learning and elicit outputs to other circuits are the *resultant* of all the decision-making processes that take place within the circuit. In particular, $[x_5]^+$ is a normalized opponent signal, whereas x_7 is not.

How can such a dissociation between LTM read-in and LTM read-out be physiologically implemented? The scheme that we apply was introduced in Grossberg (1975; reprinted in Grossberg, 1982c) for this purpose. Figure 9 schematizes this mechanism. Grossberg (1975) interpreted this formal mechanism in terms of the dynamics of large pyramidal cells which, in his application, were interpreted to occur in the hippocampus. These cells possess a large and complex dendritic tree whose activations and inhibitions generate local potentials which flow into, and are averaged by, the cell body. Due to the geometry and electrical properties of such a dendritic tree, an input which activates a particular dendritic branch may not be influenced by inputs that activate different dendritic branches. In order to maximize the functional independence of each conditionable input channel, it was assumed that the conditionable "signals reach dendritic spines. Here they produce local potentials that propagate to the cell body where they influence axonal firing. We assume that the resistance in spines are such that it is much harder for a signal to pass between spines than from a spine to the cell body ... By contrast, ... feedback ... causes a spike potential, or similar global potential change, throughout the dendritic column. This spike invades all the spines in its path and is sufficiently strong to induce transmitter level changes in active $S \to A$ [conditionable] channels. Thus a mechanism using dendritic spines and dendritic spike generators (or some formally analogous mechanism) can allow $S \to A$ signals to occur without major changes in $S \to A$ synaptic transmitter levels unless feedback invades the entire dendritic apparatus" (Grossberg, 1975, Section 21, p.320).

In Figure 9, the feedback signal which invades the entire dendritic apparatus equals $[x_5]^+$. Potential x_7 computes the cell body activation which averages $G[x_5]^+$ with the total positive conditioned reinforcer input $L \sum_k S_k z_{k7}$ that is delivered at spines distributed across the entire dendritic apparatus.

The same mechanism is used to interpret equation (13). Here term $G[x_6]^+$ is the off-channel feedback signal and term $L \sum_k S_k z_{k8}$ is the total negative conditioned reinforcer input.

Recent experiments have supported the hypothesis that synaptic plasticity may occur at the dendritic spines of hippocampal pyramidal cells (Lynch, 1986). In addition, the same functional properties which recommended dissociation of LTM read-in and LTM read-out during hippocampal learning also recommended its use during associative learning in mammalian neocortex (Grossberg, 1982a, 1987a). Recent computer simulations of the unitization, or chunking, of cognitive recognition codes have argued for the functional importance of this concept in other cortical systems (Cohen and Grossberg, 1987), but direct experimental evidence relevant to this prediction seems as yet to be lacking.

14. Decoupling the Normalization and Opponent-Processing Stages

The READ II circuit depicted in Figure 10 is mathematically equivalent to the READ I circuit in Figure 3. The READ II circuit is included to point out that the normalization and opponent processing transformations, which are carried out in a single step by equations (10) and (11), may in principle be carried out separately in two successive steps. Such a dissociation may be becessary *in vivo* because the inhibitory saturation point $-F$ in (10) and (11) is often much smaller in absolute value than the excitatory saturation point E; that is, $E \gg F$. In fact, cells are known to exist in which F is approximately zero; for example, the bipolar cells of the retina (Grossberg, 1987b; Werblin, 1971). The equations for the READ II circuit are as follows.

READ II EQUATIONS

Equations (4)–(9) are the same as in the READ I circuit. The next equation performs a pure normalization, without opponent processing, due to the choice $F = 0$ of its inhibitory saturation point.

Normalized On-Activation

$$\frac{d}{dt}x_5 = -Ax_5 + (E - x_5)x_3 - x_5 x_4 \tag{39}$$

Normalized Off-Activation

$$\frac{d}{dt}x_6 = -Ax_6 + (E - x_6)x_4 - x_6 x_3. \tag{40}$$

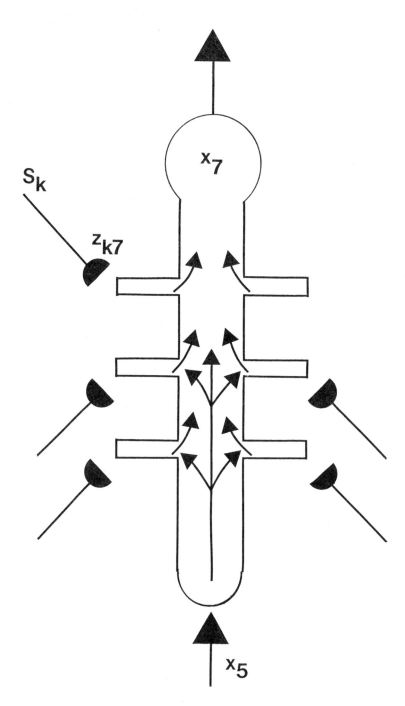

Figure 9. A possible microarchitecture for dissociation of LTM read-in and read-out: Individual LTM-gated sensory signals $S_k z_{k7}$ are read-out into local potentials which are summed by the total cell body potential x_7 without significantly influencing each other's learned read-in. In contrast, the input signal x_5 triggers a massive global cell activation which drives learned read-in at all active LTM traces abutting the cell surface. Signal x_5 also activates the cell body potential x_7.

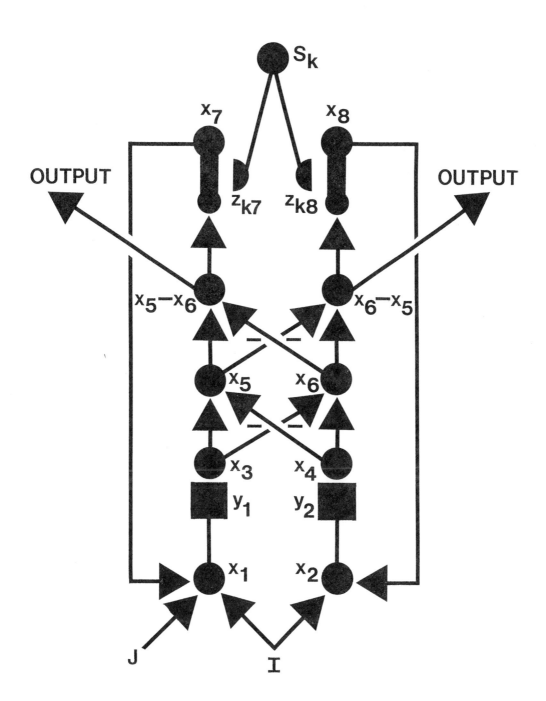

Figure 10. A READ II circuit: This circuit is mathematically equivalent to the READ I circuit depicted in Figure 3. In a READ II circuit, competitive normalization and competitive opponent processing are separated into two successive inhibitory stages, rather than being lumped into one stage, as in the READ I circuit. See text for details.

These normalized activations compete at the next processing stage to generate normalized opponent activations. Thus the variables $x_5 - x_6$ and $x_6 - x_5$ play the same role in the READ II circuit as do variables x_5 and x_6, respectively, in the READ I circuit. For notational simplicity, we do not represent the cells at which the opponent interactions occur as a separate stage, although this is implicit in the equations. The remaining equations of the READ II circuit are as follows.

On-Activation by CS Inputs

$$\frac{d}{dt}x_7 = -Ax_7 + G[x_5 - x_6]^+ + L\sum_k S_k z_{k7} \tag{41}$$

Off-Activation by CS Inputs

$$\frac{d}{dt}x_8 = -Ax_8 + G[x_6 - x_5]^+ + L\sum_k S_k z_{k8} \tag{42}$$

On-Conditioned Reinforcer Learning

$$\frac{d}{dt}z_{k7} = S_k(-Kz_{k7} + L[x_5 - x_6]^+) \tag{43}$$

Off-Conditioned Reinforcer Learning

$$\frac{d}{dt}z_{k8} = S_k(-Kz_{k8} + L[x_6 - x_5]^+) \tag{44}$$

On-Output Signal
$$O_1 = [x_5 - x_6]^+ \tag{45}$$

Off-Output Signal
$$O_2 = [x_6 - x_5]^+ \tag{46}$$

15. Comparison with Alternative Conditioning Models

Although the READ II circuit is mathematically equivalent to the READ I circuit, its equations make it easier to understand one of the circuit's key properties. In the associative equations (43) and (44), conditioned reinforcer learning is driven by the terms $[x_5 - x_6]^+$ and $[x_6 - x_5]^+$. Thus learning occurs only if the *net balance* of all inputs to the gated dipole favors the on-channel or the off-channel. Expressed in another way, LTM changes occur only if an *increment* occurs above a *baseline* of activation.

A number of models have been formulated to express this type of intuition. Whereas the Rescorla and Wagner (1972) and the Sutton and Barto (1981) models have attempted to represent all the factors which control the conditioning process by using a single equation for learning by individual LTM traces, the Pearce and Hall (1980) model uses several equations: one for computing the attentional parameters, one for excitatory associations, and one for inhibitory associations. Grossberg (1982b) has itemized a number of basic experiments which these models cannot explain because they lump too many processes together.

The READ II equations demonstrate in a real-time setting that all of these models have attempted to express an important processing insight. The READ II equations also emphasize, however, that qualitatively different type of processes, such as gated dipole opponent processes and CS-gated associative learning processes, interact with one another to generate these properties as an emergent property of the entire circuit, rather than as a direct property of a single synapse. This conclusion was also explicit in the READ circuit equations that were originally introduced in Grossberg (1972b) and further developed in Grossberg (1975). These circuits have stood the test of time and of subsequent data. Their further development in this article through systematic computer simulations demonstrates their robust ability to generate real-time conditioning profiles which other conditioning models have not yet been able to explain.

16. Presynaptic Gating versus Postsynaptic-to-Presynaptic Feedback

The READ III circuit depicted in Figure 11 is both physically and mathematically distinct from the READ I and READ II circuits, but its functional properties in computer simulations are remarkably similar, both qualitatively and quantitatively, to those of the READ I and II circuits. In the READ I and II circuits, associative learning is controlled by a correlation between presynaptic and postsynaptic influences, such as S_k and $[x_5]^+$, respectively, in equation (14). In contrast, within the READ III circuit, all of the learned changes in the LTM trace are mediated presynaptically. After describing the nature of these presynaptic influences, we also note that, in the absence of a specialized anatomical organization, their realization *in vivo* would be inconvenient at best.

The possibility that associative influences may be mediated presynaptically in some neural systems is consistent with some invertebrate data (Hawkins, Abrams, Carew, and Kandel, 1983). On the other hand, both invertebrate and vertebrate associative learning data also support the existence of postsynaptic influences (Alkon, 1979, 1984a, 1984b; Levy, 1985; Levy, Brassel, and Moore, 1983; Levy and Desmond, 1985; Rauschecker and Singer, 1979; Singer, 1983), and some associative properties, by their very definition, require a postsynaptic influence (Grossberg and Levine, 1987). Thus we present the READ III circuit to demonstrate that the simulated conditioning properties which we report herein do not, in themselves, rule out a purely presynaptic site for conditioning.

READ III EQUATIONS

Equations (4)–(9), (39)–(40), and (43)–(46) are the same as in the READ II circuit. The READ II and III circuits differ only in their equations for activation by CS inputs. In both the READ I and II circuits, the potentials x_7 and x_8 are influenced by normalized opponent signals from the prior processing stage of the gated dipole. In the READ III circuit, potentials x_7 and x_8 are influenced by normalized, but not opponent, signals from the prior processing stage.

On-Activation by CS Inputs

$$\frac{d}{dt}x_7 = -Ax_7 + G[x_5]^+ + L\sum_k S_k z_{k7} \tag{47}$$

Off-Activation by CS Inputs

$$\frac{d}{dt}x_8 = -Ax_8 + G[x_6]^+ + L\sum_k S_k z_{k8} \tag{48}$$

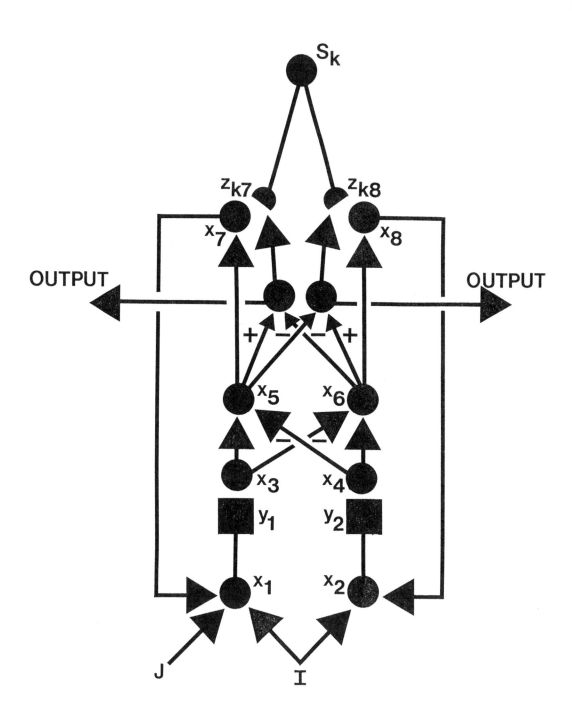

Figure 11. A READ III circuit: Unlike the READ I and II circuits, learning in a READ III circuit is driven by the correlation of two presynaptic signals, rather than by the correlation of a presynaptic signal with a postsynaptic signal. Computer simulations of both types of circuits generate similar results.

The normalization stage, defined by equations (39) and (40), assures that the potentials x_5 and x_6 compute ratios which are passed along the gated dipole on-channel and off-channel via equations (47) and (48). In addition, these nonnegative output signals activate an opponent processing stage to generate the output signals (45) and (46). As in Figure 11, these output signals are relayed along a bifurcating pathway. One branch of the pathway carries outputs to other circuits. The other branch has a presynaptic modulatory effect on the LTM trace of its channel, as in (43) and (44).

In this circuit, a single output signal, say O_1 in the on-channel, must presynaptically modulate the LTM traces z_{k7} of *all* the sensory representations whose signals S_k can sample the on-channel. In order to meet this requirement, either there exist a very large number of specific pathways branching from each READ III output pathway to the synaptic terminals of all CS-activated pathways, or all these synaptic terminals are grouped together functionally so that a single modulatory signal generated by each output pathway can spread to all the synaptic terminals which abut on its channel. Other things being equal, it seems far simpler, as in the READ I and II circuits, to allow postsynaptic-to-presynaptic signals to influence each abutting synaptic terminal via a direct local feedback process.

17. Computer Simulations with the READ I Circuit: No Passive Extinction

In each series of computer simulations, numerical parameters of the circuit were held fixed and several different experiments, characterized by different pairings of CS and US inputs, were simulated. Then individual parameters were altered, and another complete series of simulations was undertaken. In this way, an understanding of how each parameter influences network dynamics was achieved. This and the next section summarize illustrative sets of computer simulations. Although the simulation sets demonstrate the formal competence of READ circuits, they are not presumed to embody the full neural machinery engaged during conditioning. The results are, we suggest, necessary but not sufficient to explain conditioning *in vivo*. These simulation results are used in Part II, along with other modelling results, to suggest qualitative explanations of some difficult conditioning data. In particular, in Part II (Section 24) we show how the process of opponent extinction can extinguish LTM traces actively even if parameters are set, as in this section, to prevent the LTM traces from extinguishing passively.

The simulation series reported below tested the response of a READ circuit to the five experimental combinations of $CS - US$ inputs described in Figure 12. Figure 12a summarizes the CS and US inputs used to study primary excitatory conditioning and extinction. In these simulations, CS_1 onset preceded US onset for 10 acquisition trials. Then the CS_1 was presented alone for 10 extinction trials. In such a READ circuit, one mechanism of extinction is passive decay of conditioned reinforcer LTM strength when the CS is active. We show that such decay may occur in some parameter ranges, but that essentially perfect conditioned reinforcer memory obtains in other parameter ranges wherein the full range of desirable circuit properties, notably large antagonistic rebounds, prevail. Thus CS-contingent passive extinction may occur in some neural systems or species, but not others, due to evolutionary selection of a different choice of parameters. In circuits wherein passive extinction does not occur, an active extinction process may be controlled by auxiliary circuits (Grossberg, 1982c, 1987a). These auxiliary circuits match a learned expectation against the sensory events which actually occur. A mismatch may trigger a novelty reaction, which causes a burst of nonspecific arousal that can elicit an antagonistic rebound within the READ circuit. Conditioned reinforcer learning of an antagonistic rebound within an off-channel can competitively inhibit prior conditioned reinforcer learning to the corresponding on-channel due to the opponent processing that occurs between channels before the circuit elicits an output signal. This type of expectancy-mediated extinction mechanism is used to explain conditioning data in Part II.

Figure 12b summarizes the CS and US inputs used to study primary inhibitory conditioning and extinction. In these simulations, US offset preceded CS_1 onset for 10 acquisition trials. Then the CS_1 was presented alone for 10 extinction trials.

Figure 12c summarizes the CS and US inputs used to study secondary excitatory conditioning. In these simulations, the CS_1 preceded the US for 10 acquisition trials. Then the CS_1 and the CS_2 occurred together for 10 secondary conditioning trials, thereby conditioning the CS_2. Since an isolated READ circuit does not include the limited capacity attentional mechanisms that regulate blocking and overshadowing (Grossberg, 1982c, 1987a; Grossberg and Levine, 1987), the CS_2 is not blocked by the CS_1 when they are simultaneously presented. Simultaneous presentation of CS_1 and CS_2 has much the same effect on READ circuit secondary conditioning as would onset of a sustained CS_1 before onset of the CS_2. Simultaneous presentation is therefore reported here for simplicity.

Figure 12d summarizes the CS and US inputs used in secondary inhibitory conditioning. Here, the CS_1 was paired with the US for 10 acquisition trials. Then CS_1 offset preceded CS_2 onset for 10 secondary conditioning trials.

Figure 12e describes the CS and US inputs used in excitatory partial reinforcement. In these simulations, CS_1 and US pairing alternated with presentation of the CS_1 alone for 20 trials. As noted above, the conditioning which occurs within an isolated READ circuit, whether due to continuous reinforcement or to partial reinforcement, is not modulated by expectation mechanisms. Such modulation can yield higher asymptotic response levels under partial reward than continuous reward (Grossberg, 1975; reprinted in Grossberg, 1982c), as also occurs in many experimental paradigms (Boren, 1961; Brogden, 193.; Felton and Lyon, 1966; Gibbon, Farrell, Locurto, Duncan, and Terrace, 1980; Gibbs, Latham, and Gormenzano, 1978; Gonzalez, 1973, 1974; Perkins, Beavers, Hancock, Hemmendinger, Hemmendinger, and Ricci, 1975; Schwartz and Williams, 1972; Wasserman, 1974; Wasserman, Hunter, Gutowski, and Bader, 1975). This type of enhancement effect does not occur in an isolated READ circuit. The discussion in Part II describes how the interaction of expectation mechanisms with READ circuit mechanisms can yield higher asymptotes and more resistant extinction during partial reward than continuous reward.

Figures 13–17 depict a series of simulations using a fixed set of numerical parameters. Each curve depicts the real-time behavior of an activation (STM trace) or adaptive weight (LTM trace) of the READ I circuit. Due to the fact that each variable fluctuates over a different range of numerical values, each curve has been normalized to fit within an interval of fixed height. We call particular attention to the following features of these conditioning curves.

Consider Figure 13 for definiteness. This Figure depicts a simulation of excitatory primary conditioning using the inputs in Figure 12a. Because the US is presented to the on-channel, the on-transmitter y_1 in Figure 13 undergoes a series of habituation-accumulation cycles on successive learning trials, as schematized in Figure 6. Due to these reactions, the on-activations throughout the circuit undergo overshoot-habituation-undershoot-habituation cycles through time, also schematized in Figure 6. The variables x_5 and x_6 in Figure 13 illustrate these properties.

The variable CS_1-ON describes conditioning of the LTM trace within the pathway from

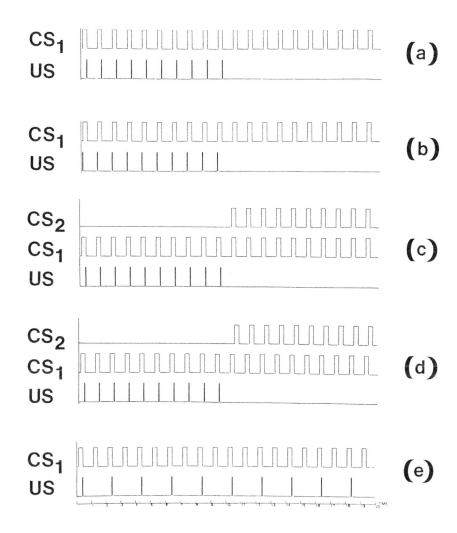

Figure 12. Input series in real-time that were used in computer simulations: (a) primary excitatory conditioning and extinction; (b) primary inhibitory conditioning and extinction; (c) secondary excitatory conditioning; (d) secondary inhibitory conditioning; (e) partial reinforcement.

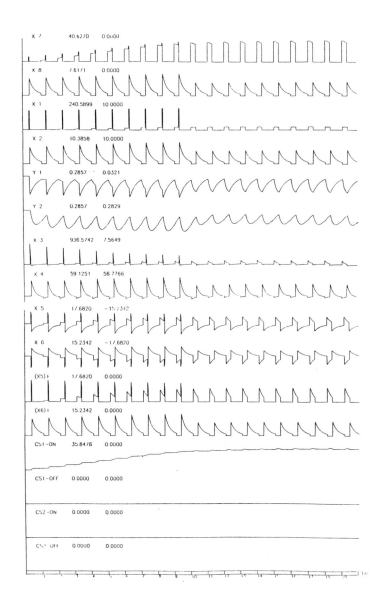

Figure 13. Computer simulation of primary excitatory conditioning and extinction with slow habituation and large feedback in a READ I circuit: CS_1 is paired with the US during the first 10 simulated trials, and CS_1 is presented in the absence of the US in the next 10 simulated trials. The numbers above each plot are the maximum and minimum values of the plot. Parameters are $A = 1, B = .005, C = .00125, D = 20, E = 20, F = 20, G = .5, H = .005, K = .025, L = 20, M = .05$.

the sensory representation of the CS_1 to the on-channel of the READ circuit. Notice that, after the 10 acquisition trials terminate, future presentations of the CS_1 alone on extinction trials do not cause delay of the CS_1-ON LTM trace. For this choice of parameters, memory is essentially perfect. Forgetting is due to active relearning, notably counter-conditioning of CS_1-off, as in the interference theory of forgetting (Adams, 1967, Grossberg, 1972b).

Another important feature of circuit dynamics is seen in the output functions $[x_5]^+$ and $[x_6]^+$ of the on-channel and off-channel, respectively. Because the output signals are rectified, they generate sustained, but habituative, on-reactions and transient off-reactions, as schematized in Figure 5.

Figure 14 summarizes a simulation of inhibitory primary conditioning obtained through a backward conditioning procedure, using the inputs depicted in Figure 12b. In this simulation, the LTM trace CS_1-OFF is the one that learns. This is the LTM trace in the pathway from the sensory representation of the CS_1 to the off-channel of the READ circuit. Conditioning of the off-channel is due to the antagonistic rebounds which occur after the US to the on-channel is terminated. These antagonistic rebounds, in turn, are caused by the habituation of the transmitter gate y_1 in the on-channel. Note that these rebounds also cause habituation of the transmitter gate y_2 in the off-channel, but that y_2 habituates during time intervals when y_1 is recovering.

An important point of comparison between Figures 13 and 14 concerns the maximum sizes achieved by the conditioned LTM traces CS_1-ON and CS_1-OFF, respectively. These maximum sizes (35.8 and 55, respectively) are commensurate. The existence of relatively large values of off-LTM traces tended to covary in our simulations with the persistence of memory during extinction trials. Large off-LTM traces and good memory went hand-in-hand. It is still too soon to say whether this is a general property of READ circuits, and thus a property upon which an experimental prediction can securely be based. On the other hand, it is an interesting correlation that deserves further study.

In order to study the covariation of extinction with large off-rebounds, we did parametric studies varying the feedback coefficient M in (31) and (32) from .01 to .07. In Figures 13–17, we chose $M = .05$. For this parameter choice, the off-LTM trace slowly decays to approximately 70% of its maximal value during successive presentation of the CS alone. A similar decay occurs given choices of M between .01 and .05.

Figure 15 depicts a simulation of excitatory secondary conditioning using the inputs summarized in Figure 12c. The LTM trace CS_1-ON grows during the first 10 trials and is then used to induce growth of the LTM trace CS_2-ON during the next 10 trials, without undermining its own LTM strength. The size (37.7) of CS_1-ON after 10 acquisition trials is larger than the size (33.3) of CS_2-ON after 10 acquisition trials. Thus secondary conditioning generates significant LTM strength in this READ circuit, but not LTM strength as great as that generated due to primary conditioning.

Figure 16 depicts a simulation of inhibitory secondary conditioning using the inputs summarized in Figure 12d. These simulations fully exploit the fact that the READ circuits contain positive feedback loops. Grossberg (1972b, 1975) was the first to note that, in order for a CS_1 to be conditionable either directly to the on-channel or to an antagonistic rebound in the off-channel, its LTM traces must contact the gated dipole at a stage *subsequent* to the habituative transmitter gates. In order for offset of a CS_1 to cause an antagonistic rebound, its LTM traces must contact the gated dipole at a stage *prior* to the habituative transmitter gates. In order for the same stage of LTM contact with the gated dipole to occur both subsequent to and prior to the habituative transmitter gates, the gated dipole must contain positive feedback pathways. In Figure 16, CS_1-ON grows on the first 10 trials

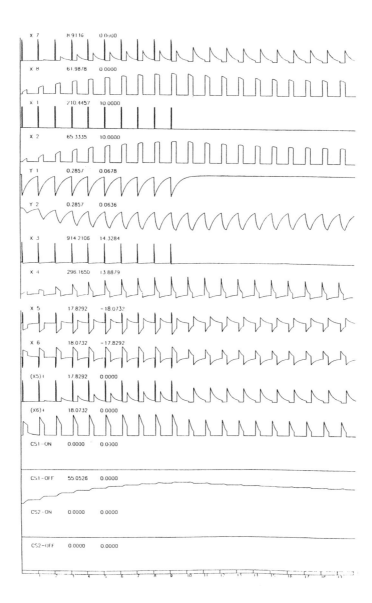

Figure 14. Computer simulation of primary inhibitory conditioning and extinction with slow habituation and large feedback in a READ I circuit: CS_1 is presented after the US offset during the first 10 simulated trials, and CS_1 is presented in the absence of the US in the next 10 simulated trials. The same parameters were used as in Figure 13.

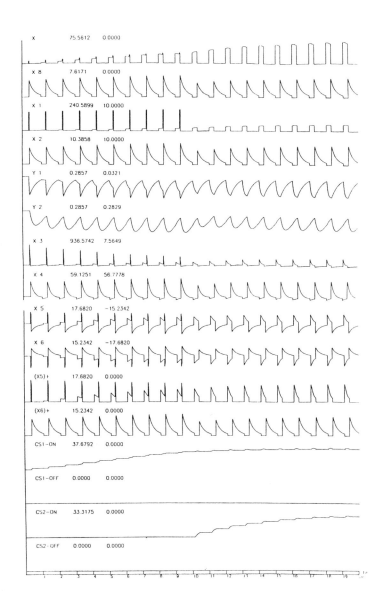

Figure 15. Computer simulation of secondary excitatory conditioning with slow habituation and large feedback in a READ I circuit: CS_1 is presented with the US during the first 10 simulated trials, and CS_1 is presented with CS_2 in the absence of the US in the next 10 simulated trials. The same parameters were used as in Figure 13.

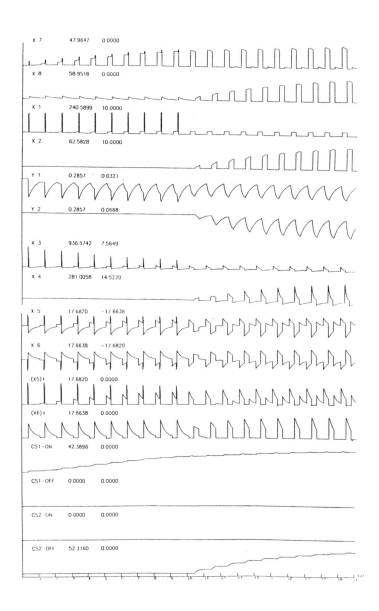

Figure 16. Computer simulation of secondary inhibitory conditioning with slow habituation and large feedback in a READ I circuit: CS_1 is presented with the US during the first 10 simulated trials, and CS_2 is presented after CS_1 offset in the absence of the US in the next 10 simulated trials. The same parameters were used as in Figure 13.

due to pairing with the US, whereas CS_2-OFF grows on the next 10 trials due to pairing with the antagonistic rebound caused by the offset of CS_1. The maximum size (42.4) of CS_1-ON during the first 10 trials is smaller than the maximum size (52.3) of CS_2-OFF during the next 10 trials.

Figure 17 describes a simulation using the partial reward schedule described in Figure 12e. The rate of acquisition is less than that in the continuous reward case of Figure 13. Because memory is essentially perfect during passive extinction trials, the asymptotic associative strength can grow to close to that achieved using continuous reward. Because this READ circuit is not linked to expectation mechanisms, the nonoccurrence of an expected US, or the occurrence of an unexpectd US, on later conditioning trials has no influence on the course of conditioning when the CS is presented alone.

Key properties of these computer simulations tend to be supported by experimental data. These simulations do not incorporate a number of the model's attentional and expectancy mechanisms used to analyse data in Part II, but their properties are consistent with data wherein such mechanisms do not play a rate-limiting role.

In the case of excitatory conditioning (Figure 13), simulations show conditioned responses (CR) of increasing amplitude over trials, as has often been described in classical conditioning (see, for example, Gormenzano, Kehoe, and Marshall, 1983).

Rescorla and LoLordo (1965) and Siegel and Domjan (1971) found that backward conditioning procedures, as in Figure 14, yield inhibitory conditioning. Zimmer-Hart and Rescorla (1974) found that inhibitory conditioning does not extinguish after presentations of the CS alone. In agreement with Zimmer-Hart and Rescorla (1974), there exists a parameter range for the READ circuit such that complete extinction of the CS-OFF association does not occur due to presentation of the CS alone.

In the READ circuit, extinction of the CS_1-ON association does not affect the CS_2-ON association. This result agrees with data obtained by Rizley and Rescorla (1972) using rats as subjects in an aversive conditioning paradigm, and by Holland and Rescorla (1975) also using rats as subjects but in an appetitive paradigm. On the other hand, there exist several experimental paradigms (Leyland, 1977; Lysle and Fowler, 1985; Miller and Schachtman, 1985; Rashotte, Griffin, and Sisk, 1977) in which extinction of a given stimulus can significantly influence the behavioral efficacy of other conditioned stimuli. In Part II, we append READ circuit mechanisms to cognitive modulatory circuits to illustrate how such an augmented circuit can be used to analyse such data.

18. Computer Simulations in Other Parameter Ranges: Responses to Stimulus Transients and Passive Extinction

The simulations depicted in Figures 18–21 show how speeding up the habituation and accumulation rates of the transmitter gates influences circuit dynamics. In Figures 18 and 19, these rates are chosen twice as fast as in Figures 13–17. In Figures 20 and 21, these rates are chosen four times as fast as in Figures 13–17. In Figures 18 and 20, the simulations are of excitatory secondary conditioning. In Figures 19 and 21, the simulations are of inhibitory secondary conditioning. These simulations illustrate the robustness of READ circuit properties within a physically plausible parameter range. The faster habituation rate causes a more rapidly falling overshoot in circuit activations and thus an accentuation of transient, rather than sustained, responses to CS and US. Otherwise, the qualitative properties of conditioning are preserved across these parameter changes.

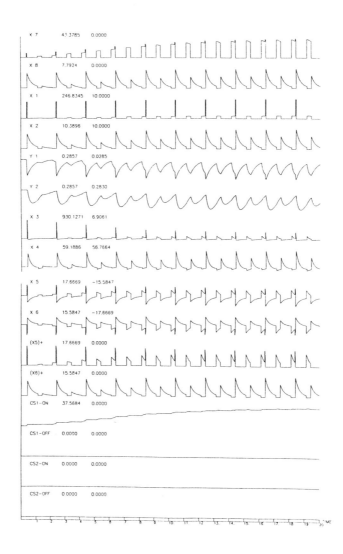

Figure 17. Computer simulation of partial reinforcement with slow habituation and large feedback in a READ I circuit: CS_1 is alternatively presented with the US and without the US during 20 simulated trials. The same parameters were used as in Figure 13.

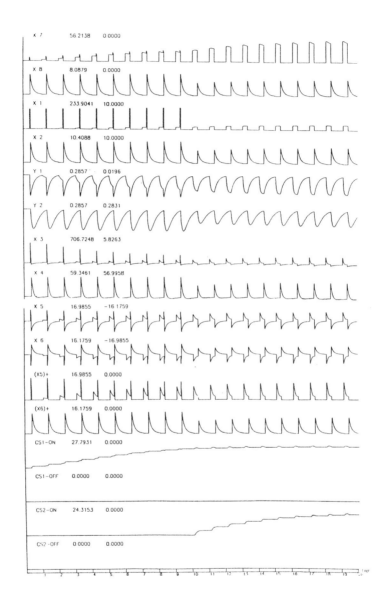

Figure 18. Computer simulation of secondary excitatory conditioning with intermediate habituation and large feedback in a READ I circuit: CS_1 is presented with the US during the first 10 simulated trials, and CS_2 is presented with CS_1 in the absence of the US in the next 10 simulated trials. The same parameters were used as in Figure 13, except for $B = .010$ and $C = .0025$.

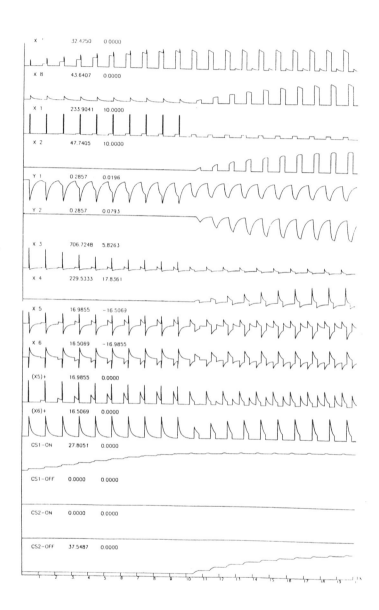

Figure 19. Computer simulation of secondary inhibitory conditioning with intermediate habituation and large feedback in a READ I circuit: CS_1 is presented with the US during the first 10 simulated trials, and CS_2 is presented after CS_1 offset in the absence of the US in the next 10 simulated trials. The same parameters were used as in Figure 18.

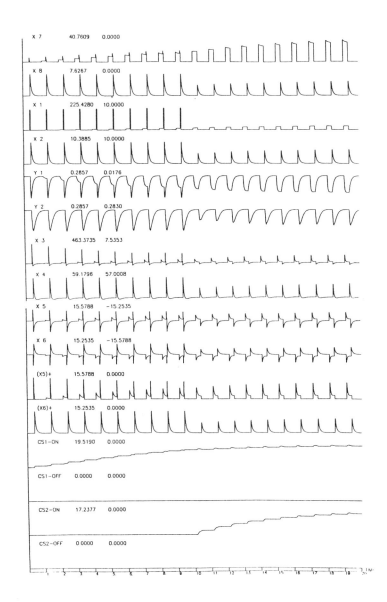

Figure 20. Computer simulation of secondary excitatory conditioning with fast habituation and large feedback in a READ I circuit: CS_1 is presented with the US during the first 10 simulated trials, and CS_1 is presented with CS_2 in the absence of the US in the next 10 simulated trials. The same parameters were used as in Figure 13, except for $B = .020$ and $C = .005$.

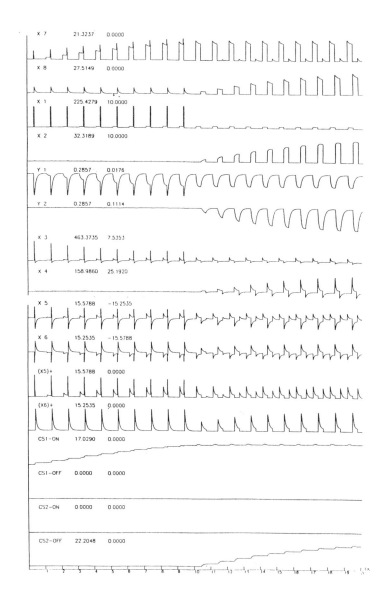

Figure 21. Computer simulation of secondary inhibitory conditioning with fast habituation and large feedback in a READ I circuit: CS_1 is presented with the US during the first 10 simulated trials, and CS_2 is presented after CS_1 offset in the absence of the US in the next 10 simulated trials. The same parameters were used as in Figure 20.

Figures 22–26 depict a complete set of simulations in a parameter range wherein passive extinction occurs when the CS is not followed by a US. The READ circuit in which passive extinction occurs has the same parameters as the READ circuit depicted in Figures 20 and 21, with one exception: In Figures 22–26, the parameter which controls the strength of the positive feedback signals from $x_7 \rightarrow x_1$ and $x_8 \rightarrow x_2$ was chosen smaller.

Several functional properties of the READ circuit changed as a result of this single change in parameters. As already mentioned, passive extinction occurs in all the Figures 22–26. In addition, antagonistic rebounds are smaller, so inhibitory conditioning is weaker (Figures 21 and 25) relative to the corresponding level of excitatory conditioning (Figures 22 and 24). Finally, due to the passive extinction that can occur on nonrewarded trials, both the rate and the asymptote of learning are less in the partial reward case (Figure 26) than the continuous reward case (Figure 22), unlike the partial reward case in which no passive extinction occurs (Figure 17). Despite these quantitative changes, the READ circuit continues to exhibit the main qualitative conditioning properties that are exhibited in its other displayed parameter ranges. These results show that the circuit's emergent properties are robust over at least 4–5 fold changes in the size of key parameters.

PART II

19. The Relationship between Conditioned Inhibition and Blocking Paradigms

When a conditioned stimulus CS_1 is appropriately paired with a shock unconditioned stimulus US in a conditioned suppression paradigm, it can become a conditioned excitor, as measured by a decreased suppression ratio, an increased response latency, or other indices of conditioned fear (Lysle and Fowler, 1985; Miller and Schachtman, 1985). If simultaneous pairing of CS_1 with another conditioned stimulus CS_2 is then followed by a no-shock interval, the CS_2 can become a conditioned inhibitor, as tested by an increased suppression ratio, a decreased response latency, and so on. Conditioned inhibitors elicit a number of paradoxical behavioral properties which have attracted intense experimental interest.

The experimental paradigm for training a conditioned inhibitor is similar to the blocking paradigm (Kamin, 1968, 1969). In a blocking paradigm, CS_1 may again be paired with a shock US. Then CS_1 and CS_2 are again simultaneously presented, but are also followed by a shock US. The key question in blocking concerns why the CS_2 does not become, at least asymptotically, a conditioned excitor. How does prior fear conditioning of CS_1 "block" subsequent fear conditioning of CS_2?

The blocking paradigm and the conditioned inhibition paradigm thus differ primarily in terms of the *consequences* of $CS_1 + CS_2$ presentations. In blocking, the consequence is a definite US event. In conditioned inhibition, it is the nonoccurrence of the expected US event. There exists a continuum of other experimental possibilities in which the compound stimulus $CS_1 + CS_2$ may be followed by a US that differs from the original US; for example, in its intensity. Then conditioning of CS_2 may undergo unblocking. From this perspective, properties of conditioned inhibition may be interpreted as a limiting case of unblocking properties. (See Note 2.)

Herein we join the computer simulations of READ circuit dynamics that are described in Part I to the additional cognitive-emotional mechanisms schematized in Figures 1 and 2 to provide a unified real-time explanation of key data about conditioned inhibition. In particular, this explanation clarifies how, despite their similarity, blocking and conditioned inhibition paradigms generate such different behavioral properties.

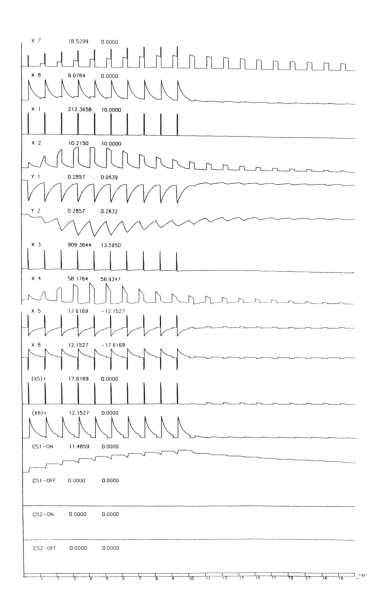

Figure 22. Computer simulation of primary excitatory conditioning and extinction with slow habituation and small feedback in a READ I circuit: CS_1 is paired with the US during the first 10 simulated trials, and CS_1 is presented in the absence of the US in the next 10 simulated trials. The same parameters were used as in Figure 20, except for $M = .01$.

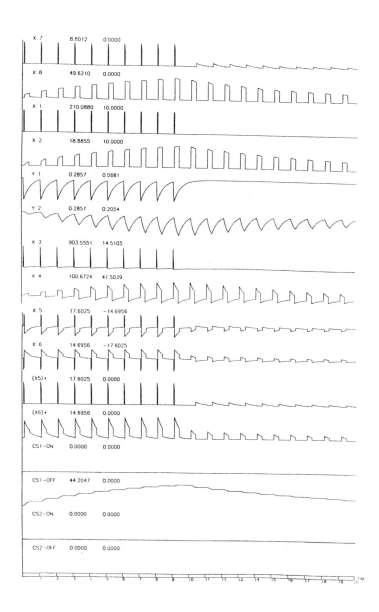

Figure 23. Computer simulation of primary inhibitory conditioning and extinction with slow habituation and small feedback in a READ I circuit: CS_1 is presented after the US offset during the first 10 simulated trials, and CS_1 is presented in the absence of the US in the next 10 simulated trials. The same parameters were used as in Figure 22.

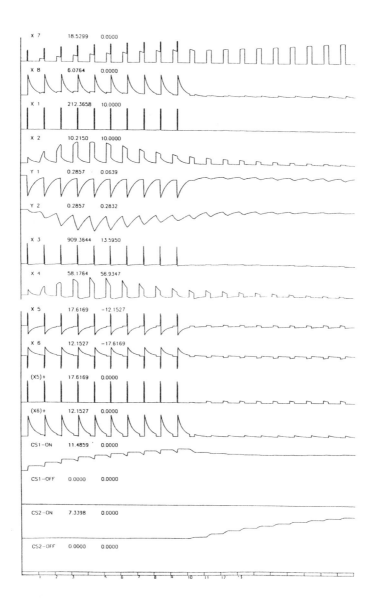

Figure 24. Computer simulation of secondary excitatory conditioning with slow habituation and small feedback in a READ I circuit: CS_1 is presented with the US during the first 10 simulated trials, and CS_1 is presented with CS_2 in the absence of the US in the next 10 simulated trials. The same parameters were used as in Figure 22.

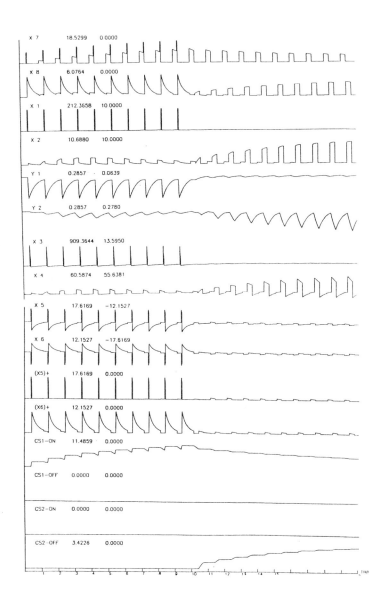

Figure 25. Computer simulation of secondary inhibitory conditioning with slow habituation and small feedback in a READ I circuit: CS_1 is presented with the US during the first 10 simulated trials, and CS_2 is presented after CS_1 offset in the absence of the US in the next 10 simulated trials. The same parameters were used as in Figure 22.

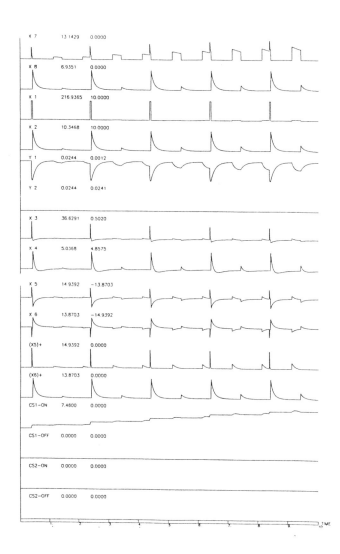

Figure 26. Computer simulation of partial reinforcement with slow habituation and small feedback in a READ I circuit: CS_1 is alternatively presented with the US and without the US during 10 simulated trials. The same parameters were used as in Figure 22.

20. Conditioned Inhibition as a "Slave" Process

Our analysis takes as its point of departure the seminal experiments, modelling concepts, and general data discussions provided by Lysle and Fowler (1985) and Miller and Schachtman (1985). Many related experiments will be clarified along the way.

One motivation for the Lysle and Fowler (1985) experiments was the fact that several predictions of the Rescorla and Wagner (1972) model have failed to be experimentally confirmed. In particular, a conditioned inhibitor CS_2 does not extinguish when it is presented alone, unlike a conditioned excitor (DeVito, 1980; Owren and Kaplan, 1981; Witcher, 1978; Zimmer-Hart and Rescorla, 1974). In addition, a neutral stimulus presented with a conditioned inhibitor CS_2 does not acquire excitatory value (Baker, 1974). The experiments which Lysle and Fowler (1985) designed to further probe these properties led them to conclude that conditioned inhibition is a "slave" process to conditioned excitation. This concept was experimentally defined and tested using the following general type of paradigm, whose many controls will not be reviewed here.

First, a CS_1 was paired with a shock US. Next, a compound stimulus $CS_1 + CS_2$ was followed by a no-shock interval. Then a number of different manipulations were carried out on several different groups of animals. In one group of animals (denoted by $CS_1[CS_2]$), the CS_1 was extinguished by being followed by a no-shock interval. In another group of animals (denoted by $X[CS_2]$), the training context X was extinguished by being followed by a no-shock interval. In a third group of animals (denoted by $N[CS_2]$), neither CS_1 nor X was extinguished. Then a retardation test was performed to discover how quickly the conditioned inhibitor CS_2 could be trained as a conditioned excitor by being randomly paired with shock on 50% of its trials. The data showed that conditioned suppression developed least rapidly for the $N[CS_2]$ group, more rapidly for the $X[CS_2]$ group, and most rapidly for the $CS_1[CS_2]$ group. Indeed, the $CS_1[CS_2]$ group developed suppression almost as rapidly as comparison groups that were tested using a novel CS rather than CS_2. In other words, prior extinction of the conditioned excitor CS_1 seemed to deactivate the conditioned inhibitory properties of CS_2 in the subsequent retardation test, as did, to a lesser extent, extinction of the context X, which had also acquired properties of a conditioned excitor.

To further analyse these properties, Lysle and Fowler (1985) tested whether fear of the CS_2 or the US was *in the test context* or *in the animal*. In the latter case "a nonassociative mechanism could be postulated whereby inhibition is motivated and thus maintained by an excitatory representation of generic form" (Lysle and Fowler, 1985, p.83). To this end they performed experiments which demonstrated that if, in conjunction with extinction of the conditioned excitor CS_1, "the animal receives presentations in a different context of the US by itself, for a novel CS, or correlated either positively or negatively with $[CS_1]$, then the inhibitory property of $[CS_2]$ will be maintained without loss ... Furthermore, if, following extinction in the original context, the animal receives US presentations for the same or a different CS in that context, then the inhibitory property of $[CS_2]$ will be restored apparently to full strength" (Lysle and Fowler, 1985, p.90). The remarkable aspect of these results is that such flexible relationships between the extinction and retraining of conditioned excitatory events and a conditioned inhibitor can have such dramatic effects upon how and whether the conditioned inhibitory property manifests itself in a test context.

The fact that extinction of the conditioned excitor CS_1 deactivates the conditioned inhibitory properties of CS_2, but reconditioning in another context reinstates CS_2 as a conditioned inhibitor, prompted Lysle and Fowler (1985) to propose that conditioned inhibition is a "slave" process to conditioned excitation.

21. Conditioned Inhibition as a "Comparator" Process

According to Rescorla (1968), excitatory conditioning is obtained whenever $P(US/CS) > P(US/\overline{CS})$, inhibitory conditioning when $P(US/CS) < P(US/\overline{CS})$, and no conditioning when $P(US/CS) = P(US/\overline{CS})$.

In a more recent exploration of contingency effects on classical conditioning, Miller and Schachtman (1985) further analysed these properties by paying particular attention to how the context X may become conditioned to the US, and the effects of such associations on conditioned inhibition and excitation. They therefore controlled both the probability $P(US/CS)$ and the probability $P(US/\overline{CS})$, where $\overline{CS}$ denotes "no CS". They noted that if $P(US/CS) = .33$ and $P(US/\overline{CS}) = 0$, then the CS became a conditioned excitor. In contrast, if $P(US/CS) = .33$ but $P(US/\overline{CS}) = .67$, then the CS became a conditioned inhibitor. Thus knowing $P(US/CS)$ alone is not sufficient to predict the excitatory or inhibitory properties of the CS. The relevance of context-US associations was vividly raised by this manipulation, since during $P(US/\overline{CS})$ trials, no CS occurred.

Miller and Schachtman (1985, p.60) explored the role of context-US associations and showed that the "critical factor was whether or not unsignaled shocks were given in the conditioning context. They did this by training two experimental groups $[P(US/CS) = .33, P(US/\overline{CS}) = .67]$ and $[P(US/CS) = .33, P(US/\overline{CS}) = 0]$ in an experimental context A. Then they broke up each group into two test groups, and tested one group's reaction to the CS in context A and the other group's reaction to the CS in a novel context B. Both groups that were trained in $[P(US/CS) = .33, P(US/\overline{CS}) = .67]$ showed short latency responses to the CS, whereas both groups trained in $[P(US/CS) = .33, P(US/\overline{CS}) = 0]$ showed long latency responses to the CS. Thus if the CS was trained as a conditioned excitor, then it preserved this property in either the training context or a novel context. The same was true if the CS was trained to be a conditioned inhibitor. This latter result is of particular interest, since it demonstrated that a conditioned inhibitor could maintain its inhibitory property in a novel context B in which no excitatory conditioning had taken place. In particular, the inhibitory effect of the CS in this situation could not be due to the unmasking in context B of a weaker excitatory effect than that which was conditioned to the training context A.

Through a variation on this paradigm, Miller and Schachtman (1985, p.61) concluded that "the training location as opposed to the test location plays the role of the associative comparator in determining whether or not a CS will be an effective conditioned inhibitor or conditioned excitor." To show this, they again chose $P(US/CS) = .33$ with CS conditioning occurring in context A, but instead of delivering unsignaled shocks in context A, for half the animals the probability of unsignaled shock in context B was .67. Testing of the CS in either context A or context B showed that it was a source of conditioned excitation, independent of the occurrence of unsignaled shocks in context B and, as in the past experiment, independent of which context was used for testing.

An interesting finer point in these results was that the total conditioned excitatory effect of the CS was not significantly increased by testing it in the fearful context B. This result is consistent with the property of associative averaging, rather than associative summation, of the total amount of conditioned fear (Section 11).

Miller and Schachtman (1985, p.63) realized that different temporal contingencies were imposed by training and testing in the same or different contexts. They particularly noted data of Kleiman and Fowler (1984) wherein "unsignaled shocks delivered in moderately close temporal proximity to a nonreinforced stimulus (but not so close as to produce excitatory conditioning) will increase the effective inhibitory strength of this stimulus relative to that produced by unsignaled shocks delivered in the middle of the intervals between presentations of the target stimulus." We will trace this temporal effect to whether conditioning occurs to a directly activated on-channel or to an indirectly activated antagonistic rebound within an off-channel.

Miller and Schachtman (1985, p.64) discovered an important asymmetry in the processing of a conditioned inhibitor when they "asked whether the comparator baseline was the excitatory value of the conditioning context at the time of conditioning or at the time of testing." To test this, they inflated or deflated the associative value of the context during the retention interval before the test began. For example, after training on $[P(US/CS) = .33, P(US/\overline{CS}) = .67]$, they deflated the context in one group by extinguishing it on $P(US/\overline{CS}) = 0$. Then the CS was tested in both the deflated group and a non-deflated group. The CS elicited a longer lick latency after context deflation than in the absence of context deflation. This is a remarkable result because it was accomplished without presenting either the CS or the US in the $P(US/\overline{CS}) = 0$ situation. Miller and Schachtman (1985, p.65) concluded that "the comparator baseline is the current associative value of the conditioning context rather than the associative value of the conditioning context at the time of conditioning ... the critical comparison does not occur until the time of testing. Thus the information retained over the retention interval is apparently the independent associative strengths of the CS, i.e., $P(US/CS)$, and the conditioning context, i.e., $P(US/\overline{CS})$, rather than solely the outcome of the comparison, i.e., $P(CR/CS)$."

We will show how a combination of an adaptation level shift, associative averaging, and antagonistic rebound properties can explain this result, in much the same way that it can explain the result of Bottjer (1982) that a novel stimulus presented just before the CS can restore the inhibitory power to the CS.

In contrast to their results on contextual deflation, Miller and Schachtman (1985, p.66) also demonstrated that "no amount of contextual *inflation* will affect the comparator role of the conditioning context." Both the effect of contextual deflation and the non-effect of contextual deflation will be explained using the same mechanisms, as will the fact that US-alone presentations either before (Holman, 1976) or during CS conditioning do degrade CS responding, but not after (Jenkins and Lambos, 1983). The present theory thus has a broader explanatory range than the comparator hypothesis, because Miller and Schachtman (1985, p.67) remarked that they "currently do not have any reasonable hypothesis as to why contextual inflation appears to be ineffective, whereas contextual deflation does influence responding ... it remains unclear why unsignaled US's following conditioning apparently fail to augment CI, whereas US's during conditioning do provide CI."

In addition, we suggest explanations of other important data that Miller and Schachtman (1985, p.69) have summarized, such as "why a conditioned inhibitor attenuates excitor behavior on a summation test far more than does a novel stimulus (Pavlov, 1927)" and why, as in the experiments of Cotton, Goodall, and Mackintosh (1982) that a "$A \rightarrow$ large shock$/AX \rightarrow$ small shock procedure renders X effectively inhibitory as measured in a summation test with a previously conditioned excitor (B) when B had previously been paired with a large shock, but *not* when B had been paired with a small shock" (Miller and Schachtman, 1985, p.69). The same mechanisms also clarify why, although conditioned excitation is retarded, conditioned inhibition is facilitated by preconditioning US-alone exposures (Hinson, 1982), why $A + /X-$ trials may produce some conditioned inhibition, but only weakly if at all, and why pretest extinction of A restores responding to X in an overshadowing paradigm (Kaufman and Bolles, 1981). These results also extend beyond the reach of the comparator hypothesis, since "the comparator hypothesis ... is silent concerning how either the nominal CS or context accrue excitatory associative strength" (Miller and Schachtman, 1985, p.81).

22. A Theoretical Review: The Synchronization and Persistence Problems of Pavlovian Conditioning

Our explanation of these demanding data about conditioned inhibition is a variant of an explanation of blocking in terms of the following types of processes (Grossberg, 1975, 1982b; Grossberg and Levine, 1987): How does the pairing of CS_1 with US in the first phase of a blocking experiment endow the CS_1 cue with properties of a conditioned, or secondary, reinforcer? How do the reinforcing properties of a cue, whether primary (US) or secondary (CS_1), shift the focus of attention towards its own processing? How does the limited capacity of attentional resources arise, so that a shift of attention towards one set of cues (CS_1 or US) can prevent other cues from being attended (CS_2 or CS)? How does withdrawal of attention from a cue prevent that cue from entering into new conditioned relationships?

Mechanisms to instantiate these processes have been derived from solutions of several simple, but basic, neural design problems, which came into view through real-time analyses of conditioning data.

The first design problem, called the *synchronization problem*, was posed in Grossberg (1971, pp.227–237). This problem asks how $CS - US$ associations can develop in a stable fashion in spite of the variability of the time lag between CS and US. The synchronization problem came into focus as a result of quantitative results from previous work (Grossberg, 1969b, 1970), which showed that each elementary sensory representation or motor command could be represented mathematically as a spatial pattern of activation across a network of cell populations. If activity at a population coding a CS was followed repeatedly by the same US, the LTM traces activated by the CS population could cumulatively learn the spatial pattern corresponding to that US. However, if the CS was followed at different time intervals by two or more events, among which only a single US occurred, the CS-activated LTM traces would not learn the spatial pattern corresponding to the US. Instead, they would learn a mixture of the spatial patterns corresponding to all the events which occurred when the CS was active, whether meaningful to the organism or not. Such a mixture would typically encode little useful information about the environment and would certainly not resemble the US pattern.

The synchronization problem hereby brought into focus two related problems of fundamental importance: How does an organism know how to distinguish significant events for encoding in LTM among all the irrelevant environmental fluctuations that never cease to occur? How are conditioning systems designed to be capable of stably operating *in continuous*, or *real time*, despite the fact that meaningful events, such as novel events and US's, occur at irregular and discrete time intervals?

The Grossberg (1971) analysis of the synchronization problem led to the proposal that there exist populations of cells, called D for drive representations (Figures 1b and 2), that are separate from the sensory representations of particular stimuli but are related to particular drives and emotions. Workers such as Bower (1981) and Bower, Gilligan, and Monteiro (1981) have called such drive representations "emotion nodes." A food US, for example, unconditionally activates the D population corresponding to the hunger drive if the hunger drive level is sufficiently high. Repeated pairing of CS with a food US thus causes pairing of stimulation of the CS sensory representation, which we denote by S_{CS}, with that of the D representation of the hunger drive, which we denote by D_H. If the $S_{CS} \rightarrow D_H$ synapses are assumed to be modifiable according to an associative rule, such as (14), then the pairing $S_{CS} \rightarrow D_H$ can become strengthened, so that eventually the CS by itself will be able to activate the drive representation D_H and thereby becomes a *conditioned reinforcer* for food. Once a neutral CS (call it CS_1) has been conditioned, it can be used as a US to reinforce responses to another CS (call it CS_2) in a later experiment. Once the $S_{CS_1} \rightarrow D_H$ synapses have been strengthened, repeated presentation of CS_2 followed by CS_1 can, in turn, strengthen the associative $S_{CS_2} \rightarrow D_H$ synapses, as in Figure 15.

Pathways $D \rightarrow S$ from the drive representations to the sensory representations were also derived and shown to be conditionable. Conditioning in the $D \rightarrow S$ pathways was related to classical concepts about *incentive motivation* and shown to overcome some serious problems involving heuristic approaches to the definition of motivation. Whereas reinforcement acts directly upon the efficacy of $S \rightarrow D$ pathways in this model, the entire conditionable pathway $S \rightarrow D \rightarrow S$ regulates motivational support for the learning and performance of conditioned responses along stimulus-response ($S \rightarrow R$) circuits (Figure 2).

In order to relate $S \rightarrow D$ conditioning, $D \rightarrow S$ conditioning, and $S \rightarrow R$ conditioning, and thereby to analyse how the $S \rightarrow D \rightarrow S$ feedback loop regulates attention towards motivationally salient cues, Grossberg (1975; reprinted in Grossberg, 1982c) defined and analysed the *persistence problem* of classical conditioning, also known as the *turkey-love fiasco*. This problem arose from consideration of another typical conditioning situation which seems problematic only when one attempts to build a real-time model.

In Figure 27b, the cues CS, and CS_2 have previously been conditioned to responses CR_1 and CR_2. Responses CR_1 and CR_2 are assumed to be motivationally incompatible, such as eating and sex. A catastrophic problem could occur in an improperly designed learning circuit if CS_1 and CS_2 were then alternately scanned in rapid succession. If only one of the cues had previously been conditioned to a response, then no difficulty would occur (Figure 27a). However, if both cues were already conditioned and if classical conditioning were merely a feedforward process which associatively links cues with simultaneously active responses, then cross-conditioning from CS_1 to CR_2 and from CS_2 to CR_1 could rapidly occur (Figure 27b). This example identifies the core issue: When many cues are processed in parallel, and some of the cues are already conditioned to motivationally incompatible responses, then why are not these associations quickly degraded by cross-conditioning? How can the ubiquity of parallel cue processing be reconciled with the persistence of learned meanings?

The persistence problem was also called the turkey-love fiasco to emphasize its basic nature and the absurd world to which it could lead if not actively prevented. During an otherwise uneventful turkey dinner with one's lover, suppose that one alternately looks at lover and turkey, where visual cues of lover are associated with sexual responses (among others!) and visual cues of turkey are associated with eating responses. Why we do not come away from dinner with tendencies to eat our lover and to have sex with turkeys? The fact that we do not illustrates that the persistence of learned meanings can endure despite the fact that sensory cues which are processed in parallel often control motivationally incompatible responses.

At least two types of mechanisms have been proposed to deal with this fundamental problem: (1) pre-wired, or innate, connections among preferred sets of internal representations, and (2) dynamic regulation of conditioned associations via attentional mechanisms. In general, a combination of both types of factors may be operative, since the

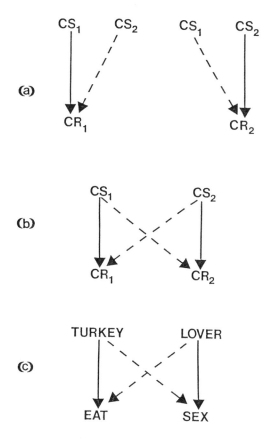

Figure 27. The persistence problem of classical conditioning: (a) A CS_j can be quickly associated with the CR_i of a distinct CS_i; (b) When each of the conditioned stimuli CS_1 and CS_2 is already conditioned to a distinct conditioned response CR_1 and CR_2, respectively, at the beginning of an experiment, alternative scanning of CS_1 and CS_2 does not always cause rapid cross conditioning of CS_1 to CR_2 and CS_2 to CR_1, as is clear by consideration of the absurd consequence depicted in (c) that would arise after dining with one's lover.

non-equipotentiality of pre-wired connections can facilitate conditioning among certain sets of events above others.

Seligman illustrated the role of non-equipotentiality during an experience when he "... felt the effects of the stomach flu six hours after eating filet mignon with sauce Bearnaise. The next time I had sauce Bearnaise, I could not bear the taste of it ... Neither the filet mignon, nor the white plates off which I ate the sauce, nor Tristan und Isolde, ... nor my wife ..., became aversive" (Seligman and Hager, 1972).

Several experiments also suggest that some combinations of stimuli and reinforcers results in faster conditioning than others. For instance, Garcia and Koelling (1966) found that when a compound gustatory and auditory stimulus are paired with agents that produce nausea, gustatory but not auditory stimuli are associated with nausea. On the other hand, when the compound stimulus is paired with a shock US, the auditory stimulus is associated with the US (Domjan and Wilson, 1972). Foree and LoLordo (1973) showed that pigeons associate visual stimuli with a food US more readily than auditory stimuli with a food US, and that this relationship is reversed when a shock US is used.

Seligman and Hager (1972) suggested that the results could be explained in terms of a selective associative difference by which a given CS is innately more "prepared" to be associated with a given US than with others. Mackintosh (1973) proposed that previous experience with the difference in the correlation of different classes of CS's and US's determines their predisposition to be associated at a later time.

Grossberg (1975) suggested a mechanistic solution of the persistence problem in which the possible non-equipotentiality of innate connections was acknowledged, but additional attentional regulatory mechanisms were invoked to deal with the case in whcih the sensory CS's were approximately equipotential with respect to pairs of motivationally incompatible responses. This solution proposed how incentive motivational feedback due to conditionable $D \rightarrow S$ pathways could shift an organism's attentional focus to preferentially process previously experienced motivationally compatible cues. Thus attention-switching between sets of motivationally compatible cues can dynamically buffer motivationally incompatible sets of cues against rapid cross-conditioning, since when a sensory representation S has a zero signal S_k in (14) and (15), no new conditioning of its LTM traces z_{k7} and z_{k8} can occur. In addition, a sensory cue which possesses a large conditioned $S \rightarrow D \rightarrow S$ feedback pathway can quickly prime the STM of motivationally compatible sensory cues while amplifying the STM activity of its own sensory representation (Figure 2). Reinforcing cues can hereby draw attention to themselves and to their entire motivational "set" via self-generated incentive motivational feedback signals (Figure 28). Killeen (1982a, 1982b) has also emphasized the importance of incentive motivation for the modelling of instrumental conditioning data.

23. Competition for Limited Capacity Short Term Memory Activity and Attention

The sensory representations which emit conditioned reinforcer signals and receive incentive motivational signals also compete among themselves for a limited capacity STM resource (Figure 2). The ubiquitous occurrence of limited capacity STM was traced in Grossberg (1973, 1980) to a more basic processing requirement: the ability of cell networks to process spatially distributed input patterns without irreparably distorting these input patterns due to either internal noise or saturation effects. This *noise-saturation dilemma* can be prevented by an on-center off-surround anatomy through which the cells interact via mass action (or shunting) laws. Such a network interaction implies, without further assumptions, that the total suprathreshold activation of the network tends to be conserved, and thus possesses a limited capacity.

When such a network is also designed to accomplish STM storage, its on-center off-surround interactions are recurrent, or feedback, interactions in which the cells excite themselves and inhibit other cells via feedback pathways (Figure 2). In addition to its noise-saturation and limited capacity properties, such a recurrent on-center off-surround network contrast enhances an input pattern before storing the contrast-enhanced activation pattern which emerges across the cells in STM (also called working memory). Thus one must distinguish between the input pattern and the more focal STM activity pattern that it generates. "Attention is paid" to those sensory representations whose cells receive a positive level of *stored* STM activity.

When incentive motivational feedback signals form part of the total input pattern to

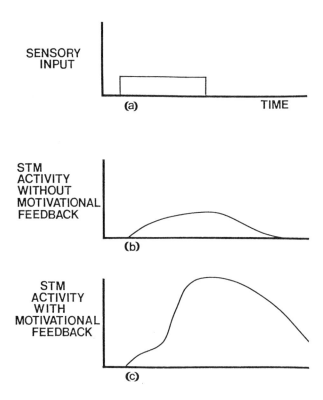

Figure 28. Augmentation of STM activation at a sensory representation S_{CS} by feedback signalling through the pathway $S_{CS} \to D \to S_{CS}$: In response to the sensory input (a) received by S_{CS}, the STM activation profile before learning is schematized in (b). After learning within the $S_{CS} \to D \to S_{CS}$ pathway takes place, the initial activation remains as in (b). However, as the feedback signals are registered, the STM activation of S_{CS} can be greatly amplified and prolonged, as schematized in (c).

the sensory representations (Figure 2), these signals can bias the competition for STM activity towards motivationally salient cues. Due to the limited capacity of STM, motivationally salient cues, in particular primary and secondary reinforcers, can draw attention to themselves via their strong conditioned $S \to D \to S$ feedback loops. In order to initiate such an attention shift, such cues must first start to be processed due to their sensory properties. After sensory processing is initiated, it can activate the learned reinforcing and motivating pathways of the cues, and can thereby help to direct the ultimate allocation of sensory and attentional resources.

Once attention shifts away from a sensory representation, its activity can become small, or even subthreshold. If, by whatever means, an attention shift causes a signal S_k from a sensory representation to become small or zero in the LTM equations (14) or (15), then the LTM traces of the representation learn very slowly or not at all.

24. Gated Dipoles and Opponent Extinction

Gated dipoles were originally derived in Grossberg (1972b) to explain how the offset of a reinforcer of positive (or negative) sign can generate an antagonistic rebound to which a simultaneous CS can be conditioned as a reinforcer of negative (or positive) sign. Using these gated dipoles, the drive representations in Figure 2 were organized into the on-channels and the off-channels of recurrent gated dipoles. These gated dipole circuits were, in turn, linked together via competitive interactions into gated dipole fields, which were designed to choose that drive representation whose combination of sensory, reinforcing and homeostatic constraints was most favorable at any given time ("winner-take-all"). The chosen channel could release incentive motivational output signals to the sensory representations and thereby focus attention upon the motivationally most favored sensory representations. These enhanced representations could thereupon generate output signals to release conditioned responses consistent with these momentary sensory and motivational constraints.

A surprising property of a gated dipole is that the unexpected nonoccurrence of an event can trigger an antagonistic rebound by causing a sudden increment in its nonspecific arousal level I (Grossberg, 1972b, 1987a). These two types of rebound-inducing events clarified how a large on-conditioned reinforcer value of a CS—that is, its on-LTM trace z_{k7} in (14)—could be extinguished by conditioning its off-LTM trace z_{k8} in (15). Such off-conditioning of z_{k8} may be due to reinforcing inputs delivered directly to the dipole's off-channel. Off-conditioning may also be due to antagonistic rebounds at the off-channel in response to either sudden offsets of on-channel inputs or unexpected nonoccurrence of on-channel reinforcers. This multiplicity of conditions leading to off-conditioning has previously been used to clarify many paradoxical properties of conditioning and extinction data, and will also play an important explanatory role herein.

A new property of extinction has been understood through the quantitative analysis of a READ circuit described in Part I. This property is called *opponent extinction*. Opponent extinction clarifies how a conditioning circuit in which passive extinction does not occur can prevent its LTM traces from saturating at maximal values due to a progressive accumulation of associative strength over many conditioning trials. Opponent extinction also shows how associative memories may be actively extinguished even if they do not passively extinguish. The opponent extinction property is based upon the dissociation of associative read-in and read-out that was related to conditioning at dendritic spines in Section 13. Opponent extinction occurs as follows.

If, by any means, off-conditioning proceeds until $z_{k8} \cong z_{k7} > 0$, then the conditioned reinforcer signals $S_k z_{k7}$ and $S_k z_{k8}$ of a conditioned reinforcer to a READ circuit become approximately equal. This circumstance can actively extinguish the LTM traces z_{k7} and z_{k8} as follows. Suppose for definiteness that only signal S_k is positive at any time. Then the difference signal $\Delta \cong 0$ in (34). Consequently $x_5 \cong 0 \cong x_6$, by (21) and (22). Thus both z_{k7} and z_{k8} approach zero, by (14) and (15). In summary, as the on-LTM trace and off-LTM trace of a conditioned reinforcer become approximately equal, these LTM traces are actively extinguished due to the fact that conditioned reinforcer learning tracks the *net imbalance* of activation across the dipole's on-channel and off-channel. This process is called *opponent extinction*. More generally, conditioned reinforcer LTM traces continually readjust themselves to track the net imbalance which they detect in all the environmental contexts within which they are activated. Opponent extinction hereby avoids the possible saturation at maximal values of both LTM traces z_{k7} and z_{k8}, no matter how many experiments activate S_k.

25. Adaptive Resonance Theory: Expectation, Mismatch, Reset, and Rebound

The gated dipole's rebound properties emphasized that cognitive, notably unexpected, events play a critical role in the modulation of reinforcement, conditioning, and extinction processes. The conceptual and data analyses generated by this cognitive-emotional connection led directly to the discovery and development of *adaptive resonance theory* (Grossberg, 1976a, 1976b, 1978, 1980; reprinted in Grossberg, 1982c). Adaptive resonance theory has, by now, been used to analyse and predict a large interdisciplinary data base and has undergone substantial technical development (Carpenter and Grossberg, 1987a; Cohen and Grossberg, 1987; Grossberg, 1987a, 1987b). Only those qualitative features of the theory which are needed to explain data about conditioned inhibition will be summarized herein.

Adaptive resonance theory suggests how internal representations of sensory events, including CS's or US's, can be learned in a stable fashion despite the potentially erosive effects of irrelevant environmental fluctuations. Among the mechanisms for the stable self-organization of sensory recognition codes are the read-out of learned top-down expectations which are matched against bottom-up sensory signals (Figure 1). When a mismatch occurs, a nonspecific arousal burst is triggered via an orienting subsystem. This arousal burst acts to reset the sensory representations of all cues that are currently being stored in STM (Figure 29). In particular, representations with high STM activation tend to become less active, representations with low STM activation tend to become more active, and the novel event which caused the mismatch tends to be more actively stored than it would have been had it been expected (Grossberg, 1982b, 1987a). These properties can be traced to the combined action of gated dipole interactions and limited capacity competitive interactions which are hypothesized to take place among the sensory representations. As a result of such an STM reset event, sensory representations which had been actively reading-out an erroneous expectation become less active in STM; hence, the expectation can be updated. Representations which were attentionally blocked before the reset event occurred can become unblocked, or dishabituated, in STM; they code sensory information that may have been erroneously unattended. Finally, the novel event which triggered the mismatch becomes more active in STM; it encodes potentially important new information.

In order to deal effectively with temporal order effects, the architecture schematized in Figure 1 needs to be augmented by mechanisms for storage of event sequences in working memory (Grossberg and Stone, 1986a, 1986b) and for the learning of temporal discriminations (Grossberg and Schmajuk, 1987).

26. Parallel Learning of Sensory Expectation and Conditioned Reinforcement

The synthesis of adaptive resonance mechanisms with conditioning mechanisms shows that the internal representation of a sensory event controls at least two distinct types of output signals: learned top-down expectations within an attentional subsystem (Figure 1a) and learned conditioned reinforcer signals to a READ circuit (Figures 1b and 3). The distinct, but interacting, properties of these signals in different learning environments are critical to our explanations of conditioned inhibition data. Notable are the interactions whereby a disconfirmed sensory expectation can cause an antagonistic rebound within a READ circuit.

Suppose, for example, that an active sensory representation of a conditioned reinforcer is reset due to a sensory mismatch with its top-down expectation. The reset event causes a rapid decrease in the STM activity of the sensory representation and, thus, in its output signal S_k to the READ circuit in (12) and (13). As a result, its conditioned reinforcer

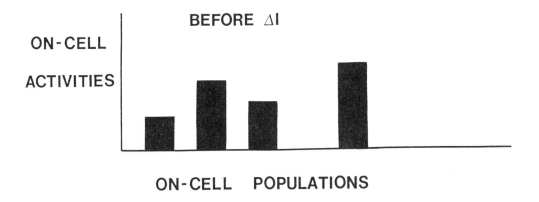

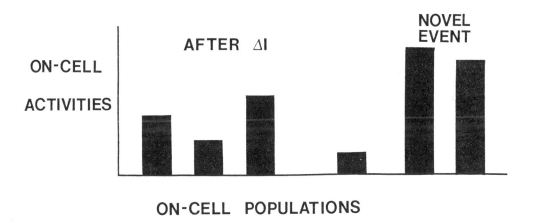

Figure 29. Short-term memory reaction to an arousal-mediated (ΔI) unexpected event. The arousal burst ΔI tends to inhibit, or reset, populations that were very active before the expected event and to enhance, or dishabituate, populations that were weakly active before the unexpected event. The novel event which triggered ΔI is also preferentially stored. Inactive populations remain inactive, but they are sensitized by a gain change. This type of global reset event gives more short term memory activity to those populations that did not control the actions leading to the unexpected outcome, including cells that code the unexpected outcome.

inputs $S_k z_{k7}$ and $S_k z_{k8}$ to the READ circuit also decrease. If the cue is an on-conditioned reinforcer (viz., $z_{k7} \gg z_{k8}$), an antagonistic rebound can hereby be elicited in the READ circuit's off-channel.

Using the above properties, we now provide a unified explanation of data about conditioned inhibition. In particular, we suggest an explanation of why a conditioned excitor extinguishes, yet a conditioned inhibitor does not extinguish. This explanation clarifies how this difference obtains, despite the facts that a given CS could be trained to become either a conditioned excitor or a conditioned inhibitor, and that during extinction trials, only the CS is presented. In addition, the explanation shows how the different *affective* properties of excitors and inhibitors are controlled, and utilizes the difference between conditioning of a CS to an affective reaction (viz., its role as a conditioned reinforcer) and conditioning of the same CS to a predicted sensory event (viz., its role as a source of conditioned expectation).

27. Conditioning and Extinction of a Conditioned Excitor

When a CS_1 is paired with shock on successive conditioning trials, several things happen in the model. The sensory representation S_1 of the CS_1 is conditioned to the drive representation D_f corresponding to a fear reaction, both through its conditioned reinforcer pathway $S_1 \to D_f$ and through its incentive motivational pathway $D_f \to S_1$. As a result, later presentations of CS_1 tend to generate an amplified STM activation of S_1, and thus CS_1 is preferentially attended. Due to the limited capacity of STM, less salient cues tend to be attentionally blocked when CS_1 is presented.

As the cognitive-emotional feedback loop $S_1 \to D_f \to S_1$ is strengthened during conditioning trials, S_1 also learns a sensory expectation of the shock. During extinction, CS_1 is presented on unshocked trials. We assume, as in Figures 13–21, that the numerical parameters of the READ circuit are chosen to prevent significant passive decay of LTM traces from occurring; that is, we assume that extinction of conditioned reinforcer learning is due to an active process of counter-conditioning, as in Section 24. When the expected shock does not occur, a mismatch occurs with the learned expectation read-out by S_1. As described in Section 26, the STM activity of S_1 is quickly reduced and an antagonistic rebound occurs in the READ circuit. This rebound inhibits the fear reaction that is regulated by the on-channel, and activates the relief reaction (Denny, 1970; Dunham, 1971; Dunham, Mariner, and Adams, 1969; Hammond, 1968; Masterson, 1970; McAllister and McAllister, 1971; McAllister, McAllister, and Douglass, 1971; Rescorla, 1969; Rescorla and LoLordo, 1965; Reynierse and Rizley, 1970; Weisman and Litner, 1969) that is regulated by the dipole's off-channel D_r.

The collapse in S_1's STM activity may be partial or complete. We assume for definiteness that it is partial, and describe in this case how conditioning within the $S_1 \to D_f \to S_1$ pathway is antagonized by rebound-contingent conditioning, which progressively extinguishes CS_1 as a source of conditioned fear.

The collapse of S_1's activity occurs prior to the rebound from D_f to D_r. Due to the hysteretic properties of a feedback competitive circuit, there exists a time interval during which D_f remains active after S_1's activity collapses. During this time interval, the incentive motivational pathway $D_f \to S_1$ is weakened due to the same conditioning mechanism (Section 24) that could lead to total extinction were S_1 to become totally inactive. If CS_1 is followed by a no-shock interval on successive learning trials, the weakening of the $D_f \to S_1$ pathway is cumulative. As a result, on a later presentation of CS_1, D_f will supply less feedback to S_1, so that S_1 will be less attended than previously, but could possibly still be more attended than an irrelevant situational cue.

In addition to conditioned weakening of the $D_f \to S_1$ pathway, the $S_1 \to D_f$ pathway can be greatly weakened or even totally extinguished. This is because S_1 remains active after it is reset. Consequently, S_1 can become associated with an antagonistic rebound at D_r. This learning may take place at a slower rate than it did when S_1 was associated with D_f, because S_1 is smaller after reset than before. On the other hand, the maximal possible LTM strength of the $S_1 \to D_r$ pathway can exceed that of the $S_1 \to D_f$ pathway, as it does in the simulations summarized in Figures 14 and 15, as well as those in Figures 16 and 17. If CS_1 is followed by a no-shock interval on successive trials, this learning process will be cumulative. Finally a time will occur when the pathway $S_1 \to D_r$ is as strong as the pathway $S_1 \to D_f$. As this time is approached, both conditioned reinforcer pathways become extinguished by the mechanism described in Section 24, and S_1 is extinguished as a conditioned excitor.

In the event that extinction of conditioned reinforcer $S \to D$ pathways occurs rapidly, it may permit residual $D \to S$ incentive motivational associations to persist. Such residual associations, including the associations which encode sensory expectations (Section 25) help to explain how, during successive acquisitions and extinctions, rate of acquisition and extinction may increase as a result of successive reversals (Davenport, 1969; Gonzalez, Berger, and Bitterman, 1967; Schmaltz and Theios, 1972).

28. Conditioning and Non-Extinction of a Conditioned Inhibitor

Suppose that CS_1 has become a conditioned excitor, thereby learning to strongly activate the $S_1 \to D_f \to S_1$ pathway as well as a learned expectation of a subsequent shock. Now present the compound stimulus $CS_1 + CS_2$ and follow it by a no-shock interval. When CS_1 and CS_2 are simultaneously presented, S_1's activity is amplified by positive feedback through the strong conditioned $S_1 \to D_f \to S_1$ pathway (Figure 30). As a result of the limited capacity of STM, the STM activity of S_2 is inhibited, or blocked. (The novelty of CS_2 can partially mitigate this blocking effect.) When the expected shock does not occur, the mismatch with S_1's sensory expectation causes both S_1 and S_2 to be reset. As described in Section 25, S_1's STM activity decreases while S_2's STM activity increases. Due to S_1's decrease, a rebound occurs at D_r. Consequently, the unexpected nonoccurrence of the shock enables S_2 to become associated with D_r in both of the pathways $S_2 \to D_r$ and $D_r \to S_2$. These are the primary cognitive-emotional conditioning events that turn CS_2 into a conditioned inhibitor.

If $(CS_1 \to$ shock$)$ trials and $(CS_1 + CS_2 \to$ no-shock$)$ trials are interspersed, then CS_1's status as a conditioned excitor can be restored against the extinction which takes place on the no-shock trials, in the manner summarized in Section 27. Intermittent restoration of the conditioned excitor properties of CS_1 enables CS_1 to motivate the cumulative training of CS_2 as a conditioned inhibitor on the intervening no-shock trials.

Why does not CS_2 extinguish when it is presented alone, unlike a conditioned excitor (DeVito, 1980; Owren and Kaplan, 1981; Witcher, 1978; Zimmer-Hart and Rescorla, 1974)? Why does not a neutral stimulus presented with a conditioned inhibitor acquire excitatory value (Baker, 1974)? Simple answers are now available.

When S_2 is unblocked by the non-occurrence of shock, it learns a sensory expectation. This sensory expectation does not, however, predict shock. It includes whatever contex-

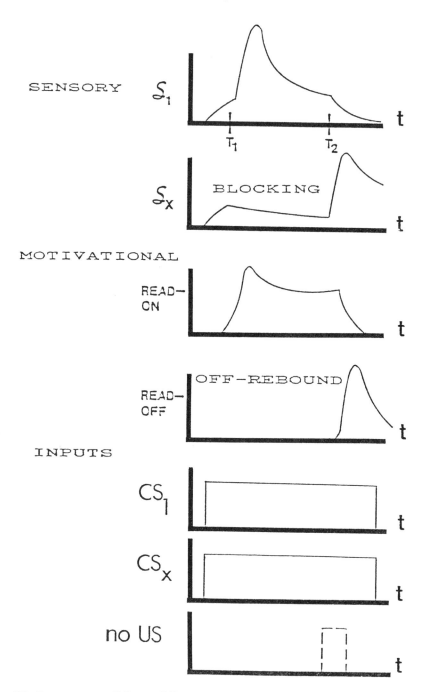

Figure 30. Presentation of CS_1 and CS_2 when CS_1 has become a conditioned excitor and the compound stimulus is followed by no-shock: During the no-shock interval between times T_1 and T_2, S_1 is actively amplified by positive feedback and S_2 is blocked. During the shock interval, disconfirmation of the expected shock causes both S_1 and S_2 to be reset. S_1's STM activity decreases and S_2's STM activity increases. Due to S_1's increase, D_f also decreases, thereby causing a rebound at D_r. This rebound becomes associated with the increased activity of S_2.

tual representations are sufficiently salient and repeatable to be cumulatively learned on successive conditioning trials. Thus presentation of the conditioned inhibitor CS_2 within a given context does not disconfirm the sensory expectation controlled by S_2. Since passive extinction does not occur, a conditioned inhibitor CS_2 does not extinguish when it is presented alone.

On the other hand, S_2 does learn to control a strong $S_2 \rightarrow D_r \rightarrow S_2$ pathway. Hence it becomes attentionally amplified and can block the processing of neutral stimuli. Thus a neutral stimulus presented with a conditioned inhibitor does not acquire excitatory value (Baker, 1974).

29. An Explanation of the "Slave" Data

Our explanation of the Lysle and Fowler (1985) data about conditioned inhibition as a "slave" process combines adaptive resonance properties of expectancy matching and STM reset with READ circuit properties of adaptation level and rebound. The following additional model properties are particularly relevant.

Extinction of a conditioned excitor CS_1 includes not only extinction of the feedback pathway $S_1 \rightarrow D_f \rightarrow S_1$, but also reconditioning of the sensory expectation associated with S_1 to anticipate a no-shock, purely contextual, sensory environment. Contextual cues X can also become conditioned excitors in a situation wherein a conditioned excitor CS_1 or a shock occurs at random times. Such contextual cues X may condition an expectation of shock and a pathway $S_X \rightarrow D_f \rightarrow S_X$ between their sensory representations S_X and the drive representation D_f, as does S_1. The fact that cues X may be attended during no-shock intervals does not, in itself, imply that the $S_X \rightarrow D_f \rightarrow S_X$ pathways will extinguish, because extinction does not occur passively (Section 17). Contextual cues extinguish only during time intervals when their expectation of shock is actively disconfirmed, thereby triggering the rebounds that enable S_X to become associated with D_r.

Consider what happens within the model in response to the conditioning experiences of the groups $CS_1[CS_2]$, $X[CS_2]$, and $N[CS_2]$ that were defined in Section 20. When CS_1 is extinguished by being followed by no-shock intervals, both its sensory expectation of shock and the sensory expectation of shock controlled by attended contextual cues X are simultaneously extinguished. Likewise, the conditioned reinforcer pathways $S_1 \rightarrow D_f \rightarrow S_1$ and $S_X \rightarrow D_f \rightarrow S_X$ are simultaneously extinguished. Thus, when CS_2 is trained as a conditioned excitor by being randomly paired with shock on 50% of its trials, the context in which CS_2 occurs is one in which no-shock is expected. Thus the occurrence of a shock after CS_2 is, in this situation, surprising. In addition, because the fearful effects of X on D_f have been at least partially extinguished, the net effect of the compound cue $CS_2 + X$ on the gated dipole is to generate a net positive reaction at D_r. When a shock occurs subsequent to a presentation of CS_2, a large mismatch occurs with the sensory expectation of CS_2 and S_2 is vigorously reset. Due to the net positive reaction of D_r to CS_2, the reset of S_2 causes a large rebound from D_r to D_f. As this rebound from D_r to D_f is forming, the shock itself generates an unconditioned input to D_f. The rebound and the direct shock input summate to generate an unusually large activation of D_f. This enhanced fear reaction is learned by S_2. Thus, we trace the enhanced suppressive effect of CS_2 in the $CS_1[CS_2]$ group to the same types of mechanisms which Grossberg (1975) has used to explain the partial reinforcement acquisition effect. It is immediately clear from this explanation why extinction of the context X in group $X[CS_2]$ should have a similar, but smaller, effect on the subsequent suppressive effects of CS_2.

In contrast, consider what happens in group $N[CS_2]$. Here neither CS_1 nor X is extinguished. Thus contextual cues X are still conditioned to an expectation of shock and to the fear center D_f when retardation testing of CS_2 commences. When CS_2 is presented in such a context X, an expectation of shock can still be maintained by contextual cues. In addition, although S_2 is conditioned to D_r, X is conditioned to D_f. As a result the *net* effect of both sets of signals upon the READ circuit is to generate a large adaptation level $\hat{I}$ in (33) and a small, possibly even zero, difference value Δ in (34). We consider the case $\Delta = 0$ to make our argument in its most extreme form. A similar qualitative argument holds for small values of Δ.

Consider what happens within the model when CS_2 is first followed by a shock. Unlike the group $CS_1[CS_2]$, an expectation of shock does exist. Thus the reset of S_2 and X will be much less in the $N[CS_2]$ group than in the $CS_1[CS_2]$ group. In addition, if $\Delta \cong 0$, this reset event may cause *no significant rebound*, since both channels of the READ circuit may receive similar conditioned input both before and after the reset event. The primary effect of the shock is to generate an unconditioned input to D_f. This input does not summate with a rebound from D_r to D_f. Moreover, this unconditioned input is received by a gated dipole with an unusually large adaptation level $\hat{I}$. The net response of a gated dipole to a fixed phasic input is reduced in the presence of a large adaptation level $\hat{I}$ (Grossberg, 1972b, 1987a). Thus conditioning from S_2 to D_f is much slower in the $N[CS_2]$ group than in the $CS_1[CS_2]$ or $X[CS_2]$ groups.

Restoration of the conditioned inhibitory properties of CS_2 by presentation of a US is readily explained by the same mechanisms if the US is presented within the same context as CS_2. Such restoration can also be explained if the US is presented in a novel context that shares cues with the original context. These cues may, for example, include similar shape of the conditioning chambers and similar procedures in the animals' handling.

This explanation of the "slave" properties sets the stage for explaining the "comparator" properties described by Miller and Schachtman (1985) by explicating the mediating role of the context X.

30. An Explanation of the "Comparator" Data

How can CS_1 become a conditioned excitor if $P(US/CS_1) = .33$ and $P(US/\overline{CS_1}) = 0$, but a conditioned inhibitor if $P(US/CS_1) = .33$ and $P(US/\overline{CS_1}) = .67$? In addition, such an explanation would also show why there exists a neutral region of values of $P(US/CS_1)$ and $P(US/\overline{CS_1})$ in which CS_1 does not become a conditioned reinforcer. This crossover region often occurs when $P(US/CS_1) = P(US/\overline{CS_1})$ (Rescorla, 1968).

In the case $[P(US/CS_1) = .33, P(US/\overline{CS_1}) = 0]$, CS_1 generates a much stronger conditioned expectation of shock and conditioned attachment to D_f than does X. In the latter case, the reverse is true. In particular, consider an early learning trial when CS_1 is presented under the $[P(US/CS_1) = .33, P(US/\overline{CS_1}) = .67]$ contingency. Because S_X is conditioned more strongly to D_f than is S_1, S_X can partially block S_1. Suppose on this trial that the shock is unexpectedly absent. When the mismatch occurs, S_X can be reset as S_1 is unblocked. Consequently, S_1 can be associated with the rebound from D_r to D_f that is caused by the reset of X. This conditioning event tends to make CS_1 a source of conditioned relief.

On the other hand, CS_1 is followed by shocks on some trials, because $P(US/CS) = .33$. Thus the above argument does not necessarily imply that the LTM trace from S_1 to D_f is weaker than that to D_r. In general, however, the *net* conditioned fear caused by S_1 alone is significantly less than the *net* conditioned fear caused by S_X alone, and S_1 may be a source of net conditioned relief in some parameter ranges. In the case where S_1 remains conditioned to fear, the ratio $\frac{z_{Xf}}{z_{Xr}}$ is much larger than the ratio $\frac{z_{1f}}{z_{1r}}$; viz.,

$$\frac{z_{Xf}}{z_{Xr}} \gg \frac{z_{1f}}{z_{1r}}, \tag{49}$$

where the z's denote the LTM traces in the indicated pathways.

On a later test trial when contextual representations S_X are alone active, they share the limited capacity STM strength (35) among themselves. We simplify this constraint by lumping all contextual representations into one and writing

$$S_X = S. \tag{50}$$

During such a time interval, the conditioned reinforcer signal $S_X z_{Xf}$ is much larger than $S_X z_{Xr}$; viz.,

$$S_X z_{Xf} \gg S_X z_{Xr}. \tag{51}$$

When CS_1 is turned on, S_X tends to partially block activation of S_1 due to the strong positive feedback $S_X \to D_f \to S_X$ implied by (51). On the other hand, because $P(US/\overline{CS_1}) = .67$, attentional fluctuations during training trials enable the animal to attach fear reactions to only a subset of the sampled contextual cues X. Thus in the moments just after presentation of CS_1, CS_1 may be sampled with neutral contextual cues and may thus begin to activate S_1. To the extent to which S_1 survives blocking by S_X, both sensory representations may share the limited capacity STM activation, so that

$$S_1 + S_X = S, \tag{52}$$

although, due to blocking of CS_1 by X, often

$$S_X > S_1. \tag{53}$$

When (52) holds, the total signal $S_1 z_{1f} + S_X z_{Xf}$ to D_f is smaller than the total signal $S z_{Xf}$ to D_f that was active in response to X alone. Consequently, a sudden decrease in total input to D_f may occur after CS_1 is presented. This decrease causes a net reduction in conditioned fear and, if it is large enough, can cause a relief rebound at D_r. Thus CS_1 can act as a conditioned inhibitor when it is presented within context X whether or not z_{1r} is larger than z_{1f}. The possibility that S_1 can act like a conditioned inhibitor even if $z_{1f} > z_{1r}$ depends critically upon the antagonistic rebound properties of the READ circuit. When a relief rebound does occur, there exists a range of parameters such that S_1 can become a source of net conditioned relief, by being associated with the rebound at D_r.

Some more subtle effects should also be noted. By (21) and (22), $[x_5]^+ > 0$ only if $[x_6]^+ = 0$ and $[x_6]^+ > 0$ only if $[x_5]^+ = 0$. On the other hand, z_{k7} and z_{k8} in (14) and (15) perform a slow time-average of these quantities, as in (38). Thus although $[x_5]^+$ and $[x_6]^+$ cannot both be simultaneously positive, z_{k7} and z_{k8} can both be positive in a probabilistically defined environment, such as $[P(US/CS_1) = .33, P(US/\overline{CS_1}) = .67]$, wherein expectations are intermittently disconfirmed. In such a situation, presentation of CS_1 can generate net positive signals $S_1 z_{1f}$ and $S_1 z_{1r}$ to both D_f and D_r. When this happens,

$$\frac{S_1 z_{1f} + S_X z_{Xf}}{S_1 z_{1r} + S_X z_{Xr}} < \frac{z_{Xf}}{z_{Xr}}. \tag{54}$$

Hence, in addition to the decrease in total input to $\mathcal{D}_f$, there may also be an increase in the total input to $\mathcal{D}_r$. When this occurs, the fearful difference Δ in (34) may decrease as the adaptation level $\hat{I}$ in (33) increases. Thus a reduction in sensitivity to shock may occur in addition to, or in lieu of, a net relief reaction.

The same type of explanation shows why the critical factor in generating conditioned excitation or inhibition was whether or not unsignalled shocks were given in the conditioning context. Once a net fear connection $S_1 \rightarrow \mathcal{D}_f$ or a net relief connection $S_1 \rightarrow \mathcal{D}_r$ is established within the conditioning context, it is carried intact to the same, or to a novel, test context. In addition, the associative averaging property defined by (35) and (36) can explain why prior unsignalled shocks in context B do not necessarily increase the conditioned excitatory effect of CS_1 in context B during conditioning.

31. The Asymmetry between Context Inflation and Context Deflation

In the context deflation experiment, training on $[P(US/CS_1) = .33, P(US/\overline{CS_1}) = .67]$ was followed by extinction on $P(US/\overline{CS}) = 0$. Then CS_1 was tested in both a deflated group and a non-deflated group. The lick latency to CS_1 was longer after deflation than in the absence of deflation. This type of effect follows from the properties summarized in Section 30. Without deflation, presentation of CS_1 in X can reduce the fearful difference Δ and increase the adaptation level $\hat{I}$ relative to the dipole's state in response to X alone. After deflation, X does not generate fearful inputs to $\mathcal{D}_f$. Hence the deflated X does not establish a large fear reaction within $\mathcal{D}_f$, and thus does not block CS_1. Presentation of CS_1 in X can therefore effectively activate S_1 which can cause an increase in the fearful difference Δ relative to the dipole's state in response to X alone. Consequently, deflating the context X can increase the conditioned excitor properties of CS_1 when it is subsequently presented in X.

In the context inflation situation, $P(US/\overline{CS})$ is chosen to be larger than the $P(US/\overline{CS}) = .67$ used during training trials, with little effect on CS_1's effect during testing. Several model properties conspire to produce this result. These properties depend upon the fact that probabilities $P(US/\overline{CS_1})$ which significantly exceed .67 define a learning situation wherein essentially all contextual cues X may be associated strongly with $\mathcal{D}_f$. The context X becomes one characterized by inescapable fear.

In such a situation, very strong, persistent activation of the $S_X \rightarrow \mathcal{D}_f \rightarrow S_X$ pathway occurs. Thus S_1 is strongly blocked by S_X whenever CS_1 is presented. This property prevents S_1 from reading out the conditioned reinforcer values that could otherwise have enabled CS_1 to act as a conditioned inhibitor. Choosing a very high $P(US/\overline{CS_1})$ can also persistently inhibit the orienting reactions (Grossberg, 1975, 1982c, 1984b) which could have enabled the model to intermittently reset fearful contextual representations and thereby facilitate the probability that initial processing of CS_1 could partially overcome the strong contextual blocking effect.

32. Some Additional Data Explanations

To explain the Cotton, Goodall, and Mackintosh (1982) data summarized in Section 21, it is only necessary to add that a large shock can cause large z_{Xf} values to be learned whereas a small shock causes only small z_{Xf} values to be learned. These conclusions follow by inspection of equations (4), (8), (10), and (14) under the hypothesis that J is large (small) when shock is large (small).

The facts that conditioned excitation is retarded and conditioned inhibition is facilitated by preconditioning US-alone exposures (Hinson, 1982) can be explained by the same mechanisms that explained CS_1 properties in response to $[P(US/CS_1) = .33, P(US/\overline{CS_1}) = .67]$, with the difference that the $P(US/\overline{CS_1})$ manipulation precedes, rather than being interspersed with, CS_1 trials. The argument did not depend upon this difference.

The classical fact that a conditioned inhibitor attenuates excitator behavior on a summation test far more than does a novel stimulus (Pavlov, 1927) can be traced to the different types of mechanisms which regulate attention through an expectancy mismatch and through the $S \rightarrow D \rightarrow S$ feedback pathways. Whereas a novel event can amplify its initial storage in STM via an expectancy mismatch, and thereby temporarily remove attentional resources from a conditioned excitor, the conditioned excitor can restore its attentional focus through persistent self-amplification via its $S \rightarrow D_f \rightarrow S$ pathway subsequent to the novel event. In contrast, a conditioned inhibitor with a sufficiently strong $S \rightarrow D_r \rightarrow S$ pathway can compete effectively with the $S \rightarrow D_f \rightarrow S$ pathway of a conditioned excitor throughout the time interval of their simultaneous STM storage, thereby causing a sustained reduction in the efficacy of the conditioned excitor.

33. Concluding Remarks

At least four types of learning process are relevant in the data discussions herein described: learning of conditioned reinforcement, incentive motivation, conditioned response, and sensory expectancy. These several types of learning process, which by their very nature operate on a slow time scale, regulate and are regulated by rapidly fluctuating limited capacity STM representations of sensory events. The theory suggests how nonlinear feedback interactions among these fast information processing mechanisms and slow learning mechanisms control data-predictive emergent properties—such as STM reset, antagonistic rebound, adaptation level shift, associative averaging, and opponent extinction—which cannot be understood using traditional concepts such as contiguity learning and associative summation.

From this perspective, the different time scales on which sensory expectancies and conditioned reinforcers may be learned becomes a key explanatory issue. This is the type of distinction that is hinted at by the observation of Gibbons *et al.* (1980, p.45) that "Perhaps intermittent reinforcement generates schedule-induced cues only later in training, and early unreinforced trial episodes are in some sense 'ignored'."

NOTE 1

In addition to being used to analyse data about conditioning, specialized gated dipoles have been used to analyse data about certain mental disorders (Grossberg, 1972b, 1984a, 1984b), mammalian circadian rhythms (Carpenter and Grossberg, 1983, 1984, 1985, 1986), eating and drinking rhythms (Grossberg, 1984a, 1985), photoreceptor transduction (Carpenter and Grossberg, 1981), cortical mechanisms of preattentive visual perception (Grossberg, 1987c, 1987d; Grossberg and Mingolla, 1985), decision making under risk (Grossberg and Gutowski, 1987), and neural and evoked potential substrates underlying the learning of cognitive recognition codes (Banquet and Grossberg, 1987; Carpenter and Grossberg 1987a, 1987b; Grossberg, 1980, 1984a). Many of these data have, moreover, received no other mechanistic explanation.

NOTE 2

The theory developed in Grossberg (1975, 1982b) provided a real-time explanation of blocking and unblocking, as well as a variety of other conditioning properties such as overshadowing, partial reinforcement acquisition effect, secondary reinforcement, latent inhibition, superconditioning, learned helplessness, vicious circle behavior, hypothalamic self-stimulation, hyperphagic eating, intragastric drinking, peak shift and behavioral contrast, differential effects of sudden versus gradual shock onsets, and dishabituation by novel cues (Grossberg, 1971, 1972a, 1972b, 1982b, 1984a). Grossberg and Levine (1987) have further developed the theory by carrying out real-time computer simulations of blocking, inverted-U in learning as a function of interstimulus interval, anticipatory conditioned responses, secondary reinforcement, attentional focusing by conditioned motivational feedback, and limited capacity short term memory processing.

REFERENCES

Adams, J.A., **Human memory**. New York: McGraw-Hill, 1967.

Alkon, D.L., Voltage-dependent calcium and potassium ion conductances: A contingency mechanism for an associative learning model. *Sciene*, 1979, **205**, 810–816.

Alkon, D.L., Changes of membrane currents during learning. *Journal of Experimental Biology*, 1984, **112**, 95–112 (a).

Alkon, D.L., Persistent calcium-mediated changes of identified membrane currents as a cause of associative learning. In D.L. Alkon and J. Farley (Eds.), **Primary neural substrates of learning and behavioral change**. New York: Cambridge University Press, 1984 (b).

Baker, A.G., Conditioned inhibition is not the symmetrical opposite of conditioned excitation: A test of the Rescorla-Wagner model. *Learning and Motivation*, 1974, **5**, 369–379.

Banquet, J.-P. and Grossberg, S., Probing cognitive processes through the structure of event-related potentials during learning: An experimental and theoretical analysis. *Applied Optics*, in press, 1987.

Berger, T.W. and Thompson, R.F., Neuronal plasticity in the limbic system during classical conditioning of the rabbit nictitating membrane response, I: The hippocampus. *Brain Research*, 1978, **145**, 323–346.

Berlyne, D.E., The reward-value of indifferent stimulation. In J.T. Tapp (Ed.), **Reinforcement and behavior**. New York: Academic Press, 1969.

Bindra, D., Neurophysiological interpretation of the effects of drive and incentive-motivation on general activity and instrumental behavior. *Psychological Review*, 1968, **75**, 1–22.

Boren, J.J., Resistance to extinction as a function of the fixed ratio. *Journal of Experimental Psychology*, 1961, **61**, 304–308.

Bottjer, S.W., Conditioned approach and withdrawal behavior in pigeons: Effects of a novel extraneous stimulus during acquisition and extinction. *Learning and Motivation*, 1982, **13**, 44–67.

Bower, G.H., Mood and memory. *American Psychologist*, 1981, **36**, 129–148.

Bower, G.H., Gilligan, S.G., and Monteiro, K.P., Selectivity of learning caused by adaptive states. *Journal of Experimental Psychology: General*, 1981, **110**, 451–473.

Brogden, W.J., The effect of frequency of reinforcement upon the level of conditioning. *Journal of Experimental Psychology*, 1939, **24**, 419–431.

Bullock, D. and Grossberg, S., Neural dynamics of planned arm movements: Emergent invariants and speed-accuracy properties during trajectory formation. *Psychological Review*, in press, 1987.

Carpenter, G.A. and Grossberg, S., Adaptation and transmitter gating in vertebrate photoreceptors. *Journal of Theoretical Neurobiology*, 1981, **1**, 1–42.

Carpenter, G.A. and Grossberg, S., A neural theory of circadian rhythms: The gated pacemaker. *Biological Cybernetics*, 1983, **48**, 35–59.

Carpenter, G.A. and Grossberg, S., A neural theory of circadian rhythms: Aschoff's rule in diurnal and nocturnal mammals. *American Journal of Physiology*, 1984, **247**, R1067–R1082.

Carpenter, G.A. and Grossberg, S., A neural theory of circadian rhythms: Split rhythms, after-effects, and motivational interactions. *Journal of Theoretical Biology*, 1985, **113**, 163–223.

Carpenter, G.A. and Grossberg, S., Mammalian circadian rhythms: A neural network model. In G.A. Carpenter (Ed.), **Some mathematical questions in biology: Circadian rhythms**. Providence, RI: American Mathematical Society, Lectures on Mathematics in the Life Sciences, **19**, 1986.

Carpenter, G.A. and Grossberg, S., A massively parallel architecture for a self-organizing neural pattern recognition machine. *Computer Vision, Graphics, and Image Processing*, 1987, **37**, 54–115 (a).

Carpenter, G.A. and Grossberg, S., Neural dynamics of category learning and recognition: Attention, memory consolidation, and amnesia. In J. Davis, R. Newburgh, and E. Wegman (Eds.), **Brain structure, learning, and memory**. AAAS Symposium Series, in press, 1987 (b).

Carpenter G.A. and Grossberg, S., Neural dynamics of category learning and recognition: Structural invariants, reinforcement, and evoked potentials. In M.L. Commons, S.M. Kosslyn, and R.J. Herrnstein (Eds.), **Pattern recognition and concepts in animals, people, and machines**. Hillsdale, NJ: Erlbaum, 1987 (c).

Cohen, M.A. and Grossberg, S., Neural dynamics of speech and language coding: Developmental programs, perceptual grouping, and competition for short term memory. *Human Neurobiology*, 1986, **5**, 1–22.

Cohen, M.A. and Grossberg, S., Masking fields: A massively parallel neural architecture for learning, recognizing, and predicting multiple groupings of patterned data. *Applied Optics*, 1987, **26**, 1866–1891.

Cotton, M.M., Goodall, G., and Mackintosh, N.J., Inhibitory conditioning resulting from a reduction in the magnitude of reinforcement. *Quarterly Journal of Experimental Psychology*, 1982, **34B**, 163–180.

Davenport, J.W., Successive acquisitions and extinctions of discrete bar-pressing in monkeys and rats. *Psychonomic Science*, 1969, **16**, 242–244.

Denny, M.R., Relaxation theory and experiments. In F.R. Brush (Ed.), **Aversive conditioning and learning**. New York: Academic Press, 1970.

DeVito, P.L., The extinction of a conditioned fear inhibitor and conditioned fear excitor. Unpublished doctoral dissertation, University of Pittsburgh, 1980.

Domjam, M. and Wilson, N.E., Specificity of cue to consequence in aversion learning in the rat. *Psychonomic Science*, 1972, **26**, 143–145.

Dunham, P.J., Punishment: Method and theory. *Psychological Review*, 1971, **78**, 58–70.

Dunham, P.J., Mariner, A., and Adams, H., Enhancement of off-key pecking by on-key punishment. *Journal of the Experimental Analysis of Behavior*, 1969, **1**, 156–166.

Felton, M. and Lyon, D.O., The post-reinforcement pause. *Journal of the Experimental Analysis of Behavior*, 1966, **9**, 131–134.

Foree, M. and LoLordo, V.M., Attention in the pigeon: Differential effects of food-getting versus shock-avoidance procedures. *Journal of Comparative and Physiological Psychology*, 1973, **85**, 551–558.

Garcia, J. and Koelling, R.A., Relation of cue to consequence in avoidance learning. *Psychonomic Science*, 1966, **4**, 123–124.

Gibbon, J., Farrell, L., Locurto, C.M., Duncan, H.J., and Terrace, H.S., Partial reinforcement in autoshaping with pigeons. *Animal Learning and Behavior*, 1980, **8**, 45–59.

Gibbs, C.M., Latham, S.B., and Gormenzano, I., Classical conditioning of the rabbit nictitating membrane response: Effects of reinforcement schedule on response maintenance and resistance to extinction. *Animal Learning and Behavior*, 1978, **6**, 209–215.

Gonzalez, F.A., Effects of partial reinforcement (25%) in an autoshaping procedure. *Bulletin of the Psychonomic Society*, 1973, **2**, 299–301.

Gonzalez, F.A., Effects of varying the percentage of key illuminations paired with food in a positive automaintenance procedure. *Journal of the Experimental Analysis of Behavior*, 1974, **22**, 483–489.

Gonzalez, R.C., Berger, B.D., and Bitterman, M.E., Improvement in habit-reversal as a function of amount of training per reversal and other variables. *American Journal of Psychology*, 1967, **79**, 517–530.

Gormenzano, I., Kehoe, E.J., and Marshall, B.S., Twenty years of classical conditioning research with the rabbit. *Progress in Psychobiology and Physiological Psychology*, 1983, **10**, 197–275.

Grossberg, S., Some physiological and biochemical consequences of psychological postulates. *Proceedings of the National Academy of Sciences*, 1968, **60**, 758–765.

Grossberg, S., On learning and energy-entropy dependence in recurrent and nonrecurrent signed networks. *Journal of Statistical Physics*, 1969, **1**, 319–350 (a).

Grossberg, S., Some networks that can learn, remember, and reproduce any number of complicated space-time patterns, I. *Journal of Mathematics and Mechanics*, 1969, **19**, 53–91 (b).

Grossberg, S., On the production and release of chemical transmitters and related topics in cellular control. *Journal of Theoretical Biology*, 1969, **22**, 325–364 (c).

Grossberg, S., Some networks that can learn, remember, and reproduce any number of complicated space-time patterns, II. *Studies in Applied Mathematics*, 1970, **49**, 135–166.

Grossberg, S., On the dynamics of operant conditioning. *Journal of Theoretical Biology*, 1971, **33**, 225–255.

Grossberg, S., A neural theory of punishment and avoidance, I: Qualitative theory. *Mathematical Biosciences*, 1972, **15**, 39–67 (a).

Grossberg, S., A neural theory of punishment and avoidance, II: Quantitative theory. *Mathematical Biosciences*, 1972, **15**, 253–285 (b).

Grossberg, S., Contour enhancement, short-term memory, and constancies in reverberating neural networks. *Studies in Applied Mathematics*, 1973, **52**, 217–257.

Grossberg, S., A neural model of attention, reinforcement, and discrimination learning. *International Review of Neurobiology*, 1975, **18**, 263–327.

Grossberg, S., Adaptive pattern classification and universal recoding, I: Parallel development and coding of neural feature detectors. *Biological Cybernetics*, 1976, **23**, 121–134 (a).

Grossberg, S., Adaptive pattern classification and univeral recoding, II: Feedback, expectation, olfaction, and illusions. *Biological Cybernetics*, 1976, **23**, 187–202 (b).

Grossberg, S., A theory of human memory: Self-organization and performance of sensory-motor codes, maps, and plans. In R. Rosen and F. Snell (Eds.), **Progress in theoretical biology, Vol. 5.** New York: Academic Press, 1978, pp.233–374.

Grossberg, S., How does a brain build a cognitive code? *Psychological Review*, 1980, **87**, 1–51.

Grossberg, S., A psychophysiological theory of reinforcement, drive, motivation, and attention. *Journal of Theoretical Neurobiology*, 1982, **1**, 286–369 (a).

Grossberg, S., Processing of expected and unexpected events during conditioning and attention: A psychophysiological theory. *Psychological Review*, 1982, **89**, 529–572 (b).

Grossberg, S., **Studies of mind and brain: Neural principles of learning, perception, development, cognition, and motor control.** Boston: Reidel Press, 1982 (c).

Grossberg, S., The quantized geometry of visual space: The coherent computation of depth, form, and lightness. *Behavioral and Brain Sciences*, 1983, **6**, 625–657.

Grossberg, S., Some psychophysiological and pharmacological correlates of a developmental, cognitive, and motivational theory. In R. Karrer, J. Cohen, and P. Tueting (Eds.), **Brain and information: Event related potentials.** New York: New York Academy of Sciences, 1984 (a).

Grossberg, S., Some normal and abnormal behavioral syndromes due to transmitter gating of opponent processes. *Biological Psychiatry*, 1984, **19**, 1075–1118 (b).

Grossberg, S., The hypothalamic control of eating and circadian rhythms: Opponent processes and their chemical modulators. In L. Rensing (Ed.), **Temporal order.** New York: Springer-Verlag, 1985.

Grossberg, S. (Ed.), **The adaptive brain, I: Cognition, learning, reinforcement, and rhythm.** Amsterdam: Elsevier/North-Holland, 1987 (a).

Grossberg, S. (Ed.), **The adaptive brain, II: Vision, speech, language, and motor control.** Amsterdam: Elsevier/North-Holland, 1987 (b).

Grossberg, S., Cortical dynamics of three-dimensional form, color, and brightness perception, I: Monocular theory. *Perception and Psychophysics*, 1987, **41**, 87–116 (c).

Grossberg, S., Cortical dynamics of three-dimensional form, color, and brightness perception, II: Binocular theory. *Perception and Psychophysics*, 1987, **41**, 117–158 (d).

Grossberg, S. and Gutowski, W., Neural dynamics of decision making under risk: Affective balance and cognitive-emotional interactions. *Psychological Review*, 1987, **94**, 300–318.

Grossberg, S. and Kuperstein, M., **Neural dynamics of adaptive sensory-motor control: Ballistic eye movements.** Amsterdam: Elsevier/North-Holland, 1986.

Grossberg, S. and Levine, D.S., Neural dynamics of attentionally modulated Pavlovian conditioning: Blocking, inter-stimulus interval, and secondary reinforcement. *Applied Optics*, in press, 1987.

Grossberg, S. and Mingolla, E., Neural dynamics of form perception: Boundary completion, illusory figures, and neon color spreading. *Psychological Review*, 1985, **92**, 173–211.

Grossberg, S. and Schmajuk, N., Neural dynamics of anticipatory timing and temporal discrimination during classical conditioning. In preparation, 1987.

Grossberg, S. and Stone, G.O., Neural dynamics of word recognition and recall: Attentional priming, learning, and resonance. *Psychological Review*, 1986, **93**, 46–74 (a).

Grossberg, S. and Stone, G.O., Neural dynamics of attention switching and temporal-order information in short-term memory. *Memory and Cognition*, 1986, **14**, 451–468 (b).

Hammond, L.J., Retardation of fear acquisition by a previously inhibitory CS. *Journal of Comparative and Physiological Psychology*, 1968, **66**, 756–758.

Hawkins, R.D., Abrams, T.W., Carew, T.J., and Kandel, E.R., A cellular mechanism of classical conditioning in *Aplysia*: Activity-dependent amplification of presynaptic facilitation. *Science*, 1983, **219**, 400–405.

Hinson, R.E., Effects of UCS preexposure on excitatory and inhibitory rabbit eyelid conditioning: An associative effect of conditioned contextual stimuli. *Journal of Experimental Psychology: Animal Behavior Processes*, 1982, **8**, 49–61.

Holland, P.C. and Rescorla, R.A., Second-order conditioning with food unconditioned stimulus. *Journal of Comparative and Physiological Psychology*, 1975, **88**, 459–467.

Holman, E.W., The effect of drug habituation before and after taste aversion learning in rats. *Animal Learning and Behavior*, 1976, **4**, 329–332.

Jenkins, H.M. and Lambos, W.A., Tests of two explanations of response elimination by noncontingent reinforcement. *Animal Learning and Behavior*, 1983, **11**, 302–308.

Kamin, L.J., "Attention-like" processes in classical conditioning. In M.R. Jones (Ed.), **Miami symposium on the prediction of behavior: Aversive stimulation.** Miami: University of Miami Press, 1968.

Kamin, L.J., Predictability, surprise, attention, and conditioning. In B.A. Campbell and R.M. Church (Eds.), **Punishment and aversive behavior.** New York: Appleton-Century-Crofts, 1969.

Kaufman, M.A. and Bolles, R.C., A nonassociative aspect of overshadowing. *Bulletin of the Psychonomic Society*, 1981, **18**, 318–320.

Killeen, P.R., Incentive theory. In D.J. Bernstein (Ed.), **Nebraska symposium on motivation, 1981: Response structure and organization.** Lincoln: University of Nebraska Press, 1982 (a).

Killeen, P.R., Incentive theory, II: Models for choice. *Journal of the Experimental Analysis of Behavior*, 1982, **38**, 217–232 (b).

Kleiman, M.C. and Fowler, H., Variations in explicitly unpaired training are differentially effective in producing conditioned inhibition. *Learning and Motivation*, 1984, **15**, 127–155.

Levy, W.B., Associative changes at the synapse: LTP in the hippocampus. In W.B. Levy, J. Anderson, and S. Lehmkuhle (Eds.), **Synaptic modification, neuron selectivity, and nervous system organization.** Hillsdale, NJ: Erlbaum, 1985.

Levy, W.B., Brassell, S.E., and Moore, S.D., Partial quantification of the associative synaptic learning rule of the dentate gyrus. *Neuroscience*, 1983, **8**, 799–808.

Levy, W.B. and Desmond, N.L., The rules of elemental synaptic plasticity. In W.B. Levy, J. Anderson, and S. Lehmkuhle (Eds.), **Synaptic modification, neuron selectivity, and nervous system organization.** Hillsdale, NJ: Erlbaum, 1985.

Leyland, C.M., Higher-order autoshaping. *Quarterly Journal of Experimental Psychology*, 1977, **29**, 607–619.

Lynch, G., **Synapses, circuits, and the beginnings of memory.** Cambridge, MA: MIT Press, 1986.

Lysle, D.T. and Fowler, H., Inhibition as a "slave" process: Deactivation of conditioned inhibition through extinction of conditioned excitation. *Journal of Experimental Psychology: Animal Behavior Processes*, 1985, **11**, 71–94.

Mackintosh, N.J., Stimulus selection: Learning to ignore stimuli that predict no change in reinforcement. In R.A. Hinde and J.S. Hinde (Eds.), **Constraints of learning.** London: Academic Press, 1973.

Masterson, F.A., Is termination of a warning signal an effective reward for the rat? *Journal of Comparative and Physiological Psychology*, 1970, **72**, 471–475.

McAllister, W.R. and McAllister, D.E., Behavioral measurement of conditioned fear. In F.R. Brush (Ed.), **Aversive conditioning and learning.** New York: Academic Press, 1971.

McAllister, W.R., McAllister, D.E., and Douglass, W.K., The inverse relationship between shock intensity and shuttlebox avoidance learning in rats. *Journal of Comparative and Physiological Psychology*, 1971, **74**, 426–433.

McCormick, D.A. and Thompson, R.F., Cerebellum: Essential involvement in the classically conditioned eyelid response. *Science*, 1984, **223**, 296–299.

Miller, N.E., Some reflections on the law of effect produce a new alternative to drive reduction. In M.R. Jones (Ed.), **Nebraska symposium on motivation.** Lincoln: University of Nebraska Press, 1963.

Miller, R.R. and Schachtman, T.R., Conditioning context as an associative baseline: Implications for response generation and the nature of conditioned inhibition. In R.R. Miller and N.E. Spear (Eds.), **Information processing in animals: Conditioned inhibition.** Hillsdale, NJ: Erlbaum, 1985.

Olds, J., **Drives and reinforcements: Behavioral studies of hypothalamic functions.** New York: Raven Press, 1977.

Owren, M.J. and Kaplan, P.S., On the failure to extinguish Pavlovian conditioned inhibition: A test of a reinstatement hypothesis. Paper presented at the meeting of the Midwestern Psychological Association, Detroit, April, 1981.

Pavlov, I.P., **Conditioned reflexes.** London: Oxford University Press, 1927.

Pearce, J.M. and Hall, G., A model for Pavlovian learning: Variations in the effectiveness of conditioned but not of unconditioned stimuli. *Psychological Review*, 1980, **87**, 532–552.

Perkins, C.C. Jr., Beavers, W.O., Hancock, R.A. Jr., Hemmendinger, P.C., Hemmendinger, D., and Ricci, J.A., Some variables affecting rate of key pecking during response-independent procedures (autoshaping). *Journal of the Experimental Analysis of Behavior*, 1975, **24**, 59–72.

Rashotte, M.E., Griffin, R.W., and Sisk, C.L., Second-order conditioning of the pigeon's keypeck. *Animal Learning and Behavior*, 1977, **5**, 25–38.

Rauschecker, J.P. and Singer, W., Changes in the circuitry of the kitten's visual cortex are gated by postsynaptic activity. *Nature*, 1979, **280**, 58–60.

Rescorla, R.A., Probability of shock in the presence and absence of CS in fear conditioning. *Journal of Comparative and Physiological Psychology*, 1968, **66**, 1–5.

Rescorla, R.A., Establishment of a positive reinforcer through contrast with shock. *Journal of Comparative and Physiological Psychology*, 1969, **67**, 260–263.

Rescorla, R.A. and LoLordo, V.M., Inhibition of avoidance behavior. *Journal of Comparative and Physiological Psychology*, 1965, **69**, 406–412.

Rescorla, R.A. and Wagner, A.R., A theory of Pavlovian conditioning: Variations in the effectiveness of reinforcement and nonreinforcement. In A.H. Black and W.F. Prokasy (Eds.), **Classical conditioning, II: Current research and theory**. New York: Appleton-Century-Crofts, 1972.

Reynierse, J.H. and Rizley, R.C., Relaxation and fear as determinants of maintained avoidance in rats. *Journal of Comparative and Physiological Psychology*, 1970, **72**, 223–232.

Rizley, R.C. and Rescorla, R.A., Associations in second-order conditioning and sensory preconditioning. *Journal of Comparative and Physiological Psychology*, 1972, **81**, 1–11.

Schmaltz, L.W. and Theios, J., Acquisition and extinction of a classically conditioned response in hippocampectomized rabbits (*Dryctolagus cuniculus*). *Journal of Comparative and Physiological Psychology*, 1972, **79**, 328–333.

Schwartz, B. and Williams, D.R., Two different kinds of key-peck in the pigeon: Some properties of responses maintained by negative and positive response-reinforcer contingencies. *Journal of the Experimental Analysis of Behavior*, 1972, **18**, 201–216.

Seligman, M.E.P. and Hager, J.L., **Biological boundaries of learning**. New York: Appleton-Century-Crofts, 1972.

Siegel, S. and Domjan, M., Backward conditioning as an inhibitory procedure. *Learning and Motivation*, 1971, **2**, 1–11.

Singer, W., Neuronal activity as a shaping factor in the self-organization of neuron assemblies. In E. Basar, H. Flohr, H. Haken, and A.J. Mandell (Eds.), **Synergetics of the brain**. New York: Springer-Verlag, 1983.

Solomon, R.L., The opponent-process theory of acquired motivation. *American Psychologist*, 1980, **35**, 691–712.

Solomon, R.L., The opponent processes in acquired motivation. In D.W. Pfaff (Ed.), **The physiological mechanisms of motivation**. New York: Springer-Verlag, 1982.

Solomon, R.L. and Corbit, J.D., An opponent process theory of motivation, I: Temporal dynamics of affect. *Psychological Review*, 1974, **81**, 119–145.

Sutton, R.S. and Barto, A.G., Toward a modern theory of adaptive networks: Expectation and prediction. *Psychological Review*, 1981, **88**, 135-170.

Wasserman, E.A., Stimulus-reinforcer predictiveness and selective discrimination learning in pigeons. *Journal of Experimental Psychology*, 1974, **103**, 284–297.

Wasserman, E.A., Deich, J.D., Hunter, N.B., and Nagamatsu, L.S., Analysing the random control procedure: Effects of paired and unpaired CS's and US's on autoshaping the chick's key peck with heat reinforcement. *Learning and Motivation*, 1977, **8**, 467–487.

Wasserman, E.A., Hunter, N.B., Gutowski, K.A., and Bader, S.A., Autoshaping chicks with heat reinforcement: The role of stimulus-reinforcer and response-reinforcer relations. *Journal of Experimental Psychology: Animal Behavior Processes*, 1975, **104**, 158–169.

Weisman, R.E. and Litner, J.S., The course of Pavlovian extinction and inhibition of fear in rats. *Journal of Comparative and Physiological Psychology*, 1969, **69**, 667–672.

Werblin, F.S., Adaptation in a vertebrate retina: Intracellular recordings in Necturus. *Journal of Neurophysiology*, 1971, **34**, 228–241.

Witcher, E.S., Extinction of Pavlovian conditioned inhibition. Unpublished doctoral dissertation, University of Massachusetts, Amherst, 1978.

Zimmer-Hart, C.L. and Rescorla, R.A., Extinction of Pavlovian conditioned inhibition. *Journal of Comparative and Physiological Psychology*, 1974, **86**, 837–845.

Psychological Review
1987, **94** (3), 300–318
©1987 American Psychological Association

NEURAL DYNAMICS OF DECISION MAKING UNDER RISK: AFFECTIVE BALANCE AND COGNITIVE-EMOTIONAL INTERACTIONS

Stephen Grossberg† and William Gutowski

ABSTRACT

A real-time neural network model, called Affective Balance Theory, is developed to explain many properties of decision making under risk which heretofore have been analysed using formal algebraic models, notably Prospect Theory. The model describes cognitive-emotional interactions which are designed to ensure adaptive responses to environmental demands, but whose emergent properties nonetheless can lead to paradoxical and even irrational decisions in risky environments. Emotional processing in the model is carried out by an opponent processing network, called a *gated dipole*. Learning enables cognitive representations to generate affective reactions of the dipole. Habituating chemical transmitters within a gated dipole determine an affective adaptation level, or context, against which later events are evaluated. Neutral events can become affectively charged either through direct activations or antagonistic rebounds within a previously habituated dipole. The theory describes the affective consequences of strategies in which an individual compares pairs of events or statements that are not necessarily explicitly grouped within the stimuli. The same preference orders may sometimes, but not always, emerge from different sequences of pairwise alternatives. The role of short term memory updating and expectancy-modulated matching processes in regulating affective reactions is described. The formal axioms of Prospect Theory are dynamically explicated through this analysis. Analyses of judgments of the utility of a single alternative, choices between pairs of regular alternatives, choices between riskless and risky alternatives, and choices between pairs of risky alternatives lead to explanations of such phenomena as preference reversals, gambler's fallacy, framing effect, and the tendency towards risk aversion when gains are involved but risk taking when losses are involved. These explanations illustrate that data concerning decision making under risk may now be related to data concerning the dynamics of conditioning, cognition, and emotion as consequences of a single psychophysiological theory.

† Supported in part by the Air Force Office of Scientific Research (AFOSR 85-0149 and AFOSR F49620-86-C-0037), the National Science Foundation (NSF IRI-84-17756) and the Office of Naval Research (ONR N00014-83-K0337).

1. Introduction: Some Previous Models of Risky Decision Making

Most environments are characterized by some degree of uncertainty. Environmental uncertainty may be inherent in some situations, such as a coin toss, or may arise due to imperfect information about the physical or social environment. Whatever the source, analysis of the structural and functional characteristics of uncertainty is a problem of considerable importance in a wide variety of research areas including mathematics, economics, and psychology.

The multidisciplinary approach to the study of decision making under risk has led to the development of two distinct types of theory: normative and descriptive. Normative theories are prescriptive in nature since they are concerned with devising decision making procedures or algorithms which are optimal with regard to some set of intuitively reasonable constraints. Descriptive theories, on the other hand, are concerned with providing an accurate portrayal of how individuals actually make decisions, independent of whether those decisions are optimal or even logical.

Historically, the distinction between the two types of theory has been blurred since normative theories, particularly Expected Utility Theory, have been widely accepted as adequate descriptions of how individuals integrate information when making risky decisions. For example, the earliest form of Utility Theory, which was developed by Daniel Bernoulli as a solution to the gambling puzzle known as the St. Petersburg Paradox, was very influential in economics for over a century (Bernoulli, 1738). More recently, the axiomatic form of Utility Theory, which was first developed by von Neumann and Morgenstern (1943), has been assumed to provide an acceptable descriptive model of decision making under risk.

Since the introduction of Axiomatic Utility Theory, a large body of evidence has accumulated which demonstrates that individuals systematically violate some of the fundamental tenets of rational choice (e.g., Allais, 1951; Tversky and Kahneman, 1981). These numerous violations of rationality have motivated a great deal of experimental and theoretical work aimed at developing a more accurate descriptive theory of decision making under risk than is provided by Utility Theory. Overall, these efforts have been quite successful in the sense that many violations of the axioms of Utility Theory and rational choice are explicable within one or more of these theoretical frameworks. For example, violations of the betweeness axiom of Utility Theory are consistent with the axiomatic framework of Portfolio Theory (Coombs, 1975).

The particular theory which has been the most successful in uncovering and explaining these violations is Prospect Theory (Kahneman and Tversky, 1979). This theory adopts a number of coding, psychophysical, and decision rule assumptions which provide a natural account of many results which are inconsistent with the axioms of Utility Theory and general assumptions of rational choice. To illustrate, Prospect Theory explains the reflection effect where choices involving gains tend to be risk averse while choices involving losses tend to be risk taking. It does so using an S-shaped value function and a decision weight function which is characterized by the properties of subcertainty and subproportionality (Section 7). These psychophysical assumptions, in combination with certain coding assumptions, also provide a plausible explanation of framing effects which involve shifts in preference depending on whether the outcomes of choices are stated positively or negatively (Section 13).

Despite the impressive array of data which is accounted for by Prospect Theory, the theory is not immune to criticism. One criticism is that Prospect Theory is a static, algebraic theory which relies heavily on psychophysical functions which are derived from analyses of group choice data. As a result, the theory provides little insight into the information processing dynamics which underlie risky decision making. A second and perhaps sharper criticism of Prospect Theory is that it does not account for all important forms of nonrational decision making. The problem revolves around the decision rule of Prospect Theory which assumes that individuals act to maximize subjective value. A vivid illustration of the difficulty with this seemingly compelling assumption is the paradoxical result which is called the preference reversal phenomenon. Preference reversals are observed when, in a binary choice situation, an individual prefers an alternative which has been judged to be worth less than the nonpreferred alternative. To illustrate, an individual might judge one alternative to be worth $10 when presented in isolation, a second alternative to be worth $8 when presented in isolation, and yet prefer the second alternative when given a choice between the two alternatives. It is important to note that the preference reversal phenomenon is a robust effect which cannot be dismissed as statistical noise, at least for the theoretically interesting cases where the alternatives are reasonably close in value (Grether and Plott, 1979; Gutowski and Chechile, 1984; Hamm, 1979; Lichtenstein and Slovic, 1971, 1973; Lindman, 1971; Mowen and Gentry, 1980; Pommerehne, Schneider, and Zweifel, 1982; Reilly, 1982; Slovic and Lichtenstein, 1983). Therefore, preference reversals violate the maximization assumption of Prospect Theory and constitute an important and as yet inadequately unexplained example of nonrational choice.

This is not to say that the preference reversal phenomenon has escaped theoretical attention. Lichtenstein and Slovic (1971), for example, assume that judgment and choice task requirements generate different information processing sequences. More specifically, their formulation assumes that judgments of the subjective value of risky alternatives follow an anchoring-and-adjustment process, where either the amount that can be won or lost serves as the anchor, while choice is primarily governed by the probability of winning. Although such a differential weighting model can account for much of the data on preference reversals (for an exception see Gutowski and Chechile, 1984), the model in its present form is not sufficiently general to predict other phenomena in the domain of decision making under risk.

Herein we describe an alternative theory of decision making under risk, which we call Affective Balance Theory. The theory is best viewed as an application of a more general theory of how cognitive and emotional processes interact (Grossberg, 1980, 1982a, 1984a). This general theory has been used to explain phenomena in such diverse areas as perception, attention, motivation, learning, and memory. Affective Balance Theory utilizes psychophysiological mechanisms and processes which have been derived from data analyses in these other areas to build a dynamic description of the affective and cognitive events which underlie risky judgment and choice. The theory clarifies how context affects the processing of risky information and provides an explanation of a number of well established phenomena in risky decision making, including preference reversals. The present work thus suggests how properties of decision making under risk may be explained as manifestations of a processing theory that was developed to explain a quite different data base. This linkage relates phenomena concerning human decision making under risk to human evoked potentials, neurophysiological and pharmacological substrates of behavior, animal discrimination learning, human memory and attentional processing, and certain mental disorders. In particular, the arguments developed herein apply the same mechanisms which have previously been used to analyse such phenomena as hypothalamic self-stimulation, secondary conditioning, asymptotically nonchalant avoidance behavior, conditioned emotional responses, superconditioning, analgesia, differential rewarding effects of sudden vs gradual shocks, self-punitive behavior, and learned helplessness (Grossberg, 1971, 1972a, 1972b), as well as partial reinforcement acquisition effect, behavioral contrast, blocking and unblocking, schedule-induced polydipsia, rebound eating, intragastric drinking, hyperphagic eating, Valenstein effect, and latent inhibition (Grossberg, 1975, 1982a, 1984a). Within the broader context of animal discrimination learning and choice behavior, all of these phenomena may be viewed as variants of decision making under risk.

Affective Balance Theory generates formal relationships which have been posited by algebraic models of decision making under risk in the form of emergent properties of real-time circuits which have been used to analyse and predict a wide range of interdisciplinary psychophysiological data. In this sense, Affective Balance Theory "explains" these formal relationships. In so doing, as an automatic consequence, it also explains the data which these formal relationships have been used to fit. In addition, Affective Balance Theory predicts a number of other data—for example, data concerning preference reversals (Section 10)—which cannot easily be accounted for by a number of other theories, notably Prospect Theory.

Rachlin, Logue, Gibbon, and Frankel (1986) have also realized the importance of concepts about instrumental behavior for understanding decision making under risk. These authors apply algebraic form factors that have been developed to fit instrumental data collected from animals to analyse human data about decision making under risk. The present article develops a real-time neural network model, rather than algebraic form factors, and thereby provides a mechanistic analysis of decision making data in the same way that this model has elsewhere suggested a mechanistic analysis of a large literature about instrumental behavior.

The present theory does not attempt to characterize all the possible cognitive strategies that individuals may invoke. Rather, it analyses the effects of a chosen strategy upon the affective values of the events to which an individual is exposed. In particular, the theory analyses the affective consequences of strategies in which a subject compares pairs of events or statements that are not necessarily explicitly grouped within the stimulus materials. The cognitive context in which individual events are embedded may alter the comparisons that a subject makes to arrive at a preference order for these events. In Section 8, we note that the same preference order can sometimes emerge from different sequences of pairwise comparisons. This result brings into a sharper focus those circumstances wherein preference order does depend upon the sequencing of event comparisons. In addition, in Section 12, we show how the cognitive context with which a neutral event, such as a zero outcome, is compared can endow the event with a positive or a negative affect, depending upon the comparisons afforded by the context. In Section 13, we discuss how the cognitive context can influence, or "frame", the set of outcomes that the subject will be inclined to process, including the pairwise comparisons that the subject constructs from the stimulus materials.

Within Affective Balance Theory, affective or emotional processing is assumed to be regulated by an opponent process which is called a *gated dipole* (Grossberg, 1972a, 1972b, 1984a, 1984b). Four main ingredients go into the design of a gated dipole: slowly accumulating chemical transmitters which are designed to generate unbiased transductions of their inputs; opponent, or competitive, interactions between an on-channel and an off-channel; phasic inputs which perturb the on-channel or the off-channel through time; and a sustained, or tonic, arousal level which equally perturbs both channels, and thereby sets the sensitivity of dipole outputs to phasic input fluctuations.

A number of other opponent processing models exist in the literature. Jensen (1970,

1971) described qualitatively some of the properties that a good theory of opponent processing should have and applied these properties to the analysis of conditioning data. Solomon and Corbit (1974) and Solomon (1980, 1982) have also used opponent processing ideas to analyse data about conditioning and, more generally, affective processing. A comparison of the gated dipole opponent process and the type of opponent process described by Solomon and Corbit (1974) is given in Section 5. We now summarize the gated dipole properties that we will need.

2. Transmitter Gates: Unbiased Transmitter-Modulated Signalling

The simplest rule whereby one nerve cell site can send unbiased signals to another nerve cell site is as follows. If $S(t)$ is the input signal to one cell site and $T(t)$ is the output signal to the next cell site, then the linear relationship

$$T = SB, \tag{1}$$

where B is a positive constant, is the simplest law of unbiased transmission. By (1), the outgoing signal is proportional to the incoming signal, and the signal is relayed perfectly.

When the output signal $T(t)$ is due to the release or inactivation of a chemical transmitter $z(t)$ in response to the input signal $S(t)$, further consideration is necessary. How is a large and sustained input $S(t)$ prevented from depleting $z(t)$ and thereby causing a progressively smaller signal $T(t)$? In other words, when $T(t)$ is due to the release or inactivation of a transmitter, the term B in (1) may not be constant. It may decrease through time as $z(t)$ is depleted, thereby reducing the sensitivity of $T(t)$ to $S(t)$. In this situation, (1) is replaced by the equation

$$T = Sz. \tag{2}$$

Our task is to analyse how $z(t)$ approximates a constant B:

$$z \cong B, \tag{3}$$

despite its depletion due to input S.

Equation (2) says that transmitter z is released or inactivated at a rate (proportional to) T in response to input S. In other words, z *gates* S to generate T, or T is caused by a *mass action* interaction between S and z. By (2), either an increase in S or in z can increase T, and no output signal T can be generated if either no input signal occurs ($S = 0$) or if no transmitter is available ($z = 0$).

Equation (3) requires that the *sensitivity* of T to S be maintained through time. If both (2) and (3) are simultaneously implemented, as in (1), then unbiased transmission by a depletable chemical is achieved. Equation (1) means that $z(t)$ is replenished instantaneously, or at least at a rate that is rapid relative to the rate of gated release or inactivation. In our applications, the rate of accumulation is slow relative to the rate of gated release or inactivation. In order to represent this type of process, an algebraic equation is insufficient. A differential equation is needed. We use the simplest differential equation that is capable of reconciling (2) and (3) when both the accumulation and gating processes take place at a finite rate relative to the rate with which the signal S can fluctuate. In this situation, (2) and (3) are not both exactly satisfied at any one time. The process attempts to achieve unbiased transmission, but can do so only approximately due to its finite reaction rates. Such a slow-down of transmitter accumulation does not reflect a system failure. It provides the basis for conditioning properties of fundamental importance (Grossberg, 1972a, 1972b, 1982, 1984a). Thus we view the slow rate of transmitter accumulation as an evolutionary specialization that has persisted due to its behavioral value. Here we suggest that it also underlies several basic properties of decision making under risk.

The simplest differential equation capable of simultaneously implementing (2) and (3) is the following one (Grossberg, 1972b):

$$\frac{d}{dt}z = A(B - z) - CSz, \qquad (4)$$

where A, B, and C are positive. In (4), the notation $\frac{d}{dt}z$ denotes the net production rate of z. Term $A(B - z)$ says that z accumulates at a rate A until it reaches the target level B, as required by (3). Term $-CSz$ says that the loss of transmitter per unit time due to gating is proportional to Sz, as required by (2). Henceforth we choose $C = 1$ for notational simplicity. This amounts to rescaling the size of S.

Term $A(B - z)$ may be physically instantiated in more than one way. For example, a passive assumulation of z may occur onto unoccupied sites whose total number is B. Alternatively, transmitter precursors may actively be produced at a rate AB, but feedback inhibition via term $-Az$ of transmitter z onto an intermediate stage of production may reduce the net production level to $A(B-z)$. Without such feedback inhibition, transmitter production would continue unabated until the cell ruptured.

In response to a constant signal of size S, (4) implies that the transmitter z approaches the equilibrium value

$$z = \frac{AB}{A + S}. \qquad (5)$$

In other words, larger signals S deactivate more transmitter. On the other hand, the output signal that is generated by an input S does not equal z. The output signal is equal to $T = Sz$, due to (2).

Figure 1 describes how the output T reacts to changes in the size of the input S. A rapid increase in S from S_0 to S_1 elicits a slow decrease in z. Multiplication of the graphs of $S(t)$ and $z(t)$ shows that a rapid increase in S generates a rapid increase in T followed by a slow decrease, or habituation, of T to an intermediate level. In a similar way, a rapid decrease in S from S_1 to S_0 generates a rapid decrease in T followed by a slow increase, or habituation, to an intermediate level. In all, rapid increases and decreases in the input S generate overshoots and undershoots in the output T due to the slow rate of reaction, or habituation, of the transmitter as it seeks to generate unbiased signals. These habituative reactions are fundamental to many of the explanations given by our theory.

3. Gated Dipoles: Tonically Aroused Transmitter Gates in Opponent Processes

Figure 2 describes one of the basic properties of a gated dipole. In such an opponent process, a phasic input (J) can elicit a sustained on-response, whereas offset of the input can elicit a transient off-rebound, or temporal contrast effect. These properties are explained as follows.

The left-hand series of stages in Figure 2 represents the on-channel, and the right-hand series of stages represents the off-channel. Both channels receive an equal arousal input, denoted by I, that is constant through time. The arousal input energizes the antagonistic rebound that occurs after the on-input shuts off. The on-input, denoted by J, is delivered

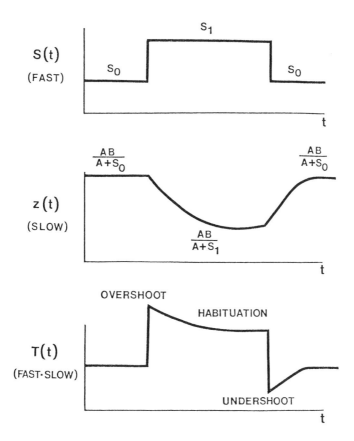

Figure 1. Reaction of output signal T and transmitter gate z to changes in input S. The output T is the product of a fast process S and slow process z. Overshoots and undershoots in T are caused by z's slow habituation to fast changes in S.

only to the on-channel. Input J is switched from zero to a positive level and held at that level long enough for gate equilibration to occur. Then J is shut off.

Inputs I and J are added by the activity (or potential) $x_1(t)$. Activity $x_1(t)$ responds quickly to input fluctuations, relative to the reaction rate of the network's slow transmitter gates. The graph of $x_1(t)$ has the same form as the top graph in Figure 1: a rapid switch from a lower positive activity to a higher positive activity, followed by a rapid return to the lower level. The activity $x_1(t)$ generates an output signal $f(x_1(t))$ in its pathway that again has the form of a double-switch between two positive values. The output signal $f(x_1(t))$ is gated by a slow transmitter $z_1(t)$ that accumulates and is inactivated from the square synapse in the on-channel. Figure 1 describes the effect of this slow gate on the input to the next stage. Consequently, activity $x_3(t)$ follows an overshoot-habituation-undershoot-habituation sequence through time. Then $x_3(t)$ relays an output signal of the same form to $x_5(t)$. Activity $x_5(t)$ also receives an inhibitory signal from $x_4(t)$. To determine what happens next, we consider the dynamics of the off-channel.

The off-channel receives only the constant tonic input I. Hence $x_2(t)$ and the slow gate $z_2(t)$ in the off-channel square synapses are constant through time. The activity

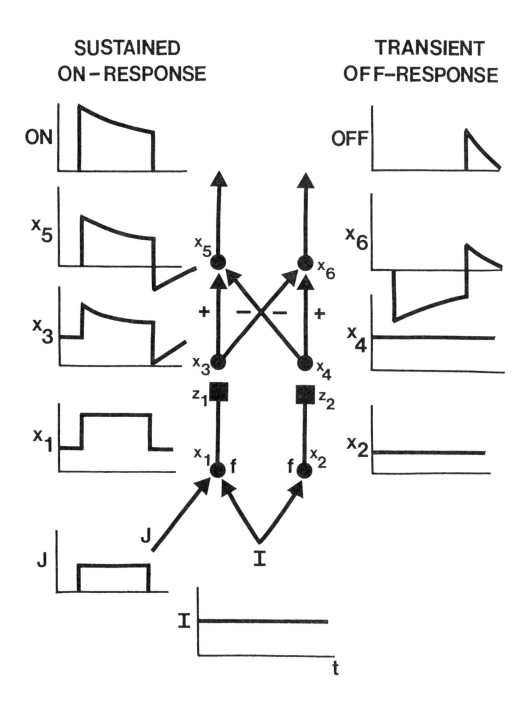

Figure 2. Example of a gated dipole. A sustained habituating on-response (top left) and a transient off-rebound (top right) are elicited in response to onset and offset, respectively, of a phasic input J (bottom left) when tonic arousal I (bottom center) and opponent processing (diagonal pathways) supplement the slow gating actions (square synapses). See text for details.

$x_4(t)$ is therefore also constant through time. For definiteness, we make the simplest assumption that corresponding stages in the on-channel and the off-channel possess the same parameters. Since the arousal input I to both channels is also equal, the size of x_4 equals the baseline activity level of $x_3(t)$. This is not always true, but its violation is easy to analyse after the symmetric case is understood.

We can now determine the reactions of activity $x_5(t)$ through time. Since the signals from $x_3(t)$ and $x_4(t)$ subtract before perturbing $x_5(t)$, and their baseline activities are the same, the baseline activity of $x_5(t)$ equals zero. Activity $x_5(t)$ thus overshoots and undershoots a zero baseline when the input J is turned on and off. By contrast, activity $x_6(t)$ responds in an opposite way from $x_5(t)$ because x_3 excites x_5 and inhibits x_6, whereas x_4 inhibits x_5 and excites x_6.

The final assumption is that the output signals caused by activities $x_5(t)$ and $x_6(t)$ are rectified: outputs are generated only if these activities exceed a nonnegative threshold. As a result, the on-channel generates a sustained output signal while the input J is on. This output signal habituates as the gate $z_1(t)$ slowly equilibrates to the input. By contrast, the off-channel generates a transient off-response, or antagonistic rebound, after the input J shuts off.

4. Mathematical Properties Leading to Antagonistic Rebound

We now describe the simplest formulas which can instantiate Figure 2 in order to set the stage for our computations about risky decision making. Let the total signal in the on-channel be $S_1 = f(I + J_1)$ and the total signal in the off-channel be $S_2 = f(I + J_2)$, where I is the baseline level of arousal which perturbs both channels, and f is a function that transforms these inputs into signals. In general, f is a nonnegative and monotone increasing function such that $f(0) = 0$. Assume that $J_1 > J_2$, and hence that $S_1 > S_2$. As in (4), let the transmitter in the on-channel, z_1, satisfy the equation

$$\frac{d}{dt}z_1 = A(B - z_1) - S_1 z_1 \tag{6}$$

and the transmitter in the off-channel, z_2, satisfy the equation

$$\frac{d}{dt}z_2 = A(B - z_2) - S_2 z_2. \tag{7}$$

Assume that the inputs S_1 and S_2 are present for a sufficient amount of time so that z_1 and z_2 equilibrate, or habituate, to S_1 and S_2. At equilibrium, $\frac{d}{dt}z_1 = \frac{d}{dt}z_2 = 0$. Thus, by equations (6) and (7)

$$z_1 = \frac{AB}{A + S_1} \tag{8}$$

$$z_2 = \frac{AB}{A + S_2}. \tag{9}$$

By (2), the gated signal in the on-channel is then

$$T_1 = S_1 z_1 = \frac{ABS_1}{A + S_1} \tag{10}$$

and the gated signal in the off-channel is

$$T_2 = S_2 z_2 = \frac{ABS_2}{A + S_2}. \tag{11}$$

After the two channels compete, the net activity in the on-channel is

$$
\begin{aligned}
x_5 &= T_1 - T_2 \\
&= S_1 z_1 - S_2 z_2 \\
&= \frac{A^2 B(S_1 - S_2)}{(A + S_1)(A + S_2)}.
\end{aligned}
\tag{12}
$$

Note that this on-activity is positive since $S_1 > S_2$. By contrast, the off-activity is negative since $x_6 = -x_5$ (Figure 2). After thresholds act, the on-output is positive whereas the off-output equals zero.

In order to understand how off-rebounds occur, eliminate the inputs J_1 and J_2. The inputs to each channel then both equal I. However, the transmitters z_1 and z_2 are assumed to change slowly, so that equations (8) and (9) are approximately valid for some time interval after the offset of J_1 and J_2. The gated signals during this interval are then approximately

$$
T_1 = f(I)z_1 = \frac{ABf(I)}{A + S_1}
\tag{13}
$$

and

$$
T_2 = f(I)z_2 = \frac{ABf(I)}{A + S_2}.
\tag{14}
$$

After competition, the net off-rebound is

$$
x_6 = f(I)z_2 - f(I)z_1 = \frac{ABf(I)(S_1 - S_2)}{(A + S_1)(A + S_2)}
\tag{15}
$$

which is positive, whereas the net on-response is $x_5 = -x_6 < 0$. Due to the output threshold, an antagonistic rebound, or contrast effect, occurs.

The rebound is transient since the transmitters z_1 and z_2 both equilibrate in response to I and approach levels $AB(A+I)^{-1}$. As a result, x_5 approaches zero. Thus the competition between on-channel and off-channel eventually shuts off both channels when they receive equal inputs for a sufficient amount of time for equilibration to occur.

5. Comparison with the Solomon and Corbit Opponent Process Model

The antagonistic rebound in the off-channel of a gated dipole is energized by an undershoot of the dipole's on-activity function x_3 (Figure 2). In a gated dipole, such an undershoot is due to habituation of the transmitter gate within the on-channel. Overshoots and undershoots have also been hypothesized to exist in alternative models of opponent processing, but the properties have not been traced to the action of a slowly habituating transmitter gate. For example, Solomon and Corbit (1974) and Solomon (1980, 1982) describe a model of opponent processing in which overshoots and undershoots occur. These authors ascribe the overshoots and undershoots to the subtraction of two opponent processes that both evolve according to similar time scales (Figure 3). Neither process, in itself, undergoes an overshoot or an undershoot. Instead, overshoots and undershoots are derived from the assumption that the off-process begins to build up only after the on-process is initiated. The model assumes, in addition, that "the second component, the b process, is aroused via the arousal of a" (Solomon and Corbit, 1974, p.126). Neither assumption is made in a gated dipole opponent process, wherein the slow habituation of the transmitter gate

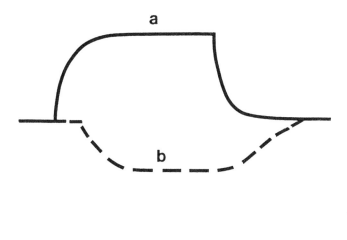

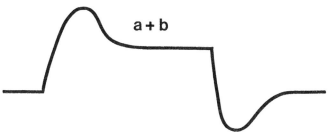

Figure 3. In the opponent process model of Solomon (1982), overshoots and undershoots are caused by an excitatory process (a) and an inhibitory process (b) that both change at a similar rate such that (b) lags behind (a) and neither (a) nor (b) separately exhibits overshoots or undershoots.

within the on-channel generates an overshoot and an undershoot within that channel. Consequently, in a gated dipole, opponent processing *per se* between the on-channel and the off-channel generates the antagonistic rebound within the off-channel without necessitating the hypothesis that on-channel activation triggers a delayed off-channel activation. The hypotheses of the Solomon and Corbit model may be challenged on several fronts. The hypothesis of delayed activation of the off-channel by the on-channel seems problematic when one asks how a direct activation of the off-channel can cause a delayed activation of the on-channel. Solomon and Corbit do not raise this question. Indeed, they do not separate the on- and off-components into two topographically distinct output pathways. More generally, their opponent process is not defined by a dynamical model. Instead their components are chosen to fit the data in different experimental paradigms. For example, the Solomon and Corbit model does not explain why the maximum size of the *a* process should sometimes, but not always, exceed the maximum size of the *b* process, or why the *b* process is delayed in time relative to the *a* process by just the right amount to produce an overshoot and an undershoot. The hypothesis that slowly habituating, tonically aroused, transmitter gates exist in an opponent anatomy provides simple answers to all of these questions, and implies other properties which enable the gated dipole model to organize data about decision making under risk.

6. The Psychophysics of Risk: Short Term Memory and Long Term Memory Interactions

The final set of assumptions of the theory may be thought of as describing the psychophysics of risk. More specifically, these assumptions describe how events, notably probabilistically experienced events, are transformed and encoded. Although the resulting algebraic properties of these assumptions are quite similar to those adopted by other theories of decision making under risk (see below for a comparison with Prospect Theory), the rationale for these assumptions is quite distinct. The properties here are based on analyses of how environmental events are coded into internal representations in order to solve inevitable dilemmas posed by a fluctuating and uncertain environment. As a result, the theory provides a dynamic, rather than static or formal, description of the psychophysics of risk. Further, the theory strengthens the rationale for these assumptions by extending the data base that motivates these assumptions beyond group choice data from studies of risky decision making. In the following paragraphs, we briefly summarize the main processing ideas about the psychophysics of risk that motivate our computations of risky decisions. We do not redevelop these processing ideas here, but refer the reader to the original sources. Our summary is intended to provide meaning to the computations, which themselves form the core of the present contribution.

The analysis of how probability information impacts on risky decisions begins with the observation that the storage of individual events and their associated affective values in short term memory is positively related to the frequency or probability of occurrence. This property follows from two interacting effects, one long-term and the other short-term. The long-term effect concerns the greater influence of familiar events than of unfamiliar events on tuning of the long term memory traces which regulate coding of an event in short term memory (Grossberg, 1980; Grossberg and Stone, 1986). Other things being equal, a better match of an event with the patterning of long term memory traces leads to enhanced activation in short term memory of the event's internal representation. Thus, to the extent that the chosen high probability events are more familiar than the chosen low probability events, the short term memory activity of an event will tend to be an increasing function of its prior probability. However, the total effect of probability is more complicated, especially when both low probability and high probability events are equally familiar.

This is because the short-term effect of probability also influences the action of cognitive expectancies. In particular, low probability events tend to be more unexpected than high probability events. They can therefore trigger a more complete reset of prior short term memory, thereby facilitating their own preferential loading into short term memory (Grossberg, 1982). The net effect of this short-term effect is often that the ratio of the short term memory activity of a low probability event to a high probability event is greater than the ratio of their respective probabilities. If we assume that the "decision weight" associated with a probabilistic event is the average short term memory activity across events with that particular probability, then we are led to the assumption that low probability events will be overweighted relative to high probability events.

Our analysis of how value or utility information affects risky decision making begins with the observation that all neural signal functions must be bounded. Consequently, the value function will be chosen to be slower-than-linear or negatively accelerated at large values of both positively and negatively valenced events. It has, moreover, been shown mathematically that the simplest bounded function capable of transducing neural activities into signals, without amplifying noise, is an S-shaped or sigmoid function (Grossberg, 1973,

1983; Grossberg and Levine, 1975). Using this sigmoid function as a starting point, the value function is computed as follows for gains and losses. It is assumed that the value, or affective magnitude, of a gain is a function of the on-response to that event, whereas the value of a loss of a given magnitude is a function of the antagonistic rebound which occurs in response to the removal of a positive event of that magnitude. If we divide equation (15) by equation (12), we see that the size of the antagonistic rebound relative to the on-response is simply $f(I)/A$, which is a function only of A and I. More specifically, the antagonistic rebound is larger than the on-response whenever $f(I)$ is larger than A. Since this inequality ordinarily holds in individuals capable of learned avoidance behavior (Grossberg, 1972b), we are led to conclude that the overall value function is not symmetric but rather is usually steeper for losses than gains. This analysis leads to the interesting and testable implication that certain underaroused individuals, for whom I is pathologically small, may show the opposite pattern (Grossberg, 1984a, 1984b).

The final psychophysical issue concerns how probability and outcome information combine or interact. In Grossberg's theory of cognitive-emotional interactions, activation of an event's short term memory representation elicits signals from this representation to the gated dipole opponent processes where emotional reactions are generated (Figure 4). Before these signals can reach the gated dipoles, they are multiplied, or *gated*, by long term memory traces which encode the conditioned reinforcer values of the event. These gated signals then activate the on-channel or the off-channel of their target dipoles (Grossberg, 1972b, 1982) thereby leading to emotional reactions and motivational signals. In other words, the net affective activity associated with an event of a given probability is the product of the (expectancy-modulated) short term memory strength of that event and the affective value of that event as read out of long term memory into short term memory.

In order to facilitate comparisons with other theories of decision making under risk, we provide a more formal summary of the main psychophysical properties of the theory. The theory assumes that each (affectively meaningful) dipole input, J$^+$ and J$^-$, is the product of two factors. The first factor, which we denote by $f(x)$, is a signal read-out from the short term memory representation x of each event. The second factor, $z^+(x)$ or $z^-(x)$, is a long term memory trace that encodes the conditioned reinforcing value, positive or negative, of an event. For positively valenced events the signal to the on-channel may then be expressed as

$$J^+(x) = f(x)z^+(x) \tag{16}$$

due to the gating of the short term memory signal $f(x)$ by the long term memory trace $z^+(x)$. Similarly, the gated signal of a negatively valenced event to the off-channel may be expressed as

$$J^-(x) = f(x)z^-(x). \tag{17}$$

The theory assumes that the function $f(x)$ is characterized by the psychometric property termed *subproportionality*, since the ratio of the expectancy-modulated short term memory activity of a low probability event to a high probability event is ordinarily greater than the ratio of their respective probabilities (Figure 5a). Finally, the functions $z^+(x)$ and $z^-(x)$ are S-shaped about the origin (or status quo), with the LTM trace $z^-(x)$ of negatively valenced events steeper than the LTM trace $z^+(x)$ for positively valenced events (Figure 5b) due to the antagonistic rebound properties cited above.

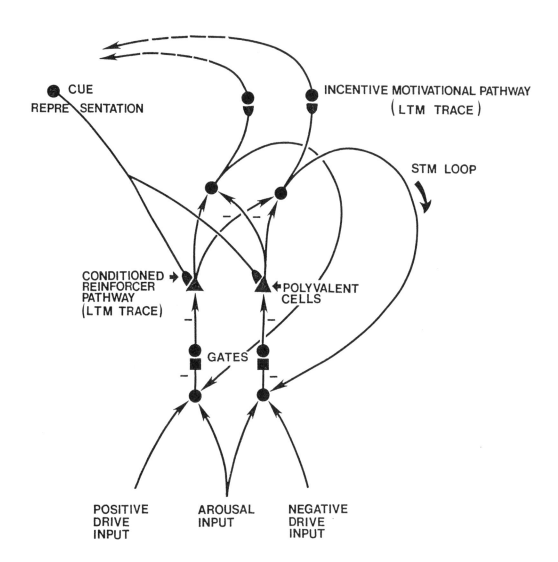

Figure 4. A cognitive-emotional interaction between cognitive, or cue, representations and a gated dipole opponent process, called a drive representation, which synthesizes reinforcing signals, internal drive inputs, and an arousal baseline into an affective response. This response generates incentive motivational feedback signals to the cue representations and can thereby cause a shift in attention towards motivationally salient information. Signals from cue representations to drive representations are multiplied by long term memory (LTM) traces which encode the conditioned reinforcing values of the cue representation. Unconditioned reinforcers can also activate the drive representation. (Reprinted with permission from Grossberg, 1982a.)

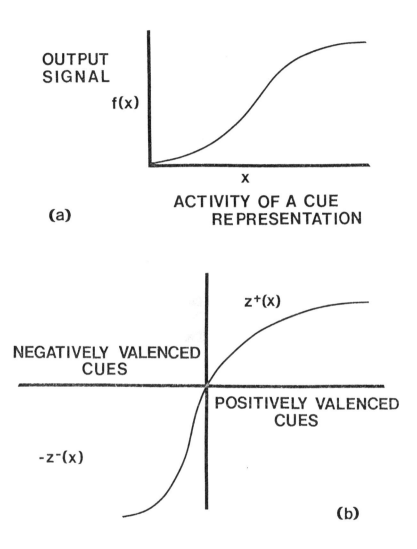

Figure 5. Relationship of dynamic neural processes to algebraic psychophysical processes: (a) A sigmoid signal function helps to achieve subproportionality, as does the modulation of short term memory by matching with learned expectations. (b) The long term memory traces $z^+(x)$ and $z^-(x)$ which input to, and learn from the positive and negative channels, respectively, of an affective gated dipole derive their shape from direct on-reactions to inputs as well as antagonistic rebound off-reactions to changes in these inputs.

7. Comparison with Prospect Theory

We now compare the psychophysical properties assumed in Affective Balance Theory with the psychophysical assumptions of Prospect Theory (Kahneman and Tversky, 1979). This summary does not provide a complete characterization of Prospect Theory, but rather focusses on the assumptions of that theory that govern the psychophysics of risk.

The first psychophysical assumption of Prospect Theory involves a scale, $v(x)$, that describes how an event x is transformed into a subjective value. The theory assumes that the value function is normally concave for positive changes in status or gains but is normally convex for negative changes or losses. That is, the marginal value of both gains and losses generally decrease with larger magnitudes. The theory further assumes that the value function for losses is generally steeper than the value function for gains. A hypothetical value function which meets these criteria is shown in Figure 6a.

The second psychophysical assumption involves a scale, $\pi(P)$, that describes how a probability P is transformed into a decision weight which calibrates the relative impact of an event with a particular probability on the overall value of a risky alternative. The theory naturally assumes that the weighting function, $\pi(P)$, is a monotonically increasing function of P with $\pi(0) = 0$ and $\pi(1) = 1$. In addition, it is assumed that small probabilities are generally overweighted but that large probabilities are generally underweighted. More specifically, the theory assumes a property called *subcertainty* so that

$$\pi(P) + \pi(1 - P) < 1 \qquad (18)$$

for all $0 < P < 1$. Prospect Theory also assumes the property of *subproportionality* that was discussed earlier. Mathematically, subproportionality can be expressed as

$$\frac{\pi(Pq)}{\pi(P)} < \frac{\pi(Pqr)}{\pi(Pr)} \qquad (19)$$

for all $0 < r < 1$. That is, for a fixed ratio of probabilities, the ratio of decision weights is closer to unity for small probabilities than for large probabilities. A weighting function which meets these criteria is shown in Figure 6b.

The third psychophysical assumption is an integration rule that describes how probability and event value information combine. Prospect Theory assumes that this integration rule is multiplicative, so that the net contribution of an event of a particular probability to the overall value of an alternative is $\pi(P)v(x)$.

On comparing the psychometric assumptions of Affective Balance Theory and Prospect Theory, we find three obvious points of correspondence. First, the value function, $v(x)$, in Prospect Theory and the long term memory functions, $z^+(x)$ and $z^-(x)$, in Affective Balance Theory both represent the positive or negative value associated with previously experienced events. Moreover, these functions are psychometrically similar, since both $v(x)$ and $z^\pm(x)$ are assumed to be sigmoidal but steeper for negative than for positive events. Second, the decision weight function, $\pi(P)$, in Prospect Theory and the short term memory function, $f(x)$, in Affective Balance Theory both represent the relative strength of an event with a particular probability in active memory. These functions also are characterized by similar psychometric properties such as subproportionality. Third, the integration rule, $\pi(P)v(x)$, in Prospect Theory and the gating law, $J(x) = f(x)z(x)$, in Affective Balance Theory both assert that probability and event value information combine multiplicatively.

These three points of correspondence illustrate our assertion that the psychophysical properties of Affective Balance Theory are similar to those of other prominent theories of

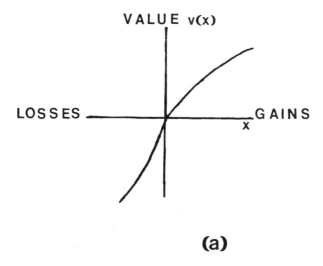

(a)

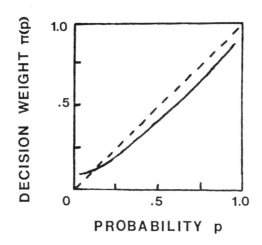

(b)

Figure 6. Psychometric functions of Prospect Theory: (a) A hypothetical value function $v(x)$. (b) A hypothetical weighting function $\pi(p)$.

decision making under risk. In addition, Affective Balance Theory provides a description of the information processing dynamics that underlie these psychophysical properties. In particular, the short term memory function $f(x)$ simultaneously reads out $J^+(x) = f(x)z^+(x)$ and $J^-(x) = f(x)z^-(x)$ into the opponent process of the gated dipole. This opponent process sometimes generates the net reaction $J^+(x) - J^-(x) = f(x)[z^+(x) - z^-(x)]$ to these inputs, thereby rationalizing a comparison between the value function $v(x)$ of Prospect Theory and the difference $z^+(x) - z^-(x)$ of the LTM traces. However, the gated dipole opponent process often does *not* merely subtract the $z^+(x)$ and $z^-(x)$ LTM functions. These deviations from additivity are, moreover, a principal source of the gated dipole's ability to explain difficult data about affectively charged behaviors.

8. The Temporal Unfolding of Risky Judgments: Generating an Affective Context

We now illustrate how different temporal sequences of event comparisons control the affective values of these events. First we consider a temporal sequence used to judge the value of a two-outcome regular alternative. Then we consider two different event sequences that may occur under conditions of risky choice, and show how both sequences can generate the same preference order.

We first observe that judgments of a two-outcome regular alternative may initially be unorderly (i.e., not monotonic in the outcome and probability variables) and require considerable practice before stabilizing (Anderson and Shanteau, 1970). The model assumes that this transition or learning phase includes development of a stable adaptation level against which alternatives may be evaluated or processed. Although no precise assumptions are made about the adaptation level, J_0, it is assumed that J_0 is a function of the previous inputs and that it perturbs both channels equally. This assumption may be relaxed when the average magnitudes of previous positive and negative inputs are not approximately equal.

The theory assumes that the judgment process begins by setting the adaptation level at J_0. Instatement of J_0 drives the transmitter levels in each channel of the dipole to levels $z_0 = \frac{AB}{[A+f(I+J_0)]}$. (Henceforth we assume for simplicity that J_0 is absorbed into the arousal level I, and that the theory is operating in the linear range of f: $f(w) = w$.) After the channels adapt, it is assumed that attention is directed to the current alternative a_i. The positive and negative inputs to the on-channel and off-channel are then J_i^+ and J_i^-, respectively. However, the transmitter levels change slowly so that the levels z_0 are maintained (approximately) for an interval after J_i^+ and J_i^- are presented. After transmitter gating and opponent processing, the dipole on-response to a_i is given by

$$
\begin{aligned}
r_i &= (I + J_i^+)z_0 - (I + J_i^-)z_0 \\
&= z_0(J_i^+ - J_i^-).
\end{aligned}
\tag{20}
$$

The theory assumes that a linear judgment function maps this affective response onto an overt response. Under this assumption, the overt response, R_i, is

$$
R_i = k(J_i^+ - J_i^-),
\tag{21}
$$

where $k > 0$ is a proportionality constant. Henceforth we assume $k = 1$ for simplicity, and describe r_i and R_i interchangeably. Hence, the theory predicts that the affective response to a risky alternative is proportional to the difference between the affectively charged inputs which correspond to attended events. Such differences provide one basis for calling the present formulation Affective Balance Theory.

We now turn to the temporal structure of the events which are assumed to influence gated dipole dynamics under conditions of risky choice. Two temporal sequences of event comparisons are considered: "between-dimension, within-alternative" comparisons and "within-dimension, between-alternative" comparisons (Payne, 1982). Conditions under which both sequences yield the same preference order are described.

In a "between-dimension, within-alternative" comparison, both events within one experimentally grouped pair are first processed before both events in the other experimentally grouped pair are processed. In these experiments, each event in a pair has a manifest affective value of opposite sign; for example, one event represents a possible gain and the other event represents a possible loss. In a "within-dimension, between alternative" comparison, one event within each experimentally grouped pair is processed before it is compared with the event of corresponding manifest value in the other pair. Then the other events in each pair are compared. In the "between-dimension, within-alternative" comparison the decision maker initially samples or attends to one of the alternatives. This sampling causes a net response to that alternative. (In Appendix A we show that choice is independent of which alternative is sampled first.) It is assumed that attention is focussed on the first alternative for a sufficient amount of time for the transmitter levels in each channel to habituate, or adapt, to the positive and negative inputs from this alternative. It is assumed that attention next shifts to the second alternative. This attentional shift causes a second net response which is also the result of competition between the gated inputs of the alternative. Since the transmitter levels are slowly varying in time, the inputs of the second alternative are gated by levels which are a function of the inputs of the first alternative. Thus the first alternative establishes an *affective context* in which the second alternative is evaluated.

To see how such an affective context influences judgments, we compute the on-activity r_1 due to the first alternative and the on-activity r_2 due to the second alternative. To accomplish this, denote by z_1^+ the habituated transmitter level in response to J_1^+ and by z_1^- the habituated transmitter level in response to J_1^-. It follows, as in (8) and (9), that

$$z_1^+ = \frac{AB}{A + I + J_1^+} \tag{22}$$

and

$$z_1^- = \frac{AB}{A + I + J_1^-}. \tag{23}$$

Thus the on-response r_1 to the inputs J_1^+ and J_1^- is

$$r_1 = (I + J_1^+)z_1^+ - (I + J_1^-)z_1^-. \tag{24}$$

As in (12), (24) may be rewritten in the form

$$r_1 = AC(J_1^+ - J_1^-), \tag{25}$$

where

$$C = \frac{AB}{(A + I + J_1^+)(A + I + J_1^-)}. \tag{26}$$

In order to compute r_2, we let transmitter levels z_1^+ and z_1^- gate the inputs J_2^+ and J_2^- of the second alternative. Thus

$$r_2 = (I + J_2^+)z_1^+ - (I + J_2^-)z_1^-. \tag{27}$$

By (22), (23), and (27),

$$r_2 = C(D - E + F), \tag{28}$$

where

$$D = (A + I)(J_2^+ - J_2^-), \tag{29}$$

$$E = I(J_1^+ - J_1^-), \tag{30}$$

and

$$F = J_1^- J_2^+ - J_1^+ J_2^-. \tag{31}$$

We assume that the decision maker senses the difference between the affective responses r_1 and r_2, and prefers the larger one. In this very limited sense, we assume that the decision maker attempts to "maximize" subjective value. Thus, letting $\Delta = r_1 - r_2$, the first alternative is chosen if $\Delta > 0$ and the second alternative is chosen if $\Delta < 0$. Subtracting (28) from (25) yields

$$\Delta = G[(J_1^+ - J_1^-) - (J_2^+ - J_2^-)] + C(J_1^+ J_2^- - J_1^- J_2^+), \tag{32}$$

where

$$G = (A + I)C. \tag{33}$$

The preceeding analysis considers the situation in which individuals engage in "between-dimension, within-alternative" processing, where the first alternative establishes the affective context in which the inputs of the second alternative are evaluated. When decision makers utilize a "within-dimension, between-alternative" processing strategy, the sampling sequence first focuses attention on one of the inputs of the first alternative and then shifts attention to the input of the second alternative with the same affective sign. For example, attention may be first focused on the positive input of the first alternative and then shifted to the positive input of the second alternative. Subsequently, attention is focused on the other input of the first alternative and then shifted to the corresponding input of the second alternative.

In these circumstances, the theory assumes that two contexts are established: a positive context in which the positive input of the second alternative is evaluated, and a negative context in which the negative input of the second alternative is evaluated. This computation is instantiated as follows. Denote the positive responses as r_1^+, r_2^+ and their difference as $\Delta^+ = r_1^+ - r_2^+$. Since r_1^+ is the first term of (24) and r_2^+ is the first term of (27), this difference is simply

$$\Delta^+ = H(J_1^+ - J_2^+) \tag{34}$$

where

$$H = \frac{AB}{A + I + J_1^+}, \tag{35}$$

Denote the negative responses as r_1^-, r_2^-, and their difference as $\Delta^- = r_1^- - r_2^-$. Since r_1^- is the second term of (24) and r_2^- is the second term of (27), this difference is simply

$$\Delta^- = K(J_1^- - J_2^-) \tag{36}$$

where

$$K = \frac{-AB}{A + I + J_1^-}. \tag{37}$$

Finally, we assume that preference is determined by the difference between Δ^+ and Δ^-. Substracting (36) from (34) yields

$$\Delta^+ - \Delta^- = H(J_1^+ - J_2^+) - K(J_1^- - J_2^-). \tag{38}$$

By (35), (36) and (38),

$$\Delta^+ - \Delta^- = G[(J_1^+ - J_1^-) - (J_2^+ - J_2^-)] + C(J_1^+ J_2^- - J_1^- J_2^+). \tag{39}$$

Since (39) and (32) are identical, it follows that preference is independent of the decision maker's processing strategy.

We believe that the mechanism which stores the value Δ^+ for later comparison with Δ^- in (38) may not be the same as the mechanism which compares r_1 with r_2 in (32). In particular, Δ^+ may be stored and later read out by a perceptual mechanism, much as a subject can discriminate and remember the intensity of an affectively charged event, such as a shock. In contrast, comparison of r_1 and r_2 can be accomplished directly within a gated dipole.

9. Risk Aversion and Preference Reversals

Evaluation of equation (32) provides some important insights. Consistent with equation (21), let us call the difference of the inputs of the ith alternative, $J_i^+ - J_i^-$, the *value* of the ith alternative. From equation (32), we see that choice is not simply a function of the difference of the values of the alternatives. Instead, choice also depends upon the cross-product, $J_1^+ J_2^- - J_1^- J_2^+$, and hence upon the ratios of the inputs. To illustrate this property, assume that the values of the alternatives are equal or that $J_1^+ - J_1^- = J_2^+ - J_2^-$. Under this assumption,

$$\Delta = C(J_1^+ J_2^- - J_1^- J_2^+). \tag{40}$$

From this expression, it is clear that $\Delta \geq 0$ if and only if $J_1^+/J_1^- \geq J_2^+/J_2^-$. By extension, if the difference between the values of the alternatives is small, then choice is primarily determines by the cross-product, or ratio, terms of equation (32).

The implications of this property represent a break with previous models, since it is possible to choose the second alternative ($\Delta < 0$) even if the first alternative has higher value ($J_1^+ - J_1^- > J_2^+ - J_2^-$). Another implication is that choice between equally valued alternatives should not be random, but rather should be determined by the ratios of the inputs. In Appendix B, we prove the following consequences of this property.

Risk Aversion and Risk Attraction

The riskier of two equally valued alternatives is chosen when both alternatives are viewed as negative, whereas the less risky alternative is chosen when both are viewed as positive.

Preference Reversal

Preference reversals occasionally occur but only when ratios of the inputs are not congruent with the differences of the inputs. That is, preference reversals do not occur when the sign of the differences is consistent with the sign of the ratios. Preference reversals occur in favor of the riskier alternative only when both alternatives are viewed as negative. Preference reversals occur in favor of the conservative alternative only when both alternatives are viewed as positive.

Together, these results illustrate how the theory predicts that individuals will tend to be risky when a situation is unfavorable but tend to be conservative when a situation is favorable. This result is a generalization of the Kahneman and Tversky reflection effect (Section 1). The reflection effect involves choices between risky and riskless alternatives. Our result applies not only to that case (Section 12) but also to choices between pairs of risky alternatives. This generalization is possible because the dynamics of affective choice described herein reveals properties which are not captured by the formal axioms of Prospect Theory.

The following constraint limits the generality of our analysis. The theory assumes that responses to risky alternatives are due only to the manner in which perceptually driven cognitive processes elicit different affective reactions. Clearly this assumption is not always justified. Certain individuals, such as professional decision analysts, may base their judgments and choices on overt mathematical computations. In these cases, the preceding predictions do not hold since responses are then a function only of the results of the computations. However, the failures of Expected Value Theory and Expected Utility Theory demonstrate that a computationally based approach to decision making under risk is often the exception rather than the rule.

10. Preference Reversal Experiments Demonstrating Interaction between Hedonic Sign and Risk Aversion

In the following section, we summarize a key result from a pair of experiments that have tested the risk aversion and risk attraction properties of preference reversals postulated by Affective Balance Theory. For a detailed discussion of experimental procedures and related results, see Gutowski (1984) and Gutowski and Chechile (1986). The general format for these experiments was a computerized card tournament during which subjects played a modified version of the game called red-dog (Epstein, 1977) and gained or lost points that were later exchanged for money. Each alternative consisted of a red-dog hand and a specification of the number of points that could be won or lost. In order to motivate careful judgments, the Marschak bidding technique was employed (Becker, DeGroot, and Marschak, 1964). Both judgment and choice experiments were carried out to provide a stringent criterion for the occurrence of a perference reversal. Judgment and choice trials were interlaced in order to avoid confounding effects due to motivational or attentional shifts.

On each trial of the judgment experiment, a subject first judged the value of the current alternative and then estimated the chance of winning. Subsequently, a random number was generated and if the number was less than the judged value, the hand was played and points were gained or lost depending on whether the subject won the hand. If the random number was less than the judged value, the subject earned that (random) number of points. This procedure was employed since it provided explicit motivation to give judgments that were exactly equal to the perceived value of an alternative.

On each trial of the choice experiment, subjects were presented with pairs of risky alternatives and asked to indicate which they preferred. On each trial, a subject first indicated the alternative he preferred to play and then estimated the chances of winning the chosen hand. After this estimate was recorded, the hand was played and feedback

TABLE 1

Preference reversal rates in favor of the riskier and less risky alternative as a function of the hedonic sign of the alternatives. V_1 is the judged value of the less risky alternative and V_2 is the judged value of the riskier alternative.

HEDONIC SIGN OF THE ALTERNATIVES

	Unfavorable	Favorable
Judged Inequality		
$V_1 < V_2$	.100	.679
$V_1 > V_2$	.528	.000

provided as to the number of points gained or lost. The overall choice set was composed of two groups in which either expected value and the probability of winning were held constant or expected value was held constant but the probability of winning varied. Many of these pairs of alternatives were chosen to fulfill a property called natural risk ordering. The notation $A_i = (a_i^+, P_i, a_i^-)$ designates an ith alternative in which an amount a_i^+ can be gained with probability P_i and an amount a_i^- can be lost with probabiltiy $1 - P_i$. A pair of risky alternatives, $A_1 = (a_1^+, P_1, a_1^-)$ and $A_2 = (a_2^+, P_2, a_2^-)$, is termed *naturally risk ordered* with A_1 riskier than A_2 if and only if $P_1 \leq P_2$ and $a_1^- \leq a_2^-$ and one of these inequalities is strict. For example, the pair $A_1 = (30, 1/3, -10)$ and $A_2 = (50, 1/3, -20)$ is naturally risk ordered since $P_1 = P_2$ and $a_1^- > a_2^-$. In contrast, the pair $A_1 = (50, 1/6, -10)$ and $A_2 = (10, 2/3, -20)$ is not naturally risk ordered since $P_1 < P_2$ but $a_1^- > a_2^-$. For such pairs of alternatives, the risk aversion and risk attraction properties of preference reversals proposed by the model can be evaluated even when psychometric judgments of risk are not available.

Differences in the values of a particular pair of alternatives were assumed only if one of the alternatives was judged to be greater than or equal to the other alternative in each replication, and if that inequality was strict in at least two of the replications. Preference, as indicated by the choice measure, was assumed only if one of the alternatives was always selected over the other alternative. Otherwise, indifference was assumed in regard to preference or differences in subjective value. Similar criteria were imposed to determine whether a particular alternative was hedonically positive, neutral, or negative. The assumption of hedonic neutrality (i.e., subjective value equal to 0) was rejected only if, for each replication, an alternative was judged to be greater than 0 or judged to be less than 0.

The primary results from these experiments are shown in Table 1, which gives the preference reversal rates as a function of hedonic sign and the judged relation between the values of the riskier and less risky alternative.

These data demonstrate that preference reversals in favor of both the riskier and less risky alternatives are strongly related to the hedonic sign of the alternatives. For unfavorable alternatives, the preference reversal rate in favor of the riskier alternative was .528, while the preference reversal rate in favor of the less risky alternative was only .100. This difference is statistically reliable, $x^2(1) = 4.80, p < .05$. For favorable alternatives, the preference reversal rate in favor of the riskier alternative was .000, while the reversal rate in favor of the less risky alternative was .679. This difference is also statistically reliable, $x^2(1) = 7.18, p < .01$. Moreover, the preference reversal rates in favor of the riskier alternative are greater for unfavorable than for favorable alternatives, $x^2(1) = 14.56, p < .01$. In contrast, the preference reversal rates in favor of the less risky alternative are greater for favorable than for unfavorable alternatives, $x^2(1) = 11.63, p < .01$.

In summary, these results show that the preference reversal phenomenon is a highly structured effect reflecting a willingness to accept risk under unfavorable circumstances and a corresponding unwillingness to accept risk under favorable circumstances. This data pattern is implied by equation (32). It provides strong support for Affective Balance Theory, since it is a natural consequence of the theory's mechanisms of opponent processing. Such data also challenge other theories of decision making under risk. Subsequent sections describe other important data properties that can naturally be derived from the theory.

11. Gambler's Fallacy: Cognitive-Emotional Dissociation or Partial Reward Effect

The gambler's fallacy is a frequently discussed phenomenon (Cohen, 1981; Diaconis and and Freedman, 1981; Skyrms, 1981) which vividly illustrates how decision making under risk may be sensitive to contextual effects generated by a sequence of positive and/or negative outcomes. In general, gambler's fallacy involves a shift in the amount of risk that a decision maker will accept after a homogeneous sequence of losses (or gains) relative to the amount of risk which will be accepted after a mixed sequence which involves both losses and gains. For example, a roulette player betting on colors might bet $10 on black after four consecutive losses whereas he might bet only $5 after a sequence of two wins and two losses.

Explanations of gambler's fallacy often assume that individuals do not appreciate the inherent variability of random processes and, thus, inappropriately shift their subjective probabilities after a homogeneous sequence of outcomes (Kahneman and Tversky, 1974). Affective Balance Theory offers two (experimentally testable) alternative explanations of this phenomenon. The first account is based on a dissociation between long-lasting emotional habituation and cognitive-emotional learning. The second account is based upon the antagonistic rebound effects due to disconfirmation of cognitive expectancies. The two accounts are not mutually exclusive in the sense that each may apply to different classes of individuals.

The first account implicates slow recovery from transmitter habituation as a primary mechanism, and a dissociation of transmitter habituation from cognitive-emotional, or conditioned reinforcer, conditioning as a secondary mechanism. This analysis assumes that each win or loss can significantly deplete the transmitter gate of the corresponding on-channel or off-channel, respectively, and that the transmitters recover at a slow rate from these losses. A sequence of wins or losses may consequently cause a cumulative habituation which acts as an affective baseline for subsequent decisions. When such a sequence is homogeneous (e.g., involves all negative outcomes), then the transmitter gate in the off-channel can habituate significantly more than that in the on-channel. When a sequence is mixed (e.g., involves equal numbers of positive and negative outcomes), then the transmitter gates in both the on-channel and the off-channel can habituate significantly. In particular, denote by M a mixed sequence and by N a sequence of losses. A natural outcome of cumulative habituation is that the depletion of the transmitter in the negative channel can be greater after a sequence of losses than after a mixed sequence. Similarly, the depletion of transmitter in the positive channel can be less after a sequence of losses than after a mixed sequence. Formally, we may express these relationships as

$$z^+(M) < z^+(N) \text{ and } z^-(M) > z^-(N). \tag{41}$$

Suppose, moreover, that these sustained habituative effects can occur without altering the conditioned reinforcer properties of the bets. In other words, the decision maker codes the event in terms of odds or other computations but does not learn from previous emotional consequences of these computations. Then the inputs J^+ and J^- that a bet generates at the gated dipole do not change over time, but the sensitivity of the dipole to these emotionally changed inputs does change through time.

Under these conditions, the gambler's fallacy occurs if the decision maker continues to bet based upon an affective "intuition." This is true because the on-response $r(N)$ to the same inputs (J^+, J^-) after a sequence of losses N is greater than the on-response $r(M)$ to (J^+, J^-) after a mixed sequence M of wins and losses. Consequently, a shift towards larger bets can occur after more losses are experienced under these conditions.

Formally, gambler's fallacy occurs when

$$r(N) > r(M), \tag{42}$$

where $r(P)$ is the on-response to sequence P. Given (41) and the hypothesis of no conditioned reinforcer learning, (42) follows from the formulas

$$r(N) = (I + J^+)z^+(N) - (I + J^-)z^-(N) \tag{43}$$

and

$$r(M) = (I + J^+)z^+(M) - (I + J^-)z^-(M). \tag{44}$$

In summary, a dissociation between emotional adaptation and cognitive-emotional conditioning can lead to the gambler's fallacy.

We now contrast this result with two examples which illustrate how conditioned reinforcer learning at cognitive-emotional synapses can counteract the tendency to make the gambler's fallacy. First let us consider the situation in which the gated dipole quickly overcomes its transmitter habituation, but a cumulative record of past wins and losses is encoded within the conditioned reinforcer long-term memory traces (Figure 4). In particular, assume that a series of wins tends to augment J^+, whereas a series of losses tends to augment J^-. Then after a mixed sequence M, these long-term memory increments may (approximately) balance out, so that

$$r(M) \cong \frac{AB(J^+ - J^-)}{A + I}, \tag{45}$$

whereas after a sequences of losses N,

$$r(N) \cong \frac{AB[J^+ - (J^- + g(N)]}{A + I}, \tag{46}$$

where $g(N)$ codes the extra conditioned reinforcer negativity due to N. In this situation, gambler's fallacy fails to hold.

A comparison of these two cases suggests that a persistent emotional desensitization in the absence of cognitive-emotional learning leads to gambler's fallacy, whereas cognitive-emotional learning accompanied by rapid emotional recovery does not. It remains to consider the case where transmitter habituation does persist, but conditioned reinforcer learning also rescales the inputs (J^+, J^-). In the simplest realization of this interaction,

$$r(M) = \frac{AB(J^+ - J^-)}{A + I + g(M)}, \tag{47}$$

whereas

$$r(N) = \frac{AB(I + J^+)}{A + I} - \frac{AB(I + J^- + C(N)g(N)}{A + I + g(N)}. \tag{48}$$

Term $-C(N)g(N)[A + I + g(N)]^{-1}$ in (48) expresses the negative conditioned reinforcer learning which can compensate for the transmitter habituation terms $g(M)$ and $g(N)$. A large value of $C(N)$ can prevent the gambler's fallacy from occurring.

What factors can control $C(N)$, apart from a simple gain control bias that favors learning over habituation? The answer to this question leads to a second explanation of the gambler's fallacy. A factor of special interest concerns the role of cognitive expectancies in modulating affective reactions. In addition to the direct effects of a win or a loss on habituation of the corresponding transmitter and conditioned reinforcer learning, disconfirmation of an expectancy can cause an antagonistic rebound, (Grossberg, 1980, 1982a).

Suppose, for definiteness, that the decision maker expects a win. Then a win causes a direct activation of the on-channel. On the other hand, a loss can activate the off-channel both directly and indirectly. The direct effect is due to the loss itself. The indirect effect is due to the off-rebound caused by disconfirmation of the expected win. Consequently, unexpected losses can be more punishing than expected losses, and can cause more negative conditioned reinforcer learning. In (48), such an effect can cause a large value of $C(N)$, and can thereby prevent the gambler's fallacy from occurring. This analysis assumes that the decision maker acts with an expectation of winning on every trial. Such a pattern of expectations works against persistent gambling after a long run of losses.

Expectations can, however, shift as a function of the temporal patterning of past wins and losses. Such a hypothesis has been used to suggest an explanation of the partial reinforcement acquisition effect (Grossberg 1975, 1982b). In this analysis, expectations shift with the pattern of wins and losses, and both direct and indirect (antagonistic rebound) effects can amplify the affective charge of an unexpected event. In the classical partial reinforcement paradigm, animals eventually run faster to partially reinforced (mixed sequence) goals than they do to continuously reinforced (positive sequence) goals. If we replace the positive sequence by a negative sequence, then we arrive at an analog of the gambler's fallacy. In this analog, continuous losses (the N sequence) may generate less negative affect than a combination of wins and losses (the M sequence). Such an effect is due to several interacting factors. An enhanced negative affect, or frustration, can be generated by losses on mixed trials, because mixed trials tend to support the maintenance of an expectation to win. This enhanced negative affect may be conditioned, for example, to situational cues, thereby creating a growing baseline of enhanced negativity in the M condition. As in the animal model of partial reinforcement, such a gambler's fallacy develops most effectively if the reinforcement probabilities are initially shaped to generate expectations capable of maintaining such performance.

In summary, the gambler's fallacy may follow either from an abnormal dissociation of cognitive-emotional learning from a persistent emotional habituation, or from a reinforcement schedule that sets up the types of correlations between expectancy-modulated antagonistic rebounds and cognitive-emotional learning which support the partial reinforcement acquisition effect.

12. Choice between Riskless and Risky Alternatives

We next describe some event groupings which may underlie the choice between a riskless alternative and a risky alternative. Suppose, for example, that the riskless alternative is

A. A sure win of $500,

and that the risky alternative is

B. A 3/4 probability of winning $800 and a 1/4 probability of losing $400.

In itself, the riskless alternative does not contain a source of negative affect. On the other hand, a choice of alternative B implies the renunciation of alternative A, and with it the possibility of a sure win. Embedding a sure win into a context of other possibilities may thus create a source of negative affect.

Expressed in another way, a riskless alternative does not, in itself, involve a comparison between pairs of outcomes in the way that a risky alternative does. The subject must create a grouping of outcomes that includes the riskless alternative in order to generate a preference order. Such a grouping may, or may not, be based entirely upon outcomes that are explicitly presented by the experimentalist, or more generally by the external environment. In particular, if the subject generates a preference order based upon pairwise comparisons, then a second outcome must be found for comparison with the riskless alternative. One possible outcome, which is not explicitly presented as part of alternatives A and B, is the denial, or disconfirmation, of the riskless alternative if the risky alternative is accepted.

In the subsequent paragraphs, we consider the preference order generated by two possible event groupings. In the first grouping, the disconfirmation of the riskless alternative is included. In the second grouping, it is not. Consider a situation wherein a decision maker initially samples or attends to the riskless alternative. Heuristically, we may think of the riskless alternative as forming a reference point or adaptation level against which the risky alternative is compared or evaluated. It is assumed that attention is focused on the riskless alternative for a sufficient amount of time for the transmitter levels in the perturbed channel to adapt to the input from the riskless alternative. As attention switches to the risky alternative, two effects occur which combine to determine the net response to the risky alternative. The first effect is an antagonistic rebound within the affective gated dipole. This rebound may occur when the subject switches from the input due to the riskless alternative to the input due to the risky alternative. Such a rebound encodes the affective residue due to a disconfirmation of the riskless alternative in order to evaluate the risky alternative. The second effect is a direct affective response to the inputs from the risky alternative. The net response to the risky alternative is then the sum of these two effects.

Let r_1 be the response to the riskless alternative, r_1^* be the antagonistic rebound, and r_2 be the response to the input of the risky alternative. We may express the net response to a riskless alternative which offers a sure gain as

$$r_1 = AKJ_1^+ \tag{49}$$

where

$$K = \frac{AB}{(A+I)(A+I+J_1^+)}. \tag{50}$$

Equation (49) is just equation (25) with $J_1^- = 0$. The antagonistic rebound which occurs in response to attention shift to the risky alternative is (approximately)

$$r_1^* = -IKJ_1^+. \tag{51}$$

After transmitter habituation occurs in response to the riskless alternative, the direct response to the inputs J_2^+ and J_2^- of the risky alternative is

$$r_2 = K[(A+I)(J_2^+ - J_2^-) - J_1^+ J_2^- - IJ_1^+]. \tag{52}$$

Due to the antagonistic rebound (51), the net affect due to disconfirmation of the riskless alternative and instatement of the risky alternative is

$$r_1^* + r_2 = K[(A+I)(J_2^+ - J_2^-) - J_1^+ J_2^- - 2IJ_1^+]. \tag{53}$$

As in Section 8, we assume that the decision maker senses or computes the difference $\Delta^+ = r_1 - (r_1^* + r_2)$ between these two net responses. By (49)–(53),

$$\Delta^+ = L[J_1^+ - (J_2^+ - J_2^-)] + K(J_1^+ J_2^- + IJ_1^+) \tag{54}$$

where

$$L = (A+I)K. \tag{55}$$

A similar analysis may be conducted for a situation where the riskless alternative involves a loss. Under these circumstances, the difference between the two net responses is

$$\Delta^- = L[(J_2^- - J_2^+) - J_1^-] - K(J_1^- J_2^+ + IJ_1^-). \tag{56}$$

One special case of particular importance involves a choice between a riskless alternative and a risky alternative which offers only outcomes which are null or of the same sign as the riskless alternative. Assume that only positive or null outcomes are possible; that is,

$$J_2^+ \geq J_2^- = 0. \tag{57}$$

In this case, the response to the riskless alternative and the antagonistic rebound are as expressed in equations (49) and (51) respectively. The response to the input from the risky alternative is

$$r_2 = K((A+I)J_2^+ - IJ_1^+). \tag{58}$$

Hence, the net response to the risky alternative is

$$r_1^* + r_2 = K[(A+I)J_2^+ - 2IJ_1^+] \tag{59}$$

so that the difference between the two net responses is

$$\Delta_0^+ = L[J_1^+ - J_2^+] + KIJ_1^+. \tag{60}$$

If only negative or null outcomes are possible, then this difference is

$$\Delta_0^- = L[J_2^- - J_1^-] - KIJ_1^-. \tag{61}$$

The implications of this analysis are applicable to two important phenomena which have been discovered during the development of Prospect Theory. Consider the following problems (from Kahneman and Tversky, 1981).

Which of the following alternatives do you prefer?

Problem 1

A. A sure win of $3000.

B. An 80% chance to win $4000.

Problem 2

C. A sure loss of $3000.

D. An 80% chance to lose $4000.

When presented with these problems, the majority of individuals prefer A to B and D to C. That is, individuals tend to be risk averse when gains are involved but risk taking when losses are involved. The previous computation accounts for this effect as the net effect of two types of factors: affective antagonistic rebounds that occur when sure events are contextually disconfirmed and affective reactions to risky events based upon prior affective adaptations. Suppose, for example in Problem 1, that attention is shifted from the riskless alternative to the risky alternative. The rebound is negative, thereby decreasing the net response to the risky alternative. Consequently, the riskless alternative will be chosen unless r_2 is considerably larger than r_1; that is, the risk averse alternative is preferred where gains are involved. In the second problem, the rebound due to an attention shift from the riskless alternative is positive, which increases the net response to the risky alternative. As a result, the risky alternative will be chosen unless r_2 is considerably smaller than r_1; that is, the risk taking alternative is preferred where losses are involved.

We consider it possible that some subjects may affectively evaluate a risky alternative by switching rapidly between its two possible interpretations. For example, an 80% chance to win $4000 may be represented as an input with conditioned reinforcer value appropriate to $4000 rapidly alternating with an offset of that input (20% chance of winning nothing). Where such rapid switching occurs, the subject creates an implicit conflict situation by generating off-rebounds to the positively valenced response. It is worth considering whether some subjects encode the 80%–20% contingency by just partially switching off the positively valenced signal, and thereby weakening the off-rebounds that compete with the positively valenced reaction before generating a net dipole output.

In the second sequence of comparisons that we will consider, the subject first adapts to the riskless alternative and then switches to the risky alternative without processing the disconfirmation that rejection of the riskless alternative could imply. All the above computations are the same, except there is no longer an antagonistic rebound r_1^*. Then (54) is replaced by

$$\Delta^+ = L[J_1^+ - (J_2^+ - J_2^-)] + J_1^+ J_2^- \tag{62}$$

and (60) is replaced by

$$\Delta_0^+ = L[J_1^+ - J_2^+]. \tag{63}$$

When (63) is used to explain why alternative A is preferred to alternative B, the psychophysical properties of the Kahneman and Tversky axioms (Section 7) bear the full burden of the explanation.

A similar type of contextual effect occurs if a positive riskless alternative is compared sequentially with the positive and negative events of a risky alternative. Then each of the comparisons may generate antagonistic rebounds due to the fact that the riskless alternative defines an adaptation level for evaluating both risky events.

In summary, this section illustrates how the additional affective values that are generated by contextually induced comparisons may explain certain properties of decision making under risk without invoking all of the Kahneman and Tversky axioms.

13. Framing Effect

Next, consider the following problems (from Kahneman and Tversky, 1981) which illustrate the framing effect.

Problem 3

Imagine that the United States is preparing for the outbreak of an unusual Asian disease, which is expected to kill 600 people. Two alternative programs to combat the disease have been proposed. Assume that the exact scientific estimate of the consequences are as follows:

If program A is adopted, 200 people will be saved.

If program B is adopted, there is a 1/3 probability that 600 people will be saved, and a 2/3 probability that no people will be saved.

Problem 4

Given the same cover story as in problem 3, a different formulation of the net effects of the alternative programs is:

If program C is adopted, 400 people will die.

If program D is adopted, there is a 1/3 probability that nobody will die, and a 2/3 probability that 600 people will die.

When presented with these problems the majority of individuals prefer A to B and D to C. That is, individuals tend to be risk averse when only positive consequences are explicitly mentioned but risk taking when only negative consequences are presented. The explanation for this framing effect is dynamically similar to that offered for problems 1 and 2. At least two different types of strategies exist which are consistent with the framing effect. In both strategies, subjects are assumed to respond to riskless alternatives by discovering other events with which they can be paired. The strategies differ only in terms of which event pairs are considered. For example, in Problem 3, the event that 600 people will be killed may be treated as a riskless alternative against which programs A and B are evaluated. Within this context, the statement "If program A is adopted, 200 people will be saved" creates a natural event pair, or contextually-induced alternative. In particular, disconfirmation of the riskless loss of 600 lives by the riskless gain of 200 lives can trigger a large antagonistic rebound. The contextual pressure to form such an event pair is substantial in this situation because the statement "200 people will be saved" is meaningless without a prior statement concerning their expected doom.

The evaluation of program B may, in principle, be made with respect to the sure event that 600 people will be killed, or the sure event that 200 people will be saved, or both. To fix ideas, suppose that the subject creates pairwise comparisons where none explicitly exist in the stimuli, but otherwise considers the events sequentially. Then, after the comparison of the sure death of 600 with program A generates a large positive rebound, comparison of program B with program A generates an additional bias towards program A, because this comparison involves a positive riskless alternative and a risky alternative (Section 11).

In subjects who use the sure death of 600 as a context for evaluating alternatives C and D, D is prefered to C for the following reasons. Disconfirmation of the certain death of 600 by instatement of the certain death of 400 people may create a small positive rebound. Comparison of program D with program C generates a bias away from program C, however, because this comparison involves a negative riskless alternative and a risky alternative. Thus, independent of parametric details, it is clear that program A is much more favored than program B, whereas there is at best a weak tendency to offset the risk seeking bias of program D over program C. In particular, there exists a range of parameters where the rebound is insufficient to offset the risk seeking bias.

If a subject does not use the sure event of 600 deaths as a context for further comparisons, then program A is again preferred to program B whereas program D is preferred to program C because the risk averse alternative is preferred where gains are involved whereas the risk taking alternative is preferred where losses are involved. Subjects may, in fact, follow this strategy more readily in comparing programs C and D than in comparing programs A and B. Unlike alternative A, the meaning of alternative C is self-contained, and does require comparison with the riskless death of 600.

14. Concluding Remarks

Affective Balance Theory provides a real-time dynamic description of some of the covert events underlying risky judgment and choice. The theory proposes dynamical explanations of decision making phenomena which have previously been interpretable only using formal axioms, such as those of Prospect Theory. This analysis clarifies how cognitive strategies may generate affective contexts for evaluating riskless and risky alternatives. In so doing, it provides an explanation of why individuals often do not act to maximize subjective value, even in simple situations where cognitive complexity is minimal, despite the fact that the mechanisms which prevent maximization have manifest adaptive functions. These mechanisms are not designed to maximize subjective value. Rather, they are designed to control the emotional processes which regulate reinforcement, incentive motivation, and affectively modulated attention shifts.

Many phenomena still lie outside the scope of the theory as presently formulated, if only because it has used only the most rudimentary ideas from the cognitive-emotional theory of which it is an application. The present results establish a bridge to that general theory, and indicate how Affective Balance Theory may be developed on a principled basis as increasingly complex situations are analysed. In particular, the present results demonstrate that psychophysiological data and theory may now be profitably applied to the domain of decision making under risk.

APPENDIX A

Relative Preference Independent of Sampling Order

Consider a choice between two alternatives a_1 and a_2. Let r_{ij} denote the response to the ith alternative when a_j is sampled first. If a_1 is sampled first, then after transmitter habituation takes place,

$$z_1^+ = \frac{AB}{(A + I + J_1^+)}, \tag{A1}$$

$$z_1^- = \frac{AB}{(A + I + J_1^-)}, \tag{A2}$$

and

$$r_{11} = AK_1(J_1^+ - J_1^-), \tag{A3}$$

where

$$K_1 = \frac{AB(J_1^+ - J_1^-)}{(A + I + J_1^+)(A + I + J_1^-)}. \tag{A4}$$

When attention is then switched to a_2, the response, r_{21}, is based upon the habituated values in (A1) and (A2). Thus

$$r_{21} = K_1[(A + I)(J_2^+ - J_2^-) - I(J_1^+ - J_1^-) + J_2^+ J_1^- - J_1^+ J_2^-)]. \tag{A5}$$

The difference $\Delta^{(1)} = r_{21} - r_{11}$ in these responses is

$$\Delta^{(1)} = K_1[(A + I)((J_2^+ - J_2^-) - (J_1^+ - J_1^-)) + J_2^+ J_1^- - J_2^- J_1^+]. \tag{A6}$$

If a_2 is sampled first, then

$$z_2^+ = \frac{AB}{(A + I + J_2^+)}, \tag{A7}$$

$$z_2^- = \frac{AB}{(A + I + J_2^-)}, \tag{A8}$$

and

$$r_{22} = AK_2(J_2^+ - J_2^-), \tag{A9}$$

where

$$K_2 = \frac{AB}{(A + I + J_2^+)(A + I + J_2^-)}. \tag{A10}$$

When attention is then switched to a_1, the response, r_{12}, is

$$r_{12} = K_2[(A + I)(J_1^+ - J_1^-) - I(J_2^+ - J_2^-) + J_1^+ J_2^- - J_1^- J_2^+]. \tag{A11}$$

The difference $\Delta^{(2)} = r_{22} - r_{12}$ in these responses is

$$\Delta^{(2)} = K_2[(A + I)((J_2^+ - J_2^-) - (J_1^+ - J_1^-)) + J_2^+ J_1^- - J_2^- J_1^+]. \tag{A12}$$

Term $\Delta^{(1)}$ compares the relative reaction to a_2 after a_1. Term $\Delta^{(2)}$ compares the relative reaction to a_2 before a_1. By (A6) and (A12), these terms differ only in their positive coefficients K_1 and K_2. Thus $\Delta^{(1)}$ is positive (negative) if and only if $\Delta^{(2)}$ is positive (negative). Hence the same relative preference exists independent of sampling order.

APPENDIX B

Risk Aversion, Risk Attraction, and Preference Reversal

Consider a choice between two equally valued alternatives a_1 and a_2. Let $D = J_1^+ - J_1^- = J_2^+ - J_2^-$. Assume that a_2 is riskier than a_1 so that $J_1^- < J_2^-$. Without loss of generality, assume that a_1 is sampled first. Then by (A6),

$$\Delta^{(1)} = K_1[J_2^+ J_1^- - J_2^- J_1^+]$$
$$= K_1[(J_2^- + D)J_1^- - J_2^-(J_1^- + D)] \qquad (A13)$$
$$= D(J_1^- - J_2^-).$$

Therefore, $\Delta^{(1)} < 0$ if and only if $D > 0$, since $J_1^- - J_2^- < 0$. This result demonstrates that the less risky alternative is chosen $(\Delta^{(1)} < 0)$ only if the positive input is greater than the negative input $(D > 0)$. That is, the less risky alternative of two equally valued alternatives is chosen only if the alternatives are favorable.

Consider a choice between two alternatives which are not equal in value. Let $J_1^+ - J_1^- = D_1$ and $J_2^+ - J_2^- = D_1 + D_2$. Assume that a_2 is riskier than a_1, so that $J_1^- < J_2^-$. Let $\Delta^{(1)} = r_{21} - r_{11}$, as in Appendix A. A *preference reversal* is said to occur if

$$D_2 \Delta^{(1)} < 0; \qquad (A14)$$

that is, if a_2 is preferred over a_1 $(\Delta^{(1)} > 0)$ even though a_1 has greater value than a_2 $(D_2 < 0)$; or if a_1 is preferred over a_2 $(\Delta^{(1)} < 0)$ even though a_2 has greater value than a_1 $(D_2 > 0)$.

By (A6),

$$\Delta^{(1)} = K_1[(A + I)D_2 + J_1^-(J_2^- + D_1 + D_2) - J_2^-(J_1^- + D_1)] \qquad (A15)$$
$$= K_1[(A + I + J_1^-)D_2 + (J_1^- - J_2^-)D_1].$$

Since $A + I + J_1^- > 0$ and $J_1^- - J_2^- < 0$,

$$\Delta^{(1)} > 0 \text{ if } D_1 < 0 \text{ and } D_2 > 0, \qquad (A16)$$

whereas

$$\Delta^{(1)} < 0 \text{ if } D_1 > 0 \text{ and } D_2 < 0. \qquad (A17)$$

The difference $\Delta^{(1)}$ may be positive or negative if

$$D_1 D_2 > 0. \qquad (A18)$$

A preference reversal does not occur in either of the cases (A16) or (A17). A preference reversal can occur only if (A18) holds. By (A15) and (A18), two possible cases obtain: either

$$\Delta^{(1)} < 0, \quad D_1 > 0, \quad D_2 > 0 \qquad (A19)$$

or

$$\Delta^{(1)} > 0, \quad D_1 < 0, \quad D_2 < 0. \qquad (A20)$$

In case (A19), the preference reversal favors the less risky alternative a_1 only if the alternatives are favorable $(D_1 > 0)$. In case (A19), the preference reversal favors the riskier alternative a_2 only if the alternatives are unfavorable $(D_1 < 0)$.

REFERENCES

Allais, M., Le comportement de l'homme rationnel devant le risque, Critique des postulats et axiomes de l'ecole Americaine. *Econometrica*, 1953, **21**, 503–546.

Anderson, N.H. and Shanteau, J.C., Information integration in risky decision making. *Journal of Experimental Psychology*, 1970, **84**, 441–451.

Becker, G., DeGroot, G., and Marschak, J., Measuring utility by a single-response sequential method. *Behavioral Science*, 1964, **9**, 226–232.

Bernoulli, D., Specimen theoriae novae de mensura sortis. *Commentarii academiae scientiarum imperalis Petropolitanae*, 1738, **5**, 175–192.

Cohen, L.J., Can human irrationality be demonstrated? *The Behavioral and Brain Sciences*, 1981, **4**, 317–331.

Coombs, C.H., Portfolio theory and the measurement of risk. In M.F. Kaplan and S. Schwartz (Eds), **Human judgment and decision processes**. New York: Academic Press, 1975.

Diaconis, P. and Freedman, D., The persistence of cognitive illusions. *The Behavioral and Brain Sciences*, 1981, **4**, 333–334.

Epstein, R.A., **The theory of gambling and statistical logic**. New York: Academic Press, 1977.

Grether, D.M. and Plott, R.C., Economic theory of choice and the preference reversal phenomenon. *American Economic Review*, 1979, 623–638.

Grossberg, S., On the dynamics of operant conditioning. *Journal of Theoretical Biology*, 1971, **33**, 225–255.

Grossberg, S., A neural theory of punishment and avoidance, I: Qualitative theory. *Mathematical Biosciences*, 1972, **15**, 39–67 (a).

Grossberg, S., A neural theory of punishment and avoidance, II: Quantitative theory. *Mathematical Biosciences*, 1972, **15**, 253–285 (b).

Grossberg, S., Contour enhancement, short-term memory, and constancies in reverberating neural networks. *Studies in Applied Mathematics*, 1973, **52**, 217–257.

Grossberg, S., A neural model of attention, reinforcement, and discrimination learning. *International Review of Neurobiology*, 1975, **18**, 263–327.

Grossberg, S., How does a brain build a cognitive code? *Psychological Review*, 1980, **87**, 1–51.

Grossberg, S., Processing of expected and unexpected events during conditioning and attention: A psychophysiological theory. *Psychological Review*, 1982, **89**, 529–572 (a).

Grossberg, S., **Studies of mind and brain: Neural principles of learning, perception, development, cognition, and motor control**. Boston: Reidel Press, 1982 (b).

Grossberg, S., The quantized geometry of visual space: The coherent computation of depth, form, and lightness. *The Behavioral and Brain Sciences*, 1983, **6**, 625–692.

Grossberg, S., Some psychophysiological and pharmacological correlates of a developmental, cognitive, and motivational theory. In **Brain and information: Event related potentials**. R. Karrer, J. Cohen, and P. Tueting (Eds.). New York: New York Academy of Sciences, 1984 (a).

Grossberg, S., Some normal and abnormal behavioral syndromes due to transmitter gating of opponent processes, *Biological Psychiatry*, 1984, **19**, 1075–1118 (b).

Grossberg, S. and Levine, D., Some developmental and attentional biases in the contrast enhancement and short term memory of recurrent neural networks. *Journal of Theoretical Biology*, 1975, **53**, 341–380.

Grossberg, S. and Stone, G.O., Neural dynamics of word recognition and recall: Attentional priming, learning, and resonance. *Psychological Review*, 1986, **93**, 46–74.

Gutowski, W.E., An opponent process theory of decision making under risk. Unpublished doctoral dissertation. Medford, MA: Tufts University, 1984.

Gutowski, W.E. and Chechile, R.A., Preference reversals and other violations of maximization. Paper presented at the 17th Annual Mathematical Psychology meeting at the University of Chicago, 1984.

Gutowski, W.E. and Chechile, R.A., Violations of maximization in risky decision making: The structure of preference reversals. Submitted for publication, 1986.

Hamm, R.M., The conditions of occurrence of the preference reversal phenomenon. Unpublished doctoral dissertation. Cambridge, MA: Harvard University, 1979.

Jensen, D.D., Polythetic biopsychology: An alternative to behaviorism. In J.H. Reynierse (Ed.), **Current issues in animal learning: A colloquium**. Lincoln: University of Nebraska Press, 1970, 1–31.

Jensen, D.D., Learning and behavior. In **Topics in the study of life: The B10 source book**. New York: Harper and Row, 1971, 307–314.

Kahneman, D. and Tversky, A., Prospect theory: An analysis of decision under risk. *Econometrica*, 1979, **47**, 263–291.

Kahneman, D. and Tversky, A., Choices, values and frames. *American Psychologist*, 1984, **39**, 341–350.

Lichtenstein, S.C. and Slovic, P., Reversals of preference between bids and choices in gambling decisions. *Journal of Experimental Psychology*, 1971, **89**, 46–55.

Lichtenstein, S.C. and Slovic, P., Response-induced reversals of preference in gambling: An extended replication in Las Vegas. *Journal of Experimental Psychology*, 1973, **101**, 16–20.

Lindman, H.R., Inconsistent preferences among gambles. *Journal of Experimental Psychology*, 1971, **89**, 390–397.

Mowen, J.C. and Gentry, J.W., Investigation of the preference-reversal phenomenon in a new product introduction task. *Journal of Applied Psychology*, 1980, **65**, 715–722.

Payne, J.W., Information processing theory: Some concepts and methods applied to decision research. In T.S. Wallsten (Ed.), **Cognitive processes in choice and decision behavior**. Hillsdale, NJ: Lawrence Erlbaum, 1980.

Pommerehne, W.W., Schneider, F., and Zweifel, P., Economic theory of choice and the preference reversal phenomenon: A reexamination. *American Economic Review*, 1982, **72**, 569–574.

Rachlin, H., Logue, A.W., Gibbon, J., and Frankel, M., Cognition and behavior in studies of choice. *Psychological Review*, 1986, **93**, 33–45.

Reilly, R.J., Preference reversal: Further evidence and some suggested modifications in experimental design. *American Economic Review*, 1982, **72**, 576–584.

Skyrms, B., Conditional probability, taxicabs, and martingales. *The Behavioral and Brain Sciences*, 1981, **4**, 351–352.

Slovic, P. and Lichtenstein, S., Preference reversals: A broader perspective. *American Economic Review*, 1983, **73**, 596–605.

Solomon, R.L., The opponent-process theory of acquired motivation. *American Psychologist*, 1980, **35**, 691–712.

Solomon, R.L., The opponent-process in acquired motivation. In D.W. Pfaff (Ed.), **The physiological mechanisms of motivation**. New York: Springer-Verlag, 1982.

Solomon, R.L. and Corbit, J.D., An opponent-process theory of motivation, I: Temporal dynamics of affect. *Psychological Review*, 1982, **81**, 119–145.

Tversky, A. and Kahneman, D., Judgment under uncertainty: Heuristics and biases. *Science*, 1974, **185**, 1124–1131.

Tversky, A. and Kahneman, D., The framing of decisions and the psychology of choice. *Science*, 1981, **211**, 453–458.

von Neumann, J. and Morgenstern, O., **Theory of games and economic behavior**. Princeton, NJ: Princeton University Press, 1944.

NEURAL DYNAMICS OF PLANNED ARM MOVEMENTS:
EMERGENT INVARIANTS AND SPEED-ACCURACY PROPERTIES
DURING TRAJECTORY FORMATION

Daniel Bullock† and Stephen Grossberg‡

ABSTRACT

A real-time neural network model, called the Vector Integration to Endpoint, or VITE, Model, is developed and used to quantitatively simulate behavioral and neural data about planned and passive arm movements. Invariants of arm movements emerge through network interactions rather than through an explicitly precomputed trajectory. Motor planning occurs in the form of a Target Position Command, or TPC, which specifies where the arm intends to move, and an independently controlled GO command, which specifies the movement's overall speed. Automatic processes convert this information into an arm trajectory with invariant properties. These automatic processes include computation of a Present Position Command, or PPC, and a Difference Vector, or DV. The DV is the difference of the PPC and the TPC at any time. The PPC is gradually updated by integrating the DV through time. The GO signal multiplies the DV before it is integrated by the PPC. The PPC generates an outflow movement command to its target muscle groups. Opponent interactions regulate the PPC's to agonist and antagonist muscle groups. This system generates synchronous movements across synergetic muscles by automatically compensating for the different total contractions that each muscle group must undergo. Quantitative simulations are provided of Woodworth's Law, of the speed-accuracy trade-off known as Fitts' Law, of isotonic arm movement properties before and after deafferentation, of synchronous and compensatory "central error correction" properties of isometric contractions, of velocity amplification during target switching, of velocity profile invariance and asymmetry, of the changes in velocity profile asymmetry at higher movement speeds, of the automatic compensation for staggered onset times of synergetic muscles, of vector cell properties in precentral motor cortex, of the inverse relationship between movement duration and peak velocity, and of peak acceleration as a function of movement amplitude and duration. It is shown that TPC, PPC, and DV computations are needed to actively modulate, or gate, the learning of associative maps between TPC's of different modalities, such as between the eye-head system and the hand-arm system. By using such an associative map, looking at an object can activate a TPC of the hand-arm system, as Piaget noted. Then a VITE circuit can translate this TPC into an invariant movement trajectory. An auxiliary circuit, called the Passive Update of Position, or PUP, Model, is described for using inflow signals to update the PPC during passive arm movements due to external forces. Other uses of outflow and inflow signals are also noted, such as for adaptive linearization of a nonlinear muscle plant, and sequential read-out of TPC's during a serial plan, as in reaching and grasping. Comparisons are made with other models of motor control, such as the mass-spring and minimum-jerk models.

---

† Supported in part by the National Science Foundation (NSF IST-84-17756).

‡ Supported in part by the Air Force Office of Scientific Research (AFOSR 85-0149 and AFOSR F49620-86-C-0037) and the National Science Foundation (NSF IST-84-17756).

1. Introduction: Are Movement Invariants Explicitly Planned?

The subjective ease with which we carry out simple action plans—rotating a wrist-watch into view, lifting a coffee cup, or making a downstroke while writing—masks the enormously complex integrative apparatus needed to achieve and maintain coordination among the thousands of sensors, neurons, and skeleto-motor units that contribute to any act's planning and execution. Moreover, recent studies of the kinematics of planned arm movements (Abend, *et al.*, 1982; Atkeson and Hollerbach, 1985; Howarth and Beggs, 1981) have shown that the integrative action of all these separate contributors produces velocity profiles whose global shape is remarkably invariant over a wide range of movement sizes and speeds. This raises a fundamental question for the theory of sensory-motor control, and for the neurosciences in general: How can the integrated activity of thousands of separate elements produce globally invariant properties?

Two broad species of answers to this question can be contemplated. The first includes theories that posit the existence of a high level stage involving explicit computation and internal representation of the invariant, in this case the velocity profile, as a whole. This representation is then used as a basis for performing the desired action. Such theories have been favored recently by many workers in the field of robotics, and at least one theory of this type has already been partially formulated to accommodate kinematic data on human movements: the "minimized Cartesian jerk theory" (Hogan, 1984; Flash and Hogan, 1985), which is a special case of global optimization analysis. The second species of answers includes theories in which no need arises for explicit computation and representation of the invariant trajectory as a whole (Sections 7 and 16). In models associated with such theories, a trajectory with globally invariant properties emerges in real-time as the result of events distributed across many interacting sensory, neural, and muscular loci.

This article describes a theory of arm trajectory invariants that conforms to the latter ideal (Bullock and Grossberg, 1986a). Our analysis suggests that trajectory invariants are best understood not by focusing on velocity profiles as such, but by pursuing more fundamental questions: What principles of adaptive behavioral organization constrain the system design that governs planned arm movements? What mechanisms are needed to realize these principles as a real-time neural network? Our development of this topic proceeds via analyses of learned eye-hand coordination, synchronization among synergists, intermediate position control during movement, and variable velocity control. These analyses disclose a neural network design whose qualitative and quantitative operating characteristics match those observed in a wide range of experiments on human movement. Because velocity profile invariance, as well as speed-dependent changes in velocity profile asymmetry ignored by prior models (Section 12), are among the neural network's emergent operating characteristics, our work shows that neither an explicit trajectory nor a kinematic invariant need be explicitly represented within a motor control system at any time. Thus our work supports a critical insight of workers in the mass-spring modeling tradition, that movement kinematics need not be explicitly pre-programmed. By the same token, our results reject a mass-spring model in its customary form and argue against models based upon optimization theory. Instead we show how a movement control system may be adaptive without necessarily optimizing an explicit cost function.

To further support these conclusions, we use the neural model to quantitatively simulate Woodworth's Law and Fitts' Law, the empirically derived speed-accuracy tradeoff function relating error magnitudes, movement distances and movement durations; isotonic arm movement properties before and after deafferentation (Bizzi, Accornero, Chapple, and Hogan, 1982, 1984; Evarts and Fromm, 1978; Polit and Bizzi, 1978); synchronous and compensatory "central error correction" properties of isometric contractions (Freund and Büdingen, 1978; Ghez and Vicario, 1978; Gordon and Ghez, 1984, 1987a, 1987b,); velocity amplification during target switching (Georgopoulos, Kalaska, and Massey, 1981); velocity profile invariance and asymmetry (Abend, Bizzi, and Morasso, 1982; Atkeson and Hollerbach, 1985; Georgopoulos, Kalaska, and Massey, 1981; Beggs and Howarth, 1972; Morasso, 1981; Soechting and Lacquaniti, 1981); the changes in velocity profile asymmetry at higher movement speeds (Beggs and Howarth, 1972; Zelaznik, Schmidt, and Gielen, 1986); vector cell properties in precentral motor cortex (Evarts and Tanji, 1974; Georgopoulos, Kalaska, Caminiti, and Massey, 1982; Georgopoulos, Kalaska, Crutcher, Caminiti, and Massey, 1984; Kalaska, Caminiti, and Georgopoulos, 1983; Tanji and Evarts, 1976); the inverse relationship between movement duration and peak velocity (Lestienne, 1979); and peak acceleration as a function of movement amplitude and time (Bizzi, Accornero, Chapple, and Hogan, 1984). In addition, the work reported here extends a broader program of research on adaptive sensory-motor control (Grossberg, 1978, 1986a, 1986b; Grossberg and Kuperstein, 1986), which enables functional and mechanistic comparisons to be made between the neural systems governing arm and eye movements, suggests how eye-hand coordination is accomplished, and provides a foundation for work on mechanisms of trajectory realization which compensate for the mechanical effects generated by variable loads and movement velocities (Bullock and Grossberg, 1987).

2. Flexible Organization of Muscle Groups into Synergies

In order to move a part of the body, whether an eye, head, arm, or leg, many muscles must work together. For example, muscles controlling several different joints—shoulder, elbow, wrist, and fingers—may contract or relax cooperatively in order to perform a reaching movement. When groups of muscles cooperate in this way, they are said to form a synergy (Bernstein, 1967; Kelso, 1982).

Muscle groups may be incorporated into synergies in a flexible and dynamic fashion. Whereas muscles controlling shoulder, elbow, wrist, and fingers may all contract or relax synergetically to produce a reaching movement, muscles of the fingers and wrist may form a synergy to perform a grasping movement. Thus, one synergy may activate shoulder, elbow, wrist, and finger muscles to reach towards an object, and another synergy may then activate only finger and wrist muscles to grasp the object while maintaining postural control over the shoulder and elbow muscles. Groups of fingers may move together synergetically to play a chord on the piano, or separate fingers may be successively activated in order to play arpeggios.

One of the basic problems of motor control is to understand how neural control structures quickly and flexibly reorganize the set of muscle groups that are needed to synergetically cooperate in the next movement sequence. Once one squarely faces the problem that many behaviorally important synergies are not hard-wired, but are rather dynamically coupled and decoupled through time in ways that depend upon the actor's experience and training, the prospect that the trajectories of all synergists are explicitly preplanned seems remote at best. In support of a dynamic conception of synergy formation, Buchanan, Almdale, Lewis, and Rymer (1986) conclude from their experiments on isometric contractions of human elbow muscles that "The complexity of these patterns raises the possibility that synergies are determined by the tasks and may have no independent existence."

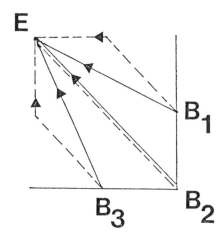

Figure 1. Consequences of two motor-control schemes. Dashed lines: Movement paths generated when a synergist producing vertical motion and a synergist producing horizontal motion contract in parallel and at equal rates to effect movements from various beginning points (Bs) to the common endpoint E. Solid lines: Movement paths generated when the synergists' contraction rates are adjusted to compensate for differences in the lengths of the vertical and horizontal components of the movement.

3. Synchronous Movement of Synergies

When neural commands organize a group of muscles into a synergy, the action of these muscles often occurs synchronously through time. It is partly for this reason that the complexity of the neural commands controlling many movements often goes unnoticed. These movements seem to occur in a single gesture, rather than as the sum of many asynchronous components.

In order to understand the type of control problem that must be solved to generate synchronous movement, consider a typical arm movement of reaching forward and across the body midline with the right hand in a plane parallel to the ground. Suppose for simplicity that the synergist acting at the shoulder is responsible for across-midline motion, that the synergist acting at the elbow is responsible for forward motion, and that the hand is to be moved from points B1, B2, or B3 to point E. Figure 1 illustrates the effects of two distinct control schemes that might be used to produce these three movements. In the first scheme, the two synergists begin their contractions synchronously, contract at the same rate, and cease contracting when their respective motion component is complete. This typically results in asynchronous contraction terminations, and in bent-line movements, because the synergist responsible for the longer motion component takes longer to complete its contribution. With this scheme, approximately straight-line motions and synchronous contraction terminations occur only in cases like the B2–E movement, for which the component motions happen to be of equal length. In the second scheme, the two synergists contract, not at equal rates, but at rates that have been adjusted to compensate for any differences in length of the component motions. This results in synchronous contraction terminations. Normal arm movement paths are similar to those implied by the second control scheme (e.g., Morasso, 1981) and experimental studies (Freund and Büdingen, 1978) have shown that contraction rates are made unequal in a way that compensates for inequalities of distance.

What types of adaptive problems are solved by synchronization of synergists? Figure 1 provides some insight into this issue. Without synchronization, the direction of the first part of the movement path may change abruptly several times before the direction of the last part of the movement path is generated (Figure 1). This creates a problem because transporting an object from one place to another with the arm may destabilize the body unless one can predict, and anticipatorily compensate for, the arm movement's destabilizing effects, which are always directional. In the same way, many actions require that forces be applied to surfaces in particular directions. The first control scheme makes the direction in which force is applied difficult to predict and control. Both of these problems are eliminated by the approximately straight-line movement paths which become possible when synergists contract synchronously. Finally, if the various motions composing a movement failed to end synchronously, it would become difficult to ensure smooth transitions between sequentially ordered movements.

In summary, the untoward effects of asynchrony place strong constraints on the mechanisms of movement control: Across the set of muscles whose synergistic action produces a multi-joint movement, contraction durations must be roughly equal, and, because contraction distances are typically unequal, contraction rates must be made unequal in a way that compensates for inequalities of distance.

4. Factoring Target Position and Velocity Control

Inequalities of distance are translated into neural commands as differences in the total amounts of contraction by the muscles forming the synergy, and thereby into mechanical terms as the total amounts of change in the angles between joints (Hollerbach, Moore, and Atkeson, 1986). In order to compensate for differences in contraction, information must be available that is sufficient to compute the total amounts of contraction that are required. Thus a representation of the initial contraction level of each muscle must be compared with a representation of the target, expected, or final contraction level of the muscle. A primary goal of this article is to specify how this comparison is made. Although information about target position and initial position are both needed to control the total contraction of a muscle group, these two types of information are computed and updated in different ways, a fact that we believe has caused much confusion about whether only target position needs to be coded (Section 7). In particular, we reject the common assumption (Adams, 1971) that the representation of initial contraction used in the comparison is based on afferent feedback from the limbs. We propose instead that it is based primarily on feedback from an outflow command integrator that is located along the pathway between the precentral motor cortex and the spinal motorneurons.

Another source of confusion has arisen because target position information is needed to form a trajectory. This is the type of information which invites concepts of motor planning and expectation. However tempting it may be to so infer, concepts of motor planning and expectation do *not* imply that the *whole trajectory* is *explicitly* planned.

A second aspect of planning enters into trajectory formation which also does not imply the existence of explicit trajectory planning. This aspect is noticed by considering that the hand-arm system can be moved between fixed intital and target positions at many different velocities. When, as a result of a changed velocity, the overall movement duration changes, the component motions occurring around the various joints must nonetheless remain synchronous. Since fixed differences in initial and target positions can be converted into synchronous motions at a wide range of velocities, there must exist an independently controlled velocity, or GO signal (Section 11). The independent control of target position commands, or TPCs, and velocity commands, or GO signals, is a special case of a general neural design which has been called the *factorization of pattern and energy* (Grossberg, 1978, 1982).

5. Synchrony versus Fitts' Law: The Need for a Neural Analysis of Synergy Formation

Our discussion of synchronous performance of synergies has thus far emphasized that different muscles of the hand-arm system may need to contract by different amounts in equal time in order to move a hand through a fixed distance. When movement of a hand over different distances is considered, a striking contrast between behavioral and neural properties of movement becomes evident. This difference emphasizes that synergies are assembled and disassembled through time in a flexible and dynamic way.

Fitts' Law (Fitts, 1954; Fitts and Peterson, 1964) states that movement time (MT) of the arm is related to distance moved (D) and to width of target (W) by the equation

$$MT = a + b \log_2\left(\frac{2D}{W}\right), \tag{1}$$

where a and b are empirically derived constants. Keele (1981) has reviewed a variety of experiments showing that Fitts' Law is remarkably well obeyed despite its simplicity. For example, the law describes movement time for linear arm movements (Fitts, 1954), rotary movements of the wrist (Knight and Dagnall, (1967), back-and-forth movements like dart throwing (Kerr and Langolf, 1977), head movements (Jagacinski and Monk, 1985), movements of young and old people (Welford, Norris, and Schock, 1969), and movements of monkeys as well as humans (Brooks, 1979).

Equation (1) asserts that movement time (MT) increases as the logarithm of distance (D) moved, other things being equal. The width parameter W in (1) is interpreted as a measure of movement accuracy (Section 27). Although movement distance and time may covary on the behavioral level that describes the aggregate effect of many muscle contractions, such a relationship does not necessarily hold on the neural level, where individual muscles may contract by variable amounts, or "distances", in order to achieve synchronous contraction within a constant movement time.

A fundamental issue is raised by this comparison of behavioral and neural constraints. This issue can be better understood through consideration of the following gedanken example. When each of two fingers is moved separately through different distances, each finger may separately obey Fitts' Law. Then the finger which moves a larger distance should take more time to move, other things being equal. In contrast, when the two fingers move the above distances as part of a single synergy, then each finger should complete its movement in the same time in order to guarantee synergetic synchrony. Thus either one of the fingers must violate Fitts' Law, or it must reach its target with a different level of accuracy. Kelso, Southard, and Goodman (1979) and Marteniuk and MacKenzie (1980) have experimentally studied this type of synchronous behavior in experiments on one or two handed movements, and have documented within-synergy violations of Fitts' Law.

Such examples suggest that Fitts' Law holds for the aggregate behavior of the largest collection of motor units which form a synergy during a given time interval. Fitts' Law need not hold for all subsets of the motor units which comprise a synergy. These subsets may, in principle, violate Fitts' Law by travelling variable distances in equal time in order to achieve synchrony of the aggregate movement. To understand how Fitts' Law can be reconciled with movement synchrony thus requires an analysis of the neural control mechanisms which flexibly bind muscle groups, such as those controlling different fingers, into a single motor synergy. If such a binding action does not involve explicit planning of a complete trajectory, yet does require activation of a target position command and a GO command, then neural machinery must exist which is capable of *automatically* coverting such commands into complete trajectories with synchronous and invariant properties. One of the primary tasks of this article is to describe the circuit design of this neural machinery and to explain how it works.

6. Some General Issues in Sensory-Motor Planning: Multiple Uses of Outflow versus Inflow Signals

Before beginning a mechanistic analysis of these circuits, we summarize several general issues about motor planning to place the model developed in this article within a broader conceptual framework. In Sections 8–13 and 27–29, a number of key experiments are reviewed to more sharply constrain the theoretical analysis. In Sections 21–28 computer simulations of these data properties are reported.

Neural circuitry automates the production of skilled movements in several mechanistically distinct ways. Perhaps the most general observation is that animals and humans perform marvelously dexterous acts in a world governed by Newton's Laws, yet can go through life without ever learning Newton's Laws, and indeed may have a great deal of difficulty learning them when they try. The phenomenal world of movements is a world governed by motor plans and intentions, rather than by kinematic and inertial laws. A major challenge to theories of biological movement control is to explain how we move so well within a world whose laws we may so poorly understand.

The computation of a hand or arm's present position illustrates the complexity of this problem. Two general types of present position signals have been identified in discussions of motor control: *outflow* signals and *inflow* signals. Figure 2 schematizes the difference between these signal sources. An outflow signal carries a movement command from the brain to a muscle (Figure 2a). Signals that branch off from the efferent brain-to-muscle pathway in order to register present position signals are called *corollary discharges* (Helmholtz, 1866; von Holst and Mittelstaedt, 1950). An *inflow* signal carries present position information from a muscle to the brain (Figure 2b). A primary difference between outflow and inflow is that a change in outflow signals is triggered only when an observer's brain generates a new movement command. A new inflow signal can, in contrast, be generated by passive movements of the limb. Evidence for influences of both outflow (Helmholtz, 1866) and inflow (Ruffini, 1898; Sherrington, 1894) has accumulated over the past century. Disentangling the different roles played by outflow and inflow signals has remained one of the major problems in motor control. This is a confusing issue because both outflow and inflow signals are used in multiple ways to provide different types of information about present position. The following summary itemizes some of the ways in which these signals are used in our theory.

Although one role of an outflow signal is to move a limb by contracting its target

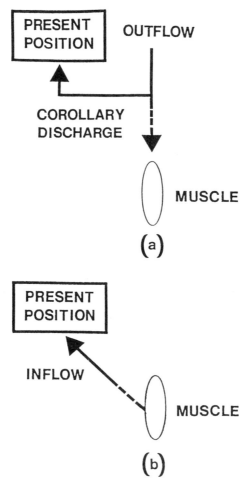

Figure 2. Both outflow and inflow signals contribute to the brain's estimate of the limb's present position, but in different ways.

muscles, the operating characteristics of the muscle plant are not known *a priori* to the outflow source. It is therefore not known *a priori* how much the muscle will actually contract in response to an outflow signal of prescribed size. It is also not known how much the limb will move in response to a prescribed muscle contraction. In addition, even if the outflow system somehow possessed this information at one time, it might turn out to be the wrong information at a later time, because muscle plant characteristics can change through time due to development, aging, exercise, changes in blood supply, or minor tears. Thus the relationship between the size of an outflow movement command and the amount of muscle contraction is, in principle, undeterminable without additional information which characterizes the muscle plant's actual response to outflow signals.

To establish a satisfactory correspondence between outflow movement signals and actual muscle contractions, the motor system needs to compute reliable present position signals which represent where the outflow command tells the muscle to move, as well as reliable present position signals which represent the state of contraction of the muscle. Corollary discharges and inflow signals can provide these different types of information.

Grossberg and Kuperstein (1986) have shown how a comparison, or match, between corollary discharges and inflow signals can be used to modify, through an automatic learning process, the total outflow signal to the muscle in a way that effectively compensates for changes in the muscle plant. Such automatic gain control produces a linear correspondence between an outflow movement command and the amount of muscle contraction even if the muscle plant is nonlinear. The process which matches outflow and inflow signals to linearize the muscle plant response through learning is called *adaptive linearization* of the muscle plant. The cerebellum is implicated by both the theoretically derived circuit and experimental evidence as the site of learning (Albus, 1971; Brindley, 1964; Fujita, 1982a, 1982b; Grossberg, 1969, 1972; Ito, 1974, 1982, 1984; Marr, 1969; McCormick and Thompson, 1984; Optican and Robinson, 1980; Ron and Robinson, 1973; Vilis and Hore, 1986; Vilis, Snow, and Hore, 1983).

Given that corollary discharges are matched with inflow signals to linearize the relationship between muscle plant contraction and outflow signal size, outflow signals can also be used in yet other ways to provide information about present position. In Sections 17–23, it is shown how outflow signals are matched with target position signals to generate a trajectory with synchronous and invariant properties. Thus outflow signals are used in at least three ways, and all of these ways are automatically registered: They send movement signals to target muscles; they generate corollary discharges which are matched with inflow signals to guarantee linear muscle contractions even if the muscle plant is nonlinear; and they generate corollary discharges which are matched with target position signals to generate synchronous trajectories with invariant properties.

Inflow signals are also used in several ways. One way has already been itemized. A second use of inflow signals is suggested by the following gedanken example. When you are sitting in an armchair, let your hands drop passively towards your sides. Depending upon a multitude of accidental factors, your hands and arms can end up in any of infinitely many final positions. If you are then called upon to make a precise movement with your arm-hand system, this can be done with the usual exquisite accuracy. Thus the fact that your hands and arms start out this movement from an initial position which was not reached under active control by an outflow signal does not impair the accuracy of the movement.

A wealth of evidence suggests, however, that comparison between target position and present position information is used to move the arms. Moreover, as will be shown below, this present position information is computed from outflow signals. In contrast, during the passive fall of an arm under the influence of gravity, changes in outflow signal commands are not responsible for the changes in position of the limb. This observation identifies the key issue: How is the outflow signal updated due to passive movement of a limb so that the next active movement can accurately be made? Since the final position of a passively falling limb cannot be predicted in advance, it is clear that inflow signals must be used to update present position when an arm is moved passively by an external force.

This conclusion calls attention to a closely related issue that must be dealt with to understand the neural bases of skilled movement: How does the motor system know that the arm is being moved passively due to an external force, and not actively due to a changing outflow command? Such a distinction is needed to prevent inflow information from contaminating outflow commands when the arm is being actively moved. The motor system must use internally generated signals to make the distinction between active movement and passive movement, or postural, conditions. Computational gates must be open and shut based upon whether these internally generated signals are on or off (Grossberg and Kuperstein, 1986).

A third role for inflow signals is needed due to the fact that arms can move at variable velocities while carrying variable loads. Because an arm is a mechanical system embedded in a Newtonian world, an arm can generate unexpected amounts of inertia and acceleration when it tries to move novel loads at novel velocities. During such a novel motion, the commanded outflow position of the arm and its actual position may significantly diverge. Inflow signals are needed to compute mismatches leading to partial compensation for this uncontrolled component of the movement.

Such novel movements are quite different from our movements when we pick up a familiar fountain pen or briefcase. When the object is familiar, we can predictively adjust the gain of the movement to compensate for the expected mass of the object. This type of automatic gain control can, moreover, be flexibly switched on and off using signal pathways that can be activated by visual recognition of a familiar object. Inflow signals are used in the learning process which enables such automatic gain control signals to be activated in an anticipatory fashion in response to familiar objects (Bullock and Grossberg, 1987).

This listing of multiple uses for outflow and inflow signals invites comparison between how the arm movement system and other movement systems use outflow and inflow signals. Grossberg and Kuperstein (1986) have identified and suggested neural circuit solutions to analogous problems of sensory-motor control within the specialized domain of the saccadic eye movement system. Several of the problems to which we will suggest circuit solutions in our articles on arm movements have analogs with the saccadic circuits developed by Grossberg and Kuperstein (1986). Together these investigations suggest that several movement systems contain neural circuits that solve similar general problems. Differences between these circuits can be traced to functional specializations in the way these movement systems solve their shared problems of movement.

For example, whereas saccades are ballistic movements, arm movements can be made under both continuous and ballistic control. Whereas the eyes normally come to rest in a head-centered position, the arms can come to rest in any of infinitely many positions. Whereas the eyes are typically not subjected to unexpected or variable external loads, the arms are routinely subjected to such loads. Whereas the eyes typically generate a stereotyped velocity profile between a fixed pair of initial and target positions, the arms can move with a continuum of velocity profiles between a fixed pair of initial and target positions. Our analyses show how the arm system is specialized to cope with all of these differences between its behaviors and those of the saccadic eye movement system.

7. Neural Control of Arm Position Changes: Beyond the STE Model

A number of further specialized constraints on the mechanisms controlling planned arm movements are clarified by summarizing shortcomings of the simplest example of a "mass-spring" model of movement generation, which we will call the Spring-To-Endpoint (STE) model, to distinguish it from other members of the potentially large family of models that exploit "mass-spring" properties of biological limbs (e.g., Bizzi, 1980; Cooke, 1980; Feldman, 1974, 1986; Humphrey and Reed, 1983; Kelso and Holt, 1980; Sakitt, 1980). As Nichols (1985) and Feldman (1986) have recently noted, past discussions of mass-spring properties have mistakenly lumped together quite different proposals regarding how such properties might be exploited during trajectory formation. Our treatment in this section is meant to serve a pedagogical function, and our criticisms pertain only to the STE Model which is explicitly specified in this section. In particular, no part of our critique denies that the peripheral motor system has mass-spring properties that may be critical to overall motor function. Indeed, in Bullock and Grossberg (1987), we analyse neural command circuits which exploit mass-spring muscle properties to generate well-controlled movements.

The components of the STE (Spring-To-Endpoint) Model for movement control can be summarized as follows. Imagine that the eye fixates some object that lies within reach. To touch the object, it is necessary to move the tip of the index finger from its current position to the target position on the object's nearest surface. The STE Model suggests that this is accomplished by simply replacing the arm position command that specifies the arm's present posture with a new arm position command that specifies the posture the arm would have to assume in order for the index finger to touch the chosen object surface.

Instatement of the new arm position command is suggested to generate the desired movement as follows. The arm is held in any position by balancing the muscular and other forces (e.g., gravity) that are currently acting on the limb. Instatement of a new command changes the pattern of outflow signals that contract the arm muscles. A step change in the pattern of contraction creates a force imbalance that causes the limb to spring in the direction of the larger force at a rate proportional to the force difference. The limb comes to rest when all the forces acting on it are once again balanced. Despite its elegance, the STE Model exhibits several deficiencies which highlight properties that an adequate control system needs to have. We briefly summarize two fundamental problems: (1) confounding of speed and distance control, and (2) inability to quickly terminate movement at an intermediate position.

The first problem, the speed-distance confound, follows from the dependence of movement rate on the force difference, which in turn depends on the distance between the starting and final positions. This might at first seem to be a desirable property, because it appears to compensate for different distances in the manner needed to ensure synchronization of synergists (Section 3). However, consider also the need to vary the speed of a fixed movement. An actor seeking to perform the same movement at a faster speed would have to follow a two-part movement plan: Early in the movement, instate a virtual target position that is well beyond the desired end point and along a line drawn from the initial through the true target position. This command will create a very large initial force imbalance and launch the limb at a high speed. Then, at some point during the movement, instate the true target position command, and let the arm coast to the final position. This example illustrates that the STE Model requires a complex and neurally implausible scheme for achieving variable speed control for movements of fixed length.

Cooke (1980) suggests that variable speed control by an STE Model can be achieved by abruptly changing the stiffness of agonist and antagonist muscles to achieve differences in distance and speed. This model has not yet been shown to produce velocity profiles with the parametric properties of the data (Section 12). In addition, Houk and Rymer (1981) and Feldman (1986) have shown that the stiffness of individual muscles is typically maintained at a nearly constant level.

A second problem with the STE Model concerns the critical need to quickly abort an evolving movement and stabilize current arm position. Such a need arises, for example, when an animal wishes to freeze upon detection of a predator who uses motion cues to locate prey. It also arises when an action, such as transporting a large mass, begins to destabilize an animal's overall state of balance. At such times, it is often adaptive to quickly freeze and maintain the current arm position. This is an easy task if the movement command is never much different from the arm's present position. Freezing could then be quickly achieved by preventing further changes in the currently commanded position. In an STE Model, this simple freeze strategy is unavailable, because a large discrepancy exists between present arm position and the target position command throughout much of the trajectory. To implement a freezing response using the STE Model, the system would somehow have to quickly determine and instate a new target position command capable of maintaining the arm's present position. But this is precisely the type of information whose relevance is denied by the STE Model.

8. Gradual Updating of PPC's during Trajectory Formation

Several lines of experimental evidence point to deficiencies of the STE Model. One line of evidence, due to Bizzi and his colleagues, demonstrates that a type of gradual updating of the movement command occurs which is inconsistent with the STE model. Earlier studies from the Bizzi lab partially supported the STE model.

The experiments of Polit and Bizzi (1978) studied monkeys who were trained to move their forearms, without visual feedback of hand position, from a canonical starting position to the position of one of several lights. The monkeys' arm movements were studied both before and after a dorsal rhizotomy was performed to remove all sensory feedback from the arm. Before deafferentation, the monkey could move its hand to the target's position without visual feedback, even if its accustomed position with respect to the arm apparatus was changed. After deafferentation, so long as the spatial conditions of training were maintained—in particular the canonical starting orientation and position with respect to the known target array—the animal remained able to move its hand to the target position. However, if the initial position of the upper arm and elbow of the deafferented arm was passively shifted from the position used throughout training, then the animal's forearm movements terminated at a position shifted by an equal amount away from the target position. Thus the movement of the forearm did not compensate for the change in initial position of the upper arm. Instead the same final synergy of forearm-controlling muscles was generated in both cases.

The fact that deafferented monkeys moved to shifted positions emphasized the critical role of the target position command in setting up the movement trajectory. The fact that normal monkeys could compensate for rotation in a way that deafferented monkeys could not indicated an additional role for inflow signals when the arm is moved passively by an external force (Section 29).

The later experiments of Bizzi, Accornero, Chapple, and Hogan (1982, 1984) carried out an additional manipulation. The results of these experiments are inconsistent with the STE assumption that the arm's motion is governed exclusively by the spring-like contraction of its muscles towards the position specified by a new target position command. In these experiments, the monkey was again deprived of visual and inflow feedback, and placed in its canonical starting position. In addition, its deafferented arm was surreptitiously held at the target position, then released at variable intervals after activation of the target light. Under these circumstances, the arm travelled back towards the canonical starting position, before reversing direction and proceeding to the target. The arm travelled further backward toward the starting position the sooner it was released after target activation. Moreover, when the arm was moved to the target position and then released in the absence of any target presentation, it sprang back to its canonical starting position. Bizzi *et al.* (1984, p.2742) concluded that "the CNS had programmed a slow, gradual shift of the equilibrium point, a fact which is not consistent with the 'final position control' [read STE] hypothesis."

The Bizzi *et al.* (1984) description of their results as a "gradual shift of the equilibrium point" carries the language of the STE Model into a context where it may cause confusion. From a mathematical perspective, the intermediate positions of a movement trajectory are not, by definition, equilibrium points. In order to explicate the Bizzi *et al.* (1984) data, we show how three quantities are computed and updated through time: a target position command (TPC) which is switched on once and for all before the movement; an outflow movement command, called the present position command (PPC), which is continously updated until it matches the TPC; and the arm position which closely corresponds to the PPC. We use these concepts below to explain data from the Bizzi lab in both normal and deafferented conditions.

We call a movement for which a single TPC (target position command) is switched on before the movement begins an *elementary* movement. Once it is seen how a single TPC can cause gradual updating of the PPC (present position command), movements can also be analysed during which a sequence of TPC's is switched on, either under the control of visual feedback or from a movement planning network which can store and release sequences of TPC's from memory with the proper order and timing (Grossberg and Kuperstein, 1986).

Our analysis of how the PPC is gradually updated during an elementary movement partially supports the Bizzi *et al.* (1984) description of a "gradual shift in equilibrium point" by showing that the arm remains in approximate equilibrium with respect to the PPC, even though none of these intermediate arm positions is an equilibrium point of the system. The only equilibrium point of the system is reached when both the neural control circuit and the arm itself both reach equilibrium. That happens when the PPC matches the TPC, thereby preventing further changes in the present position command and allowing the arm to come to rest.

These conclusions refine, rather than totally contradict, the main insight of the STE Model. Instead of concluding that the arm springs to the position coded by the TPC, we suggest that the spring-like arm tracks the series of positions specified by the PPC as it approaches the TPC. This conception of trajectory formation contrasts sharply with that suggested by Brooks (1986, p.138) in response to the Bizzi data. Brooks inferred that "animals learn not only the end points and their stiffness, but also a series of intermediate equilibrium positions. In other words, they learn an internal 'reference' trajectory that determines the path to be followed and generates torques appropriately to reduce mismatch between the intended and actual events." In a similar fashion, Hollerbach (1982, p.192) suggested that we practice movements to "learn the basic torque profiles." In contrast, we suggest that the read-out of the TPC is learned, but that the gradual updating of the PPC is automatic. A number of auxiliary learning processes are also needed to update the PPC after passive movements due to an external force (Section 30), to adaptively linearize the response of a nonlinear muscle plant (Grossberg and Kuperstein, 1986), and to adaptively compensate for the inertial effects of variable loads and velocities (Bullock and Grossberg, 1987). These additional learning processes enable the automatic updating of the PPC to generate controllable movements without requiring that the entire trajectory be learned.

9. Duration Invariance during Isotonic Movements and Isometric Contractions

Further information concerning the gradual updating process whereby PPC's match a TPC can be inferred from the detailed spatiotemporal properties of arm trajectory formation. Freund and Büdingen (1978) have studied "the relationship between the speed of the fastest

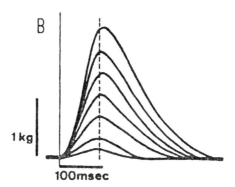

Figure 3. Curves for subjects' approach to various targeted force levels. Targeted (peak) levels are reached at nearly the same time, indicating duration invariance across different force "distances". Only the initial part of each curve represents active movement. Post-peak portions represent passive relaxation back to base-line. Reprinted with permission from Freund and Büdingen (1978).

possible voluntary contractions and their amplitudes for several hand and forearm muscles under both isotonic and isometric conditions. These experiments showed the larger the amplitude, the faster the contraction. The increase of the rate of rise of isometric tension or of the velocity of isotonic movements with rising amplitude was linear. The slope of this relationship was the same for three different hand and forearm muscles examined ... the skeleto-motor speed control system operates by adjusting the velocity of a contraction to its amplitude in such a way that the contraction time remains approximately constant ... this type of speed control is a necessary requirement for the synchrony of synergistic muscle contractions" (p.1).

Two main issues are raised by this study. First, it must be explained why, "comparing isotonic movements and isometric contractions, the time from onset to peak was similar in the two conditions" (p.7). Figure 3 shows the fastest voluntary isometric contractions of the extensor indicis muscle. Second, it must be explained why the force develops gradually in time with the shapes depicted in Figure 3. Below it is shown that both duration invariance and the force development through time are emergent properties of the PPC updating process (see Section 22).

10. Compensatory Properties of the PPC Updating Process

Ghez and his colleagues (Ghez and Vicario, 1978; Gordon and Ghez, 1984, 1987a, 1987b) have confirmed the duration invariance reported by Freund and Büdingen (1978) in an isometric paradigm which also disclosed finer properties of the PPC updating process. These authors suggest that "compensatory adjustments add to preprogrammed specification of rapid force impulses to achieve more accurately targeted responses" (Gordon and Ghez, 1987b).

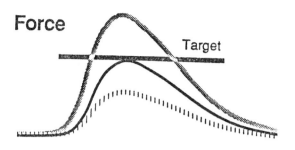

Figure 4. Overshooting (gray curve), hitting (black curve), and undershooting (dashed line) a force-level target (horizontal line) in an isometric task. Reprinted with permission from Gordon and Ghez (1987b).

In their isometric task, subjects were instructed to maintain superposition of two lines on a CRT screen. The experimenter could cause one of the lines to jump to any of three positions. Subjects could exert force on an immobile lever to move the other line towards the target line. Equal increments of force produced equal displacements of the line. Thus more isometric force was needed to move the line over a larger distance to the target line.

Figure 4 defines the major variables of their analysis. The force target is represented by the solid black horizontal line. If the subject performs errorlessly—that is, reaches target without overshoot—the value of the peak force will equal the value of the force target, as in the black curve. Overshoots and undershoots in force are represented by the gray and dashed curves, respectively. Figure 5 plots the data of Gordon and Ghez (1987b) in a way that illustrates duration invariance. The horizontal line through the data points shows that force rise time is essentially independent of peak force acceleration ($\frac{d^2 F}{dt^2}$) for all the target distances.

Gordon and Ghez (1987b) separately analysed the data for each of the three target distances, and thereby derived the three oblique lines in Figure 5. They interpreted these lines as evidence for an "error correction" process because a negative correlation exists between peak acceleration and the force rise time, or duration. Thus, if the acceleration for a small target distance was too high early in a movement, the trajectory was "corrected" by shortening the rise time. Had this compensation not occurred, the high acceleration could have produced a peak force appropriate for a larger target distance.

Gordon and Ghez (1987b) assumed that trajectories are preplanned and that their peak accelerations are a signature indicating which trajectory has been preplanned. It is from this perspective that they interpreted the compensatory effect shown in Figure 5 as an "error correction" process. In contrast, we suggest in Sections 13 and 21 that this compensatory effect is one of the automatic properties whereby PPC's are gradually updated. We hereby provide an explanation of the compensatory effect that avoids invoking a special mechanism of "error correction" for a movement which does not generate an error in achieving its target. In addition, this explanation provides a unified analysis of the Bizzi et al. (1984) data on isotonic movements and the Gordon and Ghez (1987b) data on isometric contractions.

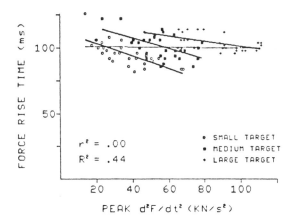

Figure 5. Duration invariance across three force target levels. Oblique lines indicate an inverse relation between rise time (duration) and peak acceleration across trials with the same force target level. These trends overlay a direct relation between target level and peak acceleration. Reprinted with permission from Gordon and Ghez (1987b).

11. Target Switching Experiments: Velocity Amplification, GO Signal, and Fitts' Law

Our explanation of the Freund and Büdingen (1978) and Gordon and Ghez (1987a) data considers how a single GO signal, which initiates and drives all movements to completion, ensures duration invariance when applied to all components of the synergy defined by a TPC. Georgopoulos, Kalaska, and Massey (1981) have collected data which provide further evidence pertinent to the hypothesized interaction of a GO signal with the process which instates a TPC and thereby updates the PPC. In their experiments, monkeys were trained to move a lever from a start position to one of eight target positions radially situated on a planar surface. Then the original target position was switched to a new target position at variable delays after presentation of the first target.

Part of the data confirm the fact that "the aimed motor command is emitted in a continuous, ongoing fashion as a real-time process that can be interrupted at any time by the substitution of the original target by the new one. The effects of this change on the ensuing movement appear promptly, without delays beyond the usual reaction time" (p.725). Figure 6 depicts movement paths found during the target switching condition. We explain these data in terms of how instatement of a second TPC can rapidly modify the future updating of the PPC.

In addition, Georgopoulous *et al.* (1981) found a remarkable amplification of peak velocity during the switched component of the movement: "the peak velocity attained on the way to the second target was generally much higher (up to threefold) than that of the control ... these high velocities cannot be accounted for exclusively by a mechanism that adjusts peak velocity to the amplitude of movement ... The cause of this phenomenon is unclear" (pp.732-733). In Section 25, we explain this phenomenon in terms of the indepen-

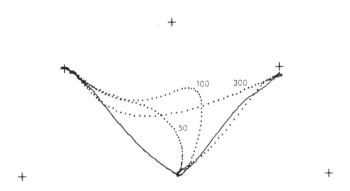

Figure 6. Monkeys seamlessly transformed a movement initiated toward the 2 o'clock target into a movement toward the 10 o'clock target when the latter target was substituted 50 or 100 msec. after activation of the 2 o'clock target light. Reprinted with permission from Georgopoulos *et al.* (1981).

dent control, or factorization, of the GO mechanism and the TPC-switching mechanism that was described in Section 4. In particular, the GO signal builds up continuously in time. When the TPC is switched to a new target, the PPC can be updated much more quickly because the GO signal which drives it is already large. The more rapid updating of the PPC translates into higher velocities.

These target switching data call attention to a more subtle property of how a GO signal energizes PPC updating, indeed a property which has tended to mask the very existence of the GO signal: How can a GO signal which was activated with a previous TPC interact with a later TPC without causing errors in the ability of the PPC to track the later TPC? How does the energizing effect of a GO signal transfer to any TPC? A solution of this problem is suggested in Section 18.

The fact that peak velocity is amplified without affecting movement accuracy during target switching implies a violation of Fitt's Law, as Massey, Schwartz, and Georgopoulous (1985) have noted. Our mechanistic analysis of synergetic binding via instatement of a TPC and of subsequent PPC updating energized by a previously activated GO signal provides an explanation of this Fitts' Law violation as well as of Fitts' Law itself (Section 28).

Our model also suggests an explanation of why the position of maximal curvature and the time of minimal velocity are correlated during two-part arm movements (Abend, Bizzi, and Morasso, 1982; Fetters and Todd, 1987; Viviani and Terzuolo, 1980). This correlation arises in the model if the second TPC is switched on only after the PPC approaches the first TPC. In the Georgopoulous *et al* (1981) experiment, in contrast, the second TPC is switched on due to the second light before the arm reaches the first target. An unanswered question of considerable interest is whether a second GO signal is switched on gradually with the second TPC in the Abend *et al* (1982) paradigm, or whether the reduction in velocity at the turning point is due entirely to nulling of the difference between the PPC and the first TPC while the GO signal maintains an approximately constant value. These alternatives can be tested by measuring the velocities and accelerations subsequent to the position of the turning point.

12. Velocity Profile Invariance and Asymmetry

Many investigators have noted that the velocity profiles of simple arm movements are approximately bell-shaped (Abend, Bizzi, and Morasso, 1982; Atkeson and Hollerbach, 1985; Beggs and Howarth, 1972; Georgopoulous, Kalaska, and Massey, 1981; Howarth and Beggs, 1971; Morasso, 1981; Soechting and Lacquaniti, 1981). Moreover the shape of the bell, if rescaled appropriately, is approximately preserved for movements that vary in duration, distance, or peak velocity. Figure 7 shows rescaled velocity profiles from the experiment of Atkeson and Hollerbach (1985). These velocity profiles were generated over a fixed distance at several different velocities. Thus both the duration scale and the velocity scale were modified to superimpose the curves shown in Figure 7.

On the other hand, Beggs and Howarth (1972) showed that "at high speeds the approach curves of the practised subjects are more symmetrical than at low speeds" (p.451), and Zelaznik, Schmidt, and Gielen (1986) have shown that at very high speeds the direction of asymmetry has actually reversed. Thus the trend documented by Beggs and Howarth continues beyond the range of speeds they sampled. Since velocity profiles associated with slow movements are more asymmetric than those associated with fast movements, they cannot be exactly superimposed. All the velocity profiles shown in Figure 7 are taken from slow (1–1.6 sec) movements, and exhibit the sort of more gradual deceleration than acceleration that Beggs and Howarth (1972) reported for such movements.

Asymmetry, its degree, and changes in its direction are of major theoretical importance. For example, the Minimum-Jerk Model of Hogan (1984) predicts symmetric velocity profiles. More generally, superimposability of velocity profiles after time-axis rescaling is a defining characteristic of "generalized motor program" models (Hogan, 1984; Meyer, Smith, and Wright 1982; Schmidt, Zelaznik, and Frank, 1978), which therefore cannot explain how the degree of velocity profile asymmetry varies with overall movement speed. In contrast, our model shows how the gradual updating of the PPC can generate velocity profiles which exhibit the type of speed-dependent asymmetry that is found in the data (Section 23).

Both the existence of asymmetry in velocity profiles and the dependence of degree and direction of asymmetry upon movement speed indicate the need for an analysis of the neural dynamics whereby a trajectory unfolds in real-time. In contrast, the Hogan (1984) model's global optimization criterion forces strict superimposability of rescaled velocity profiles because it does not represent a process of temporal unfolding. Beggs and Howarth (1972) suggested that the asymmetry reflects a learned strategy of approaching the target as quickly as possible before making corrective movements near the target. For example, these corrective movements could be made under visual guidance by instating a corrected TPC as the arm approached the target. The approach to such a new TPC would take more time, on the average, than the final approach to the previously tracked TPC, thereby causing greater velocity profile asymmetry. In our simulation results, velocity profiles become more symmetric as movement speed increases and eventually exhibit a symmetry reversal even in the absence of newly instated TPC's. Thus the greater symmetry of velocity profiles at higher speeds may be due to the combined effects of PPC updating properties as the GO signal is parametrically increased, and to the consequent elimination of corrective TPC's as

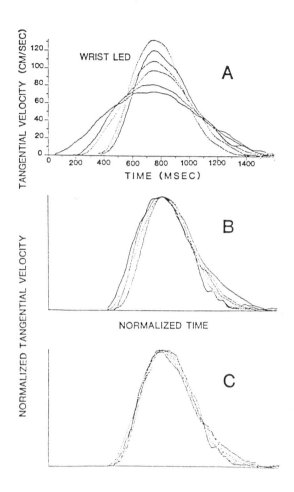

Figure 7. Velocity profiles from movements of similar duration are approximately superimposable following velocity and time axis rescaling. Reprinted with permission from Atkeson and Hollerbach (1984).

the target is rapidly approached. In support of this analysis, Jeannerod (1984, p.252) noted that "the low velocity phase is still observed in the absence of visual feedback, and even in the no-vision situation. This finding, however, does not preclude that visual feedback, when present, will be incorporated ... In the present study, movement duration and low-velocity phase duration were found to be increased in the visual feedback situation."

In summary, our explanation of these data shows how a circuit capable of flexibly binding muscle groups into synchronous synergies automatically implies the trends observed in data on velocity profile asymmetry. Thus we suggest an explanation of movement invariants, such as duration invariance and synchrony, using a control circuit which never computes an explicit trajectory and whose outputs exhibit a type of speed-dependent asymmetry which other models have not been able to explain.

13. Vector Cells in Motor Cortex

Before quantitatively developing our model, it remains to indicate how the present position command (PPC) is gradually updated until it matches a fixed target position command (TPC). Sections 15–18 motivate this mechanism through an analysis of the types of information that can be used by a developing system to learn TPC's. The summary here is merely descriptive and is made to link these introductory remarks to supportive neural data.

When a new TPC is switched on, its relationship to the current PPC can be arbitrary. Any realizable pair of positions can be coded by the TPC and the PPC. In order to track the TPC, the PPC needs to change in a *direction* determined by the difference between the TPC and the PPC. In addition, the *amount* of required change is also determined by this difference. An array which measures both the direction and the distance between a pair of arrays TPC and PPC is called a *difference vector*, or DV. At any given time, the DV between the TPC and the PPC—namely, $DV = TPC - PPC$—is computed at a match interface (Figure 8).

How does such a DV (difference vector) update the current PPC? Clearly the PPC must be updated in the direction specified by the DV. Hence we assume that the PPC cumulatively adds, or *integrates*, through time all the DV's which arise at the match interface. Due to this arrangement, the PPC gradually approaches the TPC. At a time when the PPC equals the TPC, the DV equals zero; hence, although the PPC may continue to integrate DV's, it will not further change until either the switching on of a new TPC creates a non-zero DV, or the PPC is updated by inflow information during a passive movement (Section 30). To summarize these relations, we call our model the Vector-Integration-To-Endpoint (VITE) Model.

Georgopoulos and his colleagues (Georgopoulos, Kalaska, Caminiti, and Massey, 1982; Georgopoulos, Kalaska, Crutcher, Caminiti, and Massey, 1984) have found cell populations in the motor cortex whose collective properties mirror those of the vector-computing nodes at the match interface of our model (Figure 8). The activity of each such node models the average potential of a population of neural cells with similar receptive field properties. Figure 9 shows a histogram of the average number of spikes per unit time recorded from a single such neuron. This temporal behavior closely matches that of a DV cell population in the model (Figure 18). The vector cells in motor cortex, just like the DV cell populations in the model, are very broadly tuned to direction (Figure 10a); that is, there exists a broad range of directions in which a given component of the model DV is positive.

Figure 11 further explicates these properties. Figure 11a clarifies why cells at the DV stage may be called vector cells at all. For simple movements, at increasing times $t_o < t_1 < t_2 < ...$, the relative sizes of the activities across the DV populations do not change. Hence these populations code a vector direction, even though their individual absolute activities sweep out an approximately bell-shaped curve through time. Figure 11b ilustrates that, as movement direction is parametrically changed, the relative activations of an agonist-antagonist pair of DV populations change systematically in such a way that individual populations may remain active over a broad range of directions, as in Figure 10a. Figure 11b also schematizes the fact that different agonist muscles may remain active over different ranges of direction, depending upon the movement in question. Although Figure 11a schematizes a formal DV, this DV may have many components because it controls many muscle groups. In contrast, the 3-dimensional vector which represents the direction of the arm's movement in Euclidean space has only three components. One of the major outstanding problems in arm movement control is to relate the geometry of the

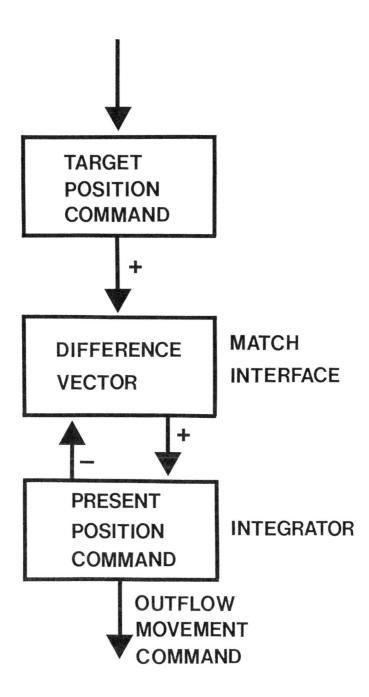

Figure 8. A match interface within the motor command channel continuously computes the difference between the target position and present position, and adds the difference to the present position command.

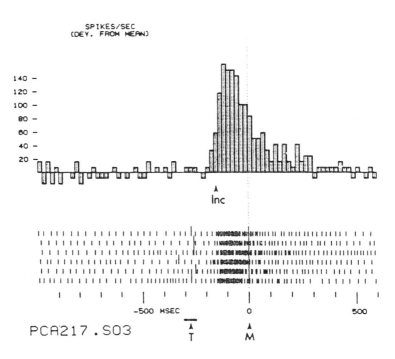

Figure 9. Quick buildup and gradual decline of activity in motor-cortical vector cells. Reprinted with permission from Georgopoulos *et al.* (1982).

high dimensional muscle space with the geometry of Euclidean space.

Due to the importance of explaining why each DV population is sensitive to a broad range of directions, we further comment on this property below. The PPC outflow channels must control several different muscle groups at each joint, and several different joints in each arm. Because of the opponent organization of the muscles (Figure 11b), up to one half of the cellular components composing the DV stage will have positive activities during a given movement.

Each initial positive-valued component, $DV_i(0) = TPC_i(0) - PPC_i(0) > 0$, of the difference vector DV corresponds to an expected change in length of one of the many muscle groups whose shortening contributes a motion component to the overall limb movement. If there were only one active agonist-antagonist muscle pair driving the movement, the movement would always tend to follow a preferred direction. Where more than one agonist-antagonist pair guides the movement, however, a muscle can facilitate motion along directions other than its preferred direction. In this case, the net direction of limb motion depends upon the relative sizes $DV_i(0) > 0$ of the cooperating agonists, so that each DV_i population can be active across a broad range of movement directions, as in Figure 11b. Since the net movement direction shifts continuously with the relative sizes $DV_i(0)$ of the

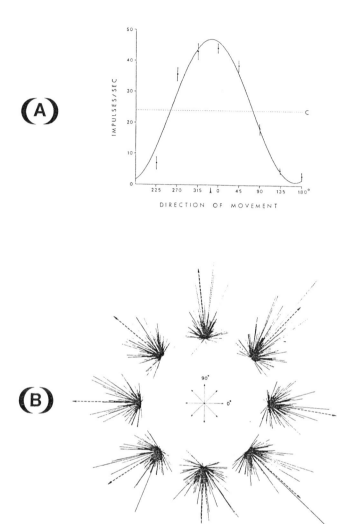

Figure 10. (A) Directional tuning curve for a motor-cortical cell exhibiting peak activity during a $0°$ (center-to-right) arm movement. Dotted line indicates control period discharge rate. Thus this cell is inhibited when movement direction falls outside the $180°$ hemisphere of movements to which it can contribute a positive motion component. Reprinted with permission from Kalaska *et al.* (1983). (B) Each dotted arrow in the central graphic indicates the direction of a radial (center-out) movement, and points to a representation of the cellular activites observed during that movement. In each plot of cellular activites, the *direction* of each solid black line corresponds to the direction of movement for which a given cell fired maximally, whereas the *length* of each solid black line corresponds to the firing rate of the same cell during the indicated movement. The single dashed line with arrowhead in each plot represents the vector sum of all the neural vectors (solid block lines) generated during the indicated movement. Note the correspondence between the direction of the vector sum (dashed line with arrowhead) and the direction of the actual movement (indicated by the dotted arrow in the central graphic). All cells were related to muscle groups acting at the shoulder, a ball-and-socket joint. Figures reprinted with permission from Georgopoulos *et al.* (1984).

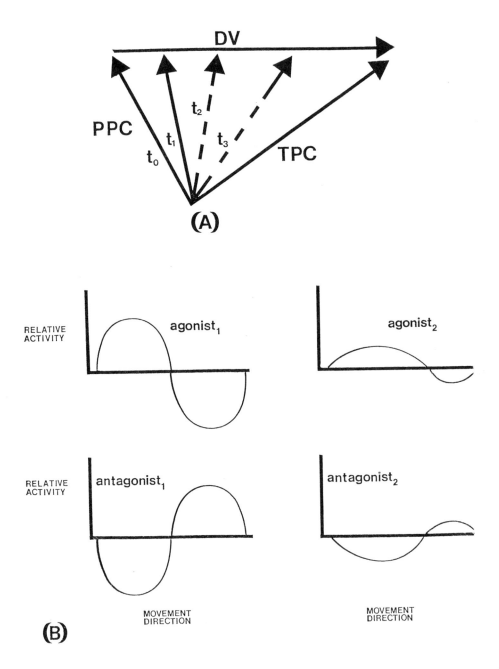

Figure 11. (A) As the movement unfolds through times $t_o, t_1, t_2, \ldots$ the present position command (PPC) approaches the target position command (TPC) in such a way that the difference vector (DV) does not change direction as its length approaches zero. (B) Over a full range of movement directions, DV cells associated with opposing muscles (AG_1 *vs.* $ANTAG_1$ or AG_2 *vs.* $ANTAG_2$) show reciprocal patterns of activation and inhibition. The zero-crossings can occur at different points along the direction scale for different opponent pairs (AG_1 - $ANTAG_1$ *vs.* AG_2 - $ANTAG_2$).

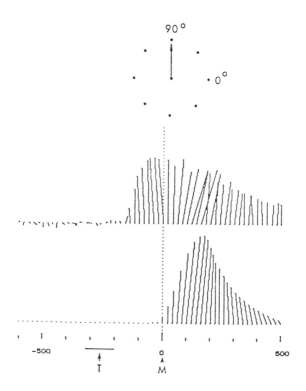

Figure 12. (A): A comparison of the population vector of 241 directionally tuned cells (upper figure) with the velocity vector of the hand (lower figure), each measured at 20 msec. intervals during the reaction time and during movement. Note the asymmetry (longer right tail) in both. Reprinted with permission from Georgopoulos *et al.* (1984).

cooperating agonists, it should be possible to predict the direction of a forthcoming limb movement.

Both of these conclusions have been supported by Georgopoulos, Kalaska, Crutcher, Caminiti, and Massey (1984) and Georgopoulos, Schwartz, and Kettner (1986). Figure 10a illustrates that vector cells in motor cortex are, indeed, broadly tuned to direction. Figure 10b illustrates that the aggregate activity of a large sample of active vector cells [read, cells from different DV_i populations] can be used to accurately predict the direction of the forthcoming movement.

Figure 12 plots data from a vector cell population *in vivo* alongside the velocity profile of the corresponding movement. Note that the asymmetry in the velocity profile is in the same direction as the asymmetry in the vector cell population profile. This correspondence suggests that the velocity asymmetry is related to the neural control circuit, as our model also suggests.

Georgopoulos *et al.* (1984, p.510) also noted that: "No obvious invariance in cell discharge was observed when the final position was the same ... these results show that, at the level of motor cortex, it is the direction of movement and not its endpoint that is the principle determinant of cell discharge during the initiation and execution of movement. Therefore, if the hypothesis be true that the endpoint of the movement is the controlled spatial variable (Polit and Bizzi, 1979) then the motor cortex seems to be distal to that end-point specifying process." In other words, if one accepts the STE Model, these data suggest that the TPC cells occur closer to the periphery than the DV cells. On the other hand, if one accepts our model, these data imply that the PPC cells occur closer to the periphery than the DV cells, but that the TPC cells occur more central than the DV cells. A combination of anatonomical and physiological experiments can be used to test this prediction. It should also be noted, however, that the STE Model on which the conclusion of Georgopoulos *et al.* (1984) is based is inconsistent with the very existence of vector cells, because the spring-like properties of the muscles themselves, rather than a neural computation of vectors, determines the direction and length of movement in the STE Model.

Several further properties of cells in precentral motor cortex, documented by Evarts and Tanji (1974; Tanji and Evarts, 1976), lend support to identifying them with the vector cells in our model. In their experiments, monkeys were trained to either push or pull a lever. During each trial (schematized in Figure 13a) animals first held the lever in a medial position for 2-4 sec. Then either a green or a red *priming* signal was illuminated. If green, the forthcoming movement required for reward was a push; if red, a pull. Finally, .6–1.2 seconds after the priming signal, the *release* signal occurred. This release signal took the form of an externally imposed push or pull on the lever held by the monkey. It both cued movement onset and perturbed the position of the lever so as to increase or decrease its initial distance from target.

Figure 13b summarizes operating characteristics of two cells. The first cell increased its activity after a "push" priming signal, but was inhibited by a "pull" priming signal; the second cell showed the opposite response. From these data alone, it would not be clear whether these cells' activities code DV's or TPC's. However, their further characteristics confirm their status as DV cells. The second bracket for each cell in Figure 13b indicates that their activities decline as movement proceeds in their preferred direction. This decline rules out the TPC interpretation. In the model, it occurs because the movement progressively cancels the difference with which DV cell activity is correlated.

The third bracket for each cell indicates that the initial position perturbations also have the effect they must have if the DV interpretation is correct: perturbations that make the starting point closer to target subtract from activity levels, whereas contrary perturbations add to activity levels. This occurs automatically in the model because PPC's, and thus the corresponding DV's, are updated by sensory feedback during passive movements (Section 30).

Though the foregoing considerations argue strongly for the existence of DV cells in precentral motor cortex, it might be argued that the DV's could be measuring force rather than positional values. Indeed, Evarts interpreted his early experimental data (Evarts, 1968) as suggestive of force coding. However, the data of Schmidt, Jost and Davis (1975) appear to rule out this alternative interpretation. After varying position and force independently, they concluded that "motor cortex cell firing patterns appear to be unrelated to the large values of rate of change of force seen in this experiment" (p.213).

The data summarized in Sections 7–13 weigh heavily against the STE Model and models based upon optimization principles. So too do the formal shortcomings of these models noted in Sections 7 and 12. We now show that the Vector-Integration-to-Endpoint (VITE)

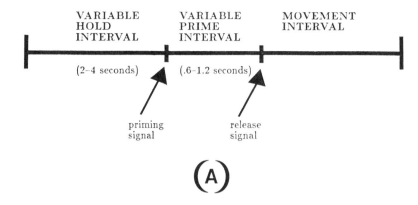

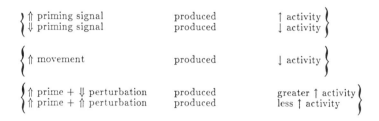

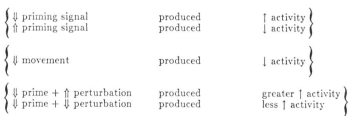

Figure 13. (A): The time course of each trial in the push-or-pull task used by Evarts and Tanji (1974). (B): Operating characteristics of two motor-cortical cells. Solid arrows indicate increases (upward arrow) or decreases (downward arrow) in cell discharge rates. Hollow arrows indicate a push-(upward arrow) or pull-(downward arrow) related event: either the push/pull priming signal, a push/pull movement, or the push/pull perturbation that also served as the release signal.

Model overcomes these formal shortcomings and provides a parsimonious quantitative explanation of all the behavioral and neural data summarized above and in the subsequent sections.

14. Learning Constraints Mold Arm Control Circuits

Rejecting the Spring-To-Endpoint (STE) Model does not entail rejecting all dependence upon endpoint commands. An analysis of sensory-motor learning during eye-hand coordination enables us to identify processes which supplement endpoint, or target position, commands to overcome the shortcomings of the STE Model (Grossberg, 1978). The central role of learning constraints in the design of sensory-motor systems has elsewhere been developed for the case of the saccadic eye movement system (Grossberg and Kuperstein, 1986).

We focus our discussion of learning within the arm movement system upon the basic problem of how, when an observer looks at an object, the observer's hand knows where to move in order to touch the object. We discuss this issue from the perspective of eye-hand coordination in a mammal, but the issues that are raised, as well as the conclusions that are drawn, generalize to many other species and sensory-motor systems. Why learning processes are needed to solve this problem is illustrated by the following example.

The movement command which guides the hand to a visual target at a fixed position relative to the body is not invariant under growth. If a young arm, with relatively short limb segments, and an old arm with relatively long limb segments, react to the same command—that is, assume equal angles at analogous joints—then the tips of the two arm's fingers will be at different loci with respect to the body frame. In short, any animal that grows over an extended period will need to adaptively modify movement commands even if its only ambition is to perform the same act earlier and later in its life cycle. Put the other way, that animals do remain able to reach desired targets throughout periods of limb growth implies plasticity in their sensory-motor commands. Because such growth is slow relative to the rate of learning, failures of sensory-motor coordination are rarely noticeable. In humans, exceptions occur during the first few months of life, prior to experiential tuning of the infant's initially coarse sensory-motor mapping (Fetters and Todd, 1987; von Hofsten, 1979, 1982).

15. Comparing Target Position with Present Position to Gate Intermodality Learning

Thus, as the arm grows, the motor commands which move it to a fixed position in space with respect to the body must also change through learning. Many arm movements are activated in response to visually seen objects that the individual wishes to grasp. We therefore formulate this learning process as follows: How is a transformation learned and adaptively modified between the parameters of the eye-head system and the hand-arm system so that an observer can touch a visually fixated object?

Following Piaget's (1963) analysis of *circular reactions*, let us imagine that an infant's hand makes a series of unconditional movements, which the infant's eyes unconditionally follow. As the hand occupies a variety of positions that the eye fixates, a transformation is learned from the parameters of the hand-arm system to the parameters of the eye-head system. A reverse transformation is also learned from parameters of the eye-head system to parameters of the hand-arm system. This reverse transformation enables an observer to intentionally move its hand to a visually fixated position.

How do these two sensory-motor systems know what parameters are the correct ones to map upon each other? This question raises the fundamental problem that many neural signals, although large, are unsuitable for being incorporated into behavioral maps and commands. They are "functional noise" to the motor learning process. The learning process needs to be actively modulated, or gated, against learning during inappropriate circumstances.

In the present instance, not all positions that the eye-head system or the hand-arm system assume are the correct positions to associate through learning. For example, suppose that the hand briefly remains at a given position and that the eye moves to foveate the hand. An infinite number of positions are assumed by the eye as it moves to foveate the hand. Only the final, intended, or expected position of the eye-head system is a correct position to associate with the position of the hand-arm system.

Learning of an intermodal motor map must thus be prevented except when the eye-head system and the hand-arm system are near their intended positions. Otherwise, all possible positions of the two systems could be associated with each other, which would lead to behaviorally chaotic consequences. Several important conclusions follow from this observation (Grossberg, 1978; Grossberg and Kuperstein, 1986).

(1) All such adaptive sensory-motor systems compute a representation of target position (also called expected position, or intended position). Thus the importance of endpoint computations is confirmed. This representation is the TPC (target position command). In addition:

(2) All such adaptive sensory-motor systems also compute a representation of present position. This representation is the PPC (present position command).

(3) During movement, target position is matched against present position. Intermodal map learning is prevented except when target position approximately matches present position (Figure 14). A *gating*, or modulator, signal is thus controlled by the network at which target position is matched with present position. This gating signal enables learning to occur when a good match occurs and prevents learning from occurring when a bad match occurs. This matching process takes place at the match interface that was described in Section 13. The DV (difference vector) controls the gating signal.

(4) In order to compare target positions with present positions, both types of data must be computed in the same coordinate system. Present eye position is computed with respect to head coordinates. Thus there is an evolutionary pressure to encode target position in head coordinates.

16. Trajectory Formation using DV's: Automatic Compensation for Present Position

The above discussion of how *intermodality* sensory-motor transformations are learned also sheds light upon how *intramodality* movement trajectories are formed. Intermodality transformations associate TPC's because only such transformations can avoid the multiple confusions that could arise through associating arbitrary positions along a movement trajectory. TPC's are not, however, sufficient to generate intramodality movement trajectories. In response to the same TPC, an eye, arm, or leg must move different distances and directions depending upon its present position when the target position is registered.

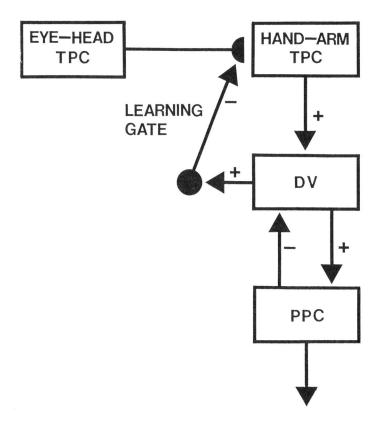

Figure 14. Learning in sensory-motor pathways is gated by a DV process which matches TPC with PPC to prevent incorrect associations from forming between eye-head TPC's and hand-arm TPC's.

PPC's can be used to convert a single TPC into many different movement trajectories. Computation of the difference between target position and present position at the match interface in Figure 8 generates a difference vector, or DV, that can be used to automatically compensate for present position. Such automatic compensation accomplishes a tremendous reduction in the memory load that is placed upon an adaptive sensory-motor system. Instead of having to learn whole movement trajectories, the system only has to learn intermodality maps between TPC's. As shall be shown below, the DV's which are computed from target positions and present positions at the match interface can be used to automatically and continuously update the PPC movement commands from which the trajectory is formed. In summary, consideration of the types of information that can be used to learn intermodality commands during motor development leads to general conclusions about the quantities from which intramodality movement trajectories are formed, and thus about the way in which other neural systems, such as sensory, cognitive, and motivational systems, can influence the planning of such trajectories.

Computation of TPC's, PPC's, and DV's is a qualitatively different approach to generating a trajectory than are traditional computations based upon a Newtonian analysis of movement kinematics. In a Newtonian analysis, every position within the trajectory is assumed to be explicitly controlled (Atkeson and Hollerbach, 1985; Brody and Paul, 1984; Hogan, 1984; Hollerbach, 1984). Such computations lead to a combinatorial explosion which is hard to reconcile with the rapidity of biological movement generation in real-time. In a vector computation, the entire trajectory is never explicitly planned. Instead, a TPC is computed which determines where the movement expects, or intends, to terminate. The subtraction of the PPC is an automatic process which compensates for the variability of the starting position. The DV which is hereby computed can be used to generate an accurate movement without ever explicitly computing a planned sequence of trajectory positions for the whole movement. In arm movements, a continuous comparison is made between a fixed TPC and all the PPC's that are computed during the movement. All of these compensations for changes in present position are automatically registered, and therefore place no further burden upon the computation of planned movement parameters. In addition, such automatic compensations for present position spontaneously generate the major invariants of arm movements that have been discovered to date (Sections 22-29). Thus the general problem of how DV's are computed is a central one for the understanding of trajectory formation in several movement systems.

17. Matching and Vector Integration during Trajectory Formation

We now specify in greater detail a model of how TPC's, PPC's, and DV's interact with each other through time to synthesize a movement trajectory. Each PPC generates a pattern of outflow movement signals to arm system muscles (Figure 8). Each such outflow pattern acts to move the arm system towards the present position which it encodes. Thus, were only a single PPC to be activated, the arm system would come to rest at a single physical position. A complete movement trajectory can be generated in the form of a temporal succession of PPC's. Such a movement trajectory can be generated in response to a single TPC that remains active throughout the movement. Although a TPC explicitly encodes only the endpoint of the movement, the process whereby present positions are automatically and continuously updated possesses properties that are much more powerful than those of an STE Model.

This process of continuous updating proceeds as follows. At every moment, a DV is computed from the fixed TPC and the PPC (Figure 8). This DV encodes the difference between the TPC and the PPC. In particular, the DV is computed by subtracting the PPC from the TPC at the match interface.

Because a DV computes the difference between the TPC and the PPC, the PPC equals the TPC only when all components of the DV equal zero. Thus, if the arm system's commands are calibrated so that the arm attains the physical position in space that is coded by its PPC, then the arm system will approach the desired target position in space as the DV's computed during its trajectory approach zero. This is accomplished as follows.

At each time, the DV computes the direction and amplitude which must still be moved to match the PPC with the TPC. Thus the DV computes an error signal of a very special kind. These error signals are used to continuously update the PPC in such a way that the changing PPC approaches the fixed TPC by progressively reducing the vector error to zero. In particular, the match interface at which DV's are computed sends excitatory signals to the stage where PPC's are computed. This stage integrates, or adds up, these vector signals through time. The PPC is thus a cumulative record of all past DV's, and each DV brings the PPC a little closer to the target position command.

In so doing, the DV is itself updated due to negative feedback from the new PPC to the match interface (Figure 8). This process of updating present positions through vector integration and negative feedback continues continuously until the PPC equals the TPC. Several important conclusions follow from this analysis of the trajectory formation process.

Two processes within the arm control system do double duty: A PPC generates feedforward, or outflow, movement signals *and* negative feedback signals which are used to compute a DV. A DV is used to update intramodality trajectory information *and* to gate intermodality learning of associative transformations between TPC's. Thus the match interface continuously updates the PPC when the arm is moving *and* disinhibits the intermodality map learning process when the arm comes to rest.

Within the circuit depicted in Figure 8, "position" and "direction" information are separately coded. Positional information is coded within the PPC and directional information is coded by the DV at the match interface. On the other hand, the computations which give rise to positional and directional information are not independent, since DV's are integrated to compute PPC's, and PPC's are subtracted from TPC's to compute DV's.

In Figure 8, the PPC is computed using outflow information, but not inflow information. This property emphasizes the need to mechanize concepts about how present position is computed. Using an outflow-based PPC clarifies how targets can be reached when sources of inflow information are eliminated (Polit and Bizzi, 1978) without being forced into the erroneous conclusion that no information about present position is needed to form a trajectory. In addition, although the PPC integrates outflow DV signals during active movements, inflow signals are used to update the PPC during passive movements (Section 30), thereby clarifying the data of Polit and Bizzi (1978) concerning failure of monkeys to compensate for passive shifts of their initial upper arm position in the deafferented state. The PPC feedback shown in Figure 8 is an "efference copy" of a "premotor" command (von Holst and Mittelsteadt, 1950). The VITE model's use of efferent feedback distinguishes it from an alternative class of models, which propose that present position information is derived from afferent feedback from sensory receptors in the limb. In particular, the far reaching consequences of its use of efferent, as opposed to afferent, feedback make the VITE model fundamentally different from the classical closed-loop servo recommended by Adams (1971, 1977) as a model of human motor performance. Further differences are introduced by the VITE model's use of the time-varying multiplicative GO signal introduced in Section 11 and elaborated below.

18. Intentionality and the GO Signal: Motor Priming without Movement

The circuit depicted in Figure 8 embodies the concept of intention, or expectation, through its computation of a TPC. The complete movement circuit embodies intentionality in yet another sense, which leads to a circuit capable of variable speed control. The need for such an additional process can also be motivated through a consideration of eye-hand coordination (Grossberg, 1978, 1982).

When a human looks at a nearby object, several movement options for touching the object are available. The object could be grasped with the left hand or the right hand. The object could even be touched with one's nose or one's toes! We assume that the eye-head system can simultaneously activate TPC's in several motor systems via the intermodality associative transformations that are learned to these systems. An additional "act of will," or GO signal, is required to convert one or more of these TPC's into overt movement trajectories within only the selected motor systems.

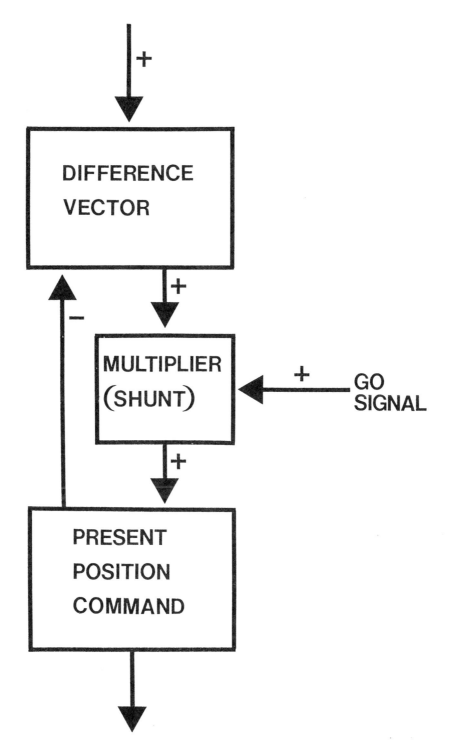

Figure 15. A GO signal gates execution of a primed movement vector and regulates the rate at which the movement vector updates the present position command.

There is only one way to implement such a GO signal within the circuit depicted in Figure 8. This implementation is described in Figure 15. The GO signal must act at a stage intermediate between the stages which compute DV's and PPC's: The GO signal must act after the match interface so that it does not disrupt the process whereby DV's become zero as PPC's approach the TPC. The GO signal must act before the stage which computes PPC's so that changes in the GO signal cannot cause further movement after the PPC matches the TPC. Thus, although the GO signal changes the outputs from the match interface before they reach the present position stage, the very existence of such processing stages for continuous formation of a trajectory enables the GO signal to act without destroying the accuracy of the trajectory.

The detailed computational properties of the GO signal are derived from two further constraints. First, the absence of a GO signal must prevent the movement from occurring. This constraint suggests that the GO signal multiplies, or *shunts*, each output pathway from the match interface. A zero GO signal multiplies every output to zero, and hence prevents the PPC from being updated. Second, the GO signal must not change the direction of movement that is encoded by a DV. The direction of movement is encoded by the *relative* sizes of all the output signals generated by the vector. This constraint reaffirms that the GO signal *multiplies* vector outputs. It also implies that the GO signal is *nonspecific*: The *same* GO signal multiplies each output signal from the matching interface so as not to change the direction encoded by the vector.

In summary, the GO signal takes a particularly simple form. When it equals zero, the present position signal is not updated. Hence no overt movement is generated. On the other hand, a zero GO signal does not prevent a TPC from being activated, or a DV from being computed. Thus a motor system can become ready, or primed, for movement before its GO signal turns on. When the GO signal does turn on, the movement can be rapidly initiated. The size of the GO signal regulates overall movement speed. Larger GO signals cause faster movements, other things being equal, by speeding up the process whereby directional information from the match interface is integrated into new PPC's. In models of cognitive processing, the functional analog of the GO signal is an attentional gain control signal (Carpenter and Grossberg, 1987a, 1987b; Grossberg, 1987b, 1987c; Grossberg and Stone, 1986).

Georgopoulos, Schwartz, and Kettner (1986) have reported data consistent with this scheme. In their experiment, a monkey is trained to withhold movement for 0.5 to 3 seconds until a lighted target dims. They reported that cells with properties akin to DV cells computed a direction congruent with that of the upcoming movement during the waiting period. These data support the prediction that the neural stage where the GO signal is registered lies between the DV stage and the PPC stage.

19. Synchrony, Variable Speed Control, and Fast Freeze

The circuit in Figure 15 is now easily seen to possess qualitative properties of synchronous synergetic movement, variable speed control, and fast freeze-and-abort. We apply the circuit properties that each muscle synergist's motor command is updated at a rate that is proportional both to the synergist's distance from its target position and to a variable-magnitude GO signal, which is broadcast to all members of the synergy to initiate and sustain the parallel updating process.

To fix ideas, consider a simple numerical example. Suppose that, prior to movement initiation, muscle synergist *A* is 4 distance units from its target position and muscle synergist B is 2 distance units from its target position. In that case, if the mean rates at which PPC's are updated for the two synergists are in the same proportion as the distance (i.e., 2:1), then the updating of synergist A will take $4/2$ time units while the updating of synergist B will take $2/1$ time units. Thus both processes will consume approximately 2 time units. Although the PPC updating process occurs at different rates for different synergists, it consumes equal times for all synergists. The result is a synchronous movement despite large rate variations among the component motions.

Changing the magnitude of the GO signal governs variable speed control. Because both of the updating rates in the example (2 and 1) are multiplied by the same GO signal, the component motions will remain synchronous, though of shorter or longer duration, depending on whether the GO signal multiplier is made larger or smaller, respectively. In general, the GO signal's magnitude varies inversely with duration and directly with speed. Finally, if the value of the GO signal remains at zero, no updating and no motion will occur. Thus very rapid freezing can be achieved by completely inhibiting the GO signal at any point in the trajectory. The fact that target position may be very different from present position when the GO signal is withdrawn does not interfere with freezing, as it would using a STE Model, because the arm position closely tracks the PPC, which stops changing as soon as the signal shuts off.

Grossberg (1978, Section 54; reprinted in Grossberg, 1982) suggested an alternative scheme whereby actively moving muscles could be opposed by properly scaled antagonist co-contractions in response to a sudden unexpected event. In this scheme, agonist-antagonist motor commands are organized as gated dipole opponent processes and the unexpected event triggers a burst of nonspecific arousal to all the command sources. Each gated dipole opponent process reacts to such a nonspecific arousal burst by causing an antagonistic rebound whose size is scaled to that of the dipole's prior on-response. The rate of antagonist contraction generated by such a scheme is thus matched to the size of the just-previous rate of agonist contraction. Both types of mechanism—inhibition of GO signal and onset of arousal burst to opponent motor controls—are worthy of further neurophysiological testing. Another role for the opponent organization of motor commands is summarized in the next section.

20. Opponent Processing of Movement Commands

Mammalian motor systems are organized into pairs of agonist and antagonist muscles. We now note a new functional role for such an opponent organization: An opponent organization is needed to convert DV's into PPC's which can eventually match an arbitrary TPC. Figure 16 depicts how opponent organization is joined to the system's other processing constraints.

The need for opponent signals can be seen from the following examples. If a target position signal is larger than the corresponding present position signal, then a positive output signal is generated by the corresponding component of the DV. Such positive output signals increase the present position signal until it matches the target position signal. Increasing the present position signal causes the target muscle group to contract. The opponent muscle group must also simultaneously relax. Inhibitory signals to the present position node of the opponent muscle instate this latter property. When these inhibitory signals are integrated by the present position node of the opponent muscle, the output signal to the opponent muscle decreases, thereby relaxing the muscle.

The need for opponent processing can also be seen by considering the case in which the

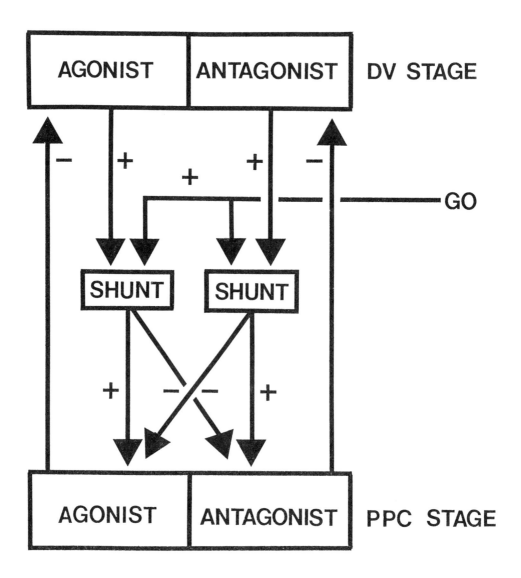

Figure 16. Opponent interactions among channels controlling agonists and their antagonists enable coordinated, automatic updating of their PPC's.

target position signal is smaller than the present position signal. Then the corresponding component of the DV is negative. Since only nonnegative activities can generate output signals, no output signal is generated by this component of the DV to its corresponding present position node. How, then, is this present position signal decreased until it matches the target position signal? The answer is now obvious, since we have just considered the same problem from a slightly different perspective: If a negative vector component corresponds to an antagonist muscle group, a positive vector component corresponds to its opponent agonist muscle group. This positive vector component generates inhibitory signals to the present position command of the antagonist muscle, thereby relaxing the antagonist muscle until its PPC equals its TPC.

21. System Equations

A quantitative analysis of movement invariants requires the development of a rigorous real-time mathematical model of the constraints summarized in the preceding sections. Qualitative algebraic analysis is insufficient because the trajectory is an emergent property of a nonlinear integration and feedback process under variable gain control. Our model defines the simplest system that is consistent with these constraints. To fix ideas, we explicitly study how the TPC to an agonist muscle group generates a trajectory of PPC signals to that muscle group. Generalizations to synergetic movement of multiple agonist-antagonist muscle groups follow directly from this analysis. Figure 17 locates the mathematical variables that are defined below. The network depicted in Figure 17 obeys the following system of differential equations:

$$\frac{dV}{dt} = \alpha(-V + T - P) \tag{2}$$

and

$$\frac{dP}{dt} = G[V]^+. \tag{3}$$

In (2) and (3), $T(t)$ is a target position input, $V(t)$ is the activity of the agonist's DV population, $P(t)$ is the activity of the agonist's PPC population, $G(t)$ is the GO signal, $\frac{dV}{dt}$ is the rate of change of V, and $\frac{dP}{dt}$ is the rate of change of P.

Equation (2) says that the activity $V(t)$ averages the difference of the input signals $T(t)$ and $P(t)$ at a rate α through time. The TPC input $T(t)$ excites $V(t)$, whereas the PPC input $P(t)$ inhibits $V(t)$ as part of the negative feedback loop between $V(t)$ and $P(t)$.

Equation (3) says that $P(t)$ cumulatively adds, or integrates, the product $G[V]^+$, where

$$[V]^+ = \begin{cases} V & \text{if } V > 0 \\ 0 & \text{if } V \leq 0. \end{cases} \tag{4}$$

In other words, the DV population elicits an output signal $[V]^+$ to the PPC population only if the activity V exceeds the output threshold 0. The output signal is a linear function of V at suprathreshold values. The output signal $[V]^+$ is multiplied, or gated, by the GO signal $G(t)$ on its way to the PPC stage. The activity $P(t)$ at the PPC stage integrates the gated signal through time.

In particular, $G(t) = 0$ implies $\frac{dP}{dt}(t) = 0$. In other words, if the GO signal is shut off within a given time interval, the $P(t)$ is constant throughout that time interval. Fast-freeze can hereby be rapidly obtained by simply switching $G(t)$ quickly to zero no matter how far

Chapter 12

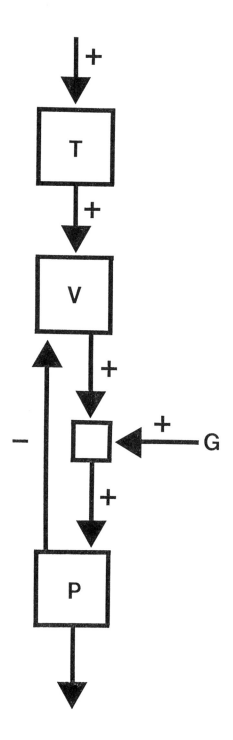

Figure 17. Network variables employed in computer simulations. See text equations (2) and (3).

$P(t)$ may be from $T(t)$ at that time. In addition, this circuit generates compensatory, or "error correcting," trajectories, as described in Section 10. For example, suppose that the GO signal starts out larger than usual or that there is a slight delay in instatement of the TPC relative to onset of the GO signal. In either case, $P(t)$ can initially increase faster than usual. As a result, $T - P(t)$ can rapidly become smaller than usual. Consequently, updating of $P(t)$ terminates earlier than usual.

This compensatory process illustrates two critical features of the VITE Model: (1) Trajectories are not pre-formed. (2) Because the GO signal feeds in between the DV stage and the PPC stage and because the DV is continuously inhibited by feedback from the PPC stage, accuracy is largely insulated from random variations in the size or onset time of the GO signal, variations in the onset time of the TPC, or momentary perturbations of the PPC due to internal noise or inflow signals.

The system of equations (2)–(4) is explicitly solved for a particular choice of GO signal in Appendix 1. In Sections 22–29, we display the results of computer simulations which demonstrate that this simple model provides a quantitative explanation of all the data thus far summarized. In most of these simulations, we write the GO signal in the form

$$G(t) = G_0 g(t). \tag{5}$$

Constant G_0 is called the GO *amplitude* and function $g(t)$ is called the GO *onset function*. The GO amplitude parameterizes how large the GO signal can become. The GO onset function describes the transient build-up of the GO signal after it is switched on. In our simulations, we systematically studied the influence of choosing different GO amplitudes G_0 and onset functions from the family

$$g(t) = \begin{cases} \frac{t^n}{\beta^n + \gamma t^n} & \text{if } t \geq 0 \\ 0 & \text{if } t < 0. \end{cases} \tag{6}$$

In (6), we chose β and γ equal to 1 or 0. If $\beta = 0$ and $\gamma = 1$, then $g(t)$ is a step function which switches from 0 to 1 at time $t = 0$. If $\beta = 1$ and $\gamma = 1$, then $g(t)$ is a slower-than-linear function of time if $n = 1$ and a sigmoid, or S-shaped, function of time if $n > 1$. In both of these cases, function $g(t)$ increases from $g(0) = 0$ to a maximum of 1, and attains the value $\frac{1}{2}$ at time $t = \beta$. If $\beta = 1$ and $\gamma = 0$, then $g(t)$ is a linear function of time if $n = 1$ and a faster-than-linear function of time if $n > 1$. We will demonstrate below that an onset function which is a faster-than-linear or sigmoid function of time generates a PPC profile through time that is in quantitative accord with data about the arm's velocity profile through time. On the other hand, if muscle and arm properties attenuate the increase in velocity at the beginning of a movement, then linear or even slower-than-linear onset functions could also quantitatively fit the data. Direct physiological measurements of the GO signal and PPC updating processes would enable a more definitive selection of the onset function to be made.

22. Computer Simulation of Movement Synchrony and Duration Invariance

In simulations of synchronous contraction, the same GO signal $G(t)$ is switched on at time $t = 0$ across all VITE circuit channels. We consider only agonist channels whose muscles contract to perform the synergy. Antagonist channels are controlled by opponent signals as described in Section 20. We assume that all agonist channels start out at equilibrium before their TPC's are switched to new, sustained target values at time $t = 0$. In all agonist muscles, $T(0) > P(0)$. Consequently, $V(t)$ in (2) increases, thereby increasing $P(t)$ in (3) and causing the target muscle to contract. Different muscles may be commanded to contract by different amounts. Then the size of $T(0) - P(0)$ will differ across the VITE channels inputting to different muscles. Thus, equations (2)-(4) describe a generic component of a TPC $(T_1, T_2, \ldots, T_n)$, a DV $(V_1, V_2, \ldots, V_n)$, and a PPC $(P_1, P_2, \ldots, P_n)$. Rather than introduce subscripts $1, 2, \ldots, n$ needlessly, we merely note that our mathematical task is to show how the VITE circuit (2)-(4) behaves in response to a single GO function $G(t)$ if the initial value $T(0) - P(0)$ is varied. The variation of $T(0) - P(0)$ can be interpreted as the choice of a different setting for each of the components $T_i(0) - P_i(0), i = 1, 2, \ldots, n$. Alternatively it can be interpreted as the reaction of the same component to different target and initial position values on successive performance trials.

Figure 18 depicts a typical response to a faster-than-linear $G(t)$ when $T(0) > P(0)$. Although $T(t)$ is switched on suddenly to a new value T, $V(t)$ gradually increases-then-decreases, while $P(t)$ gradually approaches its new equilibrium value, which equals T. The rate of change $\frac{dP}{dt}$ of P provides a measure of the velocity with which the muscle group that quickly tracks $P(t)$ will contract. Note that $\frac{dP}{dt}$ also gradually increases-then-decreases with a bell-shaped curve whose decelerative portion ($\frac{d^2P}{dt^2} < 0$) is slightly longer than its accelerative portion ($\frac{d^2P}{dt^2} > 0$), as in the data described in Sections 8, 9, 12, and 13.

Figure 19 demonstrates movement synchrony and duration invariance. This figure shows that the V curves and the $\frac{dP}{dt}$ curves generated by widely different $T(0) - P(0)$ values and the same GO signal $G(t)$ are perfectly synchronous through time. This property is proved mathematically in Appendix 2. The simulated curves mirror the data summarized in Sections 12 and 13. These results demonstrate that the PPC output vector $(P_1(t), P_2(t), \ldots, P_n(t))$ from a VITE circuit dynamically defines a synergy which controls a synchronous trajectory in response to any fixed choice $(T_1, T_2, \ldots, T_n)$ of TPC, any initial positions $(P, (0), P_2(0), \ldots, P_n(0))$, and any GO signal $G(t)$.

23. Computer Simulation of Changing Velocity Profile Asymmetry at Higher Movement Speeds

The next simulations reproduce the data reviewed in Section 12 concerning the greater symmetry of velocity profiles at higher movement velocities. In these simulations, the initial difference $T(0) - P(0)$ between TPC and PPC was held fixed and the GO amplitude G_0 was increased. Figure 20a,b,c shows that the profile of $\frac{dP}{dt}$ becomes more symmetric as G_0 is increased. At still larger G_0 values, the direction of asymmetry reversed; that is, the symmetry ratio exceeded .5, as in the data of Zelaznik, Schmidt, and Gielen (in press). Figure 20d shows that if both the time axis t and the velocity axis $\frac{dP}{dt}$ are rescaled, then curves corresponding to movements of the same size at different speeds can approximately be superimposed, except for the mismatch of their decelerative portions, as in the data summarized in Section 12.

24. Why Faster-than-Linear or Sigmoid Onset Functions?

The parametric analysis of velocity profiles in response to different values of $T(0) - P(0)$ and G_0 led to the choice of a faster-than-linear or sigmoid onset function $g(t)$. In fact, the faster-than-linear onset function should be interpreted as the portion of a sigmoid onset function whose slower-than-linear part occurs at times after $P(t)$ has already come very

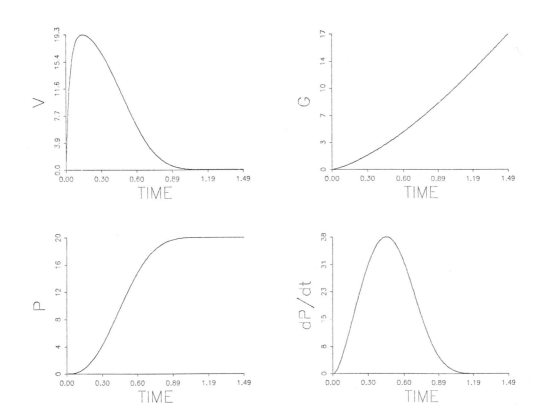

Figure 18. The simulated time course of the neural network activities V, G, and P during an 1100 msec. movement. The variable T (not plotted) had value 0 at $t < 0$, and value 20 thereafter. The derivative of P is also plotted to allow comparison with experimental velocity profiles. Parameters for equations (2), (3), (6): $\alpha = 30$, $n = 1.4$, $\beta = 1$, $\gamma = 0$.

close to T.

Figure 21 shows what happens when a slower-than-linear $g(t) = t(\beta + t)^{-1}$ or a linear $g(t) = t$ is used. At slow velocities (small G_0), the velocity profile $\frac{dP}{dt}$ becomes increasingly asymmetric when a slower-than-linear $g(t)$ is used. At a fixed slow velocity, the degree of asymmetry increases as the slower-than-linear $g(t)$ is chosen to more closely approximate a step function. A linear $g(t)$ leads to an intermediate degree of asymmetry. A faster-than-linear, or sigmoid, $g(t)$ leads to slight asymmetry at small values of G_0 as well as greater symmetry at large values of G_0. A sigmoid $g(t)$ can be generated from a sudden onset of GO signal if at least two cell stages average the GO signal before it gates $[V]^+$ in (3). A sigmoid $g(t)$ contains a faster-than-linear part at small values of t, and an approximately linear part at intermediate values of t. Thus a sigmoid $g(t)$ can generate different degrees of asymmetry depending upon how much of the total movement time occurs within each of these ranges.

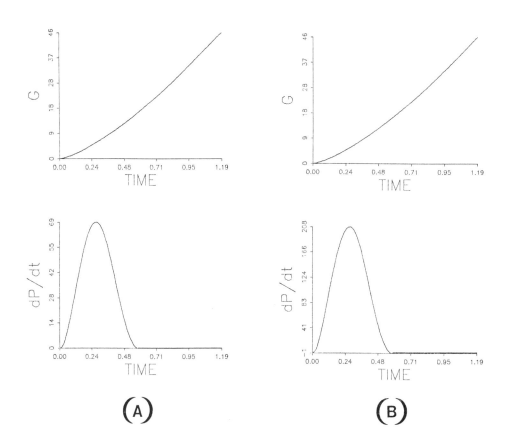

Figure 19. With equal GO signals, movements of different size have equal durations and perfectly superimposable velocity profiles after velocity axis rescaling. (A, B): GO signals and velocity profiles for 20 and 60 unit movements lasting 560 msec. (See Figure 18 caption for parameters.)

We have also simulated a VITE circuit using sigmoid GO signals whose rate of growth increases with the size of the GO amplitude. Such covariation of growth rate with amplitude is a basic property of neurons which obey membrane, or shunting, equations (Grossberg, 1970, 1973, 1982; Sperling and Sondhi, 1968). Such a sigmoid GO signal $G(t)$ can be simply defined as the output of the second neuron population in a chain of shunting equations perturbed by a step function input with amplitude G_0. Thus, let

$$G_0(t) = \begin{cases} G_0 & \text{if } t \geq 0 \\ 0 & \text{if } t < 0 \end{cases} \tag{7}$$

$$\frac{d}{dt}G_1 = -AG_1 + (B - G_1)G_0 \tag{8}$$

and

$$\frac{d}{dt}G_2 = -AG_2 + (B - G_2)G_1. \tag{9}$$

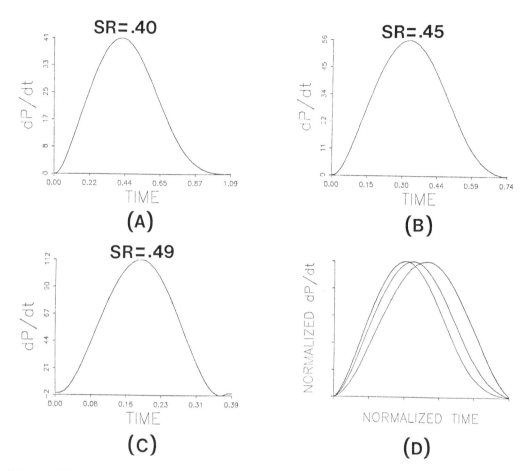

Figure 20. (A, B, C): Velocity profiles associated with a slow, medium, and fast performance of a 20 unit movement. Each SR value gives the trajectory's *symmetry ratio*; that is, the time taken to move half the distance, $.5(T(0) - P(0))$, divided by the total movement duration, MT. These ratios indicate progressive symmetrization at higher speeds. (D): The velocity profiles shown in (A), (B), and (C) are not perfectly superimposable. (See Figure 18 for parameters.)

Then $G_2(t)$ is a sigmoid function of the desired shape. The GO signal $G(t)$ can be set equal to $G_2(t)$, as we did, or even to a sigmoid signal $f(G_2(t))$ of $G_2(t)$. A typical result is shown in Figure 22. In the series of simulations exemplified by Figure 22, the range of symmetry ratios, namely .44–.50 was similar to that found in Figure 19 using a faster-than-linear signal function. Final choice of a best-fitting $G(t)$ awaits a more direct experimental determination of the PPC profile through time.

25. Computer Simulation of Velocity Amplification during Target Switching

Velocity amplification by up to a factor of three can be obtained by switching to a new value of T while a previously activated GO signal is still on. Figure 23 demonstrates this effect by comparing two computer simulations. In the first simulation, onset of $T(t)$

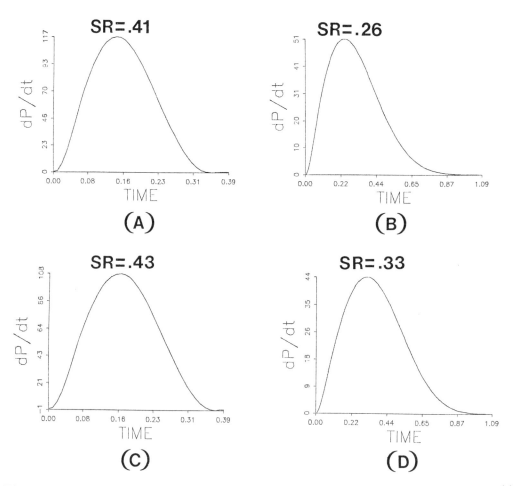

Figure 21. (A, B): Velocity profiles for a slow and a fast movement with a slower-than-linear $g(t)$: $\alpha = 30$, $n = 1$, $\beta = 1$, $\gamma = 1$. (C, D): Velocity profiles for a slow and a fast movement with a linear $g(t)$: $\alpha = 30$, $n = 1$, $\beta = 1$, $\gamma = 0$.

and $g(t)$ were both synchronous at time $t = 0$ (Figure 23a). In the second simulation, onset of $g(t)$ preceded onset of $T(t)$ by a time equivalent to about 300 msec (Figure 23b). Note the much higher peak velocity (235 versus 102) attained in Figure 23b. This effect, which matches the "anomalous" velocity multiplication observed in the target-switching experiments of Georgopoulos *et al.* (1981), is due to the prior build-up of the GO signal during response execution.

In the ensuing sections, computer simulations will be compared with a variety of data which were not reviewed in the preceding sections.

26. Reconciling Staggered Onset Times with Synchronous Termination Times

Within the context of a target-switching experiment, velocity amplification may appear to be a paradoxical property. On the other hand, such a property has an adaptive function in

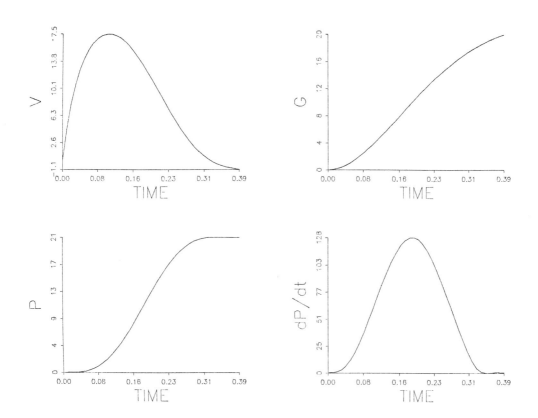

Figure 22. Simulated time course of neural network activities and $\frac{dP}{dt}$ for a 350 msec movement. Note the S-shaped growth in G (sigmoid GO signal). Parameter values for equations (2), (3), (8), (9): $\alpha = 25$, $A = 1$, $B = 25$.

the many situations where a hand will fail to reach a moving target unless it both changes direction and speeds up. In addition, we now show that the same mechanism can generate synchronous termination times of synergetic muscle components which may individually start to move at staggered onset times.

The need for this latter property has recently been emphasized by a study of Hollerbach, Moore, and Atkeson (1986), who showed that nearly straight movement paths can result from muscle coordinate planning if the onset times of muscles acting at different joints are appropriately staggered *and* if all the muscles reach their final positions synchronously. Their study did not, however, explain how a neural mechanism could generate synchronous muscle offsets despite staggered muscle onsets.

We now show that the posited interaction of a growing GO signal with components of a DV that may be switched on at different times automatically generates synchronous offsets as an emergent property of the VITE circuit. Thus the interaction of a GO signal

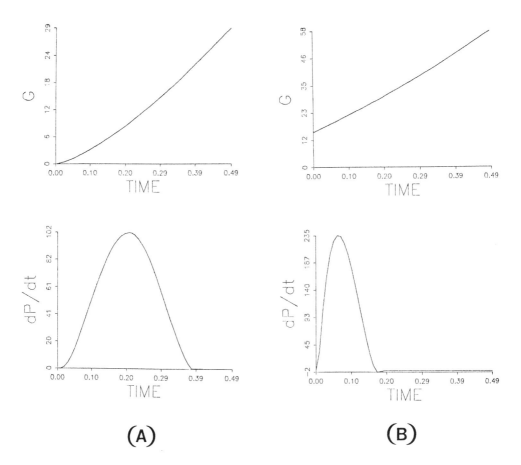

(A)   (B)

Figure 23. A much higher peak velocity is predicted by the model whenever a target is activated after the GO signal has already had time to grow. (A): The control condition, in which T and the GO signal growth process are activated synchronously. (B): Same T as in (A), but here T was activated after $G(t)$ had been growing for 300 msec. (See Figure 18 for parameters.)

with a DV both helps to linearize the paths generated by individual TPC's and, as in the target-switching experiments, enables the hand to efficiently track a moving target by quickly reacting to read-out of an updated TPC.

Figure 24 depicts the results of four blocks, labelled I, II, III, and IV, of computer simulations. Each block represents the onset time, offset time, and duration of three simulations. In the leftmost simulations of each block, onset of a DV component and a GO signal were synchronous. In the other two simulations of each block, a different DV component was read-out at successively longer delays with respect to the onset time of the GO signal. Due to duration invariance (Appendix 2), the results are independent of the initial sizes of the $T(0) - P(0)$ values of these components.

The four blocks (I, II, III, IV) correspond to four increasing values of the GO amplitude G_0 (10, 20, 40, 80). The approximate invariance of termination times across components with different onset delays is indicated by the nearly equal *heights* reached by all the bars

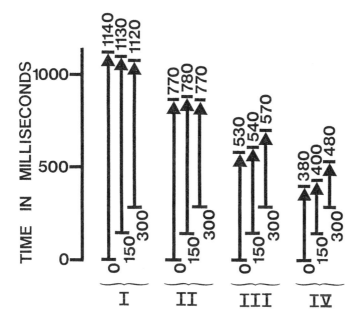

Figure 24. Simulation results showing automatic VITE circuit compensation for contraction-onset-time staggering across components of a synergy. Each block (I, II, III, IV) shows results for a different value (10, 20, 40, and 80, respectively) of the GO signal scalar, G_0. (See Figure 18 for parameters.)

within the block. The different *lengths* of bars within each block show that less time is needed to update those components whose onset times are most delayed. Thus, in block I, all the components terminate almost synchronously even though their onset times are staggered by as much as 26% of the total movement time. In block II, almost synchronous terminations occur even though onset times are staggered by as much as 39% of the total movement time. At very large choices of G_0 (blocks III and IV), synchrony begins to gently break down because the earliest components have executed over 50% of their trajectories before later components even begin to move. These and other results in the article suggest the critical importance of experimentally testing the existence and predicted properties of GO–DV interactions, notably the predicted correlations between the temporal evolution of the GO signal and the DV.

27. Computer Simulation of the Inverse Relation between Duration and Peak Velocity

Each curve depicted in Figure 25a summarizes a series of simulations in which $T(0) - P(0)$ was held constant while G_0 was varied . In this way, a series of velocity profiles were generated whose peak velocities differed even though their trajectories traversed the same distance. The duration of each movement was computed by measuring the interval between velocity profile zero crossings. The different curves in Figure 25a used different values of the distance parameter $T(0) - P(0)$.

These curves mirror the data of Lestienne (1979) summarized in Figure 25b. Figure 25b plots agonist burst duration against peak velocity. The overall shapes of the plots of simulated durations (Figure 25a) and agonist burst durations (Figure 25b) as a function of peak velocity are similar. This similarity reinforces the postulate that the VITE circuit operates in agonist-antagonist muscle coordinates (Sections 3 and 20). It also suggests that the relationship between VITE circuit outputs, motoneuron inputs, and actual muscle activities might be relatively simple (Bullock and Grossberg, 1987).

Nevertheless, two caveats deserve mention. First, were Figure 25a a plot of movement duration (MT) against *mean* velocity ($\overline{V}$), it would necessarily have the shape shown, since by definition,

$$MT = \frac{D}{\overline{V}}, \tag{10}$$

where D denotes the distance. Multiplying by different values of D generates a family of curves similar in shape to those shown in Figure 25a. The VITE model generates the curve in Figure 25a because mean velocity and peak velocity are strongly correlated in these VITE trajectories due to the duration invariance described in Section 22.

The second caveat acknowledges that the VITE circuit cooperates with several other circuits to generate a controllable trajectory in response to unexpected loads and to variable velocities (Bullock and Grossberg, 1987). For example, during medium and high speed movement, the duration of the initial agonist burst may be only one fourth the duration of the corresponding movement. If we assume that the PPC updating process consumes most of the movement time, then these short duration EMG bursts are further evidence that the PPC stage must not be identified with—and must be higher in the outflow channel than—the spinal motorneurons whose suprathreshold activities are directly reflected in the EMG bursts.

This conclusion is consonant with available data on the genesis of EMG burst patterns. In vivo, EMG activites are often sculpted into multiphasic burst patterns by several subnetworks that converge on and embed the spinal motorneurons. In particular, during high-speed movements, muscle changes lag behind neural changes early in response development. This leads to registration of "lag errors" at model regulatory circuits (Bullock and Grossberg, 1987; Feldman, 1986; Ghez and Martin, 1982; Grossberg and Kuperstein, 1986), including the stretch reflex and cerebellar circuits, which translate these error signals into large agonist activations and antagonist inhibitions. If the large agonist activations accelerate the limb so much that it begins to overshoot the intended position, this overshoot is registered as an error opposite in sign to the initial lag error, and the result is a large antagonist braking activity in concert with agonist inhibition. Such braking may slow the movement enough that a smaller lag-error is once again registered. Though this results in a second agonist burst, and transient antagonist inhibition, this last phasic modulation fades quickly and gives way to the tonic EMG pattern required to hold the arm at the final postural position. A similar analysis may be given for isometric contractions.

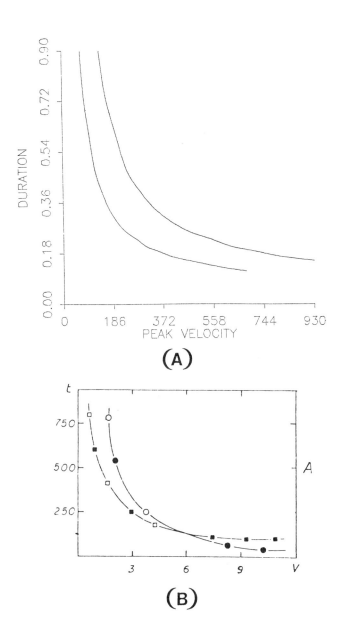

Figure 25. (A): Simulation of movement duration (sec) as a function of peak velocity (deg/sec) for a 30° (lower curve) and a 60° (upper curve) movement. (See Figure 18 for parameters.) (B): Data on agonist burst duration (squares) and antagonist burst onset-time (dots) as a function of peak velocity (rad/sec) for a 60° movement. Reprinted with permission from Lestienne (1979).

TABLE 1
FOR FIXED DURATION (MT), ERROR
GROWS IN PROPORTION TO DISTANCE

MT	DISTANCE	ERROR
.56	10	.084
.56	20	.170
.56	40	.349
.56	80	.700

28. Speed-Accuracy Trade-off: Woodworth's Law and Fitts' Law

The VITE Model circuit predicts a speed-accuracy trade-off which quantitatively fits the classical laws of Woodworth (1899) and of Fitts (1954). The existence of a speed-accuracy trade-off *per se* can be understood by considering the role of the rate parameter α in equation (1). The case of an overshoot error is considered for definiteness.

Given *any* finite value of the averaging rate α in equation (2), $V(t)$ takes some time to react to changes in $P(t)$. In particular, even if $P(t) = T$ at a given time $t = t_0$, $V(t)$ will typically require some extra time after $t = t_0$ to decrease to the value 0, and by (3) $P(t)$ will continue to increase during this extra time. If α is very large, $V(t)$ can approach 0 quickly. Consequently, by (3), $V(t)$ will not allow $P(t)$ to overshoot the target value T by a large amount. On the other hand, given *any* choice of α, the *relative* amount whereby $P(t)$ overshoots the target T depends upon the size of the GO amplitude G_0. This is true because a larger value of G_0 causes $P(t)$ to increase faster, due to (3), and thus $P(t)$ can approach T faster. In contrast, $V(t)$ can only respond to the rapidly changing values of $T - P(t)$ at the constant rate α. As a result, $V(t)$ tends to be larger at a time $t = t_0$ when $P(t_0) = T$ if G_0 is large than if G_0 is small. It therefore takes $V(t)$ longer to equal 0 after $t = t_0$ if G_0 is large. Thus $P(t)$ overshoots T more if G_0 is large. This covariation of amount of overshoot with overall movement velocity is a speed-accuracy trade-off.

Fitts' Law, as described in equation (1), relates movement time (MT), distance (D), and target width (W). The target width may be thought of as setting the criterion for what counts as an error. The law may be given two complementary readings. The first notes that for a fixed movement time, error grows in proportion to amplitude. This component of the law was discovered by Woodworth (1899). Table 1 presents simulation results based on the same parameter choices used in Figure 18. The results show that, in a parameter range where model overshoot errors occur, the model's error also grows in proportion to amplitude. In these simulations, G_0 was held fixed and $T(0) - P(0)$ was varied.

The second way of reading the law notes that in order to maintain a fixed absolute error size, or to fall within a target zone of fixed width, while increasing movement distance, it is necessary to allow more time for completing the movement. In particular, every doubling of distance will add a constant amount, b, to the time needed to perform the movement with the same level of accuracy. Allowing less than b more time for a movement of twice the distance will lead to a less accurate movement.

Table 2 presents the results of a simulation (parameters as in Figure 18) in which the rate parameter α was small enough that modest error resulted even at the smallest distance, or initial value of $T(0) - P(0)$, that was tested, namely a distance of 2 units. Then the

TABLE 2
FOR FIXED ERROR LEVEL, DURATION (MT)
GROWS LINEARLY WITH DISTANCE DOUBLING.

ERROR	DISTANCE	MT
.059	2	.39
.057	4	.49
.058	8	.59
.059	16	.70
.057	32	.80
.059	64	.91

distance $T(0) - P(0)$ was repeatedly doubled, and the value of G_0 progressively decreased, such that the error level was held approximately constant. As can be seen, movement time increased approximately linearly with each doubling of distance, as required by a logarithmic relation between MT and D. It should be noted that the "errors" shown in Tables 1 and 2 are defined relative to a mathematical point, that is a target having zero width along the direction of motion. If subjects adjust their GO signal so that expected error is no greater than the width of a physical target, then by choosing a TPC corresponding to the near side of the target, they can produce the "errorless" movements required in the Fitts task. The model's striking replication of the laws of Woodworth and Fitts, together with its other successes in experimental results, increases our confidence that the VITE Model captures some of the basic neural design principles that underly trajectory generation *in vivo*.

Woodworth's Law is a consequence of duration invariance in the model. This can be seen from the mathematical analysis provided in Appendix 2. There it is proved that the PPC value $P(t)$ can be written in the form

$$P(t) = P(0) + (T(0) - P(0)q(t))$$ (11)

given *any* continuous GO signal $G(t)$. In (11), $T(0) - P(0)$ represents the amount of contraction, or "distance" to be moved, that is mandated by the TPC value $T(0)$ and the initial PPC value $P(0)$. Function $q(t)$ is independent of $P(0)$ and $T(0)$. By (11), $P(t)$ approaches $T(0)$ as $q(t)$ approaches 1, and $P(t)$ overshoots or undershoots if $q(t)$ approaches a value greater or less than 1, respectively. Since $q(t)$ is multiplied by $T(0) - P(0)$, the amount of error (undershoot or overshoot), is proportional to distance, as in Woodworth's Law.

Whereas the proof of Woodworth's Law is a general consequence of duration invariance in the model, Fitts' Law has been mathematically proved in only one case as of the present time (Appendix 1), although our computer simulations demonstrate that it occurs with greater generality. In this case, the GO signal $G(t)$ switches on from value 0 at times $t < 0$ to the constant value $G_0 > 0$ at times $t \geq 0$. In addition, G_0 is chosen sufficiently large to generate overshoot errors. In particular, when $4G_0 > \alpha$,

$$MT = \frac{2}{\alpha} \log\left(\frac{T(0) - P(0)}{E}\right)$$ (12)

where E is the amount of overshoot error in the VITE command.

These instances of Woodworth's Law and Fitts' Law are generated by the VITE circuit itself, without the intervention of visual feedback. A number of authors have commented upon the applicability of these laws when visual feedback is inoperative. For example, Keele (1982, pp.152–153) has written: "What is the underlying nature of the movement system that yields Fitts' Law? ... One factor is the intrinsic accuracy of the motor control system when visual feedback is unavailable. When the eyes are closed during a movement (or the lights are turned off), an average movement will miss target by about 7% of the total distance moved." Schmidt (1982, pp.253–254) summarized error functions for sighted and blind movements across various movement times from studies of Keele and Posner (1968) and Zelaznik, Hawkins, and Kisselburgh (1983). A clear speed-accuracy trade-off was observed. Meyer, Smith, and Wright (1982, p.450) have reviewed data comparing the initial impulse phase of a movement, where visual feedback is unimportant, with the subsequent current-control phase, where visual feedback may be used to improve accuracy. They noted that "the initial-impulse phase was found to contribute directly to the speed-accuracy trade-off. Even when subjects had to perform with their eyes closed and relied on just this phase to execute their movements, they still produced a trade-off ... models that attempt to account for the speed-accuracy trade-off ... must include mechanisms that modulate the trade-off during the initial-impulse phase, not just during the current-control phase." The VITE circuit's ability to reproduce both Woodworth's Law and Fitts' Law as emergent properties of the PPC updating process satisfies this requirement.

It should be emphasized that the VITE circuit is also capable of generating a PPC that approaches the TPC without error in some parameter ranges (Appendix 1). In these parameter ranges, an undershoot error will occur if the GO signal is prematurely terminated or if the effects of small DV signals get lost in ambient cellular noise. A range effect has also been reported (Georgopoulos, 1986, p.151) such that "subjects tended to overshoot the target in small movements (2.5 cm) and to undershoot in large movements (40 cm)." A number of factors may influence this result. For example, during high speed small movements, auxiliary circuits for controlling the arm's inertial effects may not have a sufficient opportunity to act (Grossberg and Kuperstein, 1986, Chapters 3 and 5). During large movements, the distance to be moved may be visually underestimated, thereby leading to instatement of an incorrect TPC. The choice of GO signal amplitude as a function of target distance may contribute to the range effect. The relative importance of such factors will be easier to assess as new experiments and the theory are progressively elaborated with the aid of the quantitative VITE circuit analysis that is provided herein.

Even the definition of what constitutes a movement "error" during ecologically useful motor behavior deserves further commentary. For example, Carlton (1979) asked subjects to keep their movement errors below 5 percent. Subjects typically chose a two-part movement strategy whose first velocity component undershot the target, and whose second velocity component made the final approach to the target at a much lower speed. Such results suggest that subjects found it easier to achieve greater accuracy by breaking up the movement into parts than by launching the movement ballistically over the full distance. The first movement part, albeit strictly speaking an "undershoot error", provides the occasion for updating TPCs and choosing small GO signals during the final part of the movement, thereby achieving high accuracy without too great an increase in total movement duration. Because GO signal adjustments may also be necessary during the final components of such composite movements, these components may also obey a speed-accuracy tradeoff, as Carlton (1979) found.

TABLE 3

**A COMPARISON OF THREE MODELS' ABILITIES
TO PREDICT DATA ON PEAK ACCELERATION ($\ddot{P}$)**

DISTANCE	MT	PEAK $\ddot{P}$	PEAK $\ddot{P}$ SOURCE
20°	.554	$397°/sec^2$	Bizzi *et al.* (1984)
60°	.692	$1130°/sec^2$	(experimental data)
20°	.554	$376°/sec^2$	Minimum-jerk model
60°	.692	$722°/sec^2$	(simulation)
20°	.554	$394°/sec^2$	VITE model
60°	.692	$854°/sec^2$	(simulation)
20°	.554	$396°/sec^2$	VITE$^+$ model
60°	.692	$1127°/sec^2$	(simulation)

29. Computer Simulation of Peak Acceleration Data

Bizzi *et al.* (1984) measured the peak accelerations of medium-speed forearm movements by monkeys. They considered movements around the elbow that swept out 20° and 60°. A computer simulation is compared with their data in Table 3. In order to make this comparison, we scaled 1 time unit in our simulation to equal 10 msec. We then chose two values of the GO amplitude parameter G_0 which generated trajectories of duration approximately equal to 554 msec. and 692 msec., respectively. Due to duration invariance (Section 22), the same durations obtain given these choices of G_0 over a wide range of choices of the distance measure $T(0) - P(0)$. The fact that movements were 20° or 60° was translated into the constraint that the $T(0) - P(0)$ value corresponding to the smaller choice of G_0 must be chosen three times larger than the $T(0) - P(0)$ value corresponding to the larger choice of G_0. Then we searched for values of $T(0) - P(0)$ that gave the best fit to the peak acceleration data subject to this constraint.

The result is compared in Table 3 with the data, and with the fit of the Minimum-Jerk Model of Hogan (1984). The VITE Model fit these data substantially better than the Minimum-Jerk Model. The values associated with the VITE$^+$ model indicate that a perfect fit can be obtained (with Figure 18 parameters) if DV readout to the shunting stage, rather than being instantaneous, occurs over a brief interval whose length is proportional to the size of the DV.

As noted in Section 12, the Minimum-Jerk Model also erroneously predicts a symmetric velocity profile, at least at the level of the central controller. Moreover, it is hard to see how this model could explain the velocity amplification that occurs during target switching (Section 11). Finally, the Minimum-Jerk Model does not contain any representation that may be compared with the existence of vector cells or with the manner in which vector cell activities are integrated into outflow movement commands (Section 13). We therefore believe that the VITE Model provides a better foundation for developing a quantitative neurally-based theory of arm movements than does the Minimum-Jerk Model. The VITE model, in addition to the model circuits developed in Grossberg and Kuperstein (1986), also provides a mechanistic neural explanation of some of the types of invariant behaviors for whose analysis the task dynamics approach to motor control was developed (Saltzman and Kelso, 1983).

30. Updating the PPC using Inflow Signals during Passive Movements

Despite these successes, the VITE Model as described above is far from complete. In this section, a solution of one additional design problem is outlined. Bullock and Grossberg (1987) suggest solutions of a number of the other design problems whereby a VITE circuit can effectively move an arm of variable mass subjected to unexpected perturbations at variable velocities through a Newtonian world.

In Section 6, we noted that inflow signals are needed to update the PPC during a passive movement. For example, Gellman, Gibson, and Houk (1985) have described cells in the cat inferior olive that are sensitive to passive body displacement but not to active movement, and Clark, Burgess, Chapin, and Lipscomb (1985) have analysed muscle proprioceptive contributions to position sense during passive finger movements in humans. Two basic problems motivate our model of PPC updating by inflow signals. First, the process of updating the PPC during passive movements must continue until the PPC registers the position coded by the inflow signals. Thus a difference vector of inflow signals minus PPC outflow signals updates the PPC during passive movements. We denote this difference vector by DV_p to distinguish it from the DV which compares TPC's with PPC's. At times when $DV_p = 0$, the PPC is fully updated. Although the DV_p is not the same as the DV which compares a TPC with a PPC, the PPC is a source of inhibitory signals, as will be seen below, in computing both difference vectors.

Second, PPC outflow signals and inflow signals may, in principle, be calibrated quite differently. We will show how corollary discharges of the PPC outflow signals are adaptively recalibrated until they are computed in the same numerical scale as the inflow signals to which they are compared. We also show that this adaptive recalibration mechanism automatically computes a DV_p which updates the PPC by just the correct amount.

Figure 26 schematizes a model circuit for adaptively computing this DV_p. We call this circuit the *passive update of position (PUP) model*. In Figure 26, the PPC sends inhibitory corollary discharge signals towards the outflow-inflow match stage where the inflow signals are registered. It is assumed that this stage is inhibited except when the movement command circuit is inactive. A simple way to achieve this property is to assume that the GO signal in the movement command circuit inhibits the outflow-inflow match stage, as in Figure 25. Thus the mismatches of outflow and inflow signals that occur during every active movement do not erroneously update the outflow-inflow match stage. In addition, the GO signal is assumed to inhibit learning at the LTM traces which multiply the PPC signals on their way to the outflow-inflow match stage.

This assumption is consistent with arm movement results of Evarts and Fromm (1978) which showed greater modulation of vector cells in precentral motor cortex by inflow signals during small slow movements than during posture, and strongly attenuated modulation during large fast movements. In the model, the amount of attenuation increases with the size of the GO signal. The gating signal which attenuates the inflow process may be a nonlinear (e.g., sigmoid) function of the GO signal. Parametric analysis of the degree of inflow attenuation as a function of overall active movement speed would provide valuable information about the form of this hypothesized gating signal.

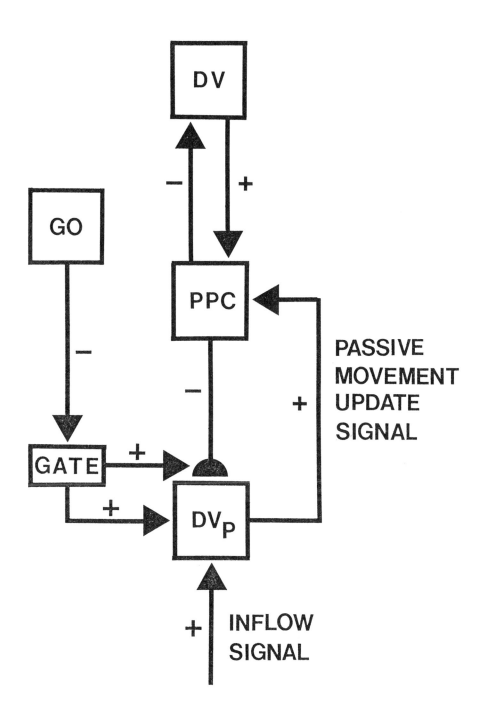

Figure 26. A passive update of position (PUP) circuit. An adaptive pathway $PPC \rightarrow DV_P$ calibrates PPC-outflow signals in the same scale as inflow signals during intervals of posture. During passive movements, output from DV equals zero. Hence the passive difference vector DV_P updates the PPC until it equals the new position caused by any passive movements that may occur due to the application of external forces.

After a movement is over, both the outflow-inflow match stage and the LTM traces are released from inhibition. Typically, the PPC represents the same position as the inflow signals, but perhaps in a different numerical scale. The learning laws described in Appendix 3 define LTM traces which change until the PPC *times* the LTM trace equals the inflow signal. After a number of such learning trials during stable posture, $DV_p = 0$ and the PPC signals are rescaled by the LTM traces to correctly match the inflow signals.

During a passive movement, the PPC does not change, but the inflow signal may change. If the DV_p becomes positive, it causes an increase in the PPC until the DV_p decreases to 0 and the PPC is correctly updated by the inflow signals. If the DV_p becomes negative, then the DV_p of the opponent muscle can decrease the PPC until a match again occurs.

31. Concluding Remarks

The present article introduces a circuit for automatically translating a target position command into a complete movement trajectory via a mechanism of continuous vector updating and integration. A wide variety of behavioral and neural data can be quantitatively explained by this mechanism. The model also provides a foundation for clarifying some of the outstanding classical issues in the motor control literature, highlights the relevance of learning constraints upon the design of neural circuitry, and may be viewed as a specialized version of a more general architecture for movement control.

The VITE circuit and the PUP circuit do not, however, exhaust the total neural machinery that is needed for the control of arm movements. Mechanisms for properly timed sequential read-out of TPC's in a serial motor plan, such as during reaching and grasping or during a dance (Grossberg and Kuperstein, 1986, Chapter 9), for adaptive linearization of a nonlinear muscle plant (Grossberg and Kuperstein, 1986, Chapter 5), and for automatically or predictively adapting to the inertial properties generated by variable loads and velocities (Bullock and Grossberg, 1987) also form essential parts of the arm control system. When all of these systems are joined together, however, one can begin to understand quantitatively how the arm system achieves its remarkable flexibility and versatility, and can begin to build a new type of biologically inspired adaptive robot whose design is qualitatively different from the algorithms offered by traditional approaches to artificial intelligence.

APPENDIX 1

Bell-Shaped Velocity Profile, Fitts' Law, and Staggered Onset Times

This Appendix solves the system of equations

$$\frac{d}{dt}V = \alpha(-V + T - P) \tag{A1}$$

$$\frac{d}{dt}P = G[V]^+ \tag{A2}$$

under the simplifying assumption that the GO signal G is a step function. Then the system can easily be integrated to demonstrate some basic properties.

In many situations, the system starts out in an equilibrium state such that the PPC equals the TPC. Then a new TPC is switched on and the system approaches a new equilibrium. Before the new TPC is switched on, $P = T$ in (A1). Since the system is at equilibrium, $\frac{d}{dt}V = 0$. Thus, by (A1), it also follows that $V = 0$ under these circumstances.

Suppose that a new TPC value is switched on at time $t = 0$. If the system represents an agonist muscle, then $T(0) > P(0)$ so that the PPC increases when $T(0)$ turns on, thereby causing more contraction of its target muscle group. Thus by (A1),

$$V(0) = 0, \tag{A3}$$

and

$$\frac{d}{dt}V(0) = \alpha(T(0) - P(0)) > 0. \tag{A4}$$

Consequently $V(t) \geq 0$ for all times t such that $0 \leq t \leq T$, where T is the first positive time, possibly infinite, at which $V(T) = 0$. While $V(t) \geq 0$ it follows by (A2) that

$$\frac{d}{dt}P = GV \tag{A5}$$

To solve equations (A1) and (A5), differentiate (A1) at times $t \geq 0$. Then

$$\frac{d^2}{dt^2}V = \alpha(-\frac{dV}{dt} - \frac{dP}{dt}), \tag{A6}$$

because T is constant. Substituting (A5) into (A6) yields the equation

$$\frac{d^2}{dt^2}V + \alpha\frac{d}{dt}V + \alpha GV = 0 \tag{A7}$$

subject to the initial data (A3) and (A4).

This equation can be solved by standard methods. The solution takes the form

$$V(t) = (T(0) - P(0))f(t), \tag{A8}$$

where $f(t)$ is independent of $T(0)$ and $P(0)$. Thus $V(t)$ equals the initial difference between the new TPC and the initial PPC multiplied by a function $f(t)$ which is independent of the new TPC and the initial PPC. By (A2),

$$\frac{d}{dt}P = (T(0) - P(0))g(t), \tag{A9}$$

where $g(t) = Gf(t)$. Integration of (A9) yields

$$P(t) = P(0) + (T(0) - P(0)) \int_0^t g(v)dv. \qquad (A10)$$

Since $\frac{d}{dt}P$ provides an estimate of the arm's velocity profile, (A9) illustrates the property of duration invariance in the special case that $G(t)$ is constant. Duration invariance is proved using a general $G(t)$ in Appendix 2. Equation (A9) also illustrates how the velocity profile can respond to a sudden switch in the TPC with a gradual increase-then-decrease in its shape, although $g(t)$ assumes a different form if $\alpha > 4G$, $\alpha = 4G$, or $\alpha < 4G$. When $\alpha > 4G$,

$$g(t) = \frac{\alpha G}{\sqrt{\alpha^2 - 4\alpha G}} e^{-\frac{\alpha}{2}t} \left[e^{\frac{t}{2}\sqrt{\alpha^2 - 4\alpha G}} - e^{-\frac{t}{2}\sqrt{\alpha^2 - 4\alpha G}} \right]. \qquad (A11)$$

Term $[\exp(\frac{t}{2}\sqrt{\alpha^2 - 4\alpha G})] - [\exp(-\frac{t}{2}\sqrt{\alpha^2 - 4\alpha G})]$ in (A11) increases exponentially from the value 0 at $t = 0$, whereas term $\exp[-\frac{\alpha}{2}t]$ decreases exponentially towards the value 0 at a faster rate. The net effect is a velocity function that increases-then-decreases with an approximately bell-shaped profile. In addition, $g(t) \geq 0$ and

$$\int_0^\infty g(t)dt = 1. \qquad (A12)$$

By (A10) and (A12), $P(t)$ increases towards T as t increases. Thus $P(t)$ either approaches $T(0)$ with an arbitrarily small error, or an undershoot error occurs if the GO signal is switched off prematurely.

If $\alpha = 4G$, then

$$g(t) = \alpha G t e^{-\frac{\alpha}{2}t}. \qquad (A13)$$

Again the velocity profile gradually increases-then-decreases, but starts to increase linearly before it decreases exponentially. The function in (A13) also satisfies (A12), so that accurate movement or undershoot occur, depending upon the duration of the GO signal.

The case of $\alpha < 4G$ deserves special attention. In this case, the rate G with which P is updated in equation (A2) exceeds the ability of the rate α in equation (A1) to keep up. As a result, an overshoot error can occur. In particular,

$$g(t) = \frac{2\alpha G}{\sqrt{4\alpha G - \alpha^2}} e^{-\frac{\alpha}{2}t} \sin\left(\frac{\sqrt{4\alpha G - \alpha^2}}{2}t\right) \qquad (A14)$$

if $0 \leq t \leq \frac{2\pi}{\sqrt{4\alpha G - \alpha^2}}$. When t exceeds $\frac{2\pi}{\sqrt{4\alpha G - \alpha^2}}$, function $g(t)$, and thus $V(t)$, becomes negative. By (A2), $[V(t)]^+ = 0$ when t exceeds $\frac{2\pi}{\sqrt{4\alpha G - \alpha^2}}$, so that, by (A2), $P(t)$ stops moving at this time. The movement time in this case thus satisfies

$$MT = \frac{2\pi}{\sqrt{4\alpha G - \alpha^2}}. \qquad (A15)$$

Within this time frame, the velocity profile is the symmetric function $\sin\left(\frac{\sqrt{4\alpha G - \alpha^2}}{2}t\right)$ multiplied by the decaying, hence asymmetric, function $e^{-\frac{\alpha}{2}t}$. Greater overall symmetry of $g(t)$ is achieved if the rate $\frac{\sqrt{4\alpha G - \alpha^2}}{2}$ with which the sine function changes is rapid relative to the rate $\frac{\alpha}{2}$ with which the exponential function changes; viz., if $2G \gg \alpha$.

Since $P(t)$ stops changing at time $t = \frac{2\pi}{\sqrt{4\alpha G - \alpha^2}}$, the final PPC value found from equation (A10) is

$$P\left(\frac{2\pi}{\sqrt{4\alpha G - \alpha^2}}\right) = P(0) + (T(0) - P(0))(1 + e^{-(\alpha\pi/\sqrt{4\alpha G - \alpha^2})}). \qquad (A16)$$

Thus an overshoot error occurs of size

$$E = (T(0) - P(0))e^{-(\alpha\pi/\sqrt{4\alpha G - \alpha^2})}. \qquad (A17)$$

In accordance with Woodworth's Law, the error is proportional to the distance $(T(0) - P(0))$. Fitts' Law can be derived by holding E constant in (A17) and varying $(T(0) - P(0))$ to test the effect on the MT in (A15). Substituting (A15) into (A17) shows that

$$E = (T(0) - P(0))e^{-\frac{\alpha MT}{2}} \qquad (A18)$$

which implies Fitts' Law

$$MT = \frac{2}{\alpha} \log\left(\frac{T(0) - P(0)}{E}\right). \qquad (A19)$$

The initial condition $V(0) = 0$ in (A3) obtains if the system has actively tracked a constant TPC until its PPC attains this TPC value. Under other circumstances, $V(0)$ may be negative. When this occurs, $\frac{d}{dt}P$ in (A2) may remain 0 during an initial interval while $V(t)$ increases to nonnegative values. Thus P begins to change only after a staggered onset time. Some properties of staggered onset times are derived below.

A negative initial value of $V(0)$ may obtain if a particular muscle group has been passively moved to a new position either by an external force or by the prior active contraction of other muscle groups. In such a situation, $P(t)$ may be changed by the PUP circuit (Section 30) even if $T(t) = 0$, and $V(t)$ may track $P(t)$ via equation (A1) until a new equilibrium is reached. Under these circumstances, (A1) implies that

$$0 = \frac{d}{dt}V = \alpha(-V + 0 - P). \qquad (A20)$$

If we assume that this equilibrium value obtains at time $t = 0$, then

$$V(0) = -P(0) < 0, \qquad (A21)$$

and equation (A2) implies that

$$\frac{d}{dt}P = G[V]^+ = 0. \qquad (A22)$$

Thus P remains constant until V becomes positive. If a new TPC is switched on at time $t = 0$ to an agonist muscle which satisfies (A21), then $T(0) > P(0)$. By (A1), V increases according to the equation

$$\frac{d}{dt}V + \alpha V = \alpha(T(0) - P(0)), \qquad (A23)$$

where $\alpha(T(0) - P(0))$ is a positive constant, until the time $t = t_1$ at which $V(t_1) = 0$. Thereafter $[V]^+ = V > 0$ so that V and P mutually influence each other through equations (A1) and (A5).

Time t_1 is computed by integrating equation (A10). We find

$$V(t) = V(0)e^{-\alpha t} + (T(0) - P(0))(1 - e^{-\alpha t}) \qquad (A24)$$

for $0 \le t \le t_1$. By (A21),

$$V(t) = -P(0) + T(0)(1 - e^{-\alpha t}). \qquad (A25)$$

Thus

$$t_1 = \frac{1}{\alpha} \, ln \left[1 - \left(\frac{P(0)}{T(0)} \right) \right]^{-1}. \qquad (A26)$$

By (A26), t_1 is a function of the ratio of the initial PPC value to the new TPC value.

For times $t \ge t_1$, equations (A1) and (A5) can be integrated just as they were in the preceding case. Indeed,

$$V(t_1) = 0 \qquad (A27)$$

by the definition of t_1, and

$$\frac{d}{dt}V(t_1) = \alpha(T(0) - P(0)) \qquad (A28)$$

by (A23) and (A28). The initial data (A27) and (A28) are the same as the initial data (A3) and (A4) except for a shift of t_1 time units. Consequently if the GO signal onset time is also shifted by t_1 time units, then it follows from (A8) that at times $t \ge t_1$,

$$V(t) = (T(0) - P(0))f(t - t_1). \qquad (A29)$$

An estimate of such a velocity profile is found by piecing together (A24) and (A29). Thus

$$\frac{d}{dt}P = \begin{cases} 0 & \text{for } 0 \le t < t_1 \\ G(T(0) - P(0))f(t - t_1) & \text{for } t_1 \le t \end{cases}. \qquad (A30)$$

Equation (A30) illustrates how a velocity profile with a staggered onset time can occur if $V(0) < 0$. As shown in Section 26, the VITE command to a muscle group can compensate for a staggered onset time if its DV is multiplied by the same GO signal as other muscles in the synergy. In this case, the GO signal onset time is not shifted to match the onset time of each component of the VITE command.

APPENDIX 2

Synchrony and Duration Invariance

Consider equations (A1) and (A2) under the influence of an arbitrary nonnegative and continuous GO function $G(t)$. As in Appendix 1, let

$$V(0) = 0 \qquad (A3)$$

and $P = T$ before T is switched to a new value. Suppose for definiteness that $T(t)$ switches from the value T_0 to T_1 at time $t = 0$, and that

$$T_1 > T_0 = P(0). \qquad (A31)$$

Consequently, equations

$$\frac{d}{dt}V = \alpha(-V + T - P) \qquad (A1)$$

and

$$\frac{d}{dt}P = GV \qquad (A5)$$

hold for an interval of nonnegative t. Define the new PPC variable

$$Q(t) = P(t) - T_0 \qquad (A32)$$

and the new target position constant

$$T_2 = T_1 - T_0. \qquad (A33)$$

Then (A1) and (A5) can be replaced by equations

$$\frac{d}{dt}V = \alpha(-V + T_2 - Q) \qquad (A34)$$

and

$$\frac{d}{dt}Q = GV. \qquad (A35)$$

By (A31),

$$Q(0) = 0. \qquad (A36)$$

Thus by (A3) and (A36), both V and Q start out with 0 values at $t = 0$.

Now define new variables

$$v(t) = \frac{V(t)}{T_2} \qquad (A37)$$

and

$$q(t) = \frac{Q(t)}{T_2}. \qquad (A38)$$

By (A34) and (A35), these variables obey the equations

$$\frac{d}{dt}v = \alpha(-v + 1 - q) \qquad (A39)$$

and

$$\frac{d}{dt}q = Gv. \qquad (A40)$$

In addition,

$$v(0) = q(0) = 0 \tag{A41}$$

by (A3) and (A36). It is obvious that a unique solution of (A39)–(A41) obtains no matter how T_2 and T_1 are chosen, if $T_2 > T_1$.

By combining (A31), (A32), (A33), and (A38), we find that

$$P(t) = P(0) + (T_1 - P(0))q(t), \tag{A42}$$

where $q(t)$ is independent of T_1 and $P(0)$. Equation (A42) proves duration invariance given a general GO function $G(t)$. Indeed, differentiating (A42) yields

$$\frac{d}{dt}P = (T_1 - P(0))\frac{d}{dt}q(t) \tag{A43}$$

which shows that function $\frac{d}{dt}q$ generalizes function $g(t)$ in equation (A9).

APPENDIX 3

Passive Update of Position

Mathematical equations for a PUP circuit are described below. As in our description of a VITE circuit, equations for the control of a single muscle group will be described. Opponent interactions between agonist and antagonist muscles also exist and can easily be added once the main ideas are understood.

The PUP circuit supplements the equation

$$\frac{d}{dt}P = G[V]^+ \tag{A2}$$

whereby the PPC integrates DV's through time. A PUP circuit obeys equations

Present Position Command

$$\frac{d}{dt}P = G[V]^+ + G_p[M]^+, \tag{A44}$$

Outflow-Inflow Interface

$$\frac{d}{dt}M = -\beta M + \gamma I - zP, \tag{A45}$$

Adaptive Gain Control

$$\frac{d}{dt}z = \delta G_p(-\epsilon z + [M]^+). \tag{A46}$$

The match function M in (A45) rapidly computes a time-average of the difference between inflow (γI) and gated outflow (zP) signals. Thus

$$M \simeq \frac{1}{\beta}(\gamma I - zP). \tag{A47}$$

If the inflow signal γI exceeds the gated outflow signal zP, then $[M]^+ > 0$ in (A47). Otherwise $[M]^+ = 0$. The *passive gating function* G_p in (A44) is positive only when the muscle is in a passive, or postural, state. In particular, $G_p > 0$ only when the GO signal $G(t) \simeq 0$ in the VITE circuit. Figure 26 assumes that a signal $f(G(t))$ inhibits a tonically active source of the gating signal G_p. Thus G_p is the output from a "pauser" cell, which is a tonically active cell whose output is attenuated during an active movement. Such cells are well-known to occur in saccadic eye movement circuits (Grossberg and Kuperstein, 1986; Luschei and Fuchs, 1972; Raybourn and Keller, 1977). If both G_p and $[M]^+$ are positive in (A44), then $\frac{d}{dt}P > 0$. Consequently, P increases until $M = 0$; that is, until the gated outflow signal zP equals the inflow signal γI. At such a time, the PPC is updated to match the position attained by the muscle during a passive movement. To see why this is true, we need to consider the role of function z in (A45) and (A46).

Function z is a long term memory (LTM) trace, or associative weight, which adaptively recalibrates the scale, or gain, of inflow signals until they are in the same scale as outflow signals. Using this mechanism, a match between inflow and outflow signals accurately encodes a correctly updated PPC. Adaptive recalibration proceeds as follows.

In equation (A46), the learning rate parameter δ is chosen to be a small constant to assure that z changes much more slowly than M or P. The passive gating function G_p also modulates learning, since z can change only at times when $G_p > 0$. At such times, term $-\epsilon z$ describes a very slow forgetting process which prevents z from getting stuck in mistakes. The forgetting process is much slower than the process whereby z grows when $[M]^+ > 0$. Since function M reacts quickly to its inputs γI and $-zP$, as in (A47), term $[M]^+ > 0$ only if

$$\gamma I > zP. \tag{A48}$$

The outflow signal P is multiplied, or gated, by z on its way to the match interface where M is computed (Figure 26).

Because z changes only when the muscle is in a postural, or a passive state, terms γI and P typically represent the same position, or state of contraction, of the muscle group. Then inequality (A48) says that the scale γI for measuring position I using inflow signals is larger than the scale zP for measuring the same position using outflow signals. When this happens, z increases until $M = 0$; viz., until outflow and inflow measurement scales are equal.

On an occasion when the arm is passively moved by an external force, the inflow signal γI may momentarily be greater than the outflow signal zP. Due to past learning, however, the inflow signal satisfies

$$\gamma I = zP^*, \tag{A49}$$

where P^* is the outflow command that is typically associated with I. Thus by (A47),

$$M \simeq \frac{z}{\beta}(P^* - P). \tag{A50}$$

By (A44) and (A50), P quickly increases until it equals P^*. Thus, after learning occurs, P approaches P^*, and M approaches 0 very quickly, so quickly that any spurious new learning which might have occurred due to the momentary mismatch created by the onset of the passive movement has little opportunity to occur, since z changes slowly through time. What small deviations may occur tend to average out due to the combined action of the slow forgetting term $-\epsilon z$ in (A46) and opponent interactions.

Equations (A45) and (A46) use the same formal mechanisms as the *head-muscle interface* (HMI) described by Grossberg and Kuperstein (1986). The HMI adaptively recodes a visually activated target position coded in head coordinates into the same target position coded in agonist-antagonist muscle coordinates. Such a mechanism for adaptive matching of two measurement scales may be used quite widely in the nervous system. We therefore call all such systems Adaptive Vector Encoders.

REFERENCES

Abend, W., Bizzi, E., and Morasso, P., Human arm trajectory formation. *Brain*, 1982, **105**, 331–348.

Adams, J.A., A closed-loop theory of motor learning. *Journal of Motor Behavior*, 1971, **3**, 111–149.

Adams, J.A., Feedback theory of how joint receptors regulate the timing and positioning of a limb. *Psychological Review*, 1977, **84**, 504–523.

Albus, J.S., A theory of cerebellar function. *Mathematical Biosciences*, 1971, **10**, 25–61.

Atkeson, C.G. and Hollerbach, J.M., Kinematic features of unrestrained vertical arm movements. *Journal of Neuroscience*, 1985, **5**(9), 2318–2330.

Beggs, W.D.A. and Howarth, C.I., The movement of the hand towards a target. *Quarterly Journal of Experimental Psychology*, 1972, **24**, 448–453.

Bernstein, N.A., **The coordination and regulation of movements**. London: Pergamon Press, 1967.

Bizzi, E., Central and peripheral mechanisms in motor control. In G.E. Stelmach and J. Requin (Eds.), **Tutorials in motor control**. Amsterdam: North-Holland, 1980.

Bizzi, E., Accornero, N., Chapple, W., and Hogan, N., Arm trajectory formation in monkeys. *Experimental Brain Research*, 1982, **46**, 139–143.

Bizzi, E., Accornero, N., Chapple, W., and Hogan, N., Posture control and trajectory formation during arm movement. *Journal of Neuroscience*, 1984, **4**(11), 2738–2744.

Brindley, G.S., The use made by the cerebellum of the information that it receives from sense organs. *International Brain Research Organization Bulletin*, 1964, **3**, 80.

Brody, M. and Paul, R. (Eds.), **Robotics research: The first international symposium**. Cambridge, MA: MIT Press, 1984.

Brooks, V.B., Motor programs revisited. In R.E. Talbott and D.R. Humphrey (Eds.), **Posture and movement: Perspective for integrating sensory and motor research on the mammalian nervous system**. New York: Raven Press, 1979, pp.13–49.

Brooks, V.B., **The neural basis of motor control**. New York: Oxford University Press, 1986.

Buchanan, T.S., Almdale, D.P.J., Lewis, J.L., and Rymer, W.Z., Characteristics of synergic relations during isometric contractions of human elbow muscles. *Journal of Neurophysiology*, 1986, **56**, 1225–1241.

Bullock, D. and Grossberg, S., Neural dynamics of planned arm movements: Synergies, invariants, and trajectory formation. Paper presented at the Symposium on Neural Models of Sensory-Motor Control at the annual meeting of the Society for Mathematical Psychology, Cambridge, MA, August 20, 1986.

Bullock, D. and Grossberg, S., Neuromuscular realization of planned trajectories: Adaptive and automatic mechanisms. In preparation, 1987.

Carlton, L.G., Control processes in the production of discrete aiming responses. *Journal of Human Movement Studies*, 1979, **5**, 115–124.

Carpenter, G.A. and Grossberg, S., A massively parallel architecture for a self-organizing neural pattern recognition machine. *Computer Vision, Graphics, and Image Processing*, 1987, **37**, 54–115 (a).

Carpenter, G.A. and Grossberg, S., Neural dynamics of category learning and recognition: Attention, memory consolidation, and amnesia. In J. Davis, R. Newburgh, and E. Wegman (Eds.), **Brain structure, learning, and memory**. AAAS Symposium Series, in press, 1987 (b).

Clark, F.J., Burgess, R.C., Chapin, J.W., and Lipscomb, W.T., Role of intramuscular receptors in the awareness of limb position. *Journal of Neurophysiology*, 1985, **54**, 1529–1540.

Cooke, J.D., The organization of simple, skilled movements. In G.E. Stelmach and J. Requin (Eds.), **Tutorials in Motor Behavior**. Amsterdam: North-Holland, 1980, pp.199–212.

Evarts, E.V., Relation of pyramidal tract activity to force exerted during voluntary movement. *Journal of Neurophysiology*, 1968, **31**, 14–27.

Evarts, E.V. and Fromm, C., The pyramidal tract neuron as summing point in a closed-loop control system in the monkey. In J.E. Desmedt (Ed.), **Cerebral motor control in man: Long loop mechanisms**. Basel, Switzerland: Karger, 1978, pp. 56–69.

Evarts, E.V. and Tanji, J., Gating of motor cortex reflexes by prior instruction. *Brain Research*, 1974, **71**, 479–494.

Feldman, A.G., Change in the length of the muscle as a consequence of a shift in equilibrium in the muscle-load system. *Biofizika*, 1974, **19**(3), 534–538.

Feldman, A.G., Once more on the equilibrium-point hypothesis (λ model) for motor control. *Journal of Motor Behavior*, 1986, **18**, 17–54.

Fetters, L. and Todd, J., Quantitative assessment of infant reaching movements. *Journal of Motor Behavior*, in press, 1987.

Fitts, P.M., The information capacity of the human motor system in controlling the amplitude of movement. *Journal of Experimental Psychology*, 1954, **47**(6), 381–391.

Fitts, P.M. and Peterson, J.R., Information capacity of discrete motor responses. *Journal of Experimental Psychology*, 1964, **67**(2), 103–112.

Flash, T. and Hogan, N., The coordination of arm movements: An experimentally confirmed mathematical model. *Journal of Neuroscience*, 1985, **5**(7), 1688–1703.

Freund, H.-J. and Büdingen, H.J., The relationship between speed and amplitude of the fastest voluntary contractions of human arm muscles. *Experimental Brain Research*, 1978, **31**, 1–12.

Fujita, M., Simulation of adaptive modification of the vestibulo-ocular reflex with an adaptive filter model of the cerebellum. *Biological Cybernetics*, 1982 (a), **45**, 207–214.

Fujita, M., Adaptive filter model of the cerebellum. *Biological Cybernetics*, 1982 (b), **45**, 195–206.

Gelmann, R., Gibson, A.R., and Houk, J.C., Inferior olivary neurons in the awake cat: Detection of contact and passive body displacement. *Journal of Neurophysiology*, 1985, **54**, 40–60.

Georgopoulos, A.P., On reaching. *Annual Review of Neuroscience*, 1986, **9**, 147–170.

Georgopoulos, A.P., Kalaska, J.F., Caminiti, R., and Massey, J.T., On the relations between the direction of two-dimensional arm movements and cell discharge in primate motor cortex. *Journal of Neuroscience*, 1982, **2**(11), 1527–1537.

Georgopoulos, A.P., Kalaska, J.F., Crutcher, M.D., Caminiti, R., and Massey, J.T., The representation of movement direction in the motor cortex: Single cell and population studies. In G.M. Edelman, W.E. Gall, and W.M. Cowan (Eds.), **Dynamic aspects of neocortical function**. Neurosciences Research Foundation, 1984, pp.501–524.

Georgopoulos, A.P., Kalaska, J.F., and Massey, J.T., Spatial trajectories and reaction times of aimed movements: Effects of practice, uncertainty, and change in target location. *Journal of Neurophysiology*, 1981, **46**(4), 725–743.

Georgopoulos, A.P., Schwartz, A.B., and Kettner, R.E., Neuronal population coding of movement direction. *Science*, 1986, **233**, 1416–1419.

Ghez, C. and Martin, J.H., The control of rapid limb movement in the cat, III: Agonist–antagonist coupling. *Experimental Brain Research*, 1982, **45**, 115–125.

Ghez, C. and Vicario, D., The control of rapid limb movement in the cat, II: Scaling of isometric force adjustments. *Experimental Brain Research*, 1978, **33**, 191–202.

Gordon, J. and Ghez, C., EMG patterns in antagonist muscles during isometric contraction in man: Relations to response dynamics. *Experimental Brain Research*, 1984, **55**, 167–171.

Gordon, J. and Ghez, C., Control strategies determining the accuracy of targeted force impulses, I: Pulse height control. *Experimental Brain Research*, in press, 1987 (a).

Gordon, J. and Ghez, C., Trajectory control in targeted force impulses, III: Compensatory adjustments for initial errors. *Experimental Brain Research*, 1987, **67**, 253–269 (b).

Grossberg, S., On learning of spatiotemporal patterns by networks with ordered sensory and motor components, I. Excitatory components of the cerebellum. *Studies in Applied Mathematics*, 1969, **48**, 105–132.

Grossberg, S., Neural pattern discrimination. *Journal of Theoretical Biology*, 1970, **27**, 291–337.

Grossberg, S., Neural expectation: Cerebellar and retinal analogs of cells fired by learnable or unlearned pattern classes. *Kybernetik*, 1972, **10**, 49–57.

Grossberg, S., Contour enhancement, short-term memory, and constancies in reverberating neural networks. *Studies in Applied Mathematics*, 1973, **52**, 217–257.

Grossberg, S., A theory of human memory: Self-organization and performance of sensory-motor codes, maps, and plans. In R. Rosen and F. Snell (Eds.), **Progress in theoretical biology**, Vol. 5. New York: Academic Press, 1978, pp.233–374.

Grossberg, S., **Studies of mind and brain: Neural principles of learning, peception, development, cognition, and motor control**. Boston: Reidel Press, 1982.

Grossberg, S., Adaptive compensation to changes in the oculomotor plant. In E. Keller and D. Zee (Eds.), **Adaptive processes in the visual and oculomotor systems**. Pergamon Press, 1986.

Grossberg, S., Cooperative self-organization of multiple neural systems during adaptive sensory-motor control. In D.M. Guthrie (Ed.), **Aims and methods in neuroethology**. Manchester University Press, 1987 (a).

Grossberg, S. (Ed.), **The adaptive brain, I: Cognition, learning, reinforcement, and rhythm**. Amsterdam: Elsevier/North-Holland, 1987 (b).

Grossberg, S. (Ed.), **The adaptive brain, II: Vision, speech, language, and motor control**. Amsterdam: Elsevier/North-Holland, 1987 (c).

Grossberg, S. and Kuperstein, M., **Neural dynamics of adaptive sensory-motor control: Ballistic eye movements**. Amsterdam: Elsevier/North-Holland, 1986.

Grossberg, S. and Stone, G.O., Neural dynamics of word recognition and recall: Attentional priming, learning, and resonance. *Psychological Review*, 1986, **93**, 46–74.

Helmholtz, H. von, **Handbuch der Physiologischen Optik**. Leipzig: Voss, 1866.

Hofsten, C. von, Development of visually directed reaching: The approach phase. *Journal of Human Movement Studies*, 1979, **5**, 160–178.

Hofsten, C. von, Eye-hand coordination in the newborn. *Developmental Psychology*, 1982, **18**(3), 450–461.

Hogan, N., An organizing principle for a class of voluntary movements. *Journal of Neuroscience*, 1984, **4**(11), 2745–2754.

Hollerbach, J.M., Computers, brain, and the control of movement. *Trends in Neuroscience*, 1982, **5**, 189–192.

Hollerbach, J.M., Dynamic scaling of manipulator trajectories. *Journal of Dynamic Systems, Measurement, and Control*, 1984, **106**, 102–106.

Hollerbach, J.M., Moore, S.P., and Atkeson, C.G., Workspace effect in arm movement kinematics derived by joint interpolation. In G. Gantchev, B. Dimitrov, and P. Gatev (Eds.), **Motor control**. Plenum Press, 1986.

Holst, E. von and Mittelstaedt, H., The reafference principle: Interaction between the central nervous system and the periphery. *Naturwissenschaften*, 1950, **37**, 464–476.

Houk, J.C. and Rymer, W.Z., Neural control of muscle length and tension. In **Handbook of physiology: The nervous system II**. Bethesda, MD: American Physiological Society, 1981, 257–322.

Howarth, C.I. and Beggs, W.D.A., the relationship between speed and accuracy of movement aimed at a target. *Acta Psychologica*, 1971, **35**, 207–218.

Howarth, C.I. and Beggs, W.D.A., Discrete movements. In D. Holding (Ed.), **Human skills**. New York: Wiley and Sons, 1981, pp.91–117.

Humphrey, D.R. and Reed, D.J., Separate cortical systems for control of joint movement and joint stiffness: Reciprocal activation and coactivation of antagonist muscles. In J.E. Desmedt (Ed.), **Motor control mechanisms in health and disease**. New York: Raven Press, 1983, 347–372.

Ito, M., The control mechanisms of cerebellar motor systems. In F.O. Schmitt and F.G. Worden (Eds.) **The Neurosciences Third Study Program**. Cambridge, Mass. and London: MIT Press, 1974, 293–303.

Ito, M., Cerebellar control of the vestibulo-ocular reflex—around the flocculus hypothesis. *Annual Review of Neuroscience*, 1982, **5**, 275–296.

Ito, M., **The cerebellum and neural control**. New York: Raven Press, 1984.

Jagacinski, R.J. and Monk, D.L., Fitts' Law in two dimensions with hand and hand movements. *Journal of Motor Behavior*, 1985, **17**(1), 77–95.

Jeannerod, M., The timing of natural prehension movements. *Journal of Motor Behavior*, 1984, **16**(3), 235–254.

Kalaska, J.F., Caminiti, R., and Georgopoulos, A.P., Cortical mechanisms related to the direction of two-dimensional arm movements: Relations in parietal area 5 and comparison with motor cortex. *Experimental Brain Research*, 1983, **51**, 247–260.

Keele, S.W., Behavioral analysis of movement. In V.B. Brooks (Ed.), **Handbook of physiology**, Section 1, Volume 2: *Motor Control*. Bethesda, MD: American Physiological Society, 1981, pp.1391–1414.

Keele, S.W., Component analysis and conceptions of skill. In J.A.S. Kelso (Ed.), **Human motor behavior**. Hillsdale, NJ: Erlbaum, 1982, pp.143–159.

Keele, S.W. and Posner, M.I., Processing of visual feedback in rapid movements. *Journal of Experimental Psychology*, 1968, **77**, 155–158.

Kelso, J.A.S., **Human motor behavior**. Hillsdale, NJ: Erlbaum, 1982.

Kelso, J.A.S. and Holt, K.G., Exploring a vibratory systems analysis of human movement production. *Journal of Neurophysiology*, 1980, **28**, 45–52.

Kelso, J.A.S., Southard, D.L., and Goodman, D., On the nature of human interlimb coordination. *Science*, 1979, **203**, 1029–1031.

Kerr, B. and Langolf, G.D., Speed of aimed movements. *Quarterly Journal of Experimental Psychology*, 1977, **29**, 475–481.

Knight, A.A. and Dagnall, P.R., Precision in movements. *Ergonomics*, 1967, **10**, 327–330.

Lestienne, F., Effects of inertial load and velocity on the braking process of voluntary limb movements. *Experimental Brain Research*, 1979, **35**, 407–418.

Luchei, E.S. and Fuchs, A.F., Activity of brain stem neurons during eye movements of alert monkeys. *Journal of Neurophysiology*, 1972, **35**, 445–461.

Marr, D., A theory of cerebellar cortex. *J. Physiology* (London), 1969, **202**, 437–470.

Marteniuk, R.G. and MacKenzie, C.L., A preliminary theory of two-hand co-ordinated control. In G.E. Stelmach and J. Requin (Eds.), **Tutorials in motor behavior**. Amsterdam: Elsevier/North-Holland, 1980, pp.185–197.

Massey, J.T., Schwartz, A.B., and Georgopoulos, A.P., On information processing and performing a movement sequence. In C. Fromm and H. Heuver (Eds.), **Generation and modulation of action patterns**, Experimental Brain Research Supplement, 1985.

McCormick, D.A. and Thompson, R.F., Cerebellum: Essential involvement in the classically conditioned eyelid response. *Science*, 1984, **223**, 296–299.

Meyer, D.E., Keith-Smith, J.E., and Wright, C.E., Models for the speed and accuracy of aimed movements. *Psychological Review*, 1982, **89**, 449–482.

Morasso, P., Spatial control of arm movements. *Experimental Brain Research*, 1981, **42**, 223–227.

Nichols, T.R., Is "the Mass-Spring Model" a testable hypothesis? *Journal of Motor Behavior*, 1985, **17**(4), 499–500.

Optican, L.M. and Robinson, D.A., Cerebellar-dependent adaptive control of primate saccadic system. *Journal of Neurophysiology*, 1980, **44**, 1058–1076.

Piaget, J., **The origins of intelligence in children**. New York: Norton, 1963.

Polit, A. and Bizzi, E., Processes controlling arm movements in monkeys. *Science*, 1978, **201**, 1235–1237.

Raybourn, M.S. and Keller, E.L., Colliculoreticular organization in primate oculomotor system. *Journal of Neurophysiology*, 1977, **40**, 861–878.

Ron, S. and Robinson, D.A., Eye movements evoked by cerebellar stimulation in the alert monkey. *Journal Neurophysiology*, 1973, **36**, 1004–1021.

Ruffini, A., On the minute anatomy of the neuro-muscular spindles of the cat, and on their physiological significance. *Journal of Physiology*, 1898, **23**, 190–208.

Sakitt, B., A spring model and equivalent neural network for arm posture control. *Biological Cybernetics*, 1980, **37**, 227–234.

Saltzman, E.L. and Kelso, J.A.S., Skilled actions: A task dynamics approach. Haskins Laboratories Status Report on Speech Research, 1983, SR-76, 3–50.

Schmidt, E.M., Jost, R.G., and Davis, K.K., Reexamination of the force relationship of cortical cell discharge patterns with conditioned wrist movements. *Brain Research*, 1975, **83**, 213–223.

Schmidt, R.A., **Motor control and learning**. Champaign, IL: Human Kinetics Press, 1982.

Schmidt, R.A., Zelaznik, H.N., and Frank, J.S., Sources of inaccuracy in rapid movement. In G.E. Stelmach (Ed.), **Information processing in motor control and learning**. New York: Academic Press, 1978, 183–203.

Sherrington, C.S., On the anatomical constitution of nerves of skeletal muscles; with remarks on recurrent fibres in the ventral spinal nerve-root. *Journal of Physiology*, 1894, **17**, 211–258.

Soechting, J.F. and Lacquaniti, F., Invariant characteristics of a pointing movement in man. *Journal of Neuroscience*, 1981, **1**(7), 710–720.

Sperling, G. and Sondhi, M.M., Model for visual luminance distribution and flicker detection. *Journal of the Optical Society of America*, 1968, **58**, 1133–1145.

Tanji, J. and Evarts, E.V., Anticipatory activity of motor cortex units in relation to direction of an intended movement. *Journal of Neurophysiology*, 1976, **39**, 1062–1068.

Vilis, T. and Hore, J., A comparison of disorders in saccades and in fast and accurate elbow flexions during cerebellar dysfunction. In H.J. Freund, U. Büttner, B. Cohen, and J. Noth (Eds.), **The oculomotor and skeletal motor systems: Differences and similarities**. New York: Elsevier, 1986.

Vilis, T., Snow, R. and Hore, J., Cerebellar saccadic dysmetria is not equal in the two eyes. *Experimental Brain Research*, 1983, **51**, 343–350.

Viviani, P. and Terzuolo, C., Space-time invariance in learned motor skills. In Stelmach, G.E. and Requin, J. (Eds.), **Tutorials in Motor Behavior**. Amsterdam: North-Holland, 1980.

Welford, A.T., Norris, A.H., and Schock, N.W., Speed and accuracy of movement and their changes with age. In W.G. Koster (Ed.), **Attention and performance II**. Amsterdam: North-Holland, 1969, pp.3–15.

Woodworth, R.S., The accuracy of voluntary movement. *Psychological Review*, 1899, **3**, 1–114.

Zelaznik, H.N., Hawkins, B., and Kisselburgh, K., Rapid visual feedback processing in single-aiming movements. *Journal of Motor Behavior*, 1983, **15**, 217–236.

Zelaznik, H.N., Schmidt, R.A., and Gielen, S.C.A.M., Kinematic properties of rapid aimed head movements. *Journal of Motor Behavior*, 1987, **18**, 353–372.

Author Index

Subject Index